A HISTORY OF AFRICA

BY W. E. F. WARD

A History of Ghana
Educating Young Nations
A History of Africa (3 volumes)
Government in West Africa

W. E. F. WARD

C.M.G., M.A.

Formerly History Master, Achimota College, Ghana

A HISTORY

OF AFRICA

BOOK ONE

THE OLD KINGDOMS OF THE SUDAN

NIGERIA BEFORE THE BRITISH CAME

SOUTH AFRICA

AURORA PUBLISHERS, INCORPORATED

NASHVILLE/LONDON

FIRST PUBLISHED 1960 BY
GEORGE ALLEN AND UNWIN, LTD.; LONDON
FIFTH PRINTING 1969
COPYRIGHT © 1970 BY
AURORA PUBLISHERS, INCORPORATED
NASHVILLE, TENNESSEE 37219
LIBRARY OF CONGRESS CATALOG CARD NUMBER: 71-125583
STANDARD BOOK NUMBER: 87695-082-9
MANUFACTURED IN THE UNITED STATES OF AMERICA

PREFACE

The ambitious title of this book requires an explanation. I have written it in the belief that there is rapidly growing up in the secondary schools and teacher training colleges of Africa (and still more so, no doubt, in the university colleges) a generation of young people who are thinking of Africa as one whole, and who refuse to let their vision be limited by the frontiers arbitrarily drawn on the map of Africa by European diplomatists.

On the other hand, Africa so far has had no historical unity; and no history of Africa can yet be more than a collection of episodes. I hope that this book will be the first of a series which, in this necessarily episodic manner, will cover all the major regions of the continent. It is written for African students in middle schools or secondary schools and teacher training colleges. Except perhaps for the history of their native land, most of them will have had little or no training in formal history while in the primary school; and many of the schools and colleges which they are now attending will have no history specialist on the staff. The book must therefore be planned so as to be useful for background reading without the help of a specialist teacher.

The general plan of the series is that each book shall contain three topics or episodes, though this first book contains a fourth, an introductory section on the nature of history and the historical outlook. One of the most important benefits from the study of history is that it helps one to see how the world came to be in its present state; which is the necessary preliminary to any effective attempts to bring it into a better state. Because of this, I approach each subject in the form of a dialogue, asking a series of questions and giving the answers by means of historical narrative. Because of this, too, I do not shrink from treating topics which are controversial. One of the uses of history should be to discipline our emotions with knowledge, and to teach us to conduct our controversies in a civilized manner. I have served at different times as an official of Her Majesty's Government in Ghana, Mauritius, and the United Kingdom. The views which I express are of course personal and not official views.

I have tried to keep the English style simple, and I have kept the vocabulary on the whole within the 2,000-word vocabulary of the *General Service List*, explaining any extra word in a foot-note. But I have allowed myself a certain latitude in this matter. There is a group of words not found in the *General Service List* which I am sure no African student nowadays will need to have explained: either common African objects like *camel, hoe, palm-tree, lorry*, or words concerned with politics or administration, such as *parliament*, *region*, *constitution*, *province*, *revenue*, *cabinet*, *missionary*, *authority*. I have used these words without hesitation or explanation.

Books Two and Three have now been published. Book Two covers modern Egypt and the Sudan, Kenya, Uganda and Tanzania. Book Three deals with the three countries of Zambia, Malawi and Rhodesia.

W. E. F. WARD

CONTENTS

ILLUSTRATIONS

*Nos. 1 and 2 courtesy of the Trustees of the British Museum
Nos. 3 to 8 Radio Times Hulton Picture Library*

MAPS

LIST OF BOOKS

These are the books which I found useful in preparing this book. I have divided them into two sections: the first consisting of books which are in print and which ought to be in the school library, the second consisting of books which can only be consulted in large libraries.

BOOKS IN PRINT

South Africa
Eric Walker: *A History of Southern Africa*
J. H. Hofmeyr: *South Africa* (2nd edition, revised by J. P. Cope)

Kingdoms of the Sudan
Basil Davidson: *Old Africa Rediscovered*
E. W. Bovill: *The Golden Trade of the Moors*
J. D. Fage: *An Introduction to the History of West Africa*

Nigeria Before the British Came
Sir Alan Burns: *History of Nigeria*
M. C. English: *An Outline of Nigerian History*

BOOKS ONLY IN LARGE LIBRARIES

Kingdoms of the Sudan
Ibn Khaldun: *History of the Berbers*
El Bekri: *Description of North Africa*
Es Sadi Abderrahman: *Tarikh-es-Soudan*
Mahmoud Kati: *Tarikh-el-Fettach*
   All these four books are translated into French, but not into English.
Ibn Batuta: *Travels*
E. W. Bovill: *Caravans of the Old Sahara*
This is the first edition of the book now called *The Golden Trade of the Moors;* but the new edition has not entirely replaced the old one.
Lady Lugard: *A Tropical Dependency*
   This book is useful also for Nigeria Before the British Came.

In drawing the maps, I have made great use of Philips' *Modern College Atlas for Africa* and J. D. Fage's *An Atlas of African History*, though I have not always followed Professor Fage blindly.

1

What is History?

The word *history* and the word *story* both come from the same Greek word, which was taken into the English language many hundred years ago. The English people took this one Greek word and made two different English words out of it, because they wished to express two different ideas.

It is not always easy to separate the idea of *history* from the idea of a *story*. Every African people has stories about its great chiefs and people of long ago: how they fought and led their people. These stories are the beginning of history, because they are about real people, and because the elders who tell them believe them to be true. But often they contain things which are hard to believe, and often they do not seem to fit well together.

Every African people has stories of another kind which are told to children, with such titles as *Why the Sea is Salt*, or *How the Crocodile Got His Teeth*. We have stories about people, like Cinderella or Sindbad the Sailor. These stories are short, and are told by word of mouth. Later on, when people are able to read, and books are printed, we have longer stories like *A Tale of Two Cities* by Dickens. And today there are hundreds of stories printed every year, some long and some short: stories about crime, or adventure, or love, or travel. We read them because they are amusing and interesting. But we know that they are not true.

What do I mean by this? What do I mean by *true*? Here we come to the difference between *story* and *history*. There is a story which tells how the elephant got his long trunk. It tells us that once upon a time, the elephant had a short nose. One day he went to the river to drink, and a crocodile caught him by the nose. The elephant's friend the snake caught hold of him, and the crocodile was not able to pull the elephant into the river; but the elephant's nose was pulled out until it became a long trunk, and since then, all elephants have had long trunks. This is a good story to tell a child. But it is not the real reason why elephants have long trunks. Those who tell this story do not know the real reason. Again, if we read *A Tale of Two Cities*, we read about people called Sydney Carton and Jerry Cruncher and others. But Dickens, who wrote the story, invented these people in his own mind. Sydney Carton never lived on earth. Dickens himself, who invented Sydney Carton and many other characters in his books, has told us that when he finished writing one of his stories, he felt sad at saying good-bye to the people in it. He knew that they were not real people, but only people whom he had invented for his story. But, he says, they had been so much in his mind for many months that they almost seemed real to him. Almost, you see: not quite.

Take another example. We may read in the newspaper that the police have discovered a murder, and perhaps some time later we may read that someone has been tried for the murder and found guilty. That is fact; that is truth. But we may buy a book which tells us the story of a murder, and how a clever policeman found out the man who did it. Not a real murder, not a real policeman; when we are reading the story we know that it is only a story written to amuse us. The writer has made it up out of his head; he has invented it. There is a word to describe such a story, a story the writer has invented. It is *fiction*. If you go to the public library, you will find many shelves headed with this word *fiction*. Your murder story which you buy, or borrow from the library, is fiction; the murder you read of in the newspaper is fact.

This difference between fact and fiction is partly what I am thinking of when I say that stories are not true. Dickens' story *A Tale of Two Cities* is fiction; it is not true. But Carlyle's *History of the French Revolution* is fact; it is true. Dickens invented Sydney Carton and Jerry Cruncher and everything they did. But Carlyle did not invent the people in his book. They were real people, who once lived; and they did the things which Carlyle says they did. Dickens was writing a story, or fiction; Carlyle was writing history. History is about real people.

Now, I had a special reason for comparing *A Tale of Two Cities* with the *History of the French Revolution*. One is fiction, the other is history, but they both describe the thing which we call the French Revolution: that is, the way in which the people of France killed their king and made their country into a republic. Carlyle describes it by telling us about the people—Danton, Robespierre and others—who made the revolution: who they were, what they said and did, and what was the result. Dickens describes it differently. He first invents Sydney Carton and the others; and then he asks himself this question: What would happen to Sydney Carton if he went to Paris at the time of the French Revolution? Before Dickens can answer this question, he needs to know what Paris was like at that time; and he himself tells us that he learned this by reading Carlyle's history. So there is some truth in Dickens' book. Sydney Carton never lived, and in that way the book is not true; but the French Revolution is a fact, which happened as Dickens describes it, and in that way the book is true.

There is another kind of truth in Dickens. Sydney Carton is fiction, not fact. But as we read about him, we ask ourselves this question: Can we imagine a man like Sydney Carton in real life? And if so, is it likely that he would do the things which Dickens makes him do? If we were to answer No to this question, we should soon lose interest in the book. But if we say Yes, then we may say that there is some truth even in Sydney Carton. There never was such a man, but there might have been. Sydney Carton is true to human nature.

So there are different kinds of truth; and when we say that a story is not true, we may mean only that the writer has invented the people in it.

What about history? In one way history is always true. It tells us about real people: what they said and did, and what happened to them. The writer tries his best to find out the truth about them. It is not always easy. If we have to be a witness in a law-court, we promise that we will tell 'the truth, the whole truth, and nothing but the truth'. The lawyer will ask us questions, and we answer them as truly as we can. Sometimes we cannot answer exactly. Let us imagine some of the questions the lawyer might ask, and our answers. Perhaps it is important for him to find out, if he can, exactly what time we left our house one morning.

—What time was it when you left your house?

—I don't know exactly; it was half-past ten when I passed the post-office, for I saw the time by the post-office clock.

—How far is it from your house to the post-office?

—About ten minutes; but I remember that I met a friend on the way, and stopped for a few minutes to talk to him. So I suppose it must have been about 10.15 when I left home.

—Are you sure you did not leave as early as 10.10?

—I don't think I left as early as that, but I may have done; I can't be sure.

—You say you met a friend on the way. Who was he?

—I am afraid I can't remember now who it was that I met.

—What, you remember that you met a friend and talked to him, and yet you cannot remember who the friend was?

—No; all this happened three months ago, and I have many friends in the town. I just cannot remember.

—Well, if you cannot remember who the friend was that you met, perhaps you can remember what you talked about; can you?

—I remember that we talked politics. My friend wanted me to go to a meeting with him that evening.

—Did you go?

—Yes.

—You talked about this political meeting. Can you remember anything else you talked about?

—I think we talked a bit about the railway accident.

—Which railway accident?

—There had been a big accident; ten people were killed. It was in the newspapers.

—But that accident was on the 26th of March. I am asking you what you were talking to your friend about on the 23rd. You cannot have been talking about the accident.

—Was that on the 26th?

—Yes; here is the newspaper of the 27th; you will see that it writes about 'yesterday's accident'.

—So it does. Then I must have made a mistake. I can't have talked about the accident on that morning; it must have been on another day, with some other friend.

This talk in the law-court shows us some of the difficulties we meet when we try and tell the truth about what happened. First of all, we cannot tell the exact truth; we cannot tell exactly what time it was when we left the house, or exactly how long we took to talk to our friend on the road. The lawyer thinks that if he can find out how long we spent with our friend, it will help him. If he could find out which friend it was, he could ask the friend to tell him how long the talk lasted. But our second difficulty is that we forget who the friend was. So the lawyer tries to find out what we talked about; he hopes that in that way he may be able to tell how long our talk lasted. But there he meets a third difficulty; we tell him something that is not true. We mix up one friend with another and one talk on the 23rd with another talk on the 27th. So we see that, although we are doing our best to help the lawyer by telling the truth, it is not easy. We have not told him the exact truth, and we have made a mistake and told him something that is not true.

We promise to tell the whole truth; but there is another difficulty here. Suppose we had a wonderfully good memory, and the lawyer asked us the question, 'What did you and your friend say?' If we told the whole truth, we might repeat every word of the conversation, beginning with our first greeting and ending with our last goodbye. But the lawyer and the judge would not want as much as that; they want only the important part of the conversation. So we should have to choose what we thought important, and leave out what we thought unimportant. Perhaps we should leave out something which the lawyer specially wants to know, and he might have to ask us more questions to find out that fact.

Now let us imagine how the lawyer feels. He is trying to find the truth of what happened on March 23rd, and he wants to find out the exact time at which this person left the house. But nobody can tell him, though everybody is trying to help. And yet it all happened only three months ago, and he has the person in front of him to answer his questions.

If it is as difficult as this to find the truth of what happened only three months ago, how can we hope to find the truth of what happened 30, or 300, or 3,000 years ago? We cannot have the people here to answer our questions, for they are dead. We have to find out what they said when they were alive. We have seen how hard it is to tell the truth, so we must remember that not all they said may be quite true, even if they were honestly trying to tell the truth. Suppose they were not honestly trying, or suppose each could see only his own side of the truth? There is a proverb which says that there are two sides to every question. If two people quarrel, each will explain his own side of the quarrel much more clearly than he will explain the other side.

If two peoples have been at war and have fought a battle, it may
not be easy to find which side won the battle. In politics, the
people of party A will tell you how foolish and wicked are the
people of party B; and if you listen to what party B will tell you
about party A, it sounds just as bad. Perhaps neither party is
quite as wise as it thinks, and neither is as foolish as its enemy
thinks. Neither has the whole truth; the truth lies somewhere
between them.

There is a special word for the story which the witness tells in
the law-court. It is his *evidence*. We use the same word for the
reasons which we have for believing that a statement in a history
book is true. Here is an example. When I was writing on page 13
about Dickens and Carlyle and their books about the French
Revolution, I asked myself this question: Where did Dickens
learn about the French Revolution? I thought it very likely
that he read Carlyle's book; but I wanted to be sure. So I looked
at both books, to see if I could find some *evidence* that Dickens
had read Carlyle. I did not know exactly when the two books
were written, but I thought that I should find that Carlyle's was
the older of the two. If so, then Dickens *might have learnt* about
the Revolution from Carlyle, but I should still need to find
evidence that he *did learn* from Carlyle. But I was lucky. I found
that Carlyle's book was printed in 1839 and Dickens's in 1859,
twenty years later. But I found more than that. At the beginning
of his book, Dickens mentions what he calls 'Mr. Carlyle's
wonderful book' and says that he cannot hope to add to it; so
here is clear evidence that Dickens did read Carlyle.

That is an easy example; it is not always as easy as that. Here
is a much harder example, which once gave me a great deal of
trouble. In 1935 I wrote a school book on the history of Gnana,
or the Gold Coast, as it was then called. Another man called
Claridge had written a big book about the Gold Coast twenty
years before, in 1915; and I used his book with others as evidence
for some of what I wrote. My evidence for the rest of what I
wrote was what African chiefs and elders told me of the history
of their own peoples, which nobody before me had written down.

In my book I had to say something about the slave trade.
Everybody nowadays sees that the slave trade was a wicked
business; but when it began, neither Europeans nor Africans
thought it wicked, and many Europeans and Africans became

very rich by it. As an example of this, Claridge says that in 1517 the Pope in Rome gave permission for the Spaniards to take African slaves to America; he said it, and I copied him. In 1958, twenty-three years after my book was printed, a man who read this wrote to me and asked, 'What evidence have you for saying that the Pope gave this permission in 1517?' I looked in Claridge's book, and what he said was quite plain. But he did not say what his evidence was, and I could not ask him, for he was dead. Then I went to a very large book, the *Encyclopaedia Britannica.* I did not find any evidence on the question; I did find that a certain bishop, named Las Casas, had advised the king of Spain in 1517 to send African slaves to America, but a bishop is not the same as the Pope. The *Encyclopaedia Britannica* gave a long list of books which would tell me more; so I read them. Most of them said nothing on this one point; and in the end I could find no evidence at all that the Pope gave any such permission in 1517. But one book which I read gave the actual words of a letter which the Pope in 1454 (more than sixty years earlier) had written to the king of Portugal (not Spain), giving him permission to take slaves from Africa. It seems that Claridge was right in thinking that the Pope gave permission for the trade, but he made a mistake in the date. Perhaps he saw that Bishop Las Casas gave his advice in 1517, and thought that the bishop would not have given such advice if the Pope had not approved. Anyway, what Claridge said and I copied from him was not the exact truth.

This shows us some of the difficulties of writing history, and it shows us, too, that there are different kinds of evidence. First of all, there is the original paper, such as the Pope's letter. Let us suppose that besides this one letter there are many others in the Pope's library in Rome all written by the same Pope Nicholas V. Now there comes a man who wants to learn about Pope Nicholas V. He will read all the letters, and will use them and other evidence to write a book. This book is called a first-hand book, because the man who writes it is the first to pick up the original papers and study them. But when the first-hand book is printed, many other writers will use it. Perhaps someone who is writing a history of Portugal, for example, will find something in the first-hand book that will help him: some letter from the king to the Pope, or from the Pope to the king. As far as that letter is concerned, the book about the history of Portugal is second-hand; he has not been to Rome to see the Pope's letter himself, but has been content to take it from the first-hand book. Some books are partly first-hand and partly second-hand. My own history of Ghana was second-hand while I was copying from Claridge and others, but first-hand when I was writing what African chiefs and elders had told me.

There are different kinds of historical evidence. Letters and other written papers are one kind. Another kind is an account given by word of mouth, such as the history which the African chiefs and elders gave me of their own people. A third kind of evidence is historical remains: buildings (whether in good condition or in ruins), graves, pottery and all kinds of tools and works of art. For example: within the last few years we have found large quantities of broken Chinese pottery in East Africa, none of it much older than about 1127 or much later than about 1450. This tells us that during that time there must have been trade between China and East Africa. Here is another example: near a certain village in West Africa is a large heap which has grown up as the people of the village have thrown away their rubbish all through the years. That rubbish heap has been carefully dug up, a few inches at a time; and everything in it was examined. Right at the bottom of the heap a broken tobacco-pipe was found, a kind of pipe which was made in England about the year 1600. This tells us that the village was built about that time. It cannot have been built much earlier, or else there would have been more rubbish underneath the pipe. It cannot have been built much later; for pipes soon wear out, and pipes were not made in this shape for very long. A broken pipe thrown away after about 1650 would have been of a different shape. The evidence of historical remains is not always as easy to understand as in these two examples, and of course there are limits to what historical remains can tell us. The Chinese pottery in East Africa, for example, can tell us when the trade began and ended, but it cannot tell us why. For that we must look elsewhere.

Sometimes the evidence that we have does not agree. People may forget, or may make mistakes, or may even try to hide the truth. If this happens, the writer has to decide which evidence he will believe; and it is not always easy to decide. When we are looking at evidence, we have to ask ourselves such questions as these: Does this evidence agree with my other evidence? On this matter, A disagrees with B; have I found either A or B to be mistaken on other matters? Has either of them any special reason for not wanting to tell the whole truth on this matter? Which of them is likely to know more about this matter?

What have we learned so far about history? We have learned:

(a) The history book tells us about real people and about things that really happened; it does not introduce imaginary people and events, as fiction does.

(b) The history book is trying to tell us the truth,· but the writer may make mistakes.

(c) It is not easy for the writer to tell us the truth and nothing but the truth; and he cannot possibly tell us the whole truth.

(d) There are different kinds of evidence, and different kinds of history books: some big, some small, some first-hand, some second-hand. When we are reading a small history book, we must remember that beneath it are the big books, and beneath them are the original papers. For example: in this book there are 49 pages about the history of South Africa. When I wrote them, I made sure of my facts by looking at a book called *A History of Southern Africa* by Eric A. Walker. That book has 973 pages, and twenty of them are filled with a list of the books and papers on South African history on which Walker has based his book.

Now there is just one more thing that we must remember about history. We have seen that it is not always easy to find the truth about what a man said or did. But even if we do find the truth about what he said or did, it is much harder still to find the truth about *why* he said or did it.

Let us take an example. I am asked if I will be secretary to a club, and I say No, because I am too busy. Is that my only reason? It is the only reason I give, but I may have other reasons. The man who is secretary now is just as busy as I am, perhaps even busier; but he has been able to do the work of secretary for some years past. Perhaps it is not that I am too busy, but I am too lazy. Perhaps there is someone on the club committee whom I dislike, and I know that if I were secretary I should have to work closely with that person. Perhaps my wife thinks I am going out too much in the evening already, and she wants me to stay at home with her and not take on any more work.

Perhaps I am beginning to lose interest in the club and am even thinking of leaving it. There may be other reasons. But when they ask me to be secretary, I shall certainly not reply, 'No, I don't want to be secretary. I am too lazy to do the work; I don't like Mr X, and I have promised my wife not to take on any more evening work. And as a matter of fact, I don't think I shall be a member of the club much longer; I don't think its meetings are very interesting.' I shall not say all this; some of it I should be ashamed to say, and some of it, I know, would hurt other members. So instead, all I say is, 'Thank you very much; no, I am afraid I am too busy'. I tell only a very small part of the truth.

And if this is so in such a small simple matter, it is much more so in big matters like affairs of state. We may see that the Government of the United States, or the Soviet Union, or Ghana makes a law, or makes a proposal to some other country, or does some action. That is a fact. But why does it do it? No doubt the Government will tell us why; but it will tell us only as much as it thinks it safe to tell us. There may be other reasons besides the reason it gives. It is like a game of chess; we see the move which the other player has just made, but we often find it hard to know why he has made it.

Now in such a case as this, we are quite free to ask ourselves, 'Is this reason which the Government gives us the true reason, or the most important reason, or is the Government hiding something from us?' And we may go further if we like, and say, 'I do not think this is the true reason; I think the true reason is something very different, as follows . . .' We may say this; and we may be quite right. But we may be quite wrong. We do not know the Government's true reason; we are only guessing. Even if our guess is a good and sensible guess, we must always be careful not to speak of what we can only guess as if it were something which we know.

Many people make this mistake, especially in politics. You will hear them say, 'Oh yes, I know that is what the Prime Minister said. But of course I don't believe him. He had to say it; but I know that he doesn't mean it. He only said it because . . .' —and then they will give you a reason which they have guessed for themselves, or which they have taken from someone else who has guessed it. If you say to them, 'What makes you think that this is the Prime Minister's real reason for saying what he did?' you will often find that they have no ground for thinking so except that they belong to the other party and are ready to think anything bad of the Prime Minister.

Let me say again, that there is no harm at all in doubting what we read or what we hear, if we have good reasons for doubting. But we must always be careful to remember the difference between what we know and what we only guess, and careful too to make the difference clear to other people when we are telling them our thoughts.

WHY SHOULD WE LEARN HISTORY?

Mr Henry Ford, the American engineer who invented the Ford car, thought that history was useless, and teachers were wasting time in teaching their classes about men and women who lived and died long ago. There are other people who think that some history may be useful, but that much of the history which is taught in schools is not. I know an English lady who complains that when she was a girl in school, her history teachers took her three times through the period of English history from 1485 to 1714, and never came near the lifetime of her mother or her grandmother, which would have interested her.

Was Mr Ford right, or nearly right? Does it help a child in any way to learn what people said and did long ago? There is so much history to learn, and every day there is more and more; for yesterday's newspaper is already part of history. We can learn so little of it; is it worth our while to learn any?

Well, let us answer this last question by saying that history is not the only subject that is increasing. This is just as true of chemistry and physics, for example, or any of the other sciences, or geography, or engineering. In every one of these subjects there is far more to be learnt than there was when I was a boy at school. People have discovered more, so that there are more books to be read, and the books are bigger. But we do not say that it is not worth while to begin chemistry or engineering because it is such a big subject and we can learn so little of it while we are in school. So why should we say this about history?

Why do we teach any subject in school? Not simply because we want children to learn facts, but because we want them to think and understand. Long ago, when he was a young man,

Sir Winston Churchill said that bullets are no use unless you
have a gun, and facts are no use unless you know how to use
them. He wanted his mind to be like a gun, not like a box of
bullets. Of course, we cannot get on without facts; but it is more
important to know how to use the facts we have than to learn
more and more facts without knowing how to use them.

We can see this in all subjects. Take geography for example.
We expect a child to learn certain facts: to know that the Sahara
is a desert and the Congo an area of heavy rainfall, and to know
where Accra and Cairo and Cape Town stand. But we think it
is more important that he should understand why the climate of
the Sahara differs from that of the Congo, and how winds and
ocean currents affect climate, and how climate affects plant and
animal and human life.

And so it is with history. A bad teacher of geography can
waste time in teaching his class lists of capes and bays and
rivers without ever helping them to understand. A bad teacher
of history can waste time by teaching his class lists of names and
dates without helping them to understand.

What is there to understand? What help will history give us?
Let me give a short answer to this question, and then discuss it
in more detail. All over Africa, and in fact all over the world,
we look to old people when we want wise advice. An old man is
able to say, 'I would advise you not to do it in that way. That is
what I did many years ago, and things went wrong. Take my
advice and do it in this way instead; I have known several people
do this, and things went better for them than they did for me.'
An old man can give us this good advice because he can look
back on fifty or sixty or seventy years of experience. But a good
history book can give us advice based on several hundreds of
years of experience. History is about people who were very
much like us; we can see what they did and what happened as a
result, and this may help us in our own affairs.

Of course it is not quite as simple as that; and of course it is
not only that. I have given a short answer, and like all short
answers, it is not exactly true; so I must go into more detail.

It is not quite as simple as that, because things are never
exactly the same as they were long ago. They may be the same
in some ways, but not in all. We sometimes say that history
repeats itself: that is to say, our position today is very much

like the position which someone else has been in before. But
history does not repeat itself exactly. For example, we say that
when Hitler attacked Russia and was beaten by the Russian
army and by the cold Russian winter, history was repeating
itself, because 130 years earlier, Napoleon, who was Emperor of
France (and, like Hitler, had conquered all the rest of Europe
except Britain), also attacked Russia and was beaten by the
Russian army and by the cold Russian winter. Yes, true; but
there were many differences. The modern armies were much
bigger than the armies of 1812, and their weapons and ways of
fighting were very different; Napoleon took the city of Moscow,
Hitler could not; the United States was helping Russia in the
modern war, but not in the war of 1812; Russia of today, after
its revolution in 1917, is very different from the old Russia
against which Napoleon fought—and so on. So if we read of
something happening in a history book which reminds us of
something that is happening today, we must be careful; the two
things may not be just the same.

Then of course, history is not written simply so that we may
learn from it what to do and what not to do. We write history,
and we read history, because it is true and interesting. We all
have an interest in learning how our fathers lived. Every child
must at some time have asked his father or mother, 'What was
it like here when you were a child?' And every father and
mother must at some time have told the children, 'When I was
your age, my parents would not have allowed me to behave like
that'. That natural interest is the beginning of history. But
although history is not written simply to teach us what we should
do and should not do, it can sometimes teach us that. When
Ghana became independent in March, 1957, Dr Nkrumah told
his people, 'The eyes of the world are upon Ghana'. What did
he mean? He meant that Ghana was the first African colony to
become independent, and all the world would watch to see how
Ghana used its independence. If Ghana was wise, people in
other countries would say, 'It is a good thing to give Africans
their independence; they know how to use it'. If Ghana was not
wise, people would say, 'It is a mistake to give African colonies
their independence; they are not yet ready for it'. Dr Nkrumah
meant that other countries would use the history of Ghana as a
lesson how to behave.

Then again, there are many questions which we ask about the world as we see it today, which history will answer for us. For example: Why are the languages of England, Holland and Germany so much alike, and so different from the languages of France and Spain and Italy? Why do the United States speak English, and the South American countries Spanish or Portuguese? Why are there so many castles along the coast of Ghana but none along the coast of Nigeria? Why does the whole of North Africa speak Arabic? Why was Ghana, and not Uganda, the first British African colony to become independent? To answer any of these questions we must look into history.

History, in fact, helps us to understand the world we live in. We see what people have done in the past, and what the result has been. We see that the world is in its present state because people in the past have made it so. If we ask, Why did people behave as they did? we may not be able to find the whole of the answer. History may tell us part of the answer, geography may tell us another part; but there may be part that remains hidden from us. For example, we may ask why the west coast of Africa remained cut off from Europe for so long, and then why it was the Portuguese and Dutch and British seamen who came to it, and not Spanish or Italian. Part of the answer is a matter of geography: the Sahara desert lay between Accra and Europe; it was difficult to cross it, and the Muslim countries of north Africa did not trade much with Europe. So Europeans could only reach Accra or Lagos by sea. Very well: but if so, why not Italians? Why Portuguese and Dutch and British? This is a matter partly of geography, partly of history. The Italians traded mainly eastward with the countries at the east end of the Mediterranean. When those countries were conquered by the Turks, the Italian trade was finished, for the Turks were not interested in trade. Europe had to look for new ways of getting to China and India; and it was easier for young countries outside the Mediterranean to look for new ways than for the old countries to change their old ways. Then, too, there were two great men: Prince Henry of Portugal sent his seamen south to explore the African coast, and Columbus discovered America and made it Spanish land, so that all the Spanish seamen went that way and did not trouble about Africa.

Well, that answer is a good one as far as it goes. It uses

geography and history; but they cannot give us the whole answer. We have to bring in Prince Henry and Columbus, and if someone asks, 'But why did Columbus go to discover America? and why did Prince Henry send his men to Africa?', we cannot answer. We may indeed find that Prince Henry talked to this man, and read that man's book, and heard about Africa from one source or another. But at one particular moment, Prince Henry made up his mind to *do* something; and I suppose he rang a bell for his secretary and told the secretary to find Captain X and send him to receive his orders. And what was it that made Prince Henry get up from his chair and ring the bell? Neither history nor geography can tell us that. We do not know.

So history cannot tell us all we want to know about what people have done, and what was the result; but if we study it carefully, it may be able to tell us a good deal. It is worth studying, because we all have an interest in asking, What was the world like before my time? Because we want to know why the world is in its present state. Because we may learn from it how to avoid the mistakes which our fathers have made, and how to follow their example when they have done wisely. Because we may learn why people who think differently from us think as they do, and this will help us to deal with them.

HISTORY IN SCHOOL

The great difficulty about history in school is that we have so little time for it: usually not more than three class periods a week. We cannot possibly do all that we would like to do; we cannot teach about every country, or about every time. Even if we limit ourselves to the history of one country, there is much in that country's history that we shall not have time to teach. We have to choose.

The most important thing is that we should enjoy the history we do in school, so that we want to read more history after we leave school. I remember very clearly the man who first made me interested in history. He was Mr Foyle, who taught me in the primary school when I was about eight years old. There were sixty-four boys in the class, and Mr Foyle had two history periods of half an hour each: both of them at the end of the afternoon when everyone was tired. We had no textbook, so

Mr Foyle's work was not easy. But he remembered that history is about people, and that children like listening to stories; so he simply told us English history as if it were one long story, and he told it so well that we all enjoyed it. It is difficult to teach history with only two periods a week; but Mr Foyle has shown that it is not impossible.

One of our problems is to understand how time passes, how long ago things happened. Even in our own life, we sometimes find it hard to remember whether something happened three years ago or five. It is much harder with things that happened before our time. Hitler, William the Conqueror, Julius Caesar— they all seem a long time ago, and we find it hard to separate them. It is made harder still, because much more is known about modern times than about earlier times. A textbook of English history, for example, may take 500 pages to cover the time from Julius Caesar to Hitler. It will not give more than twenty pages to the time from Julius Caesar to William the Conqueror. But Julius was 1,100 years before William, and William was only 870 years before Hitler. We may think that Julius and William came close together in time, because they are only twenty pages apart in the book; but we shall be making a mistake.

This is where we need a time-chart. A chart is a kind of map, and a time-chart is a kind of map which is not drawn like the maps in our atlas, on a scale of so many miles to the inch, but on a scale of so many years to the inch. Events are marked on the chart in their proper places according to the scale. There are different kinds of time-chart. The simplest is a straight line or a long narrow strip of paper, divided into equal parts. When I was teaching history in Africa, I used to have a long strip of paper pasted all round the walls of the room. It was about two inches wide, and divided by vertical lines on a scale of fifty years to one foot. It was divided into two by one horizontal line along the middle; in one half I marked events in Africa, in the other half events in other parts of the world. Whenever I was teaching about some event in history, I made the class find the date on the chart, and see what else was happening about the same time. Since events in Africa and in other parts of the world were marked on the same chart, the class did not think of African history and other history as separate things, but as parts of the same thing. It is important that I made the class find dates on

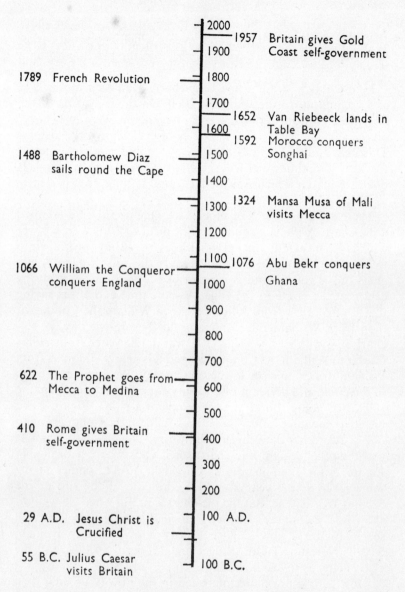

1957 Britain gives Gold
Coast self-government

1789 French Revolution

1652 Van Riebeeck lands in
Table Bay
1592 Morocco conquers
Songhai

1488 Bartholomew Diaz
sails round the Cape

1324 Mansa Musa of Mali
visits Mecca

1066 William the Conqueror
conquers England

1076 Abu Bekr conquers
Ghana

622 The Prophet goes from
Mecca to Medina

410 Rome gives Britain
self-government

29 A.D. Jesus Christ is
Crucified

55 B.C. Julius Caesar
visits Britain

Fig. 1

the chart for itself; I did not find them. My chart began about 1000 B.C. If I were talking about events which happened earlier than that, I would draw a rough chart on the blackboard on a smaller scale.

Figure 1 is a straight-line time-chart, beginning at 100 B.C. and coming up to the year A.D. 2000. On the right side of the line there are four dates marked of events in African history; on the left side there are seven dates of events in world history. This chart puts old times at the bottom and modern times at the top; sometimes you will see charts the other way round. It does not matter which way a chart runs, as long as it is clearly marked.

There are other kinds of time-chart. One useful kind is called a pie-chart. A pie is a round dish of meat or fruit with a cover which is to be eaten; you cut it in pieces by putting the knife into the centre of the circle and drawing it to the outside edge. A pie-chart too is round, and is divided like a pie by lines from the centre of the circle to the edge. A short time ago I was saying that it was longer from Julius Caesar to William the Conqueror than from William the Conqueror to the present day. A pie-chart shows this very clearly. It was 1,120 years from Julius Caesar to William the Conqueror, and it is nearly 900 years from William the Conqueror to the present day. We begin at the top of the circle and divide it into twenty equal parts, each meaning 100 years, going round like the hands of a clock. Figure 2 is a pie-chart showing Julius Caesar and William the Conqueror and one or two other dates in British history. The pie-chart is not as useful as the straight-line chart, for it ends where it began. In Figure 2, for example, Julius Caesar at 55 B.C. comes in the same place as the year A.D. 1945, the date of the end of the Second World War. But the pie-chart is useful when we want to show how a country's history is divided into periods. You will see in Figure 2 how English history is divided into Roman, Saxon, Norman, Tudor, Stuart and Modern periods, and the chart helps us to see how long each period lasted.

Most people are more interested in the history of their own country and their own time than in the history of events that happened far away and long ago. It is natural that they should ask themselves, 'What has Julius Caesar to do with me? He is dead long ago.' If indeed Julius Caesar has nothing to do with us, then we should not spend any time out of our precious two periods a week in reading about him. Our work is to show that he *has* something to do with us today; though he is dead, his work still lives. It often helps if we 'teach history backwards'. I mean that instead of starting at some event long ago—Julius

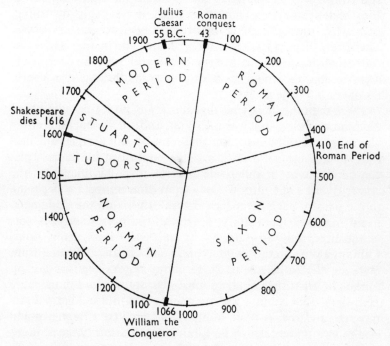

FIG. 2

Caesar for example, who took his Roman army into Britain in 55 B.C.—and working steadily forward, we can start with today and explain why the world is as we find it. For example: we may ask ourselves why the people of France speak a language very like Spanish and Italian and very different from English or Dutch or German. To answer that question we shall have to go right back to Julius Caesar; for it was he who made the country which we now call France a part of the Roman Empire, and made the people learn the language of Rome so well that they never forgot it. (Julius Caesar is only the beginning of the answer; but we cannot answer the question at all without him.)

The difference is that we have told the class, before we begin, why Julius Caesar is important to us today. We might have set out to teach the history of Europe from Julius Caesar's time onwards, and hoped that sooner or later the class would see why the subject is important. So they might, if they came with us all the way; but many of them would get tired and would think that history was not interesting. If we begin by telling them why Julius Caesar is important, and teach history backwards, it will help the class to be interested. In this book, we shall teach much of our history backwards; we shall begin by asking a question about the world today, and then go back into history to find the answer.

One last point. It is true that history is about people: what they said and did, what was the result, and—if we can find out— why they said and did so. But there is a big question here. Does a great man control events, or is he controlled by them? It is easy to see what a difference a great man has made to his country; and sometimes we may think that all history depends on the lives of such great men. I think this is mistaken. Events give a man his opportunity to act. An ordinary man does not see the opportunity, or does not know how to use it, and so does nothing; a great man sees what to do and does it, and things can never be the same again. In teaching history, we must give honour to great men; but we must also show how events gave them their opportunity. The poet Gray has told us that people may live and die as poor humble, uneducated village people, who might, if they had been given the opportunity, have been great poets or statesmen. But they had no opportunity, and nobody ever knew what great gifts they had.

Let us take an African example: Dr Nkrumah, the first Prime Minister of Ghana, the man who made the people of Ghana call for 'Self-Government Now'. We can all agree that Ghana would not have had independence so soon without him, and the people of Ghana are right to give him honour as the man who gave them their freedom. But if Dr Nkrumah had been born thirty years earlier, could he have done then what he has done now? Dr Nkrumah set up his Convention People's Party in 1949; thirty years earlier would take us to 1919. In 1919, the Gold Coast (as it then was) was not nearly so well developed. There were only 35,000 children in school (there were more than eight times as many when the British Director of Education handed over to an African Minister of Education in 1951). Takoradi harbour had not been begun. You could go to Kumasi by train from Sekondi, but not from Accra. There were no air mails, and it took six weeks to get an answering letter from England. There were very few good roads, and very few motor cars. The country was only just beginning to become rich through cocoa. There was no broadcasting, and the newspapers did not reach so many people. If Dr Nkrumah had wanted to set up his party and to ask for self-government in 1919, he would have found it much harder, if not quite impossible. Dr Nkrumah was able to give Ghana self-government in 1957 because Africans and Europeans had been making the road ready for him: by improving education, by making it easier to send news and letters and to travel by car and 'plane. Still, all this is only one side of the question. Everything was ready in 1949. The opportunity was there for someone. But it was Dr Nkrumah who took it and made such great use of it.

So a great man cannot do his work unless he is given the opportunity; and on the other hand, an opportunity may come when there is no great man ready to use it. When we teach history, we must remember that both are needed: the opportunity, and the Man.

THINGS TO DO, TO DISCUSS, OR TO FIND OUT

1. The French Revolution was in 1789, Carlyle wrote his book in 1839, Dickens wrote his in 1859, this book was written in 1959. Draw a time-chart, and mark these dates on it; and add any dates which are important in the history of your own country. (A vertical line on a scale of twenty-five years to an inch will probably be suitable.)

2. Are newspapers historical evidence? Read what two or three newspapers tell you about the same event. Do they agree entirely? If not, can you suggest any reasons for the differences?

3. Read the newspaper report of a political speech. How many times does the speaker tell you what other people (not himself) are thinking and wishing? Does he tell you how he knows? Do you think he does know? Is the news-

paper on the side of the speaker, or on the other side? What makes you think so?

4. Which is more interesting: the history of the last fifty years or the history of earlier times? Which is more important? Would your answer be the same for other countries?

5. Are there any historical remains near your school? If so, go and visit them and find out all you can about them.

6. If you are near a museum, go and visit it. See what objects it contains from your own country, and mark on a map the places they come from.

7. How many different African languages are spoken in your country? Mark on a map the area in which each is spoken. Does this give you any evidence about your country's history? Is one of these languages becoming more important than the others as a language of trade? Can you suggest why this language, rather than another, should develop in this way?

8. Think of what you did yesterday. Then write three accounts of it, as if you were writing (a) to a friend in a distant place, who says he thinks your life must be very dull and uninteresting; (b) to an old man who says that young people nowadays do not work as hard as he did when he was young; (c) to a policeman who suspects you of having committed a crime. Read your three accounts; are they all true? Are they very different?

9. What is the capital city of your country? Has it always been the capital? Why did the Government choose it?

10. Is there any part of your country which is much more thickly populated, or much more thinly populated, than the rest? Why is this? From your answers to this question and to question 9, do you think that geography has any effect on history?

11. History often repeats itself, but never repeats itself exactly. Is there any weakness in the statement, 'They have done it elsewhere so we can do it here'?

12. What written records exist as evidence for the history of your country? Where are they kept? Who looks after them? Do they all belong to the Government? If you were writing a history book and wanted to study them, to whom would you have to apply for permission?

2

The Old Kingdoms of
the Sudan

In the last few years, the British colony of the Gold Coast has become independent, and has taken the name Ghana. Since then, some of the states of French West Africa have talked of joining together and calling themselves Mali. They tell us that both these names, Ghana and Mali, are the names of great African kingdoms of the past. What were these kingdoms? How did they fall; was it the Europeans who broke them down?

No, it was not the Europeans. These African kingdoms rose without European help, and they fell again without European interference.

Before we can say who built up these kingdoms, we must say something about the different peoples who live in West Africa between the Gulf of Guinea and the Mediterranean. Ever since the Europeans began coming in their ships along the West African shores, first to trade and then to colonize, we have been very conscious of the difference between European and African, between white and Negro. But to divide people into whites and Negroes is not enough for this book. We must speak more exactly.

The Sahara has not always been a desert; and Africa has not always been cut off from Europe by the Mediterranean Sea. Many thousands of years ago, the Sahara was grass country in which men and cattle could live. And at that same time, Europe was joined to Africa from Spain to Morocco and from Sicily to Tunis, so that men and animals could pass from one to the other. One race of men spread all over the Mediterranean shores, both to the north and the south; we call it the Mediterranean race, and it still lives there, in North Africa and Spain and Italy and Southern France and elsewhere. Some of the Mediterranean people came as far north as Britain; but in

MAP 1. THE WESTERN SUDAN

This map shows the main trade routes across the desert, marked by dotted lines: from Sijilmasa to Walata and Kumbi, from Tunis to Bamba and Timbuktu, and from Tunis to Agades and Katsina. There were other routes further east, but they do not come into this book.

northern Europe they met other races coming in from the east, so in Britain and in northern Europe, the people of the Mediterranean race were few compared with those of other races.

We do not know quite how long ago this happened: perhaps about ten thousand years ago. The earliest people of Egypt very likely belonged to the Mediterranean race, and it is seven or eight thousand years since Egyptian civilization began; it is about five thousand years since the men of the Mediterranean race reached Britain. We do not know where the Mediterranean race came from. Perhaps it grew up in the country which is now the Sahara desert; perhaps it came from a little further east, such as Arabia.

The Negro race too may have come from the east, or it may have grown up in the Sahara when the Sahara was a grass land. It may be that the Negro and the Mediterranean races grew up side by side in that great country, and that when the Sahara began to dry up so that the cattle could no longer find grass to eat and water to drink, the Mediterranean men moved north and the Negro men moved south. The people of Egypt knew the Negroes five thousand years ago, and painted pictures of them; and Negro skeletons have been found which are thousands of years older still.

The Negro race, like the European, is mixed. In the Congo and in South Africa there are peoples who are small in size, such as the Congo pygmies[1] and the Bushmen in South Africa. We know that a few hundred years ago, these small people lived in much of the country which is now Negro; and very likely some of the Negro peoples have mixed with them. There is another race called the Hamitic race, taller than the Bushmen and pygmies, fairer than the Negroes, which may have grown up in Arabia, or perhaps in North-East Africa. Some thousands of years ago, the Hamitic race grew in numbers until it had to find new country to live in. Some moved westward along the North African coast and mixed with the old Mediterranean race. Some moved westward, south of the Sahara, and mixed with the Negroes living in West Africa. Others moved south-ward, and mixed with the Negroes and perhaps with other

[1] Pygmy is the name given to certain tribes in the Congo who are very much shorter than most African or European peoples.

peoples to form the Bantu of Central and South Africa. It seems probable that by the time the Hamites came into North Africa, the sea had broken through and separated Africa from Europe, and the Hamites did not cross into Europe.

So the people of Europe are mixed, and the people of Africa are mixed; and some people of Africa are dark, while others are fair. When we are speaking about the peoples who lived between the Gulf of Guinea and the Mediterranean 2,000 or 3,000 years ago, we should not speak of white and black; for nowadays when we speak of white men we mean the people of Europe and of other countries (such as America and Australia) where Europeans have made their homes. The Hamites of North Africa are often called Berbers, and in this part of the book we shall speak of Berbers when we mean Hamites and other peoples of North Africa who are not Negro.

Now for our first question: who built up the old African kingdoms, Ghana and Mali and the others? The short answer is that they were built up by Berbers from north of the Sahara and Negroes from the south, working together; neither could have done it alone.

The first of these great kingdoms, as far as we know, was Ghana, which was begun about 1,600 years ago, some time between A.D. 300 and 400. At that time the Sahara had already become a desert, though it was perhaps not quite so wide or so dry as it is now. People could live in it with camels, but they could not grow crops in it except in the few places[1] where there was water. The Berbers grew crops along the Mediterranean coast, which had more water than it has now; and the Negroes grew crops south of the desert, as they do today. There were tracks across the desert, and traders used to cross it with their camels from one oasis to another, taking salt and cloth and horses and cattle and other things from the Mediterranean to the south, and going back with gold and slaves and ivory and kola-nuts.

About A.D. 300 or 400 some parties of Berbers crossed the desert and settled among the Negro peoples on the river Niger in the country between Timbuktu and Segu. The peoples of that country were Soninke, one of the divisions of the great Mandingo-speaking people. The newcomers were farmers and

[1] Called oases.

traders, and after a time they seem to have made themselves the rulers of the Soninke. We do not know how. They did not come as a conquering army. It may be that they brought with them something new in ways of fighting, such as weapons of iron, and horses, which gave them an advantage over the Soninke. They certainly came from a country which was highly civilized, for it was part of the Roman Empire, and only a few years earlier, a man from their country had become emperor of Rome. They must have had ideas of military discipline and of government which were better than those of the simple Soninke farmers, for no people in Europe or Africa or Asia had yet been able to resist the power of Rome.

It is true that the new-comers did not have things all their own way, for the Soninke turned against them and made them move a little further west. But there they were joined by others of their countrymen, and they began to feel stronger. The country in which they were living was at one end of the main paths over the desert; salt and gold and cloth and slaves all used to pass through it. That is a sure way to become rich. London and Chicago, for example, became rich in the same way: London, because all the trade from the Continent of Europe had to cross the river Thames there; Chicago, because all the corn and meat coming from the West has to pass through Chicago on its way to the ships. Similarly, Takoradi in modern Ghana was only a tiny fishing village until its harbour and railway were built; and then it quickly grew into a city.

So, although we do not know how the new-comers made themselves rulers of the Soninke, we may guess that it was through much wisdom and much money, and a little fighting. We do know that they set up a kingdom, and we are told that there were forty-four Berber kings one after another. But the Berbers were a small ruling group of people living among a much larger number of Negroes. As time went on, two things happened: the Berber rulers took Negro wives and mixed with the Negro people, and the Negro people watched the ways of the Berbers and learned from them. And so it happened that about the year 770, four hundred years after the kingdom was founded, the Soninke rose against their kings and beat them; and a Soninke king took the power.

We read about Ghana in a book called *Tarikh-es-Soudan*, written in Arabic by an African from Timbuktu about 300 years ago, which is more than 400 years after the kingdom of Ghana had come to an end. The *Tarikh-es-Soudan* is a history of the Sudan, and the writer tells us a great deal about the Songhai kingdom and how it ended; he knows less about Mali, and he knows very little indeed about Ghana. He tells us that the first king of Ghana was called Kayamaga, and there were 44 kings of Ghana in all; 'they were all white men', he says, 'but we do not know where they came from'. The peoples whom they ruled were called Wangara.[1] Of the 44 white kings, 22 lived before the time of the Prophet Mohammed and 22 afterwards; after this line of 44 kings, Ghana was conquered by Mali, whose kings were Negro.

That is all that the *Tarikh-es-Soudan* tells us about the history of Ghana. If that is all that the writer knows, it is plain that he had not read any book about Ghana. And what he tells us about the 44 kings of Ghana raises questions. He says that 22 of them lived in the 300 years from the beginning of Ghana to the time of the Prophet, and 22 of them in the 600 years from the Prophet to the end of the kingdom of Ghana in 1240. Is it likely that the later kings lived twice as long as the earlier? He tells us that all 44 were 'white', by which he means Berber; but he says nothing about the Soninke rising in 770, and the Soninke kings were Negro. I find it hard to believe the *Tarikh-es-Soudan* on this point. I can believe that the early kings of Ghana were Berber, and it may be that there were 44 of them in all; but I do not believe that all the 44 were Berber right up to the year 1240.

I don't like this. You say It may be; we may guess; we think; I do not believe. Don't you know?

No; that is the trouble. We know very little about the history of Ghana. There are three chief kinds of historical evidence: history told by word of mouth, letters and books and other written materials, and historical remains. Now so far, none of these three is of much help to us here. We are talking of a time

---

[1] The Wangara are the Mandingo people; the Soninke are one division of the Mandingo. The name Wangara is still used today; the Akan people in modern Ghana, for example, call the Mandingo Wangara.

so long ago that no African tribe or nation living today remembers it. (In the same way, the English nation of today remembers nothing of the history of the English tribes before they came and settled in England.) Then again, these early Berbers have left no writings about their own history; we have no written papers of any kind that have come down to us from old Ghana. The *Tarikh-es-Soudan* and other Arabic books tell us very little about its early history. Lastly, very little work has so far been done in searching for historical remains, and the remains that have been found have not told us much. More work of this kind will be done, and we shall learn more; but for the present we must often say *It may be* when we should like to be able to say *It is.*

Then can we believe any of this that you are telling us? Is it worth writing?

Oh yes. The broad outline is plain enough, even if we do not know many of the details. We have several ways of knowing that the Berbers came from North Africa across the desert into West Africa. Writers of the Roman empire tell us that some of the Berber peoples left Roman Africa and went south. Many West African peoples of today, such as the Hausa and the Akan, remember something of a fair race coming from the north, though it is not easy to find from them who the fair race was and when it came. Anyone can see that the Hausa, the Yoruba, and other West African peoples of today are a mixture of dark-skinned and fair-skinned peoples. And we learn a few facts from the *Tarikh-es-Soudan* and other books. One fact from here, another fact from there; as we go on, we shall have more facts and so shall have to do less guessing.

The kingdom of Ghana, first under Berber and then under Soninke kings, grew rich and strong. We do not know where the city of Ghana was. A book called the *Tarikh-es-Fettach*, written (like the *Tarikh-es-Soudan*) long afterwards, tells us that the capital city of Kayamaga was called Kumbi; and the *Tarikh-es-Soudan* tells us that Kayamaga was the first king of Ghana. In the last few years, the French have found the ruins of a city at Kumbi Saleh, about 200 miles north of Bamako: a city of about 30,000 people, just about where we should expect Kumbi to be. But they have so far found no writings, either on paper or cut in stone, except some texts from the Koran; so we are not able to be sure that Kumbi Saleh is old Ghana, though it probably is so.

It was gold that made Ghana rich, though gold was not found in Ghana itself but in the country just south of it, in what is today the republic of Guinea. Traders from Ghana bought the gold, and sold it to other traders coming down from North Africa. This West African gold trade was one of the chief ways in which gold came to Western Europe, which had no gold of its own and always wanted more. The Soninke were pagans, but many Muslim traders from the north came and lived in the kingdom of Ghana; and the capital city itself grew into two cities, a pagan and a Muslim city side by side. Under the Soninke kings, the kingdom grew until it stretched from the Senegal river to somewhere near where Timbuktu now stands: we may say about 500 miles from east to west, and 300 from north to south. We know nothing about the wars which the Soninke kings of Ghana must have fought to conquer other peoples and bring them into the Ghana kingdom.

We do not know all the peoples whom the Soninke conquered, but it is probable that most of them spoke some form of the Mandingo language, as the Soninke themselves did. In those days, the Negro peoples living between the river Senegal and the western frontier of modern Nigeria were divided into three main groups. All the way from the Senegal to the swamps of the Niger, and from the forest in the south to the desert in the north, there were the Mandingo people, divided into many tribes and nations. The Soninke were the Mandingo people who lived furthest north, the Malinke were those who lived furthest south. All the way along the river Niger were the Songhai people. In between the Songhai and the Mandingo were the peoples from whom the Moshi and Dagomba and Gurma and other peoples of today are descended. They lived in the country of the big bend of the Niger. Perhaps the Akan of modern Ghana too come from there.

We know very little about the peoples who were living in the forest. The great kingdoms of the Sudan (Ghana and the others) never touched the forest country. No doubt there were many small tribes living in the forest; but all the great nations of the forest country, such as the Ashanti and the Yoruba, have been formed by people coming in from the north and taking power over the people whom they found there.

It may seem strange that the great kingdoms never touched the forest country, since most of the gold and all the kola-nuts came from the forest. It is because they fought with cavalry.[1] Horses move quickly; and in open country soldiers on foot, standing in a line and armed only with spears and with bows and arrows, cannot stand against cavalry. But horses were no use in the forest; there were tsetse flies to kill them and no grass for them to eat, and it is much easier to move about in the forest on foot than on horseback. Of course, Ghana and Mali and Songhai had some foot-soldiers as well as cavalry, though they did not think much of them. They might perhaps have used their foot-soldiers to fight in the forest. But they never did. Perhaps they never thought of doing so. More likely, foot-soldiers who were used to walking in grass country with the open sky above them were too frightened to go into the dark forest, where the enemy hid behind trees and shot his poisoned arrows at them.

It we remember that Ghana and the other great kingdoms fought with cavalry, we may have the answer to another question. It is plain why Ghana became so rich, with its trade in gold and slaves and so on; but why did it become strong? There have been many rich countries which have been conquered by poorer countries. The answer is that an army of cavalry is expensive. If you are king, you may perhaps have a law, as they had in Western Europe at that time, that anyone who has a horse is to bring it and fight for you whenever you call him. But you cannot keep such an army as that together for very long. If you want to make big wars and conquer many peoples, you must have an army which is paid and trained to be always ready for war. This is what the Soninke kings had; and only a rich country could afford to have such an army.

It is all very well to have a large army of soldiers on foot and on horses and on camels, and to conquer a great kingdom. But when you have conquered your kingdom, you have to govern it; and it is not easy to govern a large country when you cannot travel or send messages quickly from one end of it to the other.

---

[1] Cavalry are soldiers who fight on horseback; soldiers who fight on foot are called foot-soldiers or infantry.

We must remember that railways, motor-cars, telephones, aeroplanes, radio—all these ways of travelling and sending messages quickly—have only been invented in the last 150 years; they did not exist in Africa or in Europe at the time of the kingdom of Ghana, or for long afterwards. Printing too was unknown, so that there could be no newspapers. The king of Ghana could not have anything like a modern Government department, which carries out the orders of the central Government all over the country. He might appoint one of his own friends as governor of a province, but on the whole he had to leave the local chiefs to look after their own people. The different peoples of the kingdom kept their own languages and customs. Many of them would not feel that it had done them any good to be made part of a great kingdom. On the contrary: when they were free, they had to pay taxes to their own chief; now that they were part of a great kingdom, they still had to pay taxes to him and also to the central Government as well. They would want to become free once more, and they would remain under the king only as long as they were afraid to break away. So the king must keep moving round his kingdom with part of his army, always showing himself, showing how good his government was and how strong it was. If he became too tired or too lazy to keep moving like this, he must expect trouble; and in fact, all the kingdoms of the Sudan met trouble of this sort.

Then does it do any good to make several small tribes join into one large kingdom?

Yes, it is a good thing. It is the traders who feel the most advantage. When they have to pass through many small countries, they will have difficulties because of the different languages and laws, even if the countries are at peace and are all well governed; and if some are badly governed, or there is war, the difficulties will be greater. Every time they cross from one country to another, they will have to pay a tax (called a customs duty) on their goods. But if the small countries are joined into one large country, there will be the same law everywhere, and there will be one official language, which many people will speak. Traders will usually have fewer taxes to pay when they cross from one province to another than they paid when those provinces were independent states; though this has not always been so. In such ways as these, trade is easier in one large kingdom than in many small states. If trade is easier, there will be more trade, and so the country will become richer.

Then why were not the different peoples of Ghana happy when they became part of one great kingdom?

Because most of them were not traders; they were poor and uneducated farmers. They could see that they now had to pay two taxes instead of one; but they did not understand that if the traders became richer the whole country would become richer, and they would all be helped. We do not always understand what is good for us.

Most of what we know about the kingdom of Ghana comes from a man called El-Bekri. He was an Arab who spent all his life in Spain and wrote a big book on geography. He lived from 1028 to 1094, and did not himself visit Ghana, but learned about it from Arab and Berber traders who visited it. El-Bekri was interested in geography, not in history. He tells us a good deal about the richness of the king's court and about the trade of the place.

El-Bekri tells us about the two cities which together formed the capital; the Muslim city had twelve mosques, and was built largely of stone, while the pagan city was mainly built of mud and thatch, though the king's palace, and no doubt a few other buildings too, were of stone. When the king sat in public, there was gold everywhere: gold on the king's clothes and head-dress, on the handles of the swords, on the harness of his horses, and on the collars of his dogs. The king had one gold nugget weighing thirty pounds; he used to tie his horse to it. Before the meeting opened, the king's drums were beaten; El-Bekri gives us their name, *deba*, and we are told that the Soninke today still have drums which they call *daba* or *taba*—no doubt the same word, changed somewhat in 900 years. (Languages are always changing; no Englishman of today could understand the English which his forefathers spoke in El-Bekri's time.) Many of the king's officers were Muslims, though the king himself and most of his people were pagan. The pagans knelt before the king and poured dust on their heads, the Muslims clapped their hands.

The king had an army of 200,000 men, one-fifth of whom had bows and arrows.

We hear a little about the customs of the country. The king of whom El-Bekri speaks was called Tenkamenin, who became king following his mother's brother. When a king of 1062 Ghana died, he was buried in a great mound of earth; clothes, food and drink were buried with him, and servants were killed and buried in the same mound grave so that their spirits could serve the king's spirit in the next world.

THE ALMORAVIDES

When El-Bekri wrote, the Soninke kingdom of Ghana was nearing its end. Wherever the desert and the cultivated land meet, there is trouble. The people of the desert are poor, and they always find it difficult to get enough food. They are tempted to go down into the rich farm lands and take by force the corn or cattle that they want, and anything else they can find. So it has been in Africa. The peoples of the desert were Berbers, and there was often fighting between them and the Soninke of Ghana. But the Berbers and the Soninke needed each other. The Berbers lived by providing caravans[1] of camels for the traders crossing the desert, and without their help no trade would have been possible. Not only this. The Sahara desert produced very little food, but it produced one thing which West Africa wanted: salt. No man can live without salt, and the grass and forest country had none. In the middle of the Sahara there were salt mines at Taghaza, and all West Africa got its salt from there. Salt was what the people of Wangara most wanted in exchange for their gold, and they were sometimes so hungry for salt that they would exchange an equal weight of gold dust for it.

If the Berbers and the Soninke had been left to themselves, they would no doubt have had quarrels and wars from time to time, but they would not have allowed the fighting to stop the trade for long. They both needed the trade too much.

But they were not left to themselves. The Arabs came, and

[1] Traders crossing the desert with their camels used to travel in large parties, sometimes with as many as 30,000 camels. A party of traders with their camels is called a caravan.

made trouble for them both. The Arabs first came into Africa
very soon after the time of the Prophet. By 642 they had
conquered all the land from Persia to Egypt; and in 642 they
began to advance westward from Egypt along the Mediterranean
coast. They had much fighting with the Berbers. In 678 they
reached the Atlantic, but the Berbers defeated them and drove
them right back to Egypt. A few years later this happened again;
which makes us believe that the Arabs must have been few in
number. But in 708 the Arabs again reached the Atlantic, this
time to stay; and in 711 a Berber named Tarik, who had
become a Muslim, led an army of Arabs and Berbers across the
Straits of Gibraltar[1] to conquer Spain.

It was the Arabs who brought Islam into North Africa, and
ever since then, most of the peoples of North Africa have been
Muslims and have spoken Arabic. Many of the Berber tribes
became Muslims, but this did not make them love the Arabs,
and there was often much fighting. Luckily for the Berbers,
most of the Arabs crossed over into Spain to share in its riches,
so that in Africa the Berbers were able to remain more or less
independent.

Muslim Spain became very rich, and highly civilized; much
more civilized than Western Europe or the Berber lands in
Africa. At first, Spain and North Africa formed one kingdom,
called the Kingdom of the Two Shores; but after a time, the
Kingdom broke up, and there were several independent Muslim
states both in North Africa and in Spain. There was much trade
between Spain and North Africa, and the North African
countries learned much of Spanish civilization, though the
Arabs in Spain were far ahead of the Berbers in Africa, or indeed
of England and France and other countries of Western Europe.

**What do you mean when you talk of civilization, and say that
the civilization of Muslim Spain was more advanced than that of
Western Europe, or of the Berbers?**

Well, first of all, civilization is not a matter of riches, or of
modern inventions like radio and aeroplanes and electricity.
People were civilized before these things were thought of. A
country may be highly civilized though poor; ancient Greece

[1] Gibraltar is named after Tarik. Its name comes from the Arabic *Gebr-al-Tarik*,
meaning Tarik's hill.

was a poor country, but we of today are still learning from its civilization.

A civilized man is unselfish, and is ready to listen to other people who disagree with him. He knows the law and obeys it, even if he sees a chance of breaking it without being found out, and of making profit for himself by doing so. A civilized government makes good laws, and makes it easy for people to obey them; peace and good order are important parts of civilization.

But that is not enough. Civilized people love studying such things as science and mathematics; and they love the arts, such as poetry, music, painting, and architecture.[1] When we say that the civilization of Muslim Spain was more advanced than that of Western Europe, we mean that there was more peace and good government in Spain than in Western Europe; and that Spain had more artists and poets and mathematicians and thinkers than Western Europe, and on the whole they did better work.

In the eleventh century, just when the civilization of Spain and of North Africa was at its height, a new Arab army came from Egypt. These Arabs were poor men from the Arabian desert, and there were very many of them; one Arab writer of North Africa says that they covered the country like a swarm of locusts. And they did as much damage as a swarm of locusts. They were men from the desert, and they did not know anything about the civilized agriculture of the rich coast land. They defeated the Berbers and took all the country near the coast; they destroyed towns and dams and bridges and water-works, and their goats ate up the young trees and bushes. Much land went out of cultivation, and the desert crept forward. Life for the Berbers became harder as the desert became bigger and their trade became smaller. Some Arab tribes came south of the Sahara, others fought against the desert tribes and made them move away. And thus, the Berbers and the Soninke were thrown closer together.

The capital of Ghana was at Kumbi, and fifteen days journey west of Kumbi[2] was the town of Audoghast, which was the

[1] Architecture is the art of making beautiful buildings; the architect is the man who practises this art.
[2] Perhaps 150 or 200 miles west. We are told that Audoghast was one-third of the way from Kumbi to Arguin near Cape Blanco, which was about 600 miles.

capital of a strong Berber state. It lay on the edge of the desert, and like Kumbi, it was rich with the trade between North and West Africa across the Sahara. In the days of king Tiloutan of Audoghast (who died in 837), and again in the days of king Tin Yeroutane (about the year 960), the Berbers were very strong, and they gave much trouble to the Soninke kings of Ghana. But soon after the death of Tin Yeroutane, some of the Berber tribes rose up against the government of Audoghast, and there was a time of civil war[1] and weakness. The kingdom of Ghana took advantage of this to take back again some of the land it had lost; and by about the year 1000 the town of Audoghast itself had to pay taxes to the king of Ghana.

This meant that Ghana had pushed its boundary right up to the edge of the desert, and the Berbers had no foothold at all on the grass. The Berber tribes of the desert saw that when they quarrelled among themselves, the Soninke pushed forward; and their only hope of pushing the Soninke back was to drop their quarrels and join together.

But things did not happen just as the Berbers hoped. In the year 1048 their king Yahia ibn Omar[2] visited the holy places at Mecca, as a good Muslim should do; and he brought back with him a religious teacher called Abdullah ibn Yasin. Ibn Yasin was shocked to see how careless the Berbers were in their religion; and the Berbers were shocked when they heard the strict discipline which he preached to them. They burned his house and drove him away and would listen to him no more. Two faithful followers went with him; and the three men went and settled on an island in the river Senegal. Here Ibn Yasin went on preaching; and many Muslims from the desert and from North Africa came to join him. His followers were called in Arabic 'the people of the hermitage',[3] and the Arabic words have become softened into *Almoravides*.

As soon as they were strong enough, the Almoravides set out from the Senegal to force the Berber tribes to accept Ibn Yasin's preaching. The tribes were divided, and only wanted to be

[1] A civil war is a war between people of the same state or nation: for example, English fighting against English.

[2] The word *ibn* in Arabic means *son of;* Ibn Omar means *son of Omar.*

[3] A hermit is a man who lives all alone in order to pray to God; the place where he lives is called his hermitage. Ibn Yasin had two other men with him, so he was not strictly a hermit; but near enough.

comfortable; the Almoravides were united and strictly disciplined. Before long, Ibn Yasin had made himself master of all
the tribes of the western desert; and then king Yahia took the
Almoravide army and led it to attack other countries. In 1054
he retook Audoghast, at the southern end of the great caravan
road; two years later he took Sijilmasa,[1] at the northern end.

Yahia knew that in taking Sijilmasa, which belonged to the
king of Morocco and was not a desert town at all, he was
making trouble for himself. Sooner or later, an army would
come to throw the Almoravides back into the desert. Should
he stay where he was and wait for it, or should he go back into
the desert at once? He decided to do neither, but to go preaching
and fighting straight forward into Morocco itself. He led his
men across the Atlas mountains to the sea, and conquered the
whole country; but in 1057 he was killed in battle.

When king Yahia died, a man named Abu Bekr became
leader of the Almoravides, and he went on with the war in the
north. But he soon received news from home which made him
leave the fighting line. Two of the Berber tribes, the Lemtuna
and the Mesufa, were quarrelling. Both belonged to the Almoravides; but if the Almoravides began quarrelling among themselves, their power would soon be lost. Abu Bekr decided that
he must go south to see to this himself. He handed over the
army to his cousin Yusuf, and told him to carry on
1062   with the war. Yusuf did so; he conquered the whole
of Morocco and founded the town of Marrakech, he
crossed over into Spain and made himself master of the Muslim
kingdom there, he defeated the Christians of Spain, and extended the power of the Almoravides right up to the river Ebro.

Meanwhile, Abu Bekr soon brought the Lemtuna and the
Mesufa to make peace with each other again; but he saw that
they would not long remain at peace unless he gave them some
work to do. So he did what many other rulers have done who
were troubled by quarrels and fighting at home: he called on
his people to leave off quarrelling with one another and join in
fighting an outside enemy. This enemy was Ghana.

We have seen on page 47 that the Berbers had had trouble
with Ghana. Tiloutan was chief of the Lemtuna, and Audoghast

[1] Sijilmasa, like Audoghast and Kumbi, no longer exists; but we know where
it was.

was the Lemtuna capital. Before the Almoravide movement began, the Lemtuna and other Berber tribes had been planning to join together to push back the Soninke of Ghana. Now Abu Bekr called on them to take up this plan again. But the Berbers were not as strong as they had been, for many of their best fighting men were away with Yusuf in the north. Perhaps this is why Abu Bekr did not try and conquer Ghana with the Lemtuna and other desert tribes alone. He brought in the Fulani from Tekrur, a country near the mouth of the River Senegal. Tekrur was Ghana's western neighbour, and was also Ghana's rival in the desert trade. Both the Fulani and also the Berber tribes of the desert thus had reason to dislike the Soninke of Ghana. Moreover, most of the Soninke were still pagan, and the Almoravides were determined to destroy paganism and spread Islam.

We do not know how long the war lasted. It ended in 1076, but it is not likely that Abu Bekr waited nearly fourteen years before beginning a war which he and his men so badly wanted. In 1076, Abu Bekr and the Fulani conquered Ghana. Kumbi was destroyed; its people were killed or enslaved; many of the Soninke were forced to become Muslims; and the whole of the kingdom of Ghana became part of the Almoravide empire.

This was not quite the end of Ghana. Abu Bekr died in 1087, eleven years after taking Kumbi; and after his death the Lemtuna and the other Berber tribes began quarrelling again. This gave the Soninke their chance. They rose against the Almoravides and retook Kumbi and became free once more. But the kingdom of Ghana, like the Almoravide movement, was made up of many peoples and tribes, and was only strong while they worked together. After 1087 they did not work together. The Soninke kings were obeyed only in a small part of their old kingdom. Other parts became independent. Some of the Fulani from Tekrur built up a kingdom in the province of Kaniaga; a few years later the kingdom of Kaniaga was strong enough to conquer another province of Ghana, called Diara; and in 1203 king Sumanguru of Kaniaga was strong enough to send an army against Kumbi itself. He beat the Soninke king and took his country; and no doubt he hoped to become rich by controlling the trade across the desert, as the Soninke kings before him had done. But he was disappointed. The traders and the business men of Kumbi were not prepared to pay taxes to Sumanguru. They left the city and moved a hundred miles north into the desert to a place called Walata, where the caravans used to camp. They turned the desert camp into a city, and the trade which used to come to Kumbi now came to Walata. Kumbi, having lost its trade and most of its people, was no longer a city but a village.

The kingdom which began in Kaniaga is called the Susu kingdom because the Susu were the ruling people in it. But it did not last long. Away to the south of Kaniaga there was growing up a new kingdom called the kingdom of Kangaba. Its people, like the Soninke, were part of the Mandingo people. They had recently become Muslims, while most of the Susu were still pagans; and this may have helped them to become strong. They were fighting against the pagan tribes to the south and south-east of them; and Sumanguru, the Susu king, began to be afraid of them. He tried to weaken the Kangaba kingdom without war, by trying to make the chiefs of its different tribes quarrel with one another. In this, he had some success; and soon he saw another chance of weakening Kangaba. Its king died, and there were twelve brothers to succeed him. Sumanguru tried to kill them all, and he did kill eleven of them. But the twelfth, who was a child, and a sickly child, grew to manhood and Sumanguru could not touch him. His name was Sundiata, and he is sometimes called Mari Djata.

Sundiata could not be a friend of the man who had killed his eleven brothers and tried to kill him. But before he could fight Sumanguru, he must first make his own position safe in his own country. He must make the chiefs of all the tribes obey him as king. He did this by setting up a standing army[1], as the Soninke kings had done before him. He became king in 1230, and in two or three years he had become so strong that Sumanguru saw that he must fight. The Susu army attacked Kangaba in 1235, but Sundiata defeated them in a battle at Kirina, which was probably close to the Niger, near the town of Kulikoro. Sumanguru was killed in the battle, and Sundiata then marched into the Susu country. By 1240 he was master of all the Susu kingdom; in that year he destroyed the village which was all

[1] A standing army is an army which is paid and trained to be always ready for war.

that was left of Kumbi, and the desert crept in to cover the ruins. That was the end of Ghana.

The kingdom which Sundiata made out of the little state of Kangaba grew into a great and powerful kingdom called the kingdom of Mali or Melle, even greater than the kingdom of Ghana.

Wait a moment before you start with the story of Mali. What is the connection between the modern state of Ghana and the old kingdom of Ghana, which you say ended in 1240?

There is not as close a connection as there is between modern England and the England of a thousand years ago. The tribes who were the forefathers of the Englishmen of today came to England 1,500 years ago, and the country has been called England ever since. The English language today has changed from the English spoken by those early tribes, but it has changed gradually; and for more than a thousand years there have been English books in which we can watch the language changing. We can see, too, how the English nation has been gradually built up out of the old English tribes. The history is continuous. There is no such connection as this between old and new Ghana. The modern country of Ghana never formed part of old Ghana. The people of old Ghana were Soninke, the most northerly branch of the Mandingo people; and neither the Soninke nor any other Mandingo people have ever lived in modern Ghana. The people of modern Ghana like to think that one of their peoples, the Akan, is descended from some of the people of old Ghana who refused to become Muslims when Abu Bekr took Kumbi in 1076. The Akan themselves do not remember this. They remember coming down from a home in the north somewhere in the Niger bend. The Akan language of today is no more like Soninke than English is like French. On the other hand, although the old home of the Akan in the Niger bend was not part of the kingdom of Ghana, the civilization of old Ghana spread far outside its frontiers[1]. In their old home, the Akan certainly learnt much of the customs and civilization of old Ghana, and they brought much of it with them when they came

[1] The frontier is a country's boundary, where the laws change, and the money, and perhaps the language; where the police look at your passport and the customs officers look at your luggage. The civilization of a great country like America or China—or old Ghana—will influence land outside the country's political frontier.

south. This is the main reason why the Government of the Gold Coast changed the name of the country to Ghana; they looked back to old Ghana as the origin of their African civilization.

Another question about Ghana: is it true that the name Guinea comes from the name Ghana?

We cannot be sure; but it is probable that it does. Or it may be that *Guinea* and *Ghana* are both forms of a Berber word meaning *black*. The name Guinea was not known in Europe until after the fall of Ghana. But in a map drawn in 1375, we find the name GINYIA in big letters marked in the southern part of the desert, between Taghaza and Timbuktu; and the map shows a picture of 'Musa Mali', whom it calls 'Lord of the Negroes of *Guineua*'. (This is probably Mansa Musa, who was king of Mali from 1307 to 1332.) Some people think that the name Guinea comes from the city of Jenne. Jenne was an important city, rich and learned; but it never became the capital of a great kingdom. It seems more likely that people far away in Morocco and in Europe should hear and remember the name of the great kingdom of Ghana than that of one city. And 'Musa Mali' was *not* lord of Jenne; for Jenne, strangely enough, was independent. So I think that the name Guinea comes from the name Ghana.

THE KINGDOM OF MALI

The capital of the state of Kangaba was the town of Jeriba, on the banks of the Niger close to the frontier of modern Guinea. When Sundiata took the whole of the Susu kingdom and added it to Kangaba, Jeriba was too far to the south-west to be the capital of the kingdom of Mali. So in the same year, 1240, he built a new capital city at Niani, also on the Niger but much further down-stream, close to Segu; his new city came to be called Mali, just as the capital city of Ghana had often been called Ghana.

After 1240, Sundiata himself did no more fighting, but his generals went out conquering and extending the boundaries of his kingdom in all directions. They conquered lands beyond the Senegal which Ghana had never conquered: lands which were

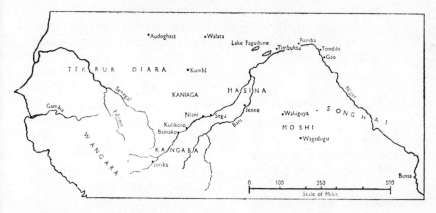

MAP 2. GHANA, MALI, AND SONGHAI

No boundaries are shown on this map, because nobody knows exactly how the boundaries ran; and we do know that the kingdoms became greater and smaller from time to time. Kumbi is marked; this was the capital of Ghana. Diara and Kaniaga were provinces of Ghana, and perhaps Kangaba too was so at one time. Audoghast was the furthest the power of Ghana ever reached in the north-west, and Tekrur was always independent.

At one time, Mali covered all the country along the Niger as far as Gao, and as far into the desert as Taghaza and Tadmekket (see Map 1). But Tekrur in the west, and Moshi in the south-east, were always independent. The Songhai kingdom was the biggest of all; it stretched eastward beyond the Niger and took in all the Mali country as well. Almost all the land on this map would be included in the Songhai kingdom except Wangara, Moshi and Tekrur.

important because it was from them that the gold came. They reached the Gambia river, and pushed far down the Senegal to the frontiers of Tekrur. No doubt they hoped to be able to increase the output of gold; but they could not. They left the work of mining the gold to the pagan tribes who had been doing it for centuries; and whenever the Mali people tried to make the miners get more gold, or tried to make them give up their paganism and become Muslims, the miners simply left off digging, and there was no gold at all.

But you said that Mali had conquered these gold-bearing lands. Could they not force the people to dig, or else turn them out and do the mining themselves?

Well, that is certainly what the Spaniards did when they conquered South America. We are told that Mali had conquered these lands of Wangara with their gold-mines; but I wonder how much that means. It must mean that they had won a battle there: but it is one thing to win a battle and quite another thing to rule a country by force. I expect it is the old story: people from the grass country did not like to live and work in the forest; they were afraid of the forest people with their poisoned arrows, and afraid too of the gods of the forest and the mines. No doubt, being Muslims, the Mali people would not believe in these gods, or worship them; but they would think of them as evil spirits, and be afraid of them. Anyway, there is the fact: although they claimed to have conquered the gold-mines, they soon left the people to go on mining in the old way, buying their gold with the salt that the miners wanted so much.

Sundiata died in 1255, and was succeeded by Mansa Ule, who ruled until 1270. Then came a time of trouble; there were seven more kings between 1270 and 1307. But in 1307 a grandson of Sundiata became king, called Mansa Musa, and ruled until 1332. Under him, the kingdom of Mali became still greater and richer. His generals took Walata far away in the north, and pushed down the Niger and conquered the country of the Songhai. The capital of the Songhai was Gao on the Niger, and their country stretched down the river on both sides as far as the frontiers of modern Nigeria. The Songhai, or at least their kings, had been Muslims since their king Za-Kosoi became a Muslim in the year 1009, that is nearly fifty years before the time of the Almoravides.

Besides Gao, the Songhai had another important city: Timbuktu. Timbuktu was founded by the Berbers from the desert in 1087, and it soon became an important trading place. It had not only a caravan trade across the desert, but trade up and down the river Niger. At some time, probably not long after it was founded, the Songhai had taken it from the Berbers, and it was now a Songhai town. This brought it more trade, for Songhai rule extended for several hundred miles down the river. It began to attract trade from Walata, and there came from Walata not only traders, but also learned men; Timbuktu was already beginning to be a centre of civilization and learning, as well as of trade. This was still more the case when Timbuktu, like Gao, became part of the kingdom of Mali, so that there was peace and freedom of trading and travelling for hundreds of miles all round. Mansa Musa brought a famous architect from Spain to build a new mosque in Timbuktu, and built himself a stone palace in the town. There was an older mosque in Timbuktu, which was the centre of what we should now call a university. Mansa Musa brought from Mecca a famous lawyer to teach at the university. But we are told that when the lawyer reached Timbuktu, he found that there were many Songhai lawyers in the city who knew more than he did; so he went away to study at Fez in Morocco for three years before he was ready to teach law in the university of Timbuktu.

Under Mansa Musa, the kingdom of Mali stretched so far into the desert that it took in the salt mines of Taghaza and the copper mines of Takedda; and it stretched very far to the west, almost as far as the Atlantic. In all the country between the Niger, the forest, and the Senegal, the only places which were not part of the kingdom of Mali were the town of Jenne, lying in the marshes of the Niger, and the Moshi kingdom which was growing up round Wagadugu and Wahiguya in the upper part of the Volta valley.

We do not know many details of the history of Mali; but it happens that we know a great deal about its riches and its customs. Mansa Musa himself, like a good Muslim, made the pilgrimage to Mecca in 1324, and we have a description of the king and his company written by a man called El-Omari, who was in Egypt some years after he passed through Egypt, and spoke to many who had seen him. And in 1352 and 1353, a famous traveller from Tangier, called Ibn Batuta, visited Mali and wrote a full description of what he saw during a stay of several months.

Mansa Musa went to Mecca by way of Walata and Tuat and Cairo, and came back through Ghadames and Gao. He took with him a very large party; some say 60,000 people, but that seems too many to believe; it would be almost impossible to feed so many people in the desert. We can easily believe the tale that there marched in front of the king a body of 500 men each carrying a gold staff weighing about four pounds. He took with him eighty camel loads of gold dust for his travelling expenses and for the gifts which a good Muslim and a great king must make to the holy places and to the poor. El-Omari tells us that the people of Egypt were impressed[1] by the generous way in which the king gave his gifts and spent his money: by the simple and well-mannered behaviour of his people (who did not know the prices of things, and would willingly pay more than a thing was worth): by the king's own piety[2] and kindness. By the time he got back from Mecca as far as Cairo, the king had spent nearly all his eighty camel loads of gold, and had to borrow more from the bankers and merchants there. One merchant of Alexandria who had lent him money came all the way back to Mali with the king to be repaid. The man died at Timbuktu, but Mansa Musa sent the money across the desert to the man's children at Alexandria. El-Omari tells us that one lawyer in Cairo asked the king how big his country was. Mansa Musa was not sure: 'about a year's journey across', he thought; but the man found this hard to believe, and after asking other people he thought that four months' journey each way would be nearer the truth. This was a good guess. Ibn Batuta, writing thirty years later, tells us that he took two months to cross the desert from Sijilmasa to Walata, and another twenty-four days to get from Walata to Niani, the capital of Mali. He did not go south of Niani, but it could easily have taken him another month to reach the southern frontier near the sources[3] of the Niger. As for the distance from east to west, it must have been about 1,000 miles from Takedda to the Gambia: three months' journey at least.

Ibn Batuta is the man who has told us most about the way in which the people of Mali lived. He was born at Tangier in Morocco in 1304, and when he was a young man he went on pilgrimage to Mecca. This journey gave him a taste for travelling; and instead of going home he went further on. He went through Asia Minor and Persia to India, and visited Ceylon, China, Sumatra and East Africa; and returned home after being away twenty-four years. After only three years at home he set out once more, this time to visit Mali. When he stayed at Sijilmasa he found that the man with whom he was staying had

[1] Impressed: that is, surprised and pleased; so surprised that they remembered what they had seen long afterwards.
[2] Many people know what their religion tells them to do, but they do not do it. A pious man is one who behaves in the way his religion tells him to behave; piety is the habit of behaving in this way.
[3] The source is the place where the river first comes out of the ground.

a brother in China, whom Ibn Batuta had met when he was there years before. As we say, it is a small world;[1] but we are surprised to find such a thing happening in those days when travelling is so much more difficult than it is now.

Ibn Batuta found both the Berber and the Negro people of Walata good Muslims; they wore fine clothes imported[2] from Egypt; the women he thought were very pretty, and they had much more freedom than he was accustomed to seeing among Muslims. He thought it very strange that (as among so many African peoples today) families descended through women: a man's heirs[3] were his sister's children, not his own.

On the twenty-four days' journey to Niani, Ibn Batuta found the road so safe that there was no need to travel in parties; there were plenty of villages, and it was easy to buy food on the way. He carried beads, spices, and salt for barter; there was no coined money. Both on this journey, and on his other journeys in Mali, he tells us that travelling was quite safe; there was nothing to fear from robbers, and if you were cheated it was easy to obtain justice. He saw a man make a complaint against the governor of Walata; the governor was brought to Niani, tried, found guilty, and punished; and the man received back the money of which the governor had cheated him. He was very impressed with the justice he found in Mali; he said that the people hated injustice more than any other people—and remember that he had been to Delhi and Peking and knew what he was talking about. He tells us of course a great deal about the gold and the richness of the king's court, though he did not like seeing people pour dust on their heads (as they used to do at Kumbi in the days of Ghana) to show respect for the king, and he could never get used to the free and easy way in which women went about in public instead of staying at home and being veiled. Having seen the beautiful buildings of India and China, Ibn Batuta did not think highly of the mud and brick buildings of Mali, but he thought highly of the music and dancing and other entertainments. He met plenty of lawyers and learned

[1] We often say this when we meet a stranger and are surprised to find that he knows a friend of ours: 'What, you know Jack Smith? I have known him since we were at college together; well, it is a small world!'

[2] To import means to bring goods into a country; to export means to send goods out.

[3] That is, the children who were in his family and would have his goods when he died.

men, judges and teachers; he saw a good deal of the army, which was strong and well trained. Children were made to learn the Koran, and there were plenty of books in the country.[1] Prices of goods were reckoned in gold dust; the unit was the *mithqal*, and eight *mithqals* made an ounce. People used gold dust for large amounts, and cowry shells (which were coming in from the East African coast) for small amounts; but in the small villages trade was carried on by barter.[2] There were slaves everywhere; some of them were educated, and educated slaves (especially women) were very expensive.[3]

That is Mali as Ibn Batuta saw it; and no doubt Ghana was much the same in its day. A large, peaceful, slow-moving country, where justice was good, and life was pleasant for the rich people with their pretty clothes and their books and music and poetry. No doubt the poor people (Ibn Batuta did not talk much to them) were illiterate and lived hard lives as farmers or porters[4] or camel-drivers; but it was a good thing for them that they lived in a country where they could complain to the king if anyone wronged them, and the king would give them justice.

THE SONGHAI

Mansa Musa died in 1332, and there were signs of trouble to come. On his way home from Mecca, he had called at Gao and taken back with him the two sons of the king of Songhai. A hundred years earlier, Sumanguru had tried to weaken the country of Mali by killing all the sons of its king; now Mansa Musa was trying to weaken the Songhai, not by killing the king's sons but by keeping them far away from their own land and their own people. As soon as Mansa Musa was dead, these two young men saw their chance; they slipped away from Niani and got to Gao. Here we see the weakness of these old kingdoms. The Government must have guessed where they would go, but once they got away it could not catch them. It sent messengers on horseback with the news that they had escaped; but all that

[1] But remember that there was no printing, so that all books had to be written by hand. When we speak of plenty of books before the days of printing, we mean books in hundreds, not in tens of thousands.

[2] Barter is trading without money: exchanging salt for beads, for example.

[3] When Mansa Musa was in Egypt, people noticed that fine cloth and women slaves were the two things that all his people wanted to buy to take home.

[4] A porter is a man who earns his living by carrying loads.

the young men had to do was to keep ahead of the messengers, and they were able to do that. They reached Gao, and called on the Songhai people there to help them; the Songhai rose against the Mandingo soldiers whom Mansa Musa had stationed there, and drove them out. Gao was again free, and one of the Songhai princes, called Ali Kolen, became king of the Songhai.

Another bad event was that the Moshi people, who lived in the upper part of the Volta valley, attacked Timbuktu, and took the city and burned it. Peace could only be kept if the king was always ready for war; as soon as he closed his eyes, there were enemies waiting to attack his country.

Mansa Musa was followed as king by his son Maghan. If families descended through women, how did the king's son become king? It looks as if there was trouble. Perhaps that is why Maghan ruled only for four years. In 1336, Mansa Musa's brother Suleiman became king. He was a strong king, and did something to restore the power of the Mali kingdom; but he could not retake Gao, and he could not hold Walata and some other northern towns against the men of the desert. Tekrur also had regained some of the land it had lost, so that Mali was smaller than it had been in Mansa Musa's time; but it was again at peace. As long as the king could keep his country peaceful, so that, as Ibn Batuta found in Mansa Suleiman's time, people could travel safely alone and find food and lodging wherever they stayed, so long would life go on: the salt and the gold, and the slaves and cotton cloth and books and all kinds of trade goods would move up and down, writers would have time and freedom to write and teachers to teach. All this life was based on agriculture and mining, on the hard work of the men with the hoe and the pick-axe. When war broke up this peaceful life, then trade was interrupted and learning went down; and if war was long and bitter, then even agriculture would be interrupted and the food supply might fail.

After Suleiman's death, Mali became weaker still; 1360 and power began to pass to the Songhai.

The Songhai were a people, mainly Negro, whose early home was on both banks of the Niger upstream from about Bussa in Nigeria. Long ago—some say about 650, others about 850—they had been conquered by Berbers from the desert. The

Berber kings began to extend Songhai power further and further up-stream; their capital lay near the place where the Niger enters modern Nigeria, but as their country grew, the capital city became uncomfortably far from the middle. Just as Sundiata had to move his capital from Jeriba to Niani, so the Songhai had to move theirs. In 1009, King Za-Kosoi became a Muslim, and next year he moved his capital to Gao, nearer the middle of his country and nearer to the trade routes.

After Za-Kosoi there were twelve more Muslim kings of Songhai before 1325, when Mansa Musa conquered the country and took away the two sons of Za-Yasiboi. It was in 1336 that Ali Kolen became king of Songhai, but for many years after that, he and the kings who followed him had to defend themselves against Mali. Ali Kolen did not take the title of Za, which all earlier kings of Songhai had used, but took the new title of Sonni. All later kings of Songhai used this title.

Sonni Ali Kolen was followed by his brother Suleiman, and a whole line of kings followed them. After a time they ceased to pay taxes to Mali, and the kings of Mali were not strong enough to make them pay again. They were attacked by the Moshi, and by the Berbers from the desert. But they held on. Their state did not grow, but it was too hard to be broken.

In 1434, the Berbers attacked Timbuktu, which was still held by Mali. This was not a short attack like that of the Moshi 100 years before; the Berbers did not want to burn Timbuktu, they wanted to hold it. They did hold it, and Mali could not take it from them again. At first it did not make much difference to life in the city. Timbuktu was ruled by a governor called a Koi, who had all the power in his hands, and who was paid one-third of the taxes which he collected for the king. When the Berbers took Timbuktu, they told the Koi to continue to rule the city in the old way; and as he was a good man, all went well. But after thirty years, he died, and the Berbers appointed a new Koi. This man seems to have been very different. The people of the town did not respect him; there was disorder and discontent; and many of the rich and learned people of Timbuktu left the city and went back to Walata to live in peace. And then a thing happened which started much trouble. The Berber chief decided that the Koi need not be paid any part of the taxes; all the revenue[1] of the city should come to the Berbers. Of course, the governor must live, and the work of government must go on; so this meant that the tax-payers of Timbuktu must pay yet more, and pay without the Berbers getting to hear of it. The Koi sent a messenger to the king of Songhai, promising to give up the city of Timbuktu to him if he would come and set it free from the Berbers.

The king of Songhai at the time was Sonni Ali, who became king about 1464. He accepted the Koi's offer, and marched on Timbuktu. He came from the south, which meant that he would need boats to take his army across the Niger; and no doubt the Koi must have promised to see that the boats were ready. But for some reason the boats were not ready, and Sonni Ali could not get across the river; he had to take his army back and cross the river lower down, so that he could come to Timbuktu from the east, marching along the left bank of the river. So the people of Timbuktu, and the Berbers of the desert, had plenty of time to prepare; the Songhai could not take the city by surprise. The Berber chiefs, and many of the scholars and learned men, and the Koi too, left the city and escaped across the desert to Walata: a journey which was long and painful for the learned men. We are told that many of them had spent all their lives in the class-room and library, and had never before been on camel-back.[2] Sonni Ali took the city in January, 1468, burnt many of the buildings, and killed many of the people, including many of the university people. For three years he went on hunting and killing the learned men, even after they had left the city. We do not know why; perhaps he thought the university and the richer merchants were not to be trusted, because they had asked him to come to help them, and had escaped to Walata when he came.[3]

Sonni Ali was a great fighter, but he was a difficult man to

---

[1] Revenue is the money which the Government collects in taxes of all kinds.
[2] They had 500 miles to go, so they had time to learn camel-riding, though many of them fell off when their camels first rose to their feet.
[3] Sonni Ali himself said that they were too friendly with the Berbers, but this does not seem enough reason for what he did. Perhaps he thought that they were just as likely to call in the Berbers against him as to call him in against the Berbers. Why did the Koi go to Walata? Was it because he thought Sonni Ali would be angry with him for not providing the boats, or did the Berbers force him to go with them?

deal with. His mother was a pagan woman from a village near Sokoto (a Hausa woman, then), and he himself, though he called himself a Muslim, cared very little about his religion. He was very hot-tempered, and would order even one of his friends to be killed if the man made him at all angry. Afterwards he would be very sorry for what he had done; so there grew up a custom at his court that if in his anger he gave orders for a man to be killed, they would take the man away and hide him until the king said, 'I wish I had not killed so-and-so; he was a good man'. Then they would confess that the man was not yet dead, and would bring him back. It seems that the king was glad when this happened, instead of being angry that his orders had not been obeyed. You had to be careful with him; but he could be a good friend, and he had many friends. If he was merciless in his killing and burning, he could also be generous. The university people of Timbuktu must have been terrified of him; but once, when he had won a war against the Moshi, he sent them as a present a batch of beautiful women prisoners. He was lucky in having a very good minister called Mohammed Abu-Bekr Et-Touri, who knew him and understood him. Abu-Bekr was a strict Muslim, very well educated, wise and kindly. It was he who started the custom of hiding a man who the king had said was to be killed. He made it his business to see that in spite of the king's hot temper and violence, the country should be wisely governed. He was not afraid to stand up to the king and tell him he was wrong; and Sonni Ali, who would listen to nobody else, would listen to him.

Sonni Ali was a great fighter. He set up a strong standing army, and for nearly thirty years he led it in one war after another to extend the Songhai kingdom. He took the town of Jenne, which had never been part of the kingdom of Mali, though the Mali kings had often tried to take it. He sat outside Jenne with his army for a long time before the city gave itself up—seven years, seven months, and seven days, we are told. As he did not have to attack the town and lose many of his men in the fighting, he treated Jenne kindly; nobody in the town was killed, and nobody's house was burnt, and when the young chief of Jenne came out to give up his city, Sonni Ali treated him with much honour and kindness.

While the king with one army was at Jenne, other armies defeated the Moshi, and took more land in the bend of the Niger. In 1480, the Moshi sent an army as far as Walata; they took the town and held it for a month, but then Sonni Ali came after them and they had to run home and leave behind them the prisoners and the property they had taken from the town. Sonni Ali would have liked to take Walata and hold it as part of his kingdom, and he actually began to cut a canal 200 miles long from Lake Faguibine to Walata, so that people could go there by boat. But he did not finish the work.

1483

The Moshi made another attack, this time against Timbuktu; and Sonni Ali, who was out in the desert watching the men digging his canal, had to leave the work and go back with his army to fight the Moshi once more. From 1483 to 1486 he fought them and won battles in their country. The Moshi, finding Sonni Ali too strong for them, turned against the kingdom of Mali. Mali, being pressed on all sides—by the Moshi, by Songhai, and by Tekrur—looked in a new direction for help. It asked the Portuguese, who were now busily trading along the coast, if they would send help against the Moshi and others. But the Portuguese wisely said no.

1482

While the Moshi, having escaped from Sonni Ali at Walata, were making their army ready to march against Timbuktu, the Portuguese were building Elmina Castle on the Gold Coast.

1487-
1513

The Portuguese had heard of Sonni Ali, and had heard also of the strong Moshi kingdom. They sent both to Sonni Ali and to the Moshi king, asking for their friendship. They wanted the Moshi to trade with Elmina, not knowing how far away Elmina was, and how difficult it would be for traders to make the journey. They asked Sonni Ali if they might open a trading station in his kingdom, and he allowed them to open a station at Wadan, a little way inland from Cape Blanco. But Wadan was too far away from the main trade roads to be worth keeping, and the Portuguese soon gave it up. They never sent their traders to Gao or Timbuktu.

Sonni Ali died in 1492. One of his sons should have followed him as king, but his great minister Mohammed Abu-Bekr decided that after serving Sonni Ali for many years it was time that he himself should be king. He fought two battles against the king's sons and beat them. When Sonni Ali's daughters were told that Mohammed Abu-Bekr was now king, they were angry, and cried out *Askia*!, which means, 'He is not!' Someone told Mohammed what the women had said. He was not angry; he smiled, and said, 'I will call myself Askia'. And he was called Askia Mohammed Abu-Bekr from that time onwards, and all the Songhai kings who followed him were called Askia.

Askia Mohammed Abu-Bekr became king in 1492, the year in which Columbus crossed the Atlantic and discovered America; and he ruled until 1528. The writers of the Sudan tell us about his wars; he fought many wars, but they say that most of his great country was at peace because the fighting was done by the king's standing army outside his frontiers. They tell us too about his markets, and about the schools at Timbuktu and elsewhere.

We learn that he improved the police, and appointed many more judges and magistrates in towns which had not had them before. When the writers Ahmed Baba and Es-Sadi (from whom we learn most of what we know about Askia Mohammed) describe a good and honest judge, they often add, 'He was one of those who were appointed by Askia Mohammed'. Under Askia Mohammed, women were no longer allowed to go about unveiled in public. Ibn Batuta would have approved of this; the Government of Askia Mohammed was stricter in such matters than the Government of Mali had been. We are told that the king was the friend of all learned men, and more and more of them came to Timbuktu and Jenne and other places to study and teach. One writer says that there was a great trade in books. They were very expensive; but we hear of one teacher in Timbuktu who had a large library of his own and was always ready to lend his books to his students, even the books he valued most. Trade went on just as it had done before; one writer says that in Askia Mohammed's time people were so honest, and the police looked after the markets so well, that a child could be sent into the market to buy, and nobody would try to cheat it.

All this depended on the character of the king. As long as the king himself was a just man, and hard-working, and strong enough to be feared by evil men and lazy officials, things would

A bronze head from Ile Ife, probably of the thirteenth or fourteenth century

An ivory head from Benin, probably of the sixteenth century

Right: The Rev. John Philip, a missionary in South Africa from 1819 to 1851

Left; Captain Lugard, first High Commissioner for Northern Nigeria

go on well. If ever the time came that the king was lazy or tired, the evil men would lift up their heads again. In a country which took six months to cross, the Government must always leave most of the work to local governors and local officials. The question was this: If a local official did wrong, would the king listen to the complaint and quickly punish the wrong-doer? In Askia Mohammed's time, the answer to this question was Yes; and Askia was such a good king that he is often called Askia the Great.

We need not spend time over the wars by which Askia conquered more and more land. He conquered Mali and Taghaza, he beat the Moshi and made them become Muslims, and he turned east and conquered the Hausa states. On the north-east, he fought against the Berbers who were in the habit of attacking the Hausa; he followed them into the desert and made their town of Agades into a Songhai colony.

By 1528, Askia Mohammed had had more than sixty years of fighting and governing, first as minister, then as king; he was old, and tired, and blind. His son Musa rose up against him and made his father give up the kingdom, and soon afterwards, the old man died at the age of ninety-seven.

Under Askia Musa and the three kings who followed him, the Government became weaker. They were Musa, 1528–31; Bengan, 1531–37; Ismail, 1537–39; and Ishak, 1539–48. Ishak was cruel but strong, and made himself king by catching and killing all his rivals. In his time, Mulai Hamed the king of Morocco asked the Songhai to give up the great salt mines at Taghaza, which had been conquered by Askia the Great. Ishak refused. 'The Hamed who asks for this', he said, 'cannot be the king of Morocco. Anyway, I am not the Ishak who can listen. The Ishak who will listen to this is not yet born.' This was the beginning of trouble between the Askias and Morocco.

In 1548 the last great Askia became king: Askia Daud, a son of Askia Mohammed. In the twenty years since Askia Mohammed had given up the kingdom, many different peoples all round the frontiers had risen up against the Songhai, and Daud had to begin by fighting against them. He had wars against Mali, Tekrur, the Moshi, and some of the Hausa states. But worse than this: at the end of his life, trouble broke out right

E

in the middle of the kingdom. The small state of Masina was peopled by Fulani. It lay in the middle of the kingdom, but it had never been conquered. It was still independent, or nearly so, though it had agreed to pay tax, first to Mali and then to Songhai. In 1581, some of its people attacked and robbed a boat on the Niger. Unluckily for them, the boat and its cargo[1] belonged to the king. We are told that such a thing had never happened before in the Songhai kingdom; and certainly it seems that travellers were no longer as safe as in the days of Askia the Great, when a child could go alone to market and nobody would cheat it. The governor of the province was the king's son, and he determined to punish the people of Masina.

1582   He did not try to find out who had robbed the boat; he simply sent an army into the Masina country to punish the whole people by killing and burning and robbing. The chief of Masina escaped, but many people were

Aug.   killed, including, we are told, many learned men. Askia

1582   Daud was very angry with his son, but he died before he could do anything to punish him or to help the people of Masina. Things were getting worse when things like this could happen; civilization was going down.

After Askia Daud came two kind but weak kings, and then in 1586 came the last of the independent Askias, Ishak II.

The trade across the desert was greater than it had ever been in the time of Mali. The Songhai kingdom was greater. It covered a wider range of climate and crops than Mali. It had iron, copper and gold; and it could get all the slaves it wanted by attacking the pagan tribes on its southern frontier. And also,

About   since the time of Askia the Great, it had ruled Taghaza and the salt mines. Gold, slaves, salt: these three were

1499   the main articles of trade between north and south.

Ghana and Mali had had two of them; Songhai had all three.

Taghaza was a poor place. There were no trees, and no sweet water. The miners were slaves, who worked for their Berber masters. They lived in houses made of blocks of salt. All their food came from far away: dates from Morocco,

---

[1] A boat's cargo is the goods which it is carrying: not the passengers' luggage but the goods in the hold which are being sent from one place to another—cocoa, ground-nuts, oil, or cotton for example.

millet and camel-meat from the south. Sometimes it happened that bad weather or some accident made the caravan arrive late with their food; and when the caravan did at last arrive it sometimes found the miners dead from hunger and thirst.

Taghaza was nearer to Morocco than to the Niger. The Berbers who managed the salt-mines kept the trade going fairly, and as long as the trade went fairly, it did not matter either to the south or to the north that the salt-mines did not belong to them. But when the Songhai took Taghaza, the king of Morocco thought it unfair. The Songhai now controlled all three of the main articles of trade, and could fix the price of them all. The king of Morocco felt just as the people of the Gold Coast felt in 1937, when they said that it was not right for one European company both to buy their cocoa and to sell them European goods.

We have seen that in 1546 the king of Morocco asked Askia Ishak I to give him the salt-mines; but Ishak would not. When Askia Daud was an old man, the king of Morocco asked him to allow Morocco to have the mines for one year and to pay rent for them, and Daud agreed. It seems that Morocco left the mines peaceably at the end of the year; but in 1585, after Daud was dead, the king of Morocco sent soldiers to take the salt-mines by force. But news had somehow come into the desert, and the Berbers had taken all their slaves away; so when the Moorish soldiers came to Taghaza there was nobody there to work the mines for them, and they had to go back home. But with all this danger from Morocco, the Taghaza mines were beginning to be a trouble to the Songhai. They found some more salt at Taodeni, much further south than Taghaza, and they made some new mines there; but Taodeni alone could not provide enough salt, and after a time they had to go back and open the Taghaza mines again. The Songhai were doing with salt just what the Wangara people had done with gold when the Mali people tried to conquer them: they left off digging. But there was one great difference: the Wangara did not need their own gold, but the Songhai could not do without their salt. When the Songhai opened the Taghaza mines again, the king of Morocco told them to pay him a tax of one *mithqal* of gold for every load of salt. But of course they would not.

A new king named Mulai Ahmed became king of Morocco

in 1578. He was very rich and strong, for his brother the late king had just won a great battle over the Portuguese at El-Ksar, and had taken thousands of Spanish and Portuguese prisoners. Many of them he used as slaves, many of them bought their freedom, so that Morocco became rich with gold from Portugal and Spain. England sold him timber for ship-building, and cannon-balls and bullets; Morocco had plenty of gunpowder, but not much iron and lead. The soldiers of Morocco had guns, both small guns for the hand, and also heavy guns.

Aug.
1578

King Mulai Ahmed determined to conquer Songhai, and to take all the gold and salt and the other riches of the country for himself. His councillors did not like the idea; they were afraid of the desert. But the king was determined to try. He said that if caravans of traders could cross the desert, surely an army could. He reminded them that the Songhai would fight with spears and swords and bows and arrows, but the Moors would fight with guns.

In October, 1590, the Moorish army left Marrakech. It was commanded by an officer called Judar Pasha, 'a little man with blue eyes', we are told. It contained about 4,000 men, all of them specially picked; more than half of them were armed with guns. They lost many men and camels and horses in the desert, but at the end of February, after a march of twenty weeks, they reached the Niger near the town of Bamba, half-way between Gao and Timbuktu. The Songhai were unlucky as well as careless. They thought that if the Moors sent an army against them, it would come from Tekrur and the west, not from the north across the desert; and they did not gather their army in time. This shows how things had changed since the days of Sonni Ali and his standing army. But they were unlucky in this way: in case the Moors *did* come across the desert, Askia Ishak sent messengers to the Berbers telling them to block all the water-holes so that the Moorish army would all die of thirst. But his messengers were taken and robbed before they crossed the frontier, and so their message never reached the Berber chiefs. In April, the Songhai army met the Moors at Tondibi near Gao, and was beaten. Askia Ishak and his beaten army crossed the Niger to the south, and the Moors, having no boats, could not follow them.

Askia Ishak hoped that if he paid the king of Morocco enough money, the king would order Judar Pasha to bring the army home again; so he sent to the Moorish commander and offered him gold and slaves. Judar Pasha answered that he had no power to make peace, but he would send a letter to his king and see what he said to Ishak's offer. He did so; and he added that the Moorish army had suffered badly in the desert march and the fighting, and that the Songhai kingdom did not seem to be as rich as he and his king had thought. 'The man who is in charge of your donkeys and their donkey-boys', he said, 'lives in a better house than the king of this country!'[1] He advised the king to accept Ishak's offer.

King Mulai Ahmed was angry, and would not believe him. He sent a new officer, named Mahmud-ben-Zergun, to take over the command of the army from Judar Pasha, and ordered him to drive Askia Ishak right out of the country and to conquer the whole of the Songhai kingdom. Mahmud-ben-Zergun began by asking Judar Pasha why Ishak had been allowed to stay safely south of the Niger: why had Judar Pasha not crossed the river and fought him again? Judar Pasha answered that he could not cross the river because he had no boats; Ishak had taken all the boats with him. Mahmud was not satisfied. He cut down all the trees in and near Timbuktu, and took all the wooden doors from the houses in the city, and he made boats with the wood. Then he went after Askia Ishak, and beat him again in a battle at Bamba; he followed the Songhai when they crossed the river, and Ishak was killed.

This was not quite the end of the war. A Songhai general called Askia Nuh kept on the fight for a little time longer, till he was killed in battle in 1594.

But it was the end of the Songhai kingdom. Not only the Moors, but all its old enemies fought against it: Moshi, Mali, Berbers, Fulani, all fighting to get what they could. There was no more peace and good government. In 1594, the king of Morocco made his soldiers collect together all the educated people of Timbuktu and send them across the desert to Morocco; their riches were taken from them, and their books and papers were burnt. One of them afterwards said to the

---

[1] We remember that Ibn Batuta, who thought Mali such a fine country in many ways, had a low opinion of its buildings.

king, 'I had the smallest library of any of my friends, and your soldiers took from me 1,600 books'. The Moorish army never went back to Morocco. After a few years, its commanders made themselves independent of Morocco and sent no more gold across the desert. They held the cities of Timbuktu, Gao, Jenne and Bamba, and the country round them; the rest of the Songhai kingdom they had to leave to itself.

Trade of course began again after a time; West Africa still must have its salt, and the north still wanted gold and slaves. But the Songhai kingdom, with its peace and civilization, was gone, and the Sudan was divided into many small states, often at war with one another. The whole of the North African coast was taken by the Turks, who were bad rulers and were not interested in trade or civilization. It was a sad thing for the world of Islam that the Turks conquered so much of it. Under Turkish rule, the Muslim countries became poor, and their wonderful civilization ceased to develop. There was often war between the Turks and the Europeans, so that traders from the Sudan no longer found North Africa a civilized country where they could meet people of other nations and learn from them. In the days of Ghana, civilization in the Sudan had been ahead of that in Western Europe; now, thanks largely to what Europe had learnt from the Arabs, Europe was advancing but the Sudan was standing still. No country can develop its civilization when it is divided into small warring states, when its educated people are taken away and its books burnt, and when it is cut off from other nations. That is why the civilization of Ghana and Mali and Songhai did not lead to anything.

THINGS TO DO, TO DISCUSS, OR TO FIND OUT

1. Make a pie-chart of the history of the Sudan from 400 to 1600. The power of Ghana lasted from about 400 to 1240, that of Mali from 1240 to about 1464, and that of Songhai from 1464 to 1594. Mark these points, and divide your chart to show the length of the three kingdoms' power.

2. On page 37 it is said that London, Chicago, and old Ghana all became rich because trade had to pass through them. This is true also of other places: Cairo, Marseilles, Cape Town, Singapore and Buenos Aires for example. Find these

places in your atlas. Why is each of them in a good place for getting rich?

3. Draw a map of West Africa, marking Kumbi and Audoghast. Find from your atlas where the desert begins today, and mark this line on your map. Is the desert as wide today as it was in the days of old Ghana? If there is a difference, can you account for it?

4. Was there in your country, before the Europeans came, one state which was stronger than the others? If so, did its rulers have difficulties like those which the kings of Ghana and Mali had?

5. On page 42 it is said that Ghana and Mali helped trade and civilization by making many small tribes join into one large state. Has European rule helped your country in this way?

6. Is it true (see page 43) that if trade increases and traders get richer, the whole country gets richer? Why is this?

7. Are there any customs in your country like those which El-Bekri describes in old Ghana?

8. Does West Africa still get its salt from Taghaza? If not, why not, and where does it get it from?

9. Do you agree with what is said about civilization on pages 45–6?

10. Read what Ibn Batuta tells us on pages 57–8 about the civilization of Mali, and compare it with the civilization of your country today. We have machines today which Ibn Batuta had never heard of; is there any other respect in which today's civilization is better than that of Mali?

11. The Koi of Timbuktu was paid one-third of all the taxes he collected for the Government. Which do you think the better arrangement: that, or a fixed salary? Why do you think the Government paid him in that way?

12. All the life of Mali, it is said, was based on agriculture and mining. Is this the same in Africa today?

13. Why do you think the Portuguese would not help Mali against the Moshi and others? Do you think they were wise not to help?

14. Do you agree that in 1582 the governor of Masina province did the wrong thing? If so, what ought he to have done?

15. Compare what Ibn Batuta thought of Mali with what Judar Pasha thought of Songhai. Can you suggest a reason for the difference?

16. Make a straight-line chart of all the important dates in the history of Ghana, Mali and Songhai.

17. Draw separate maps, on the same scale, of the three kingdoms. Which was the biggest?

18. Why do you think it was possible for the Moorish army to make itself independent of Morocco? Why could not the king of Morocco make his generals in the Sudan serve him again?

19. What difference would it have made to the history of West Africa if the Songhai kingdom had not been destroyed, but had lasted as a strong civilized state until modern times?

20. Looking back on the Moorish conquest of the Sudan, do you think that the councillors of king Mulai Ahmed were wise when they advised him not to try it?

3

Nigeria Before the
British Came

You have told us that modern Ghana was never part of any of the great Sudanese kingdoms. But Askia the Great of Songhai, you say, conquered the Hausa states of Nigeria and made them part of the Songhai kingdom. Who built up these states before his time? Why is the Northern Region of Nigeria so much bigger than the other two regions, and so different? Is it because the Northern Region was conquered by the Songhai?

Well, it is true that the North of Nigeria is very different from the South; but I do not think that the Songhai conquest had much to do with making it different. We must go further back, and must also come nearer our own time. The Songhai power over Hausa-land did not last very long. It was in 1512 and 1513 that Askia the Great conquered the Hausa states; and only two or three years later, a man called Kanta, who was king of Kebbi, rose up against Askia and would serve him no more. Askia brought an army to fight him in 1517, but the people of Kebbi drove the Songhai army away, and the Songhai were never afterwards able to break the power of Kebbi. King Kanta, having saved his own country from the Songhai, went further and tried to conquer all the other Hausa states from the Songhai kingdom. For a time he succeeded; but he was unable to hold the country he had conquered. He had a good deal of fighting with the kingdom of Bornu, which was on the other side of Hausa-land near Lake Chad; so Kebbi and Bornu fought each other in the middle of the Hausa states, and the Songhai rule over Hausa-land cannot have been very strong. Kebbi remained free after the Moorish conquest of the Songhai kingdom, and the Moorish army was never able to pass through Kebbi or round the side of Kebbi to conquer Hausa-land.

73

Very well, let us agree that it was not the Songhai conquest that made the North so different from the South. How much further back do you want to go to answer the other question: Who built up the Hausa states?

I want to go a long way back: to A.D. 600 or 700. We have seen that about that time, Berbers from the desert had conquered the Songhai and had made them into a small but strong kingdom. About the same time, more Berbers were conquering the peoples living between the Niger and Lake Chad. We know very little about it all, because about the year 1820, a long time before the British came into Northern Nigeria, one of the kings there had all the history books burnt. He did not want his people to know anything about the old times before they became Muslims and joined into one state. But we know something, from people's memories and from Arab writers outside Nigeria.

One of the earliest and strongest states that was set up in this way was the state of Bornu, which lay on both sides of Lake Chad. Bornu grew out of an earlier state, called Kanem, which drew its trade and its civilization from the east and north-east, not from Ghana and Mali. This state of Bornu was always strong, and all through the time of Ghana and Mali and Songhai, Bornu lived its own life.

West of Bornu, other Berbers coming from the north entered what is now Northern Nigeria and conquered the peoples they found there. The story is that their king was named Bawo; he came into the country of Daura and conquered it, and married its queen, and by her he had seven sons. These seven sons built the first seven towns of the Habe or Hausa-speaking people: Daura, Gobir, Kano, Rano, Katsina, Biram, and Zaria. The story goes on to say that King Bawo had other sons by other women, and these sons set up seven other states: Zamfara, Kebbi, Nupe, Gwari, Yauri, Kwararafa, and Ilorin; some say that Ilorin includes the whole of the Yoruba people.

This sounds strange. Ilorin is not the head of the Yoruba state, and never has been. How much of this story are we to believe?

Well, it all seems rather too simple to be quite true: fourteen sons of one father separating from each other, going in different

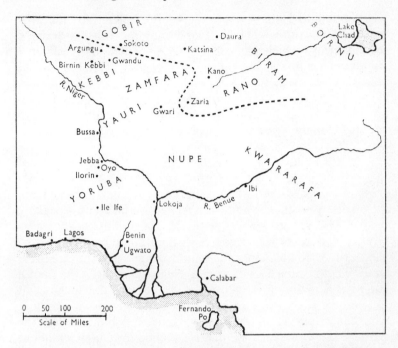

MAP 3. NIGERIA BEFORE THE BRITISH CAME

Notes on the map: This map shows all the places mentioned in Section Three of
the book, except Segu, which is shown on Map 2, and the two villages of Degel
(page 84) and Gudu (page 84). These places are both in Gobir, north-west of
Sokoto. It does not show the boundaries between the states, because nobody
knows exactly how they ran. There were fourteen Hausa states; six of them are
marked by the place of their capital town, and the other eight, whose capital town
is not marked, show the name of the state. The dotted line is drawn to separate
the seven Hausa states set up by the first invasion from the seven states set up by
the second invasion; it shows how the states of the second group lie further south
and west than those of the first group (see page 76).

directions, and each one of the fourteen being lucky and making
himself a king. We should expect the story to be less simple:
perhaps two brothers might decide to stay together and help
each other, or perhaps one of the fourteen might be unlucky
enough to be killed in battle, and have no chance of making
himself a king. And we hear nothing about the other Berbers
who helped them in their fighting. Many details of the story have
been forgotten.

At any rate, we may believe that there were two Berber armies who came into Hausa-land one after the other; the first army set up seven states—Daura, Gobir and the others—and the second army, which came later, set up seven more states—Zamfara, Kebbi and the others. The states belonging to this second group all lie further from the desert than the first seven. It looks from the map as if the second army found the first states already set up, so it passed by and went further into the Negro country to fight against the Negroes and make new kingdoms for itself.

And as for Ilorin, it is true that Ilorin was never the head of the Yoruba state. But the Yoruba people themselves say that some of the great men who began the Yoruba state came from the north or north-east and were related to the Hausa-speaking people. The Yoruba state, like the Hausa states, was set up by groups of Berbers who came down and conquered the Negro peoples they found living there, and made them into a strong state. The Yoruba language is a Negro language, the Hausa language is mainly a Berber language; perhaps this means that the Berbers who came into Yoruba country were few, and those who came into Hausa-land were many.[1] We think that the Berbers first came into Yoruba-land some time between about A.D. 700 and 1000, and that more Berbers came later, about the same time as those who set up the second group of Hausa states.

We must not think that the Berbers came from the desert and brought civilization to Negro peoples who were quite un-civilized. The Yoruba and other Negro peoples had a great deal of civilization. They were farmers, they used iron, they made beautiful things in bronze. As far as we know, the Berbers who conquered them were not specially civilized. What the Berbers knew about was fighting. In Hausa-land and in Yoruba-land, the men of the desert were able to conquer the farmers and

[1] A few hundred years before the Berbers came into Yoruba-land, other wild tribes came and attacked the peaceful people who lived under the Roman Empire in the two countries which we now call England and France. In both countries, the people spoke the same language, Latin; and the attackers spoke a language which was quite different from Latin. A few of them attacked France; they conquered it and set up their own kingdom in it, but because they were few, they soon left off speaking their own language and their children learned to speak Latin. Many of them attacked England and set up their own kingdoms in it; they killed most of the people who spoke Latin, and brought their own wives over, and so the English language today is descended from the language spoken by the attacking peoples, and is quite different from the French language, which is descended from Latin. Did something like this happen in Hausa-land and Yoruba-land?

iron-workers and bronze-workers because they were better fighters; they were an army of fighting men, with nothing to lose, coming into a peaceful country where each man had his home and family to think of and was more used to working than to fighting.

Where did the Yoruba learn their civilization, if not from the Berbers?

Nobody can answer that question properly. We know that before the time of Christ—about 900 B.C., roughly the time when David was king of Israel—there were people living in Nigeria who were making good pottery, and making also little models of men and animals with baked clay. We call them the Nok people, because these remains of theirs were first found in the village of Nok in the province of Zaria. We know very little about them, and we do not know what it was that stopped them making their pottery about A.D. 200. But it may be that the Yoruba and other Negro peoples of Nigeria learned some of their civilization from the Nok people. Then there is the Yoruba work in bronze. Some of this looks very much like bronze work which was done in the country which we now call the Sudan Republic. In that part of the Nile valley, there used to be a very civilized state called Kush, which was strong from about 800 B.C. to A.D. 300. The people of Kush worked in iron and in bronze; and we think that the people of Western Nigeria learned this part of their civilization from Kush. Trade and civilization moved along the grass land south of the desert, between the Nile and the Niger. You will see that this civilization was all African; it did not come from Europe. Perhaps when the state of Kush was destroyed about A.D. 300, some of its people moved westward to Nigeria and took their art and their civilization with them.[1]

Why must we think that the Yoruba and other peoples of Nigeria learned this sort of thing from Kush? Is it not possible that they found out for themselves how to work in iron and bronze?

Yes, it is possible, but we do not think it happened in that way. We know that Kush was making large quantities of iron tools for hundreds of years before the Berbers came into

[1] Meroe was the name of the capital city of Kush, and the kingdom too is sometimes called Meroe.

Nigeria. As for bronze, Nigeria has no copper, so the peoples of Nigeria could not have found out how to make bronze (which needs copper) for themselves; either they learned this from other peoples who had copper, or else they themselves learned it before they came into Nigeria. As far as we know, this sort of civilization began in ancient Egypt, where there was plenty of rich land, and peace, and food, and a strong Government, and priests and temples; and men had time to sit and think and find out better ways of living. We think that civilization spread out from Egypt into Europe and into Africa. While peoples are moving about, trying to find a new home, they have no time to invent new arts for themselves; they have to learn them from peoples who are settled and who have time. In Europe, so much work has been done in studying historical remains, that we can see plainly how the peoples of Western Europe learned the beginnings of their civilization from Egypt. Not nearly so much work of this kind has been done in Africa, but from what has been done, it begins to look as if Africa too, like Europe, learned from Egypt.

We do not know very much about the history of the Hausa states, except that they were always fighting each other. They were small, and never joined into one strong kingdom. While Bornu and Kanem formed a strong state in the east, and Ghana and Mali and Songhai rose and fell on the west, the Hausa states went on in their own way. At first they were pagan, but after a time Islam began to come into the country. It came from two directions. The states on the west, that is Gobir and Kebbi, received Islam from the Songhai. On the east, the kingdom of Bornu received Islam from Egypt. Both these districts became Muslim probably between 1000 and 1100, but the Hausa states in between remained pagan. It was not till about 1350 that Islam came to Kano and Zaria; it was brought by people from Mali. When some of the Hausa states were Muslim and others pagan, of course there was more fighting than ever, for the Muslim states made war against the pagans. The last Hausa state to become Muslim was Katsina, which was converted by a missionary from Egypt in 1493.

For a short time, as we have seen, the Hausa states were conquered by Songhai, though Kanta of Kebbi set them free again. But once they were Muslim, even before their conquest by Askia the Great, they were able to share in the trade and the civilization of the Western Sudan: that is, of Mali and Songhai. We hear of learned men coming to live in Kano and Katsina: some came from Songhai and others from Egypt.

But when all the seven Hausa states had become Muslim, they kept themselves separate from the pagan states to the south, even from states like Kwararafa and Nupe and Yoruba which were to some extent related to them. We have seen that these states had a civilization of their own in such matters as carving and weaving and metal-work, and no doubt took some of their ideas of government from the great kingdoms of the Sudan. And they were strong fighting states; in 1671 and 1672, for example, Kwararafa was strong enough to capture the cities of Kano and Katsina. But the Muslim states would never regard the pagan states as truly civilized.

When the Moors conquered the Songhai kingdom and the Turks conquered North Africa and Egypt, it was a great blow to the Hausa civilization. The civilization of the Sudan began to die. So did the trade across the desert. And so, Bornu and the Hausa states were left to themselves. They kept themselves separate from the pagan peoples to the south of them, except that they used to make wars and slave raids so as to take slaves whom they could sell to the Turks. Besides slaves, they sold cloth and leather-work and kola nuts; and they bought guns and silk and European goods. The Turks themselves were not great traders, but there was some trade between the Turkish lands and the rest of Europe. But there was no longer the coming and going of learned men that there had been in the kingdoms of Mali and Songhai; and civilization needs more than guns and silk and beads; it needs new ideas. No country can keep up a high civilization for long if it is out of touch with other civilized countries and is not able to learn from them.

And what happened to the Yoruba and the other peoples of the south?

They too were cut off from the civilization of Europe by the way across the desert; but they got into touch with it again by way of the sea. The Europeans came to Nigeria in their ships.

The Portuguese first reached Lagos in 1472; the name Lagos itself is Portuguese, and means a lake. It was the first natural harbour which the Portuguese had found since Sierra Leone.

The people of Lagos at that time served the king of Benin. Benin was a kingdom in the forest country which was in close touch with the Yoruba and shared the Yoruba civilization. One of the finest things in this civilization was its bronze work. We have found several wonderful bronze heads at Ile Ife in the Yoruba country which are portraits[1] of Yoruba kings; and in Benin too there was much fine work done both in bronze and in ivory. We are told that the king's house at Benin city had its walls covered with small bronze plates showing all kinds of scenes of Benin life. Some of these bronze plates still exist.

The Portuguese captain was named Ruy de Siquiera. He sent a message to the king of Benin, but he did not go there himself. A few years later, however, in 1486, another Portuguese captain named Affonso d'Aveiro did go; he sailed in his small ship up the Benin river as far as Ugwato, which was only a few miles from Benin city, and from Ugwato he found a good road to the city itself. The king of Benin was glad to have these visitors from a strange land, and when the ship returned to Portugal he sent an ambassador[2] back in it to greet the king of Portugal. Aveiro's ship went back carrying the Benin ambassador and a cargo of pepper, which was then very scarce in Europe and sold for very much money. The result of Aveiro's visit was that the Portuguese opened a trading station at Ugwato, and stayed there till 1520. Pepper was the chief thing they bought; and they paid for it with guns and cloth and metal; copper and brass and iron and lead. The African metal-workers always found it difficult to get enough metal, especially now that the Sahara trade was harder, and less copper came to them from Takedda. They had iron, but it was easier to buy iron bars from Europe than to work the poor iron-ore of West Africa with their simple tools.

All this seemed very good. The coast land might have developed its civilization by exchanging ideas with Europe, as well as goods. But the slave trade spoilt it all.

The Portuguese had been doing a little slave-trading in the Senegal for many years. Slavery existed in Europe in those days; and the Portuguese bought slaves, just as the Arabs did, to take

---

[1] That is, they were made to look just like the faces of particular men.

[2] An ambassador is a man who is sent by his government to a foreign country to represent it and to explain its point of view.

Left:
Cecil Rhodes

Right:
President Kruger

A camel caravan arriving at an oasis in the desert

An old photograph showing Market Square in Johannesburg full of oxcarts. Some of the carts have a cover over one end; sometimes the whole of the cart would be covered

to Portugal and use in their homes. When Columbus discovered the West Indies in 1492, the king of Spain began to plant colonies in America. Soon, the Spaniards found gold mines and silver mines, and they made plantations of sugar and other tropical crops. They made the native peoples of America work for them on the plantations and in the mines; but those people were not strong and they could not stand the hard work. And then the Spaniards thought of using Africans instead, for Africans were stronger. They began buying some of the slaves who were already in Portugal, but they soon came to the end of them and wanted more; and so the Portuguese began buying more slaves all along the West African coast. After the Portuguese came the Dutch and the English and many others, and the slave trade began on a large scale.

As far as Africa was concerned, the results of the slave trade were entirely bad. The trade was bad in several ways. In the first place, of course, there was the suffering of the slaves and of the people who were killed in the slave raids. Then, as more and more slaves were wanted in America, the kings of Benin and the other states sent their armies out to attack other peoples and make slaves of them; and so there was fighting everywhere, and other kinds of trade became less and less. Then, it was easier and cheaper to buy European-made goods than to make things in Africa, and so many African arts and crafts began to die out: the bronze-work and the wood-carving especially. Who knows how many good carvers and weavers and metal-workers were killed in the fighting, or sent across the seas to work at cutting sugar-cane in the West Indies? Not only this: all over that part of Africa, nobody could tell from one day to the next whether his village would still be standing tomorrow. At any time the slave-raiders might come in the night, burn the houses, and take away the people as slaves. What was the use of making plans for the future, or of taking the trouble to do good careful work? All one could do was to live from day to day. Lastly, the slave trade was bad for the character of the strong people who carried it on, both African kings and European slave dealers. The first Portuguese who came to Benin were educated gentlemen who were interested in Africa and were ready to treat the Africans they met as civilized people. But to sell guns and liquor and beads and buy hundreds of poor

F

slaves from their African masters was not work for an educated gentleman; and many of the Europeans who came to Nigeria were far from this. And the Africans too changed. People can become used to blood and cruelty, and can even come to like it. The kings and captains who spent their time in catching slaves became hard and cruel. Benin and Yoruba-land and the other coast lands became lands of fear and blood, and their old civilization died.

So we see that from about 1600 to 1800, both the north and the south of Nigeria were going through difficult times: the north, because the Hausa states were fighting each other and were cut off from the civilization of Europe by the desert and by the Turks; the south, because the country was full of slave raiding, and the European slave dealers were not interested in bringing European civilization to Africa. In the time of Ghana, African civilization had been in many respects ahead of European civilization; now, Europe was going ahead, while Africa was going backward.

You said that you would explain why the North is different from the South. You have explained that the North became Muslim while the South remained mainly pagan; but now you are telling us that both North and South spent two hundred years in constant fighting and in selling their people as slaves—northwards across the desert, or westwards across the sea. Does that not make them rather alike?

Yes; but we have only reached the year 1800. Up till then, the North was Muslim, the South was pagan; but both civilizations were being worn away by the constant fighting, so that the difference between them was growing less. But in the nineteenth century, other things happened which made the differences greater again.

THE NORTH

In the early years of the nineteenth century, the Hausa states were conquered by the Fulani. We have seen that long ago in the early days of Ghana, the Fulani were living in Tekrur near the mouth of the Senegal, and that during the times of Ghana and Mali, many of them came eastwards to live in the country in the bend of the Niger. They came in two ways. Some of them came wandering with their cattle, and settled for a time wherever their cattle could find grass to eat and the people of the country would have them. Others came as learned men; many of the judges and other learned men in Mali and Songhai were Fulani. The educated Fulani were Muslims, the cattle keepers were often pagan. The Fulani had entered the Hausa country about 1320, during the time of Mansa Musa; many of them became farmers and traders like their Hausa neighbours, but they were often stricter Muslims, and thought themselves better men.

By the year 1800, there were Fulani people living all the way from Tekrur to Lake Chad; and here and there on the long road there were Fulani states, such as Masina, where the Fulani were their own masters instead of serving the chief or king of the place where they happened to be living.

In the year 1754 there was born a Fulani named Usuman dan Fodio. He was a strict Muslim, and became a preacher in his native country of Gobir, a Hausa state in the farthest north-western corner of Northern Nigeria. Gobir at this time was still not completely Muslim, although it had had Muslim missionaries for seven hundred years. Usuman did what Ibn Yasin, the founder[1] of the Almoravides, had done nearly 700 years before: he told the people that he was ashamed of them, and preached a purer form of Islam. Large numbers of people came to listen to him, and went away determined to be better Muslims. His teaching was so famous that the king of Gobir sent his sons to Usuman to be taught. This king, named Nafata, was himself not a Muslim; he went so far as to give orders that nobody was to become a Muslim if he had not been born and brought up as one. When Nafata died, he was succeeded as king by his son Yunfa, who was one of the boys who had been taught by Usuman. Then the trouble began.

We do not know exactly what went wrong. We have only one side of the story, and that is the Fulani side. It would be interesting to hear the Hausa side of the story; but we shall never hear it. Anyway, Yunfa put some of Usuman's followers in prison, and Usuman got them set free; then the king sent for his old teacher and told him in public that he ought to keep his

[1] That is, the man who began the Almoravides, See pages 47 and 48.

people in order. Was Yunfa a pagan, and did he put the men in prison because he disliked their pure kind of Islam? Or were Usuman's people making themselves a nuisance because they thought they were above the law of the state of Gobir? This is one of the cases in which we can see what happened, but we cannot see why it happened. Anyway, Yunfa went further still; he said that he would send soldiers to arrest Usuman and to destroy the village of Degel, where Usuman lived and taught. On February 21, 1804, Usuman left Degel to escape arrest, and went to Gudu, on the western border of Gobir. There his followers gathered round him; and like Ibn Yasin with his Almoravides, Usuman dan Fodio called on them to follow him and drive out the pagan Hausa kings.

The Fulani who gathered round Usuman dan Fodio at Gudu gave him the title of *Sarkin Musulmi*, or Commander of the Faithful. There were many of Usuman's pupils living all over the Hausa country, and he called on them to rise up against the Hausa kings and kill the unbelievers. He sent some of them flags, the flag being a sign that the man who carried it was appointed by Usuman to lead the rising in his district.

And so the holy war began. Many Hausa were fighting on the side of the Faithful. No doubt these were the stricter Muslims among the Hausa people. But it is strange that some of the Fulani fought for the king of Gobir; perhaps, though Fulani, they felt that Usuman dan Fodio was so strict that he would be an uncomfortable king to serve.

In June 1804, Usuman won his first battle over the army of Gobir, and there was fighting up and down the country till 1809, in which the Fulani were not always successful. In 1808 Yunfa of Gobir was killed in battle, and all Gobir was conquered. Zamfara, Zaria, Katsina and Kano had been conquered already.

In 1809, Usuman dan Fodio retired. His son, Mohammed Bello, took the title of Sarkin Musulmi and ruled the eastern Fulani provinces from his capital at Sokoto; Usuman's younger brother Abdullahi ruled the western provinces from his capital city of Gwandu. The Fulani rulers who had conquered the Hausa states were called Emirs[1]; some of them served Sokoto and others Gwandu.

[1] Emir is an Arabic word meaning an officer who is under a king and has men under him. The English word *admiral* comes from this word.

The fighting was not yet over. In 1804 and again in 1808 the Fulani attacked Bornu, but the people of Bornu called on their brothers living east of Lake Chad to help them; and both times they were saved by an army from the east, led by a great Muslim soldier called El Kanemi. The Fulani tried again in 1810, and again El Kanemi came and defeated them. Then nearly all the Hausa states rose up against the Fulani and had to be defeated one by one; and it was not until 1826 that the fighting ended. It was no longer a holy war of Muslims against unbelievers. El Kanemi was a very great man and a learned Muslim, and there were thousands of Muslims fighting against the Fulani. Long before 1826, the Fulani themselves had admitted that they were fighting for power.

The result of the long war was that nearly the whole of Hausa-land was cut up into states (called emirates) ruled over by Fulani emirs. There were a few patches still unconquered; the most important of them was part of Kebbi. The Fulani Emir of Gwandu lived in the old capital city, Birnin Kebbi, but the Hausa ruler, the descendant of old king Kanta, still ruled over part of his country with his capital city at Argungu. Some of the Hausa states were cut up into several small emirates. As for Bornu, El Kanemi had spent so much time and trouble in fighting to keep the Fulani out of it that in the end he decided to stay there and rule it himself. Bornu is still ruled by his descendants.

The Fulani were not content with conquering Hausa-land. They pushed south-west into country where the Hausa had never ruled. The state of Nupe covered the country where the Benue runs into the Niger. Most of its people were pagan, but there were some Muslims, and some Fulani. One of the Fulani was called Mallam Dendo, and his position in Nupe was very like that of Usuman dan Fodio in Gobir. He was a teacher in the king's court, but had some disagreement with the king, and left the court and retired to a distant part of the Nupe country. In 1806 the king died, and there were two men who quarrelled over who should become king in his place. This gave Mallam Dendo his chance. The Emir of Gwandu gave him a flag, and he and the other Fulani fought to make Nupe a Fulani emirate. After many years of fighting, and after Mallam Dendo's death, his descendants became Emirs of Nupe; but some small pieces of the Nupe country were made into separate emirates, and two pieces were still ruled by descendants of the old kings.

In a somewhat similar way, the Fulani set up an emirate in Ilorin. Ilorin was a Yoruba state, and had been part of the great Yoruba kingdom with its capital at Oyo. But the fighting and slave-raiding which went on all the time had made the Yoruba kingdom very weak, and the Yoruba general in Ilorin rose up against his Government, and called on the Fulani who were in Ilorin to help him. The Fulani leader, Mallam Alimi, was given a flag by the Emir of Gwandu, and between 1817 and 1823 he and his men conquered the province of Ilorin and set up a Fulani emirate there.

By about 1850 the Fulani had made themselves strong all over the Muslim parts of Northern Nigeria, and were still fighting and slave-raiding in the pagan lands along the Niger and the Benue. But slave-raiding and slave-dealing was as bad for them as it had been for the peoples of the south. Some of the emirs and judges were good men, but as time went on, many of them became selfish and cruel. It was easy to become rich by selling other people as slaves, and many of them came to think of nothing but their own riches. After a time, some of the smaller emirates found themselves no longer strong enough to make raids against distant pagan peoples, and their emirs even began selling some of their own pagan subjects as slaves. Other kinds of trade became impossible. People became poorer, taxes became heavier. The slave trade was destroying the country: destroying peace, destroying trade, destroying justice.

Between 1901 and 1903 the British, led by Sir Frederick Lugard, fought against the Fulani emirs and stopped the slave-raiding. All over the North, the Hausa people welcomed the British; only their Fulani masters resisted. By 1903 the fighting was over, and Northern Nigeria became a British protectorate.[1]

---

[1] A protectorate is a country which the British Government protects from people outside who want to attack it and from people inside who want to make any kind of disturbance; but the British do not govern it as closely as they do a colony. Nowadays, the difference between a colony and a protectorate is not as important as it used to be; just as much trouble is taken nowadays over a protectorate as over a colony.

The British Government accepted what Lugard said about the way in which the North should be governed. He said that as far as possible, the Fulani emirs should be left to rule their people according to the customs of the country. Evil customs like slavery and slave-trading must be stopped, and if anyone thought that a Fulani judge had not given him justice, the British would consider his case. But as long as the emirs and their judges and officers ruled justly and well, Lugard thought that the British Government should not interfere. Above all, Lugard said, the British Government must not interfere with their religion; and he promised the peoples of the North that it would not.

This question of religion was important; for in those days, all schools in West Africa were run by Christian missionary societies. As soon as Northern Nigeria came under British rule, the Christian missionary societies which were already at work in the south of Nigeria asked Lugard to allow them to come and work in the North. One or two had already come in before the British arrived; Dr Walter Miller for example entered Hausa-land in 1889 and the Emir of Zaria allowed him to open a school there. But Lugard said that he would not allow Christian missionaries to come and work in the North unless the emirs allowed them; and most of the emirs would not allow them, or would allow them only on strict conditions. A Government school was opened at Kano in 1909; but even Government education was not very welcome, because the teachers were Christians, and the people were afraid that their children would be taught Christianity. So for many years, education in the North developed very slowly, and the South left the North far behind.

THE SOUTH IN THE NINETEENTH CENTURY

The slave trade was spoiling the whole of West Africa. No progress would be possible until the trade was stopped. To stop the trade, two things were needed. One was to persuade the Governments of the European countries that the trade must be stopped, so that they should make laws forbidding it. The other was to send warships to catch slave traders who carried on the trade after it was made unlawful. Britain was the most important country in this matter, for two reasons: first, that British traders bought and sold more slaves than the traders of any other nation; second, that the British navy[1] was the strongest in the world and would be able and willing to catch the slave ships.

The first country to make a law against the slave trade was Denmark. For more than sixty years, a group of people in England, of whom William Wilberforce is the most famous, worked to persuade the British Government and the British people to stop slavery and the slave trade. In 1772 the judges decided that nobody could be a slave in England; in 1807 the Parliament made a law forbidding the slave trade; in 1833 it made a law abolishing[2] the state of slavery, not only in Britain, but in all the British lands overseas. The British Parliament voted £20 million, which was a very large sum of money in those days, to ·buy the slaves from their masters and set them free.

1802

At that time Britain had no land in West Africa except for Freetown and a few castles on the Gold Coast. Luckily, Freetown has a good harbour; and for fifty years the British navy used Freetown as a base for its warships who were hunting the slave ships. One after another, the other countries of Europe made laws against the slave trade and agreed to allow the British navy to catch their slave ships as well as British slave ships. In 1862, the United States abolished slavery, and other countries in America abolished it one after the other. By the year 1850 the trade was almost stopped, though it was not till 1869 that the navy decided that its work in West Africa was done and it no longer needed the base at Freetown.[3]

It is 1,500 miles from Freetown to Calabar, and all the Nigerian coast is full of lagoons and small rivers in which ships can easily hide. As long as America wanted to buy slaves and the African chiefs were willing to sell them, the British navy could make the trade difficult, but it could not stop it altogether. A few ships would still get through, and they would sell their

[1] The navy is the whole collection of the warships belonging to a country.

[2] To abolish a custom is to stop it so that it no longer exists. From this verb *abolish* we have the noun *abolition;* Wilberforce and his friends wanted the *abolition* of slavery, and so they were called the Abolitionists.

[3] The navy still had much work to do in stopping the slave trade on the other side of Africa. That kept the navy busy for another forty years after 1869.

slaves at such a high price that they might still make a very good profit. The British Government decided that it must help the navy by persuading the African chiefs not to sell slaves. Some of the chiefs made agreements with the British that they would no longer sell slaves to the European slave traders; and though they did not always keep their promise strictly, by 1850 there was only one place in Nigeria where slaves were still being sold to Europeans. That place was Lagos.

At that time, the British Government did not wish to take any part of West Africa. It was afraid of malaria and other diseases; it did not believe that when the slave trade was finished there would be any other kind of trade; and it could see that a great deal of money and hard work would be needed if West African civilization were to be built up again. It tried to get out of the Gold Coast, and it tried not to get into Nigeria. But both in Nigeria and in the Gold Coast there were Englishmen who saw that the slave trade had done so much evil in West Africa that Africans could not repair the damage without European help. Slowly, and unwillingly, the British Government came to see that they were right.

In 1845, the chief of Lagos, named Akitoye, was driven out by his nephew Kosoko. Kosoko became chief, and he greatly increased the slave trade; and when the British asked him 1851 to stop it, he would not do so. Then Akitoye promised the British that if they would help him to drive out Kosoko, he would stop the slave trade.   The British did help him, and he did stop the trade; but he died in 1853. Then Kosoko tried to come back, but the British would not have him, and Akitoye's son Dosunmo became chief. Dosunmo did his best to rule Lagos and to stop slave trading, but he was not strong enough to stop it altogether; and in 1861 the British Government decided that the only way of stopping the slave trade was to make Lagos into a British colony. This was the beginning of British rule in Southern Nigeria.

Within a few years after Lagos became British, the slave trade ended; and a new trade began, the trade in palm oil. The British and other European traders lived on old ships stationed in the rivers, and bought oil from the African traders. The Africans on the coast would not allow the Europeans to go into the country; they made them stay on their ships at the mouth of the rivers. When people are buying and selling, they need some sort of law, and some sort of courts and judges to enforce[1] the law. From about 1840 to about 1880, the British Government made agreements with many chiefs in the coast lands; they agreed to abolish slavery and human sacrifice and to allow British traders to visit them. When African and European traders disagreed, the other traders would set up a kind of court to judge the quarrel. The British Government appointed officers, called consuls, at Lagos (until Lagos became British) and at Calabar, to help the traders, both European and African.[2]

With the traders and the consuls, there came the Christian missionaries. The Church Missionary Society began work in the west of Nigeria in 1842, and soon had a number of mission stations in Yoruba-land; the Methodists and the Baptists began about the same time. In 1846 the Church of Scotland opened its station in Calabar. The Roman Catholics began their work in 1860. The missionaries brought schools and hospitals and printing-presses, as well as the Gospel. They went where no trader could go, for anyone could see that they were not coming to Africa to make themselves rich or powerful, and so no one was afraid of them. The people of the South were pagan, and they welcomed the missionaries, even if they did not all become Christian. It was very different from the North, where the Muslims did not want Christian teaching of any kind.

Except in the Yoruba country, no Europeans had yet gone far inland from the coast. In Yoruba country, missionaries opened mission stations as far north as Ilorin as early as 1855. But there were no roads through the bush, and Europeans had not yet found the way by river. Mungo Park saw the Niger at Segu in 1796, and in 1805 he sailed down it in a boat as far as Bussa, where he and his companions were drowned. In 1823 other British explorers reached Northern Nigeria by crossing the desert from the north, and in 1830 Richard Lander and his brother went from Badagri on the coast to Bussa, where Mungo Park died, and then sailed down the Niger all the way to the

---

[1] To enforce the law is to make people obey it, even if they do not wish to.
[2] The first British consul for Eastern Nigeria was John Beecroft, who lived in the island of Fernando Po from 1829 to 1849 and was appointed consul in 1849. There was a British consul on Fernando Po from 1849 to 1873, and in that year the consul was moved to Calabar.

sea. Thus at last the Europeans found out the river way through Nigeria from north to south.

As soon as the way was found, missionaries and traders wanted to use it in the opposite direction to get into the middle and north of Nigeria. Between 1832 and 1857, both the Niger and the Benue were explored by steamships, and in 185 8the British Government appointed a consul at Lokoja. Missionaries and traders from several European countries came into the Niger valley. French and Germans and others, as well as British, sailed up the rivers of the Niger delta, and came by land from the west into the country behind Lagos. The British traders began to fear that they would lose their trade, and in 1879 they all joined into one company so as to protect themselves against French and German competition.

As late as 1865, the British Parliament said that it did not wish the Government to take any more land in West Africa or to make any agreements to protect African peoples; and it said that, far from going forward in this way, Britain should leave Africa altogether as soon as it could do so without causing the slave trade and fighting to start again. But the Government could not help itself. If Britain had not decided to set up a Government in Southern Nigeria, the French or the Germans would have done so, and British trade would have been lost. The Government did not want to come into Nigeria; but it was the British navy that had stopped the slave trade and had made the first maps of the Niger delta, it was the British Government which had sent steamships to explore the Niger and Benue, and British traders who had developed the trade in palm oil. The British felt that since they had taken so much trouble, they did not want to leave Southern Nigeria to be ruled by France or Germany, and to leave the trade to French or German traders.

In 1884, the British company bought the French company which was trading on the Niger, and about that time, most of the chiefs on the coast made new agreements with the British government, in which for the first time they promised not to make agreements with any other European country. In 1885, all the European countries that were sending traders or missionaries or explorers to Africa met in Berlin to try to agree, and they made a treaty[1] called the Berlin Act, by which they agreed

[1] A treaty is an agreement between two Governments.

that if one country could show that it had more interest than
any other in one particular part of Africa, and would promise to
set up a government in that part, the other European countries
would not interfere with it. Britain was able to show that she
had more interest than any other country in the coast from
Lagos to Calabar, and the other European countries accepted
this.

To carry out the Berlin Act, Britain now had to set up a
government in this country. In 1885, Britain set up the Oil
Rivers Protectorate covering the Niger delta; in 1887 she set
up a second protectorate over the strip of land which the British
trading company[1] ruled along the Niger as far as Jebba and
along the Benue as far as Ibi; in 1888 she set up a third protectorate covering all Yoruba-land except Ilorin.[2]

But for some time, the British did not really govern their
protectorates. They were forced in the end to govern them
because France and Germany would be very ready to protect
traders if Britain did not. Between 1891 and 1902 the British
had to send soldiers to many places in the protectorates. Many
chiefs still kept up slavery and slave-raiding and human
sacrifice and robbery, and nothing but armed force would make
them stop. It was not until 1914 that the last fighting took place
in Southern Nigeria.

DIFFERENCES BETWEEN NORTH AND SOUTH

Nigeria became one country in 1914; and during forty years of
British rule both North and South made such progress that
the country began to look forward to self-government. But
there were still differences between North and South. What
were they? The North is Muslim, the South is pagan and
Christian; we have seen how Islam has been spreading down
from the north for hundreds of years, but the Christian
missionaries arrived by sea before Islam reached the forest
country.

The North is a country of large emirates, with their laws and

---

[1] The British trading company was named the Royal Niger Company. It ended
in 1899; on January 1, 1900, its land and its government were taken by the British
Government. Lugard was an officer of the British Government, not of the Company.
[2] We have seen on page 86 that the Yoruba province of Ilorin had become a
Fulani emirate, and so had become separated from the rest of the Yoruba state.

government based on Islam; this is the result of the Fulani conquest. In the South, the large states like Yoruba and Benin were broken down by the slave trade and by civil war,[1] and in some parts of the country there were no large states but very many small tribes or even family units. Much of the civilization of the south was destroyed by the slave trade; Benin in 1897 for example was less civilized than it had been when the Portuguese first saw it in 1483.

The North, being Muslim, did not at first wish to have European education; the South welcomed it. Because of this, the peoples of the South made quicker progress after the country had come under British rule. The South had many more educated people than the North to run its government and its commerce and industry. It is easy to understand why, in modern times, the South began to ask for self-government before the North.

THINGS TO DO, TO DISCUSS, OR TO FIND OUT

1. Look at your atlas and see the countries to the east and north-east from which Kanem drew its trade and its civilization.
2. Draw a straight-line time-chart to show the times of the Nok people, the kingdom of Kush, the Berber invasion of Hausaland, the Fulani conquest of Hausaland, the coming of the British into Hausaland, and Nigerian independence in 1960. You will find all the dates in the book.
3. Can you suggest why the Hausa people welcomed Lugard and the British when they came to fight against the Fulani emirs?
4. Lugard introduced the system of indirect rule, which spread all over British tropical Africa. Find out what indirect rule was. Why did Lugard introduce it into Nigeria? Could he have governed Nigeria in any other way?
5. Draw a map of Nigeria, and mark the ways by which the Europeans explored the country, with the dates.

[1] Civil war is war between people of the same state or nation: for example, English fighting against English, or Yoruba against Yoruba. We have seen that the Fulani got hold of Ilorin because the Yoruba of Ilorin were fighting against the other Yoruba.

6. Mark Lagos, Lokoja, Calabar and Fernando Po on your map. Why are these four places important? Why was Lokoja a good place to have a British Consul?

7. This book does not tell the story of Nigeria during its 60 years of British rule. What had the British to do in Nigeria to make self-government possible in 1960? Did the differences between North and South make their work easier or harder?

8. Why were the African chiefs of Southern Nigeria so long unwilling to allow European traders to travel into the country and buy palm-oil direct from the villagers who produced it?

9. In 1865 the British Government was still trying to keep out of Nigeria; in 1885 it began setting up protectorates there. Why did it change its mind? Would it have been better if Britain had stayed out, and Nigeria had been divided between France and Germany?

10. Was Lugard right in allowing the emirs in Northern Nigeria to refuse to have schools in their emirates? Or do you think he should have forced them to have Government schools? The Christian missionaries thought that Lugard should have allowed them to travel and preach in the North; do you agree?

4

South Africa

In most parts of Africa, south of the Sahara, we see that European countries have made colonies—Britain, France, Belgium, Spain, and Portugal for example. Some African countries are still colonies, others, such as Ghana and Nigeria and Guinea, have become independent African states. But South Africa is different. It has been independent for a long time; the government is in white hands; it has two official languages, English and Afrikaans. Why is this?

IT is true that if you look at the map of Africa today you will find all the countries you mention still ruling pieces of Africa. In fact, there are two others which you might have mentioned: Italy and Germany. Italy had two colonies in East Africa. One of them is now part of Ethiopia and the other has become independent. And Togoland, the Cameroons, Tanganyika, Ruanda-Urundi, and South-West Africa used to be German colonies, and were taken away from Germany after the war of 1914-1918.

If you go to South Africa today you will find it a rich and busy country, with nearly three million whites and nearly ten million Africans, and also many Asians. But three hundred years ago it was very different.

The first European to see the Cape of Good Hope was the Portuguese sea-captain Bartholomew Diaz. In the year 1419, Prince Henry of Portugal began sending out ships to explore the west coast of Africa. In 1445 the first captain reached a land of green trees south of the Sahara; in 1460 the Portuguese found Sierra Leone; and in 1488 Bartholomew Diaz sailed round the Cape. But the Portuguese did not settle in South Africa. They settled on the Gold Coast and further south in Angola, and they settled too on the east coast from Lourenço Marques all the way northward to Mombasa; but they did not settle at the

Cape. Why was this? It was because there was nothing for them at the Cape. The Portuguese wanted gold, ivory, and slaves. They wanted to trade with people who dug gold, hunted elephants, and sold slaves. But there were no such people at the Cape.

Most of the African people who now live in South Africa belong to the Bantu race, which has filled nearly the whole of South and East Africa from Uganda to the Cape, and has pushed as far west as the Cameroons. But when the Portuguese first found the Cape, there were no Bantu people there. The people who lived in the country which we now call Cape Colony were the Bushmen. They were not Negro; they were yellow rather than brown in skin, their hair was not tightly curled, they were smaller than a Negro. They lived in family groups, hunting animals for food. They had no weaving or agriculture, they did not keep cattle, and they did not use metals. So there was no trade to be had with the Bushmen. Besides the Bushmen, there was another people called the Hottentots. They came into South Africa later than the Bushmen, but they too were not Negro. They were taller than the Bushmen, but yellow like them. The Bushmen language was full of clicks, and the Hottentot languages too had many clicks. But the Hottentots used copper and kept cattle; in these ways they were far ahead of the Bushmen.

We must not think that South Africa was as full of Bushmen and Hottentots as Buganda or Eastern Nigeria today are full of Baganda or Ibo farmers. There were very few of them. People who live only by hunting wild animals may have to travel many miles before they shoot one; they will not find enough food to be able to live in large groups. The Bushmen lived in family parties of not more than 300 people. People who live by keeping cattle can live more easily, for their meat and milk are always close by. We may expect to find them living in much larger groups than the hunters. But the cattle have to keep moving, and the people must move with them; so one group, even if it contains several hundred people, will need a great deal of land. It is when people learn agriculture that the population can increase. When you use part of your land for growing yams or maize, and turn the cattle out to feed in the bush, you will have much more food than if you lived on milk and meat alone; so

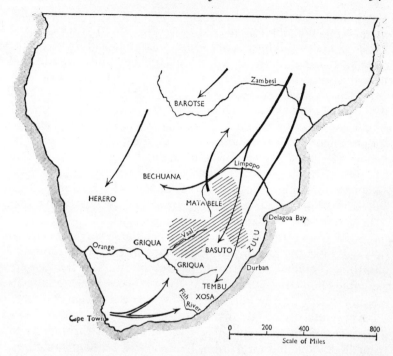

MAP 4. HOW ITS PEOPLES CAME TO SOUTH AFRICA

This map shows how the Boers met the Bantu. The white arrows show the general lines on which the Boers pushed inland from Cape Town: one along the coast (which met the Xosa on the Fish river) and the other inland, to cross the Orange and the Vaal rivers. The black arrows show the lines on which some of the most important of the Bantu peoples came south. The land shaded is the land which the Boers found lying empty because of the *Mfecane*. One black arrow points northward: this shows how Msilikazi and the Matabele were driven from their home by the Boers and moved north across the Limpopo, where Rhodes's men later found them. The Matabele were not the only people to go back north in this way; some of the Ngoni left their homes in the south and settled further north in Nyasaland.

the villages will grow bigger. Neither Hottentots nor Bushmen grew any food crops, so there were very few of them. The first three Hottentot tribes that the Dutch found when they came to settle in the Cape were very small; one had eighteen fighting men, the second had 300, the third had 600.

All the Bantu used iron as well as copper, and grew food crops as well as keeping cattle. So their numbers increased and they wanted more land, and they fought against the Bushmen

G

and drove them away and took their land. An Arab writer found Bushmen living near Zanzibar a thousand years ago, and tells us that the Bantu used to hunt them and kill them. So the Bushmen came south, the Hottentots followed them, and behind them both came the Bantu. The first of the Bantu must have crossed the river Zambesi well before 1400. We think this must be so for two reasons. One is that the Arabs from Zanzibar built the town of Sofala as a trading place about that time, so there must have been Bantu there for them to trade with. The other is that the great ruins of Zimbabwe and elsewhere in Southern Rhodesia were built by people who mined gold and kept cattle and grew food crops. They were already ruins by the time the Portuguese came; and most people now think that they were built by Bantu.

So we must think of South Africa when the Portuguese came as a land almost empty of people: perhaps three or four thousand Bushmen, eight or ten thousand Hottentots. The Bantu were coming, but they were still far away. There was nothing in South Africa for the Portuguese; they went elsewhere.

The Dutch were the first Europeans to settle at the Cape. They sent a doctor, Johan van Riebeeck, with three ships to start a colony, and on April 6, 1652, he and his men landed. In those days there was no Suez Canal, and the way from Europe to India and the East Indies was round the Cape. The Dutch were trading and building an empire in the East Indies. The voyage from Holland lasted six months or more, and sailors often became ill from bad food; so the Dutch wanted to have a colony at the Cape which could supply the ships with fresh meat and vegetables and fruit.

So the Dutch East India Company started its colony at the Cape. The Dutch soon met trouble. The Bushmen killed the Dutch cattle, as they killed the cattle of the Hottentots; and the Dutch, like the Hottentots and the Bantu, began to hunt and kill the Bushmen. The Dutch Company wanted the Dutchmen at the Cape to grow vegetables and buy cattle as its servants. But the Dutch did not want to be the Company's servants; they wanted to be free men. Van Riebeeck could not stop them buying cattle privately from the Hottentots, and going into the bush to trade with other tribes and to make farms for themselves. And they brought slaves from the East Indies and other parts of Africa. They grew wheat and maize and vines, and had sheep as well as cattle. But the wine made at the Cape was at first very bad, so that they could not sell it across the sea; the sheep were hairy, not woolly, so that there was no wool trade; and often the wheat and maize died because there was not enough rain or because they were eaten by locusts. The Dutch thought cattle the best thing for an African farm. As the cattle increased in numbers, the Dutch wanted more land; and so they began to trek[1] away into the bush to find it. They had another reason for trekking away from Cape Town; they did not like their Government, which wanted to rule them too strictly. In the bush they would be free: the father would be free to find himself a new farm and live his own life, the young son free to go hunting elephants and roaming wherever he liked in this great wonderful new country. It seemed as if the country was all ready for the white man to take. It is true that there were the Bushmen; but the Hottentots (and also the Bantu, though the Dutch had not yet met any Bantu) killed the Bushmen wherever they found them, and the Dutch did the same. The Hottentots were no trouble. Many of them were ready to work on Dutch farms for wages, but most of the bigger Hottentot tribes simply moved away when the white men came. There was plenty of room.

The Company in Holland was unhappy about its colony at the Cape. It certainly provided the ships with fresh meat and vegetables, but it cost a great deal of money, and many of the Dutch and other Europeans who went out to the Cape did not stay there, but trekked away into the bush and were lost. The Dutch had tried to grow many kinds of crops, but had had no luck; the colony manufactured nothing except its bad wine. And yet the climate was good; why should the Cape not grow into a rich colony like the colonies in America?

In 1716 the Dutch Company asked its Governor at the Cape to advise it. Was there any other crop that might be grown? Would it be a good thing to send out many more Europeans to live there? Would skilled European workmen be able to start new industries and make a living? And would it be better to send out skilled European farm-workers to work on the farms, instead of the Hottentots and slaves?

[1] Trek: a Dutch word meaning to travel, especially to travel and camp in the bush.

The Governor, though Dutch, had a French name: de Chavonnes. Many French Protestants had been driven out of France at this time, and had gone to Holland and England and other Protestant countries; some had come to South Africa. Governor de Chavonnes called his Council to help him in answering the questions from Holland. The Council could not think of any likely crop which had not already been tried in vain. They did not think that more European settlers would be any help; skilled workmen could do nothing useful at the Cape; and they did not at all like the idea of skilled European farm workers. European farm workers would be lazy and drunken; they would not do as their masters told them; and they would want high wages. Slaves they said were cheaper and more obedient, and worked harder; let us have slaves.

Only one man in the Council disagreed with this. He was the Governor's brother, Dominique de Chavonnes. He said that free men would work better than slaves, and would not need to be watched all the time. It would be better for South Africa to be divided into many small farms, each worked by one family with free white men working for wages, than into a few large farms run by slave labour. It is bad for men to think themselves too big to work; let us fill South Africa with hard-working white men, and then trade will begin.

Dominique de Chavonnes was right; but they would not listen to him. There were not many slaves, and most of them were men, so that if no more slaves had been brought in, the slave population would have died out. The Hottentots were moving away, the Bantu were still far off. The Cape might have become a white man's country, thickly settled. But the Government decided to go on with big farms and with slaves. It marked out farms of 6,000 acres and more (about three miles square) and allowed a family to live on such a farm for a year at a time for a very small rent; the Government had the right to take the land back at the end of a year, but it hardly ever did so. And so the Dutch in South Africa grew up to think that there was plenty of land for them all, and that each family had the right to hold such a big farm, which could only be worked by slaves or servants.

THE BANTU

It was in 1776, more than 120 years after van Riebeeck had landed, that the Dutch first met the Bantu. They met part of the Xosa people on the Fish River, about 450 miles from Cape Town. The Dutch Governor, van Plettenberg, came to see what was happening; he agreed with the Xosa chiefs that the Fish River should be the boundary between white and Bantu Africa, and then he went back to Cape Town.

In these 120 years, the Dutch had found a new way of life, the life of the trekker. They carried all their goods in big wagons or carts, drawn by as many as sixteen oxen; often they slept in these wagons, for they had no other home. They disliked Cape Town and wanted to be far away from the Government and its laws; they wanted to be free, to make their farms wherever they chose, to hunt elephants or Bushmen wherever they chose. South Africa belonged to them, their slaves and their Hottentot servants belonged to them. They travelled in parties, each family in its wagon; at night they would chain the wagons together in a circle with the cattle in the middle, filling the spaces between them with thorn bushes to keep away lions or Bushmen. Of course they left behind them much of their civilization. There were no schools, and very few churches, and most of the trekkers had no books except the Bible. They would come long distances, as much as six or seven weeks trek, for church services: Holy Communion, marriages, christenings; but such long journeys cannot be taken often. They were away trekking further and further into Africa; magistrates and churches followed slowly behind them.

We have spoken of the trek, and of the laager, which was the name given to the circle of wagons for defence against the enemy. We must mention another Dutch word which has meant a great deal in South Africa: the commando. Every man was compelled to bring his horse and his gun to fight if the magistrate called him to do so, and this party of fighting men was called a commando, because the men were commanded to come. But the trekkers would often make a commando for themselves, without waiting for a magistrate, if Bushmen or Hottentots (or, later on, Bantu) had taken their cattle. They would leave the women and children behind in laager with a few men to guard them, and most of the men would take their guns and ride off to get back their cattle. Trek, laager and commando, the Bible and the gathering of the big wagons for the Nachtmaal or Holy Communion; much of the history of Dutch South Africa lies in these things.

So far, the Dutch had trekked into Africa with very little trouble except for the Bushmen. But the Xosa, whom they met in 1776, were only one of many Bantu peoples who were coming southwards. About the same time as the Xosa reached the Fish River near the east coast, the Herero and others entered the country which we now call South-West Africa; the Barotse and Bechuana and others reached their present homes; and behind the Xosa on the coast were Tembu and other peoples. Trouble was coming. The Bantu had iron spears, and were well disciplined; there were very many of them, and it would be much harder for the Dutch to fight them than to fight the small parties of Bushmen or Hottentots. True, the Dutch had guns, which the Bantu so far had not; but in those days guns were not as good as they arc now; they were slower and did not shoot nearly so far. Both Dutch and Bantu were cattle-keepers, seeking new grass-lands for their animals; when they met, there was sure to be trouble.

There is one great difference between European and African custom in the matter of land which has often caused misunderstanding, in Kenya for example as well as in South Africa. To Africans, land is like air or rain, a thing which anybody may use but which belongs to nobody. You may breathe the air, but it is not your air; you may put out a basin to catch some of the rain, but the rain is not yours. Similarly, you may send your cow to feed on the land, or you may plant crops in it; it is your cow, and they are your crops, but it is not your land. If you and your people are living on the land, your cattle are feeding and your crops are growing, nobody may send his cattle or plant his crops unless you give him permission, and he will pay you for the permission; but it is still not your land. But with Europeans it is different. It may be that long ago they too had the same idea; but if they had, they have lost it. A European will agree that air and rain are free for all: but not land. In Europe, you can buy or sell land, or hire it, just as you can buy or sell or hire a bicycle. The boundaries of the land are carefully written down on paper, and you must get a lawyer to prepare all kinds of papers to show the Government; but when you have paid your money, the land is yours, and you may keep everyone else out of it.

Now when Europeans and Africans meet, and Europeans want land, it is natural for them to ask, 'How much do you want to sell this land?' They will agree on the boundaries and on the price, and when they have paid the money they think they have bought the land, and it is theirs, so that nobody else may come on it without their permission. But the Africans cannot think of selling land. They think they are giving the European permission to feed his cattle or plant his crops on the land for one year, or five or twenty years or whatever it may be. Then one day, the African says 'I am afraid I must ask you to go away and take your cattle with you; I need this land myself now'. And the European replies, 'But I have bought the land; it is mine, and I am going to stay here. You must find yourself land somewhere else'. Neither is meaning to cheat the other; it is just a misunderstanding. But it has happened very often in Africa, and it has brought much trouble.

Another matter about land is that very often in Africa, people will use land for a few years and then they will leave it for some time, meaning to come back to it later on. In West Africa, for example, farmers will leave a piece of land to go back to bush after it is worn out so that it will not produce good crops. In East Africa, it may happen that a tribe loses many of its cattle from disease, so that it cannot use all the land it once used. If a European comes looking for land for himself, he will see this land lying unused, and he will ask, 'You are not using this land; may I have it?' He will not understand that although you are not using the land now, you have used it in the past and will use it again. That is another way in which Europeans and Africans have often misunderstood each other.

So in 1776 and the years following, the Dutch trekkers met the Bantu. Very soon afterwards, they met the British.

THE BRITISH

British ships as well as Dutch called at the Cape. The British had trading stations in India, and during the years when the

Dutch in South Africa were trekking to meet the Bantu, the
British were building an empire in India as rich as the Dutch
empire in the East Indies. Sometimes during the seventeenth
century the British and the Dutch fought each other, but from
1689 onwards they were friends. Both countries were Protestant,
and they both feared France, which was the richest and strongest
country in Europe, and was Roman Catholic. The king of
France was master of his country; France had no parliament in
those days. We have seen that the king of France drove
1683   out many French Protestants (some of them came to
South Africa), and England and Holland were afraid
that France would try to conquer them and force them to become
Catholic. There were many wars in which the British and the
Dutch fought side by side against the French. So for most of
the time after Van Riebeeck landed at the Cape, British ships
calling at the Cape were treated as friends.

The French people suffered very much from the long wars
and the heavy taxes. They had no parliament which could
complain to the king, and in 1789 they made a revolution: they
killed their king and queen and made their country a republic.
They said that all peoples were their friends, all governments
were their enemies; and they wanted all other countries to make
revolutions as they had done. This led to another war in Europe,
in which England and Holland and many other countries
fought against France. Holland at first fought against France;
but some of her people wanted a revolution, and in 1795 a
French army entered Holland and the revolution was made. A
new Dutch Government came into power, friendly to France;
and Holland thus changed sides in the war.

This put the British Government in a difficult position, not
only in Europe, but also in India. For more than a hundred
years, France had held the island of Mauritius in the Indian
Ocean; there were French soldiers there, and French warships,
and whenever France and England were at war, the French
warships would hunt for British ships going to India and would
take them. Sometimes British warships were sent to fight the
French; but the French had a great advantage because they had
a safe base at Mauritius, and the British were thousands of
miles from any British base. While the Cape was friendly, the
British ships could at least buy fresh food and water there; but

if the new Dutch Government allowed its French friends to send soldiers and warships there and to put up big guns, no British ship would ever be able to reach India. So as soon as the British Government heard that Holland was now its enemy, it made up its mind that the French must not be allowed to take the Cape. In June, 1795, British ships and soldiers came to the Cape, and after a little fighting they took it. They promised to let the Dutch keep their own language and law and customs, and they did so.

In 1802 peace was made in Europe, and the British gave the Cape back to Holland. But the peace did not last long. In May, 1803, war broke out again, and lasted until 1815. Once more the British came and took the Cape, and this time they did not let it go again. In 1810 they took Mauritius; and when peace was made in 1815, they kept the Cape and Mauritius too.

The change from a Dutch Government to a British Government did not at first trouble the Dutch at the Cape as much as we might expect. The new Government did not interfere with their ways of living. The Dutch did not like any Government, and this new one was no worse than the old one; in one way it was even slightly better, because it did not try to stop them trekking away into Africa, as the old Dutch Government had done. The British tried to govern well, though of course most of them did not understand the Dutch language or customs. One of the early British Governors, Lord Charles Somerset, brought out teachers from Scotland, and missionaries as well. The Dutch Reformed Church at the Cape was short of clergy and teachers, and had no training college where clergy and teachers could be trained. The Scottish missionaries went first to Holland to learn the Dutch language, and all of them preached in Dutch. Other missionaries too came: the Moravians in 1795 and the London Missionary Society in 1799; and other societies followed soon afterwards.

But after a time there were three things which began to make many of the Dutch feel that their new British Government did not suit them. They did not like it when the Government introduced the English language and some British customs; they did not like it when the Government stopped slavery; and they were very angry indeed at the way the Government behaved about the Bantu. We must say a few words about each of these.

THE ENGLISH LANGUAGE

The new Government tried to interfere as little as it could with the Dutch ways of living. But as the country developed, it found that it must make some changes. In 1828, it set up a Supreme Court of Justice to replace the old court of justice at Cape Town, whose magistrates were often not trained lawyers. It put magistrates into the bush districts, to take over the courts of the old Dutch commissioners, who were called *landdrosts*. At the same time, the Government made English the language of the courts.

There is no doubt that the new system of justice worked better than the old, and was more suitable for a modern country. But we may think it unwise of the Government to make the courts work in English; why could they not go on working in Dutch? The difficulty here was, that the language spoken in South Africa had already changed very much from the Dutch spoken in Holland; it was fast becoming Afrikaans. Many British settlers were coming into the country, and many of the Dutch settlers were beginning to know English. Nobody at that time thought of writing in Afrikaans. The Bible was not published in Afrikaans until 1933. So the Government had to choose between English, and the Dutch of Holland. Many people already understood English, and more and more (especially the younger people) would come to understand it. As time went on, and the Afrikaans language became more and more different, fewer and fewer people would understand the Dutch of Holland. So the Government cannot be blamed for choosing English; but of course the change was difficult at first, and it is natural that many of the people should feel angry about it.

SLAVERY

When the British first came to the Cape in 1795, they found more slaves than free men; South Africa had about 16,000 Europeans and 17,000 slaves, as well as Hottentots and Bushmen who were working on the farms, though not as slaves. In 1807 the British Government made a law to stop the slave trade, and the British Navy began to hunt for slave ships and punish the slave traders. But this was not enough; people in England (William

Wilberforce and others) began to say that slavery itself should be stopped, and all the slaves should be set free. The Dutch in South Africa saw that sooner or later their slaves would be set free; and they would not mind that much if they were paid for the slaves they lost, and if they could get other workers to replace them: Hottentots or Bushmen, perhaps.

But in 1828 (the same year as the new Supreme Court) the Government at the Cape made a new law, called the Fiftieth Ordinance, which allowed Hottentots and Bushmen and free coloured persons to hold land if they could get it, and made them free to go where they wanted, without being bound to carry a pass. Many of them, it is true, were content to stay working on the farms for wages, but many went back to the old Hottentot wandering life; and the Dutch farmers complained that their men were getting lazy, and that to keep them on the farm at all they had to pay them higher wages.

And then in 1834 the slaves were set free. The British Government in London had given £20,000,000 to pay slave-owners all over the British Empire (the West Indies, South Africa, and Mauritius) for their slaves. A committee in South Africa spent nearly two years in working out how much money would be needed there, and made the sum come to over £2,800,000. But when they sent this figure to London, they were told that they would be given less than half of it: about £1,200,000. And they would not get even all of this in money; part of it would be in British Government stock. Many people in England thought that the British Government was not being fair to the slave-owners; but the Government would not pay more. Many of the slave-owners in South Africa were in great trouble. They were poor men; they had paid for their slaves, as they had paid for their horses and guns and wagons and cattle; and many of them were so poor that they had borrowed money and would find it difficult to repay the money unless they were fully paid for their slaves.

You may perhaps think that slavery was wrong; that people ought not to buy slaves, and if they did buy them they should not expect the Government to pay them when it set the slaves free. But this would be unfair. We nowadays think slavery wrong, because Wilberforce and his friends taught us to think so; but before Wilberforce had taught us that lesson, nobody thought slavery wrong. Long after the British Government abolished slavery, there were many Africans and Arabs who still thought slavery quite right. So the Dutch slave-owners, who had spent their money in buying slaves at a time when everyone thought it right to have slaves, would have been very badly treated if their slaves had been taken away from them without any payment. It was bad enough for them that they were paid so little, much less than their slaves were worth; and it is understandable that they felt angry with the British Government about it.

THE BANTU QUESTION

But it was the Bantu question which caused most trouble between the Dutch and the new Government. The real difficulty was that the colony had no boundary. Van Riebeeck had marked out a boundary just behind Cape Town in 1660; van Plettenberg tried to make the Fish River the boundary in 1778, and in 1798 the British again tried to make the Fish River into a boundary, although there were already some Xosa living south of it, and the British could not make them go back. But the trekkers did not want boundaries; they wanted to be free to go wherever they liked, right into the middle of Africa. The Dutch Government had always told them to settle down, but they would never obey it; and they would not obey the British Government either.

The British thought that the only thing to do was to mark out a boundary and make both sides—Boers[1] and Bantu—keep to it. In 1812 they called out a commando and sent British troops to help it, and they drove all the Xosa away to the other side of the Fish River. Then they tried to make the Boers come and live in the empty land. But the Boers did not want to come back to be near the Government and near the Bantu; they wanted to move on further into Africa, where there would be less trouble from the Bantu and from the Government. All this talk of making a boundary did not interest them. In this same year, 1812, the British judges went up near the boundary to try cases, and they tried many cases in which Boer farmers were accused

---

[1] The Dutch farmers in South Africa called themselves Boers, and we shall use this word from now onwards. The word means simply a farmer; but it is useful to distinguish them from the Dutch of Holland.

of ill-treating their Hottentot servants. This was a new and unpleasant experience for the farmers. Even though many of them were found not guilty, they did not like being taken to court in this way; such a thing had never happened in the old days. And three years later, in 1815, came something still worse. A Boer named Frederick Bezuidenhout refused to come to court to answer the charge against him. After waiting two years, the Government sent police to arrest him. He fired on the police and was killed. His brother and some of his friends then took their guns and fought against the Government, but were beaten at the battle of Slachter's Nek. Five of them were hanged and others punished. A Boer commando had helped the troops and police at Slachter's Nek, the judges who tried and sentenced the prisoners were Dutch (this was in 1815, thirteen years before the new Supreme Court was set up), and the law by which they were tried was the old Dutch law; but still the Boers thought that this trouble at Slachter's Nek was bad, and they blamed the British for it. The Dutch Government of the Cape had never sent police up to the boundary in the old days; the British seemed to them to be the friend of the Hottentots and the enemy of the Boers.

As the Boers would not come and live in the land south of the Fish River, the Government brought 5,000 British settlers (called the 1820 Settlers, because they came in 1820) to live there; and so the trouble with the Bantu was moved further on, to the land between the Fish and the Keiskamma rivers. Both Boers and Bantu wanted this land. There was much stealing of cattle; the Government had no police to stop it, so the Boers used to go into Bantu country and try and get their cattle back; and in 1834 the whole of the Xosa people crossed the Fish and made war on the colony. After some weeks fighting they were beaten back; and then the Government had to make up its mind what it was going to do.

The Governor was Sir Benjamin D'Urban; the big seaport of Durban is named after him. His first idea was to push the boundary forward from the Keiskamma to the Kei river and drive all the Bantu beyond the Kei. But the Bantu would not go, for the Zulu and others were behind them; and the missionaries told the Government that it was wrong to take away lands on which the Bantu had been living for many years. So the Governor changed his mind; he told the Xosa that they might stay in the land between the Keiskamma and the Kei, but they must give up their arms and come under the law of the colony. All the land south of the Keiskamma River was given to British and Boer farmers, and many farmers were given land too between the Keiskamma and the Kei.

So far D'Urban had pleased the Boers, and his peace seemed good also to the Xosa. But he was not the master; he was responsible to the Government in London, which was several weeks journey away. The Government in London did not at all like the idea of taking away land which belonged to the Bantu, or at any rate on which the Bantu had been living. The Government in London at this time was very troubled at the idea of taking African peoples under British rule. In 1828 it tried hard to leave the Gold Coast, and did in fact hand over the British settlements in that country to be ruled by the British merchants who traded there. And now in 1835 it received the news that the British border was to be pushed 100 miles further into Africa, and many thousands of Africans were to become British subjects. It said, 'No.' It told D'Urban that he must leave all the land beyond the Keiskamma to the Bantu; and D'Urban had to obey.

When this happened, many of the Boers had had enough of the British Government. They had had their farms burnt and their cattle stolen; the Government could not protect them, and it made all kinds of regulations to stop them protecting themselves. They wanted farms, and if the Bantu took their cattle they wanted to be free to go after them and take them back by force. This British Government was no use to them. They had better get out of the country and get away from it. In 1837, 2,000 Boers left the border districts and trekked northward to find new homes, away from the Bantu and away from the British. This was the Great Trek.

THINGS TO DO, TO DISCUSS, OR TO FIND OUT

1. Do not be content with the maps in this book; compare them with the maps in your atlas, and find the places in your atlas.
2. Draw a straight-line time-chart of South African history

from 1652 to the present day, and mark on it the dates given in this book.

3. Draw a pie-chart of South African history, showing the periods of Dutch rule: British rule: Dutch rule again: British rule again: the independence of the Transvaal and the Orange Free State: and the self-governing Union. The dates are all given in the book. The independence of the Transvaal and the Orange Free State can be shown on a second circle inside the first and with the same centre.

4. How many of the following plants are native to Africa? If any are not native, what country did they come from, and who brought them to Africa?

    cocoa, coffee, cotton, rubber, maize, yam, coco-yam, coco-nut, grape-vine, olive, wheat, sisal, banana, ground-nut, oil-palm.

5. On page 101 it is said that the trekking Boers left behind them much of their civilization. Compare this with what is said about civilization on pages 45-6. This was before the days of machines; which parts of their civilization did they leave behind?

6. Is what is said on pages 102-3 about African custom in the matter of land true in your country?

7. Look at your atlas to see how important Mauritius was when there was no Suez Canal and all ships from Europe to India had to go round the Cape. The people of Mauritius like to call their island 'the star and key of the Indian Ocean'; what do they mean?

8. Act a scene in which Governor D'Urban, the Xosa chiefs, the Boer leaders, and the missionaries discuss what can be done to bring peace after the war of 1834.

9. How far is it from Cape Town to the Fish river? How far can a messenger on foot and on horseback go in a day? How long would it take for the Governor in Cape Town to hear news of what was happening on the Fish river? Does this help you to understand why the Government in London, before the days of telegraph and telephone, was unwilling to stretch British power further and further into South Africa?

10. Was there anything the Government could have done to stop the Great Trek?

THE GREAT TREK

The Great Trek was something new. The Boers had always been trekking from the beginning; but so far, the trekkers had always thought of themselves as being subject to the Government at the Cape. Now, they were trekking to get away altogether from the Government and to set up independent Boer Governments for themselves.

The British Government did not know what to do. The British in South Africa did not want to see the Boers set up independent states; for they were afraid that there would be trouble with the Bantu, and that the trouble would come into the Colony. So they would like the Government to follow the trekkers, and make the whole country British. But the Government in London would not agree to this. It did not want to stretch the British Empire any further. It was having troubles of this kind in other parts of the world. In Canada there was trouble because the Canadians and the Americans were trekking further and further west, and the Government was having to stretch British rule westward so as to prevent the United States from taking all the country. In the Gold Coast, British traders were forcing the Government to protect the coast peoples against the Ashanti. In New Zealand, British settlers and missionaries were having trouble with the Maori, and the Government had had to make New Zealand a British colony. There seemed no end to it. If the Boers wanted to go right away into the middle of Africa, would it not be best to let them go?

For many years to come, the history of South Africa was troubled because the British Government in London could not make up its mind whether to rule the Boers or to let them be independent. First it would let them go; then some trouble would come, and it would change its mind and tell them that they must be British subjects again; and then it would let them go once more.

At first, the trekkers found plenty of land which was lying empty. Some years before, one of the Bantu kings had trained his army in a new way so that it became the strongest of all the Bantu in South Africa; and he fought against all the Bantu states around him. When he died, King Chaka of the Zulu followed his example, and was an even greater conqueror. For about fifteen years, Chaka and his men made war, and defeated all the peoples they came against. The defeated peoples tried to

About
1817–
1837

move further away from the Zulu; but they found other peoples living in their way, so they tried to fight their way through them. So for all these years there was fighting all over the country which now makes Natal, the Orange Free State, the Transvaal, and Bechuanaland. The Bantu call this the time of *Mfecane*, the time of crushing, because the tribes were broken and crushed together by war. Many thousands of people were killed, and much land was left empty. And then the Boers came.

The Boers crossed the Orange and the Vaal rivers, and they set up two republics, one between the Orange and the Vaal, and the other north of the Vaal. They fought against Msilikazi, king of the Matabele, and drove him and his people northward across the Limpopo river. One of the Boer leaders called Piet Retief took a few men and rode across the mountains into Zululand. Chaka was dead, and there was a new king of the Zulu called Dingaan. Retief hoped that Dingaan would give him land in what is now Natal, and he told the rest of the Boers to stay the other side of the mountains until he and his friends came back and told them what Dingaan said.

Dingaan had heard that the Boers were good fighters, and he told Piet Retief that if Retief and his men would do something for him, he would give them land. A neighbouring tribe had attacked some Zulu villages and taken their cattle; would Retief and his men help the Zulu to get their cattle back again? Retief agreed, and went with the Zulu to war; and when the fighting was over and the cattle were back in the Zulu villages, Retief and his friends went to Dingaan's town at Umgungundhlovu to be given the land which Dingaan had promised them. But Dingaan had heard bad news. The other Boers had not stayed on the other side of the mountains as Retief had told them. Before ever Retief reached Umgungundhlovu, they came across the mountains and made a laager in Dingaan's country. Dingaan had heard from Retief himself what the Boers had done to Msilikazi and the Matabele; and when he heard that the Boers had come into his country without waiting for his permission, he was frightened and angry. He invited Retief and

H

a few friends to come and see him; he gave Retief a paper which was a written gift of land; and killed Retief and his whole party while they were with him as his guests.

February 6, 1838

Dingaan then sent his army against the Boers who had come into his country. He wiped out one Boer laager, and drove the others out of the country; and the Zulu army came right down to the port of Durban and took it.

The British Government could not allow this, for Durban was not a Boer town; it was British. The settlers had bought the land, and they had an agreement with Dingaan himself, and they had done him no harm. Even the Government in London agreed that soldiers must be sent to turn out Dingaan's men and set up the Government in Durban again; and this was done. More Boers came into the country; and one of them, named Andries Pretorius, marched right into Zululand and defeated the Zulu at the battle of Blood River. The Boers set up a republic in Natal with its capital at Pietermaritzburg (named after Pieter Maritz, one of the leaders of the Trek), and the Government in London was happy to hear the news, and told the Governor to take the British soldiers away from Durban again.

December 18, 1838

As soon as the British had gone, Pretorius decided to finish with Dingaan; for Dingaan had escaped from his defeat at Blood River and still had an army. The Boers could not forgive Dingaan for killing Piet Retief and his friends while they were his guests; and they feared that he would give them more trouble as long as he was alive. Dingaan had a brother named Panda, who would like to be king of the Zulu, but feared Dingaan too much to rise up against him. Pretorius and the Boers helped Panda to rise up against his brother Dingaan; Dingaan was defeated in battle, and died; and Panda became king. But Panda was no longer quite free. The Boers had shown that they were stronger than the Zulu. The Boers had made Panda king of the Zulu instead of Dingaan, and if they wished, they could make someone else king instead of Panda. So Panda had to obey the Government of the Republic of Natal.

There were now three Boer republics: one in Natal and two (the Orange Free State and the Transvaal) on the other side of

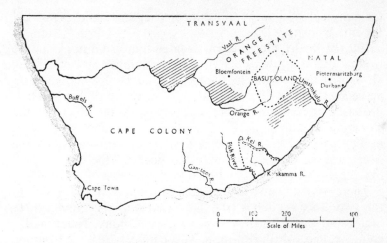

MAP 5. SOUTH AFRICA ABOUT 1850

This map shows the southern part of the country as it was about 1850. The Fish, Keiskamma, and Kei rivers are marked. (The Fish and the Kei are sometimes marked on maps as the Great Fish and the Great Kei.) The triangular piece of land, bounded with a dotted line, between the Fish and the Kei is the colony of British Kaffraria. This was a separate British colony until 1866, when it became part of Cape Colony. The shaded land lying in three pieces along the Orange and Umzimkulu rivers is the land occupied by the Griqua states. In 1829, Cape Colony was bounded on the north by the Buffels river and on the east by the Fish river. In 1847 the boundary was pushed forward so that the Colony was bounded on the north by the Orange river (all the way from the sea right up to the boundary of Basutoland) and on the east by the Keiskamma river.

the mountains. Pretorius was leader of all three. The next thing that he had to do was to persuade the British that these three new Boer republics were independent; so he sent to the Governor at Cape Town to ask him.

1840

The British Government took a long time to make up its mind, and it was fourteen years before the question was settled. Natal was the first to be decided. The republic of Natal was not happy. Its Boer population was small and poor, and it had trouble with various Bantu peoples on its borders. Even Pretorius himself admitted that it was a failure. In 1843, the British were afraid that Natal was going to have a big war with the Bantu, and that if this happened, the fighting would come down into Cape Colony; so they sent an officer to Pietermaritzburg to invite Natal to become British. Some of the Natal Boers did not like it, and trekked away; but the Natal

Government and most of its people agreed, and Natal did become British.

But the British Government decided that it did not want the trouble of ruling the other two Boer republics and of settling all their quarrels with the Bantu. In January, 1852, it made an agreement, called the Sand River Convention[1], by which it promised that it would not interfere with the Boers of the Transvaal Republic, north of the River Vaal. Two years later, in February, 1854, it made a similar[2] agreement, called the Bloemfontein Convention, with the Boers of the Orange Free State, between the Vaal and the Orange rivers.

There were now five white states in South Africa. There were the two Boer republics (the Transvaal and the Orange Free State) and three British colonies: Cape Colony, Natal, and a colony called British Kaffraria. This colony was made from the old Xosa lands between the rivers Fish and Kei; it was made a British colony in 1847, and became part of Cape Colony in 1866. The land between the Kei and the Umzimkulu was free; the Basuto were free; and along the Orange river there were some free states where the people were called Griqua, a mixture of Bantu and Hottentot with some European civilization. Neither Cape Colony nor the two Boer republics were as large as they are now; free Bantu peoples lived to the west and the north of them.

South Africa was thus divided into many states, some black, some white. For some time now the Bantu had been buying guns, so that they were able to fight the Boers with a good chance of winning. In 1837, 135 Boers with their horses and guns had defeated Msilikazi and his Matabele in a nine-day battle without losing a single man; but those days were gone. Everywhere there were Boers and Bantu wanting more land for their cattle. Could South Africa go on in this way?

GOLD AND DIAMONDS

The British thought that it could not. They thought that sooner or later, the Boer republics would get into bad trouble with Moshesh and his Basuto, or with the Zulu or some other strong

[1] A convention is really the group of people who have come together to make an agreement; but the word is often used to mean the agreement which they have made.
[2] That is, an agreement of the same kind.

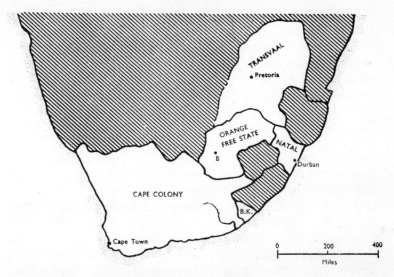

MAP 6. THE STATES OF SOUTH AFRICA AFTER THE GREAT TREK

The land shaded in this map was still occupied by free Bantu states about 1860; the land under European rule at that time is shown in white. The European states are (1) the Transvaal, with its northern boundary along the River Limpopo but its western boundary with the Bechuana and others not yet settled; this part of the boundary is marked by a dotted line; (2) the Orange Free State, with its capital of Bloemfontein, bounded by the rivers Vaal and Orange, and the mountains which separated it from Natal; (3) the British colony of Natal; (4) the small British colony of British Kaffraria, which became part of Cape Colony in 1866; (5) Cape Colony itself.

North and west of the Transvaal were the Bantu peoples of South-West Africa and Central Africa, still free from European rule. East of the Transvaal was the Portuguese colony of Mozambique, but Portuguese power did not yet go far from the coast, so there were still some Bantu people living independent north and east of the Limpopo. South-east of the Transvaal were the Zulu and Swazi and others; Zululand did not become British until 1886. There is another piece of Bantu country lying between Natal, the Orange Free State, and the Cape Colony. It is divided into two parts. The part next to the Orange Free State is Basutoland; the part near the sea was occupied by many Bantu peoples, Tembu, Pondo, Griqua and others, and did not become British until after the war of 1877.

Only two Boer republics are marked, the Transvaal and the Orange Free State. From time to time there were some other small ones, but all of them in the end joined these two important states.

Bantu people; and then the trouble would spread into the Colony. They thought that it would be better if the Boer republics would unite into one, and if Boers and British could join together in some form of united state—perhaps a federation, like the United States of America.[1]

[1] Or like Nigeria, or Malaya.

In 1865 it looked as if the British were right; for the Orange
Free State got into a big war with the Basuto. The Boers did well
in the fighting, and took a great part of Basutoland. Then
Moshesh asked the British to protect him; he said that 'he had
given his country into the hands of the Queen' of England. The
British did not want to take it. But they saw that if the Boers had
their way, they would break up the Basuto altogether and leave
them hardly any land to live on. If that happened, the Basuto
would come into the Colony to find new land; and there would
be bad trouble, because there was no land lying empty and so
they would want to turn other people out. So the British
Governor, Sir Philip Wodehouse, took Basutoland and made it
a British colony, and made the Boers give back most of the
Basuto land which they had taken away. He would not put
Basutoland under Cape Colony or Natal, for he was afraid that
the European parliaments in those countries would make the
Basuto come and work on the European farms; he kept Basutoland in the High Commissioner's own hands.[1]

We can see that the British were already finding it difficult
to stay south of the Orange river, as they had promised to do.

Very soon they found it more difficult still. In 1867 some
1870   gold (though not very much) was found in the far north,
        and diamonds were found in the Griqua lands just to the
west of the Orange Free State and to the north of Cape Colony.
At once there was a rush. The Orange Free State wanted to
take the diamond fields, the Griqua did not want to give them
up. Many white men came from Australia and elsewhere, as
well as from all over South Africa, to dig for diamonds and gold
and make themselves rich. There was quarrelling, and it seemed
that there would be fighting; and the British thought that the
safest thing to do was to make the diamond fields British
territory.

Until then, South Africa had been a country of cattle and
farm land; since then, it has been a country of gold and diamond
mines. It is much richer, but very different. The Boers had
wanted hundreds of Bantu to work on their farms; now, as the

---

[1] In October, 1846, the Government in London gave the Governor of Cape
Colony the title of High Commissioner, so that he could represent it in dealing
with Zulu and Basuto and others who were not British subjects. So Sir Philip
Wodehouse had some powers as Governor of the Cape, and others as High
Commissioner.

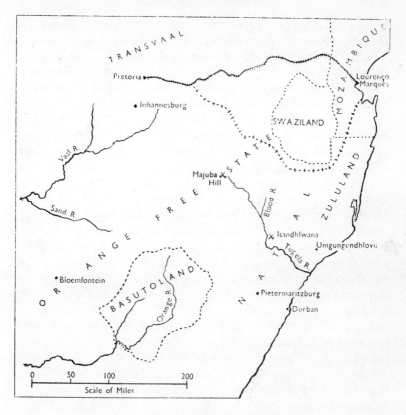

MAP 7. BOERS AND BRITISH, 1870-1901

We can see from the way in which the rivers run that there must be mountains
between Natal and the Orange Free State; and Basutoland too is full of mountains.
The map marks Dingaan's town at Umgungundhlovu, the battlefields of Majuba
and Isandhlwana, and the Blood river, where the Boers defeated the Zulu. The
Sand river is also marked, which gave its name to the Sand River Convention.
In the north-east corner of the map is the Portuguese seaport of Lourenço Marques
on the shores of Delagoa Bay; and the map shows the railway line which runs
from Lourenço Marques, north of Swaziland, to Pretoria. The Government of the
Transvaal wished to build the railway through Swaziland, but the Swazi would
not agree. Then the Transvaal thought of building the line round the south of
Swaziland and coming to the sea, not at the town of Lourenço Marques but at
some point on the south shore of Delagoa Bay. The map shows how the line would
have run. The Boers hoped that they might take a strip of land from the Zulu and
have the line running all the way to the sea through their own land, for at that
time the Portuguese had no Government posts on the south shore of Delagoa Bay.
But this would have killed the trade of Lourenço Marques; and the Portuguese
said that although they had no Government posts there, the whole of the Delagoa
Bay shore was Portuguese.

miners began to dig deeper and deeper for gold and diamonds, tens of thousands of Bantu were needed to work in the mines. The Boer republics were angry with the British for taking the diamond fields, and they were angry too when they saw thousands of strange white men coming into their country, men whose ways were very different from their ways.

Times were changing. The Governments in the Cape and Natal were beginning to build roads and railways and telegraph lines. In 1872, the British Government in London gave Cape Colony responsible self-government; that is, it set up an elected Parliament in Cape Town, with a Cabinet of Ministers. The Governor at the Cape must now govern on the advice of his Ministers, not on the orders of the Secretary of State. Many people in Natal asked for responsible self-government too, but Natal was not given responsible self-government until 1893. The new railways and roads and telegraphs were making South Africa into one country, and the Government in London thought that the different states in South Africa should agree to join into a federation.

Some of the wiser people in South Africa agreed with this; but the Parliament at the Cape would have nothing to do with the idea. The Cape Colony was the richest country in South Africa. It was busily building railways, and needed all the money it could find for this work. It was afraid that if it joined a federation it would have to help the other South African states in their troubles; and it did not want this.

The Transvaal and the Orange Free State were having great troubles. They were very poor. The diamond fields, which might have given them some Government revenue, had 1871 been taken by the British. There was a small goldfield in the north Transvaal, and many strangers were coming to look for more gold, but they had not yet found very much. The Boer farmers did not like paying taxes, and the Governments were very poor, sometimes too poor even to pay the Government staff their salaries at the end of the month. They wanted to build a railway to Delagoa Bay; this was much nearer than Cape Town, and moreover it was not British, so that a railway to Delagoa Bay would enable them to trade with other parts of the world without having anything to do with Britain. But Delagoa Bay did not belong to the Boers; it was

Portuguese, and the Portuguese naturally wanted a share in the profits of the line. There was no other suitable harbour where the Boers might build a sea-port of their own. And they had other difficulties over building their railway line. They had not enough money, and the line crept forward very slowly. The Swazi and other Bantu peoples would not allow the railway line to come through their land, so that the Boers had to take a different route from the one they wanted.[1] Then, apart from these railway difficulties, the Transvaal was already at war with Sekukuni, king of the Bapedi, and it was afraid that the Zulu too were going to make war against it. Many people in the Transvaal were coming to think that self-government was difficult and troublesome, and it would be better to become British once more.

The Government in London knew this; and it thought that if it could be done, the best thing would be for it to annex[2] the Transvaal and make peace with the Bapedi and with the Zulu. The British Government could build the Delagoa Bay railway more easily than the Transvaal Republic. If the Transvaal were British, it would perhaps be easier to set up the South African federation.

There was a British officer in Natal called Sir Theophilus Shepstone, and the British Government ordered him to go to the Transvaal and to annex it if he thought he could do so without causing trouble. Shepstone spoke Dutch well, so he went to Pretoria, the capital of the Transvaal, and spent some time there talking to the people to find out if they would rather remain independent or become a British colony. He found that most of the people he spoke to were quite ready for the Transvaal to become a British colony; so he annexed it without any difficulty.

The Government in London had now decided that the

[1] The Portuguese seaport on Delagoa Bay is Lourenço Marques. The Boers were hoping to get a strip of land on the south coast of the Bay so that they could build a seaport of their own there and run their railway line to it all the way through Boer country. But Portugal naturally would not agree to this; she said that not only the port of Lourenço Marques, but the whole coast of Delagoa Bay, belonged to her; and in 1875 the Boers had to agree that this was so, and give up their hope of a seaport of their own.

[2] That is, to take it and make it British: to raise the British flag and appoint a British Governor, to give notice to all the people of the country that they must obey the Governor, and to give notice to the Governments of foreign countries that the land has now become British.

federation must be set up. It sent out Sir Bartle Frere with orders to do two things. One was to set up the federation. The other was to try and work out a good system of government for the Bantu so that they would be contented and that there would be an end to all the trouble between the Bantu and the Boers. Frere arrived at the Cape in 1877, and two weeks after his arrival he heard that Shepstone had annexed the Transvaal.

The British Government in London thought that annexing the Transvaal would help Sir Bartle Frere in his work of setting up the South African federation; but it was wrong. The Parliament at the Cape did not want federation; and of course no federation would be possible without the Cape, which was far the richest and biggest and best developed country in South Africa. The Cape was free; it had responsible self-government; but it seemed as if the Government in London was trying to hurry it into a federation against its will. So the Cape Parliament was angry. The Orange Free State too was angry; for the Boers there thought that if the British had already annexed the Transvaal, it would not be long before the British sent Shepstone to annex their country too. So by annexing the Transvaal, the British Government had not made federation easier; it had made it harder.

Sir Bartle Frere was unlucky too in his dealings with the Bantu. Many of his ideas were good. He wanted the Bantu to have plenty of land, reserved to them by law so that European farmers could not settle in it. He wanted to set up a system of magistrates to help their chiefs to develop their country and to give good justice. He wanted to set up a good police force to stop the cattle-stealing. He wanted to stop the white traders from selling them European strong drink (brandy and rum and gin and so on) so that they drank only their own native beer. Everybody knew that most of the trouble came from drunkenness and cattle-stealing; and Frere thought that if he could stop these two things, the Bantu would be happier. All this was good; but then Frere went one step further. He told the Bantu that they must give up their guns. But the Bantu would not give up their guns, for without their guns they would be helpless against the European farmers, and now that the British Government in London had given the Cape responsible self-government, it could no longer protect the Bantu of Cape Colony against the whites. Sir Bartle Frere tried to take away the guns, and at once he found himself in a big war. Most of the independent Bantu peoples between the Cape Colony and Natal rose up against him, and they were joined by some of the peoples on the Orange river, by the Zulu, and by some of the peoples far away to the north beyond the Transvaal. The fighting began in 1877; in January 1879 the Zulu destroyed a British army at the battle of Isandhlwana, and it was several months more before the British were able to defeat the Zulu and then the other peoples, one after another.

The Boers of the Transvaal thought that the British did not know how to fight, and should never have allowed the war to last so long. At the end of 1880 they rose and declared Feb. themselves independent once more; a few weeks later 1881 they defeated a British army at the battle of Majuba.

In the same year as Majuba, the British Government made an agreement with the Transvaal, called the Convention of Pretoria. The British gave the Transvaal back its independence, but the Transvaal agreed that its foreign affairs would be managed by the British Government, and it agreed also that the British Government should have some voice in matters concerning the Bantu.

THE UITLANDERS AND THE WAR OF 1899

Why did the British annex the Transvaal and give it back only four years later? Why did so many of the Boers agree to become British, and change their minds so quickly?

The British Government in London had made up its mind that federation was the best way out of the difficulties in South Africa; and it was probably right. But you cannot 1877-80 force people into federation; they must come into it of their own free will. So the Government was wise to send Sir Bartle Frere to try and persuade the different South African Governments to agree to federation.

Sir Theophilus Shepstone too had ideas about how to help South Africa out of its difficulties. Shepstone knew the Bantu well. From 1845 till 1877 he was in charge of all the dealings which the Natal Government had with the Bantu. It was Shepstone who set aside land for Bantu reserves, and Shepstone who fought hard against other Government officers until he made the Natal Government agree that the Bantu should be ruled by their own customary law through their chiefs and European magistrates. He wanted to provide Government schools, but the Government would not give him the money for this, so he had to leave schools to the missionaries. He wanted to end the trouble with the Bantu by setting up a large Bantu state in which Europeans would not be allowed to have farms; and he would have liked other South African Governments to rule their Bantu peoples in the way that Natal did. Although he spoke Dutch well, and had many Boer friends, Shepstone's idea of how to treat the Bantu was very different from the Boer idea, and perhaps he understood better how to deal with his Bantu friends than with the Boers. So when the Government in London mistakenly decided to annex the Transvaal so as to help the idea of federation, it perhaps made another mistake in sending Shepstone to do it.

However, Shepstone went to Pretoria, and, rightly or wrongly, thought that most of the Boers in the Transvaal were ready to become British; so he annexed the country. Both Sir Bartle Frere and the Government in London promised that the Transvaal, although now British, should have self-government, but for two years they did nothing about arranging self-government, and when self-government came in 1879, it was not nearly as full as the Boers had hoped. So the Boers thought that the British had cheated them, and even those who had wanted Shepstone to annex their country changed their minds.

Why then did the British Government give the Transvaal back its independence? Not simply because of the battle of Majuba. There had been a change of Government in London. The Conservative Government, led by Disraeli, had annexed the Transvaal because it thought that this would help federation. Disraeli and the Conservatives were opposed by Gladstone and the Liberals, who thought it was wrong to annex the Transvaal. In April 1880 the Conservative Government fell, and the Liberals came into power. The Government, both under Disraeli and under Gladstone, wanted to get out of its South African troubles, for it was having trouble in other parts of the world. But if there is a change of Government in Britain, it is not the custom for the new Government to undo what the old Government has done, even if it dislikes it. Gladstone himself would have liked to give the Transvaal complete independence again, but many of his party said that this would be against the custom of the country, and they would not agree. So the Government suggested the new arrangement that the Transvaal should be independent in home affairs but that Britain should manage its foreign affairs; and the Boers accepted this.

In July 1879, some of the Boers in Cape Colony founded the Afrikaner Bond, which was a society to encourage the use of the Afrikaans language (not the Dutch of Holland), to encourage South African national feeling, and to look after the education and interests of the Boer farmers. Stephanus du Toit,[1] one of the founders of the Bond, became head of the education department of the Transvaal. Both English and Dutch were used in the Transvaal schools, but Du Toit changed that and made Dutch the only medium of instruction.[2] In 1882, the Government of the Cape allowed Dutch to be used in Parliament, and allowed Dutch to be the medium of instruction in the schools if the parents wished. This was the way in which the Afrikaans language and Afrikaner[3] national feeling began to rise.

But although they were independent again, the Boers in the Transvaal could not get away from the British. In 1872, more gold was found in the eastern Transvaal, and in 1886 the rich goldfields were found on the Rand, and the city of Johannesburg was built. This brought thousands of British and other strangers who wanted to dig gold and become rich. The Transvaal, which had been the poorest country in South Africa, now became the richest. The Transvaal Boers did not like it. They wanted to keep their old farming way of life, and they saw that these strangers wanted to change it. Many of the strangers came only for a few years, to make their money and go. President Kruger of the Transvaal asked his friend President Brand of the Orange Free State, what he should do with the Uitlanders,[4] as the Boers called them. President Brand said, 'make friends with them'. But Kruger and his people felt they could not do

---

[1] Notice that he has a French name, like Governor de Chavonnes. (See page 100).
[2] The medium of instruction is the language in which a teacher teaches his class.
[3] The Boers were beginning to call themselves Afrikaners, which simply means 'Africans'. They were as much natives of South Africa as the Bantu were.
[4] Uitlanders is the Dutch word for strangers.

that; the Uitlanders were too different. The Transvaal Government decided not to let the Uitlanders share in the government of the country. Before 1882, anyone could have a vote if he had lived in the country for one year and wanted to become a citizen. In 1882, the Government raised the one year to five years. In 1890 it did more. It set up a special council for the mining districts, and told the Uitlanders that after they had been in the country for two years they might vote for that council; but they would have to live in the country for 14 years before they might vote for Parliament.

This was a mistake. No doubt, many of the Uitlanders did not really want the right to vote, and some of them were not good citizens. But it seemed unfair to say that a man must wait 14 years for the vote, no matter how good a citizen he was and how much he wanted it. The Uitlanders of course complained, and some of them asked the British Government to help them by speaking to the Government of the Transvaal. The British Government could not give them much help, for in 1884 it had made a new agreement with the Transvaal, called the London Convention. By this agreement, the British Government gave up all the rights over the Transvaal which it had kept in the Convention of Pretoria, except that the Transvaal must not make an agreement with any foreign country without British approval.

But there was one man who was in a hurry, and his name was Cecil Rhodes. Rhodes was an Englishman, who came out to Natal as a young man to grow cotton. In 1872 he left his cotton fields and went to the diamond fields to make money. He became rich, and used some of his money to go as a student to Oxford, studying at college during term time and returning to the diamond fields in the vacations. In 1881, when he was 28 years old, he took his Oxford degree and also became a member of the Cape Parliament. He formed the De Beers Company, which controlled nearly all the diamonds in South Africa, and in 1890 he became Prime Minister of the Cape. As Prime Minister, he passed the Glen Grey Act of 1894, which was to help Bantu to get land and to keep it when they had got it.

But Rhodes looked beyond the Transvaal. He wanted to spread British rule further and further in Africa, and he dreamed of a railway from the Cape to Cairo, to run all the way through

British country. The Government in London did not want to annex more of Africa than it could help, and Rhodes saw that Germany and Portugal might push inland from east and west and cut him off from Central Africa and the north. So he formed a new company, called the British South Africa Chartered Company, to annex as much land as it could. In 1888 he made an agreement with Lobengula, king of the Matabele, that Lobengula should not deal with any other country (such as Portugal, or the Transvaal) without British permission. Two years later, Lobengula allowed Rhodes to send a small party of men through his country to Mashonaland to look for gold. Lobengula and his Matabele had been in the habit of making war on the Mashona and taking their cattle, so they did not mind if the white men too went to give the Mashona trouble. Rhodes's men occupied Mashonaland and founded the town of Salisbury, and they made agreements with the Barotse and other peoples. This was the beginning of Rhodesia, which is named after Rhodes. The party of white men was larger than Lobengula had expected; and he had not expected that they would build towns. Trouble was certain to come sooner or later. In 1893, the Matabele again made war on the Mashona; they took Mashona cattle and burned Mashona villages. Rhodes's Chartered Company made war on Lobengula and annexed the whole of the Matabele country. The king's town of Bulawayo became a European city, and Lobengula's country became the colony of Southern Rhodesia.

In 1895, Rhodes persuaded the chiefs and people of Bechuanaland to give the British Government a strip of land along the eastern edge of their country for a railway, and he persuaded the British Government to take it. The people were willing to give this land; for they feared the Boers, and now the British would be between them and the Transvaal.

What has all this to do with the Uitlanders in the Transvaal? Rhodes had now put a ring of British country all round the Transvaal, except on the Portuguese border. It is true that Portugal would not let Britain have Delagoa Bay, and true that Rhodes's dream of a Cape to Cairo railway was finished, because the Germans and the Belgians had joined hands in the north. All the same, Rhodes hoped that all South Africa would some day join together; and he thought that the Uitlanders

BELGIAN
CONGO

GERMAN
EAST AFRICA

PORTUGESE
WEST AFRICA

Zambesi R.

Salisbury

MASHONALAND

Bulawayo
MATA BELELAND

Limpopo R.

PORTUGESE EAST AFRICA

GERMAN
SOUTH-WEST
AFRICA

BECHUANALAND

TRANSVAAL

Pretoria
Johannesburg

Lourenço
Marques

Orange R.

Kimberley
Bloemfontein

Durban

Cape Town

0   100 200   400

Scale of Miles

MAP 8. CECIL RHODES'S AFRICA

This map shows how Cecil Rhodes was trying to push British power northwards. The dotted line marks the northern and western boundaries of the Transvaal and the Orange Free State. Rhodes had kept the Orange Free State from taking the diamond fields at Kimberley, so that when the Bechuana people gave him a strip of land for their railway, he was able to build the line on British land all the way to Bulawayo and Salisbury. This stopped the Germans in German South-West Africa from joining up with the Transvaal, as Rhodes feared they would. When he got as far north as Salisbury, there was no longer much danger that the Portuguese in West Africa (Angola) and in East Africa (Mozambique) might join hands and block the road north. But Rhodes's dream of a British line all the way to Cairo was stopped when the Germans in East Africa (Tanganyika) joined up with the Belgians in the Congo. The railway line is marked from Kimberley to Salisbury. It has now gone much further north, but Rhodes did not live to see it go beyond Salisbury.

in the Transvaal would be more likely to join with the rest of South Africa than President Kruger's Government would be. So Rhodes wanted to help the Uitlanders if he could.

The Uitlanders themselves talked of rising up against Kruger's Government and forcing it to give them what they wanted. They began drilling with guns. And then one of Rhodes's friends, Dr Jameson, thought he would help the Uitlanders and please Rhodes by taking an army against the Transvaal. At the end of 1895 he crossed the border with 500 men; but the Uitlanders were not ready and did not rise, and the Transvaal army defeated Jameson and took him prisoner. This attack is called the Jameson Raid. Of course everyone thought that Jameson would not have made his raid unless Rhodes had wanted him to. So there was great trouble. Rhodes had to give up his posts as Prime Minister of the Cape and as head of the Chartered Company. The Transvaal Government became harder and harder against the Uitlanders. In the end, it came to war between the Transvaal and Britain; the Orange Free State came in to help the Transvaal.

The war lasted from October 1899 to May 1902. The Boers won many battles. But the British had more men and more money, and the Boers could not hope to stand up for very long against the British armies unless some European country would help them. No help came.

The war was ended in 1902 by the Peace of Vereeniging. The Transvaal and the Orange Free State became British once more. The British Government gave £3,000,000 to repair the damage which the war had caused to houses and farms. The British gave the Transvaal self-government in 1906 and the Orange Free State in 1907.

There were many jealousies in South Africa: jealousy between miners and farmers, jealousy between Boers and English-speaking South Africans, jealousy between Boers who had fought to the end and Boers who had wanted to give up the war sooner, and (most important of all) jealousy between different states. But South Africans overcame their jealousies enough to agree to come together into one nation; and in 1909 the British Government passed the South Africa Act. By this Act the former British colonies, Cape Colony and Natal, and

the former Boer republics, the Transvaal and the Orange Free
State, were united in a fully self-governing country to be known
as the Union of South Africa. This Act also laid down the
constitution of the new country.

The war was over, and South Africa was now one country.
But there was still much jealousy between the Afrikaners and
the English-speaking South Africans. The Uitlanders in the
Transvaal before the war had hoped that, in time, English
would become the chief language of all South Africa. After
the war, the Government tried to make English the chief
medium of instruction in the schools. But the Afrikaners wanted
South Africa to have two languages, Afrikaans and English;
and they made the Government agree to have both languages
used in the schools. The Afrikaners began to act as one people
in politics also. After the war, thousands of Afrikaners came
from the farms to work in the mines on the Rand, so that they
had more votes in Johannesburg and the other places on the
Rand than the English-speaking people. It is true that the
Afrikaner Bond had changed its name, and now called itself
the South African Party; for a wise Afrikaner leader called
Hofmeyr saw that it would be a bad thing for the country if
English-speaking and Afrikaans-speaking South Africans were
enemies. Hofmeyr hoped that if he changed the name of the
Bond in this way, many English-speaking people would join
it and work for it.

For some time it looked as if Hofmeyr's idea would win, and
all white South Africans would become one people. Botha and
Smuts, like Hofmeyr, did all they could to make Afrikaners and
'English' into one nation. They had people from both races in
their party, and appointed men from both races as their Cabinet
Ministers.

But many Afrikaners, especially in the north, wanted to make
South Africa into a republic and to get back to the old Boer
ways. In 1914 and 1939, when Britain was at war with Germany,
South Africa joined the war to help Britain. But there were
many who wanted the country to stay out of the war. In 1914,
some of them even took their guns and made war on the

Government, and General Smuts had to take soldiers and fight against some of his old friends. This fighting did not last long; Smuts soon won. But some of the Afrikaners never forgave him for it. In 1948 there was an election, and Dr Malan and his Nationalist party came to power. Dr Malan chose Cabinet Ministers who were all Afrikaners.

Since then, the Nationalist Party has been in power in South Africa: first under Dr Malan, then under Mr Strydom, and now under Dr Verwoerd. It is working for two things. One is to make South Africa a republic. The other is to increase the separation between the white people in South Africa and the non-whites. It wants the whites in South Africa to have all the skilled and well-paid work and all the political power; it is especially anxious to protect the 'poor whites', that is, the whites who are less skilled and less well educated, and who have most to fear from Bantu and coloured competition.

APARTHEID

All this explains why South Africa is independent, with Afrikaans and English as its two languages. But what about the Bantu? What is *apartheid*?

Apartheid is an Afrikaans word which means 'separateness', and is a name which is given to the policy followed in South Africa to see that white and black are kept apart. The South African Government thinks that Europeans and Bantu will be better if they do not mix together but live and develop separately. It does not want South Africa to be a country in which white and black live in the same street and do the same work: a black engineer working alongside a white engineer, a black clerk alongside a white clerk.

If this is what *apartheid* means, is it a bad thing?

If the South African Government had divided the country into black areas and white areas, and had taken as much trouble to develop the black areas as to develop the white, *apartheid* would have been neither bad nor good. Just as Frenchmen live in France and Spaniards in Spain, and they do not trouble each other, so, if South Africa had been divided into

black areas and white areas, each with its colleges and industries and equal opportunities for its people, that would
not have been bad.

But it has not happened like that. The effect has been that the
whites must be the masters and must do the highly skilled work,
and the Bantu must do the unskilled or half-skilled work.

How can white and Bantu be kept apart, and why did the whites in South Africa think that they should be?

To answer these questions we must go back into history.
Van Riebeeck wanted his Dutch settlers to keep apart from the
Hottentots and Bushmen. He marked out a boundary line, and
wanted each people to keep on its own side of the line. They
would meet at the boundary line to buy and sell cattle, and
would have nothing more to do with one another. But his plan
did not work, because the Dutch would not stay inside the
line; they wanted to be free to go wherever they chose. In 1778,
Governor Van Plettenberg again tried to mark out a boundary.
He wanted the Xosa and other Bantu to stay on one side of the
Fish river and the Boers on the other. But he too failed, because
the Boer trekkers would not stay still, and the Bantu were
accustomed to move wherever they wanted to.

From that time for another hundred years the Boers and the
Bantu had trouble. The Boers filled up the land which they
found empty, and then they wanted more land, which they
could only get by taking it away from the Bantu. But the land
was no use to them unless they could find men to work on it;
for ever since the time of Governor de Chavonnes[1] the Boers
had been used to large farms which needed many men to work
them, instead of small farms which they could work with their
own family and one or two paid men. So they wanted the Bantu
to come and work for them; and it must often have happened,
as one Bantu has said, that 'My father went to sleep one night
in his own house. When he awoke next morning he found a
white man there, and the white man said, "You are on my farm,
so you must work for me".'

Some people saw that it would be wrong to take all the Bantu
land. A great missionary called John Philip said that both the
Bantu and the Hottentots must be given land which they could

[1] See page 100.

keep: enough land for them to live on and keep their tribal system working. If they had no land and were forced to spend their whole lives working on a white farmer's land, they could never hope to rise in civilization; their tribal system would break down and they would become useless. Philip worked in South Africa from 1819 to 1851, and it is very largely through him that the Government set up some of the large Bantu reserves like the Transkei, though that was after Philip's time, in 1866. Shepstone[1] too believed in this sort of *apartheid*, that is keeping enough land for the Bantu to live on. He wanted to see a large Bantu state in which no European should be able to hold any land.

The Boer republics did not try to take all the land. They left some tribes living in reserves, on condition that they paid a 'labour tax': that is, they must come and work for so many days in the year on European farms, for which they would be paid. But the Boer farmers wanted more and more workers, and so they were always tempted to take more land from the reserves.

When the mines were first opened, only the Europeans knew how to do this new work. But the mines soon became so big that there were not enough whites to work them. And so the Bantu came, and the Bantu showed that they could soon learn. After the mines came the factories; and thousands of Bantu came to work in the towns. The Europeans did not want the Bantu living amongst them in the towns; they made them live outside the towns in special Bantu settlements called locations. Long ago in the days of the Dutch settlement at the Cape, Hottentots who worked on Dutch farms had been made to carry a pass to show who they were and for whom they were working. This pass system was now made to apply to the Bantu working in the towns, and a Bantu would be punished by the law if he left his pass at home so that he could not show it to the police when they asked to see it.[2]

The thing which the whites feared most was that the Bantu would compete with them for work. They had grown up with

---

[1] See pages 123–4.

[2] The pass laws apply to all races in South Africa. A white man has to carry a pass when he goes into a Bantu reserve. But most Europeans never need to go into a Bantu reserve, whereas nearly all Bantu have to go into a town or a white man's farm at some time or other.

the idea that Europeans were more civilized than the Bushmen or the Hottentots or the Bantu, and they thought that a European must never be put in a position in which he would appear less civilized. Thus, it would not do for a white man to do unskilled work while a Bantu was doing skilled work; it would not do for a white man to work under the orders of a Bantu; and it would not do for a white man to be out of work while a Bantu was doing work which he might have done.

Not all the whites in South Africa thought like this. There were always some, Afrikaans-speaking as well as English-speaking, who knew that civilization does not depend on the colour of a man's skin, and that both among black and among white, some are good and some bad, some are wise and some foolish. But most of the whites were frightened, because there are more than three Bantu for every European; and so, if all the Bantu were given the same education and the same freedom as the whites, there would be three Bantu voters to every white voter, and every member of Parliament would therefore probably be a Bantu. The whites feared that the Bantu would govern the country for themselves only, and would take no care of the whites. This is what the whites mean when they say that if the Bantu were given power, 'it would mean the end of white civilization in South Africa'. You may think that if the Bantu had power, they would not behave like this. But when the Bantu had power over the Bushmen, they hunted and killed them just as much as the whites did. Who can tell what would happen if the Bantu had power?

Anyway, rightly or wrongly, this is what the whites feared; and they thought that if this was how the Bantu would behave when they got power, then the Bantu must not get power. They have kept the Bantu from getting power partly by laws, and partly by agreements which the employers have made with their white workers. The Mines and Works Act of 1926 says that certain kinds of skilled work are to be kept for whites only. But for many years before that, the white trade unions had an agreement with the employers, under which the employers promised to employ only white workers in certain kinds of work. If the employers had broken that agreement, all the white workers would have come out on strike.

In 1932 the Government made a law which said that Bantu

who were living on European farms must either leave them and go to the reserves, or else stay on the farms and work for the white farmer for as much as 180 days in the year if he wanted them. This may not seem so bad, because a man might choose to take his family and go to the reserves. But the reserves were not big enough. Twenty years earlier, the Government had seen this; and in 1913 it appointed a Commission, called the Beaumont Commission, to mark out bigger reserves for the Bantu. The Commission marked out land which would have made the Bantu reserves more than twice as big as they were. But much of this land was already cut up into European farms, and the European farmers would not leave, so that the Government was only able to find a little more land for the reserves, not nearly as much as was needed. Since then, more Bantu still had come into the reserves, and they were now very crowded. So the law of 1932, which said that the Bantu might go to the reserves if they chose, was no help to them; for they knew that if they went it would be hard to live there. In 1936 the Government set aside more land to make the reserves bigger. But they were still not big enough; and the Government thought that it might make bigger reserves still if it were able to take the three High Commission territories of Basutoland, Bechuanaland, and Swaziland, and to send some of the Bantu to live there. But the Bantu people in those countries did not want the South African Government to take them, and they did not want to give up some of their land to strangers, even if the strangers were Bantu. When the British Parliament was debating the South Africa Act in 1909 (see page 129), the Government promised that the administration of these three territories (whose inhabitants had asked *not* to be included in the proposed Union of South Africa) should not be transferred to the South African Government until their inhabitants had been consulted and until the matter had been discussed in the Parliament in London.[1] So South Africa was not able in 1936 to make bigger Bantu reserves by taking those three countries.

There are many South Africans who are neither Bantu nor European. There are the Coloured people, who are those of

[1] Some people think that the British Government promised not to let South Africa take those three countries if the people did not agree. This is a mistake. The Government did not promise as much as that.

mixed descent. Again, when slavery was stopped, many Indians came to South Africa to work on the farms, and others have come to trade; and there are now many thousands of South Africans who are descended from these Indians. Although these Asian people are just as much South Africans as the Europeans and the Bantu, the Government of India has always felt interested in them, and watches the way in which their Government treats them. In 1924 the South African Government proposed to make a law to make Asians live apart from Europeans, but the Government of India was angry, and the South African Government did not make the law. But in 1946 it made that law without minding what the Indian Government said.

In 1950 the Government made a new law called the Group Areas Act, which applied to the Bantu and everyone else in the country what the Government had already applied to Asians. This law gave the Government power to divide the whole country into districts (called areas), and to say that only whites were to live in one area, only Asians in a second, only Bantu in a third. There would be many areas; a large town like Johannesburg would be divided into several. If a white man had a house in an area which the Government said was to become a Bantu area, he would have to leave it by a fixed day; and the same would apply to a Bantu who had a house in a white area. Four years later, the Government made a special law to clear the Bantu out of some of the western areas of Johannesburg. Of course the Asians and the Coloured people and the Bantu were angry at the law, and they were angry too at the way in which it was applied. It would not have been so bad if the Government had applied the new law gently, and gradually. But there were cases where the Government was in a hurry, and caused more trouble and suffering than it needed to.

The Government now had powers to keep Bantu and Coloured and Asian people from doing skilled work alongside whites, and to keep them from living alongside whites. There was one more big change which the Government would have to make if *apartheid* was to be complete. It must stop Bantu and Coloured people in the Cape Province from voting alongside whites at elections for the Union Parliament. In Natal, the Orange Free State and the Transvaal, only whites had votes for Parliament; but in the Cape it had been the law ever since 1852 that anyone could vote provided he satisfied certain conditions. These conditions were not just a trick to keep out non-whites. Any man could vote in 1852 if he lived in a house worth £25 a year or earned a salary of £50 a year. In 1892 Cecil Rhodes, who was then Prime Minister of the Cape, changed the law somewhat; a man must live in a house worth £75 a year and must pass a simple test of education. These conditions applied to whites as well as to the non-whites. In modern times, about 40,000 Coloured people in Cape Colony had a vote, and about 11,000 Bantu. When the Union of South Africa was set up in 1909, the Cape said that it wanted to keep these arrangements; and it even said that it would not enter the new Union if its Coloured and Bantu people were not allowed to keep their votes. The other provinces agreed to this, but they said that they would not have non-whites sitting as members of the Union Parliament; and the Cape had to accept this. The British Government in London would have liked to see all South Africa accept the Cape system, so that (as Cecil Rhodes once said) there would be equal rights in South Africa for all civilized men. But the other three provinces would not agree to that.

So the Parliament in London passed the South Africa Act of 1909 and set up the Union of South Africa. To make sure that the South African Parliament could not easily take away the vote from the non-whites in the Cape, the Act said that this could only be done if both Houses of the South African Parliament sat together as one House and if two-thirds of the members agreed.

In 1935, the Nationalist Prime Minister, Dr Hertzog, tried to stop Bantu from voting for the lower House; but so many whites opposed him that he saw that he could not do it. In 1936 he got the Parliament to pass the Native Representation Act, which put the names of Bantu voters on a separate list. All the Bantu in the Cape were allowed to elect four members of the Senate (the upper House) and three members of the Assembly (the lower House); all must of course be Europeans. The Act also set up a Native Representative Council to advise the Government on Bantu affairs. The Act made an important change. So far, the Bantu voters in the Cape had been on the

same list as the whites, and had voted for the same candidates.[1]
Now they were on a separate list, and voted only for their three
candidates; so the other members of the Assembly need not
care at all for the Bantu.

The Native Representation Act was passed through Parliament in the ordinary way; the Government did not call the
Senate and the Assembly into one House and look for a two-
thirds majority,[2] as the South Africa Act said. When the
Government was asked why, it answered that it was not taking
away anybody's vote; it was merely changing the arrangements
under which the Bantu would use their vote. So there was no
need, the Government said, to look for a two-thirds majority;
the South Africa Act had nothing to do with this case.

In 1951, another Nationalist Prime Minister, Dr Malan,
went further. His Government got Parliament to pass a law,
called the Separate Representation of Voters Act, which did
to the Coloured voters in the Cape what the Native Representation Act fifteen years before had done to the Bantu. As
in 1936, the Government treated the Bill[3] like an ordinary Bill,
and did not call the two Houses together and look for a two-
thirds majority.

But this raised much more opposition. Four Coloured voters
brought an action against the Government in the courts of law.
They asked the Court to say that the Act ought to have been
passed in the way laid down by the South Africa Act (that is,
by a two-thirds majority of both Houses sitting together),
and that since it had not been passed in that way, it was not
lawful.

The Supreme Court of the Cape said No to them, for an
unexpected reason. In 1931, more than twenty years after the
South Africa Act was passed, the British Parliament had passed
another Act which said that South Africa, as well as Canada,
Australia and New Zealand, were all equal to Britain; none
had any power over the others. This Act is called the Statute
of Westminster. The Court said that if South Africa were

[1] A candidate is a person who is asking you to elect him.
[2] If ten men say Yes and eight say No, we say that the Yes party has a *majority*
of two. Most laws are passed by a plain majority, but the South Africa Act of
1909 said that laws on certain subjects, including any which would take away the
vote from the non-whites, must be passed by a majority of two-thirds.
[3] A law is called a Bill while it is still being discussed in Parliament; it is called
an Act when Parliament has passed it.

equal to Britain, the British Parliament could not control the way in which the South African Parliament did its work. The Statute of Westminster must have rubbed out those parts of the South Africa Act; whether or not they would have had any effect on the Separate Representation of Voters Act before 1931, they certainly would not have any effect on it now.

The four Coloured voters appealed from the Supreme Court of the Cape to the highest Court in South Africa. This court of five judges considered the case for a week, and then it gave judgment in favour of the four voters and against the Court at the Cape. It said that the South Africa Act was still in force; the Statute of Westminster had rubbed none of it out. The Separate Representation of Voters Act should have been passed by a two-thirds majority of both Houses sitting together. As it had not been passed in this way, it was not lawful and had no force.

The Government of course was angry. If this had happened in 1936 in the case of the Bantu, the Government could have got a two-thirds majority; but it knew that it could not get a two-thirds majority for putting Coloured voters on a separate list, and so it had to drop the idea. Next year, 1952, it passed an Act called the High Court of Parliament Act, which said that the courts of law had no right to question any law which Parliament had made since the Statute of Westminster in 1931. The Courts answered that the High Court of Parliament Act itself was not lawful, because it should have been passed by a two-thirds majority of both Houses sitting together. The Government could not get its two-thirds majority, and so it could not answer the judges. No good Government can go on passing laws which the judges say are not laws. It would make terrible confusion.

In 1955, the Government found a way out of its difficulty. It passed a law called the Senate Act, which increased the Senate from 48 members to 89. The old Senate contained eight members elected from each of the four provinces; in the new Senate, Natal and the Orange Free State still had eight each, but the Transvaal had 22 and the Cape 27, and there were many more members appointed by the Government, not elected. As the Government knew would happen, most of the new Senators belonged to the Nationalist party, and when the Assembly and the new Senate sat together, the Nationalist Government had

171 votes, five more than it needed for its two-thirds majority. The United Party[1] hoped that the courts of law would say that the Senate Act too was not lawful. But when an action was brought in the courts to test the matter, the judges would not say this. They said that there was nothing in the South Africa Act to stop South Africa from changing the size of its Senate or its Assembly in any way it liked; and so the Senate Act was lawful.

The Government was now able to do what it liked, for it was sure to have the two-thirds majority which it needed. In 1956, it passed a law called the South Africa Act Amendment Act: that is, a law to change the South Africa Act of 1909. This Act rubbed out the parts of the South Africa Act which dealt with the votes of non-whites in South Africa; and it repeated the old Separate Representation of Voters Act, which the Courts had stopped in 1951. Coloured voters were now placed on a separate list, and were not allowed to vote with whites.

The Government of South Africa is still going on with its system of *apartheid*. It is trying to separate white students from non-whites, to make whites and non-whites go separately to church, and to make them live their lives quite apart from each other. It is still trying to find a way of helping the Bantu to develop in their own way, apart from the whites.

There are two great difficulties. One is that the whites need the non-whites as workers in their farms and mines and offices. When people are working together all day long, how can they live apart and develop apart? The other difficulty is that even if the whites were ready to do without the Bantu and send them all away, there is not enough land in the reserves for them all. So far, the South African Government has not found the answer to these difficulties.

In 1959, the Government made a new law which it hoped would be the answer. The law was called the Promotion of Bantu Self-Government Act. By this Act, the Government will join the small Bantu reserves together to make larger reserves. In each of the large reserves, it will set up a Bantu Government, which will govern all people in its area, white as well as Bantu. The Government will set up a Bantu Development Corporation to help the Bantu to develop agriculture and mining and

[1] That is, the Opposition.

industry. The Government says that it hopes that the Bantu Government authorities will in time have full self-government.

By the same Act, all the Bantu lost their Parliamentary vote. We have seen on page 137 that in 1936, the Government changed the way in which Bantu voters in the Cape voted for members of Parliament; after 1936, they were allowed to vote for four members of the Senate and three members of the Assembly. In 1959 this was stopped. No Bantu will any longer have a vote for the South African Parliament; the Bantu must now look to their own Bantu authorities.

So the Bantu have lost their vote. Does the new Act give them a fair exchange for it?

It is too early yet to say. We are told that the Prime Minister, Dr Verwoerd, is determined that the Act shall give the Bantu a fair chance. It may possibly become a means of helping the Bantu to develop their own areas and to become self-governing. The Bantu areas make about one-eighth of the whole area of the Union, and they include plenty of minerals and of good farm land. They could be developed to be a good home for many more Bantu than there are living in them now. But it will cost a very great deal of money and hard work; new colleges and towns and factories will be needed, and most of the money for them will have to come from the white tax-payers of South Africa.

On the other hand, the Government has made it plain that the white areas of South Africa cannot do without Bantu workers. It has no intention of making the Bantu areas able to provide a home for all the Bantu. There will never be a chance for all the Bantu to live in the Bantu areas; about half of them will have to go on working in the white man's farms and mines and factories, and there, the colour bar will keep them from rising to high positions. The Act would be just if it divided South Africa into a black area and a white area, and if no Bantu needed to go into the white area to work if he did not wish to. But it does not do this. It divides the country into a black area and a mixed area, that is an area in which there will always be black and white working together. In the mixed area, the white will be on top and the black must stay below.

When we read this about *apartheid* and the colour bar, there are two things which we ought to remember. The first is that there are very many whites in South Africa who are ashamed and angry at it, and oppose their Government strongly. Members of the South African Parliament have voted against these laws. Clergy and University professors have held meetings to protest. European women have stood silently outside the Parliament buildings, wearing black sashes (which is a sign of sorrow) as a protest against the things that Parliament was doing. European men have marched in procession and have begged Parliament to change its mind. We must not criticise all the whites in South Africa for what their Government does.

The second thing we must remember is that many of the Cabinet Ministers and others who work for *apartheid* are very good men, who sincerely believe that they are doing the best thing for the Bantu and the Coloured and the Asian people. They tell us that their policy of *apartheid* has two parts. One is to separate the different races; the other is to help each race to develop in its own way. They say that we should not judge *apartheid* as if it meant only the first part, the separation; we should judge it on both. That is true. When we are judging a policy, we should always take all sides of it into consideration. But there is a difficulty here. The difficulty is that separation is much quicker and easier than development. It is much quicker and easier to stop a man from living in a certain street or from doing a certain kind of skilled work or from voting for Parliament than it is to develop education and industry and social services. That is slow and difficult and expensive. Nevertheless, these men who are working for *apartheid* think that those who now hate it will some day come to see that it is a very good thing.

Each of us is free to agree or disagree with them. I think they are mistaken, and so do many other people. But before we can agree or disagree with people, we must understand them.

THINGS TO DO, TO DISCUSS, OR TO FIND OUT

1. Find all the cases you can in this book where the Government in London did not wish to take more land or more power in Africa, but did so because it was afraid that something worse would happen if it did not. Do you think it

would have been better if the Government in London had gone in boldly, or had stayed out altogether?

2. Was Dingaan right to kill Piet Retief and his friends? If not, what should he have done? Were Pretorius and the Boers right to kill Dingaan and set up Panda as king of the Zulu under them? If not, what should they have done?

3. Why do you think that Gladstone's Government in 1880 and 1884 wanted to manage the foreign affairs of the Transvaal? What other European countries would be interested in the Transvaal, and why? Look at the atlas to see.

4. Draw a map to show why Bechuanaland was willing to give Rhodes the land he wanted for his railway.

5. Are you on the side of President Kruger, or of the Uitlanders? Do you think that peace could have been kept if it had not been for the Jameson Raid?

6. The different states in South Africa would not join in a federation in 1877, but they joined in a Union in 1910. Why do you think they changed their minds so much in less than forty years?

7. When the Union was set up, Botha and Smuts in South Africa and the Government on London all hoped that both sections of the white people in South Africa would be friendly and equal. In 1948 it seemed as if Afrikaners and 'English' were drawing apart in politics. How many reasons for this can you find in the book?

8. In all the trouble between Europeans, Asians, and Bantu, we do not hear much about the Bushmen, who are the original inhabitants of the country. What do you think South Africa should do about the Bushmen?

9. Read what is said on page 133 about the idea of *apartheid* which Philip and Shepstone held. Do you think that this kind of *apartheid* would be good, provided that the Bantu and Asian areas were as well developed as the European areas?

10. Do you think that it is wrong for one section of the people to govern the country for themselves only? If so, do you think it would be wrong for the Bantu to govern the country for themselves only? Do you think that if the Bantu got political power, they would wish to do this? If so, how do you think they could be stopped?

A HISTORY OF AFRICA

BOOK TWO

PREFACE

This is the second book of a series. The first book dealt with the king-doms of the mediaeval Sudan, South Africa, and Nigeria before it became British. As I stated in the preface to that book, I had intended to plan this book similarly, taking Ghana from West Africa, Egypt from North Africa, and Uganda from East Africa. It seems however, that most readers would prefer each book of the series to deal with one region of Africa, not to take countries from different regions. In deference to this desire, I have excluded Ghana, but have added Kenya and Tanganyika; so that this book deals with East Africa, together with the Nile Valley. This scheme has the advantage that the ex-pansionist ambitions of Egypt in the 'seventies can be seen both from the Egyptian end and from the Uganda end.

The book is written for African students in modern or middle schools and in secondary schools and teacher training colleges, many of whom will have had little or no training in formal history and will have no history specialist among their teachers. The book is therefore planned so as to be useful for background reading without the help of a special-ist teacher. At the end of each section there is a list of 'things to do, to discuss, or to find out.'

One of the most important benefits from the study of history is that it helps one to see how the world came to be in its present state; which is the necessary preliminary to any effective attempts to bring it into a better state. Because of this, I approach the subject in the form of a dialogue, asking questions and giving the answers by means of historical narrative. Because of this, too, I do not shrink from treating subjects which are controversial. The politics of yesterday are the history of today; and one of the uses of history should be to discipline our emotions with knowledge, and to teach us to conduct our controversies in a civilized manner. Much of my career has been spent in Govern-ment service; but the views I express are of course personal and not official views.

I have tried to keep the English style simple, and I have kept the vocabulary on the whole within the 2,000-word vocabulary of the *General Service List*, explaining any extra word in a foot-note. But I have allowed myself a certain latitude in this matter, using without

5

CONTENTS

ILLUSTRATIONS

MAPS

LIST OF BOOKS

Tom Little: *Egypt*

Gamal Abdel-Nasser: *The Philosophy of the Revolution*

D. C. Watt: *Documents on the Suez Crisis*

The Suez Canal Company: *The Suez Canal Company and the Decision Taken by the Egyptian Government on 26th July 1956*

Kenneth Ingham: *The Making of Modern Uganda*

E. R. Vere-Hodge: *Imperial British East Africa Company*

J. V. Wild: *The Story of the Uganda Agreement*

Carl Peters: *New Light on Dark Africa*

D. A. Low and R. C. Pratt: *Buganda and British Over-Rule*

Ronald E. Wraith: *East African Citizen*

Z. A. Marsh and G. Kingsnorth: *Introduction to the History of East Africa*

P. H. C. Clarke: *A Short History of Tanganyika*

Zoë Marsh: *East Africa Through Contemporary Records*

Basil Davidson: *Old Africa Rediscoered*

Kenneth Ingham: *A History of East Africa*

Report of the Kenya Land Commission, September 1933

Report of the East Africa Royal Commission, 1953–1955

W. McGregor Ross: *Kenya from Within*

Harold Fullard: *Philips' Modern College Atlas for Africa*

J. D. Fage: *An Atlas of African History*

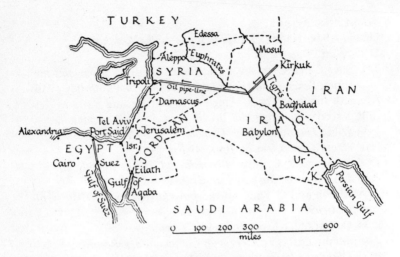

MAP 1. EGYPT AND THE MIDDLE EAST

This map shows how Egypt is related to its neighbours. Man may make railways and canals and oil pipe-lines, but mountains and rivers and deserts do not change. So this map is able to show Egypt with its neighbours both in modern times and long ago.

The boundaries of the modern states which have grown up since 1919 are marked with dotted lines. Some of them are very small: K. is for Kuwait, Isr. is for Israel, L. is for Lebanon. You will see that all the west shore of the Gulf of Aqaba belongs to Egypt, and all the east shore to Saudi Arabia; Israel and Jordan have each a very short piece of coast at the northern end of the gulf. Israel has built her port of Eilath on her coast; but you can see how easy it is (see page 62) for the Egyptians on the west shore of the gulf to stop ships from using Eilath.

The Suez Canal is marked, and so is the pipe-line which carries the Iraqi oil from the wells at Kirkuk to the Mediterranean coast at the Lebanese port of Tripoli. This was the line which the Syrians (see page 68) cut so as to stop Britain and France from getting any Iraqi oil in 1956. You will see a sharp bend in the pipe-line where it crosses the river Euphrates. When the pipe-line was first laid, it branched here, and a southern branch carried oil to the Israeli port of Haifa, which is north of Tel Aviv. But as soon as Britain left Palestine and Israel became independent, the Arabs cut this branch, and no oil flows through it now.

Now to go back to ancient times; see page 13. Much of the land shown in this map is desert: all the north of Saudi Arabia, and much of Jordan, Syria, and Iraq. Nobody would think of going direct from the Persian Gulf to the Gulf of Aqaba. The old trade route from the Persian Gulf ran up the rivers (we have marked Ur, where Abraham lived, and Babylon, though both these towns are now dead), westward from the Euphrates to Aleppo, then south to Tripoli and Damascus and along the coast (not through Jerusalem, which is in the hills) into Egypt. The country of Assyria was in the northern part of Iraq; its capital city of Nineveh was on the Tigris just north of Mosul.

1

Egypt and the Sudan

In the history of Uganda, we hear of two kings, or rulers, of Egypt who conquered the Sudan and once sent their soldiers as far as Lake Victoria. You have mentioned Egypt before. You said that long ago it was the country from which Europe and Africa learned their civilization. We notice that about 1870 and 1880 the ruler of Egypt was using British officers, and not long afterwards Britain made war on Egypt and conquered it. Today, we know that under President Nasser, Egypt is part of the United Arab Republic; but the Sudan is free and independent. It seems that Egypt has seen great changes. Why have they happened?

To begin with, all life in Egypt, as we know, depends on the river Nile. It did so in the very beginning, it does so today. Without the river Nile, Egypt would not exist. There is no other river in the world quite like the Nile, and to understand Egypt we must remember certain things about its great river.

The Nile rises in a country which has plenty of rain, and it flows to the sea through country which has hardly any rain at all, and would be quite a desert if it were not for the water of the river. As we fly over the Nile today in an aeroplane, we can see that for hundreds of miles there is just a narrow strip of green land alongside the river, and quite suddenly, on both sides, the green land ends and the brown desert begins. For many thousands of years, people have been lifting water from the river and pouring it on their fields; and the green crops will grow as far as the water can reach.

The second thing about the Nile is that it floods every year, but it never dries up. In many parts of Africa we have rivers which are big and strong in the rainy season but are nothing but a string of pools in the dry season, or even dry up altogether so that motor lorries can drive across them. The Nile is not like

11

that. It has two main streams, the White Nile and the Blue Nile, which join at Khartoum in the Sudan. The White Nile comes out of Lake Victoria, where rainfall is fairly steady all the year round; so the White Nile flows fairly steadily all the year. The Blue Nile comes out of Lake Tana in the mountains of Ethiopia, which gets fifty inches of rain from May to October, but only ten inches from November to April; so the Blue Nile floods in the rainy season and is much smaller in the dry season. North of Khartoum, where the two rivers join, the Nile water from the White Nile flows steadily, and every year the flood water from the Blue Nile comes pouring down on top of it. Like all rivers in flood, the Blue Nile brings down great quantities of mud, which the rains have washed into it.

All this has important results from the farmers' point of view. Because there is always some water in the river, even in the driest season, life in the villages of Egypt is always possible. The river enters the Mediterranean Sea by a delta built of the mud from Ethiopia, and crops can always be grown there. But the people of Egypt have not been content to lift water out of the river with buckets. As the river comes nearer the sea, it drops more and more of its mud, and the river bed is built up until it is higher than the land. Even in ancient times, the people built up the banks of the river, but when the flood came, they broke open holes in the banks and let the water and the rich mud flow over their fields. In this way, they were able to grow two crops a year: one in the dry season with the help of buckets of water, and the other in the damp new soil which was left behind as the flood water dried. The first crop was safe, but the second depended on a good flood. If the rains were poor in Ethiopia, there would be a small flood in Egypt, and the second crop would fail and there would be hunger.

So Egypt has always been a country where farmers live thickly settled along the banks of the river: where it is important for a man to be able to find the boundaries of his farm again after it has been covered with water and mud for several weeks: where it is important for people to measure how deep the water is, and to foretell, if they can, whether it will be a good flood or a bad one. Egypt was one of the first countries of the world to develop a civilization, with a strong government, with books and letters and accounts, with beautiful temples and other buildings, and a

great interest in mathematics and science. As far as we can tell,
the peoples of Europe and of Africa learnt the beginnings of their
civilization from Egypt. Many of the buildings of ancient Egypt
are still standing today, with their carvings and paintings; and
we have found thousands of early Egyptian writings: some cut in
stone, others written with a pen on paper made from the papyrus
reed which grows in the river. (The English word *paper* comes
from this word *papyrus*.)

**How long ago was this? You say that Egyptian civilization was one
of the first to develop; what were the others?**

Egyptian civilization began sometime before 4,000 B.C. There
was another civilization which began about the same time at the
mouth of the rivers Euphrates and Tigris, in what is now Iraq.
The great states belonging to this old civilization were Babylon
and Assyria. A third civilization arose in the valley of the Indus,
in what is now Pakistan; this was perhaps a little later. The civilization of China seems to have begun later than these three.

We have mentioned the civilization of Babylon and Assyria.
Though Egypt was so much cut off from the rest of the world by
deserts, it was not cut off completely. There was a very old trade
route between Babylon and Egypt; it ran up the rivers into the
north of Syria, and then turned south-west to the Mediterranean
coast, and ran between the mountains and the sea to Egypt. It
was a long and round-about way, because the deserts of Arabia
and Syria and the mountains of Sinai made the direct way impossible. Egypt has a wonderful position for trade, for nearly all the
trade between Africa and Asia had to pass through it. Traders
brought new ideas as well as goods; ancient Egypt got its first
horses and camels that way. When Babylon and Assyria were
strong, they sometimes wanted to control the whole length of
this trade route[1]; and some of the Pharaohs[2] sent their armies
right up into north Syria so as to keep the armies of Assyria and
Babylon well away from Egypt itself. We shall see that in more
modern times, the rulers of Egypt have often taken a very active
interest in the affairs of Palestine and Syria.

[1] We have seen in Book One the trouble that came because there was a trade
route between Morocco and Songhai, and both the Moors and the Songhai wanted
to control the whole length of it. So it was here.
[2] Pharaoh was the title of the ancient kings of Egypt.

What broke down this ancient Egyptian civilized state?

It lived on for three thousand years without suffering much damage. But about 1000 B.C., Egypt met new enemies. In the island of Crete and on the mainland of Greece, new peoples had set up their kingdoms. They were the Greeks: strong fighting peoples, but quick and clever and full of inventions. They soon learned the science and art and mathematics that Egypt had to teach them, and the civilized states which they set up still went on making war, both by land and sea. After a time, the Pharaohs had the idea of using Greek soldiers in their armies, and gradually there came to be thousands of Greek soldiers and traders living in Egypt.

About 350 B.C. there arose in the country of Macedon, just north of Greece, one of the greatest conquerors of the world, Alexander the Great. He conquered an empire which stretched from Macedon as far as the river Indus, and included Egypt. He built the city of Alexandria, which is named after him. He ruled for only thirteen years, and when he died, his officers fought for his empire among themselves. One of them, named Ptolemy, got hold of Egypt, and his children ruled Egypt after him.

For three hundred years, while the family of the Ptolemies was ruling Egypt, the young empire of Rome was growing. Fifty years before the birth of Jesus, Julius Caesar of Rome made war against queen Cleopatra of Egypt, and in 30 B.C. Egypt became a province of the Roman Empire.

Egypt thus became what we should nowadays call a colony, ruled by a Roman governor instead of by its own king. No longer was it largely cut off from the outside world, as it had been in the days of the Pharaohs, living its own life, developing its own civilization, and defending itself against the attacks of states away to the north-east. No longer was it an independent state, fighting and trading all over Palestine and Syria, as it had been in the time of the Ptolemies. Under Roman rule, Egypt had one main job to do: to grow wheat for the people of the city of Rome. The Government kept peace and order, not only in Egypt but on the sea, and Roman and Greek and Egyptian traders sailed down the Red Sea and across the Indian Ocean to India. But most of the people were poor farmers, living among their fields and heavily taxed. The country was ruled by Greek and Roman officials. The Roman Empire had a bad system of taxation, and as time went on, the taxes became heavier and heavier, and the mass of the Egyptian people became poorer and poorer.

Fifty-nine years after Egypt became a Roman province, Jesus Christ was crucified, and his followers began to preach the new religion of Christianity. The new religion soon spread to Egypt; as happened in many other countries, the poor people were glad to become Christians, while many of the richer and better educated people (most of whom were Greeks) thought that Christianity was foolishness.

In the year 330 A.D., the Roman Emperor Constantine moved the capital of the empire to a new city, which he called by his own name: Constantinople. Constantine was the first emperor to be a Christian; and many people who had laughed at Christianity when it was a religion of poor men and slaves were ready to accept it when it was the religion of the emperor. But there was a difference between the Christianity of the common people in Egypt and the Christianity of the educated Greeks who lived there. The Greeks had always been very interested in the exact meaning of words and ideas, and when they became Christians, they began to discuss the exact meaning of the words and ideas of Christianity. The Egyptians were not like that. They believed what Jesus told them about God, but they did not want to trouble about what the learned men told them about Jesus. The learned men went on discussing questions about Jesus. Was he only a man, or was he God? If he was God, was he man also? If he was both God and man, was Mary his mother the mother of Jesus the God and of Jesus the man, or only of Jesus the man? And so on: questions which did not trouble the poor Egyptian village people at all. But in 451, the learned men called a council, which gave the answer to some of these questions, and decided that all Christians must accept its answer and must believe what it said. The Egyptian Church refused; it said it would continue to believe what it always had believed. The Government at Constantinople supported the Council, and sent a new archbishop (he had a special title: *patriarch*) to force the Egyptian Church to obey the Council and to believe what it said. The people hated him because he was sent by the Government; and the crowd in the streets of Alexandria murdered him. From that time onwards, the Egyptian Church had two patriarchs: one whom the Church elected and obeyed, and the other whom the Government in Constantinople appointed, whom the Church would not obey.

All this is a long time ago. What have these old arguments over the Christian religion to do with President Nasser and the Suez Canal and the United Arab Republic of today?

From the time of the Ptolemies until the time of President Nasser, Egypt was never ruled by an Egyptian. It had Greek kings, Roman governors, Arabs, Berbers, Turks and British: but never an Egyptian. It was under foreign government for over two thousand years, most of the time under bad government. The people of Egypt came to hate all foreign government; they wanted to govern themselves. When the crowd in Alexandria murdered the foreign patriarch it was expressing that hate; so was Colonel Nasser when he rose up against the British. These things that happened long ago were causing the Egyptian people to feel as they now do; and it is because the people feel as they do that President Nasser has been able to do what he has done.

THE ARABS

In 641, nineteen years after the Prophet Mohammed left Mecca and went to Medina, Egypt was conquered by the Arabs. When the Arab army came, the bishop of Alexandria told his people not to fight them, for the simple religion of Islam was better than the complicated kind of Christianity which the Government in Constantinople was trying to force on the people. So Egypt became a Muslim country; most of the Christians became Muslims, though part of the Church remained Christian. The Christian Church of Egypt is called the Coptic Church. All the Muslims left their old languages and began to speak Arabic; the Copts kept on with the old Egyptian language for a time, but gradually they too came to speak Arabic.

Some of the Arab kings of Egypt were good and some bad; but even the best of them were foreigners, and their interests were outside Egypt. They made war against other Muslim states in Syria and Arabia, and they taxed the people heavily to pay for their wars and for the fine buildings which they built in Cairo and Alexandria. The worst of these Arab kings were very bad indeed. In 969, Egypt was conquered by a Berber army from the

1. Mohammed Ali of Egypt. From a drawing made in 1818

photo: Radio Times Hulton Picture Library

2. Zaghloul Pasha. A photograph taken while he was Prime Minister

photo: Radio Times Hulton Picture Library

west, and the new kings, who were called Fatimids[1], ruled it for nearly two hundred years. They conquered Palestine also, and so Cairo became for a time the capital of an empire which included the whole of North Africa, Egypt and Syria, the cities of Medina and Mecca, and the islands of Sicily and Sardinia.

The Fatimid empire lasted from about 970 till 1050. It was soon attacked by many enemies. About 1050, the whole of the western part was conquered by the Almoravides.[2] A few years later, a strong fighting people from central Asia, called the Seljuk Turks, conquered all Syria and Palestine; and about the same time, another fighting people from western Europe, called the Normans, conquered Sardinia and Sicily.

But this was not the worst. The Normans, and other Christian peoples of western Europe, began sending armies into Palestine to try and rescue Jerusalem and the other holy places of Christianity from the Muslims. The wars which they fought for this purpose were called Crusades, a word which means wars of the Cross. The first Crusade was in 1095. It was very successful; it took the city of Jerusalem, and made it the capital of a Christian kingdom.

The Muslims of course would not allow the Christian kingdom of Jerusalem to stand longer than they could help. In 1144, Zanghi the emir[3] of Mosul began from the north to conquer it. He took Edessa and Aleppo, and soon afterwards his son Nureddin took Damascus. And then the Fatimid kings of Egypt made a mistake. We might have expected them to be pleased when Nureddin went on from Damascus, as he plainly meant to do, to conquer Jerusalem. But Palestine had at one time been part of the Fatimid empire, and the Fatimids were Shiah Muslims, whereas the Muslims of Syria and Arabia were Sunni.[4] They feared that if Nureddin conquered the Christians he would not stop there, but would move on to conquer Egypt; so they decided to help the Christians against Nureddin. It did them no good. Nureddin changed his plans; he left the Christians alone for a time and sent his armies directly against Egypt. In 1171 he

[1] Because they said they were descended from the Prophet and his wife Fatima.
[2] We have read in Book One about the Almoravides and their wars against Ghana and Morocco.
[3] This Arabic title is used in Northern Nigeria; we have met it in Book One on page 84. It means a governor.
[4] The Sunni and the Shiah are the two main divisions of Islam.

conquered it, and then died, leaving his son Saladin to succeed him.

Salah el-Din el-Ayyoub, whom the Europeans called Saladin, was one of the greatest soldiers and rulers that the Arab race has ever produced. He ruled Egypt well; in 1187 he retook Jerusalem, and conquered for himself a kingdom reaching all the way from Egypt to the Euphrates, leaving the Christians only one or two coast towns in Palestine.

Unluckily for Egypt, the good government of Saladin was followed after his death by bad government at the hands of his slaves. Nureddin and Saladin had used large numbers of slave soldiers, called Mamelukes, and after Saladin's death, these slave soldiers killed his son and made themselves masters of the country. Most of the Mamelukes had no idea of how to govern; one Mameluke ruler after another set himself to make as much money as he could, following the advice of one of the early Arab kings, who said that Egypt was like a cow, which should be milked until it was dry. The best of the Mameluke kings built mosques and schools in the big cities, but they had no idea of making life easier for the poor people in the villages. There was no justice; there were robbers; there was hunger and disease; the canals became filled with mud, and land which had been cultivated was allowed to go back to bush or desert. In 1517, Egypt was conquered by Ottoman Turks, but this made very little difference. The Turkish governor ruled the country through Mameluke provincial commissioners, and the poor people suffered just as much. The Turks were not much interested in trade. Many learned men and skilled workers left the country and went to Constantinople[1], and Egypt was left to rot.

This sounds very bad; but surely the Mamelukes were not so foolish as to destroy all the wealth of the country? When Ibn Batuta and Mansa Musa visited the land of Egypt, they found rich men and learned men there. You told us in Book One that Mansa Musa was able to borrow money from a banker at Alexandria.

Yes, that is true. Cairo and Alexandria were fine cities, and traders went backwards and forwards through Egypt between

[1] In 1453 the Ottoman Turks took the city of Constantinople and made it the capital of their empire.

Africa and Asia. Not even the worst of the Mamelukes was so foolish as to frighten away traders by taking all their money, and no Muslim would make life difficult for the teachers and learned men in mosques and schools. But Egypt under the Mamelukes was not, like Mali in the time of Ibn Batuta, a land in which there was peace and justice everywhere. It was a land in which the few rich and learned men in the cities thought nothing of the poor, and took no trouble to improve life in the villages or in the poor parts of the city.

So things went on till the very end of the 18th century; and then something happened which began to bring the people of Egypt new hope.

In 1789, the people of France made a revolution: they killed their king and queen and made their country a republic. This led to a long war, in which the British fought against the French. In 1798, the French general Napoleon brought a French army to Egypt. France had no quarrel with the Mamelukes, or with the Turks, except that the French people said that all peoples were their friends, and all governments their enemies. Napoleon and his men came to Egypt because he thought it would weaken Britain if the British could no longer reach India. The French Government told him to conquer all the British possessions in Asia that he could reach (Britain had no possessions in Asia at that time except part of India); to hold the land round Suez so as to cut the direct route between Britain and India[1]; and to do anything he could to improve the life of the poor people of Egypt.

Napoleon could do very little. The Egyptian people hated him as another foreigner, and they joined the Mamelukes to fight him. They could not keep him from landing, but they fought him in the villages and in the Cairo streets. The British navy destroyed the French ships in which he had brought his men, so that the French army could get no more men or food or supplies from France; and there was very little food for the French in Egypt. Napoleon saw that he could do no good by staying there; he left his men in Egypt, got on a ship, and arrived safely back in France. The French army in Egypt was attacked by Turkish and by British armies, and had to give itself up.

[1] There was no Suez Canal at that time; but the quick way to India was by ship to Alexandria, by camel across to Suez, and by ship again across the Indian Ocean.

That was bad luck for Napoleon; but how did his coming help Egypt?

In two ways, perhaps three. In the first place, the Egyptian people saw that they had some strength, if only they used it; and the Mamelukes too saw that the support of the people was worth having. In the second place, Napoleon brought with him a group of learned men from the West, who set themselves to study the ancient Egyptian civilization, to read the ancient writings and learn the history. It is good for a people to know that it has a history behind it; a people learns to respect itself when it learns what its ancestors have done. In the third place, Napoleon brought with him something that had never before been seen in Egypt: a printing press for printing in Arabic.

It was in 1801 that the French left Egypt; and at once the Turkish soldiers and the Mamelukes began to fight each other, so that Egypt seemed to be in a worse state than ever. But there was one Turkish officer who was better than the rest. He was Mohammed Ali, who commanded a regiment of Albanian[1] soldiers in the Turkish army. Mohammed Ali and his men began by helping the Mamelukes to fight the other Turkish soldiers; then he turned round and drove the Mamelukes out of Cairo. In two years fighting he had made himself the strongest leader in Egypt; and in 1803 he went to the Turkish Governor and told him that the Turkish soldiers were behaving badly to the people, and they should be kept in better discipline. This did not do much good, but it showed the people of Egypt that there was now a man who was ready to speak for them. Two years later, in 1805, many of the leaders of the people gave the Governor a written list of their complaints against his Government. The Governor took a long time to reply; so the people of Cairo came out on strike, and marched up and down the streets of the city shouting against the Governor and the Turkish Government. Two religious leaders (one of them was head of the university of Al-Azhar) went to Mohammed Ali and said that they would obey him as their Governor instead of the Governor who had been appointed by the Sultan of Turkey. Mohammed Ali and his Albanian soldiers then joined the people, and they all marched to the castle where

[1] Albania is on the east coast of the Adriatic sea, opposite to Italy. At that time it was part of the Turkish empire; it is now an independent state, but most of its people are still Muslims.

the Governor lived. They kept him shut up inside while a messenger went by ship to Constantinople and told the Sultan what had happened; and the Sultan sent back an answer that he had appointed Mohammed Ali as Governor instead of the other man.

That must have taken a long time, I should think?

Yes; it is about 800 miles from Alexandria to Constantinople (Istanbul as the Turks call it today), and a sailing ship would take at least four days there and four days back – perhaps much more if the wind was bad.

But could they not send a telegram, or if they must send a messenger, at least send him by steamship?

No; the electric telegraph was not invented till forty years after this happened. The first small steamships were just being built at this time, but none of them were yet at sea; it was not till 1821 that steamships were put on to the short journey between England and France. Life moved much more slowly in those days.

Mohammed Ali was now Governor of Egypt, and since his own soldiers, the Albanians, were the best fighting men in the country, he was safe from any danger that the Sultan or the people might turn him out and appoint someone else in his place. He governed Egypt well. He stopped the robbery. He changed the old system of taxation, under which a business firm agreed to pay the Government a fixed sum for the taxes of a district, and then collected as much money as it could, keeping everything over and above the fixed sum as its profit. Mohammed Ali made all the village headmen collect all the crops of the village, sell them through a Government marketing board, pay the Government its tax, and give the villagers the money that remained. Taxes were still heavy, but at least people knew just how much they had to pay. There was peace and order, and so the poor people took courage. They earned much better wages, and so they went to work and cleaned out the canals which had become filled with mud. Under Mohammed Ali's Government, 20,000 new waterwheels were built to lift water into the canals, and the Government introduced a new crop, fine-quality cotton. Mohammed Ali also introduced into Egypt new industries, using steam machinery; he wanted to make Egypt a modern industrial country.

May we say then that Mohammed Ali was the first great Egyptian leader of modern times who loved the poor people of Egypt and set out to help them?

No, not at all. Mohammed Ali was not an Egyptian, and though he commanded an Albanian regiment, he was not an Albanian. He came from Kavalla in Greece. To begin with, he was just one of many Turkish officers in Egypt, and he was determined to make himself the master of the country. He did not love the poor people of Egypt, but he saw that Egypt would be richer and stronger, and better worth ruling, if the poor people worked hard and supported his Government. He wanted to make Egypt into a strong and rich kingdom, which he could pass on to his son after him. All the land, all the taxes, and all the foreign trade belonged to him; and he left the people just enough to encourage them to go on working to make more.

Mohammed Ali did not get all he wanted. Egypt was still a province of the Turkish empire, but Mohammed Ali wanted to make it independent. He fought the Sultan, and defeated him; and for a moment it looked as if he might even take Constantinople. But the European countries would not allow this to happen, and in 1841 they forced Mohammed Ali to agree to a treaty (the Treaty of London) by which he and his family were to rule Egypt; but not to rule Syria; the Egyptian army was not to contain more than 18,000 men, and the Sultan of Turkey must approve all appointments of senior officers. The treaty also had another result. Turkey was badly governed in many ways, and the European states had made treaties with the Turkish Government by which their citizens who lived in Turkey were not under Turkish law, but under their own judges. These arrangements were called 'capitulations'; and since Egypt was still part of the Turkish empire, the capitulations applied in Egypt too.

What business was it of Britain and France and Russia and the others if Mohammed Ali conquered the Sultan of Turkey?

In those days, the Turkish empire was very big, but very weak. It covered the countries of Albania, Jugoslavia, Greece, Bulgaria and Rumania in Europe. (Greece became independent in 1832). Russia wanted to rule Constantinople and to be free to send her warships into the Mediterranean; Britain and France (and some other countries) were afraid of this, and so they wanted to keep

Turkey independent. When the Egyptian army was close to Constantinople, the Sultan asked Russia to help him, and Russia sent an army and a fleet. But this frightened Britain and France and Austria, and a British fleet went to Alexandria and forced Mohammed Ali to give way. When he conquered Syria and nearly conquered Constantinople, Mohammed Ali was going too far.

The Treaty of London did not give Mohammed Ali all he wanted; but it was a good treaty for Egypt. The country could not afford to take so many men from the fields as Mohammed Ali had taken for his armies. Egypt had to give up the idea of conquering Syria, and go on with the work of developing trade and agriculture and industry within Egypt itself. After the Treaty, trade and agriculture developed very much; industry not so much, because goods from western Europe came into the country and paid a customs duty of only three per cent. Mohammed Ali built the first dam across the Nile to store up the flood water; it was a small one, and badly built so that it did not work very well, but it was the first work ever done on the river for this purpose.

In many ways, Mohammed Ali began modern Egypt; but he was not an Egyptian, and he did not use Egyptians in the higher posts of his Government. He ruled through Turks and Greeks and others, and much of the new wealth which came through the improvement of agriculture was held by foreign friends of his, who (whatever their real country) were all called 'Turks' by the Egyptian people. Much work needed to be done to educate the Egyptian people so that they could begin to run their own country.

Mohammed Ali handed over the government in 1847 to his son Ibrahim: then came Abbas, and then, in 1854, Said. It was Said who began the Suez Canal, and Port Said, the town at the north end of the Canal, is named after him.

BUILDING THE SUEZ CANAL

Engineers had been talking for some little time of cutting a ship canal through the isthmus[1] of Suez; and it was a Frenchman,

---

[1] An isthmus is a narrow piece of land with water on both sides. Suez is one, Panama is a second, Kra (in Thailand) is a third.

Ferdinand de Lesseps, who persuaded Said to let him begin the work. Britain did not want a canal. The British were content to send most of their ships to India round the Cape and to use the overland route through Suez only for the mails and for travellers in a hurry. British engineers had just built a railway from Cairo to Alexandria, and more and more people were beginning to cross Egypt on the way between Europe and India, spending money in Egypt on fares and hotels. On the other hand, although Britain did not want a canal, if it were once cut, it was certain that they would be unwilling to see it controlled by any other country – even by Egypt. The British were so anxious about the routes from Britain to India and other parts of the world that they had a large navy to protect them; and they would never allow any country, if they could help it, to cut them off from India. Neither Said nor de Lesseps saw this, and de Lesseps somehow persuaded Said that the canal would bring great wealth to Egypt, and that de Lesseps should be paid a great price for his work in cutting it.

Why were the British so anxious over their trade routes? Do not other countries also trade with India and the East?

Yes, they do. But Britain is a small country, and since about 1800 it has been unable to grow enough food for itself. It must buy food from abroad, and so it must export manufactured goods to pay for it. Other countries may export and import if they wish to; Britain must export and import, or it would starve. Britain cannot allow anyone to stop her ships on the seas. That is why Britain did not want anyone to cut the Suez Canal, but once the Canal was cut, she did not want anyone to be able to close it to her ships.

So Said made an agreement with de Lesseps, and in 1859 the work of cutting the canal began. The Egyptian Government allowed the canal company to get most of the work done by forced labour, and 20,000 Egyptians worked on it. The company was to pay no taxes; it was to finish the canal in six years; and it was allowed to own land by the side of the canal and to dig for minerals. In about a hundred years (the date was finally fixed at 1968) the Canal would become the property of Egypt. The Egyp-

tian Government was to buy one-quarter of the shares (thus
providing one-quarter of the money), and of course would receive
a dividend on its shares, like other share-holders. In addition,
as owner of the land through which the Canal passed, Egypt
would receive fifteen per cent of the profits.[1]

Said died in 1863, and Ismail succeeded him. De Lesseps and
his company thought that the canal would cost 200 million francs[2]
to build, but they were finding that it was going to cost them
much more than they had expected. They were finding it difficult to
get money to finish the work, and many people in Europe were
shocked when they saw how the poor Egyptian workmen were
suffering. The British Government agreed with Ismail and with
the Sultan of Turkey that the Company did not need so much
power: in particular, there was no reason why a canal company
should dig for minerals. With Britain and Turkey behind him,
Ismail proposed to the Canal Company that it should give up the
right to own land and dig for minerals, and also the right to use
forced labour. The Company agreed to give up these rights for an
extra payment of 84 million francs: and it sold certain buildings
and other property to the Egyptian Government for another
30 million, though this money was paid gradually; the Egyptian
Government agreed to pay it by not receiving any dividend on
its shares until 1895. With this extra money, the Company was
able to finish the work, and the Canal was opened in November
1869.

**Were Said and Ismail wise to allow the Company to cut the Canal?
I have heard it said that the Egyptian Government paid a great part,
in fact the greater part, of the cost: is this true?**

I think that Said and Ismail would have been wiser to wait a
few years longer. Britain was the country with most ships, and
Britain did not want the Canal. Much of the world's trade was
still carried in sailing ships, but more and more steamships were
being built, and people in Europe were becoming more and more
anxious to save time by travelling quickly. If they had waited a

---

[1] Egypt sold this right in 1880.
[2] The company had its offices in Paris, and used French money in its accounts.
In those days, 25 French francs made an English pound. We shall give the figures
in francs; you can divide them by 25 to get the meaning in pounds.

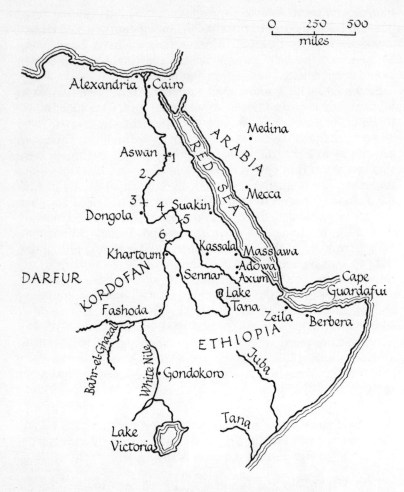

MAP 2. NORTH-EAST AFRICA

This map shows the whole of the Nile valley, with the Red Sea and Ethiopia; the middle part of the Nile valley is shown on a larger scale in Map 3. The six cataracts of the Nile are marked and numbered. The map shows the places which Ismail took: Fashoda and Gondokoro on the Nile, and the Red Sea ports. You will see how soldiers marching up the Tana river, as Ismail meant them to, would have been going towards Lake Victoria and the Nile, but soldiers marching up the Juba river would have been going further and further into the mountains of Ethiopia.

few years, perhaps British shipowners would have wanted the
Canal and would have begged the Egyptian Government to allow
it to be cut; then the Egyptian Government could have made them
pay a higher price for it. Ismail especially wanted the Canal, not
only because he thought it would bring him a profit but because
it would show the world that Egypt was now a modern state;
he invited all the kings of Europe to Egypt to see the Canal
opened, and some of them came. He was willing to pay for the
glory.

As far as I can see, this is how the arithmetic works out. The
Company expected to be able to build the canal for 200 million
francs, but it actually cost 432.8 million. Of this money, Egypt
provided 88.8 million in shares, 84 million in exchange for the
right to dig minerals, and 30 million by giving up the dividend
on its shares: total 202.8 million. As we shall see, the British
Government bought the Egyptian shares in 1875, and paid £3.97
million for them, which is about 99 million francs; so that Egypt
made a profit on the sale. However, let us ignore the profit, and
merely subtract the figure of 88.8 million francs from Egypt's
total payment of 202.8 million francs. This leaves us with 114
million francs, just over a quarter of the whole cost. In addition
to this money, Egypt also helped by providing forced labour; when
men are forced to come and work, the employer need not pay
them as much as when he has to attract them to come. This forced
labour from 1859 to 1863 is worth something, but it is difficult
to say how much: not more than the 10 million francs profit which
Egypt made by selling its Canal shares to Britain. So Egypt paid
altogether more than a quarter, but less than a third, of the cost
of the Canal.

**But did the British Government pay Egypt a fair price for the
shares?**

Yes, it paid Egypt what the shares were worth. The Canal at
that time had not begun to make very high profits. But it was a
good piece of business for Britain. Ismail badly wanted the money.
The British Government could afford to buy the shares and hold
them. It knew that if the Company did not make much profit at
first, the time would come when it would make big profits, and
Britain could afford to wait. Also, the shares gave Britain a voice
in the control of the Canal, which she wished to have. It was a

fair bargain according to the ideas of the business world. But it
is understandable that since that time, Egypt, watching the Canal
Company make bigger and bigger profits, should feel hurt that
she had no shares and so received no dividends.[1]

Ismail did much more for Egypt besides finishing the Suez Canal.
He was the grandson of Mohammed Ali, and like his grandfather,
he wanted to make Egypt rich and strong, and to make himself
king and to be independent of Turkey. Egypt was richer than it
had been in Mohammed Ali's time, and Ismail did not try to
force the Sultan of Turkey to give him what he wanted. He knew
a better way; he bought it. By 1873, ten years after he became
ruler of Egypt, he had persuaded the Sultan to sell him the towns
of Suakin and Massawa on the Red Sea, and to allow him the
title of Khedive, which was to pass to his eldest son after him,
and so on for ever. The Khedive was to have the right to hold
complete power over Egypt and the Sudan, to make treaties with
foreign countries, and to have as large an army and navy as he
liked. All this cost Ismail a great deal of money; but he thought
it worth the money.

**Was nothing said about an air force? Was Egypt now completely
independent?**

Nothing was said about an air force. There were no aeroplanes in those days; not for another forty years. Egypt was not
completely independent; for example, it had to pay a tax of
£ 750,000 a year to Turkey, and it was not allowed to have its
own ambassadors in foreign countries. But it was much more
independent than before.

Ismail did a great deal to make Egypt into a modern state. He
built harbours and began Egyptian shipping; he built railways
and canals and telegraph lines; he sent young men to study in
Europe, and built thousands of new schools. When he began to
rule, he was lucky in the same way that Dr Nkrumah was lucky
in Ghana: the price of Egyptian cotton was high and trade was
good, so that the Government had plenty of money for all these

---

[1] It is fair to the Company to point out that in 1950 it reduced its rates, so that
a ship paid less to go through the Canal than it did before the 1939 war. This of
course cut the Company's profits. The Company itself said in 1956 that they were
about 30 per cent of its total revenue; but the Company had big plans for improving
the Canal, which would have cost a great deal of money.

improvements. The business men and the civil servants were happy, for they saw their country becoming rich and modern and strong.[1]

THE SUDAN TILL 1876

You mentioned the Sudan just now. What had been happening in the Sudan all this time?

In the old days, in the time of the Pharaohs and the Ptolemies, Egypt had always ruled as far south up the Nile as she could: sometimes further, sometimes not so far. It depended on how strong the Government was. The Nile valley was a land of many different Negro and Hamitic peoples: some of them (like the Shilluk, who now live where the Bahr-el-Ghazal joins the Nile) being very like the ancient people of Egypt. As time went on, there grew up independent civilized states like Kush, which took much of their civilization (perhaps all of it) from Egypt.

We do not know very much about the history of Kush, because many of its remains are still covered with sand and have not yet been dug up and examined. Some of its kings have set up stone pillars with the story of what they did. One of them tells us of nine wars which he fought against the peoples further south; another tells us of wars which he fought against Egypt. But there is much that we do not know. We do know that Kush was conquered by Egypt some time between 1580 BC and 1320 BC, though we do not know the exact date. It rose up several times against Egypt, and finally became independent about 1050, after being an Egyptian province for about 400 years. Its first capital was a town called Napata, but about 600 BC the kings moved their capital to Meroe, sixty hours journey by camel further south. We do not know why. Perhaps it was because the Nile valley was becoming dryer and dryer, and land which was once green grass

---

[1] In Book One, pages 22 and 23, we have seen that history repeats itself, but it does not often repeat itself exactly. Here is an example. Nkrumah of Ghana and Ismail of Egypt both had good luck when they were trying to develop their countries: Nkrumah had plenty of money through the high price of cocoa, and Ismail through the high price of cotton. As we shall see, Ismail spent too much money and brought his country into great trouble. This does not mean that President Nkrumah's Government is likely to make the same mistake. History has repeated itself in giving the two countries the same kind of good luck. That is all. The two men are very different, and they behave differently.

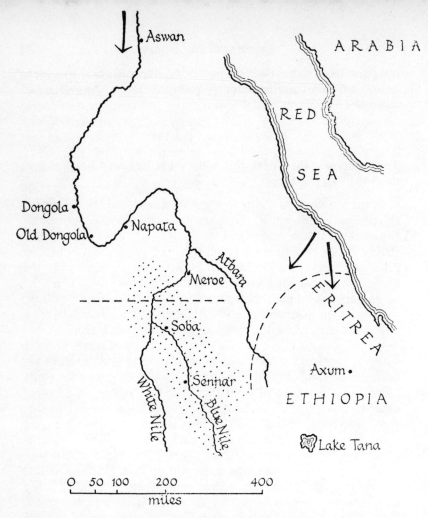

MAP 3. NUBIA AND THE MIDDLE NILE

This map shows some of the country on a larger scale. Most of the places shown are old towns, so that the map shows the history of Kush and the early Christian kingdoms. Khartoum, which stands where the White Nile and the Blue Nile meet, is not marked, because it is such a new place. All the land from Aswan to Khartoum was called Nubia, and most of it formed the kingdom of Kush. The two capitals of Kush are marked: Napata and Meroe.

The dotted line running east and west between Meroe and Soba shows roughly where the frontier was between the Christian kingdoms of Dongola and Alwa: only roughly, because we do not know exactly. The other dotted line beginning on the coast and running in a curve west and south shows roughly the frontier of the kingdom of Axum.

The long piece of country on both sides of the Blue Nile marked with dots is the Muslim kingdom of Funj with its capital at Sennar. The three black arrows, one coming up the river from the north and two coming from the Red Sea shore, show how Islam spread. It cut off the Christians in Alwa and Dongola from those in Axum, until in the end the whole of Nubia became Muslim and Christianity lived on only in Ethiopia.

was now yellow desert. Perhaps the Negro people in the south of the country were becoming more important in the government.

Kush, like Egypt, was conquered by the Romans, but Rome did not try to hold the whole country. A piece about 100 miles wide on the north was taken away, and Roman soldiers were sent to hold it. The rest of the country was left independent, but it gradually became weaker. A new state grew up at Axum, which is in the mountains of Ethiopia right away from the Nile. Axum became rich because it held the coast land of Eritrea, and so controlled the trade through the Red Sea and across to south Arabia. For a time Axum conquered part of south Arabia, but it did not hold those lands very long. About 350 AD Axum conquered Kush, and the kingdom of Kush broke down altogether. Two new states grew up to take its place: the kingdom of Dongola, and the kingdom of Alwa which, had its capital at Soba on the Blue Nile. All three kingdoms — Axum, Dongola, and Alwa — became Christian: Axum about 350 and the other two about 550. All the country from Aswan to about Khartoum is called Nubia. It is useful to have a name for the country so that we can distinguish the country from the states that grew up in it.

When I look at the map, I see that Dongola is on the Nile, below Meroe and even below Napata. If the country was drying up, why did people move back from Meroe to Napata and even further?

Yes, the modern town Dongola is 75 miles further north than old Dongola, which was the capital of the kingdom; but it is true that even old Dongola is fifty miles below Napata. But even if it is true (we are only guessing this, we do not know) that the kings of Kush moved from Napata to Meroe because Meroe was not as dry and was more comfortable to live in, this does not mean that the country down the river was so dry that people could not live there. People can live where the Nile flows. It was not that. The kingdom of Axum was making life difficult for the people further south. People could choose. If they lived in the green south they would have trouble from Axum; the people who set up the kingdom of Dongola chose to live in a dry country but to have no trouble from Axum.

The Christian kingdom of Dongola was strong from 800 or 900 years, from about 500 AD to 1351. When Egypt became Muslim, the Muslim kings of Egypt often made war on it, and sometimes they even took the city of Dongola; but it was not till 1351 that they were able to conquer the kingdom. Even then, they did not take the whole country and govern it. As the Romans had done with Kush, they took a piece in the north and left the rest to be independent. They took more than the Romans had done; they took from Aswan to the third cataract.[1] Above the third cataract there were still Christian states till long after 1351, though we do not know exactly when they fell. From about 750 onwards, Arabs crossed the Red Sea from Arabia and settled in the country round Sennar on the Blue Nile, in between the kingdoms of Alwa and Axum. They brought Islam with them; they mixed with the Negro peoples in that part of Nubia, and by about 1400 they had built up a strong Muslim kingdom called Funj or Fung. The state of Funj cut off the Christians of Alwa from those of Axum and Ethiopia; the Nubian Christians were thus shut in between the Muslims of Egypt and the Muslims of Funj, and to the west of them there were other Muslim states, Darfur and many more. Early in the 16th century, the Nubians sent messengers to the king of Ethiopia, asking him to send priests to help their Church; so there were still Christians in Nubia at that time. Late in the same century, the Turks, who had conquered Egypt, sent Muslims from Europe to conquer Nubia and to live there; and we think it must have been then that the Christian Church and what was left of the Christian states was destroyed, and all the Sudan became Muslim.

You seem to spend a lot of time on these things that happened long long ago. Does all this about Kush and Axum and Dongola help us to understand the Sudan today?

Yes, it does. When we come to 1950, we shall see that Egypt thought the Sudan ought to be Egyptian; and we have seen that Egypt has always ruled as much of the Sudan as she could. In 1950, some of the Sudanese people would have been willing to see Egypt rule the Sudan, but most of them wanted to be independent. We can understand this if we know that the country from Aswan to the third cataract was Egyptian for hundreds of years,

---

[1] Between Khartoum and Aswan there are six places where the Nile runs quickly and noisily over rocks instead of flowing quietly and smoothly. On most rivers we call such places rapids; on the Nile we call them cataracts. We number them from No. 1 to No. 6, going upstream. The first cataract is at Aswan.

but the rest of the Sudan has been fighting to defend itself against Egypt ever since the time of Kush (say 800 BC) and perhaps even earlier.

Mohammed Ali decided to conquer Nubia and all the rest of the Sudan. He had several reasons. The Sudan produced some gold, though not very much, and the pagan Negro peoples of the southern Sudan would be useful as slaves. Mohammed Ali hoped to form an army of Sudanese slave soldiers, but he was not able to; he took many slaves, but most of them died. Also, when Mohammed Ali drove the Mamelukes out of Cairo, some of them fled south and settled in Dongola; and he wanted to finish with them.

He sent his armies south in 1820. In two years fighting they reached as far as Fashoda on the White Nile; they conquered the province of Kordofan from the king of Darfur; and the king of Funj agreed to serve Egypt. (During this war, the Egyptian army made a camp at Khartoum, and the modern city of Khartoum has grown out of the Egyptian army camp of 1821.) Twenty years later, the Egyptians conquered more land near Ethiopia, and built the town of Kassala. They divided the Sudan into seven provinces, and appointed a governor-general to rule it. When Ismail got the ports of Suakin and Massawa, he had in his hands all the trade of the Sudan. But many[1] of the Egyptian officials went to the Sudan with the idea of making as much money as they could for themselves, and the poor people of the country suffered very much. A British officer, Sir Samuel Baker, went through the Sudan in 1862 and 1863 on his way to Uganda. He said that the Sudan at that time was in such a bad state that it would not have been worth while for the Egyptians to stay there if they had not been making money by slave trading.

The Khedive Ismail did not want the Sudan to remain in this state. He wanted to make it as rich and strong as Egypt. In 1863 he said that he would stop the slave trade; in 1865 he sent Egyptian soldiers to Fashoda, far to the south. Between 1870 and 1875 he conquered the whole of the sea coast from Suez as far as Cape Gardafui, and put Egyptian soldiers in the ports of Berbera and Zeila and elsewhere. He appointed Sir Samuel Baker, and after him Colonel Gordon, to push the Egyptian power further south and to stop the slave trade. Baker reached Gondokoro in May

[2] I say *many*, I do not say *all*. Some of them were good men.

C

1870, and he and Gordon stayed in the south till 1876, fighting against the slave traders and setting up Egyptian government. Gordon advised the Khedive to try and push the Egyptian power through Uganda to the Indian Ocean, and at one time he even sent a party of Egyptian soldiers to raise the Egyptian flag on the shores of Lake Victoria. Gordon wanted the Khedive to send soldiers by sea to the mouth of the Tana river, and up the Tana to Lake Victoria by the way that Karl Peters took twenty years later. The Khedive took Gordon's advice; but by some mistake the ships took the soldiers to the Juba river instead of to the Tana. The Juba was no way to Lake Victoria, and anyway the mouth of the Juba was in the country which belonged to the Sultan of Zanzibar. When the Egyptian soldiers came there in 1875, the British told them to go away again and keep out of the Sultan's country. So that plan came to nothing.

By 1876, Ismail ruled nearly all the Sudan, and his European officers (Gordon and others) were doing their best to stop the slave trade. There were 48 Egyptian stations in the Sudan, and 40,000 Egyptian soldiers. But there were not enough good officers, and some of the Egyptian officers were not as anxious to stop the slave trade as the Khedive himself was. Some of the slave traders had strong armies, which Gordon and others had difficulty in beating. In many parts of the Sudan, the power of the Egyptian Government did not stretch far from the Government station.

THE DUAL CONTROL

As for Egypt itself, Ismail, as we have seen, had not merely added to its territory, but had done a great deal towards making the country a modern state. But it had all cost a great deal of money, far more than Egypt could afford, even with the high price of cotton and good trade. The Khedive had borrowed money wherever he could, and the more he borrowed, the higher interest he had to pay. Banks and others who lend money wish to be sure that they will have their money repaid, and they always want *security:* that is, something valuable which they can keep if the borrower does not repay the money they have lent him. The security may be jewellery, or valuable legal papers; for example, if you borrow money from a bank to buy a house, the bank will want to keep the deeds of the house, that is the legal papers which say you are the owner. They will give you the deeds back when you have repaid the money, but not before; and if for any reason you do not repay the money, they may sell the house, take their money, and give you the change. So it was with Ismail; the banks asked him for security. By 1873 he had given up all the profits of the railways and the royal lands; in 1875 he sold his Suez Canal shares to Britain; he taxed his people harder and harder; but still he went on spending money, and the time came when he could not pay the interest on what he had borrowed. In 1876 he told Europe that he would pay no interest that year. At once, all who had lent the Egyptian Government their money protested, and said that Egypt must be made to pay. They formed an international committee, and British and French financial advisers went to Egypt to see what could be done.

The position was very difficult. The biggest difficulty was the capitulations.[1] The capitulations gave foreigners the right to live and trade in Egypt, to practise their own religion, to live in special districts in which the Egyptian police were not allowed, to be tried in their own law courts, and to be free of most of the taxes which Egyptians had to pay. There were many thousands of foreigners in Egypt, belonging to fourteen different nations. The system may have been suitable to the days when Egypt was under Turkish rule, and Turkey had no law at all concerning trading companies. But in a modern state such as Egypt was fast becoming, the capitulations were a great nuisance.

When a man or a Government has been spending more than it can afford, it is plain what has to be done: the first thing is to cut down expenses, and the next is to try and find fresh ways of raising money. The British and French advised both these things. They proposed to cut the Government's debts in half and to cut the rate of interest to five per cent, and to cut also such expensive things as the army. Then they proposed to raise fresh taxes, not from the poor people but from the rich land-owners. The Khedive saw his chance. He told his people that he would no longer rule them as an all-powerful king, but on the advice of Ministers. He told the army officers that the army would be smaller and many of them would be dismissed; he told the rich people that they would have to pay heavier taxes and that they (like the foreigners)

[1] See page 22.

would receive less interest on the money which they had lent the Government. He said that it was not he that wanted to do these things, but the foreign Ministers who made him. The result was that the army officers rose up against the foreign Ministers and put them in prison. The Khedive let them out, but said that he would have no more advice from foreigners. Then the German Government said that Egypt had broken its word to the foreigners who had lent it money, and the British and French Governments told Ismail that he should give up the government of Egypt. Ismail called on the Egyptian people to rise and fight for him and for their country, but they would not. At the end of June 1879 he left Egypt and went to Europe, and was succeeded as Khedive by his son Tewfik.

The real power in Egypt was held by the British and French financial advisers. They were not allowed to become Ministers again; all the Ministers were Egyptians. But they were responsible for paying the Government's debts, and they would not allow the Ministers or the Khedive to spend money as they wished. The debts must be repaid first. This system is called the Dual Control: *dual*, because it was shared by two countries, Britain and France.

It was not to be expected that the Khedive, or his Ministers, or the Egyptian people, should like the Dual Control. However selfish the rich people of Egypt may have been – and no doubt many of them were very selfish – it was natural that they should feel that their country ought not to be ruled by foreigners. There was at this time the beginning of a nationalist movement, led partly by some of the younger educated people, partly by those who listened to the preaching of a religious leader, Jemal el-Din el-Afghani. Jemal el-Din, like Usuman dan Fodio in Nigeria and Ibn Yasin in the Senegal[1] preached that Muslims should follow their religion better; but he also preached that they should all join together in one strong Muslim state. (In Islam, there is no distinction between State and Church, as there is in Christianity. Islam has never lost the idea that the whole Muslim world should be one.) The simple people, listening to Jemal el-Din's teaching, felt that the Muslims of Egypt should rise up against the foreign Christians who had so much power in their country.

[1] See Book One, pages 83, 84, 47, 48.

Even if the Khedive Ismail had spent more money than he should, does it not seem hard that Egypt should be put under the Dual Control?

Ismail was one of those people (there are plenty like him) who will spend money like water as long as they can get it without troubling about how they are to repay it. It is natural that Ismail should enjoy his work of modernising Egypt, and should feel that the rich states of Western Europe ought to provide him with the money he needed. If Ismail were alive today and still spending money, the United Nations and the World Bank would lend him money, but they would also lend him engineers and financial advisers to help him to spend the money wisely. Ismail and his Government would probably be quite glad to have the help of these international advisers. In any case, it is certain that the United Nations would not lend money to a man like Ismail unless he accepted the international advisers with it. But in 1879 there was no United Nations and no World Bank. If a Government wanted to borrow money, it had to borrow from a private bank. The bank would lend money expecting to be repaid; and if Ismail did not repay, what was the bank to do? All it could do was to go to its own Government and say, 'The Egyptian Government has borrowed our money and now says it cannot repay us. Can you help us to get our money back?' The bankers and Governments could only see one step at a time, and they had to learn by experience. So had Ismail. As a result of these experiences and others like them, we now have the United Nations and the World Bank.

Ismail was gone; but he had left behind him his debts and the Dual Control. The French and British advisers had to find ways of paying the Egyptian Government's debts, and their work was made difficult by the capitulations. It is not surprising that simple people, who understood nothing about banks and finance, should dislike seeing these foreigners holding so much power in Egypt. Trouble came in 1880, when an army officer, Colonel Arabi, led a movement in the army asking for a new constitution, a larger army, better pay for the soldiers, and three things for the villagers: no more forced labour, better arrangements for sharing the Nile water, and protection against cruel money-lenders. Arabi was himself the son of a village head-man and knew how the poor people felt. We are told that he was a big man, simple and honest, and the poor people in the villages felt that he spoke for them.

MAP 4. THE TURKISH EMPIRE

The country which is shaded is Turkey as it is today. Once upon a time the Turks ruled all the country inside the dotted-line boundary; you will see that they had the whole of the Black Sea and the south-east of Europe nearly as far west as Vienna. They also ruled all the Arabian peninsula and the whole of the North African coast except Morocco. The map marks the dates at which Turkey lost parts of her empire. Algeria is too far west to be marked on the map; this was conquered by the French in 1847.

Arabi was not simply attacking the British and French advisers; in fact, it might have been possible for him to work with them. He was an Egyptian, and all the senior posts in the army and in the Government were held by Turks; Arabi wanted these posts to be open to Egyptians. To Arabi, Turks were just as foreign as British or French, even though they were Muslims.

The Khedive and his Turkish officers saw this clearly, and they were afraid of Arabi. The Dual Control liked what Arabi said about improving the state of the villages, for they too were trying to improve agriculture and village life so as to make Egypt richer and happier. But they did not like what he said about a bigger army, for that would cost much money and make it harder to repay the debts. Both the Khedive and Colonel Arabi asked the Sultan of Turkey to send an army: the Khedive to help him

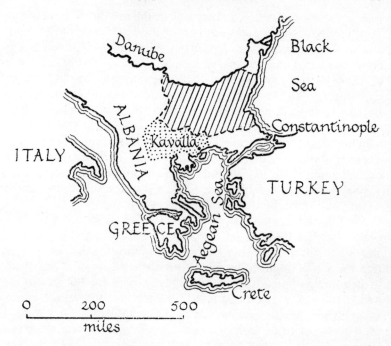

MAP 5. THE TREATY OF SAN STEFANO

In this map, Bulgaria is shaded as it was after the treaty of Berlin in 1878. The country which is dotted is the part that Bulgaria would have been given by the Treaty of San Stefano. The map shows Kavalla, where Mohammed Ali was born, and Albania, the country where his soldiers came from. Kavalla was Turkish when Mohammed Ali was born; it would have been Bulgarian if the treaty of San Stefano had come into force, and it became Greek in 1912. The country round Kavalla, north of the Aegean Sea, is Macedon or Macedonia, the country of Alexander the Great. Today it is not an independent country; it is divided between Greece, Jugoslavia, and Bulgaria.

against Arabi, Arabi to help him against the Khedive. The British and French Governments were forced to choose, and they chose to support the Khedive. They sent warships to Alexandria, and told the Egyptian Government that the Khedive Tewfik must be kept in power.

In doing this, Britain and France made a mistake; for Arabi was much the better man of the two. But Britain and France (as so often is the case in politics) had many other things to think of than whether Tewfik or Arabi were the better man. Both countries were opposed to Turkey. France was in the middle of conquering Tunisia, which (like Egypt) was part of the Turkish empire. Britain was in a more complicated position. There had just been a war between Russia and Turkey, which had come about because some of Turkey's Christian subjects had risen up against the Turkish Government. In those days, Turkey still ruled the whole of the Balkan peninsula, except Greece. Turkish Government in these countries was bad and cruel, and when the people of the countries which we now call Jugoslavia and Bulgaria rose up against their Turkish masters, Russia helped them. The Turkish armies were beaten again and again, and Russia then made a peace with Turkey which set nearly all the Balkan peoples free. This was the Treaty of San Stefano in 1877.

Most of the British people were very glad to see the Christian peoples of the Balkans set free from the Turks; and the British statesman Gladstone[1] made speeches telling the British people that the Turks ought to be driven out of their Christian provinces in Europe. But Gladstone and the Liberals were not in power; and as the war went on and Russia became stronger and stronger, many British people came to have a different feeling. They wanted the Christians to be free, but they did not want Russia to be too strong; and it seemed to them that the Treaty of San Stefano would make Russia much too strong. By the treaty, there was to be a large and strong independent country of Bulgaria, with a coast on the Aegean Sea; and Disraeli and the Conservatives (and even also some of Gladstone's Liberal Party) thought that Bulgaria would be the friend of Russia and would allow Russia to use her Aegean seaports and have a Russian fleet in the Mediterranean. And a Russian fleet in the Mediterranean was a thing which neither Britain nor France could bear to think of. So Disraeli said that the arrangements to be made in the Balkans were much too important for Russia and Turkey to settle between themselves; the other great countries of Europe (especially Britain, France, Germany and Austria) must join the discussion. This was agreed; and a conference was held at Berlin in 1878, at which the Treaty of San Stefano was replaced by a new treaty, the Treaty

[1] We have met the Liberal leader Gladstone and his Conservative rival Disraeli before when we were discussing South Africa: see Book One, pages 124, 125. Britain was having trouble in the Transvaal just at the same time as this trouble in Egypt.

of Berlin. There was still to be an independent Bulgaria; but it was to be smaller, and was to have no sea-coast on the Aegean Sea.

That was in 1878; in 1880 there was a general election in Britain, and Gladstone and the Liberals came to power: Gladstone, who had made so many speeches against the Turks. Gladstone was just as much afraid of Russia as Disraeli had been, but the danger from Russia seemed to have passed for the moment.

But what has all this about Turkey and the Bulgarians to do with Arabi and Tewfik in Egypt?

Nothing at all, really: but it shows us what was in the minds of the British and French Governments in 1881 and 1882. Neither of them wanted to see a Turkish army coming into Egypt; so unless Egypt was to fall into civil war, the French and British must use their own soldiers to support whichever they chose to support. But which was it to be? The Khedive was the lawful ruler of the country. Britain and France did not like army officers rising up against the lawful government; and Arabi would be much less easy to manage than the Khedive, and would be slower in paying off the debt. So they decided to support the Khedive. Politics is a complicated business; Britain and France could not consider the simple question of Arabi or the Khedive by itself, but must have in their minds also their fears about Russia and Turkey.

On 10 June 1882 there were riots in Alexandria, and fifty Christians were killed. It is certain now that Arabi had nothing to do with it, and his soldiers put down the rioting and brought peace again. But the British and French Governments thought that Arabi had ordered the riot. They knew that he was putting more soldiers into the city and was building forts to protect it from attack. The British admiral, acting on orders from London, told the Egyptians that they must stop building these forts or else he would destroy them with the guns of his ships. The Egyptians did stop, but after a few days the Admiral heard that they were beginning again. He gave them a further warning, and early in the morning of 11 July 1882 he opened fire. In a few hours he had destroyed the forts; the Egyptian army left Alexandria; there was more rioting; and British soldiers landed to restore order.

You speak of the British doing this, but there were French as well as British warships outside Alexandria. Did they not join in the firing?

No, they did not join. The French Government had been led by a statesman named Gambetta, who had been very strong in saying that France and Britain must keep Colonel Arabi in order; in fact, he had been stronger on the point than Britain had been. But France, like Britain, had just held a general election; Gambetta had fallen from power, and the new French Government ordered the French warships to leave Alexandria just before the British opened fire. The British were left to do the work alone. A British army, under Sir Garnet Wolseley[1] landed in Egypt and beat the Egyptian army in two battles. The Khedive went with them from Alexandria to Cairo; Arabi was exiled[2] from the country; and Egypt came under British rule.

BRITAIN IN EGYPT, 1882–1936

It is strange that it should have been Gladstone, the Liberal, who sent the British army into Egypt and took control of the country: Gladstone, who disliked Disraeli's ideas of expanding the British Empire, and who had just given the Transvaal back its independence.[3] But Gladstone had no idea of staying in Egypt. He thought that the British would stay for a short time, perhaps for a few months, perhaps a year or two, until they had set the Egyptian Government on its feet again; and then they would leave. Some people advised the British Government to make Egypt a protectorate, but the Government would not; the British hoped to be out of Egypt again in a short time, and it was not worth while taking these legal steps and arranging matters with Turkey and other countries. The British Consul-General[4], Lord Cromer, was the real ruler of Egypt, but he ruled by giving advice to the Khedive and his Ministers. The Khedive could have refused Cromer's advice at any time, legally speaking; but in fact he dared not do

---

[1] In 1874 Sir Garnet Wolseley had fought against the Ashanti of Ghana.
[2] *exiled*, that is sent to live outside the country and not allowed to come back.
[3] See Book One, pages 124, 125.
[4] In Book One, page 90, we have seen British consuls in Nigeria; they were officers appointed to look after the interests of British people living in a foreign country. Lord Cromer was — legally speaking — only the chief British consul in Egypt.

so. British rule in Egypt was in fact the same kind of indirect rule which Lugard introduced later in Nigeria and elsewhere.

Lord Cromer ruled Egypt for twenty years and more: 1883 to 1907. His government brought much good to Egypt as regards wealth and general development. He improved the life of the poor villagers as much as Arabi could have done. British engineers took hold of the river Nile and used its water as it had never been used before. They took Mohammed Ali's idea of the dam and improved it; they built new canals and dams, the biggest of which was the Aswan dam of 1902. Till then, Egyptian agriculture had been worked in two parts: a small strip which could be watered from the river all through the dry season, and a larger strip which was flooded when the river rose. The new dams kept the flow of water steady all through the year and so greatly increased the area of agricultural land. Sugar and cotton crops went up and up; the people in the villages, and the Turkish and Egyptian business men in the cities, felt that life was better than ever before. Of course there was peace and justice, and there were more roads and railways and harbour works. The British do these things well. As the Government became richer, it was able to pay off its debts. In four years, Lord Cromer produced a budget surplus; that is, the Government's revenue for the year was bigger than its expenditure. From 1887 to 1894 the surplus went on rising, and Cromer used it to reduce taxes; after 1894, as the surplus still rose, he began spending it on useful works that would bring in more money. In Cromer's position as ruler of a country that was bankrupt (that is, owed more money than it could pay), his was the only possible policy: first, make the country able to pay its way again; second, cut down taxes so as to encourage people to work; third and last, begin to spend money on improvements.

On the other hand, during the years from 1894 to 1907, Lord Cromer spent very little Government money except on works that would bring in more money, such as dams and canals and roads and railways. He spent very little on health and education, and did very little to train Egyptians to run their own country. A policy of this sort cannot last very long. People soon forget the bad times from which the new Government has saved them. Young people grow up who have never known the bad times. They begin to ask for education and for power, and later on they ask for self-government. So it was in Egypt.

The Egyptians had another reason for wanting self-government: they were unhappy over what was happening in the Sudan.

We have seen that the Khedive Ismail tried very hard to conquer the Sudan, and set up 48 Egyptian government stations in the country[1], though some of them did not have much power. But it was not long before all the Egyptian power in the Sudan was lost. In 1882 a Muslim religious leader named Mohammed Ahmed rose up and told the people that he was the Mahdi. (All Shia Muslims, and some Sunni, believe that one day, when the world is in great trouble, God will send a man, 'His Chosen One', to guide people back to truth and peace and happiness. This man is called the Mahdi.) The Mahdi soon had a large army, and destroyed several Egyptian armies that were sent against him; and it looked as though in a short time he would conquer the whole of the Sudan. Lord Cromer and the British Government decided that Egypt could not afford to fight a large war; they would just have to let the Sudan go for the time being. Colonel Gordon (he was now General Gordon), who had worked so long in the Sudan for Ismail, was sent to gather all the small parties of Egyptian soldiers from the southern Sudan and take them home to Egypt. Before he could do this, the armies of the Mahdi closed round him in Khartoum and cut him off. A British and Egyptian army, under Sir Garnet Wolseley, was sent to save him, but the Mahdi's men took Khartoum and killed Gordon on 26 January 1885, and Wolseley's army came two days too late.[2]

Wolseley had been sent only to save Gordon, not to conquer the Sudan from the Mahdi. The British and Egyptian soldiers went back down the river and left the Mahdi to take the whole of the Sudan; they held the frontier of Egypt at Wadi Halfa.

From 1885 till 1898 the Mahdi, and after him one of his officers called the Khalifa, ruled the Sudan. Under Khedive Ismail, we think there were about eight million people in the Sudan, after fourteen years of the Mahdi and the Khalifa, there were about two million. What had happened to the other six? Killed in tribal war, sold as slaves, or died of hunger and diease. In 1896 Lord Cromer decided that the time had come to re-conquer the Sudan.

[1] Not railway stations; there were no railways in the Sudan then. A place where there was an Egyptian officer and some police; what is called in East Africa a *boma*.

[2] Some of the Egyptian officers and soldiers in the far south got out by going south into Uganda. We shall see how Emin Pasha got out this way, and Lugard took some of Emin Pasha's soldiers into this army: see page 98.

A British and Egyptian army under General Kitchener marched south; the Khalifa's men fought bravely but they could not stand against big guns and machine-guns, and they were beaten in three big battles. On 2 September 1898, the British and Egyptian soldiers entered Khartoum.

The Mahdi had taken the Sudan away from Egypt, but the Sudan did not become Egyptian again after Kitchener had reconquered it. It was placed under the rule of Britain and of Egypt together; the British and Egyptian flags were flown, British and Egyptian soldiers guarded it, and British and Egyptian officials served in it. This arrangement is called a *condominium*, or joint government.

The Egyptians were not happy over the condominium; for the Sudan had been part of Ismail's kingdom, and now they had to share it with the British. As in Egypt itself, so in the Sudan: most of the senior officials were British. The Egyptians felt that the British share of the condominium was much bigger than theirs. At first, when the Sudan was poor, the Egyptians did not feel this so strongly; but the richer the Sudan became, the more the Egyptians came to feel that they should have a larger share in its government. And underneath all this was the old feeling that Egypt should govern the whole of the Nile valley, because the Nile water meant so much to Egypt.

When Lord Cromer left Egypt in 1907, there were four things that the Egyptian leaders disliked. One was the British army in Egypt and the government by the British Consul-General; they wanted to govern themselves. The second was the capitulations; they wanted everybody who lived in Egypt to be under Egyptian law. The third was the condominium in the Sudan; they wanted the Sudan to belong to Egypt. The fourth was the Suez Canal Company, which was now making good profits; they wanted those profits to belong to Egypt. It did not seem as though the British were ready to give way on any one of these four points.

In 1908, the Khedive appointed a new Prime Minister, Boutros Pasha. Boutros Pasha was a Copt, that is a Christian Egyptian; and he was the first Egyptian to be Prime Minister; all those before him had been Turks or other non-Egyptians. Boutros Pasha believed that Egypt's best way was to work with the British Government and gradually persuade the British to give Egypt more freedom. He did not believe in violent opposition. But most of his

people had made up their minds that violent opposition was the
only way of getting anything out of the British Government, and
they looked on him as an enemy of his own country. Boutros
Pasha had already done one thing which made many Egyptians
hate him; he had signed the agreement with Britain which set up
the condominium in the Sudan. Before he had been Prime Minister
many weeks, he did another. The Suez Canal Company asked the
Egyptian Government to make a fresh agreement. Under the old
agreement, the Canal would become Egyptian in 1968, and then
of course all the profits would belong to Egypt. The Company
asked Egypt to allow it to keep the Canal till 2008; after 1921,
Egypt would have four per cent of the profits, after 1961 it would
have twelve per cent, and after 1968 half the profits. Egypt would
also be paid £ 4 million at once. This proposal does not seem a
very good one from the Egyptian point of view, but Boutros Pasha
was inclined to accept it. But this made the country very angry.
There were student strikes and riots; and on 20 February 1909,
Boutros Pasha was murdered. The murderer was tried and exe-
cuted;[1] but many Egyptians praised him. The country was excited;
in many places there was disorder. Mohammed Pasha Said became
Prime Minister, and his Government refused the proposal of the
Suez Canal Company, so nothing more was heard of it.[2] The
British Government was troubled, and thought that since Lord
Cromer had gone, it had been too gentle with Egypt; perhaps it
had better govern more firmly.

In 1911 the British Government sent out Kitchener (now Lord
Kitchener) as the new Consul-General. The Egyptians knew
Kitchener and liked him; and he soon showed that he knew how
to govern. The British Government wanted him to be firm, and
he was firm; he kept the newspapers, and the secret societies, and
even the students and school-boys, in good order. But Kitchener
knew that firmness is not everything; and he gave Egypt a new
constitution. He gave more powers to the provincial councils and

[1] That is, punished with death.
[2] When the Egyptian Government told the Canal Company that it would not
accept the new proposal, but would keep to the old agreement, under which the
Canal would belong to Egypt after 1968, the Company said, 'But what good will
that do you? You will not know how to run it.' And the Government replied, 'No,
perhaps not; but we shall be able to employ foreigners to run the Canal for us if
we cannot run it ourselves.' Just what was said nearly fifty years later, in 1956. In
1936, the Suez Canal Company agreed to pay Egypt, £ 300,000 a year, and in 1949,
this fixed sum was replaced by 7% of the profits.

the town councils. He changed the legislative council so that 66 out of its 83 members were elected, and he allowed the Council to propose laws, instead of merely discussing laws which the Ministers had already agreed on in private with the British. This of course was not self-government, or anything like it; but it was a real beginning, and might have led to self-government. The Egyptians saw this, and welcomed the Kitchener constitution. But that was in 1913; next year the Great War broke out, and Kitchener never came back to Egypt.

The Great War of 1914–19 spoilt the chances of friendship between Britain and Egypt. The first thing that happened was that the British Government at last made Egypt legally into a protectorate, thus taking a step backwards, away from Egyptian self-government.

Surely that was a mistake? Why did the British do that?

They did it because Turkey, which all this while was legally the ruler of Egypt, joined the war against Britain, and sent an army through Palestine to attack the British on the Suez Canal. The British must defend the Canal; but they could not say they were defending it in the name of the Turkish Government against Turkish soldiers. So they were forced to say that they were defending it in order to protect Egypt. We can see their difficulty; but it is not surprising that the Egyptian people only saw the difficulty of their own country.

There was no fighting in Egypt; the Turks never crossed the Canal, and gradually a strong British army was built up in Egypt, which conquered Palestine. At the same time, the Arabs rose up against the Turks, and conquered all Arabia, Iraq, and Syria. So Egypt did not suffer from having enemy armies in her country. But she suffered in other ways. There were hundreds of thousands of British and Indian soldiers in Egypt. Many thousands of Egyptians served in Syria and elsewhere, and the Government forced people to sell their corn and their camels and donkeys, and even to go themselves to the war. The people felt that the British had brought all this trouble on them; and when the war ended they were more anxious than ever for the British to go. During the war, the Legislative Council did not meet, and the Government kept the newspapers under strict control. But what would happen when the war was over?

Britain and France had said that if they won the war, they would see that all the Arab countries that had fought against Turkey should become free.[1] What about Egypt? Egypt was perhaps not an Arab country, and no Egyptian soldiers had fought against Turkey; but many thousands of Egyptians had worked for the army, making roads and driving camels and motor lorries. Egypt had done all she could to help Britain, with men and animals and corn. The Peace Conference was to be held at Versailles in France, and it would be attended by the representatives of many peoples who were hoping for self-government: Czechs, Poles, Croats, Arabs and others. Why not Egyptians also?

This was what the National Party of Egypt said. It was led at that time by a man called Saad Zaghloul, who (like Arabi) came from a country village. He had been Minister of Education in Lord Cromer's time, and had later served as a Minister in the Government of Boutros Pasha. But when the British dropped the 1913 constitution because of the war, Zaghloul decided that there was nothing to be gained by working with them any longer; he went into opposition and became leader of the National Party.

Zaghloul asked to be allowed to attend the Peace Conference and to speak for Egypt, but the British Government would not allow him to. Then the Prime Minister asked to go, but the British Government would not have him either. Zaghloul wrote to the Governments of France, Italy and the United States, asking them to speak to the British Government so that Egypt should be represented at the Peace Conference; but they would not. Then there was trouble in Egypt: riots and student strikes, railway lines and telegraph lines cut, British officials murdered. Zaghloul and some of his friends were arrested and sent to Malta, and the British army restored order. In the end, the Government allowed Zaghloul to go to the Conference, but he did no good there; the peace treaty said that the British protectorate over Egypt was to continue.

All this made Zaghloul and his party[2] more bitter than ever against the British. In November 1919, the Government in London said that it would send out one of its most distinguished

---

[1] In 1914, Turkey ruled the whole of what we now call Syria, the Lebanon, Palestine and Jordan, Saudi Arabia, the Yemen, and Iraq. The British Government helped the Arabs to fight against Turkey, and all these countries became free through the war of 1914–19.

[2] Zaghloul's party came to call itself the Wafd.

statesmen, Lord Milner, to draw up a new constitution for Egypt. Zaghloul at once said that his party would boycott Lord Milner's commission, and they did so. But the Milner report was more favourable to Egypt than they had expected. It said that Britain should end the protectorate, and should make a new agreement with Egypt. In its internal affairs, Egypt would be completely independent. In foreign affairs, Egypt would agree to be guided by Britain, but the Egyptian Government would have its own ambassadors in foreign countries. The British Government would have the right to keep soldiers in Egypt, but only to defend the Canal, not to occupy the country or to have anything to do with internal affairs. The Egyptian Government would employ some British advisers, and as long as the capitulations lasted, Britain would look after the interests of foreigners in Egypt. Nothing was said about the Sudan.

This of course was not full independence, but it was a real step forward; and the British Government then did another thing which surprised Zaghloul: it invited him to go to London to discuss the proposals. Zaghloul, after discussing with his friends of the Wafd, asked for four more things. He wanted the British to end the protectorate at once, without conditions. He wanted all foreigners to come under Egyptian law; the capitulations to cease, and Britain no longer to look after the interests of foreigners, as though it could not trust the Egyptian Government to behave properly towards them. He wanted to fix a limit to the number of British soldiers in Egypt, and to move the British army away from Cairo to the land near the Canal – the Canal Zone, we call it. Lastly, he wanted the Sudan Government to employ as many Egyptians as British in senior posts; the condominium, he thought, was not a real thing, and he wanted to make it real.

Lord Milner and the British Government would not agree to these four points, and there was more trouble: more riots and bloodshed. At the end of 1921, Zaghloul was again arrested and exiled; but the British Government saw that this sort of thing could not go on and on. In February 1922, it made a declaration of independence for Egypt. Egypt was declared to be an independent state under a king; but Britain would remain responsible for defending Egypt and the Canal, and for the interests of foreigners in Egypt and the Sudan. The Egyptian Government

D

appointed a commission to draw up a constitution, and on 19 April 1923 the new constitution became law. Egypt was to have a parliament of two houses; all the members of the lower House would be elected, and so would three-fifths of the members of the upper House. The other two-fifths would be appointed by the King.[1] It was clear that the new constitution gave the King more power than the Khedive had had. Partly for this reason, partly because the British had taken no notice of Zaghloul's four points, the Wafd was angry; but Zaghloul was allowed to come back to Egypt in March, just a few weeks before the constitution came into force, and he and his party decided to take part in the coming elctions.

The elections of 1923 were as great a victory for Zaghloul and the Wafd as the 1954 elections in the Gold Coast for Dr Nkrumah and the C.P.P. The Wafd won 188 seats out of 215. In January 1924, Zaghloul became Prime Minister.

The Wafd Government hoped that in time it might be able to persuade the Government in London to agree to some of its proposals; and now that Zaghloul was in power, he hoped that there would be an end to riots and bloodshed. But it is sometimes harder to stop such things than to start them. In November 1924, Sir Lee Stack, who was the British General in command of the Egyptian army, was shot dead in the streets of Cairo. Zaghloul was shocked; of course neither he nor his party had wanted Sir Lee murdered. He apologised to the British High Commissioner[2]; the murderers were arrested and hanged. But this was not enough for the High Commissioner, who was shocked and angry at the murder of his friend. He told the Egyptian Government that it must accept several hard conditions, both as regards Egypt and as regards the Sudan. The Government accepted what he said for Egypt, but not for the Sudan; this led to fighting between British and Egyptian soldiers, and Zaghloul's Government resigned. King Fuad dissolved parliament, and new elections were held; again the Wafd was in power, and again the King dissolved parliament. There was no parliament in 1925.

[1] When the 1914 war broke out, the Khedive happened to be visiting Constantinople, so the British would not let him come back. They appointed another member of Mohammed Ali's family, and gave him the title of Sultan instead of Khedive. The new Sultan died in 1917 and was succeeded by his brother Fuad. In 1922, Sultan Fuad became King Fuad.

[2] The British Government was represented in Egypt by a High Commissioner.

We are hiring

It seems as if King Fuad disliked the Wafd; why?

Yes, he did dislike the Wafd; so much so that he dismissed the parliament of 1925 because the Wafd was in power, and when elections were being held in 1926, he stopped them merely because he saw that the Wafd was winning again. King Fuad disliked the Wafd beause the Wafd disliked him. He belonged to the family of Mohammed Ali, which was a foreign family. All through the hundred years since Mohammed Ali's time, his successors had governed Egypt with the help of the Turkish and other rich foreign families. Ever since the time of Arabi there had been a strong feeling that Egypt should be governed by the true Egyptians; but the Khedives had never been able to get in touch with the true Egyptians. Then of course, the Khedives had always been weakened by keeping in close touch with those other foreigners, the British. And King Fuad himself was very much a foreigner; he knew Europe better than he knew Egypt, and spoke Italian better than Arabic. For all these reasons, the Wafd disliked kings in general, and King Fuad in particular; and they were very angry when they saw how much power the new constitution gave the King. As we have seen, he was able to dissolve a parliament merely because he did not like the party in power, which put him in a very strong position. The Wafd so far had had only one aim, to make the British go; now it must have two aims, to make the King go as well as the British.

Zaghloul died in 1927, and was succeeded as leader of the Wafd by Mustapha Nahas Pasha. All the time from 1922 to 1936 this uneasy position continued. The Wafd won the elections and from time to time discussed with the British, trying to persuade the British Government to accept Zaghloul's four points of 1920, expecially as regards the Sudan and the position of foreigners in Egypt. The King disliked the Wafd, and from time to time tried to find another government or to govern without parliament. The British were quite determined to keep an army in Egypt to defend the Canal. They were proud of the work they were doing in the Sudan; they knew that many of the Sudanese peoples (in the south especially) had no great love for the Egyptians; and they did not want to employ many Egyptian officials there. The capitulations were not so important; the capitulations were ended in Turkey itself in 1923, and there was no special reason why Britain should be anxious to keep them in Egypt after that.

As time went on, two things happened to change the position. The first thing was that all over the world there came a time of very bad trade about 1930. It hit many countries in Africa and slowed down their development; it hit Egypt badly, because foreign countries could not afford to buy her cotton. The second thing was that Italy was becoming a strong power under her new leader Mussolini. There was a strong Italian fleet in the Mediterranean, and Italy began to think of making war on Ethiopia. Long ago, in 1889, Italy had occupied the Red Sea coast of Ethiopia and made it into the Italian colony of Eritrea. Seven years later, in 1896, an Italian army had set out from Eritrea to conquer Ethiopia, but had been completely destroyed by the Ethiopians at the battle of Adowa. For the time being, that was the end of Italy's advance, but the Italians had never forgotten it; and now Mussolini thought his country strong enough to take its revenge. In 1935 the Italians marched into Ethiopia. Ethiopia fought bravely, but no help came from other countries, and she became an Italian colony.

The growing danger from Italy, and the financial difficulties of the nineteen-thirties, showed both the Egyptians and the British that they needed each other. In May 1936, Nahas Pasha headed an Egyptian delegation of six members of his own party, the Wafd, and six members of other parties; and they came to an agreement with the British delegation headed by the Foreign Secretary, Mr Anthony Eden. Britain promised to support Egypt's application to enter the League of Nations. Britain said that her army would no longer occupy Egypt, but Egypt agreed that British soldiers should guard the Canal until the Egyptian army was strong enough to take over. Britain promised to end the capitulations as soon as the other foreign countries agreed; and they very quickly did agree. It was agreed, too, that more Egyptians should be appointed in the Sudan. The treaty was to last for twenty years, until 1956; if at that time there were still British soldiers in Egypt and the Egyptian Government wanted them to go, both countries agreed that they would invite a third country to judge between them on this point. Both the Egyptian and the British parliaments welcomed the treaty, and it seemed as if the old troubles were ended. In May 1937, Egypt was admitted to the League of Nations.

The treaty was quite satisfactory to most people in Egypt as far as the position of Egypt itself was concerned; but it still left the position in the Sudan uncertain. What was to happen to the Sudan? The Egyptian idea was that the Sudan should become part of Egypt, or perhaps that Egypt and the Sudan should be like Scotland and England, two countries with their Governments partly separate, but joined together under one King. What was the British idea? Nobody knew; the British did not want to discuss it. The Egyptians feared that the British wanted to make the Sudan a British colony or protectorate, and keep Egypt out of it altogether. Still, this was a matter which might be discussed later; for the moment, everybody was happy, and the Egyptians cheered the British soldiers in the streets of Cairo.

FROM THE TREATY OF 1936 TO THE AGREEMENT OF 1954

If this treaty of 1936 was so much welcomed, what went wrong? There has been a great deal of disagreement and trouble between Britain and Egypt since 1936.

There have been three things since 1936 to cause trouble. The first is the war of 1939–45, which again brought great trouble to Egypt. The second is the growth of the Sudan to power, and the old question, what was to happen to the Sudan? The third is the problem of the new Jewish state of Israel. Let us say a word about each of these.

The war of 1939–45, like the war of 1914–19, brought trouble to Egypt. Again there was a very large British army in Egypt; there could be no talk of keeping the British soldiers out of Cairo and Alexandria, for the Italians and the Germans were attacking Egypt from the west, and battles were fought on Egyptian soil. In Egypt, as in every other country, food and other things were scarce and dear. Egypt gave Britain all the help she could in the war, but it did not seem to the Egyptian people that Britain was grateful. Above all, it looked to the Egyptians as if their country was still occupied by the British army in 1947, eleven years after the treaty, and four years after the last German and Italian soldiers in Africa had been taken prisoners. Of course there were reasons for this; but it made the Egyptians feel that Britain was not keeping the 1936 treaty.

Now, the Sudan. In October 1946, the Egyptian Prime Minister, Sidki Pasha, made an agreement in London with the British

Government, whose Foreign Secretary was Mr Ernest Bevin. On the Sudan, this agreement said that the two countries would do all they could to develop the Sudan and prepare its people for self-government. They would work together "within the framework of the unity between the Sudan and Egypt under the common Crown of Egypt"; and when the Sudan was self-governing, it would choose for itself how it should be governed. Sidki Pasha thought that these words meant that Britain agreed to place the Sudan under the government of the King of Egypt; but he soon found that whatever Britain meant, she did not intend the King of Egypt to have any real power in the Sudan. Sidki Pasha resigned, and Nokrashy Pasha became Prime Minister of Egypt in his place. In October 1951, five years later, the Egyptian Government declared that the 1936 treaty was at an end, that the condominium over the Sudan was also at an end, and that King Farouk[1] was King of Egypt and the Sudan.

The British were helping the Sudan towards self-government. In 1946 a conference was held to discuss the next step; and as a result, the Sudan was given a Legislative Assembly in which most of the members were elected. Half of the seats on the Governor-General's executive council were given to Sudanese, and a number of Sudanese were appointed under-secretaries in the different Ministries. This constitution of 1948 is not unlike the Burns constitution in the Gold Coast two years earlier. The Egyptian Government did not like all this, for it thought that the British did not really want the Sudan to have self-government, only to cut it off from Egypt. Most of the members in the Sudanese Legislative Assembly wanted independence, but there was a party, especially in the north, which wanted the Sudan to join Egypt. In the end, the Egyptians saw that the British did mean the Sudan to be self-governing, and to choose for itself whether it would join Egypt, or join the British Commonwealth, or remain independent. But they could not help feeling that if the British had allowed Egypt a greater share in governing the Sudan all these years, the Egyptian Government would have had a greater chance of holding the Sudan. On 1st January 1956, the Sudan became independent, and both Britain and Egypt welcomed it. But it all made the Egyptians dislike the British Government.

But Israel was the biggest trouble. We have seen that after the

[1] King Fuad died in 1936, and his young son Farouk succeeded him.

war of 1914–19, the Arab countries became free. But Britain, who promised to make the Arab countries free, also promised that Palestine, the ancient land of the Jews, should be open for the Jews to make themselves a National Home there. Palestine was peopled mostly by Arabs, but there were many Jews there before the 1914 war. The British did not say that all Palestine should be Jewish, only part of it; and they did not say how large a part. After the war, thousands of Jews from all over the world came to live in their new National Home. Many rich Jews in America, Britain, and Germany, who did not themselves go to live in Palestine, gave money to help those who went there. The country was governed by Britain[1], and Britain had the difficult task of helping Jews and Arabs to live together. The position was rather like that in the Transvaal in President Kruger's time, when the Uitlanders were coming in and upsetting the old Boer ways.[2] The Arabs were quiet, old-fashioned farmers; the Jews were young, hard-working, well-educated, bringing in new ideas and new machines, and turning the country upside down. They would buy a piece of land which produced very little; and with their new methods and new machines they would make it produce a great deal. They came, and they kept coming. Palestine is a small country, and it could not possibly hold all the Jews in the world. Before long there was trouble; Jews and Arabs fought each other and fought the British. The Arabs fought the British because the British let too many Jews into the country; the Jews fought them because they let in too few. In 1947, the British said they could no longer govern Palestine, and asked the United Nations to say how it should be governed. The United Nations said that the country should be divided – and it drew the dividing line – between Jews and Arabs. The Jews at once declared their part of the country the independent State of Israel; the Arabs (led by Egypt and Jordan) made war on Israel; and the Egyptian army advanced into Israel till it came within twenty miles of Tel Aviv, the capital. But the Egyptians could not hold the ground which they

---

[1] It was not a British colony. The League of Nations (now replaced by the United Nations) asked Britain to govern it under a mandate. This made it much like a trust territory of the United Nations; the British had to give a report to the League of Nations every year. Tanganyika, Togoland, and the Cameroons were mandated territories of the League before they became trust territories of the United Nations.

[2] See Book One, page 125.

had won; the Israeli army pressed them back; and in the first days of 1949 the Israelis crossed the frontier into Egypt itself. At a village called Faluja, a young officer called Gamal Abdel Nasser still fought with his men on Israeli soil, but the Egyptian Government knew that it was beaten, and on 7 January 1949 the fighting stopped. None of the Arab states would make peace with Israel, for they all agreed that they would not recognize that there was such a state as Israel; and how can you make peace with a state which does not exist? They would not make peace with the Israeli Government; but they agreed with the Israeli army that they would not fight each other. A line was drawn which the armies agreed not to cross, and this line is still the frontier of Israel. It is not a sensible frontier. It cuts through the city of Jerusalem, and it leaves a strip five miles wide along the coast in Egyptian hands, including the town of Gaza; this strip contains many thousands of Arabs who have lost their homes in Palestine and have no hope of getting back to them unless Israel and the Arab states make peace and Israel agrees to take them back.

Ever since January 1949, Israel and the Arab states have remained in this position, and they were still in it when this book was being written at the end of 1960.

But why do they not make peace and arrange a more sensible frontier, and do something for these poor people who have lost their homes?

It is because Israel and the Arab states fear one another. Israel would like to make peace: not only because she wants peace but because she wants the Arab states to recognize her. She would like more land; she would like the Arab states to allow her to take more water from the river Jordan to irrigate[1] the dry parts of the country and make them more fruitful; she would like to make some sort of arrangement about the poor refugees[2]. But the Arab states are afraid that if they once recognize Israel as a State, she will begin asking for more and more, and in the end she will take away great areas of Arab land and fill it with her own people. The Arabs say, 'This is a poor country, but it is our

[1] irrigation is the art of watering dry land by canals and ditches filled with water from a river.

[2] refugees are these people who have lost their homes and have found shelter (or *refuge*) elsewhere.

country, and we want to go on living in it as we always have done.' The Israelis say, 'The country is a poor country now, but we know how to make it rich. Why should the Arabs occupy the land if they do not know how to use it properly?' We can see both points of view. If I were an Arab, I would not like to sell my house and my land to an Israeli for fifty pounds, knowing that with his money and his skill he will turn it into a rich farm and make twenty pounds a year out of it. And on the other hand, if I were an Israeli farmer with sons and brothers, I would not like them to have no land when there is Arab land close by which produces nothing but a poor crop of corn and a few goats and camels. It is not like the Transvaal, which is big enough for farms and for gold-mines too, so that both the Afrikaners and the Uitlanders could live there. Palestine is a small country, and there is very little land: if the Israelis come in, the Arabs must go out.

This sad story of the Arabs and the Israelis is very important for modern Egypt, which is joined in an alliance[1] called the Arab League with the other Arab states. To begin with, although Britain had helped the Arab states (Iraq, Jordan, and others) to free themselves from Turkey in 1919, they disliked her because she had allowed the Jews to enter Palestine and set up the state of Israel. If Britain was the friend of Israel, she could not, they thought, be the friend of the Arabs. Here was a new reason for difficulty between Britain and Egypt.

In the next place, the people of Egypt were naturally angry with their Government for being defeated in the war with Israel. The army felt that its defeat was the Government's fault, because the Government had not supplied it properly during the fighting. There were more riots and murders. Nokrashy Pasha, who had succeeded Sidki Pasha as Prime Minister in 1946, was murdered in December 1948. King Farouk appointed one Government after another, but none of them was able to do very much good.

As we have said[2], the Government of Nahas Pasha declared in October 1951 that the 1936 Treaty was at an end, and that the British Government should take all its soldiers out of Egypt, even out of the Canal Zone. The British Government answered that

[1] An alliance is a agreement by which countries agree to help each other in time of war.
[2] See page 54.

when two countries make a treaty, neither has the right to end it unless the other agrees. Britain and Egypt had agreed that the treaty of 1936 should last until 1956, and that British soldiers should stay to defend the Canal until the Egyptian army was strong enough to replace it. Britain had done nothing to break the treaty, and it would be time enough to talk of taking the British army away in five years time, when the treaty had come to an end. So the British refused to go. The Egyptian Government then stopped all its people in the Canal Zone from working for the British; the Egyptians stopped all fresh food for the British soldiers, and tried to stop the water supply; and there was shooting and bomb throwing. The British had to defend themselves, and in January 1952 there was some fighting. Then the crowds in Cairo rioted again, worse than ever, killing many foreigners and burning many buildings. The army decided that the time had come when the King and the Government must go. On the night of 22 July 1952, a group of army officers led their men into Cairo and took possession of the Government; Colonel Gamal Abdel Nasser planned it, but he thought it wise to have a more senior officer as head of his group of officers, and General Neguib agreed to take the command. On 26 July King Farouk left the country, and General Neguib and Colonel Nasser ruled Egypt.

It took General Neguib and Colonel Nasser a year to break the power of the Wafd and the other politicians. On 18 June 1953 they declared that Egypt was a republic; Neguib was President and Prime Minister, and Nasser was second in command. The power of the republic depended on the army; nearly all the army officers supported Nasser, and the few who did not were dismissed.

Colonel Nasser was born in 1918 in a small country town, and joined the army as a student in the army officers' college in 1937. He hated the 1936 treaty, and thought the Egyptian Government ought never to have signed it. Treaty or no treaty, Canal or no Canal, the British, he thought, must leave Egypt; and it should be his life's work to make them go. He knew that the British were strong, and that mere rioting in the streets would never make them leave Egypt. He knew too that the King and most of the politicians were thinking even more of their own comfort than of the great task of freeing their country. So, like Colonel Arabi sixty years earlier, Colonel Nasser saw that to get rid of the British he must first get rid of the politicians, and only the army could get rid of them. He set himself to persuade his fellow-officers of this, and to teach them that they must be ready for action when the time came, but that until the time came they must not waste their strength or reveal[1] their plans.

Before very long, General Neguib had ceased to be useful to Colonel Nasser. Neguib was an older man, and he disliked some of the things which the revolutionary Government did. Matters soon came to the point where either Neguib or Nasser would have to go; the army officers preferred Nasser, and on 17 April 1954, Neguib resigned the post of Prime Minister, though he stayed on for a few more months as President without any real power. He ceased to be President in November, and Colonel Nasser took his place.

President Nasser now had the whole country behind him, and could turn his mind again to the question of the British army in the Canal Zone. The British had learnt from what happened in 1952 that it was no use keeping a large army in the Canal Zone if the Egyptians cut off its food and water and shot at it whenever they could. They were willing to discuss a new arrangement, by which the Egyptian army should replace the British soldiers, but that British technical staff should stay to help the Egyptians, and that Egypt would allow the British to come back at once if there were a danger of war. The discussions took many months, but an agreement was at last signed on 19 October 1954. It was agreed that the British soldiers would all go within twenty months, but that British technical staff – civilians, not soldiers – should stay for seven years. If any country made war on Egypt, or on any Arab country, or on Turkey, the British would be allowed to come back to defend the Canal Zone.

And so it seemed at last as if Britain and Egypt would be able to understand each other and live as friends. President Nasser had won; the British soldiers were leaving Egypt. The Sudan was soon to become independent both of Britain and of Egypt and of Britain. President Nasser himself said, 'There is now no reason why Britain and Egypt should not work constructively[2] together.'

[1] That is, to allow their plans to become known.
[2] To construct is to build up; so to work constructively means to work to build up whatever needs to be built up, such as friendship, or trade.

THE BAGHDAD PACT, THE HIGH DAM, AND SUEZ

It seems as though the British were afraid that some other country might make war in that part of the world. Why should Egypt allow the British back if an attack were made on Turkey? What country was likely to attack Turkey?

It is true that the British were afraid; and not only the British. For hundreds of years, Russia had been pushing further south, conquering land from Turkey. If we look at the map, we see that the Black Sea is like a bottle with a narrow mouth; and Turkey holds the mouth. Russia would like to hold it, so that she could send her warships into the Mediterranean. If that is not possible, she would like to get control of the Persian Gulf and have a sea-port there. We have seen that in 1877 Russia fought a war with Turkey. In those days, Russia was ruled by an emperor; since 1917 she had been a communist state ruled by a Soviet or council. But her neighbours thought that Soviet Russia was just as anxious to get hold of Constantinople[1] and the mouth of the Black Sea, or to get a port on the Persian Gulf, as the old Russia of the emperors had been. Turkey, Greece, Italy and most of the countries of Western Europe, together with Britain and the United States, had formed an alliance called the North Atlantic Treaty Organization to defend each other if Russia attacked any of them.[2]

This made it more difficult for Russia to get out into the Mediterranean, and so it was likely that she might look towards the Persian Gulf. In 1955 the countries to the south of Russia began to make an alliance like the North Atlantic Treaty Organization. Turkey and Iraq began it, and Iran (Persia) and Pakistan joined. Britain and the United States supported it. This alliance is called the Baghdad Pact; Baghdad is the capital of Iraq, and the agreement was made there.

All this interested Egypt greatly. Iraq was a member of the Arab League; and we have seen that the Arab League as a whole was not very friendly either to Turkey or to Britain. Iraq was ruled at that time by a statesman called Nuri es-Said, who was strongly of the opinion that the best thing for the Arab states

[1] The Turks have shortened the name Constantinople into Istanbul.
[2] The North Atlantic Treaty Organization is often called, for short, NATO.

would be to become friendly with Britain and the West, and look to Britain and the West to support them against Russia. But President Nasser, and most of the Arab people, disagreed. They thought that the Arab states should hold together and join neither Russia nor the West. Moreover, if Iraq was friendly with Britain and the United States, she could not (so the Arabs thought) join in war against Israel, for both Britain and the United States were Israel's friends. And so President Nasser disliked the Baghdad Pact thoroughly and Egypt became the enemy of Iraq. More than that: Nasser again began to distrust the British. He thought, 'We Egyptians and Arabs want the British to go away and leave us alone. But the British do not want to go. They wanted to keep their army in Cairo and Alexandria, but in 1936 we got them to leave those towns and stay inside the Canal Zone. In 1951 we asked them to leave the Canal Zone also, and they are now leaving; but we had great difficulty in making them go. And now they are making alliances with Arabs, so that even if they leave Egypt they will have some other means of staying in this part of the world. They will want us to make peace with Israel, and to follow them in opposing Russia; but we will not do either of those things.'

How much of that is true?

It is true that the British were anxious about the Suez Canal; they did not want any other country – especially Russia – to close it to British ships, and so they did not want to take their army away unless they could make other arrangements for the Canal to be defended. It is true that they were afraid of Russia, and would like to see the Baghdad Pact made strong. It is true that they would like all the Arab states to make peace with Israel; peace is always better than war, and if there were more fighting in that part of the world, Russia – again it is this fear of Russia! – might step in and make herself a strong position there. But it is not true that Britain helped to set up the Baghdad Pact in order to weaken Egypt or to have an excuse for sending British armies into Arab countries. President Nasser thought that if the Arab countries held together, they could defend themselves against Russia or anyone else. Britain thought he was wrong. If Russia did attack the Arab states, the Russian armies would soon be in Baghdad and on the Canal. Then the Arabs would cry for help to the West, but it would be too late. It would be much better to have the plans ready made beforehand. To Britain, the main enemy was Russia; to Egypt and the Arab states, the main enemy was Israel. And so, even after the agreement of 1954, Britain and Egypt began to draw away from one another again.

There had been no fighting between Israel and the Arab states since January 1949; but the armies watched each other all along the frontier. The United Nations kept a small force of soldiers to see that the war did not begin again; and although sometimes one side or the other would fire a few shots, on the whole the frontier was quiet. But they were still at war, and Egypt had other ways of troubling Israel besides sending soldiers against her. No Israeli ship was allowed to go through the Suez Canal; Britain protested to the Egyptian Government about this, and Israel protested to the United Nations; they said that when the Canal was first built, everyone had agreed that it should be open to the ships of all nations. Neither protest did any good. Then Israel thought that she could manage without using the Canal. She had a short frontier on the sea at the Gulf of Aqaba. Here she built a port called Eilath, hoping that her trade could get into the Indian Ocean that way. But the Egyptians set up big guns along the coast of the Gulf, and said that they would shoot at any ship which tried to go to Eilath, and in July 1955 they fired on a British steamer and hit it.

During 1955, this silence along the frontiers was broken. The Israeli army began making raids on to Egyptian territory, and Egyptians made raids into Israel. President Nasser knew that the Egyptian army was not yet strong enough to beat Israel, and he did not think the other Arab armies were either; so he tried to get guns and tanks and other weapons to strengthen his army, while the Cairo radio told the people that one day the time would come for all Arabs to join against Israel and drive the Israelis into the sea. It is perhaps not surprising if the Government of Israel thought it better to fight now instead of waiting for their enemies to become stronger. The British and American Governments allowed Egypt to buy some weapons, but they were unwilling to allow her to buy very many, for Egypt said plainly that they were to be used to fight Israel. So Nasser turned to the communist countries, and he bought as much as he wanted from

Czechoslovakia. It looked as if open war with Israel was coming nearer.

President Nasser wanted other things besides weapons. The population of Egypt was growing, and he had to feed his people: either with food grown on Egyptian farms, or with food from abroad, which he would have to pay for with cotton grown on Egyptian farms. Either way, he had to bring more land under cultivation; and in Egypt, that means taking more water from the Nile. The Aswan dam (first built by the British in 1902, and raised twice since it was first built) holds enough water to provide a steady supply all through the year. But if the year's flood is poor, some farms go dry and there is hunger in the land. If the Aswan dam could be raised much higher still, so that it held enough water to provide a steady supply not for one year only, but for five years, the water would fill the ditches every year. This High Dam at Aswan would be three miles long and 365 feet high above the natural level of the river; it would make a lake 344 miles long, reaching far into the Sudan. Of course it would be very expensive; and President Nasser asked Britain and the United States to give him the money. The whole scheme was expected to cost about £250 million, but it would be carried out in stages, the first stage costing about £90 million.

Late in 1955, the British and American Governments suggested that perhaps they might between them give Egypt £25 million, provided that the World Bank lent Egypt the rest, and provided that Egypt could agree with its neighbour the Sudan over the scheme.

What has the Sudan to do with it?

For one thing, the Sudan depends just as much on the Nile as Egypt does; at least, the whole of the Northern Sudan does, where the cotton is grown. The more water that Egypt takes from the Nile, the less there is for the Sudan. For another thing, the lake which the High Dam made would drown much farm land in the Sudan: towns and villages would have to be rebuilt and new farms would have to be made.

The American Government was ready to give Egypt this money as part of its general plan for helping poor countries all over the world to develop their resources[1] and improve their standard of

---

[1] A country's resources are its minerals, its crops, its sources of electrical power and so on: things which will bring it wealth if they can be developed.

living. But the American people began to wonder if Egypt was the right country for them to help in this way. They had trouble with Egypt over oil; they did not like Egypt to be the enemy of Israel; they did not like Egypt to buy so many weapons from the communist countries and sell the communist countries so much cotton. In May 1956, President Nasser did something which the American people disliked even more: he recognized the communist Government of China, which the United States had refused to recognize. This made the United States Government, as well as its people, angry; and in July the United States declared that it would give Egypt no money for the High Dam. Britain and the World Bank followed the American example.

President Nasser of course was very angry. Very well, he said, if the British and Americans will not help us to build the High Dam, we will build it without their help. We will take the Suez Canal, and build the High Dam with the profits which now go to the Suez Canal Company.

This caused a great cry all over the world. The Company was angry; and it had shareholders in many countries, the British Government being the biggest shareholder of all. The Company said that its agreement with the Government of Egypt did not come to an end until 1968, and so the Egyptian Government had no right to take the Canal till then. The Governments of all the countries whose ships used the Canal were afraid that the Egyptians would not run the Canal properly. In particular, they were afraid of two things. One was that Egypt would close the Canal to the ships of any country that she disliked, as she had been doing already to Israeli ships.[1] The other was that Egypt would take so much money out of the Canal to pay for the High Dam that the Canal would become dangerous to ships because the Egyptians spent too little in keeping it in good condition. The British and French Governments protested to Egypt, but the Egyptian Government would not listen to them. Perhaps they were objecting, not so much to what President Nasser had done, as to the way in which he had done it. In the speech which told the world that he was taking the Canal, Nasser had said that Egypt was doing so in order to fight against the West and against Israel, because the West (he said) was trying to stop Egypt from

[1] And not only to Israeli ships, but to any ship going to a port in Israel.

developing. This sort of language would make Western Governments angry, for they had no wish to stop Egypt from developing.

Had Egypt the right to take the Canal in this way?

Yes, and No. The great reason for saying No is that the Canal
Company's agreement was not to end until 1968, and (as Britain
had said in 1951)[1], if you make an agreement to last until a fixed
date, neither side has the right to break it before the time comes.
This is true, even if conditions change meanwhile. For example,
if a firm of engineers agrees to build a bridge in three years for
£2 million, it will be no use for the firm to go to the Government after two years and say, 'We cannot build this bridge for
£2 million, for wages have gone up, and so has the price of steel
and cement. We will charge £2½ million.' The Government will
reply, 'No, you said you would build it for £2 million, and you
must do so. You are bound by your agreement.' From this point
of view, the Egyptian Government had no right to tell the Suez
Canal Company, which was carrying out its side of the agreement,
'We know that our agreement is meant to last till 1968, but it is
inconvenient for us to wait till then, so we are ending it now.'

But there is another side to the question. The Suez Canal Company was established[2] under Egyptian law, and in Egyptian eyes
it was an Egyptian company, even though many of its shareholders were not Egyptian. A Government has a right to say to
a company working in its country, 'We think that the work you
are doing is something that we, the Government, ought to do;
so we will buy your company and run it ourselves.' This is called
nationalizing a company, and it is quite right and fair, provided
that the Government pays a fair price for what it buys.

There is perhaps another thing to be said on the Egyptian side.
It is true that the Suez Canal Company had a difficult time
in its early days, and that when the British Government bought
the Egyptian shares, it paid the fair market price for them. The
Company, and the British Government, had taken the risk, and
so, by the regular custom of the business world, they were entitled
to take all the profit they could get as long as the agreement
remained in force. But there had been many changes since the
Canal was built. Trade and shipping had increased, and for many

[1] See page 57.
[2] That is, set up.

E

years the Canal had been making good profits. The Company, or the British Government, could have afforded to be generous, and give Egypt a bigger share of the profits than the old agreement promised her. But they did not; they chose to stand on their agreement.

So we see that it is not easy to give a simple Yes or No to the question. As so often happens, there is something to be said on both sides.

But whether or not he had the right to nationalize the Suez Canal, President Nasser nationalized it in the wrong way. He may have been angry because Britain and America would not help him with the High Dam, but that had nothing to do with the Canal Company. Many Governments, in Asia as well as in Europe, thought that he was wrong to take the Canal in order to pay for the High Dam; and they thought he was unfair when he told the Company's servants that if they left their work in the Canal they would lose their pension and might even be imprisoned.[1] In fact, President Nasser in his anger had gone too far; he saw this, and set himself to win over the opinion of the world. He explained that he would not punish the Company's servants for leaving the Canal if they gave proper notice; he promised that he would never close the Canal to the ships of any country; he said that he would pay the share-holders in the Company a fair price for their shares; and he said that as long as it was agreed that the Canal belonged to Egypt, he would be ready to discuss with other countries how the Canal could be properly run for the good of all.

This did not satisfy Britain and France. They did not want Egypt or any other one country to control the Canal; they wanted it to be controlled by an international body. They called meetings of the Governments whose ships used the Canal; and twenty Governments agreed to set up an international body. Russia, India and two others thought that the new Suez Canal Board should advise the Egyptian Government, but leave Egypt to run the Canal; but the other sixteen (including Britain, France and America) wanted the new Board to run the Canal. Egypt would not agree that anybody but herself should run the Canal, so the new Board came to nothing. In September, after this disagree-

---

[1] This was said in the law which nationalized the Canal.

ment, the British and French pilots[1] resigned their work in the Canal, and Britain and France thought that Egypt would not be able to manage without them; but Egypt did manage to get pilots from other countries, and the Canal stayed open.

Early in October, Britain and France brought the matter before the Security Council of the United Nations, and on 13 October the Council (including Egypt) approved a resolution which laid down: (i) the Canal should be open to all; (ii) the Canal belonged to Egypt; (iii) neither Egypt nor any other country should interfere with the Canal for political reasons; (iv) Egypt and the countries who used the Canal should settle between them how much ships should pay when they passed through it; (v) some of the Canal's profits should be kept for improving the Canal, not spent on High Dams or anything else; (vi) if the Company could not agree with the Egyptian Government about how much money Egypt should pay it, the two would ask some friend to judge between them. To these six points, Britain and France proposed to add a seventh: until all the details had been worked out, Egypt should consult with the Suez Canal Users' Association.[2] But the Security Council would not agree to that.

All this seemed fair; and it now remained to work out the details. Britain and France said that it was for Egypt to put forward detailed proposals on the lines of the six points she had accepted, and there was much discussion between the Egyptian Foreign Minister, Dr Fawzi, and the Secretary-General of the United Nations, Mr Hammarskjoeld. But before they reached any results, other things had happened.

We have seen that for some months there had been small troubles on the Israeli frontier. In September and October 1956 the troubles grew bigger. On 25 October, twelve days after the Security Council resolution about the Suez Canal, Israel said that Egyptians had been shooting people on Israeli soil; three days later, the Israeli army began to move, and on the 29th it crossed into Egypt and made war in full force.

This put the British and French Governments in a difficult position. Britain had a treaty with Israel's eastern neighbour,

[1] The pilot is the man who comes on board a ship to guide it in a specially difficult place. Every ship passing through the Suez Canal has to be guided by a pilot.
[2] The Governments had formed the Suez Canal Users' Association so as to keep in touch with each other after Egypt refused to consider any scheme for international control of the Canal.

Jordan; and the British Government warned Israel that if she made war on Jordan, Britain would be bound to help Jordan. Britain, France and the United States had agreed together in 1950 that they would not allow the frontiers of Israel to be changed, and that they would help any nation in that part of the world which was attacked by another. Israel had now attacked Egypt, so should not these three countries help Egypt? But Britain and France told the United States that there had been so much fighting on both sides of the frontier between Israel and Egypt, that they could not agree that this was a case in which their agreement of 1950 applied. So the United States took the matter to the Security Council, and proposed a resolution calling on Israel to take her army out of Egypt, and calling on all members of the United Nations not to use force or to threaten to use force. While the Security Council was discussing the United States resolution, it heard the news that Britain and France had acted by themselves. They told the Governments of Israel and of Egypt to stop fighting at once, and to take their armies ten miles away from the Suez Canal; if they refused to do so, British and French soldiers would come into the Canal Zone to force them. In addition, they asked Egypt to allow British and French soldiers to come into Suez and other places in order to protect the Canal. Israel agreed to do as Britain and France asked; Egypt refused. The Security Council meanwhile voted on the United States resolution. Australia and Belgium abstained (that is, they did not vote either way), seven members voted for it, only Britain and France voted against it.

The next day, 31 October, British and French planes began bombing Egyptian airfields, and destroyed most of the Egyptian air force. On 5 November, British and French soldiers landed at Port Said and began to fight their way along the Canal.

President Nasser knew that his army could not defend Egypt against Britain, France, and Israel; but he knew that the United Nations would help him. Meanwhile, he blocked the Canal by sinking several ships in it, took the army base in the Canal Zone, ended the Agreement of 1954, and took the property of large numbers of British and French citizens who were living in Egypt. Syria helped him by blocking the pipe-line which carried oil from Iraq to the sea-ports on the Mediterranean for export to France and Britain, and other countries in Western Europe.

The United Nations did help Egypt. Its General Assembly passed resolutions ordering Israel to take her army back inside the frontier, and ordering other nations not to put military goods into that part of the world[1] and to stop fighting at once. Most important of all, it said that these orders must be obeyed within twelve hours; it did not say what would happen if they were not obeyed, but Britain and France and Israel could see that this was a threat of some kind. A United Nations army was formed, and was sent into Egypt to restore order and to see that the foreign armies left the country.

The British Government felt that it could not go on. Britain had never before voted against a resolution in the Security Council[2] and had never before been blamed by the General Assembly. Only Australia and New Zealand voted in support of Britain and her two friends France and Israel; Canada and South Africa, with four other countries, abstained; 64 countries (including two members of the British Commonwealth, India and Ceylon) voted for the resolution against Britain. Britain explained to the United Nations that her reason for sending an army into Egypt was that she feared the fighting between Israel and Egypt might develop into a general war: that is, the other Arab states might join in. If this happened, nobody could tell what might be the result; there was a danger that the United States and Russia and other countries might find themselves in a third world war. But the United Nations did not accept this explanation; it replied, 'Even if you are right, it is not for you and France to do this by yourselves; we will all do together whatever is needed.' The strength of Britain's position in the world is that all nations (except Russia and the other communist countries) believe that Britain tries to act honestly and fairly; Britain usually has the support of world opinion in what she does. But when Britain found world opinion against her, the Assembly blaming her by 64 votes against five, her position had become impossible. The British people them-

[1] This language was used instead of the simpler words 'make war' or 'use force', so that Britain and France could not defend themselves by saying 'We are not making war against Egypt; we do not want to fight; our soldiers are going there to stop the Egyptians and the Israelis from fighting.'

[2] Resolutions in the General Assembly can be carried by a majority, but resolutions in the Security Council have to be unanimous: that is, if even one member votes against a resolution, the resolution is lost. Russia had voted against very many Security Council resolutions, and Britain had blamed her for doing so; now Britain found herself in the same position.

seives were deeply divided; the whole of the Labour Party, which
contained nearly half the voters in the country, thought that the
Government had acted wrongly. The United States was angry;
the Canal was blocked; the oil pipe-line was blocked; Russia was
threatening that she would force Britain and France to stop fighting. Britain decided that the end had come; on 22 December the
last of the British and French soldiers left Egypt.

In this way, President Nasser brought his country to complete
freedom. The Suez Canal belonged to Egypt, and the United
Nations paid for the work of clearing it and opening it to shipping
once more. The army base in the Canal Zone belonged to Egypt,
and Egypt had no longer an agreement which bound her to allow
British soldiers to use it. The Egyptian Government had taken
many British and French and Jewish businesses and driven their
owners out of the country; for the first time since the days of the
Ptolemies[1] most of the trade and business of Egypt was in Egyptian
hands. The United Nations army was keeping Israel quiet. The
British and French pilots had left the Canal, and the Egyptian
Government was free to run the Canal as it chose, without consult-
ing any other nation. The Russians were ready to help the
Egyptian Government to develop its country, even perhaps to
build the High Dam. It is true that the Egyptian army had suffered
in the fighting and had lost a great deal of its weapons; but the
Russians would replace those. All the Arab countries – their
people, if not their Governments – looked on President Nasser
of Egypt as the greatest leader of the Arabs.

**It seems from all this as if Britain and France made a great mistake
and have paid a heavy price for it. Is this so?**

It is certainly true that Britain and France have paid a heavy
price for what they did. They have lost the position which they
had in Egypt before 1956; they have lost the control of the Canal
and of the army base in the Canal Zone; they have suffered from
the blocking of the Canal and of the oil pipe-line; and most of all,
they have lost some of the respect which other members of the
United Nations felt for them. All this is a heavy price to pay. But
it is too early yet to say whether they made a mistake. They said
that they were going into Egypt in order to stop a general war;

[1] See page 14.

and there has been no general war. We do not know, and we shall not know for very many years, what evidence[1] the British and French Governments had for fearing a general war. If such a war had come about, it would have caused the whole world far more suffering than was caused by the Suez fighting in 1956. It is possible that if people all over the world knew what the British and French Governments knew, they would feel thankful to France and Britain for what they did. As I say, we do not yet know all the facts.

But even if France and Britain were right in fearing a general war, would it not have been better for them to persuade the United Nations to act, instead of acting themselves?

From their own selfish point of view, it would certainly have been better. If a strong United Nations army had landed in Egypt on 5 November instead of an army of British and French, Britain and France would be in a stronger position today. But the United Nations has no army of its own; when it needs one it has to ask its member-states to lend it soldiers to build an army, and this cannot be done very quickly. The British Government must surely have foreseen much of what would happen; it must have foreseen that the United Nations would blame it, and that Nasser would block the Canal and take the Canal Zone base. It must have foreseen that it would pay a heavy price for what it was going to do. If so, then *either* the British Government was so frightened and angry that it did not care what happened to it as long as it could hurt Egypt – and British Governments do not usually behave like this: *or* it thought the danger of a general war was so great that it was necessary to put a strong army into Egypt at once, instead of waiting for the United Nations soldiers to arrive a few hundreds at a time.

But if the British Government was so sure that there was danger of a general war, could it not have shown its evidence privately to one or two other Governments, such as India or the United States? It seems a pity that if a foreign army had to be sent into Egypt, it had to be a British army, the very army that the Egyptian Government most feared. It looked to the outside world, and to Egypt herself, as

[1] See Book One, page 16.

if the British were trying to get hold of the Suez Canal again. If Indian or American soldiers had been sent, there would not have been this fear.

That too would have been convenient for the British Government. There is an English saying about a cat and a monkey. There is a kind of nut grown in Europe, called a chestnut, which you cook in the hot ashes of a fire; the saying is that the cat was cooking some chestnuts, but did not want to burn his paws in taking them out of the ashes when they were ready, so he persuaded the monkey to take them out for him. The monkey burnt his paws, and the cat ate the chestnuts. You are suggesting that Britain should be like the cat, and India or the United States or some other country should be like the monkey. It may be that the British Government did make some such suggestion; we do not know. If so, nothing came of it. The Indian Government (let us take India as an example) may have been unwilling to play the monkey's part. But even if the Government were willing, it would have to persuade its parliament and its people to send an army to Egypt; and the Indian parliament and people had no interest in Egypt, so it would have been difficult to persuade them. The British people on the other hand were very interested in Egypt and the Canal, and'had been so ever since the Canal was built; British soldiers had fought to defend the Canal in two wars, and there was a British army in Cyprus, not far away. Britain and France could act quickly; no other country could. If action had to be taken quickly, Britain and France had to take it.

No, we cannot yet explain the Suez affair. It certainly did seem to the rest of the world as if Britain was trying to get back into the Suez Canal Zone, and if this had been all that Britain was trying to do, the British Government would have been very foolish. But if Britain went into the Suez affair with her eyes open, as we say: seeing the danger of a third world war, seeing that the whole world would misunderstand what she did, and ready to pay the heavy price which she has paid – in that case the British Government was very wise and brave.

THE UNITED ARAB REPUBLIC

So, at the age of 38, Colonel Nasser had finished his main task: he had made the British leave Egypt for good. Now he was able to think more of developing his country: of building the High Dam so as to grow more food and more cotton, of building schools and colleges, of developing mines and industry, of improving the life of the villagers with electricity and water and schemes of community development, and of breaking up the large areas of land belonging to the rich and sharing the land among the poor.

As so often happens, as soon as one problem had been solved, another arose. President Nasser had made himself the leader of all the Arab peoples, for he had stood out against the West and had won. But some of the other Arab Governments were jealous of his success, and thought that in becoming so much the enemy of the West, Nasser was becoming dangerously friendly with Russia and the communists. Nuri es-Said of Iraq thought this; so did King Hussein of Jordan and King Ibn Saud of Saudi Arabia. So, whatever the peoples of Iraq and Saudi Arabia and Jordan might think, during 1957 their Governments became rather less friendly to Egypt. Lebanon was always more friendly to the West than the other Arab states.

The exception to this was Syria, which was a republic under President Kuwatly. Syria lies between Iraq and the Lebanon, and the pipe-line carrying Iraq oil to the Mediterranean runs through it. It was therefore very important for Iraq to have the friendship of Syria; and Nuri es-Said would have liked more than friendship, he would have liked to unite Syria with Iraq into one country. The Syrians would not agree to this. Like the Egyptians, they felt that the Kings of Iraq, Jordan and Saudi Arabia were part of the old world, and that the Arab race would get on better if it joined into one great state as a republic.

In 1957, President Kuwatly of Syria and some of his ministers were frightened to see that many of their army officers were communists. The Syrian army had made more than one revolution in Syria already, and the President and his ministers were afraid that one day the army would make another revolution and introduce a communist government. Once the communists were in power, they could never be got rid of. So the President and his Government suggested to President Nasser that Egypt and Syria should join into one country. This would stop the danger from the Syrian communists, and it would weaken the influence of Nuri es-Said of Iraq, whom both Syria and Egypt hated because he was too friendly with the West and (as they thought) too willing to live in peace with Israel. Early in 1958, President Nasser agreed. The two countries were joined, President Kuwatly resigned, and President Nasser was elected, both in Syria and in Egypt, as President of the new United Arab Republic.

THINGS TO DO, TO DISCUSS, OR TO FIND OUT

1. Egypt is a very old country. Draw a straight-line time chart to cover 7,000 years, from 5,000 BC to 2,000 AD. (You will find it easier to have two or three lines parallel; then you can mark some dates on one line and some on another.) Mark the following dates: the old Egyptian civilization, 5,000 BC to 30 BC; 330 AD the building of Constantinople; Britain part of the Roman Empire, 43 AD to 410; 641 Arabs conquer Egypt; kingdom of Ghana 500 AD to 1076; 1596 Moors conquer Songhai; 1798 Napoleon in Egypt; 1805 Mohammed Ali; 1869 Suez Canal; British in Egypt 1882 to 1936.

2. Look in your atlas and find Albania, Bulgaria, Constantinople, Crete, Greece, Jugoslavia, Macedon (or Macedonia), Rumania, Sardinia and Sicily, which are mentioned between page 20 and page 41.

3. Does what you read about Mohammed Ali and Ismail help you to understand why Egypt under President Nasser is taking so much interest in African affairs?

4. In 1936 and 1946 and 1956 the Egyptian Government told the British Government that the whole of the Nile valley should belong to Egypt. Can you see anything in the work of Baker and of Gordon to encourage this idea? Where does the Nile valley begin?

5. Do you think that Britain and France were right to set up the Dual Control? If not, what ought they to have done?

6. Would it have been better if Britain and France had supported Arabi against the Khedive?

7. Why do you think that the British set up the condominium in the Sudan instead of giving it to Egypt? Write a letter in which a young Egyptian asks Boutros Pasha not to agree to a condominium, and write Boutros Pasha's reply.

8. Compare Kitchener's constitution for Egypt with any other African constitution you know.

9. What would have happened from 1921 to 1956 if the British had agreed to Zaghloul's four points? Or if Sir Lee Stack had not been murdered?

10. Why did the British want to keep an army in the Canal Zone as long as they could? Why did they agree in 1936 that they would take their army away as soon as Egypt was strong enough to defend the Canal?

11. In 1960, the British, the Egyptians, the Israelis, and the Arabs had all got less than they wanted. The British had lost the Canal. The Egyptians had lost the Sudan and the other lands which Mohammed Ali and Ismail had tried to conquer. The Israelis had failed to take any land away from Egypt. The Arabs had not driven the Israelis out of Palestine. What do you think of this position?

12. Do you think it would have been better for Egypt if the British had never ruled it? Give your reasons.

13. Find out all you can about the High Dam, the Suez Canal, and the Gezira cotton scheme. When the High Dam is finished, much of Nubia will be covered with water, and many old buildings and historical remains will be hidden. Try and find out what Unesco and others are doing about them.

14. One reason why the rest of the world is so interested in the Arab countries is that they produce so much oil. Find out all you can about the oil industry in the Arab countries.

15. Write a scene in which President Nasser and the Prime Ministers of Britain and of Israel talk together about how their three countries are to live together after 1956.

MAP 6. UGANDA AND ITS NEIGHBOURS

This map shows the boundary of the Protectorate of Uganda by a thin dotted line (running through the middle of lakes Albert, Edward, and Victoria), and the boundary of the kingdom of Buganda by a thick dotted line. It shows Tabora and Gondokoro, and the arrows show the two directions from which the Arabs came into Uganda. We can see how Karl Peters came to Buganda, from Witu up the river Tana and across to the Kavirondo Gulf. Today there are railways from Mombasa to Kisumu and Kampala and beyond, and from Dar-es-Salaam to Tabora and Ujiji; a branch goes north from Tabora to Mwanza on the south shore of Lake Victoria. You can see these and other railway lines in your atlas, but we have not marked them here.

2

Uganda

There have been very great changes in Africa in the last few years. Nearly all the lands which used to be British or French colonies have become independent. Ghana was the first of them; it became independent in March 1957. But Uganda, which is very like Ghana in some ways, was one of the last; it did not become independent until the autum of 1962, more than five years later than Ghana. Why is this?

It is true that since Ghana became independent, all kinds of countries in Africa, big and small, rich and poor, have become independent too. But when you are dealing with human beings, you cannot use such precise language as when you are dealing with numbers or chemicals. When a chemist adds one chemical to another, he knows exactly what result to expect. But with human beings it is different. You cannot say that if a colony of a given size is provided with a given amount of wealth and of education for a given time, it will become independent. Life is not as simple as that. Moreover, as we have said, Ghana is rich but Somalia is poor; Nigeria is big but Togo is small; but they have all become independent.

Uganda and Ghana are very much alike in some ways; but not in all. They are about equal in size and population. They both lie close to the Equator, and both are mainly agricultural; Ghana lives by exporting its cocoa and Uganda its cotton. Other exports are less important. Again, both countries are truly African countries. There are no white farmers in Ghana, and only a few in Uganda; and although in both countries there are Asian shop-keepers and business men, they form only a small part of the total population. These two countries do not have anything like the race problems of Kenya or South Africa.

But there are many differences between Ghana and Uganda. It is three hundred years since the British made their first settle-

ment on the coast of Ghana, but the first missionaries did not
reach Uganda until 1877, and the British flag was not raised until
1890. When the British came to Ghana – the Gold Coast, as it
was then called – there was no one strong African state anywhere
near the coast, but a mass of small states. But as soon as the
British came to Uganda, they found themselves dealing with the
strong kingdom of Buganda. They made an agreement with
Buganda; then they went further into the country and made
agreements with other states, Ankole, Bunyoro and others. Much
of the history of Uganda under British rule is the story of how
the British have tried to make Uganda into one country without
breaking their agreements with Buganda and the other kingdoms.

**Before you go any further, what is the difference between Uganda
and Buganda?**

That again is an important difference, as we shall see. The
Bantu people who live in that part of Africa express different
meanings by adding a syllable in front of a word. The word
Ganda is the name of something connected with that particular
people; but what that something is, depends on the syllable that
comes in front of it. The Ganda kingdom is Bu-Ganda; the
language is Lu-Ganda; one Ganda man is a Mu-Ganda, and
many Ganda men are Ba-Ganda. At the time the British arrived,
the kingdom of Buganda was the strongest state in that region;
and when the British made Buganda and several other states into
one British Protectorate, it was natural that they should call the
whole country by a name connected with this word Ganda. So
today, Uganda is the name of the whole British territory, and
the kingdom of Buganda is one of the states in that territory.

**Yes, but how did the name Uganda arise; did the British just invent
the word?**

Not exactly. The first British explorer to visit the country was
Captain Speke, who reached it in January 1862. He came from
the east coast; and his guides and porters[1] all spoke Swahili. It
was these Swahili-speaking people who used to drop the letter *B*
from the name Buganda and call the country Uganda. Later on,
when the British came to know the other kingdoms, Bunyoro,

[1] Porters are people who carry loads; often we call them carriers in Africa.

Toro, and so on, they needed a name for the whole country; and this word Uganda seemed useful.

Very well. But the history of Uganda did not begin with Captain Speke's visit in 1862; how did Buganda and the other kingdoms come to be set up?

We do not know as much about the history of these kingdoms as we do about some of those in West Africa. No doubt there are old men in different places whose duty is to know the history of their own chief or their own king; but what they know has not yet been written down and fitted together. So we can only tell the story without details.

There are two things about the story which remind us of West Africa. One is, that for hundreds of years at least, tribes and nations have been moving, looking for new homes. Small tribes have grown greater, and they have needed more land. Sometimes they have been lucky, and have found land that was lying empty. Sometimes they have found other peoples already living in the land that they wanted; and then there has been war. War brings about changes. Tribes are broken in pieces. People have to change their customs and their ways of living. Strong fighting chiefs arise; the Zulu in South Africa, for example, were a small weak people before Chaka's time. The story of Uganda, like the story of West and South Africa, is full of the movements of tribes and nations.

The other thing that reminds us of parts of West Africa is that there are two main kinds of life: one is the life of agriculture, and the other the life of the cattle-keeper. Some peoples are agriculturists, others cattle-keepers; it is not very often that we find one nation which is both. Now in Africa, this is an important difference. The family that keeps cattle wants to have more cattle. Cattle are wealth; a rich man shows how rich he is by the great number of cattle he owns. So the herds of cattle keep on growing, and there comes a time when there are too many for the grass. So many cattle-keeping people, like the Fulani in West Africa and the Masai in East Africa, are nomads; this means that they have to keep moving every few weeks or months to find fresh grass for their cattle.

The agriculturist on the other hand stays in one place. He finds a piece of good farming land, builds his hut, and settles there. Very likely he moves his farm every two or three years; he burns the bush, plants his crops in the ashes, and leaves last year's farm to go back to bush and get strong again. But all his farms are near his home, and he does not want to leave. He lives and dies in one place; and the longer the house or the village lasts, the more spirits of the dead are there to watch over the living people. The people pray to the gods of the land and to the spirits of their dead forefathers[1] to keep them safe and give them good crops.

These are two very different ways of living; and sometimes a cattle-keeping tribe comes into the land of an agricultural tribe and wants to settle there, and there is war. It happens over and over again, as we have seen in Book One[2], that the tribe that is hunting for new land is stronger than the tribe which is busy with its agriculture and just wants to be left alone. We have seen it happen with the Arabs and the Berbers; we have seen it happen with the Berbers and the Hausa.

Now suppose the cattle-keeping tribe conquers the agricultural tribe: what will happen? It may be that all the men of the agricultural tribe are killed, but that is not likely to happen often. The cattle-keepers will want to eat yams and millet and bananas, and someone has to grow them. The cattle-keepers will not grow them; it is against their custom. And besides, they are the masters, and they will think agriculture is fit only for servants. Not only this. It is true that they have conquered the living men; but what about the gods and the spirits? The gods and the spirits cannot be conquered; and if strangers come and dig in their land, they may be angry and bring all kinds of trouble on the people. So it is better to leave the agricultural people to grow their crops and worship the old gods; but they will be servants, and they will have to make room in the land for their new masters' cattle. This has happened in many places. It happened for example in the Northern Region of Ghana (the Gold Coast) about 500 years ago; many of the kings and chiefs today are descended from the cattle-keeping conquerers, but most of the people are descended from the original agricultural inhabitants, and their priests still worship the old agricultural gods. A chief in that region will say, 'The people belong to me, but the land belongs to the priests of

---

[1] That is, their father, father's father, father's father's father, and so on.
[2] See especially pages 44, 46, 76, 83.

the old gods.' It happened again when the cattle-keeping Fulani conquered the agricultural Hausa of Northern Nigeria, though in this case all the Fulani and many of the Hausa were Muslims, so there was no question of the old worship.

Do you mean that this happened also in Uganda?

Yes, very much so. We think that many hundreds of years ago, the people of that country were Bantu agriculturists. The Baganda today have stories about a wonderful race of people called the Bahima, great cattle-keepers and very light-colored, who came down from the north and conquered them long ago. We do not know just when this happened, but we think it was about the year 1250, when Sundiata of Mali destroyed the village of Kumbi and allowed the desert to cover it.[1] There was one large family of the Bahima, called the Bachwezi, which from about 1250 to about 1450 ruled a strong kingdom called Kitara or Kitwara, covering all the land between Lake Albert, Lake Victoria, and Mount Elgon. Further south, other Bahima families ruled the land between Lake Victoria and the lakes of the rift valley: the land which today makes Ruanda-Urundi and the Bukoba district of Tanganyika.

The Bahima lived for their cattle. They left their Bantu subjects to grow millet and bananas, while they themselves looked after their great herds. In each kingdom there was one Bahima priest-king, who held all power in his hands. The country was divided into districts ruled by Bahima chiefs, but they too were mainly concerned with looking after cattle and settling quarrels between herdsmen. They did not trouble themselves much about their agricultural subjects. No doubt, as in the Northern Region of Ghana in the old days, the agriculturists lived their own life and took their quarrels to their own priests. As long as they grew enough food for their Bahima masters and left enough grass for the cattle, their masters did not trouble about them.

About 1450 or 1500 the kingdom of Kitwara was attacked by other peoples called the Lwoo, coming down from the north as the Bahima themselves had come before. The Lwoo (sometimes called Babito) were also cattle-keepers. They conquered most of the Kitwara kingdom, and set up a new state called Bunyoro along the shores of Lake Albert. Other Lwoo states were set up

[1] See Book One, pages 50, 51.

F

south and east of Bunyoro, but further south still there were some Bahima states which were able to stop the Lwoo and to remain independent. Further east, other peoples who were not connected with the Bahima or the Lwoo set up agricultural communities in what is now the Eastern Province of Uganda. These agricultural peoples, such as the Acholi and the Teso, did not form strong states with a central government. Like some of the peoples of Eastern Nigeria, they were organized in family groups, with no central chief.

Were these agricultural peoples Bantu?

No, they were not Bantu. Their languages and customs are different, and they would not like it to be thought that Uganda today is entirely a Bantu country. This is something which we have to remember in dealing with the Uganda of today. It is a country with many different peoples, many different languages, many different customs. Can it become one country, as Ghana has done?

BUNYORO AND BUGANDA

The kingdom of Bunyoro was the strongest of the Lwoo kingdoms; in fact, it took over a good deal of the strength of the Kitwara kingdom, just as the kingdom of Bornu, 1700 miles away, took over much of the strength of the old kingdom of Kanem.[1] After a time, the kings of Bunyoro began to make war on the other states and conquer them. Bunyoro was strong, partly because its kings had the ambition to conquer other states, partly because it had two important things: salt and iron. We have seen in West Africa[2] how important salt is to people who live far from the sea: so important that people will sometimes buy it with its own weight of gold. Iron too is important; you can sell it to your neighbours and become rich, or you can use it to make spears for your soldiers, and become strong.

So the kings of Bunyoro, like the kings of Ashanti far away, set out to conquer as much as they could of the country round them. Like the Ashanti, they did conquer a good deal; but like the Ashanti again, they found that it was easier to conquer a country than to govern it. They had to keep sending soldiers

[1] See Book One, page 74.
[2] See Book One, page 44.

against some tribe which had risen up against them. When the king died, there were often quarrels between members of the royal family who wanted to become king; and this led to more fighting. From about 1750 onwards, the power of Bunyoro began to go down, and the power of Buganda began to rise.

Buganda was one of the Lwoo states, and its royal family was a branch of the royal family of Bunyoro. But it was much more thickly populated than Bunyoro. Much more of its land was used for crops, and much less for cattle; and so the king of Buganda, unlike the king of Bunyoro, was forced to take trouble over his subjects who grew the crops. The king of Bunyoro thought only of the cattle and the cattle-keepers; the king of Buganda (who is called the Kabaka) had to think of all his subjects. So Buganda grew into a strongly organized state, with the Kabaka at its head. He appointed all the chiefs, and could dismiss them. He had a council of chiefs, called the Lukiko, to advise him, but he was not bound to follow their advice. The land of Buganda might belong to the old gods; but the people were his, and their work belonged to him. Thus, the Kabaka and his kingdom were one. Without a Kabaka, Buganda could not exist. If the Kabaka were well, the kingdom would be well. Even if the Kabaka governed badly, it would usually be better to obey him than to rise up against him and bring the whole country into danger. This is very different from Ashanti and other states in Ghana, where people have always been ready – sometimes too ready – to put away a chief who governs badly and choose someone else in his place.

Buganda too began to conquer the other states around it. It conquered Busoga, which lay east of the Nile and served Bunyoro; and its armies went south-westward along the shores of Lake Victoria and conquered other states which had been part of the Bunyoro kingdom. More than once there was war between Buganda and Bunyoro; and by about 1850 it seemed as if the two kingdoms must soon fight each other again in the greatest war of all to decide which should be the master.

But things did not happen like that. We have seen[1] how long ago on the other side of Africa the Berbers and the Soninke were not left to themselves to fight their wars; the Arabs came and made trouble for them both. So it happened in Uganda. Bunyoro

[1] See Book One, page 44.

and Buganda were not left alone; new people came in from outside to take part in the affair.

These people were the Arab traders, who came into Uganda from two directions, from the east coast and from the north. The Arabs had been ruling Zanzibar and Mombasa and a long stretch of the east coast of Africa for many hundred years, and they had been trading with the Bantu peoples, selling all kinds of trade goods from Europe and India, and buying ivory and slaves. As time went on, they came further and further into the country; they set up Tabora in Tanganyika as one of their main trading post, and shortly before 1850 they came from Tabora up the west side of the Lake and reached Uganda. We have seen in Book One what trouble the slave trade brought to West Africa, and in East Africa it was just the same. The Arab slave-traders destroyed villages, killed old men and children, and drove away the women and the young men who would be worth money in the slave-market. African tribal life and civilization were broken up and spoilt.

In Buganda the Arabs could not do much damage, for the Kabaka and his people were too strong. The Kabaka sold them some slaves and some ivory, and bought guns; and the guns made his kingdom still stronger. By the time the Arabs reached Buganda, they had come nearly a thousand miles from the coast, and were far away from any strong Arab base. So the kingdom of Buganda was strengthened by the coming of the Arabs from Tabora.

Things were different in Bunyoro, which Arab traders reached from the north. Bunyoro was not strengthened, but weakened. Far away down the Nile was the kingdom of Egypt. About 1830, Egypt was ruled by Mohammed Ali, who wanted to make Egypt a great kingdom with a strong army and navy and a wide empire. He sent his soldiers up the Nile as far as Gondokoro, which is only about a hundred miles from the border of modern Uganda. After Mohammed Ali's time, Egypt became weaker, and had no real power as far south as this. But the Egyptian soldiers had shown the way to the south, and the town of Gondokoro became the base from which Egyptian and Arab traders went south into Uganda for slaves and ivory. The Acholi and other agricultural peoples, with their small family villages, could not stand against them; the traders burnt the villages and let the farm land go back to bush. In 1864 the slave traders were ready to make war on Bunyoro itself.

But why did not Bunyoro do as Buganda did; buy guns and show itself too strong for the slave-traders?

For two reasons. One is that Bunyoro was weaker than Buganda, and the other is that the Arabs coming to Bunyoro were stronger than those coming to Buganda. King Kamrasi of Bunyoro was in a difficult position, for all his life his brother Rionga was trying to make himself king. This made it easy for the slave-traders; by keeping the civil war going between Kamrasi and Rionga they made sure of their own trade. Kamrasi and Rionga ought to have seen that their quarrel was making it easy for the slave-traders to destroy their country. In 1869 Kamrasi died, and again there was a quarrel over who should succeed him. On this occasion, the slave-traders decided to help his son Kabarega against his rival, and Kabarega became king. No doubt the slave-traders looked forward to another long period of civil war in Bunyoro, with much profit for themselves.

Why were the Arabs in Bunyoro stronger than the Arabs in Buganda?

Because the Arabs in Buganda were very far from home, or even from their base in Tabora. But the Arabs coming to Bunyoro from the north had only a short distance to come from their base at Gondokoro. If things had remained as they were, and the Egyptians and the Europeans had stayed away, the Arabs from Gondokoro might have conquered Bunyoro and then gone on to make war on Buganda. Buganda would then have been in a difficult position. But luckily, the slave-traders were not left to have things all their own way.

In 1863 Egypt had a new king, Ismail, who wanted to follow Mohammed Ali's example and make Egypt a great empire. But times were changing. In 1861, on the other side of Africa, the British had taken Lagos and made it into a colony because that was the only way of stopping the slave trade, and in Central and East Africa the great missionary David Livingstone was exploring the country and telling the people of Britain what a wicked business the Arab slave trade was. So Ismail knew that if he conquered an empire, Britain and France and other European countries would expect him to do what he could to stop the slave trade in the lands he conquered.

King Ismail appointed a British officer, Sir Samuel Baker, to be his general and governor in this work of extending the Egyptian empire southwards. Baker already knew the country; he had visited Bunyoro in 1863, coming from Gondokoro by the way which the Arabs used, and he had been able to help king Kamrasi of Bunyoro against the Arab slave traders. So he seemed the right man for Ismail; he knew the country and the people, and as he was British, he would certainly do all he could to stop the slave trade.

Baker reached Gondokoro in 1871, and moved southwards into Uganda, building forts[1] and putting Egyptian soldiers to hold them. He told all the people that the country was part of the Egyptian empire and that slave trading was to stop; and for a time it seemed as if much of the northern part of Uganda would be brought under peaceable Egyptian rule. But Baker was not able to stay long enough to finish his work, and he had no good officers to help him. He was succeeded as Egyptian governor by another British officer, Charles Gordon. Gordon had a great plan for setting up Egyptian forts all the way from Uganda down to the coast at Mombasa; and he actually sent a party of Egyptian soldiers to raise the Egyptian flag on the shores of Lake Victoria. The Kabaka Mutesa was able to stop this, but he knew that Egypt wanted to make Buganda an Egyptian colony, and he was afraid.

But the danger from Egypt passed away. Egypt was poor, and its government was weak. In 1881 the people of the Sudan rose up against the Egyptian Government under a leader called the Mahdi, and in 1882 Egypt itself was conquered by Britain.[2] The British Government decided that it could not keep the Egyptian soldiers in the far south of the Sudan and in Uganda, and it told Gordon to call them back. But before Gordon could do this, the armies of the Mahdi had cut them off from Egypt, and in 1885 Gordon himself was killed by the Mahdi's soldiers. The Egyptian soldiers in the south were now cut off from Egypt, and the Kabaka would not let them move south, so they had to stay where they

[1] A fort is a strong building where soldiers can live and defend themselves if they are attacked.
[2] See pages 37–44.

were, and many of them behaved so badly that the people of the country thought them no better than the Arab slave traders.

THE COMING OF THE MISSIONARIES

The years from 1870 to 1885 were important years in Africa. We have seen in Book One that during these years European traders and missionaries were coming more and more into West Africa; and so it was in the East. European Governments were becoming much more interested in Africa; and 1885, the year of Gordon's death, was also the year of the Berlin Act, by which the European Governments agreed that if one country could show that it had more interest than any other in one particular part of Africa, and would promise to set up a government in that part, the other European countries would not interfere with it.

In 1875, Buganda was visited by an American explorer, Henry Stanley. Stanley had travelled much in East Africa; in 1871 he had marched from the east coast to see if the famous missionary David Livingstone was still alive, and had found him at Ujiji on Lake Tanganyika. So although Stanley was not himself a missionary, he was interested in missionary work. While he was in Kampala he had long talks with Kabaka Mutesa, and Mutesa agreed to ask for missionaries to be sent to his country. His letter was sent to Gordon at Khartoum, and Gordon sent it on to London, where it was published in the *Daily Telegraph*.

The missionaries soon arrived. The Church Missionary Society sent its first two missionaries in 1877, and more followed in 1879; a few days after the second party of C.M.S. missionaries, there came the first Roman Catholic missionaries, a party of the White Fathers.

The missionaries, and the Kabaka, were in a difficult position. If the Kabaka wanted Christian missionaries, it is a pity that he was sent missionaries of two different kinds, who disagreed in much of their teaching. Since France and Britain at that time were rivals in Africa, it is a pity that the C.M.S. missionaries were British and the Catholic missionaries were French. And the Kabaka too found that the new religion brought him a difficulty. The Kabaka of Buganda had always been obeyed in all things; but Christians in Uganda could not obey his Government if they thought it wrong.

Another difficulty was that the Arabs from the east coast saw the interest which the European Governments were beginning to take in East Africa. They were Muslims, and they did not like to see Christianity being preached in Uganda. They were traders, and did not want to share with the Europeans the trade in ivory, which had been all their own for so long. They owned slaves and would do as much slave trading as they could, and they did not want the Europeans to stop the slave trade and set all their slaves free. For all these reasons, the Arabs did all they could to turn the Kabaka against the Christian missionaries. For a few years, the Arabs had a plan to set up a strong Arab state in East Africa, and although this plan did not succeed, they were strong enough to cause much trouble in Uganda.

In 1884, Kabaka Mutesa died, and his son Mwanga succeeded him. Like every Kabaka before him, he wanted to be left alone to rule his people in his own way, and he found himself unable to rule in his own way because many of his people had become Christians and followed the Christian missionaries. In 1885 and 1886, he decided to stop Christianity in Uganda; he had a Protestant Bishop killed, and killed many of his own Baganda people when they refused to give up their new Christianity. In 1888 he went further; he decided to kill not only all the Christians, both Protestant and Catholic, but also all the Muslims. But the people heard of this, and Muslim and Christian Baganda joined together and rose up against the Kabaka. Mwanga left Kampala and fled to the country south of the lake; the Christian and Muslim Baganda chiefs said that they would no larger have him as their Kabaka, and they put his elder brother Kiwewa into his place.

The new Kabaka at first said that he would allow all his people to follow whatever religion they chose. But this state of things did not last long. In less than a month, the Muslim Baganda, with the help of the Arabs, rose up against the Christians; they killed many of them, and drove the rest out of the country of Buganda. There were five European missionaries, three White Fathers and two from the C.M.S.; the Baganda did not kill them, but robbed them of all they had and sent them away on the C.M.S. boat to the other end of the lake.

It seems that the new Kabaka, Kiwewa, wanted to keep himself free from Islam as well as from Christianity. When the Christians had been driven out, the Muslims thought that they would be able to do as they pleased, and they wanted the Kabaka to become a Muslim. Kiwewa would not. He arrested several of the Muslim leaders, and killed three of them; but the others rose up against him and made another brother, Kalema, Kabaka in his place. Kiwewa gathered an army and fought against Kalema, but was caught and killed. The Muslims now began to try to turn Buganda into a Muslim state by forcing all the Baganda to become Muslims. But the Baganda would not do it; many of them left their country and went to join the Christians in Ankole, where the king of Ankole had allowed them to settle.

When Kabaka Mwanga heard of all this, he thought that he might be able to get back to Kampala. He had been out of his country for more than six months, and in May 1889 he gathered an army and marched into Buganda. He was defeated in his first battle against Kalema's army, and retired to the Sese islands in the lake; he was able to do this because he had plenty of canoes and Kalema had none. He invited the European missionaries to come and join him in the islands, and they came.

Mwanga had now decided that his best chance of becoming Kabaka one more was to put himself at the head of the Christian Baganda against the Muslims. In October 1889 he once more attacked Kalema; one of his armies crossed in canoes from the islands while another advanced from the south-west. This time he beat Kalema, and entered Kampala and once more became Kabaka. Kalema and some of his men fled to Bunyoro, and king Kabarega of Bunyoro decided to help them. With an army from Bunyoro, Kalema advanced into Buganda, and at the end of November he defeated Mwanga and drove the Christians yet again to take shelter in the islands. But most of the Baganda people supported Mwanga, and in February 1890 he defeated Kalema, who fled again to Bunyoro and troubled Buganda no more.

Mwanga was again Kabaka of Buganda, but Buganda was no longer a united country as it had once been. There were now three parties: Muslims, Catholics, and Protestants. None of them trusted the Kabaka; he had begun by killing Christians, he had meant to kill the Muslims in the same way, and he got back his power by using the Christians against the Muslims. He now called himself a Catholic, and the Protestant chiefs were afraid that he might try to force them all to become Catholic. On the other hand, nobody could tell if Mwanga was a sincere Catholic, or was pretending to be a Catholic because he thought that the Catholics were the strongest party and would give him the best chance of remaining in power. One thing was clear; Buganda had been full of trouble and civil war ever since he became Kabaka. His father Mutesa had invited European missionaries into Buganda, and he, Mwanga, had killed them. The European Governments would want to make sure that Uganda was a country where white men could live in safety; and in those days, that would mean making it a colony or a protectorate. The Kabaka only wanted to be left alone. He still hoped that Buganda might again be a united country, and he tried to balance Catholics against Protestants by dividing the offices of state equally between them. As the Kabaka himself was a Catholic, the prime minister, the Katikiro, was a Protestant, Apolo Kagwa (later Sir Apolo Kagwa); the next below him was a Catholic, the third a Protestant, and so on all the way down. In Buganda, the names Catholic and Protestant were not merely names of two religions; they were at that time the names of two political parties. The Kabaka was no longer the ruler of one united country; he was the head of one of the parties in the state.

GERMANS AND BRITISH

As the Kabaka well knew, what had happened in Buganda was likely to bring one or other of the European powers into the country. The question was, which would it be? The British were one likely power. For many years the British navy had been trying to stop the slave ships that went from East African ports to the slave markets of Arabia. There had been a British consul at Zanzibar since 1841, and since 1872 there had been a regular service of British steamers between India and Zanzibar. The Sultan of Zanzibar ruled a good deal of land on the mainland of East Africa, and British missionaries and traders were working in what is now Kenya, and also further south. Between 1875 and 1880, the Sultan wanted the British to set up a trading company to take over the government of his possessions on the mainland, and develop them, and pay him a suitable rent. The great British missionary David Livingstone told the British Government that the only real way of stopping the slave trade would be to take control of the land where the Arab slave traders caught the slaves.

For all these reasons, it seemed likely that the British would soon make part of East Africa into a colony or a protectorate.

But, as we have seen in Nigeria and South Africa, the British Government at that time did not want to take over any more land in Africa. The British consul in Zanzibar and the British traders in Zanzibar and East Africa asked the Government in London to agree to what the Sultan asked; but the Government would not.

As in West Africa, what drove the British Government to act was the knowledge that if Britain did not, another European power would. In this case the European power was Germany.

Why Germany? Why not France, seeing that the Catholic missionaries in Uganda were French, and seeing that France was already busy elsewhere in Africa?

Well, if we look at the map, we shall see that East Africa, and especially Uganda, was rather out of the way for the French. The French were very busy in West Africa as far down as the mouth of the Congo, but the Belgians were opening up the Congo basin, and the land of the Belgian Congo lay between Uganda and French territory. The road up the Nile was held by Egypt, so the French had no way of getting into Uganda from the north. And it so happened that on the east coast, the British had been much more active than the French in opening up trade; partly because they were so busy in stopping the slave trade, and partly because the East African coast was opposite to India, and India was British.

Germany was in a different position. It was not till 1884 that Germany decided that she wanted any colonies, and by 1884 most of the best places on the African coast were taken by other countries. The East African coast was the only really large piece of coast still free, except for the desert coast of South-West Africa. The German Government decided that it would try and set up a German colony in East Africa.

There was a good opportunity for the German Government to get its people to support it. In 1878, Charles Gordon had appointed as governor of the southern-most province of the Sudan a German, Dr Eduard Schnitzer. Dr Schnitzer had become a Muslim, and had taken the name of Emin Pasha. He was a good governor, and the African people liked him. When the Mahdi rising broke out in 1881, Emin Pasha and his soldiers were cut off from the north, and nothing more could be heard of them. Gordon himself was killed by the Mahdi's men in 1885, and the British people were very angry with their Government for not having sent British soldiers up the Nile in time to rescue him. Surely something could be done to rescue Emin Pasha? Nobody could get to him from the north, but the American explorer Henry Stanley, who had marched from the east coast of Africa to find David Livingstone in 1871, set out in 1887 and marched up the west coast from the Congo. Nothing was heard of him for a long time, and in 1889 the German Dr Karl Peters set out to try and reach Emin Pasha from the east coast.

It was not Dr Peters' first visit to East Africa. He first went there in 1884, and made treaties with several African chiefs by which they agreed to put themselves and their people under German protection. Peters went home to Germany with his treaties, and the German Government sent warships to Dar-es-Salaam and told the world that that part of the East African coast was now a German protectorate. This made the British Government see that unless it moved in and gave British traders some help, Germany would move both north and south along the coast and take the whole country, from the Gulf of Aden right down to Mozambique. We have seen[1] that at the same time, Britain had to choose whether she would allow France and Germany to share Nigeria between them, or whether she would set up a British protectorate there. It was just the same in East Africa.

In 1886, Britain and Germany made an agreement with the Sultan of Zanzibar, by which they divided his possessions on the mainland between them. The boundary between British and German East Africa was laid down as far as Lake Victoria; it is the present boundary between Kenya and Tanganyika. The Sultan kept a ten-mile strip along the Kenya coast.

This seems unfair to the Sultan of Zanzibar. Was he angry?

It certainly was not what the Sultan had been hoping for. He had seen for a long time that he needed the help of some European nation to open up the mainland, build roads and railways, stop tribal warfare, develop trade, and make profits for him which he could not make for himself. For the last ten years, he had hoped that

[1] See Book One, pp. 91, 92.

Britain would take over the government of all his possessions on the mainland and make a good agreement with him. The 1886 agreement was not nearly as good from his point of view. The Germans had taken half his lands, and he knew that he would get very little from them. What he wanted now was that the British should form a strong company quickly and open up their protectorate and share their profits with him.

At last the British company was formed; in 1887 the Sultan made an agreement with it, and in the next year the British Government gave it a royal charter; that is, the Government would help and encourage the company in its work of opening up the country, but would control it in matters of politics. The Royal Niger Company in southern Nigeria had a royal charter, Cecil Rhodes's British South Africa Company[1] had one; and now the Imperial British East Africa Company too had its royal charter, and set to work to open up East Africa.

In 1889 the I.B.E.A. Company sent a party under Mr F.J.Jackson to Lake Victoria. Jackson was told that he was to make treaties with the chiefs in the British protectorate, and was to get as much ivory as he could for the Company. He was not to go to Uganda.

But are we not forgetting Dr Karl Peters? He did a good job for Germany in 1884; how did he get on in 1889 when he went to look for Emin Pasha?

Dr Peters was a very bold and active man. Instead of starting from German territory[2] he decided to go through British territory, though his own Government told him that it would give him no support if he did so. He went from Zanzibar north to Witu, and then up the Tana river. The 1886 agreement made the south bank of the Tana British territory, and British officers had already been 250 miles up the river. Peters did not care. He fought his way up the river against the African chiefs who tried to stop him, and in many places on the north bank of the river he raised the German flag to show that it was German territory. Then he left the river and crossed the mountains to the Kavirondo Gulf on Lake Victoria; and there too he made a treaty and raised the German flag,

[1] See Book One, page 127.
[2] That is, land belonging to someone; a bird's territory is the land in which the bird hunts, and British territory is land in which the British Government rules.

although Kavirondo was clearly British territory and Jackson's party had been there before him.

Peters arrived in Kavirondo in February 1890, and heard that Jackson had been there in November. He heard too that the Kabaka Mwanga had written to Jackson asking for his help and offering to accept British protection, but that Jackson had not accepted the offer and had given the Kabaka no help at all. Peters saw that there was a chance for Germany to set up a protectorate over Buganda, and he left Kavirondo at once to go there.

When Peters arrived in Busoga on his way to Kampala, he learned that Stanley had found Emin Pasha safe and well, and that the two men were on their way back to the coast together. He himself had been sent to find Emin Pasha, and he might now have gone back home; but instead, he went on to Buganda to see what he could do for Germany there. He arrived in Kampala on 25 February and saw the Kabaka. Mwanga made it clear that he did not intend to put his country under the protection of any European power, but he was ready to sign a treaty with the German Government by which he became the friend of the German Emperor. The Catholic chiefs agreed; the Protestant chiefs were unwilling to sign the treaty, but did so because they were afraid that there would be more civil war if they refused. The treaty was signed on 3rd March 1890; on the 22nd, a letter came from Jackson at Kavirondo. Jackson knew that Emin Pasha was found, and that Peters had been fighting and making treaties in British territory; he now wrote to say that the German Government would not take responsibility for what Peters had done, and that both the British and German Governments had told him to go to Buganda and arrest Peters. Peters of course was very angry, but he knew that if his Government did not support him he had no chance; so he left Buganda and escaped southward before Jackson arrived.

Jackson reached Kampala on 14 April 1890 and invited the Kabaka to sign a treaty; but the Kabaka liked Peters better, and would not agree. It was difficult for Jackson. His orders were that he was not to enter Buganda, and he did not know what his Company would say when it heard that he had entered it. Nor did he know what the British Government would do about Uganda. He decided to go back to the coast to see, taking with him one Protestant and one Catholic Muganda so that they could tell the Kabaka what they heard. On 1st July 1890, before Jackson and his two Baganda friends reached the coast, Britain and Germany made a treaty, by which Buganda was left to Britain.

It seems rather hard luck on Dr Peters that his Government did not support him after all his hard work.

Well, Peters at first said that he would start from German territory and march inland round the south of Lake Victoria and then past Lake Albert to where Emin Pasha was supposed to be. If he had done that, and had put up the German flag wherever he went, nobody could have objected. But he did not do this; he went north, through what he knew was British country. It is true that a German company was trying to get Witu made into a German protectorate, and Peters no doubt thought it would help Germany if he took his little army that way. But he knew that British officers had been up the Tana before him, and his own Government had told him, before ever he left Zanzibar, that if he went up the Tana it would give him no support.

But what made the German Government give up Uganda?

The German Government at that time was guided by a great statesman named Bismarck. Bismarck was afraid of France and Russia, and spent a great deal of time in trying to guard against the danger that France and Russia might together make war on Germany. At that time Britain and France were not very friendly. Both of them were extending their territory in Africa, and Bismarck thought it would help Germany if France and England were jealous of each other. He was not afraid of Britain, and he did not specially want Britain as a friend or ally; but he knew that if he allowed Britain to take Uganda, the French would not be pleased, especially as there were French missionaries working there. Also, Britain at that time held the small island of Heligoland, very close to Germany. Bismarck wanted Heligoland, and Britain was willing to give it up; so the two countries made an agreement by which they settled all kinds of small points which might have led them to quarrel. Bismarck did this sort of thing very cleverly. In 1881, all Europe knew that Italy wanted to annex Tunis, but France stepped in before her. Bismarck knew what France was going to do, but he took care that Italy should not know. Italy was surprised and very angry, and became the enemy of France, which was what Bismarck had intended. He wanted France to be without friends, and to give up Uganda was part of the price he was willing to pay.

As a result of all this, it was clear that Britain was the only European power that Buganda would deal with. Under the Berlin Act of 1885, the other European powers would stay away from Uganda on condition that Britain set up a government there. This was now the job of the I.B.E.A. Company, and Captain Frederic Lugard was the man whom the Company sent to Buganda as its representative.

Lugard had been an army officer in India, and while on leave he took a job with the African Lakes Company, a British company which was trying to put down the slave trade and open up other kinds of trade around Lake Nyasa. He was wounded while fighting Arab slave traders, and afterwards left the African Lakes Company and joined the I.B.E.A. Company.

In October 1890 the Company told Lugard to go to Buganda, and he started from Kikuyu on 1st November. He wanted to reach Kampala as soon as he could, because he knew that the Protestants and Catholics in Buganda were ready to fight each other again if only they could get guns, and he knew too that a European trader was on his way to Buganda with hundreds of guns to sell. If Lugard could get there before the guns, he might be able to stop the civil war from starting again.

What would the Baganda give for the guns?

Ivory. Slaves and ivory were the two things that East Africa had been exporting for hundreds of years. The British did not want slaves, but they still wanted ivory.

To reach Kampala, Lugard had to cross the Nile near Jinja, and it was the custom to wait here and send a messenger to the Kabaka asking for permission to enter his country. Lugard knew of the custom, but he did not follow it; it would be easy for the Kabaka to keep him waiting at the river until the trader had arrived with his guns, and then Lugard would be too late. So he crossed the Nile, and arrived in Kampala on 18 December, which greatly frightened the Kabaka. Mwanga was afraid that the

3. The Suez Canal in 1873. The white ship is taking British soldiers to India. It is a steamer but uses sails as well as engines. The Canal is wider and deeper now than it was in 1873.

photo: Radio Times Hulton Picture Library

4. British and Egyptian soldiers entering Omdurman in 1898. Fighting is still going on in the streets of the town.

photo: Radio Times Hulton Picture Library

British were coming to punish him for having killed the Bishop in 1885. Lugard had not come to do this. He had come to stop the fighting, to put Buganda under the protection of the British company, and to treat all parties (Muslims, Protestants, Catholics, pagans) fairly. The Kabaka could no longer control his own people, so Lugard saw that he must make an agreement with the Kabaka and with the leading chiefs. Lugard was in a very difficult position. He had very few soldiers, and the Protestant and Catholic Baganda had very many guns, though they had very few bullets. The Protestant and Catholic chiefs, and even some of the French and British missionaries, used their religion as a means of getting political power, and they were angry because Lugard told them that religion had nothing to do with politics.

However, Lugard was so patient and firm that on 26 December, the Kabaka and all his leading chiefs signed a treaty. Buganda accepted the protection of the I.B.E.A. Company, and the Company agreed to send an officer to act as Resident. The customs and taxes were to be collected by a committee of four members, with the British Resident as chairman; they were to be used only for the good of the country, and not for the good of the Company. The Resident must be consulted, and his agreement must be obtained, in all "grave and serious affairs and matters connected with the State." All missionaries were free to teach, and all traders free to buy and sell; but slaves, guns, and liquor were not to be bought and sold. The Company would open a road to the coast, place a steamer on the lake, and do all it could to encourage trade and good government.

But the treaty made no difference. Protestants and Catholics still quarrelled, and the Kabaka was afraid of them and of Lugard. In January, Lugard's little army of about 350 African soldiers was strengthened by the arrival of about 200 more under Captain Williams; and in February, when the trader Stokes arrived with his guns and bullets, Lugard showed him the treaty and was able to make him take them away again out of the country.

In April 1891 Lugard decided to do what other leaders have often done when they were troubled by quarrels and fighting at home[1]; he called on the Protestants and Catholics to forget their quarrels and march together against the Muslims, who were living near the boundary of Bunyoro and were robbing the

[1] See Book One, page 48.

G

Baganda farmers. They did so, and beat the Muslims, who were helped by Kabarega of Bunyoro. This did something to make Protestants and Catholics more friendly together. At the end of March, the two Baganda who had gone down to the coast with Jackson in April 1890 came back, and they were able to tell the Lukiko that the British were as strong as the Germans, and that the German Government had agreed that Buganda should come under British protection. This helped to strengthen Lugard's position. But he felt that he must have still more soldiers; and as the Company could send him no more from the coast, he went away to the country near Lake Albert. Here, there were some of Emin Pasha's old soldiers from the Sudan; Lugard invited them to come and serve under him as British soldiers, and they came.

By the middle of 1891, it looked as if Buganda was settling down more quietly: but there was trouble to come. The I. B. E. A. Company was spending large sums of money on Uganda, but was getting hardly any trade out of the country. Everything had to be carried from the coast in head loads, and the Company saw that trade would not grow very much until a railway could be built from Mombasa to Uganda. But the Company had no money to build a railway, and the British Government would not give it them.

Why was a railway necessary? Would not a motor road have been enough? It would have been much cheaper.

A road would certainly have been much cheaper; but in those days there were no motor lorries. The motor car had just been invented, but there were only perhaps fifty or a hundred motor cars in the world. They were made by hand one at a time, they were very expensive and slow, and each car needed an engineer to look after it, for they often broke down and there were no spare parts. So there could be no question of a motor road; only the steam railway engine would do the work.

So in the middle of 1891, the Company said that it could not go on with its work in Uganda after the end of 1892, and it told Lugard to prepare to leave the country. Lugard was sure that if he left Uganda, all his work would be thrown away, and other people too began to see this when the civil war broke out again in January 1892. A Catholic Muganda killed a Protestant; the Kabaka tried the man and found him not guilty. Fighting broke out; the Catholics attacked the Protestants and were winning the fight when Lugard and his soldiers joined in to help the Protestants. This changed everything; the Protestants then won, and Lugard could not stop them from burning and robbing the Catholic houses. The Kabaka, who was himself a Catholic, fled with the Catholics to the islands, and when Lugard sent soldiers to the islands the Kabaka went on into German territory.

Why did Lugard interfere in the fighting? He made it look as if the Company were supporting the Protestants against the Catholics, which was the very thing he did not want to do.

True, it did look like that, and the Catholic Bishop wrote home to Europe and said so. But what was he to do? Let us not call the two parties Catholics and Protestants, for some of us today are Catholic and some are Protestant; and as we have already said, the Catholics and Protestants in Buganda at that time were political parties. Let us speak of Reds and Greens.

The Red party, then, is much stronger than the Green. When the Reds think the time has come, they attack the Greens and defeat them. What then? They will kill many, and they will drive the rest out of the country, as the Muslims had already been driven out. The careful balance, by which half the great officers of the country are Reds and the other half Greens, will be upset; all the officers will be Reds. That is no way to make peace. The Greens will do all they can to strengthen themselves; perhaps they will go away like the Muslims to the boundary of the country and live by robbing the Red farms while they prepare for a new war. That is what will happen if Lugard does nothing. He is there to keep the peace; and he can only hope to keep the peace if he makes both sides see that they can gain nothing by fighting. Whichever side makes war on the other will find Lugard against it, just as a policeman will always help the weak man against the strong man who is attacking him. Lugard's trouble was that he was not strong enough; he was strong enough to protect the Greens against the Reds, but not strong enough to stop the Greens burning the Red houses when they had won the battle with his help. If Lugard had had the soldiers that he asked the Company to send him, he could have kept the peace better.

At the end of March, Lugard persuaded the Kabaka to come back to Kampala, and there he signed a second treaty, much like the first treaty but giving the Company rather more powers. The Catholics were allowed to settle in the province of Buddu along the western side of Lake Victoria, and the Muslims in the north; all the land in the rest of Buganda was taken by the Protestants, though Lugard would have liked them to let the Catholics have more. This shows how political the fight had become between Protestants and Catholics; the winner takes all the land, or nearly all.

The great question for Lugard now was this: Would the Company be able to continue its work in Uganda? Would the British Government take over the country? Or would the British leave Uganda to its civil wars and let the Germans come in to stop them? Most of the British Government were against the idea of annexing the country. If the Company could keep on with its work without costing the British tax-payer any money, they would be satisfied. The Company could not keep on; it had not enough money, and not much hope of trade; and it certainly could not afford to build a railway to Uganda.

Lugard left Uganda in June 1892 and went to England to try and persuade the British Government and people that whatever happened, Uganda could not now be left to itself. The Kabaka wrote two letters, one to Queen Victoria and the other to the Company, asking that his country should remain British and that Lugard should be sent back to be the British Resident. The British Government took a long time to make up its mind. In 1893 it sent out an officer, Sir Gerald Portal, to visit Kampala and advise it what to do. Portal told the Government that although Lugard had been an officer of the Company, and not of the Queen, the Kabaka and his people could not be expected to understand the difference. When the Kabaka had made treaties with Lugard, he thought he was making them with the British Government. The Company, as it said itself, could not govern Uganda; if the Company left, the British Government ought to take its place, or else there would be more civil war, and in the end Germany would take the country. Portal's advice was accepted. In June 1894 Britain made Buganda a British protectorate; and the Kabaka and the Lukiko heard the news with joy.

Lugard never came back to Uganda; there was other work for him to do in Nigeria and elsewhere. But what he had done was the beginning of British rule in Uganda, and other men continued his work. The I.B.E.A. Company soon came to an end, for the British Government took over its work in Kenya also, and bought the company for a very cheap price, so that the company's shareholders in England lost half their money.

When the British Government had once made up its mind to govern Buganda as a protectorate, things moved faster. The engineers began to build the Uganda Railway from Mombasa in 1896; the line reached Kisumu in 1902, and for many years after that the last stage of the journey was made by steamer across the lake. Kabarega of Bunyoro attacked the kingdom of Toro, but all the Baganda came to help Toro, and Kabarega was beaten and fled. This war against Bunyoro led to difficulty, because the Baganda took much of the land of Bunyoro, including a place called Mubende, which had been the capital of the kingdom and in which its kings had been buried. The people of Bunyoro have always wanted to have these Mubende lands back; they think that the Baganda ought not to keep them and that the British Government ought not to allow the Baganda to keep them. In 1896, the four kingdoms of Bunyoro, Toro, Ankole and Busoga were added to the protectorate.

In 1899, the British Government sent out an officer named Sir Harry Johnston to examine the situation in the enlarged Protectorate and advise it on how the Government should be arranged. The situation was quite different now that the Protectorate included not only Buganda but the other kingdoms as well. Johnston knew a good deal about Africa; he had studied Bantu languages and spoke Swahili well. He had worked and travelled in Angola and the Congo, Tanganyika and Mozambique, Nigeria and Tunis; he had done a good deal to stop the slave trade in Mozambique and to set up British government in Nyasaland.

Johnston soon decided on two main points. One was that as far as possible the people of the Uganda Protectorate must be encouraged to govern themselves; the British officials should limit themselves to such matters as public works, railways and steamers, revenue, and the development of mines and power stations and other such scientific matters, of which Africans at that time knew nothing. In other words, Johnston believed in indirect rule, that is ruling people through their own chiefs, or perhaps through elected councils. Nowadays, we are used to this idea, because Lugard as well as Johnston believed in it, and the

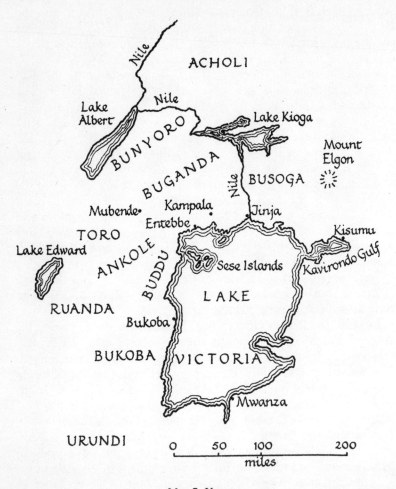

MAP 7. UGANDA

Here we see Uganda on a bigger scale, with more names but without boundaries. The Kitwara kingdom included all the land between Lake Albert, Lake Victoria, and Mount Elgon. We can see how Buganda lies in a central position, between Bunyoro and Busoga and between Bunyoro and Ankole; and it has the lake on the south so that it has nothing to fear in that direction. This is a strong position for a country that wishes to conquer its neighbours, especially before the days of telegraphs when all messages have to be carried on foot; for if Buganda suddenly attacked Busoga, for example, it would be difficult for Bunyoro to help Busoga in time. The map shows Mubende, which Buganda took from Bunyoro in 1895.

government of many British territories was arranged in this way: Nigeria, Gold Coast, and Tanganyika for example, as well as Uganda. But it was not so well known in 1900. One British officer in Uganda had already suggested that when the Katikiro or some other high official of the Buganda kingdom died, the British Government should put a British official in his place and so break down the Buganda system of government and introduce British law and customs. But the Government preferred indirect rule.

Johnston's second point was that all the fighting of the last few years had led to much confusion and difficulty over land, and if the Protectorate was to have true peace, the Government must have a policy[1] about the ownership of land.

There were long talks between Johnston and the leading chiefs of Buganda. The chiefs were especially anxious that nothing should be done to lower the position of the Kabaka, or of the Lukiko; and naturally they wanted to be sure that the chiefs and land-owners would not suffer.

Did not the Kabaka himself join in these talks?

No; the Kabaka at that time was a child. Kabaka Mwanga had fled from Kampala in 1897, and he and Kabarega of Bunyoro had joined together to make war against the Protectorate Government. There were two years of fighting, but then both Kabarega and Mwanga were caught. The Baganda people were so angry with their Kabaka for making so much trouble that they all said they would no longer have him as Kabaka, and they chose his baby son Daudi Chwa. When Johnston arrived, the new Kabaka was still only a small child, and three of the leading chiefs were governing Buganda until he was old enough to govern for himself.

Johnston told the chiefs that he wanted the Protectorate to raise enough revenue from its taxes to pay for itself, for up till then the British Government had been paying for all the cost of governing the country. He wanted the Kabaka and the chiefs to share the work of governing, and to be paid for the work they did. He wanted most of the land to belong to the kingdom of Buganda,

[1] Government policy is the general purpose which lies behind all the Government's plans. Johnston wanted the Government to make up its mind clearly what it wanted to do about the land before it made laws about it.

so that people could not sell their land to Europeans; the chiefs should have land of their own which they could sell if they liked, but the rest of the land should be controlled by the Government so that it should be used for the good of the Baganda people. He wanted the Lukiko to be strengthened so that it could take a larger part in the work of government.

The chiefs and people were satisfied, and they willingly signed a new Agreement, which replaced the two treaties which Lugard had made, and two other treaties made in 1893 and 1894 when the British Government took over from the Company.

The Uganda Agreement of 1900[1] is a long paper of 22 sections. The kingdom of Buganda was to be one province in the Protectorate, equal to the other provinces in rank; and the Kabaka gave up all his claims to any power over the other kingdoms. The laws of the Protectorate would apply to Buganda (unless any section of the Agreement made a special exception), and Buganda revenue, and the revenues of the other provinces, would be put together into the revenue of the Protectorate as a whole. The Government recognised the Kabaka as the ruler of Buganda, and recognised the Lukiko and the high officers of the kingdom; the Lukiko would consist of the three chief ministers, the chiefs of all the twenty *sazas* or counties into which Buganda was divided, and 66 other members to be appointed by the Kabaka: three from each *saza* and six from Buganda as a whole. The Lukiko would give the Kabaka its advice, but the Kabaka was not bound to follow its advice; if he wished to follow it, he was bound to consult the Protectorate Government and to do as the Government advised him.

Revenue would be raised by a tax on houses and on guns; but the Agreement provided that special local taxes such as water rates, town rates, market rates might be collected for local purposes. The Kabaka and the leading chiefs, including the twenty *saza* chiefs, were to be paid salaries at rates which were fixed in the Agreement.

Then the Agreement came to the important question of land. It estimated[2] that the Kingdom of Buganda contained 19,600 square

---

[1] The Agreement dealt only with the kingdom of Buganda, but in 1900 the Government had not yet begun to use the name Buganda to distinguish the kingdom from the Protectorate as a whole. The Agreement uses the name Uganda all through. I have used the name Buganda.

[2] To estimate is to make a careful guess when you cannot measure exactly.

miles of land. Rather more than half of this, 10,500 square miles, was put under the control of the Uganda Government. The rest[1] was divided between members of the royal family, the chief ministers, the *saza* chiefs, and a thousand "chiefs and private landowners". The size of the pieces of land given to the great people was laid down in the Agreement; the thousand "chiefs and private landowners" were to have 8,000 square miles between them, but it was left for the Lukiko to say how much each of them should have.

Two sections of the Agreement made it plain that the Kabaka and his Government must obey the laws made by the Government of the Protectorate and must work loyally with the Government in its work of administration; if ever the Kabaka and his Government ceased to work loyally with the Protectorate Government in this way, the Agreement would be broken.

Similar Agreements were made with Toro in 1900 and Ankole in 1901, though in these two countries, the Government did not give away nearly half the land to private landowners. It gave some land to the leading chiefs, but kept most of it as Government land. Bunyoro had to wait till 1933 for its Agreement; the Bunyoro Agreement was similar to those with Ankole and Toro.

Why was there this great difference between the Buganda Agreement and the others? If it was right to give so much land in Buganda to private landowners, why was this not done in the other kingdoms?

We have said on page 83 that the Kabaka of Buganda had to take much more trouble over his agriculturists than the other kings had, and his kingdom was much more closely organized. In the old days, all the land in Buganda belonged to the Kabaka, and he could give land to anyone he pleased. When he appointed a chief, he gave him some land; if he wished, he could dismiss the chief and take the land away again. But the troubles of Mwanga's time had changed this. The Protestant and Catholic chiefs had become more powerful, and each chief had got hold of as much land as he could, and had let it to farmers who were of his own religion. So there were now Catholic districts and Protestant districts, and the old idea that all the land belonged to the Kabaka

---

[1] Except for fifty square miles used for Government stations, and 92 square miles given to the churches.

was not so strong as it had been. Land had passed so often from one man to another that there was great confusion, and the Government thought that some kind of settlement must be made. It was simplest to recognise the fact that private people now did own land and look upon it as their own. The Government might have refused to recognise this fact; but in that case, the chiefs would have refused to accept the Agreement.

In the other kingdoms, there had been less fighting and confusion; land had never all belonged to the king, and was still mostly held by families or clans[1], so that the Government did not need to recognise private ownership of land.

The land settlement which was made in the Buganda Agreement weakened the power of the Kabaka, for he could not take a man's private land away from him. This private land, which was shared out by the Lukiko in square miles, came to be called *mailo* land, *mailo* being a Luganda word formed from the English word *mile*. *Mailo* land was no longer under the Kabaka's control. The 8,000 owners of *mailo* land would all wish the Agreement to work well, so they would support it. Even if the Kabaka wished to change the Agreement, it would be difficult for him to do so if this would mean upsetting the rights of the 8,000 *mailo* landowners.

Ever since 1900 and 1901, the Government of Uganda has worked on the basis of these Agreements. As a basis for modern government, the Agreements have one great weakness. As far as the Africans are concerned, they leave all the political power in the hands of the kings and chiefs and rich landowners. They make no provision for young educated people to share in political life. Nor do they provide for non-Africans; Europeans and Asians are free to live in Uganda, and are not subject to the Kabaka's Government; but the Agreements give them no chance of making their voice heard in Buganda Government affairs. There is nothing in the Agreements about a Legislative Council for the whole of Uganda; and we must remember that there are other peoples in Uganda besides those of the four kingdoms of Buganda, Bunyoro, Ankole and Toro, which were covered by the Agreements.

---

[1] A clan is a group of families who are related to one another.

THE PROTECTORATE IN MODERN TIMES

We have spent 30 pages in telling the story of how the Protectorate of Uganda began, and it may seem strange to spend only 22 pages in the story of the last sixty years. There are two reasons for this. One is that since 1900 Uganda has passed through two world wars and the bad times from 1930 to about 1935, which have slowed down its development. The other is that the difficulties of the Uganda Government today have grown out of the difficulties which faced Lugard and Johnston.

The most important of these difficulties is that the Agreements gave no chance to young educated people, who were not landowners or chiefs, of making their voice heard in politics; and it did not provide the Protectorate with a Legislative Council.

In 1919, the European business men and the small number of European cotton planters asked the Government to set up a Legislative Council, and the Government agreed. The Government proposed a council to consist of four officials and three unofficials; two of the unofficial members would be Europeans appointed by the Governor, and the third would be an Indian, whom the Governor would choose out of names suggested to him by the Indian Association. This caused trouble, for the Indians said that they wanted two members, and if they could not have two members, they would not suggest any Indian name at all. The Council met in 1921, but it was not until 1926 that the Indians agreed to suggest one of their men for the Governor to appoint. A second Indian member was appointed in 1933.

But no African members?

No, there were no African members yet. That is the weakness of the 1900 Agreements. The Government meant the four official members to look after African interests. It was not till 1945 that there were any African members.

In 1945, the Government made the Legislative Council bigger by adding three African members, one each from Buganda, and the Eastern and Western Provinces. All three were appointed by the Governor from among the Ministers of the African states. The Kabaka and his Lukiko agreed with this, though some of them feared that if a member of the Lukiko of Buganda sat in the Legislative Council, he would make promises on behalf of the

Lukiko, and so lessen the Lukiko's power. (A similar fear was expressed in the Gold Coast[1] when Governor Guggisberg invited the provincial councils of chiefs to appoint members to the Legislative Council.) In Uganda, the Government promised the Kabaka that anything which the Buganda representative said in the Legislative Council would be taken as his own personal views, and not those of the Lukiko or the Government of Buganda.

In 1946, two more unofficial members (one European and one Asian) and two official members were added to the Council, and one unofficial member was appointed to the Governor's Executive Council. In 1949, a fourth African member was added from the Northern Province, and in 1950 the four African members were increased to eight. The Council then consisted of eight African members, four Europeans, and four Asians. And then trouble began. The Government wanted the three provincial councils and the Buganda Lukiko to suggest names, from whom the Governor would pick six of the eight African members: two each from the Northern and Eastern Provinces, and one each from the Western Province and Buganda. This would leave two places empty; one of these would be filled by a member named by the Kabaka, and the other by a member named by the kings of Bunyoro, Ankole and Toro, acting in turn.

What was wrong with this? Why was there trouble?

The trouble came from the Lukiko of Buganda. It said that there was nothing in the 1900 Agreement about a Legislative Council. As far as Buganda was concerned, it was the Kabaka, and only the Kabaka, who dealt with the Protectorate Government. If the Government wanted the views of Buganda, it could get them any time from the Kabaka, and nobody else had any authority[2] to speak for Buganda. This was the same fear that had already been expressed when the first Buganda member joined the Legislative Council. We can understand the fear: "The Government began with one, now it wants two; perhaps one day it will want twenty, and then it will tell us that it prefers the advice of the Buganda representatives in its Legislative Council

[1] This happened in 1925.
[2] Authority to speak means power which you give to speak in your name; an ambassador, for example, has authority to speak for his Government. In the case of Buganda, the Lukiko felt that the Kabaka must speak for himself to the Governor; he could not give anyone else power, or *authority*, to speak for him.

to the advice of the Kabaka." The Lukiko refused to suggest any names of members for the new Legislative Council, though the Kabaka did name the one member that he was invited to name. After a time, as the Lukiko still refused to suggest anybody, the Kabaka agreed to name the second representative of Buganda, so that Buganda's voice could be heard in the Legislative Council.

The Lukiko of Buganda had its own troubles. We have seen that under the 1900 Agreement it consisted of chiefs and of members appointed by the Kabaka; there were no elected members. (And we must remember that the chiefs also were appointed by the Kabaka, they were not elected by the people or their elders, as in some parts of Africa.) But as education in Buganda improved, and newspapers and trade and knowledge increased, many Baganda began to ask that others besides chiefs should be able to sit in the Lukiko. In 1944 the Governor, Sir Charles Dundas, advised Kabaka Mutesa II and the Lukiko to find a way by which representatives of the common people could be admitted; and in January 1945, there were strikes and riots[1] in Kampala and elsewhere, showing that the matter was urgent. The great men who sat in the Lukiko then saw that it was time to set up a system by which the people could elect representatives to the Lukiko, to sit along with the 89 chiefs and others appointed by the Kabaka. In March 1946 the first elected members took their seats. There were 31 of them, and two years later the number was increased to 36. The voters elected village councils, the village councils elected *saza* councils, and the *saza* councils elected the members of the Lukiko.

But this did not mean the end of trouble. Most of the Baganda people still respected their chiefs. But there was in Buganda, as there was at the same time in the Gold Coast, a group of young educated people who did not wish the chiefs to rule the country; they wanted an elected Government responsible to the people. They opposed the Buganda Lukiko and the Government of the Protectorate; they wanted to take power into their own hands. They called their party the Bataka party. The name Bataka was a very old one. It was the name of the heads of the clans, who had ruled the people before ever there was a Kabaka, seven hundred years back. By taking this name, the men in the new party meant

[1] A riot is a disturbance made by an angry crowd, such as throwing stones, breaking shop windows, beating people, or setting fire to buildings or motor cars.

to show that they were the party of the common people against the Kabaka and the chiefs. They were not really heads of clans, and both in Buganda and in Ankole the Governments said so; but it seemed to them a useful name to take.

The Bataka party came very much to the front in 1947 and 1948, when the British Government in London set up the East African High Commission, by which the Governments of Uganda, Kenya and Tanganyika agreed to work together in certain matters, such as running the railways and posts and telegraphs. The Bataka party said that this would mean that Uganda and Kenya would become one country, the Kabaka would lose much of his power, and European farmers would take away much of the land. They were told that these things would not happen, but they would not listen, and they caused much trouble. In August 1948, the three Ministers and sixteen *saza* chiefs of Buganda met together and said that the Bataka party did not represent the Baganda people or the clans, and they asked the Government to prosecute its leader, Mr Mulumba, for causing unnecessary trouble by speaking and writing things which he knew to be false. When the Lukiko met early in 1949, the Bataka party said that the Ministers and *saza* chiefs had no right to meet without the elected members of the Lukiko, and they sent many telegrams to the Kabaka asking him to dismiss these Ministers and *saza* chiefs, and to give the Lukiko more elected members. Then the Bataka party called for a big meeting near the Kabaka's house on 25 April, so that they could march to see the Kabaka and tell him what they wanted. The meeting was held, and eight men did see the Kabaka, who said he would not dismiss his chiefs, but he would consider the people's other complaints.[1] The Bataka leaders were not satisfied, and there were riots lasting for a week, with robbing and burning of houses. When the police stopped the troubles, the Lukiko tried the leaders and punished them on a charge of trying to frighten the Kabaka.

Here then are two big questions: What would happen to the Lukiko, and to the Kabaka, if the elected members continued to oppose the chiefs? What would happen to Uganda if the Buganda

[1] One important complaint was that the farmers were not being paid enough for their cotton. Cotton is to Uganda what cocoa is to the Gold Coast (Ghana). In both countries there was a scheme by which the Government kept back some of the farmers' money in good years so as to help them in bad years.

Lukiko continued to oppose the idea of a Legislative Council for the whole Protectorate?

Presently a third big question came up: not by any means a new question, but brought up in a new way. This was the question of federation between the three territories of British East Africa. We have seen that this question came up in 1947 and made the Bataka party very frightened and angry. The Government had told them in 1947 that the bad things which they expected to happen would not happen; and in fact none of them had happened. But in 1953 some words were spoken which caused many people in Uganda to have these fears again. At that time, the British Government was setting up the Federation of Rhodesia and Nyasaland. One month before that Federation came into being, the Secretary of State in London, Mr Oliver Lyttelton, was speaking to a private meeting of people interested in East Africa; he spoke about the new Federation, and said that perhaps some day we might see more such federations, and even closer federations, in Africa; perhaps even in East Africa. Of course, he meant that Africa changes fast, and people will take today what they would not take yesterday; he certainly did not mean that the Government wanted to introduce an East African federation in 1953, or for some years to come. But Uganda was afraid of the whole idea of federation, and it is perhaps not surprising that many people in Uganda thought that Mr Lyttelton meant Federation Now.

Anyhow, they did think so; and at once trouble began. The Kabaka himself could say nothing, for he happened to be in London at the time, attending the Coronation of Queen Elizabeth II; but his three Ministers wrote to the Governor, Sir Andrew Cohen, saying that they did not want federation and asking the Governor to tell Mr Lyttelton so. The Governor wrote to the Secretary of State, and Mr Lyttelton told him that he might promise the people of Uganda that the Government did not intend to introduce federation. The Governor wrote a letter to the Kabaka and told him this; and in August he made a speech in the Legislative Council of the Protectorate and repeated the promise. But the people were too frightened to believe him. A week before the Governor made his speech in the Legislative Council, the Kabaka wrote to him and said that he did not want the kingdom of Buganda to stay any longer under the Colonial

Office; he wanted it to be dealt with by the Foreign Office. This would show that Buganda was soon to be an independent country; and indeed, the Kabaka added that he wanted the British Government to make plans for giving Buganda independence. A few weeks later, the Lukiko appointed a committee to discuss the whole matter; and the committee too wrote to the Governor making the same two requests.

There are several questions to be asked here. First: why were the people of Uganda so frightened of federation?

Mainly because they were afraid that federation would mean that European farmers would come into Uganda to take the land. In Kenya, some of the best land in the country was reserved for European farmers, and there were many European members in the Kenya Legislative Council. Uganda was an African state, and its people wanted it to remain African; and in particular, they were afraid of losing some of their land.

Then again, they knew that most of the African people in Rhodesia and Nyasaland did not want federation, but the British Government had set up the Federation because it thought it good for the country, although the Africans said they did not want it. This frightened them; they thought that if once the British Government decided that an East African federation would be a good thing, it would not care for what the African people said.

This raises the second question. You speak of the African people as not wanting federation. Most of the Africans in Uganda (and no doubt also in Central Africa) were uneducated. Did they understand enough about federation to know whether they should like it or dislike it?

That is the question which always troubles a colonial government. No doubt it is true that very few of the African people at that time had enough education to understand the arguments in favour of federation or against it. Of those few, nearly all were against federation. So here you have: on one side, the Government; on the other side, the few educated Africans; in the middle a great crowd of uneducated Africans who do not understand the question. The Government now has the job of trying to persuade the uneducated Africans: talking to them, discussing, explaining. That is a job which colonial Governments do not usually do very well; it takes a lot of time and money, and they have not time and money to spare. So the African educated leaders end by persuading the uneducated public to support them. Perhaps the colonial Government will continue with its policy for a time, saying 'These people will soon come to see that we are right.' But it cannot continue for very long; unless it can persuade the people, in the end it must give way.

Does this sort of thing happen in an independent African country?

In every independent country, in Africa or elsewhere, much of the work which a Government does is so difficult and complicated that many of the voters, perhaps most of them, do not really understand it. Every Government has the job of explaining its policy and persuading the public to support it. In this respect, independence makes no difference. But it does make one great difference; in an independent country there will be a political party which opposes the Government. The speakers of both parties will do what a colonial Government cannot do nearly as well: they will travel up and down the country explaining why the Government's policy is good or bad, and thus they will educate the public.

If the people of Uganda were so afraid of federation, and the British Government did not really mean to introduce federation, why did the Secretary of State frighten them by making that speech?

No doubt if the Secretary of State could have seen what would happen as a result of his words, he would not have spoken them. But he was speaking to a private meeting of Europeans who knew East Africa. He knew that they would favour the idea of federation, but would know all the difficulties; and they would understand that an East African federation could not come for a long time. The European audience to whom he spoke understood him; the Africans far away misunderstood him. He could of course have kept silent on this subject; but then his European audience in London might have thought that the Government was opposed to the whole idea of federation. It is very difficult to make a speech without being misunderstood.

THE KABAKA'S CASE

The Kabaka and the Lukiko had now firmly refused to have anything to do with federation; but they had done more than that. They had asked that Buganda should become a separate independent state. This was a new idea, and a difficult one. If Buganda became independent, would Ankole, Toro and Bunyoro also wish to become independent? What about the rest of Uganda, outside the four kingdoms? If Buganda were independent and the rest did not become independent, how was Uganda, without Buganda, to be governed? For fifty years, the British Government had been trying to build up Uganda into one state; was Uganda now to break up into four or five?

The British Government was especially disappointed, because only a few months earlier, it seemed as though Buganda was making a big step forward. The Protectorate Government was facing the same difficulty that Dr Nkrumah's Government was facing in the Gold Coast at the same time. Local government was in the hands of the chiefs; how could it be developed so that local councils, with elected members, could take over the work which a modern state has to leave to local government bodies? The Government, like Dr Nkrumah, wanted a system of local councils. But outside Buganda, the people wanted to organize their local government so that they would form strong kingdoms like Buganda; many people disliked the idea of handing over local matters to elected local councils. Now the Buganda Government depended very much on the Kabaka and his chiefs; so it seemed to the Governor that the Kabaka and chiefs of Buganda must show the rest of the country how local government should be organized.

Early in 1953, the Kabaka and the Governor agreed that in Buganda, the *saza* must be the chief unit of local government. The *saza* must be given more work to do, and this work must be given to it, not by the Government of the Protectorate, but by the Kabaka's Government. So the Protectorate Government handed over to the Kabaka much of the work it had been doing: primary and junior secondary schools, hospitals and other health work in the country districts, agriculture and animal health. The Kabaka appointed more Ministers, and increased the number of elected members of the Lukiko so that it had an elected majority.

It was understood that the Buganda Government would hand over much of this work to the *saza* councils. In March 1953, the Kabaka and the Governor put out a paper which explained all this, and said also that Uganda was one country, of which Buganda was a part.

All this had pleased the Government very much; and now it seemed as if it was all to be spoilt by this trouble over federation. The Governor, Sir Andrew Cohen, spent two months in talking to the Kabaka. He explained that only a few months before, in March 1953, the Kabaka had agreed to this paper which said that Uganda was one country and that Buganda was part of it. Then how could Buganda become an independent state? By asking for this in August, the Governor said, the Kabaka was breaking the agreement he had made with the Governor in March. Moreover, by the 1900 Agreement, the Kabaka and his people had promised to work loyally with the British Government; and it was not loyal to work for independence. It seemed therefore that the Kabaka was breaking, not only the agreement of March of that year, but also the Agreement of 1900.

The Kabaka was not to be persuaded. He did not trust the Colonial Office, and he wanted independence. On 30 November 1953, the Governor had no more to say. He told the Kabaka that, under the 1900 Agreement, the British Government no longer recognized him as the Kabaka, and would send him away from Buganda. A few hours later, the Kabaka arrived in London by air.

The Baganda people were shocked, but they remained calm. The British Government promised that it would not force them to accept a new Kabaka; so they knew that if they were firm in saying that nobody but Kabaka Mutesa II would do, their Kabaka must come back some day. The only questions were, When, and Under what conditions?

This was a constitutional question, like the question of the Gold Coast constitution, which caused so much trouble between the two political parties there in 1956. The British Government did for Uganda what it did for the Gold Coast: it sent out an adviser, Professor Sir Keith Hancock, to try and find a way out of the difficulty. The Lukiko appointed representatives to meet him and discuss the problem. In September 1954, the Governor and his advisers and the Lukiko representatives all agreed on what should be done, and in November the Government in London also agreed.

Sir Keith Hancock and the committee held their meetings at Namirembe, which is part of Kampala; and the recommendations on which they agreed are called the Namirembe recommendations. These are the most important:

(1) Buganda is part of the Protectorate of Uganda, and cannot be separated from the rest of the country.

(2) The position of the Kabaka must be kept as it was; he must remain the ruler of Buganda and must speak for his people when dealing with the Government of the Protectorate.

(3) He would rule his people through six Ministers. They would be elected by the Lukiko, and approved by the Governor, and would then be appointed by the Kabaka. They could be dismissed by the Lukiko if two-thirds of its members voted to dismiss them.

(4) Every Kabaka must solemnly promise the Lukiko and people of Buganda, and the Government of the Protectorate, that he will keep these recommendations and the 1900 Agreement.

(5) In order to keep the Buganda Government and the Government of the Protectorate in touch with each other on matters of education, health, local government, community development, mining and agriculture, the two Governments would set up joint committees.

(6) If the two Governments disagreed, the disagreement would be settled by a joint meeting of the Buganda Ministers and the Governor's Executive Council.

(7) The country must have time to settle down under this new system, and so there must be no more important constitutional changes till 1961, that is, seven years later.

These Namirembe recommendations then went to the Lukiko, which appointed a committee to consider them, and ended by approving them with a few unimportant changes, which were accepted by the Governor.

Surely the recommendations disagree with each other? One of them says that the position of the Kabaka is to be kept as it was;

another says that there are to be six Ministers, elected (and perhaps dismissed) by the Lukiko.

That is true. The Kabaka's position is not what it was in his grandfather's day. The Kabaka of Buganda used to rule as he pleased, appointing chiefs and dismissing them, accepting his Lukiko's advice or refusing it as he chose. The Kabaka nowadays has lost much of his power; he is becoming more and more bound to rule according to the advice of his Lukiko. But the change had been coming gradually. Even in Mwanga's time we see how the great chiefs often disobeyed the Kabaka. In modern times, as the work of Government becomes more complicated, it is not possible for one man to control everything; he has to leave much of it to his Ministers. Since 1946 there had been elected members in the Lukiko; and even if the Kabaka still had the right to go against the advice of his Ministers, he would probably find it wiser not to exercise his right. So perhaps the Namirembe recommendations did not make so much change as they appear to. Nevertheless, it is true that one recommendation which says that the Kabaka is to keep all his rights and power does not quite agree with another which says that in one respect power which used to belong to the Kabaka is to belong to the Lukiko.

When the Namirembe recommendations were accepted, the Governor took another important step towards giving the Protectorate self-government. He introduced a system of Ministers into the Legislative Council; seven were appointed, five of whom were Africans. At the same time, the number of African representative members was increased by adding two more members for Buganda. The Council now had 60 members, 30 of whom were Africans.

All this time, of course, the Kabaka was still in London, and the Lukiko and the people thought that the Governor had done wrong to send him out of the country. They brought an action in the courts to see if there was anything legally wrong in what the Governor had done. In November 1954 the Chief Justice gave judgment. He said that under the terms of the 1900 Agreement, the British Government was right in refusing any longer to recognize the Kabaka. But the Government had given the wrong reason for what it did. The Government had said that the Kabaka had broken section six of the Agreement. The Chief Justice said that this was not so, because that section dealt with the day-today organization and government of the country; and this was a matter in which the Kabaka and the Lukiko and the chiefs were all concerned. If the Government had wished, it could have acted under section twenty of the Agreement. That section said that the Kabaka must work loyally with the British Government in its general policy for the country; and this is a matter in which the Kabaka could be separately concerned. The Chief Justice said that the Kabaka had broken that section of the Agreement, and so the Government had the right to refuse any longer to recognize him.

This judgment did not mean, as many people in Buganda took it to mean, that the Government had acted illegally in sending the Kabaka away. But it was not a pleasant judgment for the Governor to hear. Governments have legal advisers, whose business it is to see that Governments not only do the right thing, but do it for the right reason. The Government and its legal advisers had plenty of time to decide what they would do if the Kabaka could not be persuaded, and under which section of the 1900 Agreement they would do it. They had made the sort of mistake that Governments ought not to make. The best thing they could do was to get the Kabaka back to his country as soon as they could; and luckily, the Lukiko and the Governor had agreed on conditions which would make it possible to send him back. The Kabaka arrived back in Kampala on 17 October 1955, and the next day he signed a new Agreement with the Governor, based on the Namirembe recommendations as accepted by the Lukiko.

A few weeks before, knowing that the Kabaka was soon coming back, the Baganda people elected the five Buganda representatives to the Legislative Council of the Protectorate. It looked as if the troubles were over.

TOWARDS SELF-GOVERNMENT

But the troubles could not be over as long as there was so much disagreement between the peoples of the Protectorate. On one side, there were the old kingdoms of Buganda and the others, wanting to keep up their position, and also chiefs and elders in other parts of the country who wanted to organize themselves into states something like Buganda. On the other side, there were people who wanted Uganda to become something like Dr Nkrumah's Ghana, one country with a strong central Government, with the kings and chiefs playing no part in the central Government but only in local government. In Uganda, there was a strong party called the Uganda National Congress, which wanted self-government for Uganda on such conditions as these. Four out of the five Buganda representatives in the Legislative Council were members of the Congress. What was the Government to do? If it took no steps towards self-government for the Protectorate, the Uganda National Congress accused it of wanting to keep power in its own hands, and refusing the Uganda people their freedom by pretending that it must not hurt the Kabaka. If the Government took any step forward towards self-government for the Protectorate, the Kabaka and the Lukiko accused it of breaking Agreements and of wanting to break up the kingdom of Buganda and its old customs.

That is a difficult position for the Government. Is there any way out?

There is no way out as long as both parties go on thinking as they do. One party blames the Government if it does anything, the other blames it if it does nothing. There is no middle way. The only hope is that one side or the other will change its mind, and will become ready to accept what it has so far refused. Things do sometimes happen to make people change their minds.

Self-government for Uganda was the Government's aim, and it hoped that if it went on pressing for this, the Baganda people would gradually move in that direction. After all, Buganda had already made great changes: elected members of the Lukiko, and ministerial government, and five Buganda elected representatives in the Legislative Council of the Protectorate.

In January 1958, more changes were made in the Legislative Council. The Governor and the Resident of Buganda left the Council. This took away three votes from the Government side, because the Governor had two.[1] So three more Africans were added to the Government side. The Council now had 15 Africans, 14 Europeans, and three Asians on the Government side, and 18 Africans, six Europeans, and three Asians on the representative

[1] The Governor had one ordinary vote, and also a casting vote: that is, a vote which was not to be used unless the Council was equally divided.

side. And in October of that year, there were to be new elections to the Council. The Protectorate was divided into 18 constituencies[1], and the people were to elect their representatives by direct election. Until that time, elections had been indirect; that is, the people elected a village council, the village council elected someone to represent it on the *saza* council, and the *saza* council elected its representative to the Legislative Council. Now there were to be direct elections; people were to vote directly for the candidate whom they wished to see representing them in the Legislative Council.

The Government knew that most people, even in Buganda, would like direct elections. But when it asked the chiefs to help in the elections by acting as assistant registration officers (that is, by making the list of voters, and by checking the voters' names against the list at election time), the chiefs refused. They said that they were officers of the Buganda Government, not of the Protectorate Government; and if they acted in the elections they would have to swear an oath of secrecy, which might perhaps go against the oath which they had already sworn to be loyal to the Kabaka. The Government asked the Kabaka's Government to allow the chiefs to help in the elections, but the Kabaka would not. So there were no elections in the five Buganda constituencies, or in three others, two in Ankole and one in Bugisu. Ankole said that it would elect its two members, but would elect them in the old indirect way. Bugisu said, like Buganda, that it would not elect any at all.

Why did the Lukiko of Buganda refuse to help in the 1958 elections, when it had helped in the 1955 elections? Was it simply because these new elections were to be direct, or was there some other reason as well?

That was one reason, but there was another reason as well. The Lukiko said that the Governor and the Resident should not have left the Legislative Council and put in three new African members instead. They said that this was the sort of important constitutional change which according to the 1955 Agreement should not be made before 1961. In other words, they thought the Governor had broken the new Agreement; and they brought another action in the courts to see if this was so. But this time, the courts decided against them.

[1] A constituency is a district whose people send a member to parliament.

So the new Legislative Council met with only ten African representative members instead of eighteen. The Governor, Sir Frederic Crawford, thought that the change which he made in January 1958 (putting in three Africans on the Government side of the Council instead of the Governor and the Resident) was small and unimportant; and the courts agreed with him. He knew that by the Agreement of 1955 he must not make any large and important changes until 1961; but he wanted to lose no time after that. So he set up a committee, with Mr J.V.Wild as chairman, to consider what changes should be made in 1961: how to arrange for direct elections all over the country, how many seats there should be in the new Legislative Council, how many members should represent each part of the country, how to make sure that there should be some representation of Asians and Europeans.

Did the Governor think that Buganda would agree to this?

The Governor of course knew that if the Kabaka and the Lukiko still thought in 1961 as they thought in 1958, they would not agree. But he hoped that some way might be found, during those three years, of persuading them to agree. When he set up the Wild committee, he said that he knew there was a "strong feeling throughout the country" – that is, in Buganda too – "that there should be more Africans on the representative side of the Legislative Council". And he repeated the Government's promise that "whatever constitutional and democratic developments there may be in Uganda, the dignity and prestige of the traditional rulers, which the people themselves so clearly desire, shall be maintained." [1]

All this did not satisfy the Lukiko. The judgment of the courts was given at the end of November 1958; in the middle of December, the Lukiko drew up a petition [2] asking that the kingdom of Buganda should be given independence, and that the Agreements of 1894, 1900, and 1955 should be ended, as soon as arrangements could be made (a) for handing over to the Kabaka and his Government all the powers which the Protectorate Government still held

---

[1] That is to say, whatever new arrangements there might be for helping the people of Uganda to govern themselves through their elected representatives in parliament, nothing should be done to lessen the respect which the people felt for the Kabaka and the other kings and chiefs. That sounds very good; but how is it to be done? That is the great question.

[2] A petition is a humble request.

within Buganda; (b) for settling the position of Asians and Europeans within an independent Buganda; (c) for settling the relations of an independent Buganda with the other parts of the Uganda Protectorate, and with Britain. A month later, on 21 January 1959, the Kabaka approved the petition, and sent it to the Governor, asking him to send it on to the Queen.

It sounds as if the Lukiko were frightened of something. What was it?

There were great changes going on in Uganda, and I think the Lukiko were afraid that the result of the changes would be to weaken the power of Buganda compared with the rest of the country. It was quite plain, for example, that if the Protectorate had a strong parliament like the one in Ghana, the real power of the Kabaka and his Government would be lessened, just as the power of the Asantehene and the other great chiefs in Ghana had been. So far, there was no Dr Nkrumah in Uganda, with his party all over the country; but if such a man arose, he would have more power than the Kabaka. If Buganda became independent now, before such a man arose, it would be safe from him.

There was another thing which frightened the Lukiko. The big new Owen Falls electricity station, by which the river Nile was made to generate electricity as it left Lake Victoria, was nearly finished. The small village of Jinja had grown into a big town, and there was talk of building many factories to use the electricity which was now being produced. There were many European business men and engineers coming into Uganda. The Lukiko were afraid that these men would introduce a colour bar like the one in South Africa, so that the Baganda and the other peoples of Uganda would be kept down in the lower positions in industry. The Protectorate Government, they thought, would allow this to happen, but an independent Government of Buganda would not. They were feeling rather as President Kruger and his Afrikaners in the Transvaal felt when they saw all the Uitlanders coming into their country and upsetting the old ways.[1] Kruger and his people wanted to go on governing their own country as before; they did not want the strangers to take the government out of their hands. So it was with Buganda.

And, apart altogether from the question of fear, we must remember that Ghana was already independent; so was Uganda's

[1] See Book One, pages 125, 126.

northern neighbour, the Sudan. It was natural that the Baganda should feel that they were just as ready for independence as the Ghanaians or the Sudanese.

You said that there was nothing yet in Uganda like Dr Nkrumah's party, the Convention People's Party, with a strong leader like Dr Nkrumah himself. But there was the Uganda National Congress; was that not much the same?

No, the U.N.C. was not nearly as strong as Dr Nkrumah's C.P.P., and it had not yet found a leader like Dr Nkrumah. In December 1958, just at the time of the Lukiko's petition, the Uganda National Congress got into difficulty; its leaders quarrelled, and the party split up. A new party was formed called the Uganda Nationalist Movement. The first thing it did was to call on all the people of Uganda to boycott[1] all Asian and European shops and businesses, as so to drive Asians and Europeans out of the country. The boycott was very effective in Buganda, not so effective elsewhere. It caused trouble: beating, burning, rioting. And of course it did a great deal of damage to the trade and the wealth and the revenue of the country: so much so that the Protectorate Government was even forced to stop bringing more British teachers into the country because it was afraid that it might not be able to pay them.

Why did it do so much damage?

For two reasons. One is that if the European and Asian firms could not sell their goods, they could not buy the cotton and other things that Uganda had to sell. There were very few African business firms to take the business. The other reason is that the revenue of the Protectorate Government depends largely on customs duties, and if there are no goods crossing the frontier, no duties can be charged.

In April 1959, the Secretary of State in London replied to the petition from the Lukiko, saying that he could not advise the Queen to agree to independence for Buganda. He suggested that the Kabaka should appoint representatives to discuss how the kingdom of Buganda should be given more power, without breaking away from the rest of Uganda; and he asked the Kabaka's Government to allow the election of the five Buganda members

[1] That is, to refuse to trade with them.

to the Legislative Council, and to stop the trade boycott. The Lukiko agreed to hold talks about the constitution, but asked that they should take place in London, not in Uganda. They would not agree to allow the elections, and they would not ask the Baganda people to stop the trade boycott, though the Kabaka and the Katikiro asked the people to stop using violence, to stop the beating and burning and rioting.

Just before Christmas 1959, the Wild Committee made its report. It recommended:

(a) The Legislative Council should be changed into a National Assembly of at least 79 members, 76 of whom should be elected.

(b) All voters should be registered in one list; there should not be separate lists for Africans, Asians, and Europeans.[1]

(c) There should be no special care taken to see that Asian and European members were elected to the Assembly, since questions of race ought not to enter into politics, and the three races ought to be so sensible and friendly that nobody cared to which race a candidate for the Assembly belonged.

(d) The majority party in the Assembly should be invited to form a Government; the Executive Council should be replaced by a Council of Ministers, three of whom should be senior officials, and the other eight or nine should be members of the majority party in the Assembly.

(e) The committee did not agree on the powers of the Council of Ministers. Most of its members thought that the Council should be responsible to the Assembly from the beginning, but some thought that for the time being it should be responsible for advising the Governor, as the old Executive Council was.

(f) The position of the Kabaka and other kings and chiefs should be kept as high as it was.

(g) Uganda should be one country, not a federation; but the committee thought that after the new National Assembly

[1] There is a special term for this. The list of voters is called the electoral roll; and the one list, on which the names of all voters are written without making any difference according to race, is called the common roll. The question whether there should be a common roll, or separate rolls for the different races, is an important one, which is much discussed in Kenya and Central Africa.

had been elected, a special conference should be held to discuss this.

These recommendations are very like those of the Coussey Committee in Ghana[1]; if they were followed, Uganda would be travelling towards independence by the road which Ghana had taken. The difficulty, however, lay in recommendations (f) and (g): how was it possible to keep Uganda as one country with a unitary[2] Government, without lessening the position of the Kabaka and the other chiefs?

This difficulty was plainly shown when the report was published. Many African politicians at once said that they welcomed the recommendations, and they would oppose anybody who tried to give the central Government less power than the Wild report recommended. The Buganda Government said it could not accept the recommendations. The Kabaka, it said, could not deal with a Council of Ministers, for by the Agreement he dealt direct with the Queen. If Uganda was to be self-governing, there must be a federal Government, and Buganda would be prepared to consider taking part in a federation. But if Uganda was to be self-governing with a unitary Government, Buganda could not take part. In that case, Buganda must be completely independent.

So the independence of Uganda has been delayed by the same question which delayed – though only for a very short time – the independence of Ghana: is the government to be unitary or federal? The Kabaka and his Government in Buganda, like the Asantehene and the National Liberation Movement in Ghana, said it must be federal; the political parties in Uganda, like the C.P.P. in Ghana, said it must be unitary.

Does it really matter very much?

Well, Dr Nkrumah thought it mattered very much in Ghana. He said that Ghana was too small for a federal government; and Uganda is no bigger, in fact, if you do not count the lake, it is smaller. Federations are suitable for big countries like Nigeria or the United States, where parts of the country are very far away from the central Government; or for small countries like Switzerland or Malaya, which are formed by joining together many small independent states. A unitary Government is better for small

---

[1] An all-African committee which reported in 1949.
[2] *Unitary* is the opposite of *federal*.

countries, if they can agree to it; it is stronger and cheaper and more effective. Ever since the Agreement of 1900, Uganda has been developing as a unitary state, and it would be a step backwards to make it a federation. Still, it would be better to make Uganda a federation than to split it into four or five tiny independent states.

But the real difficulty is that the Government must be either unitary or federal; it cannot be both. Someone must choose; and this means that the Buganda Government and the political parties in Uganda must agree. In 1960, neither side was ready to give up anything for the sake of the independence of Uganda; but we hope that both sides will come to see that independence will only work if all the citizens are ready to give up something to make it work.

On the last day of 1960, the Lukiko passed a resolution asking the Kabaka's Government to declare that Buganda was an independent country. The resolution was carried by a large majority: 79 to 8, with one member abstaining. But the Governor refused to approve the resolution, and so it could not become law. The Uganda People's Congress and the Democratic Party opposed the idea of an independent Buganda; so did the other states, Ankole, Bunyoro, Busoga and Toro. And the king and parliament of Bunyoro (the Omukama and the Rukurato) added that it was time for Buganda to give back to Bunyoro the six counties which Buganda had taken in the war against Kabarega of Bunyoro.[1]

In March 1961, general elections were held for the new legislative council of Uganda. The Buganda Government had told its people not to register their names as voters, and most of them obeyed. Only about 35,000 Baganda did register as voters, and most of these were members of the Democratic Party, which on the whole opposed the policy of the Kabaka and the Lukiko. So when the votes were counted, twenty out of the 21 seats for Buganda were filled by members of the Democratic Party. The total strength of the Democratic Party was 43, the Uganda People's Congress had 35 seats, and other parties had 4. When the new legislative council met, it elected nine more members: six of these were Democratic Party and three from the Uganda People's Congress. The leader of the Democratic Party, Mr Benedicto Kiwanuka, became leader of the legsislative council; in July he was given the title of Chief Minister.

[1] See page 101.

In April 1961, the Governor's executive council was replaced by a Council of Ministers, as the Wild Committee had recommended. The Council consisted of the Governor, three ex-officio members, nine African members and one Asian, all these last ten being members of the Democratic Party.

All this time, from November 1960 till June 1961, a Commission was sitting to discuss the difficult question whether Uganda should have a unitary or a federal government. The commission was headed by Lord Munster, so it is called the Munster Commission. As we have seen, the Kabaka and most of the Baganda people were asking for a federal government, but most other people in Uganda preferred a unitary government. So the British Government thought, at any rate; and the British Government thought that a unitary government would be better, if the people of Uganda as a whole could be persuaded to accept it.

The Munster Commission recommended that Buganda should not become an independent country. On the other hand, it said that Uganda should have a federal government; the country should be divided into two units, Buganda being one and all the rest of the country being the other. Buganda should exercise many of the powers which the central Government exercised in the rest of the country. The other states, Ankole and the rest, should have no more power than they already had under their Agreements; they should not be given powers equal to those of Buganda. Uganda, the Commission recommended, should be fully self-governing in internal affairs on 1st March 1962, and completely independent on 9 October 1962.

The Munster Commission had done its best to satisfy Buganda and the others as well. The question now was, would the Commission's recommendations be accepted? In September and October, a constitutional conference was held in London to try and settle the question. The conference agreed that Buganda would be represented in the National Assembly (the name of the legislative council was to be changed) by 21 members; it would be for the Kabaka and the Lukiko to decide whether these members would be directly elected by the people, as elsewhere in Uganda, or elected by the Lukiko itself. The conference agreed also on ways of safeguarding the position of the other states. The constitutional position of Ankole, Bunyoro and the others could be changed only if (a) the Government of the state wished it, (b) a two-thirds majority of the state council agreed, (c) all the people in the state were asked to vote, and a two-thirds majority of the people agreed, (d) a two-thirds majority of the Uganda National Assembly also agreed.

The great point which was gained at this London conference was that the Kabaka's Government agreed at last to take its full share in the government of Uganda, allowing its people to vote for the National Assembly. For a long time now, the Uganda Government had felt that the Kabaka and the Lukiko were against it; and it would be a very happy change to have their full help and support once more.

On 1st March 1962, Uganda became internally self-governing, as the Munster Commission had recommended. Mr Benedicto Kiwanuka, the Chief Minister, was named Prime Minister; and the Council of Ministers was replaced by a Cabinet, all composed of members of his party chosen by himself. There were no longer any ex officio members. His Cabinet of 14 members included one European and one Asian. A few days later, the Lukiko decided that the members from Buganda should be chosen by indirect election; that is, the Lukiko itself would elect them. The way was now clear for new elections to the National Assembly.

But before the elections, the Prime Minister said that he would prefer to see Ankole, Bunyoro and Toro placed on the same footing as Buganda: that is, given the same powers. This would make Uganda a fully federal state, with at least five units instead of two: Buganda, Ankole, Bunyoro, Toro, and the rest of the country. He asked the National Assembly to vote in favour of this, and the Assembly did so. In April, there were more talks in London on this question, and the British Government said that if the Government of Uganda wished this, it would not object.

At the end of April, the general elections were held; and this time, the Baganda people voted in large numbers. This changed the composition of the Assembly. Outside Buganda, people voted much as they had done before. But the Baganda who had been told not to vote in the last election now came out and voted; and most of them voted for two parties, both opposed to Mr Kiwanuka's Democratic Party. They were the Uganda People's Congress, and a new party, the Kabaka Yekka. The Kabaka Yekka was a Buganda party which supported the Kabaka; in national affairs, the U.P.C. and the Kabaka Yekka usually voted together.

The new Assembly was composed of 43 U.P.C. members, 24 Kabaka Yekka, and 24 Democratic Party. Mr Benedicto Kiwanuka thus found himself in a minority, with only 24 votes to 67. He and his Cabinet resigned, and his opponent Mr Milton Obote formed a new Cabinet to govern the country.

But what about the six counties which Bunyoro wanted Buganda to give back?

The question of the six counties was a difficult one. Bunyoro said that most of the people there wished to belong to Bunyoro, and the area included certain places which were specially sacred to the Bunyoro people. Buganda said that the land had belonged to Buganda for more than sixty years, and most of the people there were content to stay in Buganda; there could be no question of giving the land back to Bunyoro. The British Government was anxious to get the question settled, for it thought there was quite a chance that when Uganda was independent, Buganda and Bunyoro might come to fighting in the six counties. So the Government appointed another Commission, the Molson Commission, to try and settle the question before independence day.

The Molson Commission studied the position on the spot; and early in May it reported. It said that in two counties, Buyaga and Bugangazzi, most of the people were Banyoro, and wished to be governed as part of Bunyoro. In these two counties there were 49,600 Banyoro and only 6,500 Baganda; and the Commission recommended that these two counties should go back to Bunyoro. In the other four counties, the position was different. In those four, there were only 8,200 Banyoro but 97,300 Baganda; and the Commission recommended that those four counties should stay part of Buganda.

On 9 October 1962 Uganda became an independent state, with Mr Milton Obote as Prime Minister.

THINGS TO DO, TO DISCUSS, OR TO FIND OUT

1. Do you agree with what is said on pages 79–81 about agriculture and cattle-keeping? Or are things different in your part of Africa?

2. Draw a map of the country round Lake Victoria, and shade the country which was occupied by the Bahima.

3. Draw a straight-line time chart of the history of Uganda from 1250 to 1900, and mark on it: the coming of the Bahima; the coming of the Lwoo; the date (1750) when Buganda began to grow strong; the coming of the Arabs; the death of Kamrasi of Bunyoro; the death of Gordon; the coming of the missionaries; the coming of Jackson; the Agreement of 1900.

4. Read what is said about the Berlin Act on pages 91 and 92 in Book One and on page 81 in this book.

5. What would have happened if the Arabs had succeeded in their plan of setting up a strong Arab state in East Africa? What difference would it have made to Uganda and Kenya?

6. On page 91 it is said that Uganda was rather out of the way for the French. Look in your atlas to see where the French set up their colonies in Africa, and see if you agree with this.

7. Write a scene in which Kabaka Mwanga and his chiefs agree to sign a treaty with Karl Peters.

8. Try to find out the value of the cotton crop in Uganda and the cocoa crop in Ghana. How many people are there in the two countries? If you divide the value of the crop by the number of the people, this will give you a rough estimate of the country's wealth. Compare the two countries.

9. Uganda and Ghana produce other things besides cotton and cocoa. What are they, and how much are they worth? Would it make much difference to your answer in Question 8 if we counted them in?

10. Do you think that Governor Dundas was right in adding elected members to the Buganda Lukiko, or would he have been wiser to push on with building up an elected Legislative Council for the whole Protectorate?

11. It is not good to riot and rob and burn houses; but do you think that the ideas of the Bataka party were good, even if they were too violent in expressing them? Or do you think the Lukiko was right to punish the Bataka leaders?

12. If you think that the Lukiko was right, do you think that the Gold Coast Government was right in 1950 to punish Dr Nkrumah because his followers rioted? If not, why not?

13. Do you think that Governor Cohen was right to send the Kabaka to England? If not, what ought he to have done?

14. Write a scene in which the Governor and the Kabaka find that they cannot agree, and the Governor tells the Kabaka that he is to be sent to England.

15. Do you think that the people of Uganda should be given the kind of Government that they want? If so, how is the Government to know what they want? Does the Kabaka know? Do the politicians know? When the Kabaka and the politicians disagree, how is the Government to know which is right?

16. We have said much about Buganda, but little about the other three kingdoms, and almost nothing about the people who do not belong to the four kingdoms. Write two speeches for an Acholi leader to make to the Kabaka and to the Governor.

17. Find out from your atlas all you can about the altitude, temperature, rainfall, population, minerals and industries of Uganda and of Ghana; and compare them.

18. Where do students in Ghana and Uganda go for (a) university education, (b) technical education? Find out all you can about these colleges.

19. Do you agree with (c) of the Wild Committee's recommendations on page 124? If so, do you think that African voters ought to be willing to vote for a European candidate? And if so, would you think it wrong if an African candidate said, 'Do not vote for that white man, vote for me because I am your brother African!'?

20. The Baganda people were very much afraid of the idea of an East African federation when Mr Lyttelton spoke about it in 1953. Do you think they will still be afraid of it when Uganda, Kenya and Tanganyika are all independent under African Governments? Would it make a difference if Kenya and Tanganyika were independent, but their Governments included European and Asian Ministers as well as African?

3

Kenya

When you were writing about Uganda, you mentioned the Imperial British East Africa Company. You said that the Company was mainly interested in Uganda. Why was it not much interested in Kenya?

This is a question of geography. We must remember that in those days there were no motors and there was no railway; the Company wanted to build a railway to Uganda, but it had not enough money, and the British Government would give it no help. So everyone going inland from Mombasa or anywhere else on the coast had to go on foot. What would they find on the way?

First of all, they went for two or three days through the coastal plain, where there is plenty of rain. Then the path began to climb, and for about ten days they walked through a region where there is much less rain – less than ten inches a year in places – and very few people live even today. Much of this region is covered with bush and is full of tsetse fly: a bad country for men and for cattle. The Swahili people call this bush country *nyika*.

Then, after finishing with the *nyika*, they would come to a better country: a great wide grass land with low hills rising out of it here and there. The grass land was the country of the Masai, who moved up and down it with their cattle; the hills were the home of the Kamba. A little way further still was the Kikuyu country, partly farm land and partly forest; some of the Kikuyu farm land was so well cultivated that one of the Company's men said it was like a large garden. But the Kamba and the Kikuyu were both at war with the Masai; every night the Kamba and Kikuyu fighting men had to watch over their villages and their cattle for fear that the Masai would come to steal them. Everyone was afraid of the Masai, and the I.B.E.A. Company could see that it would be difficult to stop the fighting. The Kikuyu country grew good crops, but it grew nothing that the white men wanted

132

for trade. From the Company's point of view, Uganda was a
country with a settled Government and with ivory for trade; but
Kenya was only a bush country which you had to go through to
reach Uganda. The *nyika* country was no good at all, parts of the
high land might be made useful, but only with a great deal of
trouble and money; and the Company had not the men and
money to do the job.

**You say that the Company thought that parts of the high land
might be made useful. How: by taking land away from the Kikuyu
or the Masai and giving it to Europeans?**

No, the Company had no thought of taking land away from
any African farmers; in fact, in 1891 it made a law that no
European was to buy or lease any land from Africans. But it did
seem to the Company that there was plenty of land which was
not being used, both in the high lands and on the coast; and the
Company thought that if enough land was left for the African
farmers, there would be no harm in letting other people use land
which was empty. The Company was not thinking mainly of
Europeans, it was thinking of Asians. Its first idea was to bring
over Indian farmers to settle in the empty lands in the coastal
plain and grow such crops as cotton, rubber, ground-nuts, and
copra, as well as food-crops. But hardly any Indians came.

Why was there so much land lying empty along the coast?

Because the land along the coast belonged to the Sultan of
Zanzibar. Some of the rich Arabs in Zanzibar had farms on the
mainland which they worked with slave labour, but they had
never covered the whole of their country with these slave farms.
Now that the British had stopped the slave trade and were trying
to stop slavery itself, it was harder for the Arabs to find men to
work on their farms; so agriculture was going down.

It is true that the Company thought also that later on, if a
railway were built, Europeans might come and make plantations
in the high lands, and might perhaps even settle there. But it was
not until 1894 that the Company first allowed any empty land
in the highlands to be leased to Europeans or Asians. And less
than a year later, on 1st July 1895, the British Government took
over Kenya from the Company and set up the East Africa
Protectorate.

You speak of empty land. As we all know, much of the best farm land in Kenya has been in European hands for a long time; and the Kikuyu and the Kamba and some other African peoples have not nearly enough land for themselves. Do you mean that all the land now being farmed by Europeans was empty when the Government leased it to them?

That is a big question. The short answer is this: No, it was not all empty, but the Government thought it was all empty, for it could see nobody living on it or using it. But a short answer is not enough for such a big question; we shall have to explain at more length.

In other words, the Government made a mistake, and gave away land which did not belong to it. How did the Government come to make such a mistake?

It is true that some of the land which the Government leased to Europeans was land which Africans said was theirs; and the Government agreed that it had made a mistake in letting the Europeans have these pieces of land. But this land was only a small part of the land now being farmed by Europeans. Most of the European land was really empty. Let us see what the Government did.

There could be no European settlement until the railway was built; for nobody would come to grow wheat or pyrethrum or anything else as long as everything he wanted to sell had to be carried down to Mombasa in head loads. The railway was built between 1895 and 1902; it was called the Uganda railway because its purpose was to make trade easier between Uganda and the coast. Uganda in those days was larger than it is now; the Uganda border came where the railway line dropped down into the Rift Valley. The Rift Valley and Nyanza provinces of Kenya were called the Eastern Province of Uganda until 1st April 1902, when the British Government took them away from Uganda and handed them over to the East African Protectorate, as Kenya was then called.

The Uganda railway had not been built in order to bring in European settlers. It had been built because the countries of Europe – Britain, France, Germany and others – had met together in Brussels in 1890 to discuss how to stop what was left of the slave trade, and had agreed that one of the best ways of stopping the trade would be to build roads and railways and establish peace and order. It was because of this agreement that the Germans began to build their railway from Dar-es-Salaam and the British began to build theirs from Mombasa. The railway was built and paid for by Britain; it cost nearly eight million pounds, which was a very large sum in those days, when a clerk in a London office earned one pound a week. So it is not surprising that when the railway was finished, the British Government hoped that it would pay its way. But the railway did not pay its way, and the Government wondered what it could do to increase trade. It there was land empty, would it not be a good thing to bring in European settlers to grow crops for export and to buy manufactured goods from Europe?

If there was land empty: but that was the question. Was there empty land?

Yes, there was. All the early European travellers said that they found large areas of land without any people: forest country in which the big trees were still standing, grass country which was full of antelope and other wild animals. It is true that in 1898 and 1899 thousands of people and cattle had died. There had been no rain for eighteen months, and no food for man or for beast; and people and cattle had died not only from hunger but from disease. The Kikuyu, the Kamba, and the Masai had all been hit by this disaster . The Masai took the cattle they had left far away to the south; the Kikuyu left their farms in Kiambu and other districts near Nairobi, and went back north towards Fort Hall. There were fewer people, and fewer cattle, and they did not need so much land. Some of this land which had been used by the Kikuyu and the Masai, and which now seemed empty, was taken by Europeans; and that was a mistake. But apart from this, there was land which nobody's cow had ever trodden, land which nobody's hoe had ever broken. Africa was a country which was too big for its people, as England used to be only three hundred years ago. In England, up to 1600 and even later, there were great areas of forest and other land lying empty, which by law all belonged to the King; if anybody wanted to go and build or farm there, he would have to get the King's permission. It seemed to the British Government that East Africa was in the same state; there was empty land, so the Government had better take hold of it and make sure that when the time came, the land would be properly used. That is how the idea came that empty land in Kenya should be Government (or 'Crown') land.

It was in 1902 that the Crown Lands Ordinance was passed. The Government took power to sell or to lease Crown lands, but the Ordinance said that no land which Africans were occupying could be leased or sold. If there was any doubt, the district commissioner was to hear the case; and the Government of course was sure that its district commissioners would be careful to see that no injustice was done to the Africans. In 1904 the Government appointed a committee to make sure that enough land was left for Africans to use; and in those early years, the Government did not think that Europeans and Africans need ever disagree over land.

Before 1914, European settlers did not come into Kenya in very large numbers; in that year there were only three thousand Europeans in the country, counting settlers, missionaries, Government officials and business men together. Was Kenya a country where Europeans could make a living?

The one man who did more than anyone else to answer this question was Lord Delamere. Delamere Avenue in Nairobi is named after him. Lord Delamere was a rich Englishman, who used to spend his holidays hunting in East Africa, mainly in Somaliland. In 1896 he crossed the border into Kenya and loved the country; and in 1903 he decided to leave England and make his home there. Lord Delamere was rich, and he was also determined. He leased land from the Government at Njoro, and brought English sheep to feed there. This was land which the Masai had never used; it was empty, and so Lord Delamere leased it for £ 200 a year, on condition that he spent £ 5000 on developing it within five years. He spent much more than that. Four out of every five sheep died, because the soil lacked some mineral which sheep must have. Delamere gave up sheep and tried cattle; but his cattle died from East Coast fever, which is a disease carried by a tick.

But was there no agricultural department to analyse the soil, and to tell Lord Delamere to dip his cattle?

No, that is the point. Kenya had no trade, and so no money to pay technical staff like agricultural officers. People did not know in those days that East Coast fever of cattle was carried by a tick. There was nobody to warn Lord Delamere; he had to learn his lesson the hard way, by trying and failing, and trying again until he succeeded.

Lord Delamere had failed with sheep, and failed again with cattle; so he tried growing crops. He grew wheat. But the wheat crop too was a failure, because it was attacked by a disease called rust. That was nearly the end for Lord Delamere, for he had spent all his money. But he was determined to make agriculture succeed in Kenya. He borrowed more money by mortgaging[1] his lands in England; he brought out a scientist of his own, and set him to work to breed a new kind of wheat which would resist the rust disease. Three years later he was able to grow a clean crop. Gradually, too, he found out how to raise good sheep and cattle in Kenya. But it cost him eleven years hard work, much of the time living in a small mud hut; and it cost him £ 40,000, which in those days was worth four or five times as much as it is today. All Kenya farmers, whether African, Asian, or European, who breed good sheep and cattle and grow good crops in Kenya today are profiting by Lord Delamere's hard experience.

But when Lord Delamere had shown that there was money to be made in Kenya, many other Europeans began to come out hoping to obtain farms from the Crown land. Some of them were from South Africa; and the South African fashion came into Kenya of having large farms which needed many Africans to work on them instead of small farms which a man could work with his own family and perhaps one or two paid men.[2]

In every group of people there are some who are good and others who are not good. So it was with the European settlers: some were good men, others were not. Some of them in the Machakos district were so good, and helped their Kamba neighbours so much, that in 1953, when the Queen sent out a Royal Commission to East Africa, the Kamba told the Commission, 'Europeans have too much land in Kenya, and we Kamba have not enough. But we make no complaint against these European neighbours of ours; they are our friends, and we want them to stay.' But some of the Europeans were selfish; they came to Kenya

---

[1] To mortgage a house or land is to borrow money and to give the man who lends the money the right to take the house or land if the money is not repaid.
[2] See Book One, page 100.

to make money and live a comfortable life; so they wanted land, and they wanted Africans to work on the land. So it came about that the Kenya Government found itself being pressed to find more land for the new European settlers, and to find people to work on their farms for them. The Europeans were not content if an African came and worked for a few months and then took his money and went home, and did not come back for a long time, perhaps not at all. They wanted to have people always with them, so that they could teach them European ways of farming. Some of them began to say that the Government ought to do more to make Africans work on European farms. It could take land away from the Africans, so that there would not be enough land for all the Africans to live on and some of them would have to come to live and work on European farms. Or the Government could put a heavy tax on Africans, so that they would have to go to work to earn money to pay their tax. Or, it could introduce a system of labour passes like the one in South Africa.[1] The Government did not want to do any of these things; and so Lord Delamere and some of the Europeans began to say that Kenya ought not to be a colony under the Colonial Office in London, but it ought to be independent, or nearly independent, with a Government elected by the Europeans in Kenya.

In those early days, before the 1914 war, the Government would not think of giving Kenya its independence, or anything like it. Even in 1914, there were only about 3,000 Europeans in the country, and Kenya as a whole was very poor. Until 1912, the British Government in London had to pay Kenya about £250,000 a year, because the revenue was not enough to pay for even the most necessary Government expenditure. It would be no use to give independence to such a small group of people when their Government had no money to do anything. In 1907 the first Legislative Council and Executive Council were set up; but all the members of the Legislative Council were nominated by the Governor, and most of them were officials. There were no elected members.

The Kenya Government was in a difficult position. The railway was built; it reached Nairobi in 1899, and Kisumu in 1901. It had been built, and was being largely run, with the help of Indians brought over from India. The Government of India looked after

[1] See Book One, page 133.

its people well. It made the Kenya Government promise that everyone who came should be sent home to his village in India after three years if he wished to go, but that he should be allowed to stay and settle in Kenya if he wished to stay. At one time there were as many as 20,000 Indians working on the line, and there were never more than 2,600 Africans. Most of the Indian labourers went home to India at the end of their three years; but some of them stayed in Africa, and a good number of the better educated Indians also stayed, some to work on the railway line as signalmen and station-masters and so on, and some to go into trade. By the time that there were 100 Europeans living in Kenya, there were already 6,000 Indians – or Asians, as we call them today. In 1905, the railway earned enough money to cover its expenses, but it was not for some years more that it made enough profit to help Kenya as a whole. So the Government wanted European settlers to come into East Africa, for the more European farmers and business-men there were, the sooner the railway would pay. But it did not want to take away African land. Was it possible to bring in more European farmers without taking away African land?

Wait a moment. Why did the Government build the railway with Asians? Why did it not use more Africans?

Because at that time there were very few Africans who had seen a wheel, or a spade or a pick-axe; and in India there were thousands of miles of railway, and thousands of people who knew how to build a railway and how to run it. The Government wanted the railway built quickly and well; and it would have been very slow, and there would have been much bad work done, if the Government had used Africans who had to learn the work from the beginning. And if the Government had asked Africans to come to Mombasa to begin the work, many would have stayed at home on their farms, and of those that did come, many would have become tired and would have left the work after a few months, just as they were becoming useful.

But when railways were built in Ghana and Nigeria, they were built with Africans, and the railway clerks and signalmen and station-masters were African. If this could be done in West Africa, why could it not be done in East?

For two main reasons. One was that the people of West Africa had been in touch with Europeans for hundreds of years; they knew European ways and European tools, and had some education. Ghana, for example, had had sixty years of primary schools and twenty years of secondary schools when it began to build its railway in 1898. But East Africa was far behind. We have seen that one reason for building the railway was to stop the last of the slave trade; and it was not until 1897 that slavery was stopped in Zanzibar. Primary education began in Uganda in 1895, sixty years later than in Ghana. Secondary education was just beginning in Uganda while the railway was being built, and the first secondary school for Africans was not opened in Kenya until 1926. In other words, there were Africans in Ghana and Nigeria who could quickly learn railway work; there were none in East Africa.

The second main reason is that East Africa had a much bigger job to do, and was in a hurry. The Ghana railway took three years to get from Sekondi to Tarkwa, about forty miles, and two years more to get to Kumasi, 120 miles further. The Nigerian railway took nearly four years to build from Lagos to Ibadan, about 100 miles. But the Uganda railway was built all the way from the coast to Kisumu, nearly 600 miles, in five years. Ghana and Nigeria took their time, and were able to train their men; East Africa had to have its railway quickly, and had to use people who already knew the work.

Anyway, now the railway was built; and the Government thought that it would only begin to pay its way when there were European farmers growing wheat and other crops for export. The difficulty was that the Europeans naturally wanted to have their farms close to the railway line, but the railway line ran through African country – Kamba, Kikuyu, Nandi, and Kipsigis country – as well as through country which looked as if it were empty of people. It was to be expected that there would be trouble between Europeans who wanted land near the railway, Africans who said that the land belonged to them, and the Government, which tried to be just to both.

There was one tribe which was a specially difficult problem, the Masai. The Masai were cattle-keepers, wandering with their cattle up and down country in Kenya and Tanganyika which was about 400 miles from north to south and 100 to 150 miles wide.

The Masai, like the Kikuyu and the Kamba, had suffered from disease and famine[1], and thousands of men and of their cattle had died. It seemed as if part of their land was empty, and Europeans were soon asking for it. The railway cut across the Masai lands, and when the Masai and their cattle came back, they found that some of their land had been taken for European farms. Not very much: there was still plenty of room for them to move. But this was only the beginning; if more Europeans came into the country they might lose more. In 1904, the Masai chiefs and people made an agreement with the Government, by which they gave up some of their land in the Rift Valley, and were given two reserves, one in Laikipia to the north of the railway, and another south of the railway. The two reserves were joined by a road half a mile wide, so that the Masai and their cattle could pass from one reserve to the other. The agreement was to last 'so long as the Masai as a race shall exist.'

Like all such agreements, the Masai agreement of 1904 did not give either side all it wanted. The Masai wanted to be left alone; they did not want the railway or the Europeans in the country at all. The Europeans did not like seeing so much good land shut up so that no European could ever make his farm there; and the European farmers on either side of the half-mile road did not like the Masai cattle passing up and down just outside their fences and perhaps bringing disease to their own animals.

The agreement did not work well. Some of the Masai in the south who had agreed to go north to Laikipia did not go; they stayed in the south and spread out far beyond the boundaries of the reserve. The northern Masai too spread out beyond Laikipia. It was their habit to move; they could not keep still. Then again, the half-mile road became full of ticks and of tick-borne disease, so that the Masai did not like to take their cattle along it. So in 1911 the Masai were becoming divided into two groups.

Why did the Masai spread out beyond the boundaries of their reserve? Were the two reserves not big enough?

The Laikipia reserve contained 4,500 square miles and the southern reserve 4,350 square miles. There were about 45,000 Masai, with about 50,000 cattle and 600,000 sheep; so there were

[1] Famine is a great hunger which kills people, caused perhaps by lack of rain or by plant disease.

about five people to each square mile, with six cattle and 70 sheep. The reserves were big enough in 1904.

But was it good land, with plenty of grass and water?

Laikipia is now full of European farmers, who find it very good land. The southern reserve was not all as good as Laikipia, but much of it was very good land indeed, with plenty of water. No, the Masai and their herds did not spread out beyond the boundaries of the reserve because they had not enough land, but simply because they had always wandered wherever they liked, and they did not understand why they should now settle down. Of course, it is true that their herds were increasing, but there was still land enough.

However, it was plain that the 1904 agreement was not good enough. The paramount chief of the Masai, named Lenana, did not like seeing his people divided into two. So in 1911 the Masai made a new agreement with the Government to replace the agreement of 1904. They gave up the Laikipia reserve, and the Government increased the size of the southern reserve from 4,350 square miles to just under 15,000. But this agreement caused trouble. Some of the northern Masai did not wish to leave Laikipia. The Government took some chiefs and elders round the new land in the south; some of it they liked and some they said was no good. The Government in London said that the northern Masai must not be made to go south if they did not wish to, and some of them, including one great chief, said that they did not wish to. In the end, they all agreed to move, but it was a sad affair: they had more cattle than the Government thought, and many died from hunger and disease on the way south.

Why did the Government make that mistake: could it not count the Masai cattle before it made the arrangements for moving the Masai?

The Masai and their cattle were spread out over hundreds of miles of bush, and I do not suppose that even the paramount chief, Lenana, could have made more than a very rough guess at the numbers of cattle. It would have taken several men and months of work to find all the Masai herds and count them. The Government had not the men to do it. And what would the Masai have thought if they had seen Government men coming to count their cattle and write down the numbers in note-books? They would surely have thought the Government was planning to take away their cattle; and they would probably have taken their spears and killed the men. It was all very unfortunate. It is easy for us, fifty years and more later, to say that when the Government was told how many cattle the Masai were believed to have, it ought to have multiplied the figure by two or three so as to be on the safe side. But it was not so easy for the Government, with very few men and very little experience, to see it in 1911.

Anyway, it left the Masai feeling unhappy; and a few years later there was more trouble, when the Government wanted them to supply carriers and fighting men for the war against the Germans in Tanganyika. The Masai would not leave their cattle; nor would they sell cattle and sheep to the Government for meat. One or two people were killed over this.

Then did the Government treat the Masai fairly?

It tried to. In 1932 the Government appointed a Commission to go into the whole question of land in Kenya: to see if any Africans had been unjustly treated and to recommend how any injustice could be compensated[1] and to recommend what land should be reserved for African use in the future. The chairman was Sir Morris Carter, and the commission is often called the Carter Commission. One of its members was Mr Hemsted, who was the officer in charge of the Masai from 1912 to 1923. The Commission heard evidence from over 700 witnesses, including 487 Africans; also, it received about 400 letters from Africans, and about 200 Africans made statements to district officers, which the officers sent to the Commission. As its report says, the Commission had 'no lack of material on which to work.' The Carter Commission said that[2] the Masai were probably the richest tribe in Africa in land and in cattle. They had one square mile of land for three people, while Kikuyu-land had one square mile for 283 and Kavirondo-land had one for 145. It was true that some parts of the Masai land were dry, and some were bad because of tsetse-fly; but most of their land was as good, both for

[1] If you do wrong to a man, you compensate him if you give him something, or do something for him, equal to the wrong you have done.
[2] See paragraphs 658–663 of its Report.

cattle and for growing crops, as any land in Kenya. The Masai were not interested in growing crops, and the Commission thought it would be a pity if the Masai agreements of 1904 and 1911 kept out Kikuyu and other African farmers, who could make good use of the land. Moreover, tsetse-fly was spreading in the Masai land, and if the Masai would allow Kikuyu and others to come in and cultivate some of their land, the cultivation would keep down the tsetse-fly and so would be good for the Masai and their cattle.

It seems then that in the end the Government arranged for the Masai to have as much land, and good land too, as they needed. But we can understand if the Masai in 1911 felt angry when they saw thousands of their cattle die and when they saw the land which they left in Laikipia being taken over by European farmers. As we said in Book One[1] it is easy to see what people do, but not so easy to see why they do it. Very likely some of the Masai in 1911 thought that the Government wanted their cattle to die; but they were wrong.

You mentioned the Kikuyu. They too have lost some of their land. What did the Carter Commission say about the Kikuyu?

The Carter Commission took a great deal of trouble to find out how much land the Kikuyu held before the great famine of 1898–99. In those days, the Kikuyu land was surrounded by thick forest, and when the people wanted more land for farms or for their cattle, they had to get it by cutting down the forest. Much land which now is bare grass land was then thick forest in which the sun did not shine and it was difficult to travel. Some of the forest was inhabited by the Dorobo, a people who lived by hunting; and as the Kikuyu came to need more land, they had to get it from the Dorobo. Of course, they had to arrange it so that the spirits of the Dorobo ancestors would allow them to live there. Sometimes a Kikuyu family adopted a Dorobo, so that his land would still belong to the same family, although it was being used by Kikuyu farmers instead of by Dorobo hunters. Very often the Kikuyu paid in goats; but the Carter Commission found that many Kikuyu said they had paid goats and bought the Dorobo land, while the Dorobo said that land could not be bought with goats or anything else. Some of the Dorobo witnesses said that

[1] See Book One, pages 19–21.

5. Kabaka Mutesa II of Buganda. A photograph taken in 1951

photo: Radio Times Hulton Picture Library

6. Masai cattle on the move

photo: Camera Press, Ltd.

they had received very many goats from the Kikuyu; but as long as the Kikuyu were farming the land they had bought, the Dorobo still had the right to receive more goats if they asked for them.[1]

Still, whether they bought the land, or rented it, or adopted the Dorobo so that they belonged to the same family, one way or another the Kikuyu got the land. Then came the great famine, and some of the Kikuyu died and left the land empty; and the Europeans came and the Government saw no harm in letting European farmers take this 'empty' land. The Carter Report reckons that in 1895 the Kikuyu held 1519 square miles, and between then and 1902 they got 275 square miles more, making their total in the year 1902 to be 1794 square miles. It was between 1902 and 1907 that the Government took most of the 'empty' Kikuyu land; and in this way the Kikuyu lost 109 square miles; but when the Government saw its mistake, it gave the Kikuyu 265 square miles of land which were really empty. So, if we look at the area only, the Kikuyu gained 156 square miles.

Yes, but area is not everything. Was the land which the Government gave them as good as the land which it took away?

The Commission asked that question, and answered No. They thought that the 265 square miles of new land which the Government had given the Kikuyu were worth as much as 79 square miles of the land which it had taken away; so the Kikuyu had lost altogether the value of 30 square miles of land. The Report advised the Government of Kenya to compensate the Kikuyu people for this loss by adding land to the Kikuyu reserve, and by paying money to some Kikuyu who had lost their land and were not living in the reserve.

The Commission thought that the real difficulty in Kikuyu land did not come because 109 square miles were taken by Government, but because when the railway was built and the city of Nairobi grew up just outside the Kikuyu reserve, more and more people wanted to come and live there. If the Kikuyu had remained nothing but a people of farmers, they would have had enough land; the Government did not foresee the changes which education and industry would bring.

---

[1] See the evidence of Karanja Waweru in paragraph 276 of the Carter Report. For the rest of this discussion on the Kikuyu land, see paragraphs 214–290, 481–486.

J

It is true that 109 square miles is not very much: about six per cent of the land which the Kikuyu held in 1902. But 109 square miles is a very small part indeed of the land which was reserved for European farmers, the 'White Highlands'.

That is true. As a result of the Carter Commission, the Government enlarged the African reserves until they totalled 52,000 square miles, and set up a Native Lands Trust Board to look after them. The Government gave up the idea that there was Crown land which it could give or lease to anyone it liked. But the Government also set up the European area in the highlands, and fixed its boundaries just as it had fixed the boundaries of the African reserves. The White Highlands totalled 16,000 square miles; though nearly 4,000 square miles, a quarter of the whole, was forest reserve, and nobody was to make farms there.

But why was it necessary for Kenya to have European farmers at all? West Africa has no European farmers, but it has got on very well without them.

Parts of West Africa certainly have: Ghana and Nigeria, for example. Sierra Leone was very poor until a few years ago when iron and diamonds were found there; and parts of French West Africa are still poor. If we take Ghana and Nigeria, and compare them with Kenya, there are two main reasons why they have been able to get on so well without European farmers. One reason is, as we have said already, that they had been in touch with Europe much longer than Kenya, and had learned a great deal. The other reason is that they have been producing things that Europe wanted to buy: cocoa, palm oil, tin, gold, ground-nuts, aluminium, diamonds, manganese, timber. This means that Ghana and Nigeria are rich enough to develop their roads and railways, their schools and hospitals, their trade and industries. But Kenya had no minerals, and no crops which Europe wanted to buy; and so there seemed no chance that it would ever be able to develop in this way. It would never be able to pay for teachers or doctors from England, or to send Africans to be trained in England; nor would it be able to pay for agricultural officers to teach African farmers how to grow new crops (even if the African farmers would have wished to learn) or for geological surveyors to look for minerals.[1] The coming of the European farmers has brought problems. But it is difficult to see how Kenya could have begun to develop without them. It is true that coffee was introduced into Kenya by missionaries; so were potatoes and wattle trees and eucalyptus. Bus it was not until European farmers had begun to make money by growing coffee on a big scale that the export of coffee began to help the country to become rich, and Africans too began to grow the crop. The same is true of tea and sisal and pyrethrum: they were all developed by Europeans who hoped to make money out of them, and when Africans saw that there was money to be made, they too began to grow them. Whether Africans or Asians or Europeans, we are alike in this: we can learn far better from someone who says, 'Look at me. I was poor, but now I am rich, and you too can be rich if you do what I did.' than we can from someone who says, 'I am paid to show you how you could become rich; if only you would do as I say, I assure you that you would become rich.'

But the United Nations would have helped the African people of Kenya, would it not? Or America would have helped.

Not at the time we are speaking of, from 1900 to 1940 or so. In those days there was no United Nations. There was a League of Nations from 1919 to 1939, but the League did not send technical advisers all over the world as the United Nations does nowadays. And it was only from 1945 onwards that America began to give the help she now does to countries that need it. In the world of 1910, with people thinking as they did in those days, the only way for Kenya to get started was to get European farmers to produce crops for export. And they would not come to Kenya unless they thought they would make money by doing so.

We have already said that some of the Europeans in Kenya were selfish. But we must not think that all Europeans were selfish who wanted Africans to come and work for them on their farms. Most of them had been taught as children that it was wrong to sit idle without working; and people in Western Europe do work very hard indeed. When they came to Africa, they found

[1] Geology is the science which teaches us how the earth and the rocks are made. A geological surveyor is a man who knows where to look in order to find useful minerals such as coal or oil or copper or tin.

the women still doing their work of cultivating the land as well as looking after the home and the children; but the men no longer had to go to war and watch against enemies who might attack their villages or their cattle. So it seemed to the Europeans that for part of their time the men had nothing to do; and in Europe they had been taught that it is wrong for a man to have nothing to do.

But why did the Government set aside so much land for Europeans? Not all of it was used. Why were Africans not allowed to use land in the Highlands?

As we know, there are great differences between farming in the European way and farming in the old-fashioned African way. Africans in the old tribal life grow their crops with shifting cultivation, and they try to have as many cattle as they can, which they send to graze all mixed up with other people's cattle. A European farmer surrounds his land with a fence; he cultivates inside his own fence, and keeps his cattle too inside the fence.[1] He does not pay cattle in *lobola* or bride-price, and he is not so much interested in having large numbers of cattle. He thinks it better to have strong healthy animals giving much milk or meat than to have more animals of lower quality. The two ways of farming do not mix; fences are contrary to African custom, and a European farmer does not want poor diseased cattle grazing among his strong healthy animals. But it was a mistake for the Government to say that the land in the Highlands was to be reserved for Europeans. What it really meant was that the Highlands were to be kept for farming of the European kind; but there were no African farmers who farmed in the European way, and in 1902 the Government did not think there ever would be. So the Government spoke carelessly of reserving the land for Europeans when it really meant for farming in the European way.

The Government in those early days was not thinking of keeping out Africans; it was thinking of keeping out Asians. The I.B.E.A. Company, as we have seen, had plans for bringing over farmers from India to cultivate the low lands of Kenya. The

[1] Until about five hundred years ago, farming in England was rather like African farming: there were no fences, and all the village cattle grazed together in the bush. The change to the modern way came gradually, and it certainly means that better use is made of the land. But it also means that most people in England today have no land at all: and that change caused much trouble.

Government thought that, since Europeans would only be able to make their farms in the highlands, where it was cool, the Asians, who were used to a tropical climate, ought to stay lower down, where it was hotter. In 1906 the Government said that it would not allow Asians to lease Crown lands between Kiu and Fort Ternan; these places are both on the railway line, Kiu where it climbs above 5000 feet on the way up from the coast, and Fort Ternan where it drops below 5000 feet again, about fifty miles from Kisumu. But no proper boundaries of the highlands were laid down until the time of the Carter Commission.

Of course, there were many Africans in the highlands. The European farmers could not have run their farms without them. A census in 1945 counted over 200,000 Africans living on European farms. Not all of them were working for Europeans; some of them had been living there before the Europeans came. But most of them were people who had left the reserves to come and live on a European farm and work for the European. While the man was working on his employer's farm, his wives would be growing crops, and his children would be looking after his cattle. In some ways, it was a good system: good for the European because he had a man to work for him, good for the African because he had a home and a farm and cattle of his own, besides the money he earned by his work.

But there were other things about the system which were not so good. The African had a home; but it was not on his family's land; and if he left his work or were dismissed, he lost his home and had to take his cattle away. The European had men to work for him; but if he had the men he had to have their cattle – too many animals, and too much disease. No doubt many European farmers were good men and were kind to their African workers; but nobody likes to feel that if he loses his job he will lose his home as well.

Three things happened to weaken the system. It was not long before the European farmers began to ask if they could not keep down the numbers of animals which their African workers kept on their farms; and the first thing was that the Government made laws to help the Europeans in this matter. The Europeans in the highlands had had district councils for their local government since 1928; and a law of 1940 allowed the European district councils to limit the numbers of animals that might be kept by

African workers on European farms. In 1946, one district council limited the African workers to 15 sheep (no cattle) and two acres of food crops for each family; and many workers said they would not accept these limits, and left the farms. Another district council said that, however many African families were living on one European farm, they must not have between them more than 40 cattle and 20 sheep or goats. That district council got rid of 20,000 cattle from its farms in one year. So by about 1950, the system was ceasing to be attractive to the African workers, and many Africans were leaving the European farms and going to the African reserves, or even out of Kenya altogether.[1]

The second thing was that when the Government appointed the Carter Commission, and asked it to lay down proper boundaries for the European Highlands, it told the Commission that nobody but Europeans was to have the right to buy or sell or lease land there. For the first time, the Government decided to keep out Africans, as well as Asians.

We do not know why the Government made this change. There were of course many more European farmers in Kenya in 1932 than there had been twenty years earlier, and no doubt some of them would have liked the sort of colour bar which existed in South Africa[2]. But the Government, both in London and in Nairobi, would not agree to that sort of colour bar. The probable reason is that the Kamba and the Kikuyu and others had far more cattle than their land could carry, and they would not listen when Government agricultural officers begged them to change their way of living: to have fewer and better cattle and go in for mixed farming, collecting the manure from the animals and using it to feed the crops. We can understand the Africans' answer: 'Cattle are part of our life, and each family wants to have as many cattle as it can. For you white men, money is part of your life, and everyone wants to have as much money as he can. It does not matter to you if a pound note is new and clean, or old and dirty; it will still buy the same amount. Similarly, to us a cow is a cow, whether fat or thin. If one family has to pay five cows to another, it will not be allowed to say, "We can pay only three cows, but

[1] See the Report of the East Africa Royal Commission of 1953–55, pages 59–61 and 163–170.
[2] See Book One, pages 131–142.

they are very healthy and fat." Why should we change this custom? Customs are not meant to be changed. You tell us that we have too many cattle for our land. We say that we have not enough land for our cattle. There is plenty of land which is not being used, but you will not let us go there; and one European family has as much land as twenty African families. Give us more land, and then there will be no more trouble.'

All that is understandable. But we can understand the Government too, if it thought, 'It is true that there is land lying empty and unused in the highlands. But if we can get more good European farmers to take it, we know that it will produce good cattle, or wheat, or pyrethrum, or other things for sale; and the Europeans will manure it, so that it will stay fertile for ever. The Africans are ruining their own land; if we let them into this empty land, they will soon fill it up and ruin it like the rest. They will turn Kenya into a desert, and then they will have to change their customs, whether they like it or not. So let us keep this land in the highlands for farmers who know how to look after it properly; and we will hope that gradually, with more education, African agriculture will improve.'

No doubt that is what the Government thought; and it is a good answer to the Africans. But unfortunately, it is not what the Government said. It did not say that the land in the highlands was to be kept for farmers (of whatever race) who knew how to look after it properly. It said that the land was to be kept for Europeans; which was a mistake.

The third thing which weakened the land system was a result of this Government decision. The Carter Commission, as we have seen, found that there were other Africans living in the highlands as well as those working on European farms. Some were living there because they or their families had been living there before the land was leased to a European. These people were protected by the law; they had a right to stay there, and the European could not make them work for him or turn them away. The Commission said that if, as the Government had just told it, this land were to be reserved for Europeans, the law must be changed, and these Africans must lose their rights; though of course the Government must not take away their rights without giving them compensation. The Government did change the law, and it did give them compensation. About 4,000 Africans were moved out of the highlands, and they were given about £ 6,000 in money[1] and about 6,000 acres of good land.

It was these last two changes which did most to make Africans unhappy over land. Nobody likes being turned out of his home, even if he is given compensation in money and land somewhere else. And worse than that, nobody likes being told that, however good a farmer he is he will not be allowed to lease a farm because the land is reserved for people of a different race. For over twenty years there was trouble over this.

In May 1954, the Government accepted the advice of Mr Swynnerton, who drew up a plan for improving African agriculture. Mr Swynnerton said that there were six million cattle in Kenya, most of them in the drier parts of the country. If a cow was killed, it was worth about £ 2, but there was no reason why the value of a cow should not be raised to £ 10 or £ 15. If the Africans could be persuaded to kill 650,000 cattle a year at that price, Kenya would become much richer. Moreover, he said that Africans should be persuaded to exchange their small scattered pieces of land so that each family had its land in one piece; then they could grow more crops for sale, such as coffee, pyrethrum, tea, sisal, sugar, cotton and so on. Of course, the Africans could not be made to do this; they would need to be persuaded to do it willingly, and the Government would need at least 170 more agricultural officers to go round and explain the scheme. The Government in London also approved of the Swynnerton scheme, and gave Kenya five million pounds to help to carry it out.

At last, in October 1959, after the Swynnerton scheme had been running for five years, the Kenya Government agreed that land in the highlands ought to be open to farmers of every race; and in May 1960 it made its proposals. It would invite Europeans in the highlands to sell some land; and with this land and with other land that was lying empty it would make a number of fifty-acre farms for Africans. African farmers who applied for one of these farms would be given a course of training. In November 1960, the Legislative Council passed the Agriculture (Amendment) Bill, which made these proposals law. Under this scheme, about 8,000 African families would be settled in the highlands.

This was good as far as it went; for the Government had now

[1] This was before the war of 1939–45. Before the war, £ 6,000 was worth as much as £ 20,000 would have been twenty years later.

agreed that questions of race had nothing to do with land. In fact, the Minister of Agriculture said that this should be true of all land in Kenya; if non-Europeans were able to hold land in what had been the white highlands, non-Africans ought to be able to hold land in African reserves. But there was nothing about this in the new law.

The African leaders said that the new law did not go nearly far enough. They said that there ought to be many more than 8,000 African families settled in the highlands; and when Kenya became independent, the independent Government would increase this number very greatly. Some of them went so far as to say that all the land should be taken away from Europeans and given to Africans. But most of them did not go as far as that; they said that Kenya needed good European farmers with their skill and capital, and those who were friendly to Africans should be allowed to stay.

In September 1961 the Government said that it would raise the number of African families in the highlands from 8,000 to 25,000; each family would have only 25 acres instead of fifty. We shall see later on[1] other plans which the Kenya Government had at that time for improving African agriculture in ways suggested in the Swynnerton scheme.

Kenya in 1900 seemed a big country, with land enough for everybody; but it was a very poor country. The Europeans and Asians had come with their skill and their capital; they had stopped the fighting and the slavery, and they had made the land much richer. Peace, wealth, and modern medicine are good things; but they bring as their result an increase in population, and that means erosion and land-hunger. Kenya today seems smaller than in 1900, for it is easier to travel by road and railway, and there are many more people wanting land. Kenya cannot afford to drive away people who can help it with their skill and capital. On the other hand, the East Africa Royal Commission[2] in 1955 said that Europeans appeared 'as a tribe hanging on to their tribal territory instead of pooling it for the common territorial need'. Both Africans and Europeans, said the Commission, must get away from thinking of land in a tribal way: this for the Kikuyu, this

[1] See page 178.
[2] Report of the East Africa Royal Commission, chapter 5, paragraph 19 and elsewhere; chapter 25, paragraph 10.

for the Europeans, this for the Masai, and so on. The land of
Kenya, with the crops that grow and the cattle that feed on it, is
the country's great wealth; and it must be used, not for the good
of one tribe or another, but for the good of all Kenya. Africans,
Asians and Europeans must all learn to think of themselves – and
to think of each other – as Kenyans.

TOWARDS SELF-GOVERNMENT

We have spent a great deal of time in discussing the question of
Kenya land, for the land question has been at the bottom of so
many of Kenya's difficulties. Much of the political trouble has
come because the Africans thought that the Europeans wanted to
keep all power in their hands so that they could do what they
liked with the Africans' land: and because the Europeans on their
side thought that their own farms, into which they had put so
much money and hard work, would be taken from them and
given to Africans who would ruin them. Because of these fears,
political questions could never be discussed with an open mind.
But we must now turn to see what these political questions were.

It was in 1921 that Africans in Kenya first began to enter
politics; and it was because of trouble on the land that they did
so. The war of 1914–18 was over, and thousands of Africans had
served in it, either as soldiers or as porters; many had died or
been killed in battle. After the war there were bad times for
everyone, not only in Africa but in Europe. The world had spent
its money for four years on guns and on fighting, and it was much
poorer than before. In Kenya, nearly two Europeans out of every
three had joined the army; their farms had gone back to bush,
their cattle had died from disease or hunger. Those who came
back found that all the work they had done before the war was
thrown away, and they had to start again from the beginning.
We must not blame them too much if they asked, 'How are we
going to live and pay our men until we can get our farms into
order again?'

But what they did was unwise. The European farmers joined
together, and agreed that they would cut the pay of all their
African workers by one-third. They hoped that the Government
would agree to cut the pay of its own African workers in the
same way, and that it would force people to go on working at the

new rates of pay. But things were not as simple as that. As we have seen, the Government was unwilling to force people to work[1]; it was having enough trouble in registering them and making them carry their certificate of registration, the *kipandi* as they called it. And the Europeans soon found that their African workers left the farms, rather than work for so much less money. And, since the Europeans had joined together to reduce wages, the Africans for the first time joined together to resist. Their leader was Harry Thuku, who was a Kikuyu working as a telephone operator in the Treasury at Nairobi. He formed an association called the Young Kikuyu Association, which sent a copy of its rules to the Government asking the Government to approve them, and asked the Government to meet it to discuss the things that troubled it.

The Government agreed to the meeting, and it was held on 24 June 1921 at Dagoreti, a little to the west of Nairobi and to the south of the railway line. There came to it some Kikuyu chiefs and headmen (we must remember that these were appointed and paid by the Government); many young Kikuyu men, members of the Association or not; some missionaries, some district commissioners, and some senior Government officials from Nairobi. Harry Thuku of course was there. The young men made their complaints. They complained of the cut in their pay; they complained of the registration system and of the way in which it worked; they complained that men and women were forced to go and work on European farms when they did not wish to; they complained that there were no Government schools, but only mission schools; and they complained too that Europeans had written papers to show their right to occupy land, but that no Africans could have such papers. Harry Thuku asked the Government not to force them to work at reduced wages, as the Europeans wanted the Government to do; and the acting Chief Native Commissioner promised that the Government would not. That was all that the young men got from the meeting; but it was something.

The next thing was that the Government told Harry Thuku that he must either give up all this business of politics or resign from the Government service. That is understandable: Government

---

[1] Lord Delamere was not at all satisfied with the Government over this; see page 138.

servants are not allowed to be politicians. But Harry Thuku was not attacking the Government's policy; he was complaining to the Goverment about injustice, but he was sure the Government did not mean to be unjust, and he thought that when the Government heard what he and his people thought, it would put matters right. It seems a pity that the Government did not say to itself, 'We do not like this young man, and we do not think that he has any right to talk to us like this; but if what he says is true, there is something wrong, and we must put it right.' However the Government merely said, 'Keep quiet, or else resign.' He resigned. Now of course Thuku and the Y.K.A. had something else to complain about: the Government would not listen to them. Thuku and his people held meetings up and down Kikuyu country, and at Kisumu, complaining of the pay cut, the increase in taxation[1], and the registration system. He sent cables to London, expecting that the Colonial Office and the King would tell the Kenya Government to do what his Association wanted. The Government became afraid, and in March 1922 it arrested Harry Thuku in Nairobi.

Thuku was arrested quietly enough; but then the Government managed matters very badly. It did not put him in prison to await trial, but kept him in the police barracks, a row of one-storey tin buildings. That same day, the Governor left Nairobi and went down to the coast. A crowd of Africans gathered outside the police barracks to see what would happen to Thuku, and the police were kept up all night in case of trouble. Next morning, there was some shouting and some stone-throwing; one tired policeman fired without orders, and at once the other police fired too. More than twenty people were killed, and the crowd at once ran away. We should not blame the police too much. It is hard for the police to stand still, hour after hour, while the crowd is laughing and shouting and throwing stones, especially if they are tired through having been on duty all night. It is one of the most unpleasant positions that a police officer can find himself in. If the Government had managed better, the police need not have been in that unpleasant position at all; expecially if Harry Thuku had

[1] In 1916, the hut tax and poll tax was raised from 4 s. to 6 s. 8 d., and in 1920 to £ 1, though people who were really too poor to pay the full tax were allowed to pay less. The registration system was introduced in 1920; there had been earlier laws in 1915 and 1918, but they were not enforced.

been put in the strong Nairobi prison, as the commissioner of police advised, instead of in the police barracks, which (as the commissioner said) the crowd could have pushed down.

But was the Government right to arrest Harry Thuku?

Yes, things had gone so far that the Government had to arrest him. All Governments have sometimes to arrest political leaders; President Nasser for example has done it in Egypt, and President Nkrumah in Ghana. Harry Thuku's crowds were getting bigger and bigger, and his language was getting stronger and stronger. He was telling his people to burn their *kipandi* and not to obey the Government, because he was stronger than the Government. No Government can allow that kind of talk.

But was not Harry Thuku right to complain about higher taxes, and the registration, and the cut in pay? And could not the Government have done something to keep things from going so far that he had to be arrested?

Even at that time, there were some Europeans – and many Asians – who thought that Harry Thuku had a good deal of right on his side; and they thought, too, that the Government ought to have handled the young man more sympathetically when he first started his Association. Most people would probably think so today. But the same can be said of all Governments. No doubt the political prisoners in other countries think that they have a good deal of right on their side and that their Government ought to have handled them more sympathetically. In politics, there is usually something to be said on both sides. But as things were in March 1922, the Government had to arrest Harry Thuku; there would have been worse trouble if it had allowed him to go on talking as he was doing.

Anyway, that unhappy morning was the end of Harry Thuku, and for the time being it was the end of the Kikuyu political movement. The Government tried and punished some of those who were the leaders of the crowd. Harry Thuku himself was not tried; he was sent away to Kismayu in the north of Kenya to live under police supervision.

We have seen that before the 1914–18 war, Lord Delamere was asking that the Europeans in Kenya should elect their Government. During the war, as we have said, two Europeans out of every three joined the army: and the Government in London was so grateful to them for the help they had given, that after the war it decided to allow Europeans to elect members to the Legislative Council, though not to elect the whole Government, as Lord Delamere wished.

Kenya had had a legislative council and an executive council for some years, as nearly all British colonies had: the executive council since 1905 and the legislative council since 1907. The Governor's executive council was composed of some of the senior officials, and the legislative council consisted of eight Europeans, all nominated by the Governor: six officials and two (Lord Delamere and another) unofficials. There were no elected members. In 1918, two European unofficial members were added to the Governor's executive council, and in 1920 eleven European members were elected to the Legislative Council, all European men and women having the vote. There were also of course official members.

But what about the Asians? The Government in London proposed that there should be two elected Asian members of the Legislative Council. An Asian had been nominated as a member a early as 1909; but he soon resigned from the Council, and no other Asian was nominated until 1920.

The Asians were feeling unhappy about many things in Kenya. As we have seen, although the law did not forbid them to hold land in the highlands, yet the Government would never allow them to buy or lease land there; and they felt as unhappy over this as Africans have felt for so many years. The next thing was that there was talk of limiting the number of Asians that were allowed to come and settle in Kenya. There were already many more Asians than Europeans, and some of the Europeans were saying that Kenya ought not to admit any more. The third thing was that in Nairobi and other towns, Asians were not allowed to have their houses or their shops and offices in the same street as Europeans; there was a European part of the town and an Asian part. Lastly, Europeans were allowed to elect members to town councils, but Asians were not; the Governor nominated Asian members. All these things made the Asians in Kenya feel that the Government was not treating them fairly; and in 1919 they complained to the Government of India, which was the country from which most of them had come. The Government of India sent one of its senior officials, Sir Benjamin Robertson, to visit Kenya and see for himself how its people were treated there.[1]

On 21 May 1920, the Government in London proposed: (a) Asians should be allowed to elect members to town councils; (b) there should be no limit to the numbers of Asians allowed to come into Kenya; (c) the Asians should elect two members to the Legislative Council; (d) Asians should still not be allowed to live in the part of a town which was reserved for Europeans; (e) if possible, Asians should not be allowed to have their offices and shops in the same streets as Europeans, but it might not be possible to arrange this; (f) Asians should still not be allowed to hold land in the highlands, but the Government of Kenya should look to see if it could find land suitable for Asian farmers lower down, nearer the coast, without taking land away from Africans.

Five months later, the Government of India, having heard what Sir Benjamin Robertson had to tell it, told the Government in London that it could not agree to these proposals. Naturally, it was pleased at (a) and (b). But on (c), it said that if 8,000 Europeans needed eleven elected members in the Legislative Council, two elected members were not enough for the 22,000 Asians in Kenya. On the other three proposals, the Indian Government said[2], 'You say that Asians must not live or work next door to Europeans, because they are dirty. We cannot agree; some may be, but not all. It ought to be enough if you have strict rules about keeping houses and compounds clean and tidy. Similarly, you say that Asians must not have farms or houses in the highlands because the climate does not suit them. If the climate does not suit them, they will not want to live there; but it is wrong not to allow a man to live in the highlands because of his race.'

The Government in London was now in a difficult position, and the Colonial Office and the India Office consulted together to see if they could find a way out of the difficulty. In September 1922 they sent out fresh proposals to Kenya; these are called the Wood-Winterton proposals, because Wood and Winterton were

[1] You will notice that this official was an Englishman. In those days, India had not reached full self-government. There was a special Government department in London, the India Office, responsible for it, with a Secretary of State for India. But India had a good deal of self-government, and was quite able to defend its people in Kenya against the Kenya Government and the Colonial Office.

[2] These are not the actual words of the Indian Government's letter; but they contain the sense.

the names of the two Under-Secretaries of State who worked them out.

From the Asian point of view, the Wood-Winterton proposals were better than the proposals of May 1920, which are called the Milner proposals, because it was Lord Milner who made them. Like the Milner proposals, they agreed that there should be elected Asian members on town councils, and that there should be no limit to the numbers of Asians coming into Kenya: though the Colonial Office said that if ever there were so many that Kenya looked like becoming an Asian country, it might have to reconsider this. They agreed with the Milner proposals too that the highlands should for the present be closed to Asians; the Government of India said it would agree to this for the time being, but one day it might raise the question again. But the Wood-Winterton proposals said that Asians and Europeans should be allowed to live and work side by side, as the Government of India wished. On the Legislative Council, the Wood-Winterton proposal was that instead of there being eleven elected Europeans and two elected Asians, there should be seven Europeans and four Asians. European and Asian voters should be in the same list; everyone should be entitled to vote if he had certain qualifications, and the qualifications for a vote should be arranged so as to include all the Europeans and about one Asian in ten. The Legislative Council should continue to have an official majority.

When the Wood-Winterton proposals were sent out to Kenya, they satisfied nobody. The Asians would not accept them because 4 Asians to 7 Europeans, though better than 2 Asians to 11 Europeans, was still not good enough; they wanted at least as many elected members as the Europeans had, if not more. After all, there were nearly three Asians in Kenya for every European. The Europeans would not accept the proposals for a similar reason. They were afraid that if the Asians were given even four members, they would soon ask for more; and Kenya would soon become an Asian country, in which the Europeans would have no political power. The Europeans liked the Milner proposals better than the Wood-Winterton.[1]

[1] We speak of what the Europeans wanted or did not want. We can only go by the speeches that were made by their elected members and other European leaders. To be fair, we must remember that among the Europeans in Kenya, as among all groups of people in all countries, there were many quiet people who did not agree with much of what their leaders said.

So the Government of Kenya told the Government in London that the Wood-Winterton proposals would not end the difficulty. European and Asian delegations went to London to see the Secretary of State; and in July 1923 the Government in London said what it would do. The paper is called the Devonshire White Paper, because the Duke of Devonshire was the Secretary of State for the Colonies who issued it. The Devonshire White paper was not a set of proposals; it was a statement of the way in which Kenya was to be governed, and it was an order to the Governor.

The Devonshire paper is in two parts. The first part sets out the ideas which ought to guide the Government in all its actions; the second part sets out a scheme which puts those ideas into practice. The ideas are important; in following years, the Government in London applied them in other parts of Africa as well as in Kenya. In 1919, the Governor of Kenya, General Northey, told the Asians that Kenya was to be mainly a European country, and that although Asian interests would not be forgotten, European interests were more important.[1] The Devonshire paper disagreed with General Northey. It said[2], 'Kenya is first of all an African country, and the Government has made up its mind that the interests of the Africans are the most important. If ever African interests are opposed to the interests of Europeans or Asians, so that the Government has to choose between them, it must favour the Africans. Of course the Government must help the Europeans and Asians as far as it can; it will not undo what it has already done to help them. But the British Government feels that it should govern Kenya mainly in the interests of the Africans; and the Government cannot give this responsibility to anyone else[3]. It must educate the Africans until they are able to govern themselves, and as far as it can, the Government will do this; though lack of money may make it unable to do as much as it would like to do. Kenya is no different from Uganda and Tanganyika; in all three countries, the British Government is responsible for govern-

[1] The Governor's words were, 'His Excellency believes that, although Indian interests should not be lost sight of, European interests must be paramount throughout the Protectorate.'
[2] Here again, we are giving the sense of the Devonshire paper in simpler language. But the exact words are given in a foot-note on page 162.
[3] That is to say, it cannot give it to the elected European or Asian members of the Kenya Legislative Council.

K

ing the country in the interests of the Africans, and nobody can take away that responsibility.'[1]

That sounds fine. When the Europeans and the Asians were quarrelling over their position in Kenya, the Government in London was right to remind them that they must not forget the position of the Africans. But did it make very much difference?

It did not make as much difference as we might expect. For one thing, the Devonshire paper warns us that Kenya would be too poor to do all it would like to do; and a few years afterwards Kenya did become very poor indeed, as we shall see later on. For another thing, the paper speaks of African interests and European or Asian interests being opposed, or perhaps being opposed. But in practice, it was difficult to say what this meant. For example, we have seen that European district councils made rules which limited the numbers of cattle which Africans might keep on Europeans farms. An African who was told that he had too many cattle, and he must get rid of some of them, might perhaps say that this was against African interests. But the European farmer might reply that his farm was being eaten up by African cattle, so that he could not live and pay his taxes; and it would be against African interests if Europeans could not pay taxes so that the Government should have money to provide African schools and

[1] 'Primarily, Kenya is an African territory, and His Majesty's Government think it necessary definitely to record their considered opinion that the interests of the African natives must be paramount, and that if, and when, those interests and the interests of the immigrant races should conflict, the former should prevail. Obviously the interests of the other communities, European, Indian, and Arab, must generally be safeguarded. Whatever the circumstances in which members of these communities have entered Kenya, there will be no drastic action of reversal of measures already introduced, such as may have been contemplated in some quarters, the result of which might be to destroy or impair the existing interests of those who have already settled in Kenya. But in the administration of Kenya, His Majesty's Government regard themselves as exercising a trust on behalf of the African population, and they are unable to delegate or share this trust, the object of which may be defined as the protection and advancement of the native races... There can be no room for doubt that it is the mission of Great Britain to work continuously for the training and education of the Africans... Within the limits imposed by the finances of the Colony, all that is possible for the advancement and development of the Africans, both inside and outside the native reserves, will be done... As in the Uganda Protectorate, so in the Kenya Colony, the principle of trusteeship for the natives, no less than in the mandated territory of Tanganyika, is unassailable. This paramount duty of trusteeship will continue, as in the past, to be carried out under the Secretary of State for the Colonies by the agents of the Imperial Government, and by them alone.'

hospitals. There was always room for arguments of this kind. Still, the Devonshire White Paper was never forgotten, and the Kenya Government did its best to govern according to the Devonshire ideas.

After thus setting out its general ideas on the problem of governing Kenya, the Devonshire paper went on to discuss the special questions about the position of the Asians, which had brought the Kenya Government to ask for help from London. It discussed the Legislative Council and its elections. The Wood-Winterton paper had proposed that European and Asian voters should have their names on one list: there should be one *common roll* of voters. The advantage of the common roll system would be that each elected member would be elected by the votes of both races, so that he would have to think of the interests of both races. The Devonshire paper considered this proposal, but it did not agree. It said that Europeans and Asians in Kenya were so much afraid of each other that if a candidate tried to win the friendship and the votes of the other race, his own people would leave him, and would find another candidate who would promise to do all he could for the help of his own race against the other. If this was so, the Devonshire paper said, the common roll system would not work. It therefore decided in favour of a *communal roll* system: that is, separate lists or rolls for each race, Europeans voting for European candidates, Asians for Asian candidates – and one day, perhaps, Africans voting for African candidates. It proposed a Legislative Council with an official majority, with eleven elected Europeans, five elected Asians, one elected Arab (this would make two Arab members, for there was already one nominated Arab member) and one nominated European missionary to represent African interests.

On the other matters, the Devonshire White Paper generally followed the Wood-Winterton proposals. The highlands were to be closed to Asians. Europeans and Asians were to live and work sidy by side. There were to be elected Asian members on the town councils, elected on the system of the communal roll. No limit would be set to the numbers of Asians coming into Kenya, unless they came in such great crowds that Kenya seemed likely to be no longer an African country. All this, except for the communal roll, was the same as the Wood-Winterton proposals.

From the Asian point of view, the Devonshire paper was on the

whole a step backwards. The Milner scheme had proposed a
Legislative Council of 11 to 2; Wood-Winterton a Council of 7
to 4; Devonshire a Council of 11 to 5. The Devonshire scheme
gave them the communal roll, and because this meant that Asian
votes could never keep a European out of the Council, it was
ready to allow far more Asians to have the vote than one in ten,
which was all that Wood-Winterton would have given them. But
the Asians wanted to be treated equally with the Europeans; and
they would not accept the five elected seats on the Legislative
Council. There were 15,000 Asian men and women who might
have registered as voters, but only about 200 did so. This was an
uncomfortable position for everybody; some way had to be found
getting Asians back as members of the Legislative Council without
of their feeling ashamed. The Government in London asked the
Governor to nominate Asian members, and five took their seats in
this way. In 1927 one Asian agreed to be a candidate for election,
and he was elected; so there were then five Asian members, one
elected and four nominated.

THE YEARS OF POVERTY

So far, except for the years of the war, Kenya had been growing
richer. More land was being cultivated, and more crops were
being exported. The Government's revenue was rising, and so the
Government was able to spend more on developing the country.
But after the war there came a time of poverty. We have seen that
the European farmers tried to cut the pay of their workers by
one-third. The Government also found itself poor. In 1920 Kenya
changed its money; until then it had used rupees, the money of
India, but now it changed to pounds, shillings, and cents. The
change was not well managed; the value of the rupee in shillings
changed a good deal, and before the new money settled down, a
good deal of suffering was caused. In 1922 the Government was
so poor that it had to dismiss over 240 officials because it could
not afford to pay them. From 1925 to 1929 things were better.
Europe was at peace, trade was improving, and the world was
willing to buy the crops that Kenya produced. People in Kenya,
and in other countries too, thought that the world was beginning
to get over the effects of the 1914–18 war.

But they were wrong. From 1929 to 1937 the whole world went through a time of terrible poverty, which nobody who saw it can ever forget. There were many causes, and it is difficult to explain it shortly.

Before 1914, the world as a whole was growing richer through trade. Britain, for example, imported all kinds of raw materials (such as iron, cotton, wool, rubber) and manufactured them into goods of all kinds. Then Britain sold the manufactured goods all over the world at a profit. Part of the profit was used to pay for more imported raw materials, part to buy food and clothes and sther things for the people of Britain; but there was always some left over. Britain used this third part to lend money to foreign countries – for example to build railways in the United States and South America – and those who borrowed it paid Britain interest.[1] Other countries did the same thing; each country exported whatever it could produce, and imported what it needed from abroad. For example, before 1914 Britain imported from Germany nearly all her dye-stuffs for dyeing cloth, and nearly all the fine glass for cameras and telescopes. And all the countries did well by this trade.

Now it is plain that such a complicated system of trade cannot be carried on unless buyers and sellers trust each other. There must be *credit* as well as cash. If Britain imports raw cotton from Egypt, and dye-stuffs from Germany, and hopes to make a profit by making both into fine coloured cloth, there can be no trade unless Egyptian cotton-growers and German chemists are prepared to wait for their money. And so, before 1914 there was a complicated system of banks and cheques and other ways of providing *credit* for people who were not prepared to pay cash. The whole system worked because buyers and sellers and bankers in different countries knew and trusted each other.

But the war changed it all. *First:* during the war there had been no trade between Germany and Britain. Britain was no longer able to buy German glass and dye-stuffs, so British chemists had to learn how to make them. Thus, new industries grew up in Britain; and when the war was over, the people in Britain who

[1] Anyone who borrows money has to pay the lender every year for the use of it. What he pays is counted as so much per cent of the sum he has borrowed. This payment is called interest. If a company borrows money by selling its shares, the money it pays is not called interest, but dividend.

lived by making glass and dye-stuffs were not willing to give up their new industry and allow Britain once more to depend for these things on Germany. Exactly the same thing happened in other countries: new industries grew up, and each country tried to produce as many different kinds of goods for itself as possible, instead of producing some kinds for itself and buying the others from abroad. This meant that there was much less trade between one country and another than there had been before the war; and less trade meant less wealth.

Second: Britain and the other countries of Western Europe came out of the war much poorer; the United States, which was in the war for only a short time, was not much affected. It so happened that the United States, which was a young country and had borrowed large sums of money from Britain and elsewhere to build its railways and develop its mines and industries, was now grown up and ready to begin lending money in its turn to other countries. The war gave the United States its chance. All Western Europe bought guns and other material of war from the United States on credit, and hoped to be able to repay after the war was over. Now, there are three ways in which Europe could repay a debt of this kind. It could pay in gold, in goods, or in services. In gold, by paying America for the goods in bars of gold. In goods, by exporting goods to the value of the debt. Or, lastly, in services such as shipping or insurance: by carrying American goods and passengers in its ships, or by insuring American lives or property against fire or danger of any kind. But none of these three ways was possible. Europe could not pay much in gold, for it had not enough gold. Europe has no large gold-mines, and without trade it could not buy gold from South Africa or other countries where it is produced. Europe could not pay much in goods, because the United States could make for itself nearly everything it needed, and refused to import goods from Europe for fear of throwing its own people out of work. Lastly, Europe could not pay much in services; for the most important service was shipping, which depended on world trade. World trade was growing smaller and smaller, and in any case, the United States wanted its own goods to be carried in its own ships. The result was that the countries of Western Europe owed America money which they were not able to pay.

Third: It was partly because of this that in 1928, the United

States, now the richest country in the world, decided to invest[1] no more money overseas but to leave the countries of Europe to themselves. All the profits which Americans made in their business were now invested in buying shares in American companies. Naturally, when so many people wished to buy shares, the price of shares went up; one company found the price of its shares rise from 40 to 450 dollars even at a time when it had paid no dividend at all. People were investing their money hoping that it would be safe, and that one day it would bring them in a good dividend. In the autumn of 1929, people began to ask themselves, 'Is our money safe?' When that question is asked, trouble is near. The whole of this complicated system depends on confidence; as long as people are confident that the system will work, it does work; when people lose their confidence, the system breaks down. In October 1929, American confidence broke. Everyone wanted to sell shares, nobody wanted to buy. Thousands of people were ruined. We can imagine what a shock this was to the other countries of the world when they saw this happen to America. If America could break down like this, who could hope to be safe?

Fourth: Germany was in a specially difficult position. Germany had lost the war, and she had agreed to a peace treaty which bound her to pay very large sums of money to the countries which had won the war – Britain, France, and others. Germany found the same difficulty in paying this money to Britain and France as those countries found in paying their debts to America. She borrowed millions of dollars from Britain and America to build new factories, and then found she could not sell the goods which those factories made. In 1931, those who had lent money to Germany began to lose their confidence; they became afraid that Germany might not be able to repay them, and they all began trying to get their money out of Germany at once. This brought about the very thing they feared. German banks and business firms closed their doors and said they could not pay their debts, and the Ger-

---

[1] In Western Europe and America (it is different under communism) a man who has saved money often *invests it in* shares; that is, he buys shares in some company, and expects the company to pay him every year a dividend on his money. If a company makes good profits and pays good dividends, many people will want to buy its shares, and the price of the shares will go up. If a company does badly, and pays only a small dividend or none at all, nobody will want to buy its shares, and those who already have its shares will try and sell them. Then the price of its shares will go down.

man Government said that it could pay no more under the peace
treaty.

These are four of the most important causes of the poverty
which came upon the world from 1929 to 1937. Since all countries
were closely bound together in trade, when one suffered, they all
suffered. In Britain, nearly three million people were out of work,
roughly one in eight of those usually employed.

**All this was very sad for Europe and America; but has it anything
to do with Kenya?**

Yes; Kenya suffered too. People in Europe and America not
only found themselves poor, but feared that they were becoming
still poorer; so they spent as little as they could. They would not
buy as much cotton and wool and coffee and cocoa and copper
and other raw materials from overseas as they had been doing.
When people who have something to sell find that nobody wishes
to buy, they cut their price. This is what happened in Kenya, and
in all the other countries which lived, like Kenya, by exporting
their products to Europe and America as raw materials. Australia
suffered because the price of wool fell to less than half; Canada
suffered because the price of wheat fell to less than a third;
the Gold Coast, because cocoa fell to less than a half; and Kenya,
because cotton fell to 36 per cent and coffee to 52 per cent. Even
at these low prices, the producers could not sell all that they grew.
In Canada, thousands of tons of wheat which could not be sold
were burnt instead of coal to drive steam-ships; in Brazil, whole
ship-loads of coffee which could not be sold were taken out to
sea and thrown into the water.

**But surely there were people in the world who needed these things?
Was it not wasteful to throw away good food like this?**

Yes; there was actually at the time a famine in China, and if the
wheat which was burnt could have been taken to China and given
to the hungry people there, it would have saved many lives. But
it would have cost money to do this; the wheat-growers and the
ship-owners were all unhappy and afraid, and they could not
think of doing such a thing.

So Kenya suffered, like the rest of the world. The Government
had to give up its plans for developing the country, for building
more roads, hospitals and schools. These things could not be done

without money, and since Kenya was getting so much less for its cotton and coffee and pyrethrum, the Government had not the money to do them.

Education in Kenya was specially unlucky. There was a Government education department, but most of the schools were run by the Christian churches; the education department inspected the schools and paid grants of Government money to help the schools and to pay the teachers. The Christian churches in Europe and America sent out missionaries to teach and to preach; their salaries, which were much smaller than Government salaries, were paid by the churches in Europe and America which sent them. When these bad times came to Kenya about 1930, there had been mission schools in Kenya for eighty years, but many Africans were still not interested in European education, so most of the schools were small. The war and the bad times hit the missionary societies hard. Some Christians in Europe and America lost their faith and left the Church. Those who remained were all much poorer and gave much less money to the missionary societies. So it happened in Africa that European missionaries who died or retired could not be replaced. At the same time, the Government found that it could not afford to pay so much in grants to schools, and it could not afford to pay so many education officers and inspectors. And it so happened that just at this time, Africans were at last beginning to take more interest in sending their children to school: the Kikuyu especially, who lived so near Nairobi and who had listened to the political speeches of Harry Thuku. So as more and more African children began coming to school, the numbers of European missionaries and teachers and education officers, instead of going up as they should have done, began to go down.

In 1929 there was trouble among the Kikuyu, when two missionary societies told their people that girls should not be circumcised. Some Christian Kikuyu were angry at this, saying that they could see nothing un-Christian in this Kikuyu custom. They left the mission churches, and set up the Kikuyu Independent Schools Association: independent, because they wished to be independent of the missions. The Association soon set up its own schools all over Kikuyu country and into the Rift Valley province, and it set up its own training college to train teachers for its schools. The Association was poor, and most of its schools were not good enough to qualify for a Government grant; but in 1937 the Government appointed an inspector of schools with the special duty of helping the Independent schools. So when the second war broke out in 1939, education in Kenya was in an unhappy position; there were more children in school, but fewer Europeans to teach and to manage the schools. During those years, the Kikuyu leaders did not follow the example of Harry Thuku and take part in politics; they thought it more important to develop their own schools. But the political feeling was still there. In 1922 Harry Thuku's Young Kikuyu Association was replaced by the Kikuyu Central Association under the leadership of Jomo Kenyatta.

KENYA FROM 1927 TO THE MAU MAU

We have seen that from about 1929 onwards until the second war (1939–45) Kenya was too poor to develop very much. After about 1937, Britain began to fear that a second war was coming, and began to build more war-ships and aeroplanes and make more guns and other material of war so as to be ready for war if it came. This was a great help to countries like Nigeria, Nothern Rhodesia and the Gold Coast, which had metals (tin, copper, manganese and aluminium) which were needed for these manufactures; but it was no help to Kenya, which had no metals. During the war, Kenyans of all races joined the army, and thousands of Africans saw other parts of the world and other ways of living. They earned good money, and they sent much of it home to Kenya; hundreds of new schools were built with the money which was sent home in this way. But though money can buy building materials, and a village can build itself a school in a few weeks, it is not so easy to find teachers. Many of the new schools were of little use because the teachers who taught in them were not properly educated for the work they were doing.

The Legislative Council of Kenya in 1927 consisted of 38 members. Eleven were senior officials, who were members because of the posts they held in the Government; they were all Europeans, because no Asian or African had yet been appointed to such high posts.[1] Nine members were nominated by the Governor; eight

---

[1] Members who are members because of the position they hold are called *ex-officio* members.

of them were European officials and the ninth was an Arab official. There were eleven elected Europeans. Five were Asians, one elected and four nominated; if the Asians had wished, they could all five have been elected, but the Asians would not elect members on a communal roll. One Arab was elected to represent Arabs; and one European missionary was nominated by the Governor to represent African interests.

In 1944 the first change was made in this Council: an African member was nominated by the Governor. Four years later, there was a bigger change, as we can see if we compare the Councils of 1927 and 1948 in a table:

	1927	1948
European ex-officio	11	7
European official nominated	8	9
Arab official nominated	1	1
European elected	11	11
Asian elected	1	5
Asian nominated	4	–
Arab elected	1	1
European to speak for Africans	1	–
African nominated	–	4

The two Councils are the same size. But in 1927 there were 20 officials to 18 unofficials, an official majority of two; in 1948 there were only 17 officials but 21 unofficials, so that the unofficial members had a majority of four over the Government. The Gold Coast Legislative Council had already been given an unofficial majority two years earlier, in 1946.

Although the Legislative Council of 1948 had an unofficial majority, it could not control the Government. The Government policy was in the hands of the Governor and of the Secretary of State in London. The Governor was advised by his senior officers and by his Executive Council, which was mainly composed of officials. If the unofficial members of the Legislative Council disliked Government policy and passed a resolution against it, they could not make the Governor or any of his officers change the policy or resign. Kenya in 1948 was still far from responsible government; a country has *responsible government* when its parliament or legislative council can make the Government carry out whatever policy it wishes – when the Government is *responsible* to parliament. The Kenya Legislative Council of 1948 could make speeches and give advice, but it could not make the Governemnt take its advice.

In 1948, as we have seen in our history of Uganda[1], the British Government set up the East Africa High Commission. Ever since 1926, the Governors of the three British countries of East Africa – Kenya, Uganda and Tanganyika – had been meeting regularly to discuss together. In 1929, the Government in London had appointed a Commission, the Hilton Young Commission, to consider whether these countries should be joined more closely in any way. The Commission did not think that they could be joined into one country; but it did think that they ought to act together in matters which concerned them all, and it thought that Nyasaland and Northern Rhodesia too might act with them. Nothing was done until after the war, and by that time the British Government was beginning to think of joining Nyasaland and Northern Rhodesia in some way with Southern Rhodesia. So the High Commission, when it was set up in 1948, did not include these two countries, but only the three countries of East Africa.

The East Africa High Commission governed all three countries a one country in certain matters. It ran the posts and telegraphs (that is why all three countries use the same stamps), the railways and harbours, income tax, money (all three countries use the same money), the East African literature bureau, and other matters. Locusts or tsetse flies do not know when they cross from Kenya to Tanganyika; so the High Commission was in charge of the work against these insects. The Commission also made maps of the whole of East Africa; and did other kinds of work which are needed by all three countries equally. But it did not run education or health services. The Commission had its own legislative assembly, with seven of its own officials, one official member nominated by each of the three countries, and thirteen unofficial members, six of them being Europeans. Here too, as in the Kenya Legislative Council, there was a unofficial majority: 13 unofficials to ten officials. We have seen that there was some trouble in Uganda when the High Commission was set up; but there was none in Kenya.

[1] See page 110.

When Tanganyika became independent at the end of 1961, the British Government saw that the High Commission of three Governors could no longer continue, and must be changed. So it closed the East Africa High Commission, and put in its place the East Africa Common Services Organization. The new Organization does the same work that the Commission used to do. But instead of the three Governors, there are now the three prime ministers of Kenya, Uganda and Tanganyika. There is a central Legislative Assembly, which is made up of four ministers from each territory of the three countries, and nine members from each country, elected by the country's parliament. The Secretary-General and the Legal Secretary of the Organization are also members of the assembly. The first Secretary-General was Mr A.L.Adu, an African from Ghana.

When the war ended in 1945, the Government of Kenya felt more hopeful than it had done since 1929. The African people of Kenya had learnt a great deal from the war, and they were calling for more and more schools for their children. The prices of cotton and coffee and of all other products had risen, and it seemed as if they were likely to remain high; so the revenue was good. Kenya now had money to develop its roads, its schools, its health services, and all the other things which it had been unable to develop during the years of poverty. Moreover, in 1945 the Government in London had passed a Colonial Development and Welfare Act, which for the first time gave the colonies money from Britain to carry out this kind of development. Under this Act, Kenya was given money from Britain to build the Royal Technical College at Nairobi, the Muslim Institute at Mombasa, and many secondary schools and teacher training colleges; and also for other things not connected with education. The Kenya Government appointed a Commission, the Beecher Commission, to advise it on how to improve its education. The Commission said that Kenya needed many more secondary schools for boys and girls (there was only one full secondary school for African boys, the Alliance High School, founded in 1926, and there was no full secondary school for African girls), and many more colleges to train teachers for primary schools. But it was not enough to train teachers in college; they needed help when they had left college and were teaching. There should be many more education officers and school supervisors to help the teachers in all schools.

It did not matter, the Commission said, whether teachers were working in Government schools, or in mission schools or independent schools; wherever they were working, they needed help, and they should have it.

In 1950, the Legislative Council accepted the advice of the Beecher Commission. The Government sent to Britain and appointed nearly forty British teachers to help the primary schools, and many more to teach in training colleges and in secondary schools. Between 1945 and 1958 the number of trained primary school teachers rose from 1,980 to 10,500; and while in 1945 there was one African secondary school with 400 pupils, in 1958 there were 31 African secondary schools with 4,500. The numbers of children in primary and middle schools too rose very greatly. But these numbers would have risen in any case; the importance of the Beecher report is that it did so much to raise the quality of the schools.

But there were many things in Kenya which were very bad, and which the Government could not hope to put right by bringing more teachers or officials from Britain. European medicine, both for people and for animals, had stopped much of the disease which used to kill, and so there was a great increase in population, both of men and of cattle. Some of the land in the African reserves was being ruined because too many crops were being grown and too many cattle were grazing. Africans would not change their old ways of farming; they would not listen to the advice of Government agricultural officers, because they thought the Government wanted to take away their land. Thousands of young men left the land altogether and came to Nairobi or other towns to look for work. There was not enough work for them, and there were not enough houses for them to live in. They could not bring their wives and children; even those who did find work could often not afford to rent a place to sleep in, and they slept where they could, under verandahs or in buses. But they could not go back home to the old-fashioned life of the village and tell their people that they had failed, that city life was too hard for them. To live like this, out of work and poor and without a home while all round you are other people who are busy and happy and comfortable, is one of the hardest things in the world to endure. We must not be surprised if some of these young men came to think that it was not their fault that they were poor, but that all the world was against them: the Government, the Nairobi City Council, the Asian and European business men who would not give them work, their own chiefs and elders in the village who were content with the old ways and did not understand the modern world, the European farmers with their long grass and their fat cattle. They felt angry; if this hard world would not make a place for them, they would break it to pieces. And so the Mau Mau began.

The Mau Mau was a movement among the Kikuyu and two other tribes, the Meru and the Embu, who were related to the Kikuyu and lived near them. Nobody knows what the name means; it was first used by the Government in 1949. The Mau Mau movement began among the Kikuyu of the country districts as well as among those of Nairobi. Some of the members of the Kikuyu Independent Schools Association, including the chairman, were glad to have their schools helped by the Government, as the Beecher Commission advised. But there was a part of the Association, called the Kikuyu Karang'a, which wanted to have nothing to do with the Government. As time went on, the Kikuyu Karang'a became stronger; in August 1950 it was able to remove the chairman of the Association from this position; and before long it was able to get most of the Kikuyu Independent schools into its hands. This meant that the Kikuyu Karang'a schools turned their backs on the Government; they would not accept help or advice; and some of them were used to spread Mau Mau teaching.

But what was Mau Mau? It was opposed to the Government, opposed to Christianity, opposed to Europeans, opposed to the Kikuyu chiefs. It was a movement of some of the Kikuyu (and Meru and Embu) who were trying to get control of the rest of their people. The Kikuyu had had political societies before, but this was a society of a new kind. It believed in killing. Its leaders made the members take an oath to obey them and to kill anyone whom they were ordered to kill. There were many kinds of oath; like the old tribal oaths, they were based on fear of the old gods[1], but some of the oaths and the oath-taking ceremonies went far beyond anything in the old tribal life. The Mau Mau leaders did

[1] The general sense of the oath is, 'If I am ordered to kill someone and I do not obey, may the god of this oath kill me.' The person taking the oath really believes that the god will kill him, so he dares not disobey; and no doubt, if the god did not kill him, his fellow-members would.

not want their people merely to turn away from the Government back to the old tribal life; they wanted them to have no life except that of membership of Mau Mau and obedience to the Mau Mau leaders. They must say and do things which were so bad that neither the Kenya of today nor the Kikuyu of the past would have any place for them; Mau Maù would be their only home.

We must suppose that the Mau Mau leaders meant first to get control of the whole of the Kikuyu people, and then perhaps to turn the whole Kikuyu people against the Europeans and Asians, and the Government. But they never succeeded in getting control of all the Kikuyu. Many chiefs and elders opposed Mau Mau because they said it was an evil thing and against Kikuyu custom. Many young people opposed it because they too said it was an evil thing and against Christianity. Many Kikuyu teachers went on with their work although they had to sleep each night in a different place in the bush so as not to be killed by the Mau Mau. The Mau Mau killed over 30 Europeans, mostly farmers living alone far from their neighbours, and over twenty Asians, mostly in Nairobi. But it killed over 1,800 Africans. Two things beat the Mau Mau. One was that the Kikuyu and other African men formed a guard to defend their homes so that the Mau Mau could not come and get food there. The other was that police and soldiers from other parts of Kenya and from outside the country came to help this home guard. Together they drove the Mau Mau into the bush and hunted them until all the leaders were killed or taken and the rest gave up the fight. It took four years, from 1952 to 1956; and it took a great deal of money and labour which might have been spent better. The Mau Mau did not shake the Kenya Government; but it made the country much poorer in money, and poorer too by the death of many good men.

KENYA SINCE THE MAU MAU

The Mau Mau danger ended in 1956, when the last important leader in the bush was taken; but it was not till 1960 that the Government ended the state of emergency[1] which it had declared

---

[1] An emergency is a sudden great danger. The Government in 1952 declared that Kenya was in a state of such emergency that it must have special powers to do things, and to do them quickly, which in ordinary times the law would allow it to do only slowly, or not at all.

in 1952 when the Mau Mau began. Since the ending of the Mau Mau, there are two subjects of interest in Kenya history: one is what the Government is doing to remedy the evils which caused some of the Kikuyu to start the Mau Mau. The other is Kenya's progress towards self-government. We will take them one by one.

So you think that the Mau Mau had something to complain about?

Certainly they had something to complain about. There were many things in Kenya that needed putting right. But what the Mau Mau did was no way to put them right. If a man has no work, no house, no land, and thinks that Africans ought to have more power in the Government, he cannot change these things by burning schools and villages and killing 1,800 Kikuyu men and women.

Some of the things in Kenya that needed putting right were things which the Government had wanted to change before Mau Mau, but had been unable to. Now, when all Kenya was thankful that the Mau Mau trouble was over, the Government hoped that people would allow it to make changes which they would not have allowed before. We have mentioned[1] the East Africa Royal Commission of 1953-55. That Commission, which included one African member, Chief Kidaha Makwaia of Tanganyika, went up and down Kenya in the middle of the Mau Mau trouble; and its report gave the East African Governments a great deal of advice on what the country needed if it were to enter the modern world. The report contains nearly 500 conclusions and recommendations[2]; and it will take the East African Governments a long time to work them all out.

The most important changes concern the land. European farmers in Kenya have used their land mainly to produce crops for sale; Africans have had their family land scattered in small pieces among the land of other families, and have used it to grow food. As long as land is scattered in this way, no one can improve his farming. The Kikuyu, moreover, did not live in villages but in houses dotted in ones and twos all over the farm land, so that it

[1] See page 137.
[2] A conclusion is an opinion which you form after hearing evidence and arguments. The first 25 chapters of the report contain the arguments; chapter 26, on pages 390–433, is a list of the conclusions and recommendations. The evidence is not published.

L

was impossible to provide water or electricity supplies and make life on the land more comfortable. During the Mau Mau troubles, the Government forced the Kikuyu to come and live together in villages, which could be surrounded with a fence and guarded against the Mau Mau. The villages can be provided with schools and community centres, and with piped water or even electricity. The cattle can be kept in kraals and the fields manured. Not only this. Many African farmers, not only among the Kikuyu but among other peoples, have come to see that it is a good thing to have one large farm instead of many small ones. In 1959, the Legislative Council passed the Native Lands Registration Ordinance and the Land Control (Native Lands) Ordinance. These laws made it possible for African farmers to exchange their small pieces of land with one another so that each has all his land together in one piece; then each man can be given a written certificate of his land. This would have pleased Harry Thuku[1]. When a man has all his land in one piece, he can farm as he likes; he can grow coffee or other crops for export, as the Europeans do, or he can grow food to sell in Nairobi market. The Government has a scheme to train Africans to farm in this modern way, and many Africans are now making a very good living from their agriculture. We have seen on page 153 that there are schemes for settling successful African farmers on land in the Highlands which used to be reserved for Europeans but is reserved no longer. In September 1961 there were already about 145,000 African farmers who had been given written certificates for their land.

In the last few years, Kenya has been making great progress towards self-government. In 1948 the Legislative Council was changed so that it had an unofficial majority. Three years later, just before the Mau Mau began, a new step was taken. The Government in London increased the size of the Legislative Council: there were to be six African members instead of four; six Asians instead of five; two Arabs, as before; and 14 elected Europeans instead of 11. The 16 official members should be increased to 26; one at least of them should be an Arab. Thus there would still be an unofficial majority of two. The six African members would all be nominated by the Governor, the six Asians

---

[1] We have seen on page 155 that Harry Thuku and his young men complained that Europeans were given written certificates for the land they held, but that Africans could not have them.

all elected; one of the two unofficial Arab members would be elected and the other nominated.

In March 1954 the new Secretary of State, Mr Lyttelton, proposed very much bigger changes: not merely in the membership of the Legislative Council but in the form of government. The real power of the government should be put into the hands of a Council of Ministers: the Governor and the deputy Governor, six official Ministers, and six Ministers chosen from the unofficial members of the Legislative Council; one African, two Asian, and three European. In addition to the Ministers, there should be at least three under-secretaries, one Arab and two Africans.

What was to happen to the Governor's executive council?

The executive council would continue to exist. It would consist of all the 14 members of the Council of Ministers, with one more Arab and two more Africans. Thus, there could never be any disagreement between the Council of Ministers and the executive council. All the Ministers and Under-Secretaries, said Mr Lyttelton, must be members of the Legislative Council. A general election would be held, though it could not be held until the fight againt the Mau Mau was over. Meanwhile, the Ministers would be appointed by the Governor. If, when the election was held, the voters elected these men as Ministers, the new constitution would continue; if not, the proposals would fall to the ground. If the new constitution did continue as a result of the election, there would be no more changes before 1960, either in the balance between the races, or in the balance between officials and unofficials.

Those were the Lyttelton proposals. The question was, what would the politicians say to them?

The Arabs accepted them. The Asians too accepted them, though they said that they thought the Africans should have more than one Minister. As for the Europeans, they were divided. Mr Michael Blundell and seven other unofficial members accepted them; three more said that they would accept them if those who had elected them to the Legislative Council agreed; the remaining three said No.

But the Africans said that the proposals were not good enough. It was not enough to give only one Ministry to an African; there should be two African Ministers, if not three. And they thought that the Ministers of agriculture, local government, health, and works should be officials, who could be trusted to be fair to all races: not European elected members, who (the Africans said) would do more for their own people than for people of other races.

In April 1954 the new Government was set up, though the Mau Mau was still going on and elections could not be held until September 1956. The six unofficial Ministers were appointed by the Governor: Mr Blundell and two other Europeans, two Asians, and one African, Mr B.A.Ohanga, who was appointed Minister of Community Development. At the same time, as Mr Lyttelton proposed, two more Africans and one Arab were appointed to the Governor's executive council.

When the new Government was formed, Mr Blundell and five of his European friends in the Council formed the United Country Party. They said that there were three opinions among the Europeans over the Lyttelton proposals. Some thought that Kenya should be mainly ruled by the Europeans. Others thought that the country should be divided into European, Asian, and African areas, each area self-governing. There was a third group which thought that Kenya should be governed as a whole by a government which included Kenyans of all races. We, said the United Country Party, belong to this third group. We will work for a truly multiracial government which will be fair to all people in Kenya. We will oppose anyone who wants to divide Kenya into racial areas, or to consider a man's race before deciding to give him power. And lastly, we will do all we can to help Africans to take a bigger share in the work of government.

In February 1956, the Council passed a law to enable Africans to elect their members to the Legislative Council. The idea behind the law was that the vote should be given only to a man who had shown himself to be a man of good sense; and a very good man should be given more votes than one. The law said that to be given the vote, a man must be 21 years old, and must also satisfy one of these seven conditions: (i) he has finished an intermediate school course; (ii) he has a degree or a diploma or some professional certificate; (iii) he has an income of £ 120 a year or has property worth £ 500; (iv) he has served the Government or some other employer for many years; (v) he is 45 years old, or is an elder of his people; (vi) he has received a decoration from the

Government; (vii) he is, or has been, a member of the Legislative Council or of some other government body. If a man satisfied more than one of these conditions, he might be given extra votes up to three. Voting was to be by secret ballot.[1]

The elections were held between September 1956 and March 1957. There were three European parties; the United Country Party, the Independent Group and the Federal Independence Party. The Independent Group wanted Ministers to be chosen without considering their race; this would probably have meant that there would be no African Ministers, because at that time the Europeans and Asians were better educated and more experienced than the Africans. The F.I.P. wanted Kenya to be a federation of self-governing racial areas.

What about African political parties?

African political parties were having a difficult time because of the Mau Mau. Politics began, as we have seen, among the Kikuyu. Harry Thuku's Young Kikuyu Association was followed by the Kikuyu Central Association, of which Jomo Kenyatta became president in 1922, and in 1929 Mr Kenyatta came to Britain on behald of the K.C.A. to put forward the Kikuyu complaints over the land question. From 1931 to 1947 Mr Kenyatta lived in Britain; these were the years of poverty and of war, during which there was very little political activity among the Kikuyu. At that time, as we have seen, the Kikuyu leaders were putting their main work into their independent schools. In 1947 Mr Kenyatta came back to Kenya and took charge of the K.C.A. once more. The Association soon changed itself into the Kenya National Union, trying to unite all Africans, and not to be merely a Kikuyu organization. But when Mau Mau began, the K.N.U. was stopped by the Government because it was supposed to be connected with the Mau Mau. Mr Kenyatta himself and some of the leaders of the K.N.U. were tried on a charge of being connected with the Mau Mau; they were found guilty and imprisoned, and after their imprisonment they were sent to live in the north of Kenya, well away from Kikuyu country.

In December 1955 there was a meeting in Nairobi which was

[1] Voting by secret ballot is voting by marking a paper and putting it into a box so that nobody can tell how you have voted. This system was introduced in England in 1872; before then, voters had to show openly how they were voting.

attended by Africans from many tribes. The meeting formed a new party, to replace the K.N.U., called the Kenya African National Congress. But the Government at once said that it could not allow the new party: because until the Mau Mau trouble was over there must be no African political parties covering the whole of Kenya, only district parties.

Why did the Government say there must be no African political parties covering the whole of Kenya?

Because the Government was afraid that the Mau Mau leaders might use such a party as a way of making their plans. The Government knew that the Mau Mau leaders were trying to get the Kamba and others to join their movement; and if there were political meetings held up and down the country, it would make things easier for the Mau Mau. Let us finish with the Mau Mau first, said the Government; and then we will see.

So the result of all this was that when the 1956 elections came on, there were no properly organized African political parties. But that of course did not stop Africans from being elected, or from acting together as a group after they had been elected.

In the elections, six out of the eight Africans who had sat in the old Council were defeated, including the Minister, Mr Ohanga. The leader of the new African members was Mr Tom Mboya, who was general secretary of the Kenya Federation of Labour. Among the Europeans, the Independent Group won eight of the 14 seats, and the U.C.P. won the other six; the F.I.P. did not win a seat. The new Council was made up like this:

	Elected	Corporate	Nominated	Ex-officio	Total
European	14	2	15	7	38
Asian	6	–	2	–	8
Arab	1	–	1	1	3
African	8	–	2	–	10
	29	2	20	8	59

The two corporate members were elected to represent commerce and agriculture. Counting the elected and the corporate members together, the Council had not merely an unofficial majority, but an elected majority of three over the nominated and ex-officio members.

When the Council met, all the eight African elected members said that they regarded the Lyttelton constitution (under which the Council had been elected) as dead, and they would take no part in the work of government. They said that their constituencies[1] were so large and so many of their voters were illiterate, that an African elected member could not possibly keep in close touch with all his voters and explain things to them, as he should do. They wanted smaller constituencies; which would mean, they said, 15 more constituencies and so 15 more elected African members. Also, they said, they could not agree to Mr Lyttelton's proposal that there should be no more changes until 1960[2], four years ahead. So the Government had to be set up without an African Minister.

So matters stood from March to October 1957: the Africans would not help, and the Government was in an impossible position. In October 1957 the new Secretary of State, Mr Lennox-Boyd, came from London to Kenya to discuss the position. The African leaders told him that they wanted five things: (i) All adults should have the vote, and each should have only one vote; (ii) elections should be held on a common roll; (iii) all empty land in the highlands should be opened to African farmers, either to separate families or to co-operative societies; (iv) there should be eight years schooling for every child; (v) Africans should have a bigger share in local government.

After hearing what every party in Kenya had to tell him, Mr Lennox-Boyd decided that the Lyttelton constitution would not work, and he made new proposals of his own. He proposed: (i) there should be 14 elected African members instead of eight; (ii) there should be two African Ministers instead of one, and four unofficial European Ministers instead of three; (iii) there should be twelve new non-Government seats in the Legislative Council, four each for European, Asian and African members; these twelve members should be elected by the Legislative Council itself; (iv) if the Legislative Council were in future to be made still bigger, all the new seats should be filled by elections on a common roll; there should be no more new communal seats; (v)

[1] A constituency is a district whose voters elect a member to represent them.
[2] See page 179.

there should be a new body called the Council of State, whose work would be to examine all new laws and say whether they were unfair to any race; if they were, the Government would be bound to re-consider them; (vi) the Governor's executive council should be abolished and its powers should pass to the Council of Ministers.

The Asians and most of the Europeans accepted the Lennox-Boyd proposals. But the Africans would not. Mr Mboya made a speech, in which he said: (i) it was unfair that six million Africans should be represented by the same number of elected members as 50,000 Europeans; (ii) since most of the members of the Legislative Council were Europeans, the four extra Africans who were to be elected by the Council itself would be elected mainly by European votes, and so would not really represent African opinion; (iii) he saw no need for a Council of State.

In spite of this African opposition, the Government went forward with the Lennox-Boyd proposals. In January 1958 a bill was introduced to increase the number of elected African members from eight to 14. The African members of the Legislative Council would take no part in discussing the Bill, but it was passed without them. In April the new constitution came into force. All the African candidates disliked it, and when they were elected and the new Council was to elect twelve new members, they would take no part in the election. But twelve members were elected according to the Lennox-Boyd proposals: four Africans, four Asians, and four Europeans. In May, the Council of State was set up, consisting of a chairman and ten members from all races, none of them members of the Legislative Council.

In June, Mr Mboya asked the Secretary of State to give the Africans more than 14 elected members, to make more changes in the Council of Ministers, and to drop the Council of State. Mr Lennox-Boyd said No to this. He asked the Africans to join the new Legislative Council and the Council of Ministers and help to carry on the Government: and while they were doing this, to discuss with the Governor and the other groups in Kenya and try and agree on the next step forward towards self-government.

The Africans did not like this idea. They said that a proper conference would be better, a conference called by the Secretary of State with the object of drawing up a new constitution which all could accept. At the end of January 1959, Mr Ronald Ngala, who was secretary of the African elected members' organization, said that until the Secretary of State agreed to the idea of such a constitutional conference, all the African members of Council would stay away from its meetings and take no part in the work of government; and Mr S.G. Amin, who was president of the Kenya Indian Congress, said that the Asian members would do the same. For the next three months they all stayed away; and then at the end of April, a group of Council members (four Africans, three Asians, and an Arab, led by Mr Oginga Odinga) went to London and talked to the Secretary of State, and he promised that there should be a constitutional conference of the kind the Africans wanted before the 1960 elections. Mr Oginga Odinga said this was satisfactory; 'we are moving in the right direction', he said. Mr Michael Blundell also approved.

Why was the Government in London so slow in agreeing to the idea of a constitutional conference?

There are two different points of view here. The Africans thought that the Kenya Government was too much under the control of the Europeans in Kenya, and that the Kenya Europeans would do all they could to keep the Africans from getting any more political power. They therefore wanted to reach an agreement with the Government in London which that Government would compel the Kenya Government and the Kenya Europeans to accept. They thought that this was possible, for they knew that the Government in London had already given self-government to Africans in Ghana and the Sudan, and would soon be giving it to Nigeria and Sierra Leone. That is the African point of view.

But there is an English point of view. Englishmen are more interested in seeing how something works than in looking to see how it is made. When Africans say that the Lyttelton constitution will not work, and the Lennox-Boyd constitution will not work, any Englishman will reply, 'But you have not tried them!' The work of government is not easy, and it has to be learnt with practice. If the 14 elected African members and two African Ministers took their share in the work, it need not stop the Africans from asking for a bigger share. All Governments make mistakes, and the more practice Ministers have, the fewer mistakes they will make. Meanwhile, it is not wise to give more power to people who refuse to use the power they already have.

That was how the position seemed to most Englishmen. They did not understand why Africans in Kenya would not do as Dr Nkrumah had done in Ghana. The Legislative Council in Ghana had been given an unofficial majority in 1946, and there were new constitutions in 1951, 1952, and 1954, each a step towards full independence, which came in 1957. Dr Nkrumah in Ghana did not like the 1951 constitution; but he agreed to work it, and he worked it so well that in six years time his country was independent.

That is why the Government in London was slow in agreeing to the idea of a constitutional conference.

But why was the British Government unwilling to agree to the idea of 'One man, one vote'? That is surely a better form of government than one in which most people have no vote, and some have more than one vote? 'One man, one vote' is the rule in Britain itself.

It would take a long time to discuss this question fully. No country yet has had a perfect government, in which (i) all the people holding power are wise and good, (ii) all the voters are well educated and understand the questions on which they have to vote, (iii) all the voters use their votes wisely and unselfishly. A vote is a good thing if it is wisely used. If a man really has good reasons for preferring party A to party B, it is good that he should have a vote and be able to choose between them. But if he does not know one party from another: or if he is afraid to vote for the party he prefers: or if he simply votes for the party which makes him the biggest promises – in cases like these he is not using his vote wisely.

If we cannot yet have the perfect government, there is something to be said in favour of two kinds of imperfect government. When most people are poor and uneducated, you may say that you will give votes only to those who seem likely to understand politics, and even perhaps more votes than one to those who understand best. This is especially the case where many of the Ministers too are inexperienced, as nearly all of them – Europeans and Asians, as well as Africans – were in Kenya. Then you will hope that sensible voters will prevent an inexperienced Government from making many bad mistakes.

It is different when the Government is very experienced, when everyone can read, and when there are plenty of newspapers and radio, so that people have opportunities of discussing politics with understanding. Then you may say that everyone should have the vote, because everyone ought to be able to use it wisely. This is the position in Britain today, where, as you say, the rule is, 'One man, one vote'.

But Britain has only come to this position recently. There were laws in 1832, 1867, 1884, 1918, and 1927 which gave the vote to more and more people; and since 1927 each man and woman in Britain has had a vote. But it was only in 1948 that a law was passed which took away from university graduates the second vote which they held; so it is only since 1948 that Britain has reached the position of 'One man, one vote'.

We cannot say that 'One man, one vote' is always the best form of government. It depends on the condition of the country; and the British Government may have been right in thinking that 'One man, one vote' was not the best form of government for Kenya in 1960.

THE LANCASTER HOUSE CONFERENCE

It was only in July 1959 that the Government said it would allow political parties to be formed covering the whole country. Even then, it made one condition: it would not allow any party which was openly racial. At that time, the elected members of the Council had divided into three groups. The United Country Party had become the New Kenya Group under Mr Blundell, still working for multi-racial government. Four elected European members refused to join the Group, saying that they wanted no African farmers in the highlands, no inter-racial schools, and no common electoral roll. The third group was the Constituency Elected Members Organization, led by Dr Kiano: it included all 14 elected African members, six Asians, one Arab, and one European. It agreed with the New Kenya Group in wanting a multi-racial government, but it thought that the New Kenya Group would be too slow and gentle in working for it. The African members in the C.E.M.O. wanted (i) twelve more elected African members, (ii) all parties to be multi-racial, and (iii) Ministers to be responsible to a multi-racial electorate. We must remember that at that time, the Council of Ministers was not responsible to the electorate; it was responsible to the Governor. If the Legislative Council disapproved of the policy of any Minister, or of the whole Government, it could not make the Minister or the Government resign.

When the Government gave permission for new parties to be formed, the New Kenya Group changed its name to the New Kenya Party. The group of four European members who disagreed with the N.K.P. called itself the United Party. The C.E.M.O. set up the Kenya National Party, though Dr Kiano and Mr Mboya and a few other African members left it and set up a new party of their own. The Kenya National Party, under Mr Masinde Muliro, had as its chief aim the common electoral roll. It wanted the seats which were reserved for one race or another to be gradually opened to candidates of any race, until by 1968, all seats would be elected filled by candidates elected on a common roll under a system of 'One man, one vote'.

Mr Mboya, Dr Kiano and their friends tried to form a party called the Kenya Independence Movement. Their policy was: (i) the common roll, (ii) land in the highlands was to be opened to Africans[1], (iii) no more European farmers were to be allowed to come into Kenya to settle, (iv) all British military bases were to be removed, (v) Jomo Kenyatta and all who were in prison or in camp because they had been connected with Mau Mau should be set free. But the Government said that the K.I.M. was openly racial, and so it would not register it as a party.

The constitutional conference which the Africans had been asking for was held at Lancaster House in London in January and February 1960. The constitution to which the members of the conference[2] agreed by a large majority was this: (i) The Legislative Council would have 65 elected members, 53 of them elected on a common roll and 12 elected (four from each race) by the Council itself, as under the Lennox-Boyd scheme. Of the 53 elected members, twenty were reserved for different races: ten European, eight Asian, two Arab. In these twenty constituencies, there would have to be two elections. In the first election, candidates would have to get at least 25 per cent of the votes belonging to the voters of their own race. For example, in an Asian consti-

[1] It was opened next year: see page 152.
[2] The United Party would not accept the new constitution.

tuency, an Asian candidate must first show that 25 per cent of the Asian voters in the constituency have voted for him. Then, all candidates in that constituency who have been able to show this will go through a second election, in which all voters, of all races, will take part. (ii) The vote would be given to all adult Kenyans who could satisfy one of these conditic ns: they could read and write in their mother-tongue, they were 40 years old, they had an income of £ 75 a year, or they had held office. (iii) The Council of Ministers would consist of four officials and eight unofficials: four African, three European, and one Asian. (iv) The judges must not be controlled by the Government. (v) There would be a Bill of Rights, that is to say a list of rights which belonged to every Kenyan and which no Kenya Government must take away. One of these rights was the right to keep his property.

But this Lancaster House constitution is not yet responsible government.

No, it was not responsible government because the Governor could still nominate Ministers, and in any case four of the twelve were not elected members of the Legislative Council. Still, it was a step forward. Mr Ronald Ngala said that the constitution 'falls short of African hopes, but a big step forward has been taken.' The Africans would not be fully content with anything but 'One man, one vote', without any conditions; and they did not like the idea that European farms might be regarded as European property and protected by the Bill of Rights, so that the Kenya Government could not touch them. This, they feared, might mean that it would be difficult to get land in the highlands for African farmers.

However, everyone agreed that the new constitution was an advance; and Dr Kiano, Mr Ngala and Mr Muimi became Ministers in a new Government which was to hold office till the elections in February 1961.

Before the elections, two new parties were formed. One was the Kenya African National Union. Its president was Mr James Gichuru, who had been president of the Kenya African Union in 1944 while Mr Kenyatta was in Britain, but had resigned to let Mr Kenyatta take his place in 1947 when he came back. The secretary of the party was Mr Mboya. The party's main strength was among the Kikuyu.

A few weeks later, several small groups came together to form the Kenya African Democratic Union, with Mr Ngala as president and Mr Masinde Muliro as vice-president. The five groups were: the Kenya National Party, which had turned out its non-African members and re-named itself the Kenya African People's Party; the Masai United Party; the Coast African Political Union; the Somali National Association; and the Kalenjin Political Alliance, which was made up of several peoples (the Suk, Kipsigis, and others) speaking similar languages.

The new Legislative Council of 53 members was elected in February 1961. This is the strength of the parties:

KANU	16 (all African)
KADU	10 (all African)
New Kenya Party	4 (all European)
Kenya Coalition	3 (all European)
Kenya Indian Congress	3 (all Asian)
Kenya Freedom Party	1 (Asian)
Independent	16 (different races; two support KANU)

Next month, the twelve extra members (called 'national members') were elected by the Council. All the four Europeans belonged to the New Kenya Party; of the four Africans, three belonged to KADU and one to KANU. In August 1961, Mr Kenyatta was set free, and soon afterwards he became president of KANU, Mr Gichuru giving up his place to him as he had done fourteen years before.

Now that Mr Kenyatta was back, the whole situation in Kenya politics was changed. He was so outstanding among the African leaders in Kenya that politics without him had seemed unreal. Even his political opponents of KADU recognised his greatness.

Mr Kenyatta's problem was to unite the people of Kenya into one nation. He had to convince the Asians and Europeans that they had nothing to fear if they gave up their separate claims. He had also to convince the other African tribes that they had nothing to fear from his own people the Kikuyu. It was this fear which gave KADU its strength. It would be dangerous if Kenya politics became a struggle for power between the Kikuyu and the rest. Mr Kenyatta proposed to solve this tribal problem by making Kenya, like Uganda, a federal state: the regions would have enough powers of self-government to take away their fear that they would be at the mercy of a central government under Kikuyu control. He began more talks with the British Government to work out a new federal constitution for Kenya, and in 1963 the new constitution was ready.

The legislative council of 53 members was replaced by a parliament of two Houses: a Senate of 41 and a House of Representatives of 129. The Senate would represent the 41 districts; the House of Representatives would be elected by the voters. They would elect 117 members, and these 117 would elect twelve more, as in the Lancaster House scheme. But there was a great difference. Nothing was said about race, and if the 117 members chose to do so, they could elect twelve more Africans. There were no reserved seats. There were to be six regions. The coastal strip was to be taken over from the Sultan of Zanzibar, and he was to be given compensation. The constitution listed some powers which were reserved to the regions, and others which either the regional or the federal government might exercise.

The elections under the new constitution were held in May 1963. There were three parties: KANU and KADU, and a third party called the African People's Party, led by Mr Ngei. The APP supported KADU. The result of the elections was that the Senate had 20 KANU members and 18 from the Opposition; the House of Representatives had 67 from KANU, 40 from the Opposition, and five independent members.

But that makes only 38 in the Senate instead of 41, and only 112 in the House of Representatives instead of 117. What about the others?

The three empty seats in the Senate and the five in the House of Representatives were all in the northern region, which was mainly inhabited by Somali people. The Somali chiefs and people held a meeting before the elections and decided to take no part in them. They did not want to belong to Kenya, they wanted to be allowed to join Somalia, which had been independent since 1960. But the Kenya Government was not willing to hand over part of its northern region to Somalia.

After the elections, the 112 members of the House of Representatives elected the twelve additional members. They elected eleven
members of KANU, including two Asians and two Europeans,
and one European member of KADU. Politics in Kenya had now
become multi-racial; Kenya was independent, and Mr Kenyatta
was prime minister.

After the elections, Mr Ngei and his APP changed sides and
came over to support the KANU Government. In December 1964
there was another change in the constitution: Kenya became a
republic, with Mr Kenyatta as president. The 1963 constitution
had already given Kenya its independence; it was no more
independent with Mr Kenyatta as president than it had been
with him as prime minister. But the Kenya people liked it better
so. When the republic was proclaimed, Mr Ngala the KADU
leader did a great thing. He dissolved his party and led his supporters over to join the Government. He did so, he said, 'to
strengthen the national front and to speak with one voice on all
issues that confront our nation. We consider the cause of Kenya
to be greater than any of our personal pride, gains or losses.
This is one of the times when we must be prepared to sacrifice our
political dignity for the peace and harmony of Kenya.'

(For exercises on this chapter see page 247)

4

Tanganyika and Tanzania

Most of what we know about the history of East Africa has come from books written by strangers from other parts of the world who have visited the country. As we saw in Book One (page 18) there are different kinds of historical evidence: *first*, books or letters or other writings; *second*, accounts given by word of mouth; *third*, historical remains. So far, none of these three kinds of evidence has given us very much help in the early history of East Africa. In the Western Sudan, we can learn a good deal, though not as much as we should like, from books like the *Tarikh-es-Sudan*, written by Africans about their own history. But there are no books or writings of any kind which have come down to us from the interior of East Africa. The East African peoples can tell us something of their own history by word of mouth, but it does not take us very far back: never further back than about 1500 AD, and often not as far.

It looks as if the most important kind of historical evidence for the early history of East Africa will be the third kind of evidence, historical remains. But we are only just beginning to study the historical remains of East Africa; no doubt there are remains which have not yet been found, and perhaps the remains which have already been found will tell us more when they have been more carefully studied. Although we have found stone tools, stone walls and towns, canals, wells, roads, and terraces for agriculture, we have found hardly any human remains; and without these we cannot know what sort of people made these stone buildings, or what sort of life they lived.

In East Africa, as in West Africa and Europe, there were people long ago who used arrow-heads, axes, knives, and other tools of stone. This stone age lasted for thousands of years; in East Africa it began perhaps 500,000 years ago and ended less than two thousand years ago. During that long time, people learned to

M

improve their stone tools very much; and no doubt they improved their civilisation in other ways. We have found very few bones to tell us what the people looked like; and although we have found thousands of their stone tools, we know nothing of the tools they made of wood, or of their clothes or their houses. The oldest stone tools in East Africa are older than any in Europe. When the first stone tools were being made in East Africa, the Sahara was a green country with big rivers, and Africa was joined to Europe through Spain and Italy.

Let us jump from these first men, of whom we know so little, to a time which is almost like yesterday, about 7,000 years ago. Most of the people then living in East Africa were people rather like the Bushmen of South Africa today, small men who lived by hunting, who did not grow crops or keep cattle. But about 7,000 years ago, two new kinds of men appeared in East Africa. One was the Hamite, the other was the Negro. No one knows where these two races began: perhaps in the green country which is now the Sahara desert, perhaps in North-East Africa or Arabia. We do not know which race is the older, and we do not know exactly when they began; we have suggested 7,000 years ago, but they may be older than that. Most of the African peoples of today are descended from these three races, Bushman, Negro and Hamite. The Bushman was certainly the first, and filled up the whole of East and South Africa; the other two moved slowly after him, taking many hundreds of years on the journey. It is only 200 years since the Bantu met the Dutch at the Cape.

About 6000 BC, people in Western Asia – perhaps in Syria or Iraq – made a great jump forward in civilisation. Until then, men had gone out to hunt for meat, and women had gone out to search for fruit and roots and leaves and insects to eat. Now, they began to plant food crops and to keep cattle. This change meant that they had more food, and had less trouble in getting it; they were able to stay longer in one place, and had more time to spend on other matters besides the business of finding food. It was not long before they invented the arts of making clay pots and of using metals. Once these arts were invented, they spread to other parts of the world: southwards into Africa and westwards into Europe, as well as into the east of Asia. Between 4500 BC and 4000 BC, agriculture and cattle-keeping spread along the banks of the Nile, and later, they spread into East and Central Africa.

Pottery and agriculture began in Britain about 2500 BC. Here are some of the dates shown in a table:

	Agriculture	Bronze	Iron
First invented	6000	5000	1500
Reached Britain	2500	1900	500
Reached East Africa	2000?	–	100 AD
Reached West Africa	?	1200	300 BC

But this table of dates raises questions. First of all: since all the dates are rough, and none is exact, why do you put a special? after the date when agriculture reached East Africa?

For two reasons. One reason is that East Africa is a big country, and agriculture may have begun in one part of it long before it began in another. The other reason is that we know agriculture began in Egypt about 4500 BC, and we must allow some time for it to spread south. In Kenya and in Northern Rhodesia there were stone age peoples from about 3000 BC onwards who did not practise agriculture when they first settled, but did later on. But how much later on, we do not know. So we guess about 2000 BC; it may have been somewhat earlier.

And why is there no date for the beginning of agriculture in West Africa?

Because we know nothing about the life of the people of West Africa at that time. If Negroes brought agriculture from Egypt, it cannot have begun in West Africa till long after 4500 BC, but we have no evidence at all.

Why is there no date for bronze in East Africa?

East Africa had no copper, and the first metal it knew was iron. In Europe and in West Africa there was a long bronze age before the iron age began; but East Africa went straight from stone to iron. When the Bantu got as far south as Rhodesia and the Transvaal, they found both copper and gold, and they mined for both; but they had no bronze age.

Both in Europe and in Africa, these new arts made it possible for people to live more settled lives, to eat better food, and to develop their civilization. So both in Europe and in Africa, tribes began to grow bigger, richer, and stronger. Instead of living as the Bushmen did, in parties of fifty or a hundred, people began to live in tribes of several hundreds or even thousands. This led to fighting, in which the large tribes with bronze or iron weapons beat the small tribes with stone weapons. Africa began to fill up with peoples of different kinds. Bushman, Negro and Hamite peoples were moving about over East Africa, meeting and fighting each other, and often joining together to from new peoples.

About 1000 BC, Negro and Hamite peoples mixing together formed a new race, the Bantu. Like other peoples, the Bantu increased in numbers, and split into many tribes. They moved southward, driving the Bushmen before them, and filled up the whole of Central and Southern Africa from the Great Lakes to the Indian and Atlantic Oceans. The Bantu practised agriculture, kept cattle, and used iron. About 500 AD there grew up a Bantu civilization in East and Central Africa, which lasted a thousand years, till about 1500. It was not one large kingdom like Songhai, but was made up of several different states, which sometimes fought against one another. But just as the civilization of the Western Sudan was one civilization, whether Ghana or Mali or Songhai was the ruling power, so the Bantu civilization of East and Central Africa was one, whichever Bantu state happened to be the strongest.

These Bantu people built in stone. At Engaruka, near Lake Natron in north Tanganyika, there are the remains of a town with over 6,000 stone houses, and at Zimbabwe and other places far away to the south in Southern Rhodesia, they built not only stone houses but also very large stone buildings. They dug deep wells through solid rock to reach water beneath the rock. They cultivated steep hillsides, building stone walls to hold up the earth so that the rain should not wash it away. They built stone channels to carry water from a spring or a stream gently to their farms on the hill side. A few Bantu people in East Africa, the Chagga for example, still do this; but most have forgotten the art. They built roads, sometimes cutting through a hill and building an embankment over a swamp to keep the road dry and level. All this building in stone was possible because they had iron tools, which they made from the iron-stone which is found all over East Africa.

We do not yet know when all this work was done. One writer thinks that Engaruka may be only about 300 years old, another thinks it may be 2,000 years old. So far, we have found nothing.

there to help us to fix a date: no coin, or bead, or piece of pottery, not even a wooden door-post.

How would a wooden post help to fix the date?

Pieces of wood are helping to fix the date when Zimbabwe was built. Nowadays we have all heard of radio-activity. The atom bomb is dangerous, not only because of the force and heat of its explosion, but because of its fall-out, which goes on long after the noise and heat have ended. Every substance is made of atoms, and each atom is made of a nucleus and a number of electrons; some substances have more electrons in their atom, some have fewer. It is possible for the atoms of a substance to have more electrons than they can keep; when this happens, they throw out the spare electrons till they have the right number. This is what makes the fall-out from an atomic explosion dangerous: unwanted electrons are being thrown out and damaging our bodies.

In studying radio-activity, scientists have found that many substances exist in atoms of more than one kind. One such substance is carbon, of which every living body is made, whether of animals or of plants. Most carbon atoms have 12 electrons, but a few have 14; and carbon-14 atoms (sometimes called radio-carbon) are radio-active, throwing out the extra two electrons. Scientists have measured the number of carbon-14 atoms mixed with the ordinary atoms; and they have measured the rate at which the extra atoms are thrown out. Now every living thing uses carbon to build up its body, and goes on doing so until it dies. At the moment of death, therefore, its body is made up of a large number of ordinary carbon atoms[1] and a much smaller number of carbon-14 atoms. After death, the ordinary carbon atoms remain unchanged, but the carbon-14 atoms go on steadily throwing out their spare electrons, neither hurrying nor resting. If a scientist finds this dead thing – a bone, or a piece of wood, or a piece of cloth – a thousand or five thousand years later, he can measure how many carbon-14 atoms still remain radio-active. He knows how many there would have been when the thing was alive and growing, and he knows how long it must have taken for the whole number of carbon-14 atoms to be reduced to the number he finds still work-

[1] Besides carbon, living things use other substances: hydrogen and oxygen and others. But it is the carbon that interests us here.

ing. And so he can make a very good guess at the age of the dead thing — how long it is since it died.

At Zimbabwe, this carbon-14 test has been applied to two pieces of wood which were found. One of them is dated between 471 and 711 AD, the other between 610 and 794 AD. It looks as if Zimbabwe was built about 600 or 700 AD. But at Engaruka we have so far found nothing to test by the carbon-14 test.

It seems that the carbon-14 test is not very exact, if all it can say about the first piece of wood is that it was cut down some time during a stretch of 240 years.

No, the carbon-14 test cannot be exact. The bigger the pieces that we are given to test, the more exact we can be. But even this result at Zimbabwe is much better than anything we had before. All the objects found at Zimbabwe which could be dated — Chinese pottery, Indian beads and so forth — showed that the buildings were in use about 1400 and 1500 AD. Some people thought that Zimbabwe might have been built as long ago as 2000 BC, but nothing at all was found which could certainly be dated as long ago as that. Moreover, the style of the buildings suggested that they were built by Bantu people, perhaps about 800 or 1000 AD. But some people did not agree with that. And in any case, it may not be likely, but it is possible, that a building might stand for a thousand years or more without containing any object of that age to be found by later scientists; and that it might then stand for another thousand years, and during that latter time collect a number of objects which the scientists could date. In other words, the fact that all the beads and pieces of pottery and other objects found at Zimbabwe were young did not prove that the building itself was not much older. The scientists were only able to say that the building was probably not much more than a thousand years old; they could not say that it was certainly so. But now comes this carbon-14 dating, which — as far as it goes — is certain, not merely probable. The older of these two pieces of wood from the drainage cannot be older than 471 AD, the younger cannot be younger than 794 AD; somewhere between those two dates the building was put up and its drains were laid. Carbon-14 is helping historians all over the world to fix dates which had been uncertain. We hope that it will help us at other places in Africa as well as Zimbabwe.

At present, there is still — as in the case of Engaruka — a great deal of uncertainty about dates.

Let us suppose, then, until someone proves us wrong, that the Bantu civilization of East and Central Africa lasted roughly from 500 AD to 1500 AD, and that Engaruka, Zimbabwe, and many other ruined towns and buildings were part of it. Two questions then arise: *first*, How did it live? and *second*, Why did it die? We will take them one by one.

This iron-using, stone-building Bantu civilization did not use ships, except of course for small fishing canoes. It did not need ships of its own, for it was able to trade with other peoples who came to the East African coast by sea. There had been foreign sea-captains sailing their ships down the East African coast for very many years. From about 1000 BC onwards, there were strong and highly civilized kingdoms in the south of Arabia, whose people were great seamen. They traded with India as well as with Africa, and their countries became rich with the profits of the trade. Arabia, like the Sahara, may perhaps have been not quite so dry then as it is now, but it still was dry enough to make agriculture difficult. They took great care of their water; they built dams to store it, they built terraces on their hills and carried the water in channels; and like Egypt today, they kept the desert back by carrying water to their fields and gardens. The kingdom of Saba, or Sheba, whose queen visited king Solomon of Israel (about 950 BC) and brought him so much gold and spices and precious stones, was one of these kingdoms of southern Arabia.[1] We read that Solomon had his own ships, which brought gold from Ophir; and he made himself a great chair of ivory. The ivory must have come from Africa. We do not know where Ophir was; some think it was another kingdom of south Arabia, some think it was somewhere in India or further east, some think it was Sofala in Mozambique.

The Arabs were not the only seamen to trade in the Red Sea and the Indian Ocean. When Egypt was a great power, Egyptian ships too used to sail down the African coast and bring back spices and gold and ivory — and sometimes slaves. The Greeks too were great seamen, and we know that they used to come this way; the first of them is said to have sailed the Indian Ocean in 510 BC. We still have a sort of sea-captain's guide-book to the East

[1] See I Kings 9, vv 26–28; 10, vv 1, 2, 10, 18.

African coast which was written in Greek and published about 60 AD; it goes as far as a town called Rhapta, which was twenty-five days sailing from the mouth of the Red Sea. From Rhapta, it says it was fourteen days journey inland to a mountain covered with snow. This guide-book is called the *Periplus;* the word is Greek for 'going round'. It says that the African peoples do not form one large kingdom; you will find a separate chief at each market town. Some of them are independent, some of them are under the Arabian kingdoms. They import things made of iron, and they export a great deal of ivory and smaller amounts of other things, but no gold.

The *Periplus* tells us that the Arabs were not content to send their ships to a strange country. Like other trading nations, they wanted to have their own people living there to help their sea-captains, and so they had Arab agents living in the African ports, who often married African wives and learnt the local language. In this way, Arabs and Africans came to know each other, and the trade could be better organized.

So the trade went on for 1500 years or more. Like so many other things, the East African trade was changed by the coming of Islam. The Prophet died in 632 AD. There was much fighting in Arabia and Persia, and many Muslims who were defeated in the wars left their country and came to settle along the East African coast. This was a great change. Before then, the Arabs had lived in East Africa in much the same way as Englishmen live in Nigeria or India today: going there to work and make money, but not to govern. Now they were coming to settle and to govern. Often they settled on islands off the coast; Mombasa, Zanzibar, Mafia and Kilwa Kisiwani are islands which became the homes of Arab settlers. But they settled also on the mainland, for example at Mogadishu, Malindi, and Sofala far away in the south. For the Arabs, now that they were living in East Africa, were sending their ships further than Rhapta, which was the end of the *Periplus*. At Sofala, they found something else to buy besides ivory and tortoise-shell and rhinoceros horn. They had reached a country which was able to export large quantities of gold, and of iron. The writer of the *Periplus* found the people of what is now Somaliland and Kenya ready to import iron goods from Arabia; now, six or seven hundred years later, the Bantu of what is now Mozambique and Rhodesia had iron to spare for export.

And so there grew up all down the East African coast from the
Red Sea down to Sofala a trading civilization. The Arabs were
masters of the trading settlements, and in them, there grew up an
African society whose civilization was strongly influenced by
Arab civilization, and whose language, Swahili, shows this mixture of Bantu and Arab. The Arabs of the coast did not trouble
to learn much about the interior of the country. They were content to buy the iron, gold, ivory, tortoise-shell and other African
goods – sometimes slaves as well – and to sell to the Africans the
goods they received from over the sea: spices from Arabia and
Indonesia, cotton and silk from India and China, and Chinese
pottery. The Arab settlements became rich; and the Arabs spent
their riches in building beautiful stone houses and mosques, with
carved wooden doors and beautiful Chinese pottery hung on the
walls. Their buildings are different from those at Zimbabwe; it seems
as though Arab civilization did not much influence the Bantu civilization of the interior, at least as far as building is concerned.

There was no Arab empire. The different Arab towns were
independent, and sometimes they fought against one another;
and even when they were at peace, they were always competing
against one another for the trade. For a long time, Kilwa was the
most important town on the coast: from about 1100 to about
1350; the Sultan of Kilwa made his own copper money, which
was used up and down the coast as well as in Kilwa itself. But after
a time other towns became stronger and Kilwa was no longer the
richest or most powerful.

Much of what we know about the Arabs of the East Coast
comes from Arab writers. The first important writer is El Masudi,
who was born in Baghdad and died in 956 at Cairo. He visited
East Africa some time not long after 900, about a hundred years
before El Bekri[1] wrote about Ghana from what the traders told
him. El Masudi did not need to ask traders about East Africa;
he went to see the country for himself. He tells us not only about
the Arab towns on the coast, but about the powerful people of
the country behind Sofala. Their capital city was somewhere on the
Zambesi river. Their king was called the Waqlimi, which, says
El Masudi, means 'son of the great god'; his people chose him to
be king, but if he did not govern well, they killed him. The people
thought highly of good speaking. Although they called their king

[1] See Book One, pages 43, 44.

'son of the great god', most people did not worship the great god, but worshipped plants or animals or other such things – remember that this is a Muslim writing, who would not take much trouble to understand the religion of unbelievers. These people hunted elephants, but did not use the ivory themselves; they sold it to the Arabs. They also had plenty of gold and iron; they used both, but had plenty to sell to the Arabs as well. They kept cattle, and used them not only for meat and milk, but for carrying loads. El Masudi tells us that the ivory was mostly sent to Oman in Arabia, from where it was carried further on to India and China.

Two hundred years after El Masudi, we hear about the East African trade from another Arab writer, Edrisi. He was born in Spain when the Almoravides[1] were ruling it, and he wrote his book about 1154. Unlike El Masudi, Edrisi does not seem to have been down the East Coast himself; but he is a most careful writer and took great trouble to get at the truth. Like all the Arabs, he calls East Africa the land of the Zanj; we do not know exactly what this word Zanj means or what language it comes from, but it has been taken into the Arabic language to be a name for dark-skinned Africans, Hamite, Negro or Bantu – but not Bushman. We know the word in the name Zanzibar, which means the coast of the Zanj. Edrisi tells us that in his day the trade in gold and ivory and slaves was still important, but the trade in iron was more important still. He mentions Malindi as a town of the Zanj whose people have iron mines and sell a great deal of iron; he mentions other towns as well which do the same thing. Even Sofala, which has so much gold for sale, does even more trade in its iron. And where did the Arab ships take the iron from Sofala and Malindi and other East African towns? They took it to India; the iron of Sofala, says Edrisi, is the best iron in the world, and the iron-workers of India are the best iron-workers.

After nearly another two hundred years, the towns on the East African coast were visited by another Arab traveller, an old friend of ours[2]: Ibn Batuta. He came along the coast about 1330, and

[1] See Book One, page 48.
[2] See Book One, pages 55–8. Ibn Batuta, we remember, did not think very much of the buildings he found in Mali when he visited that country, twenty years after he came to Kilwa, the buildings in Kilwa and other East African towns seem to have pleased him more. They were built of wood and of stone, and the Mali buildings were of mud and brick, the bricks probably not fired in a hot enough oven and so rather soft.

visited (among other places) Kilwa, which was then still the leading city on the coast, though its time was nearly over. Ibn Batuta
found it a beautiful and well built town; most of its people were
'Zanj', dark-skinned with tribal marks on their faces. No doubt
the Sultan's senior officials were Arabs and spoke Arabic; but
most people would probably speak the mixed language, Swahili.

The Arabs were not the only seamen who sailed the Indian
Ocean. The Chinese sailed their ships to Oman in Arabia and
Basra in Iraq and other ports in that part of Asia in the time of
El Masudi, and may have been there now and again even earlier.
Some time after 1000 AD the Chinese invented the compass, and
with this they were able to sail straight across the open sea instead
of along the coast. For a long time they did not come further
south-west than Ceylon; they were content to sail in the Bay of
Bengal and up the west coast of India. But in the 15th century,
between 1417 and 1500, they came several times to the East African
coast. In 1417 a great Chinese sea-captain named Cheng Ho
brought his ships to Malindi; for the people of Malindi had sent
a live giraffe as a present to the emperor of China, and Cheng Ho
brought the Malindi people who had gone with it back to their
own home in his ships. But most of the trade with China was
carried on by Arab ships, whose captains met the Chinese in the
Persian Gulf or in south India or Ceylon.

**But if the Chinese had once found the way by sea to East Africa,
and wanted to trade silk and cotton, spices and pottery for African
gold and ivory, why did they not come again and again? Why
leave the African trade to the Arabs?**

China is a very large country, and in those days it was governed
by an emperor, whose orders had to be obeyed. There were two
parties among the Chinese emperor's ministers. One party wanted
to build bigger and bigger ships and to sail further and further
across the seas; Chinese ships at that time were bigger and better
than any ships in Europe. The other party thought this a waste
of effort. They thought that China had nothing to learn from
foreign countries, and did not need the African gold and ivory;
or at any rate, it could get the gold and ivory from the Arabs
without the trouble of sending its own ships far away. Let China,
they said, be content, and keep all its strength at home to defend
itself against enemies who might attack it from the north and west

by land. About the year 1500, the emperor made up his mind to take the advice of this second party. Laws were made forbidding Chinese to build big ships and to sail in them. China turned its back on the rest of the world.

That was surely a mistake?

Yes, it was a mistake; but it was a natural mistake. China had a very long history, and so far had learned very little from the rest of the world, except in the matter of religion. Buddhism had come into China from India, and Islam from Arabia. But from what the Chinese could see of the rest of the world, they had at that time little to learn from it. The Chinese had invented paper, printing, silk, gunpowder, rockets, and the magnetic compass[1]; and as we have seen, they knew much more about ship building than Europe or any other part of the world. The Chinese knew that there were civilised states in India, but they knew of no others. The Arab civilization had taken much of its ideas from China. If the Chinese had visited Western Europe, they would have found there builders, poets, painters and goldsmiths and carvers in wood and ivory as good as their own. But Western Europe was divided into small states who were constantly fighting one another; and before about 1400 Europe was behind China in mathematics and science. The Chinese never came into touch with Western Europe, for there were thousands of miles of country in between which were inhabited by peoples with much less civilization.[2] They did not know that the peoples of Western Europe were learning fast.

For hundreds of years, then, there was this civilization on the east coast of Africa: a string of trading cities, founded no doubt by Arabs but inhabited mainly by 'Zanj', their harbours full of ships from India and Arabia and China. Inland, there was the Bantu civilization, with its stone buildings, its roads, its stone water-channels, and its exports of gold, ivory, and iron. About 1200, the trade seems to have grown much bigger, and the East African cities became richer. Kilwa was visited by Ibn Batuta, who says that all its buildings, though very fine, were of wood; later on we hear that many of them were built of stone. In Kua, which is on a small island off the mouth of the Rufiji river, we can

[1] The compass which points to the Poles, and shows us north and south.
[2] Mongols, Tatars, Turks and others.

still see the ruins of more than thirty stone houses and seven mosques; at Gedi, Mombasa, and other cities up and down the coast, stone building came in more and more.

Was this Bantu civilization like the civilization of old Ghana, Mali and Songhai?

As far as we can tell at present, it was not as highly developed as that civilization in the Sudan. For one thing, we know that in the kingdoms of the Sudan there were many learned men and many books, some of which we can read today. But there was no writing in East Africa; and a civilization without reading and writing cannot possibly develop as well as one which has books. For another thing, the Bantu in East Africa had no horses, so they had no cavalry soldiers; and we know that the kings of Ghana and Mali were able to hold their power because they had armies of cavalry which could move quickly over the country. Again: as far as we know, the Arabs from the towns on the coast did not visit the inland kingdoms except in small trading parties. Ibn Batuta visited the coast, but he did not go inland. Islam did not reach the Bantu; they kept their old religion. A fourth point: the stone buildings at Zimbabwe and elsewhere are not at all like the mosques and other buildings in the coast towns. They are purely African; there are no straight lines in them and they seem to be built by Africans who were used to building in mud and thatch. The beautiful arches and decoration of the buildings on the coast have had no influence inland.

The Bantu civilization of East and Central Africa was a real civilization, as far as it went. It covered a wide area, and for a long time its peoples seem to have lived at peace; it had some skill in mining, in building water channels, and building stone walls. We should guess, even if Masudi had not told us, that its people, like Bantu peoples today, loved polished speaking. A few examples have been found of its goldsmiths' work, from which we may guess that its workers in gold and ivory were as good as those in West Africa; no doubt much of their work was sent out of the country and lost by Arabs and Portuguese. But the peoples of the Sudan learned from the Muslims of North Africa how to read and write, and so were able to develop their civilization; the peoples of inland East Africa, though they too were in contact with Muslim traders, never learned this.

That will do for the first question. The civilization of East Africa, both on the coast and inland, lived by its trade with Arabia, India, and China.

What about the second question: Why did this civilization die?

It was killed by war, just as the civilization of the Songhai was killed. From about 1250 onwards, the Bantu peoples of East Africa began to suffer attacks from other peoples coming from the north and north-east. In Uganda, as we have seen[1], the Bahima came down from the north and conquered the country; and about 1450 the Bahima were followed by the Lwoo. The Galla and the Masai were other peoples who came down conquering from the north: Hamitic peoples, light-coloured and cattle-keeping, and great fighting men. We have seen[2] that it often happens in Africa and all over the world that a settled peaceful people which has developed a high civilization is conquered by a wandering people which is less civilized but is well organized for war. It happened in Europe when the northern peoples – Franks, Angles, Goths and others – broke down the Roman empire, and it happened a second time when the Turks conquered the Greeks and other peoples of south-eastern Europe. It happened in West Africa when the Almoravides[3] conquered Ghana. And now we see that it happened also in East Africa. We do not know if it was the Masai that destroyed the town of Engaruka; at any rate, Engaruka lies in what is now Masai country.

The Hamitic and Nilo-Hamitic peoples did not go very far to the south; the Masai went furthest, and they did not quite reach as far south as the line from Dar-es-Salaam to Dodoma and Tabora where the railway now runs. But not all the Bantu peoples stayed where they were to lose their freedom and be ruled by Hamitic or Nilo-Hamitic kings. Some of them moved away south-ward and attacked other Bantu peoples and tried to conquer new lands for themselves to replace those they had lost. The Sotho and the Shona and the Rozwi and others set up strong kingdoms, and they built for themselves not only stone walls to stop erosion on their hillside farms, not only stone houses, but also stone castles or forts to defend themselves in time of war. Further south still, the Ngoni and other Bantu peoples became so warlike that fighting

[1] See page 81.
[2] See page 80; also Book One, pages 44, 46, 76, 83.
[3] See Book One, pages 48, 49.

and conquering became an important part of their life. South and East Africa, which had been a peaceful land, became a land of war and conquest; and that is always bad for civilization.

But war came to this East African civilization from another direction as well. In 1498 the first Portuguese ships arrived on the East African coast.

We have seen in Book One that in the fifteenth century, the Portuguese began to explore the coast of Africa. In 1419 Prince Henry of Portugal began sending ships southward along the west coast. In 1446 they reached the mouth of the Senegal river, in 1460 they came to Sierra Leone, in 1471 they reached the Gold Coast, and a few years later built their first castle there.[1] One of the ships in the fleet which went out in 1482 to build Elmina was commanded by a captain named Bartholomew Diaz; and four years later, in 1486, Diaz reached the most southerly point of Africa and saw the land beyond running away to the north-east. The weather was bad, so he went no further, and named the Cape the Cape of Storms; but when he returned home and told what he had seen, the king of Portugal changed its name to the Cape of Good Hope.

In 1498 (six years after Christopher Columbus had crossed the Atlantic and discovered America for the king of Spain) the Portuguese captain Vasco da Gama sailed round the Cape and up the east coast of Africa. He called at Sofala, and found Arabs trading there; at Mozambique he picked up four men and made them guide him as he sailed further up the coast. On 7 April 1498 he arrived at Mombasa, after passing Kilwa and other places without stopping.

The Arabs were not pleased to see the Portuguese, for they could see that the Portuguese wanted to join in their trade to India. And the Portuguese did not behave in a way to make people welcome them. Like other peoples of Western Europe at that time, the Portuguese had fought for four hundred years against the Muslims of Palestine and North Africa. Portugal itself was a country which had been conquered from the Muslims, and the Portuguese were beginning to try to conquer Morocco. So when they met Muslim Arabs on the East African coast, they called them 'Moors' and looked on them as enemies. Vasco da Gama tells us how he took people prisoner, and tried to make them

[1] Elmina Castle, as it is called today; it was built in 1482.

tell him what he wanted to know by dropping burning oil on their skin. It is not surprising that the 'king' of Mombasa, though he sent the Portuguese fresh meat and fruit, would give them no help in finding their way to India. In fact, da Gama was told that what the Portuguese had done at Mozambique had made the Mombasa people so angry that they would take the Portuguese ships if they could.

Leaving Mombasa, da Gama sailed on to Malindi. Here he was more fortunate. He took prisoner some of the Malindi people, and they promised that if he would let them go free, they would give him a pilot[1] to show him the way to India. Da Gama went ashore at Malindi and met the 'king', who was wearing a robe of fine white cotton and green silk, sitting on two chairs[2] with cushions, beneath a red silk umbrella. Malindi was not friendly with Mombasa, and welcomed the Portuguese because they might help the Malindi people against Mombasa. Da Gama set all his prisoners free, and in return the king of Malindi found him a pilot to show him the way to India. After visiting India, Vasco da Gama went back home to Portugal by the way he had come.

The Portuguese were not really interested in Africa for its own sake; they had not expected to find much civilization there, and were only looking for a way to India. The people in Europe had heard wonderful tales of the wealth and civilization of India; the Turks had closed the direct way to India by land, so Columbus and Da Gama hoped to find a new way by sea. The Portuguese expected to find all Africa savage, except that there was a story in Europe that somewhere in the middle of Africa there was a Christian kingdom whose king was named Prester John. No doubt this story came from the Christian kingdom of Ethiopia, which as we have seen[3] was shut in by the Muslims and had lost touch with the rest of the Christian world. When the Portuguese came to Mozambique, they heard of a great civilized kingdom some distance inland, from which came the gold and ivory they saw at Sofala. They thought this must be the kingdom of Prester John, and the news, says Da Gama, 'made us so happy that we cried for joy.' This southern kingdom was not Christian; it was the kingdom of the Waqlimi, which Masudi told us about.

[1] A pilot is a man who shows the way to a ship's captain in a harbour or a part of the sea which is new to him. We have read on page 67 about the Suez Canal pilots.
[2] How can a man sit on two chairs? But that is what Da Gama says.
[3] See page 32.

The wealth and civilization of the East African coast towns depended on their trade with India and the East. But the Portuguese did not wish this trade to continue; they wanted all the trade of India for themselves. They were not content to have their agents on the Indian coast, living and trading there by permission of the Indian kings, and depending on ships coming all the way from Portugal. Their great statesman Albuquerque made a much better plan. He wanted to conquer a piece of India large enough to be made a strong place for a Portuguese Governor; and for this he chose Goa. Then he picked three important trading towns, whose position made them able to control important trade routes: Ormuz at the mouth of the Persian Gulf; Malacca, at the entrance to the Straits and the spice islands of Indonesia; and Socotra, at the entrance of the Red Sea. With those three places in their hands, Albuquerque thought that the Portuguese would control all the trade of the Indian Ocean and could take what taxes they chose out of every ship that passed. Lastly, Albuquerque planned to use the East African coast for supplying fresh food and wood for repairing the Portuguese wooden ships. If he could be sure of this, the Portuguese position in the Indian Ocean would be safe.

This meant that it was not enough to depend on the friendship of the East African towns. The Portuguese must be masters of the East African coast. Between 1500 and 1510 they made themselves masters; they attacked Kilwa, Sofala, Zanzibar, Brava, Mombasa, and Zeila. Here and there they allowed the Arab sultan to rule, provided he paid taxes to Portugal; in Mombasa and some other places they built Portuguese forts with Portuguese governors in command.

Why were the Portuguese able to conquer the whole of the coast in ten years?

Because, though few in number, they had guns: not only small guns fired from the hand, but big guns fired from the ships. In 1503 a Portuguese ship attacked and took some small ships from Zanzibar; the sultan of Zanzibar sent four thousand men in canoes to attack the Portuguese ship, but the Portuguese captain sent two of his ship's boats against them, armed with guns, and defeated them. The Portuguese had guns, and Arabs and Africans with spears and swords and arrows could not stand against them.

N

MAP 8. THE ARAB COAST FROM OMAN TO SOFALA

This map shows the Arab settlements on the East African coast which are mentioned
in the chapter on Tanganyika. It shows the Arab state of Oman, and marks the two
Portuguese settlements of Ormuz and Socotra, and the islands of Mauritius, Réunion,
and Nossi Bé. For a short time in 1875–76, the Khedive Ismail of Egypt, who already
held the coast past Massawa and Zeila as far as Cape Guardafui, even sent his
soldiers to hold Brava and Kismayu; this was when he hoped to use the river Tana
as a way to Lake Victoria and the southern Sudan.

Whether there was an Arab sultan left to rule his town or not, the Portuguese wanted all the trade for themselves. They themselves would bring goods from India and wait for the Africans from the interior to bring gold and ivory in exchange. But the Arabs had been in the habit of sending men into the interior to buy and sell, and the Africans did not come down much to the coast. If they did not care to come down to the coast towns under Arab rule, they liked still less the idea of coming to meet the Portuguese, for they feared and hated them. The Portuguese on the other hand never had enough men to go into the interior as the Arabs had done. All they could do was to send a party now and again with guns to see why the supply of gold – it was gold that the Portuguese most wanted – was running out. The settled civilised states of the interior were broken up by civil war, the Portuguese sometimes fighting on the side of some African chief who had promised to pay them in gold. By 1719, the king of Portugal saw that the strong African states of the interior had been broken in pieces, and the chief of each small piece had made himself independent, so that there was no longer any law and order, and no longer any trade. The Portuguese Governor of Sofala had been richer, as long as the trade lasted, than the Governors of Ormuz and Malacca; but the trade did not last long.

Some of the Portuguese saw the mistakes they were making. In 1667 a Portuguese named Manuel Barreto, who knew the gold-bearing country between the Zambesi and the Limpopo, says there are three main reasons why less gold is produced now than formerly. One is that the African chiefs do not want gold to be mined in their land; for if they do, the Portuguese will come and take the land, and the chiefs will become poor labourers. The second reason is that there are not as many people living there now as there used to be. And the third reason, says Barreto, is that everyone fears the Portuguese and runs away from them into the bush; that is why there are fewer people living there now.

Here then is the second reason why the civilization of East and Central Africa died. While African peoples, helped by the Portuguese, attacked and broke down the strong civilized states of the interior, the Portuguese cut off the Indian Ocean trade on which the civilization had fed. No more Chinese pottery came across the sea to be proudly shown on the walls of houses in Kilwa or Mombasa; as a Swahili poet said about the town of Paté, 'The hollows in the walls which were made to hold pottery now hold wild birds' nests.' The cities of the coast, having lost their trade, became smaller and poorer; many of them were left empty altogether and the bush came in and covered them until they were forgotten.

If some of the Portuguese, like Manuel Barreto, could see the mistakes they were making, why did they go on making them? The Portuguese were very strong and bold in conquering the coast; why did they not hold it properly and develop the trade wisely?

There were several reasons for this. One is that Portugal was a very small country; and although Portuguese captains made a wonderful effort in exploring the world between 1420 and about 1520, they had not enough men to be strong everywhere. They conquered Brazil and built up an empire there, so that Brazil speaks Portuguese to this day. As we have seen, they did not want East Africa for its own sake; they only wanted it as a step on the way to India. It was in India and Indonesia and Brazil that the Portuguese made their main effort. Then again, in 1580 the kingdom of Portugal came into the power of the king of Spain; and Spain had many other places to think of than East Africa, or even India. Spain held the whole of America from Florida southwards, and was getting gold and silver from the mines there, using African slaves to work them. That is why Mexico and all the other countries of Central and South America today speak Spanish, except Brazil, which speaks Portuguese. So as far as East Africa is concerned, the Portuguese were too weak to do much good. There were probably never more than one or two hundred Portuguese along the whole coast north of Mozambique; and it is only natural to guess that the best men would want to go to Brazil or India where they could be most useful.

THE SEVENTEENTH AND EIGHTEENTH CENTURIES

Although the Portuguese conquered the coast quickly, they had much trouble with the people; especially at Mombasa. There was fighting between the Portuguese and the Mombasa people in 1528, and again in 1586 and 1589. In 1589 the town was attacked by a Bantu people called the Zimba, who had left their home near

Zululand[1] and had been marching northward. They had taken Kilwa two years earlier, and now they took Mombasa; then they went on to Malindi, but there they were defeated by the Bantu people who lived near by. In 1598 the Portuguese built a strong castle at Mombasa and named it Fort Jesus; and they hoped that after this they would have no more trouble there. On the other side of Africa, at Elmina on the Gold Coast, they had built a castle just as big and strong, and they felt quite safe behind the big guns of Elmina Castle. So they hoped it would be at Mombasa.

But Elmina Castle had been standing for more than a hundred years when Fort Jesus was built, and during these years the Portuguese had been growing weaker on the African coast. In the west, the English and the Dutch were beginning to send their ships to trade with the Africans, and to fight against the Portuguese if the Portuguese tried to keep them away. In the east, the Portuguese found that they had not broken the power of the Arabs. The Portuguese held the small island of Ormuz at the mouth of the Persian Gulf, and several other islands: Socotra, Mombasa, Kilwa and others off the coast of Africa, and Bombay off the coast of India. Now an empire like this, which is made up of a string of islands along a foreign coast, will only be safe as long as there is a strong fleet to defend it against attack by the people of the mainland. Albuquerque knew that. His plan was that Goa should be a strong base, defended by a strong army; and that a fleet should be based on Goa to defend the islands of the Portuguese empire. But Portugal no longer had a fleet in the Indian Ocean strong enough to defend these islands. In 1622, the Arabs of Oman drove the Portuguese out of Ormuz. In 1631, the sultan of Mombasa collected a party of three hundred men and managed to take Fort Jesus by surprise, though he could not hold it against the Portuguese fleet which came next year from Goa to retake the place. In 1698, the Imam[2] Seif bin Sultan of Oman took Fort Jesus from the Portuguese after a siege[3] of nearly three years; next year he took Kilwa and Pemba. By 1700, the

[1] The Zimba had come a long way. Who knows what made them leave home: famine, cattle disease, war, or a witch doctor?

[2] The Arabic word Imam means a religious leader. At that time, the Imam of Oman had political power as well. This often happens in Muslim countries, for Church and State are not so clearly distinguished in Islam as they are under Christianity.

[3] An army *lays siege to* a town, or *besieges* it, when it sits down outside the town to keep off any army coming to help the townspeople while it is attacking the town.

Portuguese had been driven out of all the towns they held on the East African coast north of Mozambique colony, which they still hold today.[1]

The East African coast thus came under the rule of the Imam of Oman, but he was not strong enough in his own country to set up a strong empire in Africa. His people were ready to unite in order to drive out the Portuguese from Oman, but as soon as the Portuguese were gone, the Arabs began to quarrel again among themselves. So the East African towns were left to themselves, much as they had been before the Portuguese arrived. The difference was that the Portuguese had destroyed the Indian Ocean trade, and though driven out of the Swahili coast, they were still strong in India, so that the trade could not start again. Moreover, the fighting among the Bantu peoples in the interior of East Africa was breaking up the civilization there. There was no more trade in gold, and very little in ivory. The only trade left was in slaves; whom the Arabs took to Arabia and the Portuguese took to Brazil. For nearly a hundred years after 1700 the Swahili coast towns slowly decayed. They had come into being, and had lived, by the Indian Ocean trade; when the trade ceased, they died.

It seems as if the Portuguese did much harm to East Africa, and very little good?

They introduced maize and cassava, and perhaps pineapples, all of which were native to America. They may perhaps have introduced bananas, which were native to tropical Asia. This was part of their plan for making East Africa useful as a place where their ships could get fresh food for the voyage across the Indian Ocean; but of course it was a great help to the people of East Africa. Apart from this, they did very little good. It is probably fair to say that the Portuguese did not go to East Africa with the idea of doing good to the country; they went to East Africa only to use it. In some other parts of the world, such as Goa, Brazil and the Congo, it was different. There, the Portuguese did work hard to improve the country. But they could do nothing with the Muslims of East Africa, who did not want the Portuguese as missionaries, or as traders, or as governors. So the Portuguese merely used the

---

[1] In 1723, the sultan of Pate asked the Portuguese to help him against some of the other coast towns. The Portuguese came in 1728 and took Mombasa, but they were driven out again next year.

East African coast for what they could get out of it: gold and ivory as long as it lasted, and afterwards slaves; and all the time food, and wood for mending ships.

What was happening in the interior of the country while the Portuguese and Arabs were fighting on the coast?

The two hundred years from about 1500 to about 1700 were the time when many of the peoples who live in Tanganyika today arrived there. Or perhaps we should say the time when many of the states of modern Tanganyika were built up; for sometimes it happened that a small group of newcomers settled among a large group of people who were already living there, and built them up into a new kind of state. We have seen this happening elsewhere; for example[1] the Berbers mixed with the Soninke and built old Ghana, and they mixed with other Negro peoples and built the Hausa states. In Uganda too, the Bahima and the Lwoo and others mixed with the Bantu people and built new states.

So it was in Tanganyika. The Bahima, and people like them, passed down through Uganda, coming west of Lake Victoria, and entered Tanganyika. Some Bantu peoples too were coming down from the north; for example, the Chagga people may have been built up from small groups of Kamba and other Bantu people coming down from what it now Kenya. Everywhere there was movement and change. Wherever the Bahima came, they built small groups of agricultural people into larger groups of people among whom cattle-keeping was the work for the upper class, and farming and such crafts as iron-working were regarded as lower work. Sometimes the change came peacefully, when small family groups saw that they could not stand against the new-comers, or when people were moving into country that was empty, as Kilimanjaro was empty of people before the Chagga came. Sometimes there was war, as we have seen in the case of the Zimba, who did so much damage in Kilwa and elsewhere along the coast. The last people to arrive in Tanganyika were the Masai, who settled in Kenya about 1500, but did not spread south into Tanganyika for another three hundred years.

All this movement and change, both on the coast and inland, was bad for the civilization of East Africa. About 1500, Zimbabwe

[1] See Book One, pp. 36, 74; and page 81 in this book.

was brought into use again by Shona people[1] after lying empty for
a time; and about a hundred years later, the Rozwi, who are related to the Shona, made it the capital of a strong kingdom. But the
Rozwi kingdom of Zimbabwe was quite destroyed by the Ngoni,
coming from the south, in 1834 and 1835; and the stone buildings
were left empty.

BRITISH AND GERMANS AND THE SULTAN OF ZANZIBAR

For most of the eighteenth century, the East African coast was
supposed to belong to the Imam, or Sultan, of Oman; though he
had very little real power there. In the latter half of the eighteenth
century, the Indian Ocean began to be troubled by the quarrels
between two European countries, Britain and France. Both countries were extending their trade in India, and both were finding
that it was easy to pass from being mere traders to become governors. It so happened that at that time, the great Mogul Empire,
which had governed most of India from its capital at Delhi, was
becoming weak. Many of its local governors were making themselves independent, and some of them were governing their people
badly. There was much fighting and disorder, and some of the
Indian rulers asked the French or the British to help them against
their enemies. So there was war in India between the French and
the British, and the French and the British fought each other also
by sea.

In the land fighting in India, the British beat the French, and
more and more of India began to come under British rule. But
at sea the French were very strong, and they won more than one
sea battle with British ships. One thing that helped the French at
sea was that they held the island which today is called Mauritius.
Mauritius had good harbours and plenty of timber, and was very
useful as a base to which French ships could go for repairs. Britain
had no base nearer than Gibraltar, two months journey away. In
the eighteenth century, a great French Governor of Mauritius
(the Ile de France, as the French called it) called Labourdonnais
began to grow sugar in large plantations; and at once the sugar
planters began to ask for slaves to work in the sugar cane fields.

[1] These are the same as the Mashona who live in Rhodesia today. *Ma-* or *Ama-*
or *Ba-* or *Wa-* in front of a Bantu name means *people*; for example, Ama-Zulu,
Ba-Ganda, Wa-Kamba, Wa-Ngoni.

The French got some slaves from Madagascar, but they soon found the people of Madagascar too strong for them, and so they looked to East Africa. In 1776 the Sultan of Kilwa agreed to sell a thousand slaves a year to the French, and to sell slaves to no one else. It looked as if France was setting up an important trade in the Indian Ocean; and even if the British became the rulers of India, their ships could only sail between India and Britain by the permission of the French.

In the year 1798, the French general Napoleon, as we have seen[1] landed in Egypt with an army, and he had the idea of marching overland to India. If he could not do this, at any rate he would block the short way between Britain and India, which was by sea to Egypt, overland to the Red Sea (there was no Suez Canal at that time) and by sea to north India. If the French held Egypt, all British people going to India would have to pass round the Cape, and when their ships entered the Indian Ocean they would be in danger from the French in Mauritius.

The British saw the danger. The British fleet destroyed the French ships at the battle of Aboukir off the Egyptian coast, and a British army landed in Egypt and beat the French, though Napoleon himself got back to France. But the British Government did more than this. It made a treaty of friendship with the Sultan of Oman. The Sultan agreed not to trade with the French, and not to allow French or any other ships to attack British ships passing the Arabian coast on their way to and from India. The British agreed to help the Sultan against his enemies. His ships were being attacked by Arab pirates[2] in the Persian Gulf, and his lands were being attacked by Arabs from the deserts of Saudi Arabia.

Is it because of this treaty that the British are still interested in Oman and other Arab states in the Persian Gulf?

This treaty began the British interest in Oman; though as we shall see, there have been other treaties since between Britain and Oman.

Were the British thinking about the oil in Kuwait and other places in that region?

No, not at that time. There were no motors or aeroplanes or other machines using petrol, so there were no oil-wells and nobody was

[1] See page 19.
[2] Pirates are sea-robbers.

interested in oil from Arabia or anywhere else. Times have changed. In those days, all the Arab lands were ruled by the Turks, and the Indian Ocean was not safe for ships because of the pirates. Today, there are no more pirates in the Persian Gulf, and Iraq and Saudi Arabia and other Arab lands are independent. But Britain is still bound by the treaty which she made in 1798; and when the people of Saudi Arabia attack land (such as the Buraimi oasis) which the Sultan of Oman says is part of his country, he still has the right to ask Britain for help, and Britain is bound to help him. Of course, there is oil in the Persian Gulf; but not in Oman. The oil is further north, nearer the head of the Gulf.

In 1806 there came a new Sultan of Oman, a boy of fifteen named Seyyid Said. Seyyid Said was a much stronger ruler than most of the Sultans in the hundred years before him. He came to power by killing with his own hands another man who claimed to succeed the previous Sultan. He saw how dangerous his position was, with the pirates on the sea and the Saudi Arabia[1] people attacking him by land. But at least he did not have to choose between the British and the French; for since 1798 the British had been growing stronger and stronger by sea, and in 1805 – the year before Seyyid Said came to power – they had destroyed the last French fleet at the battle of Trafalgar near Spain. British ships came to help Seyyid Said against the pirates, and in a few years the pirates were finally defeated. Seyyid Said beat back his land enemies without the help of British soldiers; but he knew that by clearing the sea of pirates, so that he could be free to think of the land war, the British had helped him, although no British soldiers had landed in Oman. By 1814, Seyyid Said's country was safe; and he felt thankful to Britain for what she had done.

Britain too was much stronger in the Indian Ocean than she had been a few years earlier. As we have seen,[2] during the war with Napoleon she had taken the Cape and made it into a British colony. In 1810 she had taken Mauritius, after trying more than once in vain to do so. Both the Cape and Mauritius remained British when the long was ended in 1815. Britain ended the war with the strongest navy in the world; and she began using her ships to stop the slave trade.

[1] The name Saudi Arabia is modern; the name comes from the name of the country's first independent king, Ibn Saud, who became king after the Arabs and the British together had broken the Turkish power in the war of 1914–18.
[2] See Book One, page 105.

This was unlucky for Seyyid Said, for he and his people were great slave-traders and were becoming very rich by the trade. But he thought it so important to keep the friendship of Britain that he was even prepared to limit the slave trade, though it probably did not come into his mind that the time was coming when the slave trade would be stopped altogether.

The British were in a difficulty. Although the British Governments of Mauritius and of British India wanted to stop slaves being brought in from Africa and Madagascar, there were Indian states which were not yet under British rule which still wanted slaves; and the French sugar-planters in Mauritius too would buy as many as they could get, in spite of the Government and the law. The British war-ships could not be everywhere at once; so the Government decided that the trade would never be stopped until the Arabs stopped bringing ship-loads of slaves for sale. In 1817 the British made a treaty with king Radama of Madagascar, by which Radama said he would do all he could to stop slaves being taken in Madagascar for sale overseas. In 1822, the British Captain Moresby signed a treaty with Seyyid Said. The Sultan agreed that he would not allow his ships to sail south of Cape Delgado, or east of a line from Diu in India to the island of Socotra. As Mauritius was south of Cape Delgado, and the British lands in India lay east of the Diu line, this treaty made it unlawful for slave ships to come to British India or to Mauritius. But it was still the job of the British navy to stop the Arab ships; the Arab captains woud not obey the law and give up their rich trade if they could help it. Seyyid Said also agreed that he would not allow slaves to be sold to any Christian; this meant that no Europeans, such as French or Portuguese, would be able to help the Arab slavers by buying their slaves from them on the East African coast and taking them to Mozambique or further south.

Seyyid Said gave up a great deal. What did he get out of the Moresby Treaty?

Seyyid Said got the friendship of the British, who were the strongest power in that part of the world; and more than that, the British recognised him as ruler of the whole East African coast as far south as Cape Delgado. Seyyid Said thought that the time had come for him to make himself ruler of the coast. Oman was quiet, and the British had stopped the pirates in the Persian Gulf; this was his chance.

There was only a small part of the coast which still obeyed the Sultan of Oman; Zanzibar, which was then an unimportant place, was the chief town which did so. The Arabs in Mombasa were trying to build up an empire of their own, and they were very strong because they held the Portuguese Fort Jesus. Seyyid Said decided to attack Mombasa. The Arabs there were afraid, and when a British war-ship happened to visit the town, they even asked the captain, whose name was Owen, to take Mombasa and make it British. Captain Owen would have liked to do so, for he thought that Mombasa would be a useful harbour in the British navy's work of stopping the slave trade. But the British Government in London at that time (1824-26) was quite determined that it would not take any land in East Africa[1], and it told Captain Owen that he must say No to the Mombasa people. The Government had a special reason for saying No, apart from the general reason that it did not want the trouble of governing any part of East Africa. It knew that the Mombasa Arabs did not really want to become British; they only wanted to fly the British flag so as to keep Seyyid Said away. But Seyyid Said was the friend of the British, and if he was to stop the slave trade, he must be able to rule Mombasa and the other coast towns from which the slaves were sent oversea.

Seyyid Said had a great deal of trouble with Mombasa and other Arab towns on the coast. He sent armies several times between 1819 and 1837, and it was not till 1837 that all the Swahili coast obeyed him. In 1840 Seyyid Said took a very important step. He liked Zanzibar so much that he decided to leave Oman and live in Zanzibar. He knew that he might find it just as difficult to govern Oman from Zanzibar as he had found it to govern East Africa from Oman; but he thought Zanzibar the better place. When he was dead, no doubt the two countries would have to be separated; but Seyyid Said hoped to be able to hold them both during his life-time. He set out to develop Zanzibar. It had great advantages: plenty of good water, a deep water harbour, good climate and fertile soil, and a position right in the middle of the Swahili coast.

[1] In 1828 the Government in London decided to leave the Gold Coast, to pull down the forts and take all the British people away. The Government in those days did not want colonies.

Seyyid Said introduced cloves; he planted much of his own land with cloves and made other Arabs do the same, and by the time he died, the value of the Zanzibar crop of cloves was so great that cloves came next to ivory and slaves as the chief exports of the island.

The Moresby Treaty had of course lessened the value of the export of slaves; and the British Government still kept pressing the Sultan to limit the slave trade even more. In 1845, Seyyid Said agreed to another treaty, which stopped the export of slaves from East Africa to Oman. Slaves could only be bought and sold along the African coast; they could not be sent to any other country by sea. The British officer who made this treaty was Captain Hamerton, so the treaty is called the Hamerton Treaty. If it were enforced, it would bring about a big drop in the revenue which the Sultan gained from the tax he received on each slave who was exported from Zanzibar; so the British promised to pay him £ 2,000 a year in compensation until the trade in other things increased to as to make up for this drop in revenue.

But could the Hamerton treaty be enforced? Seyyid Said could not stop Arabs in the other coast towns, or even Zanzibar itself, from loading ships and slipping out of harbour in the hope of getting across the sea without been seen by a British ship. Probably both he and his people thought that the treaty would not make very much difference, though the Sultan himself did what he could — which was not very much — to enforce it. Still, the British ships were doing something to lessen the trade and its profits; and the Arabs disliked both the Moresby and the Hamerton treaties.

Why then did the Sultan agree to the Hamerton treaty? Not because he wanted to stop the slave trade, nor because he loved the British. He had another reason: the French were again becoming active in the Indian Ocean, and the Sultan needed British help against them, as he had done forty years before. The French had lost the island of Mauritius, but they still had the island of Réunion near by. Réunion[1], like Mauritius, grew sugar and needed slaves; and the French sugar planters tried to get slaves from Africa. The French Government said that if the British wanted to stop the slave trade, they would not supply Réunion with slaves, but with 'free labourers'; and although the British knew that it was difficult to tell the difference between a ship-load of slaves and a ship-load

[1] At that time, the island of Réunion was called Bourbon.

of 'free labourers', they did not see what they could do to stop this new trade. The French did more. They took the island of Nossi-Bé near the north end of Madagascar, and they asked the Sultan if they might build forts at Brava and Mogadishu. The Sultan did not allow them to do so; but he could see that the French were thinking of building up an empire in East Africa, and so he could not afford to lose the support of the British, even if he had to buy their support by limiting the slave trade.

If the slave trade was to be limited, it was all the more necessary for other trade to be developed; and Seyyid Said did a great deal to develop general trade. He encouraged Indian traders to come and live in Zanzibar; and he sent caravans of traders from Zanzibar and other towns into the interior of Africa to bring back ivory and skins. These caravans went further and further, and some of the Arab leaders became not only rich men, but something like kings. For Seyyid Said never tried to govern the interior of Africa. He gave the caravan leaders a flag as a sign that they were under his protection[1], but he did not want the trouble of building an empire. As long as the ivory and other goods came back to Zanzibar or the other towns, and paid their tax to his Government, the Sultan was content. Even along the coast, he was content to leave his governors in the towns from Warsheikh in the north down to the river Rovuma in the south almost independent, provided they paid him his proper share of the tax on ivory and other goods coming down from the interior. A narrow strip along the coast was settled by Swahili-speaking Arabs, and was cultivated by slaves; here they grew coco-nuts and exported copra and other palm produce. Further inland, the Sultan had no power; and yet his trading caravans so opened up the country, and Zanzibar had become so important as a market, that the saying grew, 'When men whistle in Zanzibar, people dance on the shores of the great lakes.'

The trouble in all this was that ivory tusks are very heavy, and someone had to carry them. This meant that the Arabs were not content to buy ivory; they must also buy slaves to carry the ivory. There were two main reasons why they used slaves, not free porters. One was that they would never have been able to get enough porters to come willingly for pay. The other was that (whatever the British might think) the Arabs saw nothing wrong in slavery,

---

[1] In the same way, Usuman dan Fodio gave flags to the Fulani whom he appointed to lead armies against the Hausa; see Book One, pages 84, 85.

and there was always the chance that they could sell the slaves as well as the ivory. And so East and Central Africa was ruined by the slave trade. Hundreds of miles of country which had been full of villages were left quite empty. Thousands of slaves started on the long road down to the coast; very many of them were left to die by the road side and many more died in the slave ships, unless they were lucky enough to be stopped by a British ship and set free.

Seyyid Said made commercial treaties with the United States and France as well as with Britain, and these three countries all appointed consuls in Zanzibar to look after their traders there: the Americans in 1837, the British in 1841, and the French in 1844. Trade increased very greatly; and one result of this was that more and more Europeans and Americans came to Zanzibar and saw the slaves being sold in the market there. The idea began to grow in Britain that it was not enough to send war-ships to catch the slave ships on the sea; the trade would never be stopped until police were sent to stop it in the interior of Africa as well.

In 1856, Seyyid Said died while he was returning from Oman to Zanzibar. His fourth son, Majid, was governor of Zanzibar, his third son, Thuwaini, was governor of Oman. There was a younger son, Barghash, who was a bold and ambitious man, who did not like the way in which his father had stuck to his friendship with the British and had agreed to limit the slave trade. He would have liked to bring in the French to weaken the British, so that the Arabs could remain independent of both. Seyyid Said knew this, and when he went on his last visit to Oman he took Barghash with him so that there should be no trouble while he was away. When Barghash came back to Zanzibar with his father's body, he did try to make himself sultan and to kill his brother Majid, who had been recognised as sultan by most of the people, and by the British and American Governments. But the British Government stopped the fighting. It arrested Barghash and sent him to live in India; it persuaded Thuwaini and Majid to invite the Governor-General of India to judge between them so as to avoid a war between the two brothers; and it persuaded the French Government (which did not at first recognise Majid, and favoured Thuwaini) that Zanzibar was not worth quarrelling over. Lord Canning, the Governor-General of India, decided that Oman and Zanzibar should be separated; each should be independent; and because Zanzibar was so much richer than Oman, Sultan Majid of Zanzibar should pay Sultan Thuwaini of Oman about £9,000 a year. This was agreed to, and for ten years the money was paid; then Zanzibar decided that it would pay no more. Barghash was allowed to come back from India after a time, and succeeded his brother Majid without trouble in 1870.

All this trouble over Zanzibar made it plain that the Sultan of Zanzibar was no longer really independent. The British would not allow him to export slaves; they would not allow him to encourage the French. Sultan Majid never felt really safe, for he knew that some of his people would like the bold Barghash as their ruler; so this made him lean more than ever on British help.

What happened over the question of 'free labourers' for Réunion, which you mentioned on page 221?

This was settled in 1859, just at the time when Barghash and Thuwaini were making so much trouble for Sultan Majid. The British and French Governments made an agreement with the Government of India that Indian labourers would be allowed to come to Réunion under the same conditions as to Mauritius. The Indian Government looked after its people very well, and made sure that the Governments of Mauritius and Réunion treated them properly. So there was no need after that of any slaves or 'free labourers' from Africa.

All this time, Europe knew nothing about the interior of Africa beyond what it learned from the Arabs and from ancient writers. The travels of Mungo Park and of the Lander brothers in West Africa[1] had taught people in Europe that the Nile and the Niger were two different rivers; they had heard tales of great mountains and lakes in the middle of Africa, but no European had ever seen them. But in the first years of Seyyid Said's government in Zanzibar, the travels of European explorers began.

The first Europeans to go inland from the East Africa coast were two missionaries, Krapf and Rebmann, both Germans but members of the Church Missionary Society of Britain. Krapf arrived at Mombasa in 1844, and Rebmann two years later. In 1847, Rebmann went inland from the mission station at Rabai near Mombasa as far as the Taita hills, about a hundred miles away, and next year he went to the Chagga country and was the first European to see Kilimanjaro. In 1849 the other missionary, Krapf, went

[1] See Book One, page 90.

7. Kenya constitutional talks. A meeting in Nairobi in 1961, with European, African and Asian Kenyans taking part

photo: Camera Press, Ltd.

8. Ruins of the Mosque in Kilwa

photo: Camera Press, Ltd.

to the Kamba country and saw Mount Kenya and the Taną river. Krapf and Rebmann were missionaries first of all; they produced the first Swahili grammar and dictionary, and this language work and their geographical work were carried out so as to help themselves and other missionaries to preach Christianity in the interior of Africa.

Meanwhile, another great missionary, David Livingstone, was working up from the south. Livingstone was a great man in every way. He had no easy advantages. In his time there was no compulsory education in Britain, and he had to leave school at the age of ten because he could not pay the school fees. He went to work in a cotton factory, working fourteen hours a day; but he bought himself a Latin grammar and studied Latin in his spare time, and educated himself in this way until the London Missionary Society accepted him. In 1841 the society sent him to Bechuanaland. He arrived there at an important time. We have seen in Book One that in 1836 and 1837 the Boers of South Africa trekked away into the interior of the country and set up the independent states of the Transvaal and the Orange Free State. The missionaries in Bechuanaland felt that they too must push further into the interior to set up new mission stations. This job exactly suited Livingstone. During his first ten years he crossed the Kalahari desert and went further north to the country of the Makololo in the Zambesi valley; and in 1851 the Makololo showed him the Zambesi. He wanted to set up a mission station in the Makololo country, and the people themselves wanted him to do so. But the way by which he had come, across the desert, was too hard; he must find an easier way. So he set out on his first great journey, which took him right across Africa from the west coast at Luanda to the east coast at Quelimane. On this journey he met the slave trade; and he decided that the rest of his life must be given to the work of saving Africa from the suffering it caused. He thought it would not be enough (as many people in England thought at that time) to preach Christianity; the missionaries must introduce schools and teach agriculture and crafts, and must develop honest trade in something better than the beads and cloth and gunpowder which the Arabs brought to pay for their ivory and slaves. He went back to England in 1856 (the year of Seyyid Said's death) and preached his ideas up and down the country /ith great success. A new missionary society, the Universities' Mission to Central

o

Africa, was set up to work on the lines that Livingstone suggested, and the Government provided money for Livingstone to lead a party into Central Africa to find a good place for the sort of mission station that he wanted.

These travels of Krapf and Rebmann in the north and of Livingstone in the south started great interest in Britain in the work of exploring the interior of Central Africa, and many parties were sent between 1856 and in the next twenty years after 1856. Burton and Speke set out in 1857 from Zanzibar and went by way of Tabora to Ujiji on lake Tanganyika; and Speke alone went north and found the southern end of lake Victoria. In 1860, Speke and Grant, starting again from Zanzibar, went all round the west side of lake Victoria and round the north end of the lake till they saw the Nile at Jinja. At Gondokoro they met Sir Samuel Baker, and they went home to England down the river to Egypt.[1] Baker, after leaving Speke and Grant, explored the country round lake Albert.

Meanwhile, Livingstone was at work again. His second journey, which lasted from 1858 to 1864, explored the lower Zambesi and its tributary the Shiré, and Livingstone then left the water and went on by land to see lake Nyasa. All this country was being turned into a desert by the slave trade, and Livingstone thought that if a steamer could be placed on lake Nyasa and a mission station set up in the high land of what we now call Nyasaland, it would be a good way of stopping the slave trade in that part of Africa. Livingstone's third and last journey, from 1866 to 1873, began at the mouth of the Rovuma river. His idea was to go westward to see if there were any river flowing into lake Victoria which might be called the true source of the Nile; people in Britain still thought that perhaps a river flowed from lake Tanganyika into lake Victoria, and they were not sure whether lake Victoria was one big lake or a group of smaller lakes. Livingstone went down to lake Nyasa, and then explored the country south and southwest of lake Tanganyika. He rested at Ujiji for a time, and then spent more than two years exploring the country west of the lake, finding rivers which flowed into the Congo, and not into the Nile. He spent seven years on this journey. Much of the food and medicine that was sent him from Britain was stolen before it reached him; many of his letters were stopped because the slavers were

[1] We have met Speke and Baker in Uganda: see pages 78 and 86.

afraid that he would tell his people too much about the slave trade. But the African people whome he met loved him so much that when he died near lake Bangweulu, his African friends and servants carried his dead body seven hundred miles down to the coast so that it might be buried in his own country.

Livingstone died in 1873. Next year, another great explorer named Stanley travelled from the east coast to lake Victoria; sailed in a boat all round the lake; went down to lake Tanganyika and sailed round that lake also; and then went westwards and down the Congo till in 1877 he came out on the Atlantic Ocean. On this journey, as we have seen[1], Stanley visited Buganda and spoke to Kabaka Mutesa about Christianity.

All these travels between 1851 and 1877 taught the people of Europe two lessons. The first was, that it was possible for Europeans to live and travel in the interior of Africa, and to win the friendship of Africans. Until then, most people had thought that a European would certainly die of disease or be killed by lions or snakes or by African spears and arrows. The second was that, as Livingstone kept preaching, the slave trade was an evil thing that must be stopped; and it could only be stopped by bringing East Africa under European rule, and introducing education and trade to replace the trade in slaves.

While Livingstone was exploring round lake Tanganyika, a war was being fought in Europe between France and a group of German states, of which the greatest was Prussia under its great statesman Bismarck. France was beaten, and Prussia and her German allies joined after the war to make one new and powerful state: Germany.[2]

It was not long before Germany began to think of taking part in the new European study of Africa. German missionaries, explorers, and traders began to work in Africa, and German warships as well as merchant ships began to visit the African coast. Societies were set up in Germany for the study and the exploration of Africa, and before long many Germans, especially among the younger men, were thinking that it was time for Germany to set up colonies of her own. It seemed to them that Britain had taken

[1] See page 87.
[2] We have met Bismarck before; on page 95 we have seen how he was willing to let Britain take Uganda, because it suited him just then to have Britain for a friend and to make the French more jealous of Britain.

much of the best land in the world, such as India, Canada and Australia; France was taking North Africa; and East and Central Africa was the last region left in which Germany might have a chance of building a colony that would be worth having. Bismarck himself at first was not interested, and the societies felt that without the Government's help they could not set up colonies in Africa. But there was a young man, Dr Karl Peters, who was not content with this. Like Dr Nkrumah in Ghana more than sixty years later, he decided that if the old societies were afraid to move faster, he would form a new society of his own.[1]

In 1884, Peters and some of his friends founded the Society for German Colonization; and in that same year, Peters came to East Africa to set up a German colony there. In November he came to Zanzibar, and although the German consul there tried to stop him, he crossed to the mainland, and made agreements with a number of chiefs in the country behind Dar-es-Salaam. He was in Africa only a few weeks; then he went quickly back to Germany, set up a company called the German East African Company, and gave the new company all the agreements he had made.

Of course, this made trouble. The Sultan of Zanzibar was angry, for he looked on all the Tanganyika coast as part of his kingdom, and looked on the chiefs who had made agreements with Peters as his people. The British consul in Zanzibar was Sir John Kirk, and he too was angry. He was angry because he had been working hard to get the slave trade stopped, and hoped to develop other and better kinds of trade in the Sultan's East African lands. But if the Sultan were to lose his lands, Kirk's years of work would be wasted. Moreover, there were some British traders who were doing a little further north just what Peters had done in Tanganyika. Only a few weeks before Peters made his agreements, a British officer had made agreements with some chiefs in the Kilimanjaro district, and a British East African Association had been formed with the idea of setting up a British colony in what is now Kenya. So the British East African Association too was angry when it heard what Peters had done.

[1] On pages 93 to 95 we have seen how Dr Peters did his best to make Uganda a German colony, in which he might have succeeded if his Government (especially Bismarck) had supported him.

It seems then that the British were just as bad as the Germans?

No, there was a difference. Peters had been busy in the country close to Dar-es-Salaam and had gone there secretly, knowing well that the Sultan did not want him to go. The British were making agreements in country 200 miles away, where the Sultan had no real power; moreover, they asked the Sultan's permission before they went there, and he gave it. As we have seen[1], Sultan Barghash of Zanzibar would have liked to lease all his mainland country to the British, if they would develop it for him and pay him a good rent and a good share of the trading profits. Sir John Kirk hoped that the British Government would one day agree to do this, but the Government was unwilling. The British Government in those days was doing its best to limit its colonial responsibilities. The year 1884, in which Peters made his agreements, is the year in which the British gave the Transvaal back its self-government[2]. Lord Cromer was just beginning his great work[3] of putting Egypt in order, and the British Government was still hoping that in a year or two he would have finished the job and the British could leave Egypt again. In Nigeria, the British trading company bought the French trading company, and the Government saw that it would soon have to set up a protectorate there.[4] On the Gold Coast, the Government was afraid that more trouble was coming with the Ashanti. Once you set foot on Africa, it seemed, you had to go on walking; it was difficult to stop and sit down. The Government was determined that it would not set foot on the land of East Africa if it could help it.

The German statesman, Bismarck, had so far been as unwilling as the British Government to set up colonies in Africa; but now he changed his mind, and he agreed to accept not only the land covered by Peters' agreements, but also the district of Witu at the mouth of the Tana river. Witu also belonged to the Sultan of Zanzibar, but a chief there named Simba had broken away from the Sultan and said that he was independent. Another German officer visited Simba and said that if he wished, Germany would protect him against the Sultan; and Simba made an agreement asking for German protection.

[1] See pages 92 and 93.
[2] See Book One, page 126.
[3] See page 42.
[4] See Book One, page 91.

Why did Simba do that? Did he not see that he would be losing his independence?

No; Simba was afraid of the Sultan, who had an army and might make war against him. He did not know the Germans well enough to be afraid of them. The Germans gave him guns which would be useful if he were attacked by Zanzibar; that was enough for Simba.

The Sultan protested at all this, and said that he would never agree to give his lands to the Germans. But in August 1885 a German fleet sailed into Zanzibar harbour, and the commander told the Sultan that if he did not agree, the ships would destroy his palace. Britain would do nothing to help him, so the Sultan had to agree. The Germans said that they would set up no colonies in the Sultan's lands; but they must first find out how far the Sultan's lands reached. In 1886 a commission, composed of British, German and Zanzibari members, agreed that the Sultan's country on the mainland stretched from Tunghi Bay in the south to the Tana River in the north, in a strip ten miles wide. Beyond the Tana, Kismayu and Mogadishu and two other towns belonged to the Sultan, each with a small piece of land surrounding it. The land behind this ten-mile strip was divided between Britain and Germany, the boundary being the present boundary between Kenya and Tanganyika. The Sultan agreed to all this; though he was angry when the Germans agreed with the Portuguese of Mozambique to move the Tanganyika border a little north from Tunghi Bay to the Rovuma River. The British East African Association agreed with the Sultan that they would govern the British section of the ten-mile coastal strip for him, paying him the same customs revenue that he was then getting from the mainland ports, and sharing equally with him any extra revenue that might come from increased trade. This agreement was made in 1887, and next year the Germans made a similar agreement over their section of the strip.

The British Government still wanted to keep out of East Africa if it could. We have heard[1] of Emin Pasha, who had been cut off from Egypt by the armies of the Mahdi. Emin Pasha offered to make the southern part of the Sudan a British colony if the British Government would help him; but the Government said No. Emin Pasha, it said, was a German; he had better ask his own Government.

[1] See page 91.

So there were now two companies, a British company in what is now Kenya and a German company in what is now Tanganyika. The difference between them is that the German company was supported by its Government, the British company was not. So development went ahead much faster in Tanganyika than in Kenya.

It went on much too fast for the people of Tanganyika. In August 1888 the Arabs and the Swahili-speaking Africans rose up against the Germans under a chief called Bushiri of Pangani. The German company had to call on the German Government for soldiers to help it fight the African people. Bushiri was caught and killed in December 1889, but the last of the fighting was not over until the middle of 1890. The German Government decided that the company ought not to have any responsibility for governing the colony; it made the company limit itself to matters of trade, and the German Government itself governed the new colony. The German agreement with the Sultan of Zanzibar was only a few months old; but Germany now proposed that instead of leasing the coastal strip from the Sultan, she should buy it from him altogether; and the Sultan agreed. That is why the Sultan still had in 1961 a coastal strip in Kenya, but none in Tanganyika.

We have read[1] about Karl Peters and his journey up the Tana to Uganda, which happened in 1889 and 1890, while the Germans were fighting against Bushiri and his men in German East Africa. The 1890 agreement between Britain and Germany, which so disappointed Peters because it gave Uganda to Britain, also fixed the boundary between German East Africa and the British lands in Central Africa; and Zanzibar and Pemba, and Witu as well, became British protectorates.

The German Government now settled down to develop its new colony. The Germans are very hard-working and careful, and they set to work to see what East Africa could produce. As early as 1902 they set up an agricultural station at Amani to study the animal and plant diseases of East Africa and to find out what crops could best be grown there. They made plantations of rubber, cotton, and coffee. The first rubber was exported in 1907, but only a few years later, the big new plantations in Malaya and other countries in south-east Asia produced so much rubber that

[1] See page 93.

the price fell and the East African plantations were ruined. The Germans tried hard with cotton. They set up cotton stations to teach the African people how to grow it; they printed text-books on cotton-growing in several African languages; they gave cotton-seed free to Africans, and made them plant it whether they wished to or not; and they did a great deal to see that the cotton was of good quality. They were unlucky, because after a few years the world price of cotton fell, as the world price of rubber did; and it was difficult to make the Africans grow cotton when they got so little for it. But up to 1914, the cotton crop in German East Africa was still increasing. Coffee began behind Tanga, but the Germans soon found that it grew better on the slopes of Kilimanjaro, and they made large plantations there. Some of the Chagga people of Kilimanjaro began to grow coffee for themselves, and away in the Bukoba district near Lake Victoria other African peoples grew coffee in among their plantain trees. The railway from Tanga to Moshi was built between 1896 and 1912 to help the coffee industry.

But the best thing the Germans did in the way of agricultural crops was when they introduced sisal from America in 1892. Sisal did very well in Tanganyika, and large areas of land grew sisal which could grow no other crop of any value. Sisal, like coffee, needed a railway; and in 1907 the Germans opened the railway line from Dar-es-Salaam to Morogoro; it reached Tabora in 1912 and Kigoma in 1914.

How did the Germans find the land for all these crops? Were there German settlers, and did they have the same difficulties that Kenya had?

Yes, many German settlers came to East Africa. In 1895, the German Government said that all the land of East Africa was Crown land, and it appointed commissions to see how much land the African people needed and how much could be set aside for Europeans. The Germans saw that they must be careful to leave the Africans enough, and they thought that it would be wise to leave the Africans four times as much land as they were actually using at the time. But even this, as they afterwards found, was not enough. Many Germans came and settled in the good part of the country (especially from Tanga to Moshi), and like the British settlers in Kenya, they complained that their Government did not do as much as it should do to help them to get labour on their farms and plantations. German East Africa was not heavily populated, and the German Government was trying to do many things at once: to build railways, to set up plantations, and to make the African people themselves grow cotton and other crops. By 1914, just over 3,000 square miles of land were in the hands of European settlers. (The land set aside for Europeans in Kenya was 16,000 square miles, though one-quarter of this was forest reserve, not to be used.)

The Germans did very good work in education. Most of it was carried on by the missionary societies, but there were several Government schools as well. By 1914 there were 60,000 children in primary schools, and there were a few receiving secondary education. When the British came to Tanganyika in 1920 after the war, they thought that education in Tanganyika was the best in East Africa.

But in all their determination to develop the country from the economic point of view[1], the Germans rather neglected to work out a proper system of government. Some of their district officers were good men, who tried to understand the people; but many were content as long as the people were quiet and worked hard. There were not many European district officers, and the Germans continued the Zanzibar system of appointing African chiefs to rule over districts where they were strangers. These chiefs were called *akidas;* they were responsible to the German district officers for law and order, and they collected the poll tax. As an *akida* did not rule over his own people, but over strangers, he could be no help to the Germans in understanding what the people were thinking; and no doubt many an *akida* collected much more than the proper amount of tax and kept the balance for himself.

All this new hard government and the new hard-working way of life was disliked by the African people. Bushiri's war ended in 1890, but there was much more fighting to come. As the Germans pushed inland from the coastal strip, they had much fighting against the Chagga, the Wanyamwezi, the Wahehe and other peoples; but this was finished by 1903. But just as the German Government was hoping that all trouble was over, it found itself faced by a new rising. In July 1905, the people south of the Rufiji

[1] That is, to develop its agriculture and its wealth; the Germans did more for Tanganyika's *economic* development than for its *political* development.

River rose up against the Germans in a war called the Maji-Maji war. This name means 'water-water', and the war is called by this name because the medicine-men mixed a medicine for the fighters, which, they said, would turn the German bullets to water so that they would do no harm. The war soon spread to other peoples, until all the south-eastern part of the country was full of fighting, from Dar-es-Salaam to Kilosa in the north and from Songea to Lindi in the south. The Maji-Maji people began by killing every German in the area: officials, settlers and missionaries alike. The Germans were surprised. Their first effort was to keep the Wahehe and the Wanyamwezi from joining in the war, and in this they succeeded; then they slowly broke down the Maji-Maji fighters, partly in battle but very largely by burning all the villages and all the crops. By January 1907 the fighting was over, and 120,000 Africans were dead, many of them from famine.

The Maji-Maji rising had one good result: it made the German Government see that it must take more trouble to understand the African people. A few weeks after the fighting was over, the Government set up a separate Colonial Office in Berlin, and appointed a Minister for the Colonies. The first Minister, Dr Dernburg, came out to East Africa to see things for himself, and found much that needed putting right; the German Parliament was angry at the stories it heard of bad government by the *akidas* and by some of the German district officers. Under Dr Dernburg, the German Government came to see that plantations were not everything. It did much to encourage Africans to grow cotton for themselves; it made it harder for Europeans to get Crown lands; it stopped forced labour except for public works such as repairing roads; it punished officers who had been cruel; it made much better rules for protecting African workers against their employers. It was a time of great improvement.

But Germany did not have long to make these improvements. In 1914, Germany and Britain went to war. For a time, the Europeans in East Africa, both Germans and British, hoped that the war would be fought in Europe and that there would be no fighting in Africa. But in Tanganyika there was a very great German General, Paul von Lettow-Vorbeck, who thought different-ly. He was not the Governor, but he persuaded the Governor (who at first had been one of those who hoped that there would be no fighting in Africa) to agree with him. General von Lettow-Vorbeck knew that the British fleet was much stronger than the German, so that Germany could send him no help. On the other hand, the German army in Europe was much stronger than the British and the French. It would therefore suit Britain if East Africa remained at peace; then Britain could take all her soldiers to strengthen her army in Europe. If it would suit Britain for East Africa to remain at peace, then, argued von Lettow-Vorbeck, it must suit Germany for East Africa to go to war. He could not hope to conquer Kenya and Uganda; but he could give the British so much trouble that they would need thousands of soldiers to guard British East Africa against his attacks: soldiers who would be much more useful fighting in Europe.

Von Lettow-Vorbeck was a fine general and a great man; and he played this game all through the war, from August 1914 to November 1918. As he foresaw , thousands of soldiers came against him: British, Belgians, Indians, Africans, and South Africans. The fighting went up and down Tanganyika from one end to the other, and the General was still free at the head of his little army when the war ended. They could not catch him.

But the war had ruined Tanganyika. Tens of thousands of men had to leave their villages and carry loads for the soldiers, and thousands and thousands of them died, not so much from bullets as from malaria and dysentery. Villages were destroyed, farms were left empty, the armies ate all the food, and women and children died of hunger.

TANGANYIKA UNDER BRITISH RULE

When peace was made, one of its conditions was that the German colonies in Africa and elsewhere should not be returned to German rule. The new League of Nations, which was set up under the peace treaty, set up a special commission to look after the former German colonies. Britain was given a *mandate* to govern Tanganyika: that is to say, was invited to govern Tanganyika but to give a report every year to the League of Nations. The League of Nations commission was called the Mandates Commission, and the Mandates Commission discussed the reports which the British Government sent it on Tanganyika.

Very much like the Trusteeship Council of the United Nations, it seems?

The idea is the same, but it was differently carried out. The members of the Mandates Commission did not represent their Governments; they were men chosen because of their experience in government. They did not visit the mandated territory, but discussed the territory's reports with the representatives of the Tanganyika Government, and gave advice to the League, which passed it on to the British Government. Another difference is that in those days, even the African people themselves were not yet thinking of independence; they still remembered the days of hunger and civil war and slavery, and they wanted peace and food and good government and education. The Mandates Commission did not, like the Trusteeship Council, begin with the idea that Tanganyika and the other countries must be given independence as soon as possible. The world has changed since 1920.

In 1920, Sir Horace Byatt was appointed the first British Governor of Tanganyika, and the usual British type of government was set up; an executive council of four officials – but no legislative council yet – and Government departments of education, agriculture, and so on. Sir Horace Byatt made as few changes as he could. He saw that what the country most needed was rest, so that the people could go back to their farming and trading, and the country could make up some of the wealth it had lost in the war. It was a difficult time; we have seen[1] that in 1921 and 1922 Kenya was suffering badly. But during the five years that Byatt was Governor, things improved, and before he left Tanganyika, the country no longer needed money grants from Britain.

The next Governor was Sir Donald Cameron, who had served in Nigeria, and had seen Lugard's system of indirect rule working there. What he saw in Tanganyika made him think that indirect rule would be good for the country.

What is indirect rule?

Indirect rule is the opposite of direct rule. The Germans had ruled Tanganyika on a system of direct rule. The German district officer gave his orders to the *akida*, and the *akida* passed them on to the people; both the *akida* and the district officer were strangers,

[1] See page 154.

whose power depended on the Government. When Lugard went to Northern Nigeria[1] he found strong Fulani emirs ruling the country; and he decided that it would be best to leave them to continue ruling their people, but to watch them and see that they ruled wisely. More than this: Lugard said that since people everywhere were accustomed to obey their own chiefs and elders, it would be better for a colonial Government to work through the chiefs and elders whom the people knew and obeyed. If changes had to be made, it would be easier for the Government to make them by explaining them to the chiefs and leaving the chiefs to explain them to their people. Gradually, Lugard thought, chiefs and their councils could be educated into becoming modern local government authorities. That was indirect trule as Lugard thought of it. The idea of ruling through chiefs and elders was taken up in many British colonies; though not all British governors and commissioners were as interested in the idea of educating the chiefs and elders as Lugard had been.

Some people have said that the British used indirect rule because they wanted to keep Africans divided into tribes and to keep them from developing into independent nations? Is this true?

That was certainly not Lugard's idea; nor was it Cameron's idea in Tanganyika; nor has it ever been the idea of the best British Governors and commissioners. According to Lugard and Cameron, there were two parts in the idea of indirect rule: one was to use the chiefs and their councils to rule their own people, and the other was to teach the chiefs and their councils to rule wisely and to use modern methods. This second idea must certainly lead to wider and wider co-operation between tribes. Roads, secondary schools, hospitals, electricity schemes, cannot be limited to one tribe; by co-operating in such schemes as these, different tribes will come to feel themselves members of one nation. That was what Lugard and Cameron hoped, and all the best British officers.

But there were two difficulties. One was that the chiefs' councils were full of old men, and old men are not interested in new ideas. It was easy for a British officer to say to a chief, 'This is a matter which you and your council must settle according to the custom of your people'. But is was very difficult to make the chief and his

[1] See Book One, page 87.

council see that there were some matters which they ought to handle themselves, but on which the custom of their people would give them no help. It was so difficult, that some British officers never succeeded, and after some years they gave up trying. In such a case, the chief and his council simply went on in their old way, and certainly did nothing towards making an independent nation.

The other difficulty was that because the chiefs' councils were full of old men, young men who were educated found no place in them. The educated young men were thinking of building up a modern nation, the old men were thinking of keeping up the old customs. If only the British could have found a way of bringing the two sides together, indirect rule would have been successful in helping Africans to develop into independent nations. But although in different parts of Africa the British tried to get educated young men to share in the work of the chiefs' councils, they never had very much success. As the British had promised to rule, and had ruled for so long, through the chiefs and their councils, the British could not turn back to find another way of ruling; and so some of the young men said that indirect rule was simply a way of keeping all the power in the hands of the old men and of slowing down independence. That was not what Lugard and Cameron meant it to be.

Sir Donald Cameron arrived in Tanganyika as Governor in 1925, and next year the Government passed the Native Authority Ordinance, which began the system of indirect rule. The Ordinance gave the Government power to recognize a chief and his council as a Native Authority; and when a Native Authority had been recognized, it was given powers to hold courts of law, to collect taxes, to maintain peace and good order and to make regulations on various matters. The British officers were told to find out who in their districts was accepted by the people as a traditional chief. They found that all the years of German direct rule had not made the people forget their chiefs; the chiefs had not been recognized by the German Government, but their people still obeyed them. Under Sir Donald Cameron's Government, the traditional chiefs were recognized, and the system of native authorities soon became a success. The authorities began to run schools and dispensaries and other things which were outside traditional African custom.

Cameron found that many of the native authorities were too

small and too poor to have much hope of developing into really effective local government bodies. He tried to persuade some of them to join together into larger bodies. In this way the Sukuma Federation and the Nyamwezi Federation were set up, and there were other smaller bodies formed by grouping chiefs together.

It was Cameron, too, who first gave Tanganyika its Legislative Council. It met for the first time in December 1926, with fourteen official members and seven unofficials; five Europeans and two Asians. All the members were nominated. Cameron thought that the time had not yet come for elections, and he thought too that Africans had enough to do for the moment in getting their native authorities to work. Moreover, very few Africans understood English, and those who did were mostly young men. He hoped that the African native authorities would one day send represent-atives to provincial or regional councils; and later still there might be a central African council for the whole of Tanganyika. When that had happened, it would be time enough to think of African members of the Legislative Council. Till then, the Governor and his senior officials on the Council would look after African interes-ests.

In 1929 the seven unofficial members were increased to ten; there were now seven Europeans and three Asians, all of them still nominated.

Cameron saw that the country needed economic development as well as local government and a legislative council. The railway line from Tanga to Moshi was pushed up to Arusha to help the European planters who were growing coffee there, and the Central line was extended from Tabora to Mwanza on the southern shore of Lake Victoria. In German times a few of the Chagga people had tried growing coffee, but the German Government had not encouraged them, and they gave it up. The British district com-missioner, Mr Dundas (later Sir Charles Dundas) had the idea that the Chagga might grow coffee in the shade of the plantains which they grew for food; and he persuaded many of the Chagga to start doing this and to set up the Kilimanjaro Native Planters' Association to market their coffee. Coffee (of a different kind) was also grown in the Bukoba district; so coffee was now added to sisal and cotton as an important export crop, though sisal was far the most important.

Tanganyika had few minerals. The Germans had found nothing

except a little mica. Soon after the war, gold was found near Lake Victoria and in the far south of the country, but there was not much; later on, a little tin and silver and tungsten were found, all useful but all in small quantities. In 1940 diamonds were found at Shinyanga, and diamonds soon became Tanganyika's most important mineral. Another of Cameron's wise acts was to set up a strong Labour Department to look after the workers in plantations and mines: to see that proper arrangements were made for housing and feeding them, for helping them to travel from their villages to their place of work, and for providing medical help.

Tanganyika, like Kenya and every other country, suffered badly in the bad times of poverty from 1929 to 1937. The revenue from African hut and poll taxes dropped from £750,000 to £450,000 in two years. Africans who were beginning to grow crops for export lost courage when they saw the prices falling. Much of the Government's plans for developing education and health and other services had to be given up because there was no money to pay for them. Tanganyika was just beginning to make a little economic progress once more when the war came in 1939.

The war of 1939–45 affected Tanganyika in the same way as it affected other African countries. Its men joined the army and fought overseas, so that they saw other countries and other ways of living, and came home with wider experience and with more money than if they had stayed at home. Tanganyika's exports, the gold and sisal, coffee and cotton and diamonds, earned the country much more money; so that at last the Government saw the chance of doing some of the things it had wished to do before the war but had been too poor to do. Just after the war, the Government in London tried to start a big ground-nut industry in Tanganyika. It would have been a great help to Tanganyika if it had succeeded, for ground-nuts are an important export crop in Nigeria and some other African countries. But the scheme did not succeed.

Though not as poor as it had been, Tanganyika was still poor. But its education and other services received help from the British Government under the Colonial Development and Welfare Act of 1945.[1]

After the war, four African members were nominated to the Legislative Council; and in 1949, the Government thought that it would be wise to enlarge the Council further, so that Africans

[1] See page 173.

could take a larger share in the work of government. The year before, there had been trouble in the Gold Coast, and one cause of the trouble was that Africans had not enough share in the government, and ex-soldiers had many complaints which the Government did not take seriously enough. So the Tanganyika Government decided to learn from the Gold Coast experience. It formed all the unofficial members of the Legislative Council into a committee, and asked them to go round the country and see if Africans had complaints and wanted to have changes made in the central Government. The members went round the country, and were surprised to find that most people seemed to take no interest in the affairs of the central Government; their problems and complaints were all local affairs. So they came back to Dar-es-Salaam and said that if the Legislative Council were bigger, it might have more influence. They proposed that instead of 7 European, 4 African and 3 Asian unofficial members, the Council should have seven from each race.

In 1955 a new Legislative Council was set up as the committee had proposed. It had thirty nominated unofficial members: three from each of the eight provinces, three from Dar-es-Salaam, and three others. The eight *ex-officio* members of the Council became Ministers, and six unofficial members (four Africans, one European, and one Asian) became Assistant Ministers. Tanganyika was moving quickly towards self-government.

But it is not self-government when all the members are nominated by the Governor; there must be elections.

True: elections were the next step, and in 1956 an election law was passed. There was to be a common voters' roll, on which African voters would be in a large majority over Asians and Europeans. Each area would be represented in the Council by three members, one from each race; and each voter would have three votes, which he must use by voting for one candidate from each race. In this way, all three races would share in the work of government.

Many people were afraid that this complicated system of elections would not make a good Council, for voters of one race would not be able to choose candidates of another race, whom they did not know. But the system did work very well. In 1954 Mr Julius Nyerere, a former school teacher, founded a political party

P

called the Tanganyika African National Union. Although it was
an African Union, Mr Nyerere was so wise, and so friendly to the
Asians and Europeans, that they had a great respect for him, and
many agreed to serve under him. When the elections were being
held, Mr Nyerere was able to tell the African voters that if they
voted for the European and Asian candidates whom he named,
they would be voting for men who were willing to serve under him.
The result was that in the 1958 elections, Mr Nyerere's party, the
T.A.N.U., won most of the seats.

But Mr Nyerere said, and the European and Asian members of
his party agreed with him, that because Tanganyika was mainly
an African country (it had eight million Africans to about 20,000
Europeans) it was wrong that there should be as many European
and as many Asian members in the Legislative Council as African
members. The Government set up a committee, called the Ramage
Committee because its chairman was Sir Richard Ramage, to see
what further changes should be made. The Ramage Committee
reported in 1959. It proposed that there should be a large majority
of elected African members in the Legislative Council, but that
some seats should be reserved for Asian and European members.
The Government accepted the proposals, and new elections were
held in September 1960. The new Legislative Council had fifty
seats for African elected members, with eleven seats reserved for
Asians and ten for Europeans. In addition, the Governor had
power to nominate a few extra members. Again, Mr Nyerere and
the T.A.N.U. won the election. Most of his candidates were not
opposed; and of those that were opposed, only one lost his seat.
Forty-nine out of the fifty African elected members thus supported
Mr Nyerere; and so did many of the Asian and European members.
Mr Nyerere became Chief Minister, and next year was called
Prime Minister; ten out of the 14 members of the Council of
Ministers were chosen by him.

We see, then, that Tanganyika's central Government made
great progress in ten years, although its local government was still
being run on the system of indirect rule. There were 435 native
authorities, with 28 town councils and the council of Dar-es-Salaam.
After the war, the Government thought that something ought to
be done to try and develop local government on more modern
lines. In 1953 the Legislative Council passed the Local Government Ordinance, which provided that there should be three kinds

of local government bodies: local councils, town councils, and county councils. The local councils would be developed out of the native authorities, with extra members added, Europeans or Asians as well as Africans. When the first local councils and county councils were set up, the local councils, which covered a smaller area, had more success than the county councils. This made the Government think that it would be wise to encourage councils which covered the area of one administrative district; and a new law was passed to provide for these new district councils. Some of the chiefs were afraid that all these changes meant that there would be no more room for them, but the Government promised that the chiefs would be allowed to continue in the work of local government, and that people who preferred to go on with a council of the old type should not have a council of the new type forced on them. The new district councils will take over some of the work which used to be done by the central Government, and they will draw their revenue partly from local rates[1] and partly from money paid to them in grants from the central Government. But it will take some time before all local government in Tanganyika is reorganized on these new lines.

In December 1961, Tanganyika became fully independent, with Mr Nyerere as Prime Minister.

But what about Zanzibar? You have told us nothing about Zanzibar since it became a British protectorate.

There is not much to tell. The Sultan continued to govern his dominions. He was assisted by a British Resident, and of course employed British officials. There was no British Governor. The Sultan's dominions included not only the islands, but the coastal strip of Kenya; this strip was leased from him by the Kenya Government, and was treated as part of Kenya. Zanzibar was moderately prosperous; it was the world's chief producer of cloves, and its only serious worry for a long time was a disease ('sudden death' it was called) of the clove trees.

But below the surface, things were not so happy. Zanzibar could not expect to be free from all the political trouble on the mainland. Like Kenya, it was a multi-racial country. There were

---

[1] Local taxes are called rates.

no British there except a few officials and business men; the ruling class consisted of the Arabs. There were 45,000 of them, and 16,000 Asians, but there were 240,000 Africans. To the Africans, the Arabs were just as much foreigners as the British were. They had been there much longer than the British, but they had been slave-owners and slave-dealers until the British stopped them. The Africans did not see why three per cent of the population should hold all the political power.

And so politics began in Zanzibar mainly as a movement against the rule of the Sultan and his Arabs. The main party called itself the Afro-Shirazi party. It took this strange name because there was a tradition that some of the people of Zanzibar in the early days had come from Shiraz in Persia. The name meant that the party stood for the original inhabitant of Zanzibar against the Arabs.

The British advised the Sultan to allow parliamentary government and a ministerial system; and he did so. The Arabs of course formed their own party to fight for their own governing power. Elections were held in July 1963. The Afro-Shirazi party, under its leader Mr Karume, won 13 seats, and its opponents won 18. No party likes losing an election; and the Afro-Shirazi party was especially bitter at this result, for it had received 13,000 more votes than the winning party. It complained that there must have been trickery to produce this election result.

The British however were anxious to end their responsibilities in East Africa. Uganda and Tanganyika were already independent, and Kenya was about to become so. If there was trickery in the Zanzibar election, it was well hidden, and the British did not feel that they could refuse to accept the election result as a fair test of public opinion. In December 1963, Zanzibar became independent; the Sultan was head of the state, and there was a cabinet formed from the majority of the assembly.

One month later, on 12 January 1964, there was a revolution in Zanzibar. A small group of armed men took possession of the secretariat building, the radio station, the Sultan's palace, and other public buildings. There was not much fighting, except at one or two police stations, where the police fired at the men who told them to come out and give up their guns. The Sultan's Government was taken by surprise, and it had no soldiers. It was soon over. The Sultan got on a ship and escaped to Dar-es-

Salaam. The rebels[1] proclaimed that Zanzibar was now a republic, with Mr Karume (leader of the Afro-Shirazi party) as president. The Afro-Shirazi party had lost the elections six months earlier; it had now taken power by force.

The new Government in Zanzibar made it plain that Zanzibar was no longer an Arab country; it was an African country. The Minister for Home Affairs, Mr Muhammad Babu, said that the revolution had been brought about because of the old Government's 'stupid administration and favouritism to the Arabs'. The old Arab ruling class very soon lost all power. Three months after the revolution, in April 1964, Zanzibar and Tanganyika joined together into one state, to be called Tanzania. President Nyerere of Tanganyika was to be president of Tanzania, and there were to be two vice-presidents: Mr Karume of Zanzibar and Mr Kawawa of Tanganyika.

THINGS TO DO, TO DISCUSS, OR TO FIND OUT

1. We are told that Rhapta was 25 days sailing from the mouth of the Red Sea, and that from Rhapta it was 14 days journey by land to a mountain covered with snow. Find how far an Arab sailing ship could go in one day, allowing for ocean currents. Take your atlas, start from the mouth of the Red Sea and measure this distance 25 times along the East African coast. (Remember that the ship would keep in sight of the land all the way, so follow the bends in the coast-line.) Where do you think that Rhapta was? There are two mountains in Kenya and Tanganyika which are covered with snow: which are they? How far is each from the sea? Could either of them be reached on foot from the sea in 14 days? If so, where does this suggest that Rhapta was? Can you make the two answers agree?

2. We still find in East Africa Indian beads and Chinese pottery imported by the Arabs several hundred years ago. Why do we not find Chinese and Indian silks and cotton goods and Arabian spices?

---

[1] A rebel is a man who overthrows, or tries to overthrow, the Government of his country by force.

3. Even Ibn Batuta was content to go from one East Coast town to another; he did not go inland. Can you suggest why the Arabs of East Africa did not go far inland until the days of the 19th century slave trade?

4. Draw a map of the Indian Ocean to show the Portuguese settlements and trading posts.

5. How would the history of East Africa and India have been different if the Chinese had kept up their sea-power and had been able to keep the Portuguese out of the Indian Ocean?

6. This is a list of some African crops and food-stuffs, showing where their real home is and who first brought them to Africa.

Plant	Home	Brought by
Banana	S.E. Asia	Arabs
Cassava	Eastern Brazil	Portuguese
Cocoa	Central America	Portuguese
Coconut	Tropical Asia	Indonesians?
Cotton	India	Arabs
Egg-plant	India	Arabs
Groundnut	Brazil	Portuguese
Lime	S.E. Asia	Arabs? Indonesians?
Maize	America	Portuguese
Okro	N.E. Africa and Arabia	Arabs
Peppers	Central America	Portuguese
Plantain	India	Arabs
Rice	Tropical Asia	Arabs?
Sweet-potato	Caribbean	Portuguese
Sugar-cane	India	Arabs
Tomato	Mexico	Portuguese
Yam	China	Arabs

(There may have been some kinds of rice and of yam native to Africa; but the kinds now used were brought from overseas.) What did Africans eat before the Arabs, Indonesians and Portuguese came? Coffee is not in this list; where is the home of coffee?

7. Would Britain ever have made colonies in East Africa if there had been no Arab slave trade? If you say Yes, what do you think would have brought the British into East Africa?

8. Write and act scenes in which: (a) Captain Moresby and Sultan Seyyid Said are discussing the treaty of 1822; (b) The Sultan of Zanzibar and Sir John Kirk are discussing Dr Karl Peters; (c) General von Lettow-Vorbeck and his Governor are discussing what they should do in 1914.
9. Do you think direct rule in the German fashion or indirect rule in the British fashion the best kind of government for a colony? Which would have done more for economic development? Which would have done more to prepare the colony for independence?
10. Do you think that the chiefs and their councils have any useful part to play in modern local government? Give your reasons.
11. Was it right to take Tanganyika away from Germany in 1919 and place it under a British mandate?
12. Why did Tanganyika, the poorest of the three countries of East Africa, gain its independence so much more quickly and easily than Kenya and Uganda?

KENYA

THINGS TO DO, TO DISCUSS, OR TO FIND OUT

1. Write and act a scene in which the Carter Commission is trying to find out from its witnesses whether a piece of land belongs to the Kikuyu or the Dorobo.
2. Most people in England today have no land at all. Suppose the population of Kenya doubles itself in the next hundred years, and that many factories are built in the towns. Will all the African people of Kenya still be able to have land, or will Kenya become like England?
3. How long will the Masai be able to live as they now do, wandering with their cattle over hundreds of miles of country?
4. Do you think the Swynnerton scheme, or something like it, is the answer to Kenya's land question? If not, what would you suggest?
5. Write and act two scenes: (a) The European farmers after the 1914 war discuss how to get their farms working again, and agree that they must cut the pay of their African workers; (b) They explain this to the Africans.

6. Draw a map of Kenya, and mark on it (a) the land which is suitable both for cattle and for agriculture, (b) the land which is suitable for cattle but not for agriculture. (It depends on rainfall.) Measure the areas. What proportion of Kenya is suitable for (a) both agriculture and cattle, (b) cattle only, (c) neither?

7. Make a time chart of the history of education in Kenya, using the dates given in this book and any others you can find.

8. Find out when the first Christian missionaries came to Kenya, and make a list of the dates when the important missionary societies began their work.

9. Make a time chart of the progress of Kenya, Uganda and Tanganyika towards self-government. Put all three countries on one chart so that you can compare them.

10. On page 179 we read that Africans disliked the Lyttelton proposals because they thought that European ministers would do more for Europeans than they would for Africans and Asians. Were the Africans right in thinking so? If so, do you think that African ministers will do more for Africans than for Asians and Europeans? Is it possible to find ministers who will be fair to all Kenyans, of whatever race?

11. How far is it true to say that KANU means the Kikuyu and their relatives, and KADU means the rest of the African peoples of Kenya? Ought political parties to be based on tribal feeling? If not, on what should they be based?

12. Find out all you can about the Swynnerton plan for Kenya agriculture, and how far it is working in Kenya. Do you think that some such plan would help Uganda and Tanganyika?

13. On pages 184 and 185 we read that the African leaders refused to help in the work of Government because they disliked the constitution. Is it the custom among your people to walk out of a tribal council if they disagree with what is being done? Do you think, generally speaking, that an independent African Government will mind if some members of Parliament walk out and refuse to share in its work? Find out what President Nkrumah's Government in Ghana does to members of Parliament who do this.

14. Find out the value of the goods exported from Kenya last year: coffee, cotton, pyrethrum, hides and so on. Make a table of the figures. Mark on a map the parts of Kenya where each item comes from. Which countries buy these Kenya products?

15. Find out what goods are manufactured in Kenya. How much of Kenya manufactures is sold in East Africa, and how much is sold overseas? Can you suggest any other kinds of goods which could be manufactured more cheaply in Kenya than imported from overseas?

16. Would it be a good thing for Kenya, Uganda and Tanganyika if, when all are independent, they joined together into an East African Federation?

17. If a cow was worth £ 2 in 1954, how did Mr Swynnerton think its value could be increased to £ 10 or £ 15?

18. If the Somali people living in the north of Kenya wish the boundary of Kenya to be altered so that their part of Kenya is added to Somalia, do you think that an independent Kenya Government ought to do what they ask? If not, why not?

A HISTORY
OF AFRICA

BOOK THREE

PREFACE

This book, which deals with the three countries formerly combined in the Federation of Rhodesia and Nyasaland, is the third book in a series written for African students in modern or middle schools, secondary schools and teacher training colleges. Many of these institutions will have no history specialist on their staffs; the book is therefore planned so as to provide useful background reading without the help of a specialist teacher. There is a list of 'things to do, to discuss, or to find out.'

Bearing in mind that English is a second language to my readers, I have tried to keep the English style and vocabulary simple. But though the style may be simple, the matter is not. The book is designed for readers with a keen interest in the political and economic problems of the region, and I hope it will be useful to School Certificate and G.C.E. candidates studying the history of Central Africa. I have taken more pains to simplify the style than the vocabulary; African students are familiar with the everyday political terms, though they are not found in the 2,000-word vocabulary of the *General Service List*.

Anyone writing about the history of the Bantu peoples has to face the difficulty of tribal names. I have not tried to be completely consistent over this. As a rule, I write of Shona, Zulu, Lovale, not of amaShona, amaZulu, baLovale. I refer to Msilikazi's people as Ndebele, not as Matabele; but I use the European terms Mashonaland and Matabeleland. There is the further difficulty that names of countries change. When writing of pre-colonial days, I try to use geographical expressions such as 'north of the Zambesi' or 'the lake country' or 'the country which is now called Zambia'; when dealing with the colonial period I use the terms then officially current; since independence I write of Zambia and Malawi. Here again, I cannot hope to have been completely consistent.

As in the other books of the series, I do not shrink from treating subjects which are controversial; indeed, the whole history of the region, from Rhodes's first dealings with Lobengula to Ian Smith's declaration of independence, has been a matter of acute controversy. The politics of yesterday are the history of today. One of the uses

5

of history should be to discipline our emotions with knowledge, and to teach us to conduct our controversies in a civilised manner. It is partly for this reason that I approach the subject sometimes in the form of a dialogue, allowing an imaginary interlocutor to raise queries and objections. This is a convenient device for introducing differing opinions on controversial points. Much of my career has been spent in Government service (though not in Central Africa); but all the views I express are of course personal, not official views.

There is a list of books for further reading, many of which have helped me; but I must make special acknowledgement of my debt to A. J. Wills's *An Introduction to the History of Central Africa*. I have also to thank Mr E. Wightman, Press Attaché in the Zambia High Commission in London, for his courteous help in answering my requests for information about his country.

W. E. F. WARD

CONTENTS

Page

ILLUSTRATIONS

Nos. 1, 13–16 courtesy of Camera Press; nos. 2–11 Radio Times Hulton Picture Library; no. 12 High Commission for the Republic of Malawi

NOTES ON ILLUSTRATIONS

2. They are attacking a village. Some are shooting down the fighting men who resist. Others are driving away the young men and women slaves, yoked together at the neck.

3. This drawing was made in 1861. The march might take some weeks, and very many slaves died before reaching the slave market.

4. The *indaba* in the Matopo hills, at which Rhodes listened to the grievances of the Ndebele. Rhodes is sitting with his hands on his knees, while the white man with the beard interprets what he has just said and the chiefs sit listening.

5. Rhodes was much criticised in England, and had to appear before a committee of the House of Commons to explain his policy. Rhodes is speaking at the small table in the middle. The map on the wall shows the Transvaal and the Orange Free State as still independent; everything north of the Limpopo, including the modern country of Malawi, is called Rhodesia.

6. The Mashona, like their forefathers, have built their village on a rocky hill-top for greater safety; but the Ndebele have set the houses on fire and are now killing the people. This raid took place just after the British had settled in Salisbury in 1890.

7. The drawing was made by Sir Harry Johnston. Some of Jumbe's ships can be seen tied up to the shore.

8. No machine has yet been invented for harvesting tea. In every country where tea is grown, the young leaves have to be picked by hand. Notice how the bushes are planted in rows along the contour of the hill to prevent erosion.

11. Sunflower seed is valuable for its oil. Modern machinery is greatly increasing Africa's agricultural wealth.

12. Dr Hastings Banda, first President of the Republic of Malawi.

13. The President is seen making a speech against Mr Ian Smith's Government in Rhodesia.

14. Zambia has valuable forests, which are being developed by modern machinery.

15. This photograph was taken when the dam was newly finished and the lake was just beginning to fill. A road runs along the top of the dam. You can see how big the dam is if you compare it with the cars and lorries on the road.

16. These transformers pick up the electricity which is generated at the Kariba power station, and start it on its journey to the copper-belt. If you look at the workmen on the right of the picture, you will see how big the transformers are.

MAPS

LIST OF BOOKS

L. H. Gann: *A History of Northern Rhodesia*
J. R. Gray: *The Two Nations*
A. J. Hanna: *The Story of the Rhodesias and Nyasaland*
Colin Leys and Cranford Pratt: *A New Deal in Central Africa*
Philip Mason: *The Birth of a Dilemma*
R. Oliver: *Sir Harry Johnston and the Scramble For Africa*
Margery Perham: *Lugard – The Years of Adventure*
W. Rayner: *The Tribe and Its Successors*
E. A. Walker: *A History of Southern Africa*
B. Williams: *Cecil Rhodes*
A. J. Wills: *An Introduction to the History of Central Africa*

1

EARLY DAYS IN CENTRAL AFRICA

It is harder to learn the early history of East and of Central Africa than the early history of West Africa. The West African kingdoms of Ghana, Mali, and Songhai were visited by Arab travellers like Ibn Batuta, and the travellers have left us descriptions of what they saw. The African peoples learned to read and write, and they produced historians and learned men like Es Sadi and Leo Africanus, whose books we can still read. But things were different in East and Central Africa. The Arab travellers like El Masudi visited the Arab coast towns, but they do not seem to have gone inland, and they do not tell us much about the African peoples who lived there. Moreover, the African peoples did not learn to read and write, so they have left no written records of their own. There was no one in East and Central Africa like Es Sadi, the African historian who tells us much of what we know about the history of the Songhai. In East and Central Africa we have to depend on what we can learn from historical remains, and from African traditions handed down by word of mouth.

In Central Africa, we have both African traditions and historical remains; but neither tell us as much as we should like. There are plenty of stone buildings, of which Zimbabwe is the most famous; and there are ancient gold workings, and some pottery and beads and other small objects. But we are not yet able to say exactly who built Zimbabwe, or when it was built, or what the different buildings were used for. As for the traditions, there has been so much coming and going, and so much mingling of peoples, that the traditions do not take us back very far.

The Arabs did not go further south than Sofala. There they could get iron and gold, but beyond Sofala there was nothing to attract them. From what the Arab traveller El Masudi tells us, it seems that the people who sent their gold down to Sofala must have been Bantu. He says that they kept cattle and used both gold and iron. They hunted elephants, but did not use the ivory; they sold it to the Arabs. They thought highly of good speaking; they had a king, who they thought was the son of a god; but although he was the son of a god, they killed him if he did not govern them well.

El Masudi visited the coast in the year 912, about 150 years before Abu Bekr conquered Ghana. It is of some importance to know that the people of the Sofala region at that time were probably Bantu. We believe that the different Bantu-speaking peoples advanced southward through Africa. Some scholars think that they came from somewhere near the great lakes, others think that they came from further west, near Cameroun. They took hundreds of years over their march, and as they came, they drove the Bushmen and other earlier peoples out of their way. The Bantu had iron spears and hoes, and some of them kept cattle; the Bushmen had no metals, did not grow crops, and regarded the Bantu cattle as easy game for hunting. To the Bantu (and much later, to the Dutch in South Africa) the Bushmen were merely a nuisance: just as much of a nuisance as elephants or baboons or locusts who spoil the farms today. When the Bantu came, the Bushmen had to go.

We do not know if the Bantu had gone beyond Sofala in El Masudi's day. Perhaps not: it may be that the Arabs, and El Masudi himself, stopped at Sofala because the people further south were all Bushmen, and there was no gold or ivory or iron to be bought. But this is only a guess; we do not know. The southernmost of the Bantu peoples, the Xosa, first met the Dutch at the Fish river in South Africa in 1776; that was about 850 years after El Masudi's time, and 1200 miles away.

We must not think that these early Bantu tribes of 1000 or 1500 years ago were large and powerful nations like the Zulu or the Bemba or the Baganda of today. They began as very small groups: perhaps only three or four families, two or three hundred people. But though the groups were small, they were stronger than the Bushmen and other peoples whom they found already in central Africa. The Bushmen too lived in small groups; they had to, because they lived by hunting and by gathering wild leaves and fruits and roots. The Bushmen made their tools of stone; the Bantu had iron. With their iron hoes and pangas, the Bantu grew better crops (the Bushmen did not grow crops at all, but some other peoples did); and so the Bantu had better food. The Bantu kept sheep and cattle, which the other people did not; and of course the Bantu had iron spears, which made them stronger in war.

So we must imagine East and Central Africa gradually becoming dotted with small groups of people. Bantu clans were moving south, pushing aside most of the Bushmen and others, but perhaps here and there taking wives from them. With their iron pangas and hoes they were cutting and burning the bush and planting their crops in the rich ashes: beginning to change the vegetation of Africa in a way which the older peoples with their stone tools could never do. All the time from about 500 BC – no one can say exactly when – until about 1000 AD, this slow advance was going on. By about 1000 AD the Bantu were mining the gold; some of it they sold to the Arabs at Sofala, and some of it their own goldsmiths made into beautiful ornaments. And by about 1000 AD too, some of the buildings at Zimbabwe were probably standing; at any rate, some of the wood used in the building dates from before 800.[1]

THE FIRST BANTU INVASIONS

It seems likely that the first Bantu invaders, including the forefathers of the Nguni and the Sotho, came south across the Zambesi some time between 1000 and 1200, and lived in what is now Rhodesia for two or three hundred years. Behind them came the Shona; they arrived about 1450, and drove out the earlier Bantu.

[1] There is still much uncertainty over the date of the buildings at Zimbabwe. It is certain that the site was inhabited about the year 300 AD by a people who used iron; that many of its stone buildings were standing by about 1400; and that those who built them were local Africans – not Egyptians or Phoenicians or other foreigners, as was once believed. (Egyptians of course are Africans, but they would be quite foreign to that part of Africa, and their buildings were quite unlike those of Zimbabwe.)

MAP 1. SOUTHERN AFRICA

The following rivers are marked, all of them mentioned in the book:

Congo	1	Limpopo	11	Luena	4
Fish	12	Lualaba	2	Rovuma	9
Kabompo	6	Luangwa	8	Shire	10
Kafue	7	Luapula	3	Zambesi	5

The Sotho moved southward and westward. One section
of them settled just south of the Limpopo in what is now the
Transvaal. Another moved into the mountains and became
the forefathers of the Basuto people of today. A third went
further west, and mixed with earlier peoples living on the
edge of the Kalahari desert to form the Tswana people. The
early Nguni people took a more easterly route, and settled
between the mountains and the sea, in what is now Natal.

1. The Victoria Falls

They stayed there until the time of the Mfecane[1] and the wars of the early nineteenth century. Then, as we shall see, many of the Nguni peoples left that region of Africa altogether and fought their way back northwards. We shall hear more of these northward journeys of the Nguni in Chapter Three.

It seems that for some hundreds of years, from the time that the first Bantu peoples crossed the Zambesi until about 1600, central Africa was fairly peaceful. The population was small, and there was room for everybody – once the Bushmen had been pushed away. The Shona peoples themselves caused a disturbance when they arrived about 1450, but the country settled down again after a time.

We say the Shona peoples, not people; for there were many different Shona clans or small groups. There were already

[1] See pages 33–38 of this book.

some Bantu peoples living in the Zambesi valley; they did not all move south with the Sotho when the Shona arrived. After a time the Shona conquered them, and these peoples (the Tonga and the Tavara) became subjects of the Shona. The Shona chief who led his people on this war of conquest was called Mutota. The Tavara people whom he conquered did not call him by his own name. They spoke of him as Mwene Mtapa, 'the great plunderer'. As often happens[1], Mutota and his people took this name and used it as a title of honour. All Mutota's successors bore the title of Mwene Mtapa.

It seems then that for something like five hundred years, the land between the Zambesi and the Limpopo was gradually settled by various Bantu peoples: first by the early Sotho and Nguni and others, and then by the Shona. Other Bantu peoples such as the Ila and the Tonga stayed north of the Zambesi. The kingdom of the Mwene Mtapa and his Shona people was rich and strong, largely because it exported gold to the Arabs at Sofala.

In 1486, about the same time as the Shona were settling down, the first Portuguese sea captain found his way round the Cape of Good Hope into the Indian Ocean; and a few years later, Vasco da Gama sailed right up the east coast and found the way across the ocean to India. As we shall see in the next chapter, the Portuguese brought trouble to central Africa. For the moment, we will simply notice that they are arriving on the coast, and we will continue with the story of the coming of the African peoples.

THE MALAWI AND LUBA PEOPLES

A new group of peoples was coming down from the north at that time. The early Portuguese traders met them in the country round lake Nyasa, and called them Maravi; they called the lake too lake Maravi because of the people who lived there. Maravi or Malawi: it is the same word. As far as the Portuguese could learn, the Malawi peoples arrived in the country between lake Nyasa and lake Tanganyika about the year 1500, and

---

[1] There was another such case in West Africa. The king of Songhai called himself Askia; the word was an angry exclamation uttered by women who did not want to see this man become king.

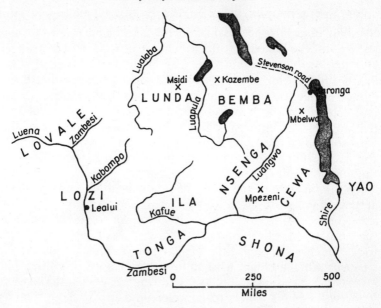

MAP 2. THE PEOPLES OF CENTRAL AFRICA

This map shows where the principal Bantu peoples mentioned in Chapter One settled north of the Zambesi. The Luyi are given their later name of Lozi.

Four places are marked with a cross instead of a dot: Msidi, Kazembe, Mbelwa, Mpezeni. These are the villages where the four chiefs of those names lived, and we mark them with a cross because we do not know exactly where they were. The map marks the Stevenson road from lake Nyasa to lake Tanganyika.

they stayed there more or less peacefully for about two hundred years.

As they came south, the Malawi seem to have kept fairly close to the two lakes. Other Bantu peoples were moving in the same direction, further to the west of the Malawi and a little behind them. These were the Luba.

The Luba did not keep cattle; they lived by their crops and by hunting. They came up from the Congo valley, perhaps fifty years behind the Malawi; and they found land to live in which was fairly empty, except for some Bushmen, whom of course they drove out. They lived peacefully in their new home until their numbers grew and they became too crowded. Then some of them moved to find new homes.

About 1600, a woman called Lueji became chief of the Luba. She had three brothers, who did not like being ruled by their sister; and they liked it still less when Lueji married a stranger and her husband began to act as if he were the chief. One brother took some of the people and moved westward into the Congo valley. Another brother also took some of the people and settled on the banks of the Luena river. This river is a tributary of the Zambesi; it flows through what is now Angola. This section of the Luba people became the Lovale tribe, who still live in that area, though it is now divided between Angola, the Congo, and Zambia.

The main part of the Luba people stayed where they were, and were ruled by Lueji and her husband. As time went on, they too grew in numbers, and they began to call themselves the Lunda. One of their later chiefs, who was Lueji's grandson, took for himself the title of Mwata Yamvwa, 'master of wealth'. All the chiefs who followed him bore this title, and it is still in use today. Some time during the 1600s, the Mwata Yamvwa sent out chiefs to conquer land further south, so as to enlarge the Lunda territory. In this way the Luapula valley became Lunda country; the capital of the Mwata Yamvwa was west of the Luapula, in what is now the Katanga province of the Congo, but his people lived also well east of the river in what is now the north-eastern part of Zambia.

We shall end this chapter on 'early days' about the year 1700. Many of the peoples who live in central Africa today had not then appeared in the region. We shall describe them in Chapter Three. In Chapter Two we shall speak of the Portuguese, and what happened in the region because of them.

Let us sum up this story of how the early Bantu peoples came into central Africa. They came in three big waves. First came the forefathers of the Sotho and the Nguni, who settled between the Zambesi and the Limpopo some time about the year 1000 or 1200: we do not know quite when, but about the time of the fall of old Ghana.

The second wave was the Shona, who came about 1450, about the time of Sonni Ali of Songhai, and pushed the Sotho and Nguni southward across the Limpopo. The Shona kingdom was ruled by kings who called themselves Mwene Mtapa.

The third wave consisted of the Malawi peoples, who

settled round the lake (lake Malawi or Nyasa) and the Luba, who came a little behind the Malawi and settled in a wide strip of country reaching from the border of Angola right across the north-west of the modern country of Zambia into Katanga and again into the north-east of Zambia. By the year 1700, all these three waves of people had arrived and settled in their homes.

2

THE PORTUGUESE

Portugal is a small and poor country on the Atlantic coast of
the Spanish peninsula. Like Spain, it was conquered by the
Arabs and the Berbers, about the time when the kingdom of
Ghana was first becoming strong. For hundreds of years, the
Muslims of Spain, and Portugal were in close touch with the
Muslims of Africa: with Morocco, and beyond Morocco,
with Ghana and then Mali. It took the Christians several
hundred years to reconquer Portugal from the Muslims. As
they gradually conquered the land of Spain and Portugal,
they began to hope that as the Muslims had crossed from
Africa to Europe, so they themselves might one day cross from
Europe to Africa and conquer the rich kingdoms of Morocco
and Mali.

In the fifteenth century, Prince Henry of Portugal made up
his mind that it should be possible to find a way by sea to the
country beyond the Sahara. He sent out his sea-captains with
orders to follow the African coast and to make maps and
reports of all they found. In the year of Prince Henry's death,
1460, the Portuguese first reached Sierra Leone; in 1486 the
Portuguese captain Bartholomew Diaz rounded the Cape and
sailed as far as the Fish river before turning back home.

So far, the Portuguese had been disappointed in the results
of their voyages. They had found a fair amount of gold on the
Gold Coast, and here and there some ivory and spices. They had
begun a small-scale trade in slaves, whom they sold for domestic
servants in Portugal and Spain and Italy. But they were hoping
for something more striking. They were hoping to sail their
ships into the harbour of a country belonging to a great and
wealthy king: a country where gold and jewels were plentiful,
where there were fine cities and colleges, much learning, and

much trade. A country something like the Mali of Ibn Batuta, but even better: they hoped for fine stone buildings (Ibn Batuta did not think much of the mud buildings of Mali) and they hoped for a Christian country; Mali was Muslim. They believed that somewhere in Africa there was such a country, if only they could find it. They admired the civilization of Benin in West Africa: its wide streets, its bronze carvings, the order and dignity of its king and his court. But Benin for them was not the real thing: it had no stone buildings, no literacy, and no Christianity. The country they were seeking must be in some other part of Africa: but where could it be?

While Bartholomew Diaz was on his voyage round the Cape, another Portuguese traveller called Pedro da Covilhao was exploring Africa from the north. Covilhao entered Egypt and took a ship down the Red Sea. He followed the Arab trade routes, and visited the whole of the East African coast as far as Sofala. And more than that: he went inland and found the Christian kingdom of Ethiopia. From Ethiopia he sent letters home to Portugal, telling the Portuguese sea captains to find their way to Sofala, and to get Arab pilots who would take them across the Indian Ocean to India itself.

Ten years later, Vasco da Gama sailed from Portugal to follow this advice. His fleet rounded the Cape in the last few weeks of the year 1497. On Christmas Day, sailing beyond the point where Diaz had turned homeward, he came ashore at a place which he named Natal, and that part of the coast still bears the name Natal today.[1] He touched at Sofala and Mozambique; at Mozambique he picked up four men and made them guide him on his northward voyage. In April 1498 he arrived at Mombasa, and from Malindi, a little further north, he obtained an Arab pilot who guided him to Calicut in India.

On this first voyage, Vasco da Gama was mainly interested in finding the way to India. But he came back again. In 1502 he stayed longer at Sofala, and he satisfied himself that there really was gold to be had there. Three years later, in 1505, the Portuguese sent troops to occupy the town; the Arabs and the Bantu people tried to stop them, but the Portuguese

---

[1] He gave it the name because *dies natalis* is the Latin for "Birthday", and he landed on the birthday of Jesus.

were too strong. Between 1500 and 1510 the Portuguese conquered all the other Arab towns and became the masters of the whole of the east coast of Africa.

The Portuguese did not like the town of Sofala as a place to live in. It was surrounded by swamps and was full of malaria. But still, it had gold, and gold was what the Portuguese most wanted. The Portuguese heard of the Mwene Mtapa; they were told that he was king of a strong and wealthy country inland, and the gold at Sofala came from his country. This seemed to fit with what they had always believed. Could it be that this 'Monomatapa' (as they called him) was the great Christian king who they heard lived somewhere in the interior of Africa? As a source of gold, Sofala was very important: so important that the post of Governor there was looked on as one of the best posts in the Portuguese service. It was a fine thing to be Governor of Sofala; you would soon be a rich man – if you did not die of fever first.

For some time the Portuguese were content to strengthen their position on the coast and buy the gold that came to them. They built posts at Quelimane on the Zambesi delta, and also at two posts up the river, Sena and Tete. At Tete they were about 250 miles from the sea, but they were still in the coastal plain, and had not got away from the malaria. For more than fifty years they could do no more. They were very lonely, and if they wrote a letter home they would have to wait two years for a reply. It is true that from time to time some bold man would make the journey into the interior. As early as 1514 a Portuguese named Fernandez reached the Monomatapa's country. He brought back reports of the healthy climate, the many stone buildings, and the plentiful gold; and he urged his Government to leave the malarial lowlands and make settlements on the high veld. But the Government had not the men to spare, and nothing was done.

By the time the Portuguese did come into the Shona country, the power of the Monomatapa was no longer what it had been. The grandson of the first Monomatapa lost control over one section of the Shona people. These were the Rozwi, the more westerly section; they lived in Matabeleland. The chief of the Rozwi was called Changa, and when he became independent of the Monomatapa, he called himself Changamire, which became the title of all his descendants. For a long time the Rozwi lived side by side with the Shona as an independent people. This split in the kingdom of the Monomatapa happened about the time that the Portuguese took Sofala.

Soon afterwards, the Shona kingdom suffered greatly from the attacks of a tribe called the Zimba. The Zimba seem to have come from the south, but we do not know from where, nor do we know why they came. They were great fighters, and they were much feared because it was said that they ate their prisoners. They spent some years in fighting and marching all over the country between the Limpopo and the Zambesi; and then they moved further north, and gave trouble to the people at Mombasa and Malindi. But they had greatly weakened the Shona kingdom.

Then there was civil war. In 1565 the Monomatapa, whose name was Mokamba, had to fight against a rebel chief. Both were killed in battle, but the new Monomatapa could not crush the rebellion, so that the Shona kingdom was again divided. A few years later there were more quarrels, and two more sections of the kingdom broke away. The old Shona kingdom of the Monomatapa was now divided into five parts: one big part, that of the Rozwi, and four small parts. It may have been in all this fighting that so many stone forts were built on hill-tops, so that villages or clans might take refuge there.

Do we know why all this fighting broke out? Why could not the Shona people have continued to live in peace?

No, we do not know. We can only guess. The Shona people were increasing in numbers and in wealth. It was worth something to be king of such a people. People seek for wealth and power. One of the tribes that rebelled was the Manyika, whose land was rich in gold. Perhaps the Monomatapa tried to make the Manyika chiefs and people pay him part of their gold, and they refused to do so. Perhaps another strong chief fought against the Monomatapa because he himself wanted the position. But this is only guessing; we do not know.

It was fifty years before the Portuguese made a serious attempt to get into direct touch with the Monomatapa. In

1560 the Catholic Church sent its first missionary to Central Africa, a Portuguese priest named Gonçalo da Silveira. He brought some other priests with him, and set up a mission station on the coast. He himself spent only a few months there, and then he left the other missionaries and went inland to the capital of the Monomatapa.

The Monomatapa welcomed him, and listened to what he had to say; and he even accepted Christianity. But after a time, when he came to know more about Christianity, he found that Silveira was preaching ideas which he could not accept: it was wrong to have more than one wife, to inherit your dead brother's wife, to use magic for making rain. There were people around the Monomatapa who warned him that Silveira was a dangerous man. These were the Arab traders. They hated the Portuguese – with good reason – and warned the Monomatapa, 'If you allow the Portuguese to send priests, you will find that they will send soldiers as well.' The Monomatapa was afraid, and told Silveira to leave the country. He refused to go; the very next day he baptized fifty new Christians; and that same night he and all the fifty were killed. The missionaries on the coast stayed longer, but they too found the same: the people at first welcomed them, but afterwards turned against their preaching. Two years after they had arrived, the missionaries decided that it was useless to stay any longer, and they went back to India, from which they had come.

The Portuguese and the Monomatapa

When the Arabs warned the Monomatapa not to trust the Portuguese, they were right. Nine years after Silveira was killed, an officer called Francisco Barreto[1] left Sofala with a strong force to go to the Monomatapa and get his permission to mine for gold. He failed. His force went up the river to Sena, losing many men from fever. Barreto sent a messenger asking the Monomatapa's permission to come into his country, and the Monomatapa said they might come, if they would promise to help him against the Manyika people who were rebelling against him. Barreto agreed, and the Portuguese

[1] There was another Portuguese officer named Barreto, from whose writings we learn about the Portuguese doings in this part of Africa. This was a different man, Manuel Barreto, who lived a hundred years later.

moved on. They fought three battles against the Manyika people, but they could not force a way through to join the Monomatapa. So they had to go back to Sena, and Barreto died there.

In 1571 the Portuguese tried again. This time they went straight inland from Sofala, so as to avoid the fever in the Zambesi valley and get quickly into the healthy country on the high veld. They reached a part of the Manyika country where gold was being mined. They had heard so much about the riches of the Monomatapa that they expected to find the gold lying on the ground in heaps and ready to be poured into sacks. They were disappointed when they saw how hard and dangerous the work of mining the gold was. They did not stay long; they made a treaty with the Manyika chief and then went back to Sofala. By the treaty, the Portuguese promised to make the chief an annual payment, and he promised to allow Portuguese traders to come into his country. As a result of this treaty, many Portuguese traders went there during the next few years, though some of them had a difficult time because of the civil wars that were going on.

The position of the Monomatapa was becoming more and more difficult. Only a small section of the Shona people still obeyed him. The Portuguese seemed determined to force their way into his country. The Zimba people had done great damage. Some of the Shona chiefs were joining together in an alliance to fight against him. What was he to do?

In 1599 the Monomatapa Gatsi Rusere thought of a new plan. The Portuguese with their guns were the strongest people in Africa, and if they fought on his side, they would help him to beat his enemies. He invited the Portuguese to help him, and promised in return to allow them to trade and to mine for gold as they pleased. The Portuguese came, and they delivered Rusere from the fear of his rebel chiefs. Then they claimed their reward. The Monomatapa's country became full of Portuguese traders and miners. In 1616 a Portuguese officer named Bocarro went north across the Zambesi to look for silver. He found no silver, but he found people wearing copper bracelets and using copper bars as money. He cut across country to Lake Malawi and saw the Shire river leaving the lake; he already knew the lower part of the river where it flows into the Zambesi, but no Portuguese had previously seen the upper part. Bocarro crossed the lake and found his way to the river Rovuma; he went down the Rovuma and reached the sea again at Kilwa.

The Monomatapa Gatsi Rusere died in 1627, and his successor, Kapararidze, thought he had made a mistake in inviting the Portuguese into his country. Their price was too high. He told all the Portuguese traders to leave the country again. They had to go; but they complained to their Government, and in 1632 the Government sent a force under Diogo da Meneses to compel the Monomatapa to do as Rusere had done. Meneses marched straight to the capital, fought against the Monomatapa and killed him, and then set up a new Monomatapa called Mavura.

Mavura owed his position to the Portuguese, and he had to pay them the price they asked. He had to admit that he was no longer an independent king, but was subject to the king of Portugal. Portuguese traders and miners were to move freely in his country. Missionaries were to be allowed to preach and to build churches. Portuguese officials were no longer to be expected to bow and clap their hands when they greeted the Monomatapa. The Portuguese captain at the trading station at Masapa, close to the capital, was to have authority not only over the Portuguese in the Monomatapa's country, but over all Africans who visited Masapa. Mavura himself became a Christian, and all the Monomatapas who followed him were baptized as long as the Portuguese were strong in the country. Though no separate Portuguese governor was appointed, the Monomatapa's country had really become a Portuguese colony; the Portuguese allowed the Monomatapa to rule his people, provided he did everything they told him.

For a few years, the Portuguese made great profits. The gold trade had been interfered with by the civil wars, but it revived again; and again it was worth a good deal to be the Portuguese Governor at Sofala. Several trading stations were opened in the Monomatapa's country, and it seemed to the Portuguese that the good days had come at last.

But there was one thing that the Monomatapa and his people could do to protect themselves against the Portuguese. They did just what the West African gold-miners did when the people of Mali tried to compel them to produce more gold[1]. Instead of producing more, they produced less. They left the mines and ran away and hid in the bush where the Portuguese could not catch them. It was one thing to mine for gold and sell it to the Arabs; it was quite another thing to have the Portuguese take it from them for any price the Portuguese chose to pay. Thirty years or so after the Monomatapa Mavura was baptized, the Portuguese officer Manuel Barreto reported that the gold trade was worth very little. The chiefs, he says, do not want their people to mine for the gold; for if they do, some Portuguese officer will come and take the land, and will make the chief himself work like an ordinary labourer. When the people hear that the Portuguese are coming, they leave the mines and go and hide in the bush.

But why should the Portuguese not do their own digging? If the African miners hid in the bush, could not the Portuguese take up the work where the Africans had left it?

One reason was that the Portuguese had not enough men. The Portuguese were strong because of their guns; but there were very few of them: perhaps only three or four hundred in the whole of east Africa. They could not spare a hundred men or more to dig for gold.

Even if they had the men, they would very likely not have used them as miners; for the Portuguese were full of the idea that digging and labouring was not work for white men. White men in the tropics could be traders, or soldiers, or officials, or planters; but not labourers.

There was a moment when it looked as if the Portuguese might set up a real colony in the Shona country. When they had killed Kapararidze and set up Mavura as a Monomatapa of their own, they did make a plan to send out a thousand Portuguese settlers with their wives and children. But the plan was never put into effect.

But if they wanted the gold so much, why was the plan not put into effect? Why were there so few Portuguese in east Africa?

There were several reasons. Portugal is a small country, and at that time it had a small population. If there were 500 Portu-

[1] This happened nearly 400 years earlier.

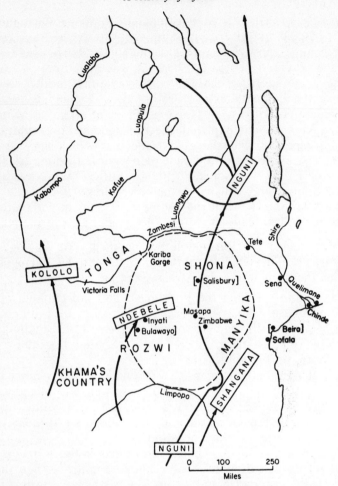

MAP 3. MONOMATAPA AND THE SOUTHERN BANTU

This map shows the places named in chapter Two. The dotted line marks roughly
the boundary of the Monomatapa's kingdom before it began to break up. We do not
know the exact boundary line. Three towns (Salisbury, Bulawayo and Beira) which
did not then exist are marked; they are put in brackets to remind us that they did not
exist in the Monomatapa's day.

The four main peoples of Southern Bantu (Kololo, Ndebele, Shangana and Nguni)
are shown in the new homes they occupied in the 19th century. The arrows show
roughly the lines of their march. When the Nguni had settled west of lake Nyasa
they split up, and the arrows show where the three sections went.

The map shows the Chinde and Quelimane mouths of the Zambesi.

guese in east Africa, it probably means that one Portuguese man in every 700 was working there. East Africa was only one of many overseas countries where the Portuguese were working: India, Indonesia, the Congo, West Africa, and Brazil were the chief. Since 1580, Portugal and Spain had become one country, and the new Government was more interested in the Spanish settlements in America than in the Portuguese settlements in Africa. For these and other reasons, the Portuguese in East Africa received very little help from home. Their Government decided not to send its thousand settlers to Africa; it sent them instead to India, where it thought they would be more useful.

And the gold trade of Sofala died away. Small quantities still came through: but so small that it was no longer worth much to be Governor of Sofala.

Still, these small quantities of gold were enough to attract the greed of Portuguese traders and soldiers. If there was not much gold, they hoped for silver, or ivory, or slaves. They interfered in the civil wars; they offered their help as fighting men now to one side, now to the other. In the end, the Monomatapa and his people decided it was time to make an end of the Portuguese. They called in the Rozwi to help them. The Rozwi came. In the last few years of the 17th century (from 1693 to 1700) they attacked and destroyed all the Portuguese stations on the high veld, and pushed the Portuguese down into the hot malarial Zambesi valley. But they were not content with that. Under their chief, the Changamire, the Rozwi conquered all the Shona states, and put an end to the kingdom of the Monomatapa altogether. For more than a hundred years, the Rozwi ruled the high veld. They probably enlarged and improved Zimbabwe, and built many other stone buildings, whose ruins still stand.

That was the end of Portuguese influence on the high veld. On the coast itself, north of Mozambique, the Portuguese power did not last much longer. The Arabs become strong again and drove them out. They still held Mozambique and the Zambesi posts at Sena and Tete; but they held nothing more.

The 18th century, the time of the Rozwi rule on the high veld, was not a peaceful time. We know nothing of the wars and fighting; but there are so many stone forts built on hili tops that it is plain that the people lived in fear of being attacked. No doubt the people sometimes had to leave their homes and drive their cattle up the hills to take shelter in the stone forts. They continued to live in much the same way as they had done before the Portuguese came. But the Portuguese had broken up the trade on which their civilization depended; and so they were poorer.

You blame the Portuguese for breaking up the trade in the Indian Ocean. Should you not blame them also for breaking up the Monomatapa's kingdom?

The Portuguese must take all the blame for breaking up the trade in the Indian Ocean, but for breaking up the Monomatapa's kingdom they are only partly to blame. When they arrived, Mutota's grandson no longer ruled the whole country; he was quite unable to crush the rebellious chiefs. The Portuguese were not to blame for this early rebellion. But the Monomatapa's weakness suited them; and like the Arabs, they used his weakness to get wealth and power for themselves. The Portuguese destroyed any chance that the Monomatapa might have had of defeating his enemies and restoring the power of the Shona kingdom. But to be fair on the Portuguese, we must admit that his chance of doing this seemed a small one. As soon as the Rozwi had thrown out the Portuguese, they turned on the Monomatapa and conquered his kingdom. It seems likely that if they had not done this in the 1690s, they would have done it a few years later. And as we shall see, the Rozwi in their turn were later overthrown by other Bantu peoples, whose warfare was not caused in any way by the Portuguese or other Europeans.

After the Rozwi conquest, the Portuguese lost touch with the people of the high veld, and knew nothing of what went on there. They still remembered the days of the Monomatapa; they remembered the gold and the stone buildings at Zimbabwe and elsewhere. A hundred years later, when men in Europe began to think of exploring the interior of Africa, they heard of Monomatapa — they were not sure whether it was the name of a king or of a country — and marked it on their maps. They were disappointed when they reached it.

3

LATER AFRICAN MOVEMENTS

As we have seen in the first two chapters, two important things happened about the same time, in the year 1700 or thereabouts. One was that the Mwata Yamvwa, the paramount chief of the Lunda people, fixed his capital in the Luapula valley, so that his people had reached their permanent home. The other was that the Rozwi drove the Portuguese off the high veld and conquered the Shona kingdom of the Monomatapa.

The Bemba

Soon after this, other Bantu peoples began coming down from the north. While the Portuguese and the Monomatapa were fighting and making treaties together, the Bemba were living further north in the valley of the Lualaba river, in what is now part of the Congo. In the last years of the 17th century, just a little time before the Rozwi drove out the Portuguese, two sons of the paramount chief led a large section of the Bemba people away from their old home. They moved south and east, and crossed from the Lualaba to the Luapula valley.

The Lunda people were already living in the Luapula valley, and the Mwata Yamvwa had his capital there. But it was forty or fifty years before the incoming Bemba met the Lunda. This shows us how small the young Bantu nations were in those days. The Luapula valley is about 250 miles long, and the Bemba were able to live in it for forty or fifty years before meeting the Lunda; there must have been very few villages in each tribe.

The Bemba did not stay very long in the Luapula valley. They moved eastwards, going north of lake Bangweulu. They were evidently increasing in numbers, for at several places in their journey, different clans left the main body to settle down. The main body of the people moved across the hills into the Luangwa valley, and then turned northward again and settled on the high ground near the present border between Zambia and Tanzania. Their travels took them nearly a hundred years, but by 1800 they were ended. The whole of the country between the three lakes Tanganyika, Mweru and Bangweulu was occupied by different sections of the Bemba people. Sometimes they were all ruled by one paramount chief, whose title was Chitimukulu.

The Nyanja and the Cewa

The Malawi peoples lived in the country between lake Malawi and lake Tanganyika. Some time during the 18th century, the Malawi peoples split into two main divisions. One division stayed near lake Malawi; it came to be called the Nyanja or 'lake people'. The other division, which came to be called the Cewa, moved onwards, and different sections settled along the hills which today form the border between Zambia and Malawi, and across the modern border into Mozambique. By about 1800 they were all settled. The Portuguese knew that this large block of country was all occupied by Cewa people. They thought that it might be one large and strong kingdom, as the Shona kingdom had been; but it seems that the Cewa peoples never united in this way. After 1800, the only move made by the Cewa was that one section reached into the Luangwa valley, into country which is now part of Zambia.

The Luyi

One other important Bantu people, the Luyi, came down from the north during the 18th century. The Lüyi had been living in the Congo basin, and they came down into the Zambesi valley down the Kabompo river. They found other Bantu peoples living there, as well as some Bushmen; they drove out the Bushmen and conquered the other Bantu, and by about 1800 they had built up a strong state in what is now Barotseland. Their greatest paramount chief, Mulambwa, ruled from 1812 to 1830. In his time, the Luyi were strong in war, and were able to gather large herds of cattle from their weaker neighbours. And Mulambwa was a wise ruler. He

made one very important decision: when slave dealers came
to him, he refused to have anything to do with the slave trade.
His successors followed him in this.

After their great chief Mulambwa died in 1830, the Luyi
were not left long in peace. The whole of central Africa was
soon invaded by strong Bantu peoples coming back northward
from the country further south.

THE RETURN OF THE SOUTHERN BANTU

Between about 1450 and 1750, a whole series of Bantu states
had been set up on the high veld of what is now the South
African republic, in the Transvaal and the Orange Free State.
Most of them were Sotho-speaking, and the Sotho peoples
who made them drove the Bushmen and the Hottentots west
into the Kalahari or south-west towards the Cape.

On the other side of the mountains, in Swaziland and Natal,
there were Nguni-speaking states. In 1776 the most southerly
of the Nguni-speaking peoples, the Xosa, reached the Great
Fish river in the Cape Province. There they met the white men,
the Dutch settlers, who were pushing eastward and northward
from the Cape.

When the herd-boys of the Xosa people were driving their
cattle to drink in the Great Fish river, great things were happening three or four hundred miles behind them. There lived in
Natal a Nguni-speaking nation called the Mtetwa; all round
the Mtetwa lived other Nguni-speaking peoples, only loosely
linked together. About 1780, a paramount chief of the Mtetwa,
named Dingiswayo, decided to organise his own people, and
as many of the neighbouring peoples as he could, into one
strong kingdom. He organised his army into regiments, and
set out on his wars of conquest. One of his officers was named
Chaka. He was a man of the Zulu people, which at that time
was one of the smaller and weaker of the tribes that served
Dingiswayo. Chaka made such a name for himself in the army,
that when Dingiswayo died, Chaka succeeded him as king of
the Mtetwa.

When Chaka became king, the whole of the Mtetwa nation
took the name of his own people, the Zulu. Chaka carried on
the work that Dingiswayo had begun, and was even more

successful. Before his time, the Mtetwa had gone into battle
with a light throwing spear and a longhandled stabbing spear.
Chaka made them give up the throwing spear, and he shortened
the handle and widened the blade of the stabbing spear. This
meant that the men fought in close ranks and could be better
drilled; and it meant too that their spears made more dangerous
wounds. Chaka set out to enlarge his army. When he conquered
another tribe, he did not kill all the fighting men, or sacrifice
them to the gods. He knew a better way than that: he made
them serve in his regiments. Men, women, cattle were brought
in to add to the strength of the Zulu nation, and nobody could
stand against them.

Chaka's first great victory was in 1818, and for about
fifteen years he and his Zulu fighting men were constantly at
war. Most of the country which now makes the Transvaal,
the Orange Free State and Natal was laid waste: homes and
crops were burnt, cattle were driven away, and any people
who were not taken into Zululand were left to die of hunger.

Two sections of the army which Chaka had defeated in
1818 fled northward towards Mozambique. One chief called
Soshangane led a people called the Shangana; another called
Zwangendaba led a people who called themselves simply the
Nguni. We shall hear more of these people.

Meanwhile, other tribes in fear of Chaka broke away
westward on to the high veld. They had lost their homes, their
grazing land, their cattle; they had to become wanderers,
fighting and plundering to keep themselves alive. As they
went, they followed Chaka's example and gathered in fighting
men for their armies from many different tribes. Their only
hope of avoiding death or slavery was to bring death and
slavery to others.

The Kololo

One strong party went westward across the Vaal into the Cape
Province, and there they attacked a mission station. But
their spearmen could not stand against gunfire; they were
defeated and broke up into groups; and one group of them
set out for the north. This group was led by a young Sotho
chief called Sebetwane, and called itself the Kololo. It fought
its way across the Tswana country, the modern Botswana:

and in 1831, after years of wandering and fighting, it crossed the Zambesi and entered Zambia.

The Ndebele

Another group of Chaka's enemies took a different route. In 1821, one of Chaka's officers named Msilikazi rebelled against him and left Zululand, taking a large division of the army with him. His people came to be called the Ndebele (the Europeans called them Matabele), and they continued Chaka's policy of taking the best of the young fighting men from the tribes they defeated, and putting them into their own regiments. They settled for some years in the Transvaal, raiding and plundering the peoples near them, and twice they attacked small trekking parties of Boers. But here they made a mistake. The Boers sent up a commando against them, and Msilikazi's spearmen could do nothing against the Boers with their horses and their guns. This was in 1837. Msilikazi and his people moved away; they crossed the Limpopo and settled in the country round the Matopo hills, and built a capital at Inyati, not far from Bulawayo.

Thus, in the 1830s there were four new Bantu peoples who had escaped from Chaka and his Zulu government and had arrived north of the Limpopo. They were the Kololo under Sebetwane, the Ndebele under Msilikazi, the Nguni under Zwangendaba, and the Shangana under Soshangane. All these peoples had learned from Chaka and the Zulu to be strong disciplined fighting men. They lived by fighting, and like the Zulu, they took the best of the young fighting men from the peoples they defeated, and put them into their own regiments. When they came pouring over the Limpopo and the Zambesi into central Africa, none of the peoples they found there could stand against them.

We are not concerned in this book with the Shangana, who stayed in Mozambique and built up a strong state there. Zwangendaba and the Nguni followed them there; but they could do nothing against the Shangana, so they turned westward, and came into contact with the Kololo and the Ndebele.

The Kololo

The Kololo arrived at what was for them a lucky moment.

The great Luyi chief Mulambwa had just died, and there was
a dispute over who should succeed him. The Kololo defeated
the Luyi in four battles, and by 1838 the whole of the Luyi
state was under Kololo rule. Sebetwane was a wise chief:
when he had conquered the Luyi (or the Lozi, as the Kololo
called them) he treated them like his own Kololo, and he set
out to make Luyi and Kololo into one people. He had great
success. The Luyi adopted the language and customs of the
Kololo, and began to call themselves Lozi instead of Luyi.
Sebetwane, who lived until 1851, was the founder of the Barotse
state of today. After his death, his successor was unwise enough
to change his policy; he treated the Kololo as the masters and
the Lozi and others as their servants. In 1865 this brought
about a Lozi revolt; it was led by a son of Mulambwa, and
the Kololo men were slaughtered. But the women and children
were spared, and the process of adopting Sotho speech and
customs continued.

The Nguni

After being defeated by the Shangana in Mozambique, Zwangendaba and the Nguni went up into the plateau. Here they
met the Shona and the Rozwi.[1] There was still a Rozwi king
calling himself the Monomatapa; the Nguni killed him, and
spent a year or two in plundering his country. Then in 1835
they crossed the Zambesi into the Nsenga country, and by
1845 they had marched, fighting and plundering as they went,
all the way past lake Nyasa and nearly as far as lake Tanganyika.
In that year, Zwangendaba died, after leading his people
more than two thousand miles from their old home in Natal.

After their great chief was dead, the Nguni split up into
three groups, each led by a son of Zwangendaba. One went
north into the country now called Tanzania and settled near
Tabora. The second went up the west side of lake Tanganyika
into the Congo. The third, under a chief called Mgai, stayed
where it was for a few years, until Mgai too died in 1850.
Then this group too broke up. One section turned south into
Malawi, and brought death and destruction to the people in
the lake country there. Another section crossed the Luangwa

[1] See pages 29, 30

river into the Bemba country; but by that time the Bemba
had obtained guns from the Arab traders, and the Nguni
found it wiser to leave them alone. So they recrossed the
Luangwa and conquered the Cewa, and it was not until after
1870 that they settled down.

The Ndebele

The Ndebele settled in their new home around the Matopo
hills about the same time that the Kololo broke the resistance
of the Lozi and became rulers of Barotseland. The new home
of the Ndebele was the plateau country of the Shona and the
Rozwi, the country which had been the kingdom of the Monomatapa. The last Monomatapa had been killed by the Nguni
a year or two earlier, but the Nguni had not stayed to settle
down there; they had gone further north.

Msilikazi did not follow the wise policy of Sebetwane. He
made no attempt to build up a peaceful settled kingdom in
which his Ndebele and Rozwi and Shona subjects should be
equal. To the end of his days – he died in 1868 – he kept up
the old custom of keeping his Ndebele separate as a people
for fighting and plundering, and every year he sent his regiments
out to raid the peoples round them. The Shona especially
were reduced to utter misery. At any time a Shona village
might be attacked by a party of young Ndebele spearmen
who wanted to 'wash their spears' and show their manhood.
The Shona remembered the great days of Zimbabwe, and they
tried to find safety by building stone fortified villages on the
hill-tops. But stone walls could not keep out the Ndebele; the
Ndebele despised the Shona, and they came to despise themselves. So it went on through the days of Mzilikazi and his
successor Lobengula, until the fighting Ndebele met a power
stronger than themselves, and were defeated by the machine-
guns and rifle-fire of the Europeans.

These armies of Kololo, Nguni and Ndebele were very
different from the earlier armies of invading Bantu. When the
Shona or Sotho people came looking for a new home, they
were content as soon as they had found one. All they wanted
to do then was to settle down to plant their corn and graze
their cattle. Of course there was some fighting; some men
would be killed, and maybe some clans would move away so

as to remain free instead of staying on as slaves or lower-class citizens. But the fighting was not heavy.

But the newcomers from the south had learnt to enjoy fighting or raiding for its own sake. To them, fighting was the only life for a man; herding cattle or tending crops was work for women or young boys or slaves. So when they had conquered a home for themselves, they did not settle down in peace, but remained a nuisance to their neighbours. Every year the regiments went out to raid and kill; and they wrecked the peaceful Bantu civilisation and laid large parts of Africa waste. All this fear and suffering was not at all typical of the old Bantu way of life. It was the work of Dingiswayo and Chaka, who had first taught their peoples to give up peace and live by war.

4

SLAVERS AND MISSIONARIES

Our story so far has been concerned almost entirely with the doings of the Bantu peoples of central Africa. It is true that a few hundred Portuguese with guns had been able for a time to have some influence in the kingdom of the Monomatapa; but they were unimportant compared with the Rozwi, the Kololo, the Ndebele and the Nguni. The Portuguese were important in the coastal towns of east Africa, but not in the interior of Central Africa.

But we have now reached a time – towards the middle of the 19th century, between 100 and 150 years ago - when this old African world was broken into by strangers whose influence was far deeper and more lasting than that of the Portuguese. These strangers were the Arab slave traders from the north, and the Christian missionaries from the south. As we know, other Europeans followed behind the missionaries: traders, settlers, miners. We shall tell their story later. The missionaries were the first Europeans to come, and they often disapproved strongly of what the traders and settlers did.

THE SLAVE TRADE

There used to be a very large slave trade carried on by Europeans. The slaves were taken across the Atlantic to work in mines and plantations in America; they came mostly from West Africa, but a few were taken from Angola and Mozambique. But this trade had been stopped long before the time we are describing, and it had never touched the lands of Malawi, Zambia and Rhodesia. Before the time of Chaka and Msilikazi, the British and some other nations of western Europe had quite made up their minds that slavery and the slave trade were evil, and they were prepared to spend a great deal of time and

2. Arab Slave Raiders at Work

money in stopping them. We are not concerned in this book
with the European slave trade.

As far as central Africa is concerned, the slave trade was
run by Arabs from the east coast. After the Arabs had driven
the Portuguese out of East Africa, they continued the slave
trade. Sultan Seyyid Said of Zanzibar sent his caravans further
and further into the interior of Africa, though the British
gradually persuaded him to stop exporting the slaves by sea.

Seyyid Said ruled until 1856. By the end of his long reign,
the slave trade was in full swing all over east and central Africa.
Although the British warships were making it difficult for the
Arabs to export slaves by sea across the Indian Ocean, some
traders were still managing to send occasional ship-loads,
and many more slaves were being shipped across the narrow
waters between the Sudan and Somaliland on the African
shore, and the ports on the Arabian shore of the Red Sea and
the Gulf of Aden. In the coastal lands of East Africa, where
rich Arabs held large estates, thousands of slaves were needed
to work on the land. The Portuguese too, at that time, used
slaves to work on the plantations in their African colonies.
The coastal tribes had long since been worked to death;

there were no more slaves to be obtained near the coast. The slave caravans had to go further and further into the interior, and many Arabs became rich by capturing and buying slaves, whom they·sold at a large profit when they arrived back on the coast.

In those days, when every step of the journey into the interior of Africa had to be made on foot, it would not have been possible for the Arabs themselves to capture all the slaves they needed. The Arabs were traders; they had cloth and manufactured goods of all kinds for sale, and they were prepared to buy all the slaves and ivory they could find. Many African chiefs were prepared to capture slaves and sell them to the Arabs, in order to obtain the goods which the Arabs had to offer.

Neither Arabs nor Africans in those days thought slavery wrong, and they could not understand why the British should see any harm in it. Many African peoples had domestic slavery, though this of course was a very different thing from plantation slavery in a foreign land. Some African peoples found it natural to sell slaves to the Arabs. The Bemba for example were often short of food, and if they took prisoners in their wars they sometimes could not feed them. In the early days, the Bemba used to kill their prisoners; when the slave trade began, it seemed more convenient, and even perhaps kinder, to sell the prisoners instead of killing them. Others used to sell criminals from their own people; thus they got rid of the criminal and received value for him. Some peoples, such as the Lozi and the Nguni, would never touch the slave trade. The Nguni would never sell their prisoners. They knew a better way than that: they kept them and made them serve in the regiments. Moreover, the Nguni were so strong that they could take any land they wanted; so they were able to find fertile soil and feed their people well.

When African chiefs began to organize their people for the work of capturing slaves, it made the business much easier for the Arab traders, and of course it spread the horrible trade over a much larger area. The Yao people of Malawi were great slave raiders all over the Shire valley and the southern parts of Malawi and Zambia. They sold some of their slaves to the Arabs from the east coast, and some to the Portu-

guese of Mozambique. The Yao had not long come down into
the Shire valley from further north. We do not know what
made them leave their old home, which was east of lake
Nyasa. They moved down to the Shire valley about 1850. By
then they had obtained some guns from the Arabs, and many
of them had become Muslims; and so they set out on their
new life of slaving and plundering.

While the southern part of the lake country was being
raided by the Yao, the northern end of the lake was being
raided by Arabs (or men of mixed Arab and Bantu blood)
from the east coast. South of the Zambesi there was no slave
raiding. The Ndebele kept that country for themselves; they
raided the Shona whenever they wanted to, and they would
have no strangers hunting in their land.

Other slave raiders worked from the north-west, from
Angola. The chief raiders here were the Mbunda people, and
other people of mixed Portuguese and Bantu blood whom
the Bantu called Mambari. The Mbunda and Mambari used
to buy slaves from the Lovale and other peoples, and they
also used to raid on their own account. The Lunda people
especially suffered severely, and the raiders used sometimes
to go as far as the Luapula. The Lozi would have nothing to
do with the trade, and Barotseland was always peaceful. 'I do
not sell my people like cattle', said their great chief Lewanika.
This slave trading on the Angola side of the country went on
long after the eastern trade had been stopped. The Portuguese
needed men to work in the cocoa plantations on their island
of San Thomé, and there was still a little slave raiding in this
part of the country as recently as 1910. By then, of course, the
Portuguese did not call them slaves, they called them 'free
labourers'; but the poor Lunda men in the San Thomé plantations would not notice much difference.

THE MISSIONARIES

We have seen that in the early days, the Portuguese sent
missionaries to the country of the Monomatapa, but without
much success. While the Portuguese were strong, the Monomatapa called himself a Christian; but after the Portuguese
left the high veld, Christianity died out there. When Christian-

ity came back to central Africa, it came from a different direction: from the south.

Christian missionaries began working among the Bantu in South Africa at the very beginning of the 19th century. On many occasions the missionaries interfered to protect the Bantu both against the Boers and against the Government. It was the missionaries, for example, who told the Government that it would be wrong to push the Xosa people out of land they had lived in for some years; and it was one of the greatest of the missionaries, John Philip, who persuaded the Government to set aside large areas of land for Bantu reserves. Because of such things, the Bantu came to look on the missionaries as their friends, and were glad to have their advice and help when the Boers or the Government, or white traders, were making life difficult for them.

David Livingstone

In 1816, the London Missionary Society opened a station at Kuruman in Bechuanaland, north-west of Kimberley; and it was from here that the greatest missionary of all, David Livingstone, set out on his travels of preaching and exploration. In 1847 he opened a station at Kolobeng, three hundred miles further north, and two years later he crossed the Kalahari desert and reached Lake Ngami. In 1851 he reached the Zambesi and met Sebetwane, paramount chief of the Kololo. Sebetwane was then an old man; it was nearly thirty years since he and his people had been defeated near Kuruman and had moved northward. He and Livingstone liked each other, and Livingstone hoped to be able to found a mission station among the Kololo; but before anything could be arranged, Sebetwane fell ill and died; and Livingstone thought it better to return to the south.

He was back again the next year, and Sebetwane's son Sekeletu welcomed him. But the swampy Barotse country did not seem suitable for a mission station, so Livingstone decided to explore further to the west. Sekeletu lent him 27 men to go with him. The party pushed up the Zambesi, and across the plateau into the Congo basin; and after a journey of more than two thousand miles they reached the Atlantic Ocean at Luanda. Then they went back to the Kololo country; and then onward again, down the Zambesi to Tete, and so to the Indian Ocean at Quelimane. From Quelimane, Livingstone himself, who was very sick, went home to England by ship; but he promised his Kololo men that he would come back, and the faithful Kololo, who had marched with him from sea to sea, insisted on waiting at Quelimane until he came.

On this journey, Livingstone had seen something of the effects of the Arab slave trade. Both when going through Angola towards Luanda, and when going down the Zambesi towards Tete, he found the people frightened of strangers, and ready to attack him until they found that he was a new kind of white man, 'Inglesi'. On his next journey, Livingstone saw much more of the trade. He landed at Quelimane, where he found his Kololo men still waiting for him. He went up the Shire river and saw Lake Nyasa; and then he went along the north bank of the Zambesi and took his Kololo followers back to their homes. Again, Sekeletu welcomed him, and invited him to open a mission station in his country. Sekeletu was not specially interested in Christianity; but he greatly revered[1] Livingstone, and hoped that Livingstone would be able to protect him from enemies such as the Ndebele. But Livingstone would not stay in Barotseland; he went back eastward and tried to set up a mission station in the Shire highlands. But the missionaries who came there died of fever, and were constantly attacked by Yao slave raiders. The station was abandoned, and the missionaries left the Shire valley and settled in Zanzibar.

On his last journey, which lasted from March 1866 until May 1873, Livingstone started from Zanzibar and went round the southern end of lake Nyasa. Then he turned north to explore lake Mweru, and pushed still further north to Ujiji on the shore of lake Tanganyika. Then he crossed to the west side of lake Tanganyika and found the river Lualaba. He decided to turn back to find the source of the Lualaba, and then to follow the river all the way to its mouth, to see whether

[1] That is, he not merely admired him, but thought him one of the greatest men he had ever met. All Africans felt like this about Livingstone. Imagine what it must have meant for the little group of Kololo men to wait for him two years at Quelimane, among Portuguese and strangers a thousand miles from their home; and for his African servants to carry his dead body all the way from lake Bangweulu to Tabora and then to Zanzibar.

3. The Slaves on Their Way to the Coast

it flowed into the Nile or the Congo. But he had not the strength to do this; near lake Bangweulu he died.

The further Livingstone walked over Africa, the more convinced he became that the most important thing for Christian men to do there was to stop the slave trade. But he saw that preaching alone would not stop the trade. Africans wanted European goods; and ivory, with the slaves to carry it, was all that the African villages had to offer in exchange. The slave trade was an evil thing, but it was a trade; and Livingstone thought that the only way to stop an evil trade was to start a good one. He felt sure that Africa could produce other things besides ivory, and if the African people could be helped to produce other materials that Europe wanted, a healthy commerce would spring up and the slave trade would die away. He thought that Christianity and commerce were both needed. Before his last journey, he told an audience in England, 'I go back to try to open up a path to commerce and Christianity. Do you carry on the work that I have begun.'

That is all very well; but European commerce has done a good deal of harm to Africa, as well as good. Was Livingstone hoping for something like the mining compounds on the copper-belt?

There was nothing in Britain at that time like this large-scale industry, and we can be sure that Livingstone never imagined anything of the kind in Africa. Like all his countrymen, Livingstone believed that hard work was good for people. But he saw, too, that if the slave trade and the tribal warfare were stopped, African men would have nothing to do while the women worked on the farm and the boys herded the cattle. If the men could be employed in some work and earn the money they needed to buy European goods, Livingstone thought they would be happier. At the same time, they needed Christianity; without this, there would be selfishness and injustice. When Livingstone went through the Nyanja country, he was pleased to see what a busy and useful life the blacksmiths lived, smelting the iron ore and making all kinds of useful tools. This was the sort of thing that Livingstone would have liked to see developed all over Africa: this, or such industry as that of the cotton-growers in Uganda and the cocoa-farmers in Ghana and Nigeria. Livingstone could never have imagined anything like the Kariba or the Jinja hydro-electric schemes, for there was nothing of that kind in Europe in those days. While Livingstone was on his last journey, the American inventor Edison was trying to find a way of using electricity to make light, but he did not make his first successful electric light bulb until six years after Livingstone died. Electric machinery came later still.

People in Britain were shocked to hear what Livingstone told them of the slave trade. From Livingstone they learned, too, that the people of central Africa were friendly and trustworthy; they admired the Kololo who waited so long at Quelimane for Livingstone to return, and they admired still more the brave men who carried his dead body over hundreds of miles to the sea. If this is what Africans were like, they thought, they deserved the help that Britain could give them. People in Britain accepted Livingstone's idea that Christianity and commerce must go together, and so they decided to send out missionaries and to introduce commerce, so as to carry on the work which he had begun.

But no doubt they hoped to make a great deal of profit as well?

No, not at the time we are describing, say from 1875 to

1890. The commercial men who wanted to make great profits went to the diamond and gold fields in South Africa. As far as central Africa was concerned, Livingstone had told them that there was a certain amount of iron ore there, but no one in Britain was interested, for Britain had all the iron ore she needed. As far as anyone knew, there was nothing else; and it was certain that trade would be very difficult and dangerous, for the Arab and other slave traders would do all they could to stop it. So people in Britain thought that there would be very little profit to be made out of the trade in central Africa for many years to come. Consequently, rich people did not want to invest their money in it; and the company that was started to trade in central Africa was always short of capital.

New missionaries began their work before trade was started. In 1859, Livingstone's own missionary society, the London Missionary Society, sent missionaries to work among the Kololo. The scheme was a failure. The Kololo chief, Sekeletu, wanted Livingstone, but he did not want these strangers, and he did nothing to make their life comfortable. The mission consisted of two men, with their wives and six children. Six of the party died of malaria, and only one man and two children lived to struggle back to Kuruman.

As a result of Livingstone's preaching in Britain, a new society had been founded, the Universities Mission to Central Africa; and in 1860 this society sent out its first party of missionaries. But many of these missionaries too died of malaria, and the Yao slave traders made their work impossible. In 1863 the missionaries who were left alive decided to give up their work in Malawi and settle at Zanzibar.

These two efforts had ended in complete failure. The mission to the Ndebele was able at any rate to continue its work, but the missionaries did not feel that they were having much success. The mission was led by one of Livingstone's friends in the London Missionary Society named Robert Moffat. Moffat had been many years in Africa, and met Msilikazi while the Ndebele were still living in the Transvaal. The two men became friends, and in 1859 Moffat thought the time had come to send a mission to Msilikazi's new capital at Inyati. Msilikazi made them welcome, and allowed them to stay and preach. But he would not allow any of his people to learn to read, or to become Christians. The missionaries stayed at Inyati all through the time of Msilikazi and his successor Lobengula. The king liked to have them as advisers; and in the later years, when other Europeans were beginning to come into the country, he consulted them whenever he had to deal with the new strangers. But they had no success in preaching the Gospel.

In those early days, most paramount chiefs looked on missionaries in the way that Sekeletu looked on Livingstone and Msilikazi on Moffat. Africans were coming to know the white men better, and to understand that they were different from the Arabs, and had different ways of trading. They felt that the missionaries, unlike some white men, were truly their friends, and were not trying to get anything out of them. A paramount chief valued the advice of his missionary; he wanted the missionary to live near him, and would not hear of allowing any of his sub-chiefs to have a missionary.

The missionaries in Nyasaland

There were three other important missionary settlements in central Africa in the early days. In 1875, the Free Church of Scotland sent out a mission to Nyasaland; Dr Robert Laws, who came with it, stayed in Nyasaland for fifty years. The missionaries brought a small steamer and launched it on the lake, and they built their mission station on the western shore. The people here were being constantly raided by the Nguni from the hills, and the Nguni chief, Mbelwa, was very angry with the missionaries for settling down among the lake people. He wanted them to go and live with him; but Dr Laws explained that they must have a station on the lake shore because their supplies came by steamer. After a few years, Laws was able to send some missionaries to live with Mbelwa, and gradually the Nguni came to listen to them. Mbelwa died in 1891; his successor died in 1897; the chief who succeeded in that year was himself a Christian.

Other Scottish missionaries began working in the Shire highlands in 1875; they named their station Blantyre, after the small Scottish village in which Livingstone was born. The missionaries at Blantyre had great difficulties. The Portuguese did not want them there at all, for they said that the whole of the Shire valley was Portuguese territory. The African people there had suffered so much from the Yao slave raiders that they had lost all order and discipline. All they wanted was peace and safety, and it was not easy for a few missionaries to help them in this way.

The Scottish missionaries at Blantyre in the south and Livingstonia in the north were helped when their friends in Scotland set up a trading company to develop trade in the lake country, as Livingstone himself had wanted. The company was at first named after Livingstone, but soon changed its name to the African Lakes Company. It began work in 1878. The company hoped to make a profit, even if only a small one. But profit was not its chief aim. The men who founded it were supporters of the missionaries, and their chief aim was to provide the sort of trade which Livingstone had wanted. They might have made big profits if they had sold guns and ammunition and drink, all of which were eagerly desired by the Africans. But they would not touch any of these things.

The company worked under great difficulties. The rapids on the Shire river made it impossible for a steamer to go right up from the sea to the lake. The company had to provide two steamers, one for the journey from the sea up to the rapids, and another from the rapids to the lake; and all the goods had to be unloaded and carried past the rapids from one steamer to the other. Then there were the Arab and Yao slave raiders, who were doing very well out of the slave trade, and did not want the company to interfere with their profits. They were ready to drive out the company and the missionaries by force, and the company had to raise a small army of its own to defend itself. Trade was very difficult, and not at all profitable.

Meanwhile, the London Missionary Society (Livingstone's own society) had opened a station at Ujiji on lake Tanganyika. The journey from lake Nyasa to lake Tanganyika was much shorter than the overland journey from the east coast, and it would be much easier to send goods by water to the north end of lake Nyasa and then to lake Tanganyika. In 1881 a Scottish business man named Stevenson gave some money for making a road between the lakes, so that the missionaries at Ujiji could get their supplies from the African Lakes Company. This route was named the Stevenson road.

The Paris Evangelical Mission

The third important missionary society which helped to open
up central Africa was the Paris Evangelical Mission, which
had been working for some years in Basutoland. In 1877 the
society sent Francois Coillard to visit the Ndebele and try
and establish a mission station in their country. Coillard was
unlucky. He first visited a Shona clan, who hoped that he
would give them guns to defend themselves against the Ndebele,
and had no use for him when they found that he had no guns.
Then he found himself in trouble with Lobengula, the king
of the Ndebele, who was angry that Coillard should have
gone to his subjects the Shona before coming to him. Lobengula
would not allow Coillard to work at all among the Ndebele,
so he went on into Barotseland. Here he found that the king
would be glad to have him, but not just at that moment; the
political situation was too difficult.

We have seen on page 36 that in 1865 the Lozi had risen up
against their Kololo rulers and killed the Kololo men. The
Lozi chief who led the rising was named Sipopa; he was a son
of the great chief Mulambwa. Sipopa did not live long to
rule the Lozi, and in 1870 a grandson of Mulambwa, named
Robosi, rose up against the government and made himself
paramount chief. Robosi was a strong ruler and a hard one,
and he had much difficulty. When Coillard arrived, he was
building a new capital at Lealui, and was not by any means
out of his troubles; in fact, he had to put down a serious
rebellion in 1884.

In the end, Coillard was not able to settle in Barotseland
until 1885; in that year he set up his first mission station near
Lealui. By that time, Robosi had changed his name to Lewanika;
and like other paramount chiefs, he was glad to have the
missionaries as advisers. Unlike Lobengula and Msilikazi,
Lewanika listened to their preaching and allowed his people
to become Christians. He allowed his own son to be baptized,
he put a stop to many customs connected with the old religion,
and after 1897 he would never allow his army to raid the neighbouring peoples. Coillard lived in Barotseland until 1904,
Lewanika ruled until 1916. It was largely because of Coillard
that Lewanika accepted British protection; but that story
belongs to a later chapter.

There were other missionary societies of course, both Protestant and Catholic, which came to work in central Africa; the White Fathers and the Methodists were early in the field. But the Paris Mission in Barotseland and the Scottish missions in Nyasaland were the most important of the early missionary settlements for the work they did in opening up the country and in preparing the chiefs to meet the new dangers that were coming from white traders and settlers.

5

ANNEXATION BETWEEN LIMPOPO AND ZAMBESI

Before the year 1880, only a small part of Africa had come under European rule. The Portuguese still had their weak settlements in the coast lands of Angola, Mozambique, and Guinea. The French had occupied the coast of Algeria and the Senegal, and in both regions they had pushed two or three hundred miles inland. The British had two tiny colonies at Freetown and Lagos, and had recently pushed forty or fifty miles inland along the Gold Coast (the modern Ghana). Only in South Africa did white rule stretch very far inland; it was more than a thousand miles from the Cape to the northern frontier of the Transvaal on the river Limpopo. It was more than four hundred years since the Portuguese explored the African coast, and nearly a hundred years since Mungo Park and others began to explore the interior. Yet, except in South Africa, colonization had been very slow.

But in the twenty years from 1880 to 1900, nearly the whole of Africa was quickly brought under white rule, and the colonial period began.[1]

There are reasons why colonization was so slow before 1880. One reason is that until Livingstone showed them differently, Europeans were afraid of the interior of Africa: afraid of fever, of lions and snakes, and afraid above all of the people. A second reason is that it was difficult and expensive to travel in Africa. You could not go far up the rivers in a steamer because of the rapids. You had to travel on foot. You had a long slow journey through hot country with mosquitoes and tsetse flies; and you had to travel with large numbers of carriers, for not only must you carry all your food and medicine

[1] Ethiopia and Liberia remained independent. Tripoli became Italian in 1911, Morocco lost its independence in 1912. But all the rest of Africa was divided up by 1900, though here and there there was some fighting after that date.

and ammunition, but every chief you came to would want a present before he would 'give you the road', that is, allow you to pass through his country. These presents too you had to carry with you.

A third reason why colonization was slow is that in the first half of the 19th century, Britain was the country which could most easily have colonized Africa, and Britain at that time did not want African colonies. As late as 1865, the British parliament told the Government that it did not want any new colonies in Africa, and the Government should leave the few colonies it already had, as soon as it could conveniently do so.

This raises a good many questions. First: why did not Britain want African colonies before 1880? The British were quick enough afterwards! Second: if Britain really did not want colonies earlier, why did not other countries such as France and Germany and Italy colonize Africa? Third: you have given reasons why colonization was slow before 1880; why was it so quick afterwards?

We can answer these questions one by one. First, the reasons why Britain did not want African colonies. The British were busy in settling and developing Canada, Australia and New Zealand, as well as some other countries which were not British, such as the United States and Argentina. They had all the work they needed in these countries; the climate was pleasant and healthy, there was plenty of trade there, and British engineers could build railways and harbours and make money by doing so. But Africa did not seem much of a country for white men, and it did not seem as if there was much trade there. Ivory, yes: some gold here and there[1]: palm oil on the west coast; but nothing else. The gold, ivory and palm oil were all being brought down to the coast for sale; by going inland and colonizing the country, the white men would not get any more of these things than they were already getting. The Portuguese had tried that with the Monomatapa's country; and we have seen that instead of getting more gold, they got less.

---

[1] The South African diamond fields were not opened until 1870, the goldfield of the Rand not until 1886.

But there is a great deal in Africa besides gold and ivory and palm oil. Look at the things which Europe buys from Africa today: cocoa, coffee, cotton, sisal, manganese, copper, tin, diamonds, uranium, timber, and much besides! How can you say that there seemed to be not much trade in Africa?

That is how it seemed in 1870. All these other exports have begun since then. The Gold Coast did not begin exporting cocoa until 1891. Copper was not exported from the Congo until 1899, and from Zambia until 1925; Nigeria began exporting tin after the 1914 war. It is true that there is a great deal of wealth in Africa, and very likely there is a great deal more which we have not yet discovered. In 1870 the white men did not know what they would find in Africa, but they did know that it would be a slow and expensive matter to search.

So even business men in Britain were slow to ask for colonies in Africa. The British Government was even more determined not to colonize Africa if it could help it. The British statesman Gladstone was four times prime minister, and had much influence for fifty years. Gladstone was not interested in Africa. In 1884, Harry Johnston, whom we shall meet later on in central Africa, was making treaties with African chiefs near Kilimanjaro in East Africa. Some of Gladstone's colleagues in the Government pressed him to recognize those treaties, and to declare the Kilimanjaro region a British protectorate. But he would not; he was not interested in what he called 'the mountain country behind Zanzibar with an unrememberable name'. He agreed that Britain should do what she could to stop the slave trade; and he agreed with Livingstone that it would be a good thing if more healthy trade could be introduced. But such trade, he thought, could be introduced without colonizing Africa; and Gladstone did not see why Africans should be brought under British rule; they should be left alone to govern themselves. In 1881 he gave the Transvaal and the Orange Free State their independence.

So much then for the British slowness; but what about the other countries?

Well, France was not very slow; the French pushed inland from Algeria and Senegal, though it is true they pushed inland much faster after 1870. Germany and Italy could do nothing before 1870, for those two countries did not exist. Many small German-speaking countries were joined together in 1871 to make the one country of Germany. Italy too became one country in 1870; before then it had been a group of independent states. Portugal already had settlements in Africa; but Portugal is a small country, and had not the strength to fight long colonial wars against such strong peoples as the Ndebele and the Nguni. As long as other countries left the interior of Africa alone, Portugal was content with her settlements on the coast.

Then why did the position change so quickly after 1880?

That is the story we are now going to tell. There are one or two general things we can say. Europe had learned from Livingstone and other explorers that Africa contained plenty of land where white men could live and remain healthy; white men were no longer afraid of going into the interior. When diamonds and gold were found in South Africa, it became clear that there was money to be made there, and miners and business men began to make their way into central Africa to see what they could find.

In 1882, Mr Gladstone, much against his will, occupied Egypt. He did so because the country seemed to be in disorder and its finances were in a complete mess. Its ruler had borrowed money all over Europe and could not repay it. British and French financial advisers were appointed, but there was an army rebellion against them, and many people were killed. Gladstone hoped to put things straight in a few months, and then leave Egypt to itself again; but as we know, the British stayed in Egypt for more than fifty years.

When the other European Governments saw the British do this in Egypt, they too began to think of Africa as a country suitable for European rule. They did not think the British would stay in Egypt if it did not pay them to do so; and if the British were to make money in Africa, why should not other countries? The French especially were jealous of Britain, and they determined to push ahead with their colonization in north and west Africa. King Leopold of Belgium became interested in the Congo. He set up a company to explore and open up the Congo, and before long the Belgians were growing rubber and mining copper there. Carl Peters and others began working to secure colonies for Germany: for why, they thought, should Germany be left out? In this way a scramble for Africa began. The business men and the miners of different European nations tried to get control of African minerals, and each man looked to his own Government to protect him against his rivals from other countries. Sometimes the missionaries thought that the traders were cheating the Africans, and they asked their Government to make the country a colony so as to protect the Africans from bad treatment. By the 1880s, the business men of Europe had decided that Africa was not as dangerous a country as they had thought, and that the profits to be made there might be well worth the risk. When one man led the way, others followed; and the competition made the pace grow faster and faster until all Africa was divided up.

We can see this process very clearly in Central Africa. From the 1850s onwards, white men began coming into Matabeleland and Barotseland and elsewhere to hunt elephant and look for gold. In the 1870s, they found Zimbabwe and saw the signs of old gold workings. They found a little gold at Tati near Bulawayo: not very much, but enough to encourage them to go on searching.

CECIL RHODES

And now Cecil Rhodes comes into the story. Rhodes was a great man in South Africa. He controlled the Kimberley diamond mines and became prime minister of the Cape, and he had dreams of a railway to run all the way from the Cape to Cairo on British soil. The Transvaal was trying to expand westward across the old route by which Livingstone and others had gone north from Kuruman into the interior. If the Transvaal expanded westward until it touched the new German protectorate of South-West Africa, it would block Rhodes's way to the north and his dream of the British railway would be ended. In 1885, Rhodes succeeded in stopping the Transvaal from expanding westward; the southern part of Tswana country became the colony of British Bechuanaland, and the northern part became a British protectorate. (The colony is now part of the Cape Province of South Africa, the protectorate is the independent state of Botswana.)

President Kruger of the Transvaal, stopped from pushing westward, tried to push to the north. In 1887 he sent one of his men named Piet Grobler to make an agreement with the Ndebele king, Lobengula. Lobengula accepted the invitation and signed the agreement. It provided that the Ndebele and the Transvaalers should be friends, and that there should be a Transvaal representative at Bulawayo. Rhodes was angry, and he persuaded the British Government that this move by the Transvaal must be stopped. The missionary John Moffat, whom Lobengula knew well, had recently been appointed a Government commissioner in Bechuanaland, and he was ordered to tell Lobengula that the Transvaal had no right to make an agreement with him. (We need not go into the reasons why the British Government thought so.) Lobengula believed his friend Moffat, and made a fresh agreement with the British Government. It was a stronger agreement than the one which Piet Grobler had made, because Lobengula now promised not to make any fresh agreement with the Transvaal, the Portuguese, the Germans or anyone else, without the permission of the British Government.

Rhodes now saw his way clear. He expected to find Lobengula's country full of gold, and maybe of diamonds too. What he now wanted was Lobengula's permission to search and dig for minerals. But he was not the first in the field; there were other white men already in Bulawayo asking for this permission. Rhodes sent three of his own men to persuade Lobengula to deal with him and not with his competitors. Lobengula would much rather have been left alone; he did not want the white men in his country at all. But he saw that he would not be able to keep them all out, so it was a question of deciding which of the white men he would do business with, and then of getting the best terms he could. He chose Rhodes, and in October 1888 he signed an agreement with Rhodes's representative Charles Rudd. He granted no land for settlement, but he gave Rhodes full charge over all metals and minerals in his kingdom, with power to do whatever mining he thought fit; and he promised to make no other grants to anyone without Rhodes's consent. He was not as wise as Lewanika of Barotseland, who was careful to keep the Lozi country itself clear, and to make grants only over the land of the other tribes whom the Lozi ruled.

And what did Rhodes give Lobengula in return for this valuable grant?

Very little: a salary of £100 a month[1], and a gift of a thousand modern rifles with a hundred bullets for each. Though he did not know it, Lobengula had sold his country's freedom.

As soon as Lobengula had signed the paper, he wished he had not done so. Some of the other white men in Bulawayo told him he had made a mistake. He wrote to Queen Victoria in London, asking what he was to do, and received a reply advising him to be very careful in dealing with white men who asked him to sign agreements. He turned on the chief who had advised him to make the agreement with Rudd, and 'ate him up', as the Ndebele used to say; that is, he sent soldiers to kill him and his whole family and clan and destroy his village. But this could not save him.

Rhodes was already in London, and he asked the Government to give his British South Africa Company a royal charter: that is, to give it authority to act in the name of the British Government, not only to mine and trade, but to occupy territory and hoist the British flag over it. With all the wealth of the Kimberley diamond mines behind him, it was easy for Rhodes to buy out the opposition of the other white men who were his rivals at Bulawayo. There were a good many people in Britain who did not approve of what Rhodes was doing. Some did not approve of bringing rifles into Africa (we remember that the African Lakes Company would never trade in them); some, like Gladstone and his followers, wished that Rhodes would leave the Ndebele and all Africa north of the Limpopo alone; some thought that if the country between the Limpopo and the Zambesi were to become British, it should come directly under the British Government, and not under the control of a commercial company. But Rhodes persuaded the Government to support him; he got his Charter

---

[1] To be fair to Rhodes, we should remember that £100 a month then was worth quite £1,000 a month today. But the price is still cheap.

in October 1889, and at once began preparing to put it into effect.

The Pioneers of 1890

Rhodes planned to send up a group of white settlers who would make their homes in Mashonaland and work the goldfields which they expected to find there. There were nearly two hundred of these 'pioneers', as they were called, with a force of four hundred mounted soldiers, commanded by a British army officer, to protect them from attack. Though one of Rhodes's men in Bulawayo had assured Lobengula that Rhodes did not want land, each pioneer was promised a farm of 3,000 acres in Mashonaland, as well as fifteen gold claims.

The pioneers began their journey in June 1890. Lobengula had promised to allow a party of miners to come and look for gold, but he had not expected as big a party as this. The British Government's High Commissioner in South Africa promised him that the pioneers would not attack the Ndebele, and would not cross Ndebele country. This promise was kept; but the High Commissioner also told Lobengula that the pioneers were coming only to look for gold; he said nothing about farming. Lobengula and his people were afraid, and his chiefs wanted him to let them attack the white men and kill them all. But Lobengula knew that this would mean the end of the Ndebele nation, and he would not let them. On 12 September 1890 the pioneers made their camp at the end of their march, and named it Salisbury in honour of the British prime minister, Lord Salisbury. The pioneers at once scattered over the veld to peg out their mining claims and their farms.

By his agreement with Rudd, Lobengula had granted the Company mining rights over the whole of his kingdom. But the boundaries of his kingdom had never been laid down. Some people said that Mashonaland, where the pioneers were at work, was not part of it. And the Portuguese now remembered the days of the Monomatapa, and they said that Mashonaland had certainly been part of the Monomatapa's country, and they had rights in it because of their old agreements. Rhodes on the other hand wanted to include Mashonaland in Lobengula's kingdom, and to push its boundaries as far to the east as he could. Rhodes would have liked if possible to obtain a port on the Indian Ocean. But the British and Portuguese Governments made an agreement, and fixed the frontier between Mozambique and Mashonaland in the hill country just east of Umtali. Rhodes was angry, because he did not get his seaport; but it was a reasonable frontier line, much more reasonable than some frontier lines in Africa.

Lobengula now saw what he had done. In spite of Rhodes's promises, the Company's men were taking farm lands in Mashonaland, which Lobengula, rightly or wrongly, regarded as part of his territory. True, they had so far kept away from Matabeleland itself, but Lobengula guessed that sooner or later they would come into Matabeleland also. Even if they found gold in Mashonaland, they would come into Matabeleland in the hope of finding more. He wished with all his heart that he had never made the agreement with Rudd. He now tried (not for the first time) to play off one European against another: he made a fresh agreement with a man called Lippert. The new agreement said that the Rudd agreement gave the Company mining rights, but no farming rights; the only European who had any authority to handle farm land was to be Lippert. No doubt Lobengula hoped that Lippert and the Company would quarrel, and while quarrelling would leave him alone. He did not know Rhodes; Rhodes had already agreed with Lippert that if Lobengula made him any grant, Rhodes would buy it from him, and Rhodes did buy it. The Company had thus bought the right not only to the minerals but also to the land over the whole of Lobengula's kingdom. In April and May 1891, the British Government declared a British protectorate over the whole of the land between the Limpopo and the Zambesi, and between the boundaries of German South-West Africa and Mozambique.

The Annexation of Matabeleland

Two years later, the end came. In June 1893 the Ndebele raided the Shona country, as they had so long been in the habit of doing. Some of the Mashona fled to take shelter with the Europeans at Fort Victoria, and the Europeans refused to give them up to the Ndebele army when it came for them. The leader of the European settlers was Dr Jameson, a close friend of Rhodes. He came from Salisbury to Fort Victoria, and found the Ndebele army still there. He told the chiefs in command that they must leave the place in an hour and begin marching back to their own country; if they did not go, he would make them. They went; but a few in the rear who were slow in starting were killed by European troops.

Even this did not provoke Lobengula to war, and he told his people that the white men living in Bulawayo were his guests and must not be harmed. But Jameson had now made up his mind that the time had come to finish with the Ndebele kingdom. The white men had found very little gold in Mashonaland, and they hoped that there might be much more in Matabeleland. The whole of the Company's work was based on the idea that it would make money from gold mining and would be able to pay dividends to its shareholders. So far, the shareholders had not received a penny, and none of the pioneers had become rich.

In October the Company's army was ready, and the invasion of Matabeleland began. In spite of their new rifles, the Ndebele could do nothing against the Company's machine-guns and artillery, and were heavily defeated in two battles, although they did succeed in cutting off and destroying a small party of white troops which had become separated from the main body. Lobengula fled northwards towards the Zambesi, but he died of small-pox before reaching it. The Company's men took over Matabeleland, but they did not find another huge goldfield like the Rand, as they had hoped.

Surely all this is a very sad story, and shows the white men at their very worst? They took Lobengula's country, partly by cheating and partly by force, although Lobengula had done them no harm. Is this an unfair way of putting it?

It certainly is a sad story, and the white men do not come well out of it. It is true that Lobengula did the white men no harm; he was always honest with them, and protected the few white men in Bulawayo to the very last. The pioneers went to Salisbury with the promise from Rhodes that they would be given homes and farms, although Lobengula was told that they were coming only to look for gold, not for land and cattle.

We should perhaps draw a distinction between Rhodes and Jameson and the Company on one hand, and the British Government on the other. The Government was in a difficult position. It knew that if central Africa did not soon come under British rule, it would come under the rule of Germany or Portugal, or possibly the Transvaal. Lobengula had no hope of keeping his independence much longer. The Government would have preferred to occupy and govern the country itself; but it knew that the British parliament would never agree to the expense. The Chartered Company, with Rhodes's immense wealth behind it, seemed the answer to this difficulty. But if the Company paid all the expenses, the Government had not much hope of controlling what it did. The British High Commissioner was at the Cape, a thousand miles away. The Government approved of occupying Mashonaland, but not of occupying Matabeleland. But it could not stop Jameson, and all it could do was to make the peace terms a little less severe than Jameson would have made them.

But could not the Government have said to Jameson and Rhodes, 'If you make war on the Ndebele without our permission, we shall take away your Company's royal charter?'

The Government would have had the legal right to do this. But it would have been a very strong step, and it would have brought on a first-class political row. British Governments have a tradition of 'trusting the man on the spot' as much as they can. Rhodes and Jameson and their political friends in England would have told the Government, 'You don't know the Ndebele; we do. What right have you, so far away, to tell us that we are doing wrong?'

And this brings us to the weakness of Lobengula's position. True, he had done no harm to the white men; but he and his Ndebele had done a great deal of harm to the Tswana and the Mashona and the Lozi and all their other neighbours. Rhodes could say with a good deal of truth, 'The Mashona are longing to be delivered from their fear of the Ndebele. We have nearly finished putting down the slave trade, but Lobengula's men do just as much harm as any slave raiders. We cannot allow this to go on any longer.' The Ndebele would not listen to the Christian missionaries; they were not interested

4. Rhodes Talking to the Ndebele Chiefs in 1896

in schools or in new ideas; they lived for nothing but raiding and war. For the sake of all their neighbours, their way of life had to be stopped. But it is a great pity that it was stopped not merely by force but by cheating.

The British High Commissioner at the Cape did not think that Rhodes and the Company were the best people to govern the Ndebele. He advised the Government to treat Matabeleland as it had treated Bechuanaland: to make it a colony or a protectorate, and to rule it by a Governor appointed from London. But the Government allowed the Company to take control, and Matabeleland was placed under the same kind of government as Mashonaland.

The Ndebele were angry. They were fighting men and they were not willing to become farm labourers: they disliked the Mashona police who were given authority over them: they saw some of their land and cattle taken away: and they blamed the white men also for two things which were not the white men's fault, plagues of locusts and of cattle disease. In March 1896 they rose in rebellion, and three months later even the peaceful Mashona joined them, so much did they hate the Company's government. The Matabele rebellion was stopped

5. Rhodes Defending Himself in London in 1897

by Rhodes himself, who went unarmed into the Matopo hills, where the Ndebele had their camp. He listened to their complaints, and agreed that they were justified. He was able to satisfy the Ndebele on one or two matters, so the Ndebele chiefs made peace. But the Mashona had no powerful chiefs who could order them to make peace. Like the Kikuyu of Kenya and the Ibo of Nigeria, they lived in small clans, governed by clan elders. Like their ancestors, they took refuge in rocky hill-tops and in caves, and there they fought on in small groups. It was a horrible business, and it was not until October that the last of the fighting ended. It was an unhappy beginning to the colonial period.

6

ANNEXATION BEYOND
THE ZAMBESI

The story of the British advance from the Limpopo to the Zambesi is simple. Rhodes's Chartered Company was dealing with Lobengula, and the British Government had very little to do with the affair. The Ndebele and the Mashona were the only two peoples concerned, and their homeland was a compact country with two great rivers as its boundaries. Once the eastern boundary with Mozambique had been fixed, that chapter in the story was ended.

But it is a very different matter north of the Zambesi. It is 800 miles between Angola and lake Nyasa, and there are many different African peoples living in that large area. And there were many people concerned: Rhodes and his Chartered Company, the Arab slave traders, the Scottish missionaries and the African Lakes Company, and the British Government.

The British Government could not stand aside from the affairs of the country north of the Zambesi as it had stood outside those of Rhodesia. For one thing, the Scottish Churches and business men would not allow it to forget the work they were doing in the country which we now call Malawi. For another thing, the Government could see that the Belgians, the Germans and the Portuguese were all actively pushing in from different directions. The Belgians were busily exploring the Congo basin; they had set up a Congo Free State in 1876, and were now extending its boundaries as fast as they could. The Germans began making treaties with the east African chiefs in 1884, and had occupied nearly the whole of Tanganyika by 1890. The Portuguese were active both in Angola and in Mozambique, and still hoped that they might be able to join the two territories together, so that there would be a wide strip of Portuguese country stretching from east to west right across

Africa from sea to sea. Rhodes and his Company could not deal with these foreign Governments; only the British Government could deal with them. And even so big a man as Rhodes might find that he had to take less than he had hoped to get.

So this is not one story, but several stories. We must tell them one at a time, and notice where one story touches another.

LAKE NYASA AND THE ARAB WAR

The Scottish missionaries began working in the lake country in 1875, and the African Lakes Company was set up in 1878. But they could do very little against the Arab and Yao and other slave raiders. The African Lakes Company would not sell guns and ammunition, which was what the Africans most wanted; nor would it buy slaves, which was what the Africans had to sell. The slave trade grew and grew, and the Arab and half-Arab slave dealers came to look on the Europeans as more of a nuisance. In 1887, one of them called Mlozi attacked the Company's trading station at Karonga. He was driven back, and the local people moved forward and burned Mlozi's village. The Europeans recruited more African troops; and they were lucky in finding a good leader, Captain Lugard of the Indian Army, who was on leave from India and had come to Africa to see the country and gain experience. What they badly needed was weapons. Rifles and ammunition were being sent out from Britain, but the Portuguese customs officers at the mouth of the Zambesi were slow to allow them to be sent inland. The British thought, rightly or wrongly, that the Portuguese did not want the western shore of the lake to come too much under British influence, and would be content to look on while British and Arabs fought and weakened each other.

The war went on through 1888 and 1889. Lugard was seriously wounded and had to go back to England; but when he was there he did a great deal to explain to his countrymen what the position was like in the lake country, and he begged the Government to give the missionaries and the Company some real help against the slave raiders.

The Government was still unwilling to take any part in African politics. It was easier and cheaper to leave to Rhodes

6. The Ndebele Raiding a Village in Mashonaland

the work of conquering and governing Mashonaland and
Matabeleland. But the Government could not very well take
this easy and cheap way north of the Zambesi river. There
was an active and increasing slave trade, and for over eighty
years the British Government had been doing its best to stop
the slave trade. There was also Scottish missionary work, now

fourteen years old, with the honoured name of Livingstone
behind it. And in 1889, two new things had happened. One
was that the Mahdi, who had conquered the Sudan and
killed Gordon, began to attack Egypt. Lord Salisbury's
Government had hoped that the Mahdi would be content
with the Sudan, and was prepared to leave it to him. But if
he was going to attack Egypt as well, it would give the British
and Egyptian Governments much trouble and expense, and
it might be better for them to try and reconquer the Sudan
and kill the Mahdi.

But what have the Mahdi and the Sudan to do with Malawi?

Lord Salisbury noticed that since 1885, when the Mahdi
conquered the Sudan, the Arab slave traders in the country
near Lake Nyasa had become much bolder. He thought that
perhaps the two things were connected: perhaps the Mahdi
in the Sudan was telling the Arabs in the lake country to drive
the missionaries and the other white men into the sea and
conquer the whole region for Islam. If so, it might be wise
for Britain to fight the southern Arabs as part of her plan to
reconquer the Sudan from the Mahdi. For this reason, Lord
Salisbury was more ready to listen to Lugard than he might
otherwise have been, and he was prepared to consider plans
for helping the Scots on Lake Nyasa.

For this reason: but you said there was another reason as well?

The other reason was quite different. One great difficulty
about doing anything in that part of Africa was that to get to
it, you had to go up the Zambesi and the Shire rivers. The
Portuguese at the mouth of the Zambesi made everyone stop
at their port of Quelimane, which stood on the only branch
of the delta where the water was deep enough for a steamer
to enter. But in 1889 another deep-water branch of the delta
was discovered, so it was now possible to enter the Zambesi
and steam up it without being stopped by the Portuguese. This
meant that the British could get to the lake country without
troubling the Portuguese or asking Portuguese permission;
which made the situation much easier.

But there was still one great difficulty. The British people
would never have agreed to send troops to Central Africa,

and Salisbury's Government knew that it would be useless to come to parliament and ask for such a thing. A chartered company would be the easiest way. But Rhodes's British South Africa Company had only just received its charter, and was busy with its preparations for the invasion of Mashonaland; it could be no help in the lake country. The African Lakes Company was too small and weak to be given a charter, and its leaders in Africa were not men of the Rhodes type. The situation in the lake country needed a man; and Lord Salisbury sent Harry Johnston.

Harry Johnston in Nyasaland

Harry Johnston was no newcomer to Africa. He had worked in Tunisia, Angola and the Congo, the Cameroons and the Niger delta, and in the Kilimanjaro region. He was a keen student of African languages and easily made African friends; during the seven years he was in Nyasaland he learned Swahili and three local Bantu languages. Johnston sometimes made mistakes: Nigerians of today dislike him because of the way in which he treated Jaja of Opobo. But he was a good friend to Africa, and Malawi and Uganda especially owe him a great deal. Johnston had another useful qualification for work in Nyasaland: he spoke Portuguese.

Johnston was appointed British Consul at Mozambique, and he was told to make any treaties he could with the African chiefs who were independent of Portugal. Just before leaving London, he met Cecil Rhodes. Rhodes was full of his plans for dealing with Lobengula; but he was already looking beyond Lobengula to a time when his Company would be ready to push beyond the Zambesi. Rhodes thought that he might use Johnston, and he actually paid part of Johnston's travelling expenses in Nyasaland, although Johnston was a Government official. Johnston was prepared to work with Rhodes. His idea was that if Portugal would give up all her claims to Mashonaland and Matabeleland, and give up too all her idea of joining Angola and Mozambique from west to east, Britain in return should allow Portugal to expand up the Shire river and occupy the south end of lake Nyasa. This would have allowed Rhodes's Chartered Company to push as far north as it liked until it met the Germans in Tanganyika; in fact, there was still a chance that it might push as far as lake Victoria. Johnston talked over his idea with the Portuguese, and was sure they would accept such a scheme. But Salisbury felt that it was politically impossible to leave the Scottish missionaries in the Shire highlands to come under Portuguese rule; and he told Johnston that he must resist all Portuguese claims in the Shire region.

What do you mean when you say that it was 'politically impossible' to abandon the Scottish missionaries in this way?

The missionaries and the African Lakes Company had so many powerful friends in Britain that many members of parliament – even perhaps members of Salisbury's own party – would have voted against the Government. Lord Salisbury was English, and the cry would have been raised that an English prime minister was sacrificing Scottish interests. As one writer[1] has said, Salisbury 'knew very well that he would rather face the wrath of Portugal than that of Scotland.'

Johnston arrived in Nyasaland in July 1889. He found a Portuguese party, led by Major Serpa Pinto, ready to march into the lake country and make treaties with the chiefs between lake Nyasa and the Zambesi. The chiefs on the lower Shire were unwilling to let Pinto's party through, and Pinto thought that the African Lakes Company was encouraging them to stop him. Johnston told Pinto that if he tried to force his way through, there would be heavy fighting; maybe European lives would be lost, and there would be serious trouble between Britain and Portugal. This rather alarmed Pinto and he decided that he had better go back to his Government in Quelimane and get fresh orders. The moment Pinto was gone, Johnston himself went north into Nyasaland to begin his work. He met an English ivory-hunter, Alfred Sharpe, appointed him a vice-consul, and sent him off into the interior with the power to make treaties. The two men separated, Johnston going north up the lake shore, and Sharpe westwards towards lakes Bangweulu and Mweru. Before leaving, Johnston told Mr Buchanan, one of the staff of the African Lakes Company, that if the Portuguese tried again to enter the Shire highlands, he was to declare a formal British protectorate over the area.

[1] Roland Oliver, *Sir Harry Johnston and the Scramble for Africa*, p. 150

From August to December 1889, Johnston was busily making treaties, He had the help of the Scottish missionaries in interpreting and explaining to the chiefs what the treaties meant. They did not mean very much. A chief who signed a treaty declared that he was at peace with Britain, that he would allow British people to travel in his country and would submit any disputes he had to the decision of a British representative, and that he would not place his country under the protection of any other European country without British consent. The treaty did not give the chief British protection, and of course it gave Britain no rights at all over his land. It merely secured that Britain should have the first chance of giving him protection at some future time.

Johnston went up the whole length of lake Nyasa and on to the southern end of lake Tanganyika, making treaties all the way. He made a larger agreement than usual with one of the half-Arab slave traders, Jumbe Kisutu, whose headquarters were at Kotakota on the western shore of lake Nyasa. Jumbe was a far-sighted man. He had seen that the slave-trading days were coming to an end, and for some time past he had been getting out of the trade in slaves and limiting himself to the trade in ivory. Johnston found Jumbe so powerful that he thought it better to offer him full British protection at once, and Jumbe agreed. Further north, at Karonga, Johnston made a short-term peace agreement with Mlozi and his friends, who had been making life so difficult for the missionaries there. With Mlozi, there was no question of giving him British protection; the slave traders merely agreed not to attack the mission station again, and not to attack any tribe which had signed a treaty with the British.

In December, when he was on the shores of lake Tanganyika, Johnston heard news which brought him hurrying back south. The Portuguese had sent another party inland and there had been a little fighting. Buchanan had thereupon carried out his orders and had declared a British protectorate over the Shire highlands; but in spite of this the Portuguese had come on, and had actually hauled down the British flag. This was serious; but luckily for Johnston, the matter had already been reported in Europe, and the British and Portuguese Governments had come to an agreement. Britain threatened to occupy Mozam-

7. Jumbe's Village on Lake Nyasa

bique if the Portuguese troops were not withdrawn from the
Shire highlands, and the Portuguese gave way. This happened
in January 1890, and the agreement was confirmed by the
treaty of June 1891, by which Portugal gave way to Britain
here and Britain gave way to Portugal further south, so that
Rhodes did not get the seaport he wanted.[1]

Johnston was disappointed at having to leave lake Tanganyika in a hurry, for that area had not yet been reached by
the Germans, and he had hoped to make many more treaties
with the chiefs there. But Sharpe went up to the Tanganyika
region next year and made more treaties. By the Anglo-German
Treaty of July 1890[2] these treaties were accepted; the Tanganyika boundary was fixed so as to leave the northern end

[1]See above, page 60
[2]By this treaty, Germany also agreed to give up her claim to Uganda; Johnston
of course would have liked to make treaties all the way up the rift valley to Uganda.

of Lake Nyasa to Germany, but to leave the whole of the Stevenson Road to Britain.

After leaving lake Tanganyika, Sharpe went west and south-west, hoping to make treaties in the Luapula valley and Katanga. Kazembe, the chief of the Lunda people in the Luapula valley, made a treaty with him readily enough; but his rival Msidi in Katanga would not. Sharpe accepted Msidi's decision and went away. Msidi held out for another year; in 1891 a Belgian party arrived from the north, hoisted the Belgian flag, and shot Msidi when he tried to resist. Katanga thus became part of the Belgian Congo.

How was this great area to be governed, in which Johnston and Sharpe had been making treaties? The African Lakes Company could not govern it. When Rhodes's Chartered Company was clear of its troubles in the south, it might be able to govern it; but not just yet. The British Government was not yet ready to take on such a large responsibility. In the end, a compromise was reached. A boundary line was drawn along the mountain ridge west of lake Nyasa. All the country west of the line would be governed by the British South Africa Company – by Rhodes's Company. East of the line, the British Government would take control; but the British South Africa Company would have the right to any minerals, and in return would pay £ 10,000 a year towards the expenses of governing the country. The boundary line we have described is today's frontier between Zambia and Malawi.

In May 1891, the British Government proclaimed the lake region a British protectorate under the name of the British Central Africa Protectorate, and appointed Johnston as Com-missioner. Two years later the African Lakes Company was wound up; Rhodes's company took over its land and mineral rights, and a new company called the African Lakes Corpora-tion was set up to carry on its general trading. In 1894 the British Government stopped the arrangement by which Rhodes's company paid part of the expenses of the new Protectorate; the Company was restricted to Zambia, and the British Govern-ment became entirely responsible for the lake country.

Johnston arrived to take up his post as Commissioner in July 1891. He had very little money, and fewer than two hundred troops. The Yao chiefs, in spite of living in a British protectorate, were still slave raiding. Johnston's first business was to show that his Government meant to govern. With his few soldiers, he set out to attack the slave raiders, and in a few weeks he had made seven of the Yao chiefs agree to give up slave raiding and accept British rule. The strongest of them, Makanjira, escaped, and gave serious trouble for five more years. In 1894, the Government in London saw that it must give Johnston more troops, and more money for the expenses of his administration. It provided also several gunboats on the lake and on the Shire river. With these extra forces, Johnston was able to make his authority more felt, and by 1896 all the Yao chiefs had given up their slaving and become peaceful citizens.

Meanwhile, Johnston had also to look after the north. In 1889 he had made a short-term agreement with Mlozi and other slave traders there. But Mlozi and his friends had now built up their strength again; they had plenty of rifles and ammunition, and were hard at work again, selling the slaves they took in Portuguese and German territory. In September 1895 Johnston set out with more than 400 men and seven guns to punish Mlozi. They went by steamer up the lake and took Mlozi by surprise; they besieged him in his village for two days and then took the place by storm and hanged Mlozi for his long years of cruelty and slave raiding. A few months later, Johnston became ill; he had to leave Nyasaland, and (like Lugard before him) he never returned.

Johnston did much more for Nyasaland than conquer the slave raiders and bring the country peace. We leave to the next chapter the work he did in setting up a peaceful administration.

THE NORTH-EAST

In telling the story of Nyasaland we have already touched upon part of the north-east. After 1894, the British South Africa Company was left in charge of the whole of modern Zambia, but there were large areas in which the African chiefs were still independent. If the Company wished the Belgians and the Portuguese to recognise its authority, it had to enforce its authority on all the African chiefs in the area. There were three in the north-east who were specially important: Mpezeni of the Nguni, Chitimukulu of the Bemba, and Kazembe of the Lunda.

Mpezeni was now growing old, and the young men of the Nguni were angry when they saw the white men coming into their country to look for gold. Mpezeni could not control them, as Lobengula had controlled his Ndebele. In 1897 they killed two white men, and attacked some others. Troops were sent from Blantyre to help the white men, and the Nguni were defeated. Mpezeni was allowed to remain as chief, but his son Nsingu, who was the real head of the attack, was shot as a murderer, and the Nguni were fined large numbers of cattle. After this, the Nguni gave no more trouble.

It seems as if this affair, like that of Lobengula, was caused by the white men's greed for gold?

That is largely true. If the white men (British and Germans) had not gone into Mpezeni's country looking for gold before the Government had had time to send a commissioner to talk things over and make an agreement, Nsingu and the young men would not have made this war. But Nsingu should not have killed the two white traders. Lobengula was wiser; he would not let his young men kill the white men in Bulawayo.

But it made no difference; the Ndebele had to accept British rule, just as the Nguni had.

True; but by 1897 things had gone so far that the Nguni would have had to accept some colonial rule. If it had not been British, it would have been Belgian. And the Nguni, like the Ndebele, had for years been a terror to all their neighbours with their raiding. They had to be made to stop it.

The Bemba so far had had nothing to do with the white men. They had some rifles, but they lived in terror of the Arab slave raiders. Their villages were strongly fenced, and surrounded with a deep ditch, and they would allow no strangers to enter their country.

After Johnston had destroyed Mlozi, some of Mlozi's Arab friends moved westwards, and they set up a new slave-raiding state in the upper part of the Luangwa valley. They got some of the Bemba to help them, just as in the Shire valley they had got help from the Yao. This led to disunity among the Bemba, and the paramount chief. Chitimukulu, asked the Company's officers for help against one of his sub-chiefs. Troops were sent, and in 1898 the Arab and Bemba raiders were defeated. Next year, the last of the Arab slave traders was defeated in the Luapula valley, and by 1900 the whole of the north-east had peace at last.

THE NORTH-WEST

In the north-west of the country, the strongest paramount chief was Lewanika of Barotseland. His people the Lozi, though much stronger than the Mashona, were sometimes raided by the Ndebele. In fact, when Lobengula had to face the European attack in 1893, he had six thousand men already across the Zambesi on their way to raid the Lozi, and he had to call them back. Lewanika wanted to save his country from these Ndebele raids. He knew that a neighbouring chief, Khama of the Bamangwato[1], had saved his country from the Ndebele raiders by making it a British protectorate. In 1883, Lewanika sent to ask Khama how he liked living under British protection, and whether it would be a good thing for the Lozi to ask the British to protect them too. Khama replied that it would be a very good thing; but Lewanika had too much trouble at home for the moment to follow Khama's advice. In 1885 things began to settle down, and Lewanika then asked the missionary Coillard to write to Queen Victoria for him and ask for British protection. Coillard did not like to interfere in politics, and would not write the letter; but in 1889 Lewanika feared another Ndebele raid, and this time Coillard did agree to write. He wrote, not to Queen Victoria in London, but to the British Commissioner in Bechuanaland, telling him that Lewanika would like to be given British protection.

It was now 1889, and Lewanika had not only the Ndebele to fear; like Lobengula, he had to fear the white hunters and miners who came begging him to grant them hunting and mining rights over his country. He gave a grant to a man named Ware; but Lewanika was careful to keep the Lozi country out of it. He gave Ware the right to mine gold or any

[1] Khama's country was in the north-east of what is now Botswana.

other minerals all over the country of the other tribes who obeyed him, but not in Barotseland itself. Very likely some of the Ila and Tonga and other people in the area would say that Lewanika had no right to make this grant; but he made it.

The next thing that happened was that Ware sold his grant to Rhodes's Company, just as Lippert had done in Matabeleland. Rhodes sent a representative named Lochner to see Lewanika, and in June 1890 Lochner and Lewanika came to an agreement. The Company would exercise the mining rights that had been granted to Ware; in return, the Company would protect the country from an attack by the Ndebele or anyone else, would pay Lewanika £2,000 a year (worth ten times as much in today's money), and would pay him also a royalty[1] on all minerals it exported. The Company promised to send a representative to live at Lewanika's capital, Lealui; but it was seven years before Rhodes had anyone to send there.

This Lochner agreement of 1890 was replaced by a new agreement in 1898. Barotseland, as before, was kept clear; there was to be no mining there. Lewanika gave away only one new thing: he allowed the Company to judge all disputes where white men were concerned. He gave no farming rights. On the other hand, the Company agreed in return to provide African education; and it was made quite plain that the Company was acting merely as the representative of the Queen.

Two years later, in 1900, the whole of north-western Rhodesia, including Barotseland, was proclaimed a British protectorate. The Resident appointed by the Company was to be under the orders of the British High Commissioner in South Africa. The western boundary with Angola was settled by an agreement with Portugal in 1903.

Lewanika seems to have been luckier than Lobengula; why was this?

Partly, no doubt, because he was wiser. Lobengula and his Ndebele wanted to be left alone to raid the Mashona and other people in the old way; Lewanika, like Khama, saw that the

---

[1] A royalty is a tax, reckoned as a percentage of the value of the goods. Thus, the more the Company exported, the more it would have to pay Lewanika. Lewanika and his adviser Coillard were wise; not many African chiefs in those days were paid a royalty on mineral exports.

old ways would have to stop, and he was ready to change. Partly too because Lewanika was able to say, 'You may go and dig as much as you like in Ila or Tonga country, which all belongs to me; but you are not to come and dig in Lozi country.' Partly again because much of Barotseland is flooded every year when the Zambesi rises; it is not the sort of country to attract gold-miners. But the first of these reasons is the most important: Lewanika was a wise man. You can see the difference between him and Lobengula when you compare the prices they asked. Lobengula asked for £1,200 a year, with a gift (once only) of a thousand rifles and ammunition; Lewanika asked for £2,000 a year, with a royalty on exports. Lobengula gave rights over his whole country, Lewanika only over the outer part, where his subject tribes lived. Lobengula granted farming as well as mining rights; Lewanika would not.

By 1900, the whole of the area which today makes Rhodesia, Zambia and Malawi had come under British rule. It is not so very long ago. In 1967, when this book was written, there were many people still living in England who were old enough at that time to read about these events in the newspapers. My own memory of the newspapers goes back to 1904, one year after the Angola boundary line had been drawn. When we read of this old Africa: the Africa of Ndebele raids and Arab slave traders, of British and Portuguese exploring and treaty-making, of independent chiefs who made every traveller pay them a tax before they would 'give him the road' – it seems very far away. It is difficult to realise that poeple still alive can remember it.

One other thing we should notice is that from the beginning, Malawi (the Central African Protectorate, as it was then called) was different from the other two countries. They were governed by the British South Africa Company, which had rights not only to minerals but to farm land; Malawi was a British protectorate directly under the Queen, and governed by the Queen's officers. The Company was first of all a commercial company, which hoped (though it never succeeded) to make a profit after paying the expenses of government. The Government of Malawi was free from that disadvantage.

7

BRITISH CENTRAL
AFRICA TO 1924

The whole of this great country, nearly nine hundred miles each way, had now become British, and the British now had to decide how to govern it. The country was not thickly populated. Much of it was poorly watered or infested with tsetse fly, and much of the lower ground was full of malaria. The African population was much smaller than it is now; it was supposed that were about half a million Africans in Southern Rhodesia, and fewer than a million in Northern Rhodesia.[1] Here, as in East Africa, there were large areas which were empty of people: land which had never been broken by a hoe and grass which had never been grazed by a cow. We can hardly blame the white men if they thought there was room for their farms as well as for the African villages and their grazing land.

Both the British Government and the British South Africa Company saw that the land question was one of the most important questions they had to settle. In 1898, the British Government ordered the Company to see that the Africans in Southern Rhodesia always had enough land for their farms and their cattle, including enough drinking water. The Company set to work to mark out reserves, and in the next four years it set aside about 21 per cent of the total area of Southern Rhodesia. In 1915 it appointed a commission to revise this settlement; the commission reduced the area of the reserves from 21 percent of the country to 17 per cent, but improved the quality of the land.

Why did the commission reduce the area?

The Company was in a difficulty. It wanted to reserve enough land for the Africans, but it also wanted to attract

[1] These names were given to the two territories in 1897; the British Central Africa Protectorate was renamed Nyasaland in 1907.

European settlers. It was a commercial company, and it wanted to make a profit. It was not a bad thing that some skilful European farmers should come into the country (if there was room for them) to grow crops for export. This would provide revenue for the Government, and without revenue the Government would never be able to provide schools and hospitals and other services. But Europeans wanted big farms of 2,000 or 3,000 acres, after the South African fashion; if they were offered small farms, they would not come. So the Company naturally tried to make as much land available as possible for European settlers. We must be fair. The reserves that were set aside in 1902 were comfortably big enough for the African population at that time. The Company of course knew that the African population would increase. But at this point it made a mistake: it said that African agriculture was inefficient, but that African farmers would soon learn modern methods of farming, so that as the population increased, the reserves would still be able to support it. As we know, African farmers (for various reasons) have been slow to adopt modern methods; the result is that reserves which used to be quite big enough are now too small.

In the western part of Northern Rhodesia, the position was still governed by the grant that Lewanika had made in 1898. In 1904 he went further and allowed the Company to make grants of farm land to European settlers in the outlying parts of his country: not in Lozi country itself. But not many Europeans came. When the railway was built from the Victoria Falls to Broken Hill, a few came to take farms along the railway line. But there were so few African people living there that the white men found it very hard to get enough labourers. There was plenty of empty land, but what was the use of land if there was no one to work on it? In the eastern part of Northern Rhodesia the position was much the same. This was out of Lewanika's control, but there was no railway, and it was tsetse fly country, so very few Europeans went there.

Johnston's Land Policy in Nyasaland

In Nyasaland the position was quite different. Here, the slave trade had made such a mess of the country that there were no strong chiefs left like Lewanika. As soon as Johnston had

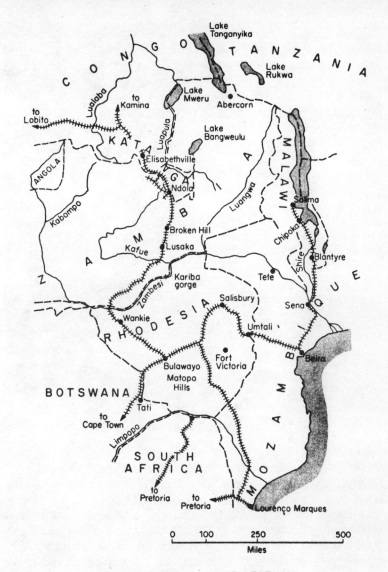

MAP 4. CENTRAL AFRICA TODAY

The modern boundaries are marked, and the main railway lines. Notice how the railway to the north, instead of going north-east by Salisbury and Abercorn, turns north-west by Wankie and goes on to the mines at Broken Hill and the copper-belt. The main line enters the Congo (Katanga) soon after leaving Ndola, but branch lines connect the Zambian copper towns. It is easy to see that the quickest route for the produce of north-eastern Zambia to the sea is through Malawi to Beira.

8. Picking Tea in Malawi

brought some peace and quiet into the country, white men came in to try and make their fortunes. They brought with them trade goods – guns, powder, cloth, and so on – and tried to persuade the chiefs to grant them land. The white men meant to buy land. The chiefs of course did not understand this. They thought the white men were trying merely to lease the land; for how could anyone buy land? Land was not a thing that could be bought and sold. Some chiefs did make grants of land, but because of this misunderstanding it was likely that there would be trouble later on

Johnston meant to stop this. He understood how Africans thought about land. He was determined that they should not be cheated by putting their mark to a written paper which they could not read or understand, and then being told that they had given away their land in exchange for a few pounds worth of trade goods. He was determined also that white men should not be granted long leases at low rents. He preferred to lease the land for 14 or 21 years, and at the end of the lease the rent could be increased if the land were worth more.

What Johnston did was to inspect every grant that was shown him. He went to see the land for himself, and spoke to the chief who had made the grant to find out whether he knew exactly what he was doing. (We must remember that Johnston spoke Swahili and three Nyasaland languages.) If Johnston thought that the white man had not paid a fair price for his grant, Johnston told him that he must either pay more or take a smaller grant. And he added that all African villages and farm lands were outside the grant: that if any minerals were found on the land, the Government must get a five per cent royalty: and that if the Government later on needed to build a road or a railway through the land, it must be allowed to do so without any charge. He explained to the villagers that if the white man ever told them that they must pay him rent or work for him without pay, they were not to believe him; for there was nothing about this in the grant.

But what power had Johnston to make the white men agree to all this?

Well, after all, Johnston was the Governor[1]. But he had something to offer them if they accepted his conditions. Once the grant was satisfactory to him, he would give the white man an official Certificate of Claim. This was a paper to say that the Government recognized and approved the grant. With this Certificate, the white man could prove that he had the right to occupy the land. Without it, no one would be able to sell his grant to anyone else. So the Certificate was well worth having, even if Johnston made you pay the African chief more for your grant than you had hoped.

Johnston followed this system all over Nyasaland. The African Lakes Company came to him with very large claims, but Johnston decided that many of them were not genuine, and he cut them down very severely. He also had to deal with

[1] His actual title was Commissioner, but he had the powers of a Governor. Nyasaland became a Governorship in 1907.

the British South Africa Company, which had many grants of land in the western part of the country. Johnston would have liked to cut down the Company's claims as he had cut down others. But here he was not able to be as severe as he wished, because Rhodes and the Company had been paying such a large share of the cost of Johnston's administration. Still, the people of Malawi today owe it to Johnston that so much of their land remained in African hands throughout the colonial period. The land situation in Nyasaland was like that in Uganda or West Africa: not like that in Kenya or Southern Rhodesia.

Mining and Railways

Most of the Europeans at that time did not come to central Africa for farm land, and the British South Africa Company was not specially interested in farming. The Company and most of the white men were interested in minerals: in gold first, and if they could not find gold, in any other mineral there was. As we have seen, they found no large gold deposit in central Africa to compare with the Rand, but they found several small deposits which were worth mining. In 1899, copper was found in Katanga, and some copper was found also in Northern Rhodesia. But the Rhodesian copper ore seemed to be much less rich than the Katanga ore, and the rich Katanga ore was also cheaper to work. So for many years, Rhodesian copper could not compete with copper from across the Congo border in Katanga. In 1902, lead and zinc were discovered at Broken Hill.

When it was known that Rhodesia contained copper, lead and zinc, as well as gold, it became plain which way Rhodes's railway must run. The first train steamed into Bulawayo from the south in 1897. Two years later the new line from Beira reached Salisbury, and in 1902 Bulawayo and Salisbury were linked. Rhodes hoped to build the line north-west from Salisbury, to cross the Zambesi near where the Otto Beit bridge now carries the road towards Lusaka, and then to run the line northwards towards Abercorn and lake Tanganyika. He had spoken of his plans, and some white men had already taken farms near Abercorn to wait for the railway line to reach them. But the Government in London refused to share the cost of the line, so that line was never built. Instead, a line was built from Bulawayo north-west to the new coalfield at Wankie (very useful for the steam railway engines); it reached Wankie in 1903 and crossed the Zambesi at the Victoria Falls in 1904. By 1910 the line had been built through Broken Hill and the copper-belt to the Congo border.[1]

All this did nothing to help Nyasaland. As early as 1902, trains could run from Salisbury to Cape Town, but there was no railway line from Rhodesia into Nyasaland. In Rhodes's day, the way into Nyasaland was by two steamers up the Shire river, changing steamers at the rapids. In 1915 a railway line was built from Blantyre down the lower Shire valley to Chindio on the Zambesi, so there was an end of the trouble with the rapids. But this railway merely linked Blantyre with the Zambesi steamers, so that people and goods still had to come by river from the small ports of Chinde[2] or Quelimane in the Zambesi delta. The journey from the sea into Nyasaland was a little easier and quicker, but it was still very slow.

The next improvement was to replace the slow Zambesi steamer by another railway. The Portuguese had built their big new seaport at Beira, and in 1899 a line had been built from Beira to Salisbury. Beira was clearly the port which was going to grow; the day of Chinde and Quelimane was over. In 1922, a new line was built from Beira to the bank of the Zambesi at a point opposite Chindio, but the wide river still had to be crossed by a ferry. It was not until 1935 that the British Government helped to pay for bridging the Zambesi; then the railway was extended northward from Blantyre to Chipoka on the lake shore, and began to pay its way.

Organizing the Government

British central Africa was thus divided into three territories: two of them ruled by the British South Africa Company and the third ruled by the Crown as a protectorate. Everyone could see the disadvantage of having a commercial company to govern. The Africans and the European settlers could see it, because the Company was trying to make a profit out of its

---

[1] The railway from Salisbury to Lourenço Marques was not built until 1955.

[2] Note the difference between Chinde, the port in the delta, and Chindio, the terminus of the new railway on the north bank of the river.

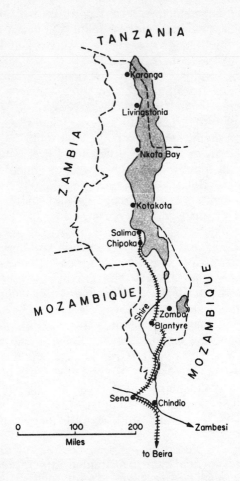

MAP 5. NYASALAND OR MALAWI

This map shows the places mentioned in chapter Six and in chapter Ten, and shows the modern railway line and the frontiers which were settled in the 1890s. Notice that the railway line does not cross the Zambesi at Chindio, but higher up the river at Sena.

The Shire highlands, over which there was so much trouble between Johnston and the Portuguese, are south of Blantyre. The Shire river makes a bend to the west (and that is where the rapids are) and the railway avoids the highlands by making a bend to the east.

government. The British Government could see it, because whatever the Company did, people were likely to blame the British Government. The Government had handed over much of its authority to the Company in the two Rhodesias, but it felt that it must have some powers to supervise what the Company did in its name.

To settle how the territories should be governed, the Government issued a series of Orders in Council. An Order in Council is an order which the Government issues under power which is given to it by an Act of Parliament. The most important Orders of Council concerning these territories are four which were issued between 1898 and 1902: one for Southern Rhodesia, one for the North-East, one for the North-West, and one for the Central African Protectorate. The general effect of the Orders was (i) to say that the country was under the protection of the British Government; (ii) to divide the country into administrative districts; (iii) to provide for the administration of justice; and (iv) to say that the Government had the right to control the way in which land was sold or leased for farming or mining. As far as the North-West was concerned, the Government consulted Lewanika, and he agreed. In 1911, North-East and North-West were joined into one territory of Northern Rhodesia. Matabeleland and Mashonaland had already been joined into the one territory of Southern Rhodesia by an Order in Council in 1898.

Did the Orders in Council say anything about setting up a legislative council in the territories?

In Southern Rhodesia, the Order of 1898 gave the Company's Administrator a legislative council of nine members, five to be appointed by the Company and four to be elected. The vote was given to anyone who was literate enough to fill in an application form, and who lived in a house worth £75 or had an income of £50 a year. There was nothing said about restricting the vote to Europeans; but no Africans at that time lived in such a house or had such an income, so there were no African voters. The Government appointed its own Resident Commissioner, whose duty was to represent the Queen and tell the Government in London if any laws were passed in Southern Rhodesia which seemed to him unfair to the Africans.

Any such law was not to come into force until the Government
in London had approved it. The Commissioner used his
powers more than once, and the Government in London did
sometimes refuse to approve the proposed laws.

The legislative council of Southern Rhodesia was modified
three times before the 1914 war. By then, it consisted of 18
members, twelve of whom were elected. There were still no
African members.

No legislative council was set up in Northern Rhodesia
for many years afterwards. The country was governed by the
Company's Administrator; he was appointed by the Company
with the approval of the Government in London. He, like
the Administrator in Southern Rhodesia, had to submit for
the approval of the Government in London any law which
the Resident Commissioner thought was unfair to the Africans. For many years there were very few Europeans in Northern Rhodesia, so the Government did not think it right to
appoint a legislative council; and nobody at that time thought
of appointing African members. In 1918 the Administrator
was given an Advisory Council of five elected European members. This was not a legislative council. It could not make
laws. All it could do was to give the Administrator advice,
and he was free to ignore its advice if he wished.

In Nyasaland, the Order in Council of 1907 changed
the title of the Commissioner to Governor, and gave him an
executive council and a legislative council. The legislative
council was small: it must contain at least two European
members nominated by the Governor. Nothing was said, of
course, about African members.

**But could not the Government have made a beginning and
appointed one or two African members, even if at first they
could not take much share in the discussion?**

It is true that British colonial Governments in Africa have
been slow to appoint African members to the legislative
councils; and Africans today blame them because they relied
too much on the chiefs and not enough on educated African
men in the towns. But in those far-off days there were no
Africans in Rhodesia who had been taught English. Schools
were only just beginning. In Nyasaland, the missionaries had

been running schools for twenty years; but they had been working mainly in the local African language, and they were only just beginning to go beyond primary education. In central Africa, there was no convenient African language like Swahili, which all Europeans and Africans would understand. The council meetings must be held in English; and in those early days the Government could not have found suitable African members who understood English.

The labour question

Later on, there was to be trouble between Europeans and Africans over land, but in 1900 there was room for both races. But from the very beginning there was trouble over labour. The large European farms could not be worked without African labour, and as time went on the mines too needed more and more men. But apart from this, the white men were accustomed in their own country to the idea that a man must work to earn money and maintain his wife and family. They had been taught as children that it was wrong to be idle. Britain was a country in which very few people had land of their own; they expected to buy food in the shops, not to grow it for themselves. But these ideas were quite strange to the Africans. Every African family had land, and the women farmed it to grow food for the family, while the young boys looked after the goats and cattle, and the men sat in council and did the fighting. Now that the British had stopped the slave raiding and the wars, the men had no more fighting to do, but they were still not willing to go out to work for money. The white men could not understand this attitude, which was so very different from their own.

But they were wrong if they thought that the men did no work in time of peace. They hunted, and they did the heavy work, such as building houses and clearing the bush for a new farm.

True: but the men's heavy work did not go on all the time, like the women's work on the farm and in the home. The men did seem to have a good deal of time for sitting around. As for hunting, in England nearly all hunting is done for sport, so the white men would not think of hunting as work. Here again, the ideas and customs of the two races were different, and so they misunderstood each other.

So the white men began to ask themselves how they could make the African men take up paid work on the farms and in the mines. One method was to make them pay a tax; this would not only make them work so as to earn money for their tax, but would bring in revenue, out of which the Government could begin to develop the country.

The Nyasaland chiefs had agreed with Johnston that their people should pay a tax of three shillings a house, to be increased later on to six shillings when the Government thought fit. The people were allowed to pay their tax either in money or in goods. After a few years, the rate of tax was increased to six shillings in the richer parts of the country.

In Southern Rhodesia, the Company first imposed a tax at the rate of ten shillings a house, and in 1901 the tax was increased to a pound, not per house, but per man. Instead of paying his tax in money, a man might if he chose work for four months. North-Eastern Rhodesia was poorer, and there the tax was only three shillings. The Company tried after a time to increase the tax in Southern Rhodesia from one pound to two pounds, but the Government in London said this would be too much, and did not allow it to do so.

Gradually, the tax had its effect in bringing the men out to work. The Government expected that the people would do all they could to avoid paying, and was surprised to find how willing the people were. They were willing to pay the tax, for they could see that British rule had brought them peace from the wars and slave raiding. On the whole, the men would rather go to work in the mines of the Rand[1] than work on the white man's farm nearer home. The big mining companies had more money to spend in housing their African workers. People could go there in hundreds, and be sure of finding friends and relatives from their own villages in the big mining compounds. And the young men came to think that work in the mines was work for a man, whereas working on the white man's farm was too much like the work which the women had always done.

So after a few years, thousands of men from all three terri-

---

[1] We must remember that in the time we are talking of, the Rhodesian copper mines were not yet working.

tories – especially from Nyasaland – went south every year: so many, in fact, that it caused great difficulty at home. The women stayed at home to look after the farm and the children. Sometimes the villages were empty of young men, and village life suffered.

African village life suffered also in other ways. People were beginning to use money, instead of making payments in the old way, in fowls and beer, cloth and goats and cattle. They were beginning to think of the things that money could buy, and so were beginning to think more of getting things for themselves. The schools too were introducing new ideas: boys who were learning to read and write did not want to go back to the village and herd cattle. In our own day we have seen these changes go very far; in the first twenty years of the 1900s they were only just beginning, and very few people could understand what was happening.

In 1914 the first world war broke over Africa. It was a great shock to the Africans. Only a few years earlier, the white men had come into their country and made them stop fighting and raiding; and now the white men were enlisting them as soldiers and sending them off to fight in a war which had nothing to do with them. If it was wrong for Africans to make war, how could it be right for Europeans to do so? There was very little fighting in Central Africa itself, but large numbers of men from Central Africa (Africans and Europeans) took part in the fighting in Tanganyika.

All these great and rapid changes made many Africans feel that life was becoming difficult to understand. In 1915 there was trouble in Nyasaland.

John Chilembwe

A man named John Chilembwe, a Yao from the Shire valley, had been educated not only in Nyasaland but in the United States. When he returned to Nyasaland in 1900, he did not settle down to help the mission which had sent him to America. Instead of that, he founded a church of his own, and by 1914 he and his followers had set up several congregations and had built several church buildings. Chilembwe was a strong man and a natural leader. When he was in America he had seen how badly the Negroes there were sometimes treated.

He did not mean to come back home merely to be an assistant to the white missionaries. There were many things in Nyasaland that troubled him. The schools were not good enough, and there were not enough of them. There were many different missionary societies working in central Africa, and they did not always agree. What were Africans to believe? The white missionaries taught that all Christians were equal in God's sight; but not all white men treated them as equals. In addition to these things, there were other troubles: drought, hunger, high prices, and – as always – trouble over land.

There were not many European farms in Nyasaland, but the same difficulties arose there as in Kenya and Southern Rhodesia and South Africa. The white farmer had Africans living on his land. He called them 'squatters', a word which means people who come and live on someone's land without permission. But many of these so-called 'squatters' had lived there before ever the white man came into the country. They were not squatters on his land, he was a squatter on theirs. However, an African chief had granted the white man the right to live there, and Johnston had given him a Certificate of Claim; so the white man had the law on his side. He was content to allow the Africans to live on his land: but, he said, they must work for him one month in every year. He would not take a money rent; he needed their work. Since the seasons are the same for every farmer, black or white, and since the Africans also had to work to earn money for their tax, they had to work for the white man and neglect their own farms just in the busiest time of the year. This system caused a great deal of discontent, and Chilembwe protested against it. There was one European settler who was specially hard on his African squatters; and when Chilembwe gave him trouble, he took the very strong step of burning some of Chilembwe's churches.

So it came to fighting. Chilembwe and his people rose in rebellion in January 1915, while many police and all the troops were away on the Tanganyika border to guard the country against German attacks. Chilembwe and his people killed three European men, but they were careful to treat European women and children well. Chilembwe hoped to set up an independent African state. But the Government brought troops and police back from the border and defeated Chilembwe and his people. Chilembwe himself was shot dead in the fighting, and some others were punished by death or imprisonment.

It seems as if Chilembwe, like Harry Thuku in Kenya, was unlucky. He had a good deal of right on his side, and the Government surely did not handle the affair well?

Yes: both Chilembwe and Harry Thuku had good reason to complain. Both of them were troubled because there was not enough education: because people were being made to go and work on European farms: because taxes were rising: and generally, because the African peoples, who had been independent only a few years earlier, were now being made servants in their own country. The Kenya and the Nyasaland Governments were unwise in the way they handled these affairs; though it is true the Nyasaland Government's attention was much taken up with the war against Germany. The two Governments did not take enough trouble to develop African powers of leadership.

The Chilembwe rising passed away without making much impression on the Nyasaland Government. Some Europeans said, 'This is what happens if Africans are educated.' Some of the missionaries were wiser; they said, 'This is what happens if we do not listen to African complaints, and if Africans who are capable of leading their people are not given the chance to lead.'

THE END OF COMPANY RULE

When the 1914 war was ended, people all over the world hoped that they could go back to business again and be happy and prosperous once more. But they were wrong. For more than four years, all the trading nations of the world had been spending their wealth, not on making more wealth but on destroying it: on guns, shells, bombs. Millions of the best young men had been killed; railways and factories and houses had been destroyed. Trade had been upset. The world was far poorer than it had been before the war; people were angry and frightened and did not trust one another. So trade did not revive as people hoped it would, and the whole world went through some years of poverty. People wanted goods, but they could not afford to pay the price; so the world price of all raw materials fell. All countries which lived by exporting raw materials suffered from this fall in prices Australia suffered because the price of wool fell to less than half; Canada because the price of wheat fell to less than a third; Kenya and the Gold Coast suffered in the same way because the prices of cotton and coffee and cocoa fell to a half or a third of what they had been before the war. Central Africa too was hit in just the same way. Its farmers found that no one would buy their maize or tobacco at pre-war prices, so they had to reduce their price, and found themselves poorer. The British South Africa Company had less chance than ever of making a profit, and it had no money to spend on developing the country. The European settlers wanted to see the Company go. They did not like being governed by a committee of business men in London, and they were already beginning to think of asking for self-government.

The Company's charter had been granted in 1890 for a period of 25 years, and this period ran out in 1915. The British Government was too busy with the war at that moment to give proper attention to African affairs. It was content to extend the charter for the time being; but it did so with one important alteration. This provided that if the legislative council of Southern Rhodesia asked for responsible government, and was able to satisfy the British Government in London that the country was ready for it, the Government would grant the request. This of course would end the Company as a governing body, as far as Southern Rhodesia was concerned: in that country, the Company would continue merely as a commercial company. Nothing was said about Northern Rhodesia; and there was no need to say anything about Nyasaland, for Nyasaland was not governed by the Company.

The British South Africa Company would not be sorry to give up the burden of governing the two Rhodesias. In the 25 years of its life, it had not so far paid a penny of dividend to its shareholders. Instead of making a large profit every year, as it had hoped, it had lost money. In 1915 the Company thought of saving money by joining the two Rhodesias into one country, paying one Administrator and one chief justice instead of two, and so on. But the Europeans in Southern Rhodesia would not agree to this. They thought of Southern Rhodesia as a 'white man's country', but they did not think of the North in the same way. The South had 33,000 Europeans and 770,000 Africans; the North had over a million Africans, but only about 3,000 Europeans. Thus, the white men in the South thought that they would have a much better chance of self-government if they remained separate from the North.

There was another matter which made the Company ready to give up its burden of government. Much of the land in Southern Rhodesia was still unoccupied. It was not African reserve, but no white farmer had yet applied for it. To whom did this land belong?

This was a difficult question. The Company said that Lobengula had granted the land to Lippert, and the Company had bought the grant from Lippert; so the land now belonged to the Company. The white settlers said that this land belonged to 'the people' – that is, to the white people, those who were hoping soon to be given self-government. In England, there were some friends of the Africans who said that this land belonged to the Africans. They said that Lobengula had not granted all his land to Lippert. He had granted only the right to lease land; and any land which Lippert or the Company had not yet leased still belonged to the African people. Lastly, there were some who said that the land belonged to the Crown: the Company had been governing the country on the Crown's behalf, and if the Company ceased to govern, the Crown would step in.

All this was a legal question, and the lawyers in England argued it for three years, from 1914 to 1917. Then they gave judgment: the land, they held, belonged to the Crown. This judgment had two results. One was, that it made the Company still more anxious to get rid of its burden of governing the country. The other was, that the settlers were greatly encouraged to press for responsible government. If they joined South Africa, that land would be taken over by the South African Government; if they got responsible government and remained a separate country, they would control it themselves.

The British Government had now offered responsible government to the settlers in the South. What were they to do?

Responsible government as a separate state was not the only possibility. Cecil Rhodes had always supposed that sooner or later, the whole of Rhodesia (South and North) would join South Africa. General Smuts, who was prime minister of South Africa, would have been very glad to welcome it. He believed that the English-speaking people and the Afrikaners in South Africa should join into one nation and forget their differences and their old quarrels. Many of his fellow-Afrikaners did not agree with him in this, and Smuts would have been very glad of the Rhodesian votes. He offered to give Southern Rhodesia ten seats in the South African parliament, which was more than such a small number of voters had the right to expect. He offered also to buy the land which had not so far been leased to white settlers, and to pay the Company nearly £7 million, which was much more than the Company had any hope of getting from the British Government. Smuts was prepared to pay a high price for Southern Rhodesia: not only for its votes, but also for the chance it would give South Africa of extending her influence up to the borders of Tanganyika and Katanga.

Separate and responsible government was one possibility, to join South Africa was a second. There was a third possibility: that Southern Rhodesia should become a British Crown Colony. But the settlers would not have this: they did not want the Colonial Office in London to interfere in their affairs.

But would that not have been better for the Africans?

Yes, it would. That is one reason why the settlers would not have it. Like Lord Delamere in Kenya, they wanted self-government for themselves, and they feared that if they were under the Colonial Office, they would not be allowed to do as they liked in the matters of land and labour. The British Government might of course have made Southern Rhodesia a colony against the wish of the settlers; but it thought it would be unwise to do this. Instead, it offered them responsible government.

Thus, only two choices were really practical politics: separate and responsible government, or joining South Africa. In 1917 a political party was formed in Southern Rhodesia to work for responsible government. It was led by Charles Coghlan (later Sir Charles), and in 1920 it won the elections to the legislative council. The new council naturally passed a resolution asking the British Government to grant it responsible government. In 1922 a referendum was held. in which all voters in Southern Rhodesia were asked whether they preferred to join South Africa or to have separate responsible government. Six thousand voted for joining South Africa, and nearly 9,000 for separate responsible government.

Why was there such a strong majority for responsible government?

The decision about the land had a good deal to do with it. The settlers would rather have the land controlled by their own Government in Salisbury than by the Government in Pretoria or Cape Town. But another reason was that they felt themselves British, and they wanted to stay British, not become South Africans. Smuts was still in power in South Africa, but the Nationalist party, the party of the Afrikaners, was getting stronge and stronger. In the very next year, 1924, the Nationalist Party under its leader General Hertzog defeated Smuts in the elections and formed a Government.

The question was thus settled. The Company gave up control over Northern and Southern Rhodesia. The Government in London paid it compensation for the money it had lost, but not much more than half of what Smuts would have paid it. Southern Rhodesia was given a constitution. There was to be one house of parliament of thirty members; the prime minister would govern with a cabinet of six Ministers. Elections were to be held at least every five years. The Company was to keep its rights over minerals, and the Crown could not interfere with these. The Crown was to be represented by a Governor, who would have to follow the advice of his Ministers. Everyone could vote who had an income of £200 a year; this figure was so high that very few Africans had the vote.

There was one limitation on this self-government. Any law which did not treat Africans just as it treated Europeans must be sent to London for the approval of the British Government before it took effect. This duty, which had previously been carried out by the Resident Commissioner, was now laid upon the Governor.

Southern Rhodesia became a self-governing state under this constitution on 1st October 1923, with Sir Charles Coghlan as its first prime minister. In the first elections held under the new constitution, Coghlan's party won 26 out of the thirty seats in parliament.

Northern Rhodesia

There was no talk of responsible government for Northern Rhodesia. The British Government thought that responsible government was possible in the South, where there was one European to every 23 Africans, but not in the North, where there were 300 Africans to every European. In April 1924 Northern Rhodesia became a Crown colony. The Government took over control of all the land (except that Barotseland, as usual, was kept separate); the Company kept its land in the north-east, and all its mineral rights. There was to be a legislative council of 14 members, nine nominated by the Governor and five elected. There were no African members. But under the Crown colony system, Africans might hope that as education developed, African members would come to sit in the legislative council, as they were already doing in West Africa; the British Government would not allow the settlers to block their way.

Nyasaland

Nyasaland, the smallest and poorest of the three territories, continued as a protectorate. It had a legislative council, with some official and some European unofficial members. All members were nominated by the Governor; there were no elected members, and no African members. Nyasaland had very few European settlers compared with the two Rhodesias. One reason for this was that, before the railway was extended, the country was so difficult to reach. Another reason was that only a small part of the country was suitable for them, and in that part it was difficult to get African labourers. The Government wanted to attract more European settlers, for it knew that they would develop the country and bring in revenue.

But at the same time, it was determined to follow Johnston's advice, and was careful not to let land on long leases at low rents.[1] In 1912 it passed a Crown Lands Ordinance, which said that leases were usually to be for 21 years only. This was too short a term to attract many settlers. In 1917 the Government went further and passed an Ordinance to stop white farmers from refusing to accept a money rent from their African 'squatters' and making them work instead. The Government had at any rate learned that lesson from Chilembwe's rising. So, compared with the Rhodesias (especially Southern Rhodesia) Nyasaland was not a country to attract many white settlers. In 1924 there were still fewer than 1,500 white men in the country – settlers, business men, officials and missionaries together.

AFRICA IN THE 1920s

Our story has now reached 1924. The early 1920s were an important period in the history of British Africa. New ideas were being discussed in the Colonial Office in London. In 1922, Lord Lugard published his book *The Dual Mandate in British Tropical Africa*, which set forth his idea of the way in which Britain should govern her African colonies. He said that the mineral and agricultural produce of Africa should be developed both for the sake of the world that needed it and for the sake of Africa herself. The Governments in Africa should work as far as they could through the African chiefs and elders, but at the same time should educate those chiefs and elders, and develop their councils, so that they might become able to lead their people into modern ways. In 1922 and 1924, the Phelps Stokes Fund of America sent its two commissions all round Africa to study African education.[2] Their reports were published; and when the British Government read what they had to say,

---

[1] See above, page 83.

[2] One of the commissions visited central Africa and South Africa. The great African teacher Dr Aggrey was a member of the commission. He gave a public lecture, which was heard by Dr Banda, then a very young man. It was this lecture by Dr Aggrey which gave young Banda the idea of going to America for education, as Aggrey himself (and Chilembwe) had done.

9. Lugard

it determined that it must do much more in education, and
not leave everything to the missions. By 1924, the Colonial
Office had set up an advisory committee on African education;
and in the Gold Coast (Aggrey's native land) and Uganda,
Achimota and Makerere colleges had been begun. The British
were becoming used to the idea that they should rule their

colonies so as to prepare them for self-government, and should grant self-government as soon as they were ready for it.

These new ideas would not have much influence in Southern Rhodesia, with its new responsible government and parliament of thirty white men. But they were sure to have much influence in Northern Rhodesia and Nyasaland, whose Governors were responsible to the Colonial Office.

8

CENTRAL AFRICA, 1924–1945

Central Africa in 1924 thus consisted of three territories: one colony which was very nearly self-governing, one colony which was poor and was very far from self-government, and one protectorate which was if possible even poorer. It was an accident that the region was divided into three territories; it might have been governed as one, or divided into more than three. As we have seen, the settlers in Southern Rhodesia had refused to allow the Company to join the two Rhodesias together. They intended to develop Southern Rhodesia as a white man's country, and did not want to spend money on the worthless North. In the other two territories, the British Government intended to follow its usual policy and prepare the Africans for self-government.

In 1925 something happened which made a great change in the position. A new deposit of copper ore was found in Northern Rhodesia, of the same type as the rich ores of Katanga. A Rhodesian copper-belt was opened; mining companies poured men and money into the country. Northern Rhodesia, which the settlers in the South had scorned as not worth having, suddenly became a most desirable country. The whole attitude of the settlers changed.

The European population of Northern Rhodesia rose from about 3,000 in 1920 to 13,000 in 1939, and 49,000 in 1953. Three thousand white men in 1920 could not reasonably expect to be given responsible government. But 33,000 white men in the South had been given it in 1923, so 49,000 in the North might reasonably hope for it in the 1950s.

The African population of the copper-belt also increased enormously, as men came flocking to it from all parts of central Africa. New mines were opened, new towns built. The Africans at first came to work for a few months, meaning then to go home to their villages to rest and to spend the money they had earned. But as time went on, more and more of them decided to stay and make their homes in the mining towns. Tribal life in the villages became weaker and weaker, as first the strong young men, and then more and more of the women too, left their village homes and made new homes for themselves in the copper-belt.

INDIRECT RULE

Since Northern Rhodesia was a colony, controlled by the Colonial Office in London, its Governor, Sir James Maxwell, introduced the new idea of indirect rule, which the British Government then thought was the best way of governing its African colonies. The Government got this idea from Lugard, whose book we have mentioned on page 99. When Lugard went to Northern Nigeria, he found strong Fulani emirs ruling the country; and he decided that it would be best to leave them to continue ruling their people, but to watch them and see that they ruled wisely. More than this: Lugard said that since people everywhere were accustomed to obey their own chiefs and elders, it would be better for a colonial Government to work through the chiefs and elders whom the people knew and obeyed. If changes had to be made, it would be easier for the Government to make them by explaining them to the chiefs, and leaving the chiefs to explain them to their people. Thus, the British district commissioner should not give orders to the people; he should try and persuade the chief to give orders to his people. Gradually, Lugard thought, chiefs and their elders could be educated in modern ways, and would become modern local government authorities. That was indirect rule as Lugard thought of it. This idea of ruling through chiefs and elders was taken up in many British colonies; though not all British governors and district commissioners were as interested in the idea of educating the chiefs and elders as Lugard had been.

But if the tribal system in Northern Rhodesia was becoming weaker and weaker, because so many people were leaving the villages and going to live in the copper-belt, was indirect rule likely to work well in Northern Rhodesia?

Not as well as it did in countries like Uganda and Northern Nigeria. Indirect rule was difficult everywhere. If it was to help Africans to govern their country in modern ways, the African chiefs must be able to rule their people; and they must also be able to learn new ideas of government – about roads, schools, hospitals, agriculture, water supplies, taxation, and so on. Indirect rule would not work well if a chief could not rule his people, or if a chief took no interest in such modern ideas. In other parts of Africa where the British introduced indirect rule, there were some chiefs who could not rule, and others who could not learn, so that indirect rule did not work in every district.[1]

But in Northern Rhodesia there were special difficulties. First, the chiefs were losing their powers as the tribal life became weaker. Many a young man who came back to his village from Ndola or Mufulira said to himself, 'I have seen the world. I have worked deep underground. I have used modern machinery. I know about electric light and water that comes from a tap. And here are these old men still sitting under the tree and drinking beer and talking, just as they did before I went away. How can they understand things? And if they do not understand, why should I respect and obey them?'

Second: how were Ndola and Mufulira and the other big towns to be governed? There were no chiefs there. True, there had been chiefs. But they were chiefs of the small tribes whose land had been taken to build the big mining towns. There was no chief whom the thousands of Bemba, Cewa, Lovale, Nguni, Nyanja and others who now lived there could be expected to obey.

For these reasons, indirect rule did not work very well in Northern Rhodesia. It was introduced in 1929 by two ordinances, the Native Authorities Ordinance and the Native Courts Ordinance. These ordinances provided that when an

[1] We have been speaking only about chiefs. This is merely to keep the description short and simple. When we speak of chiefs, we mean to include also the elders and councillors who share with the chief the work of governing. Some African peoples have never had powerful chiefs like Lewanika or Mpezeni; they have governed themselves in small clans with councils of clan elders.

African chief had been elected by his people in the customary way, the Government would call him a Native Authority, and, would give him power to make rules and orders for his people, and the power to sit in court to try offenders. In 1936, the system of indirect rule was improved. One new ordinance provided that a Native Authority, instead of consisting only of the chief, might consist of the chief and his councillors. Another new ordinance provided that a Native Authority might run its own treasury, collecting taxes from its people and spending the money on the ordinary work of local government.

This was all very well for the country districts; though, as we have said, if people did not respect their chief, they would not respect him any the more because the Government had given him a title and a uniform and a new set of duties. But it was no help at all in the big mining towns. The land there was owned by the mining companies; the people belonged to many different tribes and came from all over central Africa. How could there be a chief without land, and without the right to speak to the ancestral spirits of his people?

Could each tribal group in the town have its own elder or headman?

The Government thought of that, and so did some of the mining companies. As early as 1931 the idea was tried at Mufulira, but the mine-workers did not give the elders much respect. Later on, the district commissioners in the mining towns appointed councils of Africans to advise them on tribal matters; later on still, they allowed the Africans themselves to elect these council members. But the councils had no power to do anything; they existed only to give advice to the district commissioner, who sat on the town council to speak for the Africans. But this was not really indirect rule at all; it was direct rule by the district commissioner.

Indirect rule in Nyasaland

Indirect rule was tried in Nyasaland also; and since Nyasaland had no copper-belt, and few European settlers, it worked much better there. Nyasaland had a system of district councils for some years before indirect rule was begun in Northern Rhodesia. In 1933 the councils were improved by the Native Authorities Ordinance and the Native Courts Ordinance, which were very similar to the two Ordinances with the same names passed in Northern Rhodesia four years earlier. But the Native Authority Ordinance of Nyasaland gave the Native Authority power to raise taxes and spend the money; .this power, as we have seen, had to be given in Northern Rhodesia by a separate ordinance in 1936.

Southern Rhodesia

Indirect rule of this kind was never introduced in Southern Rhodesia. It could not be; for indirect rule was intended as a means of preparing Africans for self-government, and the Europeans in Southern Rhodesia did not intend that their country should ever be governed by Africans.

But is it true that indirect rule was intended to prepare Africans for self-government? I have heard it said that the British intended it for quite the opposite reason: they supported the chiefs because they were usually uneducated, and so were likely to give the Government less trouble than the educated Africans in the towns.

It may sometimes have seemed so. Indirect rule did not work out as the British had hoped. Both in Africa and in London, the Governments hoped that the chiefs and their councillors – the 'Native Authorities' – would learn new ideas: they would come together in tribal or district councils and then in councils of provinces or regions: and lastly, they would form a majority in the legislative council and so take over the government of the colony. Of course, the Native Authorities who did this would be very different from the group of 'old men sitting under the tree and drinking beer and talking' of the old days. The British hoped that educated men would join the councils, and bring their knowledge and experience to help the chiefs. If this had happened, the members sitting in the legislative council would have included chiefs and elders and educated men, all representing the Native Authorities. In that case, there would have been no split between chiefs and educated men; and indirect rule would have led smoothly and easily to self-government. That was what the British hoped. It would take us too long to discuss the reasons why it did not happen. It is much easier to think of a plan than to provide, year after year, the men, the money, and the wisdom to carry it out.

So there was no indirect rule in Southern Rhodesia. But even there, the Government encouraged the chiefs to work towards a system of local government, and the first steps which it took were much like those in the other two territories. There was a Native Councils Act in 1937, which allowed Africans in a district to set up a district council; and in the same year there was a Native Courts Act, which gave a chief and two of his councillors the power of judging cases according to African customary law. But these courts had no power (as they had in the other territories) to try offenders: only to judge in civil cases. In 1943 the Native Councils were given power to raise taxes and spend the money, and for every pound they raised from their people, the Government gave them a pound from its own revenue. In Southern Rhodesia, there was no idea that Native Authorities might so develop that in time they would form a majority in parliament. The idea there was that Europeans and Africans should develop separately. A few European leaders thought it possible that one day, in the distant future, there might be some African members of parliament; but they must always be in a minority. Real power must always be in white hands.

All these developments took place in the country, especially in the African reserves. There was nothing in the big towns of Southern Rhodesia like the African advisory councils in the mining towns of the North.

LAND AND LABOUR

Although two of the countries were under the rule of the Colonial Office and the third was nearly independent, they were all multi-racial countries; each had a minority of Europeans living among a great majority of Africans. In each country there was some land set aside for Europeans, and some for Africans. But the principles on which the division was made were very different.

Northern Rhodesia

In Northern Rhodesia, the British Government's agreement

with the British South Africa Company provided that when
the country became a colony, the British Government should
take control of all the land, and administer it 'as it thinks best
in the interest of the native population and in the public
interest generally.' We notice that the Government thought
first of African interests. But it took the Government some
time to work out its land policy. The Company had already
sold or leased nearly seven per cent of the land to Europeans,
though a great deal of this land was not being used: some
was being used for cattle, and a little was growing maize or
tobacco. The Government could not upset these agreements
which the Company had already made. But it set out to see
what could be done to administer the rest of the land 'in the
interest of the native population and in the public interest
generally.'

The first thing it did was to set aside land for African reserves:
rather more than one-third of the country, 100,000 square
miles out of 288,000. All the rest of the country was called
Crown land, and the Governor would have control over it.
Crown land was meant to be used for agriculture of the European type. Africans were free to buy it if they wished; there
was no rule against it, as there was in the 'white highlands'
of Kenya. But of course hardly any Africans could afford to
buy Crown land, or had the skill to farm it in the European
way. No African villages were allowed on Crown land; Africans who wanted to live in the old village way must live in
the reserves. After 1929, about seven per cent of Northern
Rhodesia was European land, 34 per cent African reserve,
and 59 per cent Crown land.

During the next twenty years, the copper mines prospered;
there was money in the country; the miners needed food;
and so more land was needed to grow it. The African reserves
had seemed amply large enough in 1929, but they were not
large enough now. The Government could have taken some
of the Crown land and added it to the African reserves; but
this, it thought, would do little or nothing to feed the hungry
mouths in the copper-belt. African villages grew enough food
for their own people, but no more. Or, the Government could
have leased more Crown land to white farmers. But this, it
thought, would not be administering the land 'in the interest

of the native population and in the public interest generally.'
We shall see in the next chapter what the Government did in
1947, and what the Africans thought of it.

Nyasaland

While the two Rhodesias were developing their farms and
their mines, Nyasaland remained poor. It had no important
minerals, and less than a third of the country was suitable
for agriculture. The Government had to pay large sums of
money every year as interest on the money spent in building
the railway; and the railway did not begin to pay its way until
1935. In the fifteen years from 1924 to 1939, the European
population increased from 1,500 only to 2,000.

On the other hand, the country was much more thickly
populated than either of the Rhodesias. About 14 per cent of
the land had already been leased to Europeans, and the Nyasaland Government thought it should lease no more. There
was no empty land to set aside as Crown land. Nyasaland
was not, and never could be, a white man's country in the
way that the settlers in Southern Rhodesia meant their country
to be.

In 1936, the British Government put this into a law, called
the Nyasaland Protectorate (Native Trust Lands) Order in
Council. The Order said that no more land was to be sold
freehold. All land which had not already been sold or leased
was to be called Native Trust Land, and was to be used for
the benefit of the African people. The Governor might allow
it to be used for African villages, with their farm land and
grazing land. Or, under certain strict conditions, he might
lease it to a European.

**But if he leased land to a European, would that be for the benefit
of the African people? Was this a trick to cheat the Africans
out of their land?**

No, it was not a trick. The conditions were very strict. The
Governor must first consult the Native Authority, and ask
if it had any objection to seeing the European use this piece
of land. If it had no objection, the Governor would fix the
rent which the European had to pay, and that rent would be
paid to the Native Authority. But the Native Authority

might object: it might say that it needed the land for village farms; or it might not like the white man, or it might not like the use he proposed to make of the land. If it did object, that would end the matter. In fact, the Nyasaland people did not feel that they were in danger of losing their lands.

Thus, both in Northern Rhodesia and in Nyasaland, the Governments were trying to limit the amount of land held by Europeans, and to administer the rest of the land as well as they could for the benefit of the Africans. In Southern Rhodesia, the position was very different.

Southern Rhodesia

We have seen that in 1902 and again in 1915 land was set aside in Southern Rhodesia for African reserves, amounting after 1915 to about 17 per cent of the whole country. This area was big enough at that time to provide homes for all the African people; but none of the reserves was near the railway, so that most African farmers could not, like the Europeans, grow maize for export.[1] By 1930, the African population had increased to about a million, and the reserves were no longer big enough. In that year, there were about 50,000 Europeans in the country, and they had bought or leased over 31 million acres of land, nearly a third of the whole country. Anyone, African or European, was legally free to buy or lease land outside the reserves; but very few Africans could afford to do so, and only 45,000 acres outside the reserves were in African hands.

The Government became anxious. It saw Africans moving into the towns, and the white men were beginning to complain that Africans ought not to be allowed to live there: they ought to live in the reserves. On the other hand, the Government saw nearly a third of the country already in European hands, with more European settlers coming in. It would not be long before Africans who were told to go back to the reserves would reply, 'We cannot go back; there is no room for us there.' What was the Government to do? In 1926 it appointed a commission of inquiry, the Morris Carter commission, to study the problem and advise it.

The commission reported that something must be done to

[1] Though some of them did so; see below, page 113.

limit the land available for Europeans settlement: the white men must not be allowed to take all the land that was still free. On the other hand, it said, Africans were farmers and cattle-keepers, and they must continue to be so. They might come and work in the towns, but they should not be allowed to settle there permanently. Many Europeans agreed with this. One European leader said, 'The native is a visitor to our white towns for the purpose of assisting the people who live in towns; and no other native should be present.'

The Land Apportionment Act

In 1930, the Government made a new law, the Land Apportionment Act, to give effect to the recommendations of the Morris Carter commission. It divided the land of Southern Rhodesia afresh into four classes. One class was the European Area, which was limited to 49 million acres, just over half the country. The next was the African reserves, which the Act increased from 17 per cent of the country to 22 per cent. The third class was a Native Purchase Area amounting to eight per cent. In this area, land was to be available for sale to Africans in small farms, at cheap prices which the Government hoped Africans would be able to pay. The Government thought that there would in time be many Africans who had learnt something of modern methods of farming, but could not afford to buy a large farm; these men would be able to settle in the Native Purchase Area and practise their agricultural skill without being limited by village custom. These three classes of land together totalled 81 per cent of the whole country. The remaining 19 per cent was called unassigned land, and the Government might later on grant it either to Europeans or to Africans as it thought fit. But even if all this unassigned land were to be granted to Africans, they would still have less than half the country. The European area included all the towns, and nearly all the agricultural land which lay conveniently near the railway lines.

The Land Apportionment Act also laid down that Europeans were not to live in the reserves or in the Native Purchase Area unless they were working for the African people, for example as teachers or doctors. But – much more important – it laid down too that Africans were not to live in the European

area unless they were working for a European employer; if
they left their job and did not find another, they must go back
to the reserves. They need not go back at once; but by the
end of 1936 – six years hence – there must be no Africans left
in the European area unless they were working for a white
man. There were many African villages ih the land which
was now declared to be the European area, and over the next
ten years, the police came to one village after another and
made the people move: either to find work with a white
employer or to go back to the reserve.

Did the Africans protest against the Land Apportionment Act?

There was not much open African protest at the time,
mainly perhaps there were not enough Africans with sufficient
education to understand what was happening. Even in 1939,
when the Bledisloe Commission visited Central Africa[1] to
discuss whether the three countries ought to be joined, the
Bantu Congress, which complained to the Commission about
the Maize Control Act and other matters, said that it had
no complaint over the Land Apportionment Act. But we can
be sure that the villagers who were made to leave their villages
must have protested to the police, even if their protests never
came to the ears of the Government. The worst thing about
the Act was the hard way in which it separated Africans and
Europeans and prevented them from ever living together and
becoming one community. It was this idea of separateness,
rather like the South African *apartheid*, which made the
Africans feel that their Government did not care for them.

The protests against the Land Apportionment Act came
from the Europeans. The Europeans in the towns were pleased
that the Act stopped Africans from coming to live there. But
many white farmers objected to the Act because it made the
African reserves bigger and set a limit to the amount of land
that might be granted to Europeans. These people hoped that
the European population would quickly increase; and they
feared that the time would come wnen new settlers would
arrive and be told that there was no land for them. The Government was wiser than this. It knew that one day the Land

[1] For the Bledisloe Commission, see page 117; for the Bantu Congress, see page 125;
for the Maize Control Act, see page 113.

Apportionment Act would have to be revised, and that the time would come when African professional and business men would live in the towns. But no white politician in 1930 dared say this in public; it would have been the end of his political career. However, for various reasons, the Government put back from the end of 1936 to the end of 1940 the date by which Africans were to leave the European area. There was no proper census of the African population, there was drought, and there was cattle disease; the Government thought it would be cruel to keep to the date which the Act fixed.

The Maize Control Act

Another Act which the Government passed about the same time caused much more bad feeling among the Africans. Times were hard, and the price of maize (which was not only Rhodesia's main food crop but also one of the country's main exports) was falling and falling. The Government made a law called the Maize Control Act. It set up a maize marketing board to buy all the maize grown in the country at fixed prices. The most important thing, the Government thought, was to keep the incomes of the farmers, both African and European, from falling too sharply. Oversea countries were unwilling to buy as much Rhodesian maize as they had been buying; and the Board decided to buy as much maize as the Rhodesian people themselves would eat, and to sell the rest for export at whatever price it would fetch. So far, so good; but the Board decided to supply the home market mainly from maize grown on European farms, and let most of the African-grown maize go for export. This meant in effect that the Board bought at two prices: a high price from the European grower and a low price from the African. No doubt most of the European farmers grew better maize than the Africans; but not all of them did, and the Africans thought the Maize Control Act very unfair.

The Industrial Conciliation Act

In 1934, the Government passed another Act to protect the position of the white workers in the towns against African competition. The Industrial Conciliation Act of 1934 seemed at first to be an innocent law for regulating trade unions and

10. Harvesting Maize With Modern Machinery

settling industrial disputes. The trouble was that Africans
were excluded from the Act. They were not allowed to form
trade unions of their own, and of course the white trade unions
would not admit African members. This meant that the
Africans were unable to organise so as to obtain better pay
and working conditions. The white men took it for granted
that Africans were to remain unskilled labourers. By two other
Acts in 1936 and 1937, a strict pass system was set up for
African workers, much like that in South Africa. Africans
had to carry their passes with them at all times, and show
them to the police whenever they were asked. Of course, they
went in constant fear of losing these precious bits of paper,

and of finding themselves in trouble because they could not produce them.

POLITICS IN SOUTHERN RHODESIA

Sir Charles Coghlan became the first prime minister of Southern Rhodesia in 1923, and his party held 26 seats in parliament out of 30. Coghlan died in 1926, and was succeeded by one of his Ministers named Moffat, a member of the famous missionary family of that name. In 1930, Southern Rhodesia, like every other country, felt the effects of the depression in world trade – the years of poverty, as we have called this period on page 94. The prices of maize and tobacco fell, and we have seen that the Government passed the Maize Control Act to try and protect the maize farmers from the drop in the price. The prices of minerals also fell; and as in many other countries, the voters blamed their Government for not giving them better protection. A new man came to the front to lead the parliamentary opposition to the Moffat Government. This was Dr Godfrey Huggins; he had been one of Coghlan's party, but he bitterly criticised the way in which the Government handled the troubles. Huggins formed a new party, which he called the United Party; and in the elections of 1934 he and his United Party won 24 seats, only two fewer than Coghlan had held in 1923.

Huggins was perhaps lucky; he spent the worst of the bad years (from 1931 to 1934) in party warfare, and had little chance of showing what he could do to save the country. By the time he came to power in 1934, the worst of the trouble was over, without his help. The outside world was beginning once more to buy Rhodesian products. South African money helped to improve Rhodesian roads and to bridge Rhodesian rivers. Huggins wanted to bring in thousands more white settlers, to link the two Rhodesias into one country, and to persuade the British Government to grant responsible government to this greater united Rhodesia.

The idea of uniting the two Rhodesias was not new. It had been suggested before the copper-belt was opened, but the settlers in the South had then said no to it. With the copper-belt open, the position was quite different. In 1928 the British

Government sent out the Hilton Young commission to consider whether any of the British territories in East and Central Africa should be joined together. Some people suggested that Northern Rhodesia, or at any rate the north-eastern part of it, should be joined to Tanganyika. But the white settlers in Northern Rhodesia would not hear of this; they preferred to join Southern Rhodesia. Southern Rhodesia would gladly have taken them; but only on condition that land and labour policy over the whole of the united Rhodesia should be controlled by the Government at Salisbury. The Hilton Young commission advised the British Government not to allow the Southern Rhodesian labour policy to be introduced into the North. The British Government accepted this advice; so for the time being, there was an end to that scheme.

In 1930, the British Government issued a statement called the Passfield Memorandum, named after Lord Passfield, who was then Secretary of State for the Colonies. The Memorandum said that Britain was responsible for helping forward African development; and so, even if the white settlers came to be a majority in the Northern Rhodesian legislative council, Britain would not give them self-government. The Passfield Memorandum was on the same lines as the Devonshire White Paper of 1923, seven years earlier. In 1923, the Europeans in Kenya were pressing to be given more self-government, and were complaining that there were too many Asians in Kenya. The Devonshire White Paper told the Kenya Government that it must govern Kenya mainly in the interests of Africans. The British Government thought that Kenya was first of all an African country, and African interests must come before Asian and European interests. Now, seven years later, the Passfield Memorandum said just the same about Northern Rhodesia. African interests in Northern Rhodesia must come before the interests of Europeans. Africans must be prepared for self-government; and until they were ready for it, Britain would not hand over its responsibility for them to anyone else.

The Passfield Memorandum was a great shock to the European settlers in Northern Rhodesia. They had very different ideas about African development from Lord Passfield's. Lord Passfield and his Government soon went out of office, and some of the Government that followed were not quite so strongly in favour of supporting African interests against European. But the white settlers in the North had taken fright. If this was the way the Colonial Office thought, they had better escape from Colonial Office control and join with the South.

All through the 1930s, the Europeans in both the Rhodesias were agreed in demanding that the two countries should be united: but always with the condition that the united Government should be given control over land and labour policy, and to this condition the British Government would never agree. Huggins asked the British Government to send out another commission to look into the problem, and in 1939 the Bledisloe Commission was sent to visit all three territories. The Bledisloe Comission agreed with one recommendation which had been made by the Hilton Young commission: this was that Northern Rhodesia and Nyasaland should be joined at once. It recommended that a joint council should be set up to keep the three Governments in touch with one another. But on the question of uniting the two Rhodesias, it did not say what Huggins hoped it would say. It said that if the two Rhodesias could be united, it would be a very good thing; but land and labour policy in the two countries differed so much that the two countries could not be united yet.

So once again, Godfrey Huggins was disappointed. That same autumn of 1939, the second War broke out, and the British Government had very little attention to give to politics in central Africa.

But the war made a great difference. Both the Rhodesias became richer because their copper and chromium and other products obtained such high prices. Thousands of Africans joined the army and fought in Ethiopia and Burma; they came home at the end of the war, determined (like the soldiers in Britain) that their country must not merely settle down to its old ways. Another thing was that in 1944 a committee was set up to organise the three countries for war. The Bledisloe Commission had recommended such a committee, but many people had said that it would never work. Now, because of the war, it had to be made to work, and it did work. The committee consisted of the three Governors, and of three members nominated by each Government. These men were all white; there was no talk yet of African members. It began to look as if union, which Huggins so much desired, might be coming closer.

POLITICS IN NORTHERN RHODESIA

Politics in the North was very different from politics in the South, for one plain reason: the South had self-government, the North had not. In the South, there were rival parties and rival leaders. In the North, the rivalry was between the official and the unofficial members of the legislative council. The Government made policy; the unofficial members criticised it. The new legislative council in 1924 had eight official and five elected unofficial members, all Europeans. The Governor presided. The unofficial members naturally wanted to get more power, so that they could run the country more in the way of Southern Rhodesia and one day unite the two countries. The official members were there to carry out the policy of the Passfield Memorandum and see that Africans were helped to develop their education and their general way of living.

As in Kenya, the white settlers demanded more seats on the legislative council. In 1938 one official member was removed and another unofficial member added, so that instead of having eight officials to five unofficial members, the council now had seven officials to six. This additional unofficial member was appointed by the Governor to represent African interests. The man chosen was Colonel Stewart Gore-Browne (later Sir Stewart Gore-Browne). Gore-Browne had a farm in the Bemba country and was a good friend to the Africans. He first joined the council as an elected member in 1935. At that time, most members of the council were badly frightened by riots on the copper-belt, in which six Africans were killed and over twenty wounded. Gore-Browne was not frightened. He said that the riots would never have happened if the Africans had not had grievances, and that they must be given some way of expressing their grievances peacefully and having them listened to. He saw that, sooner or later, the Government would have to admit that Africans did not all come to the copper-belt merely as 'visitors'; more and more, they were coming to stay. After being on the legislative council for three years as an elected member, Gore-Browne was appointed to the new place for a member to represent African interests. This left his elected seat vacant, and his place was filled by a young railwayman and trade unionist called Roy Welensky.

The legislative council in 1944 consisted of nine officials, eight elected European members, two nominated unofficial Europeans, and three Europeans nominated to represent African interests: a total of 13 unofficial members to nine officials. It was not until 1946 that the first African members were elected.

Gore-Browne and Welensky disagreed over policy. Welensky was a trade unionist, and his first thought was to look after the interests of his fellow trade unionists, who of course were all white.' He formed a new party, the Labour Party, which joined most of the other Europeans in saying that Northern Rhodesia ought to unite with the South; it would be the best way of keeping European interests safe. Gore-Browne took quite another view. He said that Africans in the North should be allowed to form trade unions; they should be given some way of making their views known to the authorities in the towns; and they should even be given seats on the legislative council. This of course would be impossible in the South; so Gore-Browne said that the North should not try and unite with the South. It should work instead for responsible government as a separate country, in which Africans and Europeans could live side by side on equal terms.

Gore-Browne had one great success: it was he who persuaded the Government to set up Native Courts to try cases among Africans living in the towns, and also the African Advisory Councils which we have mentioned on page 105. He did in fact persuade the Government to recognise that Africans were living permanently in the towns, and were not merely 'visitors', as the white settlers (in the North, as well as in the South) liked to think. But when he spoke about African trade unions and African members of the legislative council, he frightened his fellow-Europeans. They turned away from him, and looked to Welensky as their leader.

Nothing was done until after the war about African trade unions or African membership of the legislative council. In

1940, the European miners in the copper-belt went on strike for higher pay. They got it, and the African miners then rioted. Seventeen Africans were killed, and nearly seventy wounded. Of course, there was a commission of inquiry. It reported that African rates of pay were much too low, and that there was still no way in which African workers could discuss their affairs peaceably with the management. The commission in fact said just what Gore-Browne had said five years before. Nothing happened until after the war. But it was plain that as soon as the war was over, the Northern Rhodesian Government would have to answer the questions which Gore-Browne had asked: Were Africans to be allowed to form trade unions? and were Africans to be allowed to sit on the legislative council?

EDUCATION UNTIL 1939

In all British African colonies, schools were begun by the missionaries, and after a time the Governments began to help the mission schools with grants of money. In Nyasaland (the Central African Protectorate, as it was then called) there were 720 primary schools in 1904, with 36,000 boys and 19,000 girls attending them. They belonged to seven different missionary societies, and the missionaries reckoned that all parents who wanted schooling for their children were able to get it. In those early, days, Nyasaland was one of the most advanced countries in Africa in respect of the number of children attending school; but other countries which were richer caught it up and left it far behind. The Nyasaland Government paid its first grant to the schools in 1907; it came to £1,000. Southern Rhodesia passed its first education ordinance as early as 1899, and in 1901 it paid a grant of £134 to four schools.

In Central Africa and in other parts of Africa, education developed slowly because the Governments were poor. All African Governments have suffered because their revenue has depended on the price of their cotton, tobacco, copper, tin, cocoa, coffee and other raw materials. If the price of these things goes up in London or New York, the producers in Africa have money in their pockets, and the Governments take some of it in taxes; if the price goes down, everyone is poor and unhappy, and the Governments wonder if they will be able to balance their budgets.[1]

It is important to remember that from the financial point of view, schools and hospitals are very different from such public works as roads and bridges and power stations. Once the road or bridge or power station has been built, it does not cost much to keep it in order. But it is no use building a school or a hospital unless you are ready to go on year after year providing books and medicines and equipment, and paying teachers and doctors and nurses and other staff. The result has often been that if there is a good year and the Government finds it has £10,000 to spare, it says, 'Good.' This will be enough to build a bridge over that river; so let us build the bridge now while we can.' But if the director of education comes to ask for a new school, the Government is likely to tell him, 'We would like to let you have your new school; but it is going to mean the salaries of twelve extra teachers next year, and every year afterwards. We are told that the price of copper is almost certain to fall next year, and if so, we shall not be able to pay those extra teachers; so we dare not build the school.' This has always been the great financial difficulty in developing education in Africa.

This poverty of the Governments was the main reason why progress in education was slow until after the war of 1914. There was very little money, and there would have been hardly any schools at all if it had not been for the missionaries, who collected money from churches in Britain and other countries, and used it to provide schools and pay teachers. We have mentioned the Phelps Stokes commissions[2], which visited Africa in 1920 and 1924, and gave the British Government such new ideas about African education. One of these new ideas was that the Governments in Africa should not leave the missionaries to provide education according to their own ideas; the Governments should pay them grants and should supervise the work they did. We can see these new ideas beginning to work in the 1920s.

Northern Rhodesia had over 48,000 children in primary

[1] To balance the budget means to collect enough revenue to pay for all the expenditure which the Government has undertaken.
[2] See pages 99, 100

schools in the year 1924, but nearly all of them were in mission schools. The Government was not satisfied with the work being done; it said that some were good, but others were far from good, and it was time that the Government began to supervise the schools. There were two teacher training colleges, one run by the Paris mission and the other by the Methodists; but the Government said that more colleges were needed. Next year, 1925, the Northern Rhodesian Government set up a department of African education and paid its first grant, amounting to £2,000. Nyasaland too set up its department of education in 1925, though as we have seen, it began paying grants to schools many years earlier. In the year 1920, Nyasaland had 2,000 schools with 100,000 children; we notice that the schools were small, with only fifty children each on the average. Things were much the same in Southern Rhodesia; in 1924 it had 1,216 schools with over 77,000 children. But there was one big difference here: Southern Rhodesia at that time was far the richest country of the three, and paid a grant of £23,000 for African education. Its department of African education was opened in 1927.

During the later 1920s, the educational position in all three countries was very similar. There were many thousands of children in school, but the schools were small and nearly all the teachers were untrained. Most of the children left after one or two years of school; very few stayed as long as four years. There was no secondary education, and no hope of any secondary education until more money could be found. There were special difficulties over girls' education; most parents did not believe in sending their daughters to school, and so there were hardly any women teachers. The young education departments with their newly appointed directors must have wondered which of all these problems they ought to tackle first.

In all three countries, they came to much the same conclusion. Children who left school after only one or two years had no time to learn anything of value. The Governments must persuade parents to let their children stay for at least four years; in this time they would learn to read and write, and would be able to go on learning from books after they had left school. The teaching must be improved; more training must be provided for teachers. Somehow, girls must be brought into the schools. If mothers could be given some sort of adult education, they might send their daughters to school.

Northern Rhodesia and Nyasaland took from America the idea of the Jeanes school. This was a training college where men would bring their wives and children, and both husband and wife would receive training. When they went back to their villages, not only would the husband be a better teacher, but the wife would be able to help other women and would encourage them to send their children – even their daughters – to school. (In those days there were many parents who did not wish to send even their sons to school, and district commissioners had to try and persuade chiefs and elders that education was a useful thing.) Jeanes schools were established in Nyasaland in 1929 and in Northern Rhodesia in 1930.

During the 1930s, progress was slow because of the poverty which came about all over the world. There was a heavy fall in the price of copper; in 1932 and 1933, two-thirds of the Europeans and Africans working on the copper-belt left it and went to look for work elsewhere. The revenue of the Northern Rhodesian Government was badly hit, for a fall of £10 a ton in the price of copper meant a fall of half a million pounds in Government revenue. The Northern Rhodesian Government spent £18,000 on African education in 1933 and £29,000 in 1937. Nyasaland and Southern Rhodesia suffered similarly. Many thousands of children were already attending primary school; in each of the three countries, roughly two children out of every five were getting some kind of schooling. But the directors of education were far from satisfied. They wanted more teacher training, more girls in school and more women teachers; they wanted all children to stay at school for at least four years; and they were beginning to ask for secondary education. But they had to wait for progress of this kind until after the 1939 war.

But do you mean to say that however hard they tried, the colonial Governments could not possibly have found any more money than they did for this important matter of African education?

No, we cannot say that. There is no doubt that the independent African Governments are prepared to take more trouble and spend more money than the colonial Governments. For example, Malawi on the eve of independence was spending £ 900,000 on education; and two years after independence that figure was doubled. Again, in 1966 and 1967 the independent Government of Zambia was recruiting hundreds of teachers from Britain, both for primary and for secondary schools; and the Northern Rhodesian Government had not done this in colonial times. The colonial Governments might have placed heavier taxes than they did on copper, tobacco, asbestos and other industries, and if so, they could have spent more than they did. But before the 1939 war, the prices of all their products were much lower than they are today, and as we have said, their revenue was not steady, but jumped up and down according to the world price of copper and the other things. They would not have been able, however hard they tried, to find anything like as much money for education as the independent Governments are now finding.

Moreover, education needs time as well as money. It takes years to train a teacher; and if you decide to double the money you are spending on teacher training, you will get twice as many teachers, but you will not get any of them any sooner. So educational development always begins slowly, and gets faster as time goes on. The fast progress that is being made today would not have been possible without the slower progress that was made before 1939.

9

THE FEDERATION
IS ESTABLISHED

Politics in British Central Africa were greatly influenced by what happened in Britain at the end of the war in 1945. There was a general election, and the Labour Party, the party to which Lord Passfield had belonged, came to-power. It believed in trade unions, and it sympathised more with workers than with employers: thus, in central Africa it sympathised more with the Africans working on the farms and in the mines than with the European farmers and the big mining companies who employed them.

It soon became clear that there were going to be changes. In all three territories, African congress movements were formed. In Southern Rhodesia, there had been a Bantu Congress as early as 1938, but it was a small body. During the war, the Bantu Congress changed its name to the African National Congress, and it began to grow. Africans who had served in the forces joined it, and the Congress began to say how much Africans disliked the pass laws and the bad housing. In Northern Rhodesia, the African National Congress grew out of a number of African welfare societies in the towns; it was first formed in 1948, and Mr Harry Nkumbula became its leader in 1951. The Nyasaland African Congress was formed in 1944, and kept in close touch with the chiefs. These three African congress movements however were not at first the strong fighting organisations that they afterwards became. They were small; they grew slowly; they were content to protest in a quiet and moderate way against evils which they were sure could be put right. It was only when they found that their protests were not listened to that they made up their minds that strikes and boycotts and even stronger measures were the only way of making the Europeans pay attention to them.

We have seen that at the beginning of the war there was a strike of the European miners on the copper-belt, and this was followed by serious African rioting. When the Government was told that African wages were too low, it appointed two commissions to find a remedy. The Forster commission was asked to follow up Gore-Browne's suggestion and find some way in which African workers could let the mining companies know their grievances; the Dalgleish commission was asked to consider whether any jobs (in the mines or elsewhere) that were then reserved for Europeans could be opened to Africans.

The Dalgleish report gave the Africans a good deal of hope. It recommended that there were some posts in the mines which Africans could quite well take over from Europeans at once, and there were others which Africans could easily be trained to take over before long. The Dalgleish commission did not wish to frighten the European mine-workers with the idea that they would be thrown out of work, so it did not recommend that any European should be turned out of his job to make way for an African, but merely that when the European left his job, an African should be appointed in his place. But this did not satisfy the European union of mine-workers. The union had an agreement with the companies which clearly stated that certain kinds of work were to be reserved for Europeans; and the union simply stood firm on this agreement and refused to move.

As we shall see, although when the war ended there was no African trade union, African trade unions began to appear in Nyasaland and Northern Rhodesia in 1948 and 1949. The strength of the European union had been that if it called its members out on strike, the mines could not work; whereas the Africans, not being organised in a union, would probably not all have come out on strike. But when the new African union was organised, the Europeans saw that their position was weakened; for the mining companies would have been just as much troubled by an African strike as by a European. It would not do for the European union to appear opposed to the idea that African mine-workers might be promoted to more responsible posts. There might be a serious strike by the African union; and – who knows? – the Government in Lusaka or in London might support the Africans. So the

European trade union leaders were cunning, and they made an agreement with the leaders of the African union. They said, 'We are not against the idea that Africans should take over European jobs in the mines – not at all! All we say is, that it would be unfair to ask an African to take a European job but to pay him low African wages. If an African takes over a European job, he should be paid the same as the European, and he should live in the same kind of house.'

This was a clever move. It sounded quite fair to the Africans, as if their fellow-workers were trying to protect them against an employer who would try and under-pay them. It is not surprising that the Africans agreed to this. At the same time, it was difficult for the companies not to accept it; for it was the sort of language that trade unionists use all over the world. 'The rate for the job,' they say; you should pay a worker what the job is worth, and not make any differences because of age or sex or race or religion or anything else; if the worker can do the job, he is entitled to the pay and conditions that go with it. Yes: but, as the union well knew, there were difficulties in Northern Rhodesia. The white workers were skilled and experienced; the Africans, newly appointed to a job, would be nervous and inexperienced. The employers would get better work – to begin with – from the experienced European worker. And how was an African to be housed in European style, when he was not allowed by law to live in the European area? The companies would have to begin building expensive new European-type houses in the African areas. In other words, the companies would lose money by appointing Africans; and companies do not like losing money. The result of this agreement was that hardly any Africans were appointed to European jobs in the mines for several more years – which was what the European union intended. It was not until 1953 that the companies found the African unions becoming so strong that they decided it was impossible to continue this equal pay agreement any longer. Thus, although the Dalgleish report raised African hopes, it was a good many years before those hopes were fulfilled.

The European settlers saw the Africans beginning to organise themselves, and they felt that somehow or other they must get the two Rhodesias united into one before it was too late.

There were two things that specially frightened them. One was that the new Labour Government in Britain sent out advisers from the British trade union movement to help Africans to organise themselves in trade unions. Both in Nyasaland and in Northern Rhodesia, African unions were formed in 1948. The African Mine-workers Union in the copper-belt, under its president Lawrence Katilungu, was specially important. No union could be formed in the South, for the Industrial Conciliation Act in that country made it impossible; it was not until 1960 that multi-racial trade unions were allowed in Southern Rhodesia. The British Government would have liked to see African unions formed in the South too immediately after the war; but it had no power to send advisers there, because Southern Rhodesia was self-governing in such matters.

The other thing that frightened the Europeans also happened in 1948. There was a general election in South Africa, and General Smuts fell from power. He was replaced by Dr Malan, leader of the Nationalist Party. General Smuts had always tried to unite the Afrikaner and the English sections of the South African people into one nation, and on page 96 we have seen that he was ready to give a good deal in order to bring Southern Rhodesia into his Union of South Africa. But Dr Malan's policy was quite different. He believed in a South Africa in which the Afrikaners should rule. He did not want the Rhodesian voters, for most of them would be English. And so the whites in Southern Rhodesia saw that there was now no hope for them in joining South Africa. In 1923, they had voted by only three to two in favour of being a separate country; after the 1948 elections in South Africa they all turned away from the idea of joining South Africa and made up their minds instead to press to be allowed to unite with the North.

The white settlers were still as determined as ever that if the two Rhodesias were united, the Rhodesian Government (not the Colonial Office) must control land and labour policy. But they could see that if they did not unite soon, it would be too late to hope for this. Both in Northern Rhodesia and in Nyasaland they could see the British Government helping the Africans to advance. The Africans there now had trade unions; they also had provincial councils, and even national councils. The African Representative Council in Northern Rhodesia was set up in 1945, and in 1948 it was invited to submit the names of two Africans for the Governor to nominate to the legislative council. In Nyasaland, the African Protectorate Council was set up in 1946, and two of its members were nominated to the legislative council in 1949. The African population was growing fast, and African education too was beginning to develop.

Education had been backward hitherto, because it had been too much left to the missions, and the missions had not enough money to provide a full system of schools for the whole country. The Colonial Governments spent some money in giving grants to the missions, but their grants were not large; in 1937, for example, Northern Rhodesia spent only £ 24,000 of Government money on African education. But in 1945, the British Government[1] passed a new law called the Colonial Development and Welfare Act, which provided money from the British taxes for such things as schools and hospitals in the colonies. This was a great help; in 1948, Northern Rhodesia spent £ 300,000 on African education, more than twelve times what it had been spending eleven years before. Primary schools improved a great deal, but there was still very little secondary education, and no higher education. All the same, things were beginning to move. If the whites did not get the two Rhodesias united quickly and keep the Africans from gaining power, they would soon be too late.

But it did not seem likely that the British Government would allow the two countries to unite. It was pressing ahead with African advance in Northern Rhodesia; it would surely never agree to put the Africans in that country under the control of the Government in Salisbury. So the Europeans dropped the idea of uniting, or amalgamating, the two countries. Instead of this, they took up the idea of federation, which they thought the British Government might possibly accept.

What was the difference between amalgamation and federation?

Federation is a system of government which is often used

[1] Not the new Labour Government; this Act was passed by the war-time Government under Winston Churchill.

when two countries wish to join together, but do not wish to give up all their differences. If they amalgamate, they form one country, with the same laws and with one central Government which controls everything. But if they join in a federation, they accept a written constitution, which gives some powers to the central or federal Government, and reserves other powers for the provincial or regional Governments. When they are drawing up the constitution, they can make it as tight or as loose as they like: they can give most of the power to the federal Government, or they can leave the federal Government weak and give most power to the provincial Governments. Both the federal and the provincial Governments have to obey the constitution; if they try to do what the constitution does not allow them to do, their action is unlawful.

WORKING TOWARDS FEDERATION

In October 1948, representatives of the Europeans in both the Rhodesias met, and they agreed that federation, and not amalgamation, should be their aim. Sir Godfrey Huggins did not much like the idea; he preferred amalgamation. He feared that in a federation, the Northern Rhodesian Government would still control land and labour policy, and he and his people wanted to control this policy from Salisbury. But the proverb says that 'half a loaf is better than no bread', and Huggins decided to accept federation. Perhaps, after the federation had been set up, the federal Government in Salisbury would find means of increasing its power.

In February 1949 a conference was held at Victoria Falls to work out a federal scheme. The Southern Rhodesian delegation was led by Sir Godfrey Huggins, that from Northern Rhodesia by Roy Welensky. Sir Stewart Gore-Browne also came; he had lost his place as leader of the unofficial members of the Northern Rhodesia legislative council, but he still sat there to represent African opinion. There were two African members in the Northern Rhodesia legislative council, but they were not invited to Victoria Falls. Three European settlers, but no Africans, came from Nyasaland.

This conference at Victoria Falls did not succed in working out a scheme. There were two main points on which the parties could not agree. One was the question which always has to be discussed in planning a federation: how much power is to be given to the federal Government, and how much to the provincial Governments? Huggins wanted a very strong federal Government; the Northern Rhodesian representatives thought it would be useless to ask for a federation of that kind, for the British Government would never agree to it. It would be better, they thought, to begin with a federation in which the provincial Governments had most of the power. They hoped that later on, the provincial Governments might agree to give up some of their powers to the federal Government.

The second main point on which the conference could not agree was the question of the federal parliament. Huggins was quite firm; he would have no Africans in the federal parliament. African members might sit in the provincial parliaments if the provinces wished: but not in the federal parliament. Here again, the Northerners thought it useless to propose to the British Government a federal parliament with no African members; the British Government would never accept it.

The Colonial Office in London had not been consulted beforehand, and the Northern Rhodesian and Nyasaland Governments were not in any way bound by anything that had been said at Victoria Falls. As for the Africans, what would they think of a conference to which not one African had been invited, not even the African members of the Northern Rhodesia legislative council? The Africans did not know much about federation; but they learned from Huggins that it was a kind of government which would give them no members at all in the federal parliament. Of course, they opposed the idea of federation. Africans in Northern Rhodesia made up their minds that their country must stay under Colonial Office rule until they were ready to govern themselves.

If only these political questions could be settled, there was a great deal to be said for setting up a federation. It is a good thing to get rid of frontiers and customs barriers and have a few large countries instead of many small ones: to have large areas in which law, money, taxes, postal arrangements, and so forth are everywhere the same. It is bad for trade when a

11. Harvesting Sunflower Seeds With Modern Machinery

continent is cut up into many small countries, with different laws and different money and taxes. We have seen that the boundaries of the three territories in central Africa were drawn by the Europeans to suit themselves, by a process of bargaining: 'If we give you this village, then you must give us that one.' Africa has suffered a great deal from being divided in this way.

In central Africa, there were special reasons for joining the three territories together. Nyasaland was long and narrow and very poor, but the natural way for the tobacco from the northeastern part of Northern Rhodesia was down the Nyasaland railway to Beira. It would help Nyasaland a great deal if some of the wealth that came from Northern Rhodesia's copper and Southern Rhodesia's tobacco and chromium could be spent on improving its roads and schools and hospitals. Again the river Zambesi and some of its tributaries (such as the Kafue) could be dammed so as to produce electricity; it would be much better to have one Government to plan the electricity schemes for the good of the whole country than to have three Governments trying to reach agreement, but each thinking only of its own people. In fact, the federal Government did build a great dam on the Zambesi at the Kariba gorge, and the electricity which was produced there was shared between Southern and Northern Rhodesia.

All these are economic arguments: that is, arguments about money and wealth. The economic arguments in favour of federation were very strong. But people think of other things besides wealth; and it would be no use to set up a federation for economic reasons unless it could satisfy its people, African as well as European, from the political point of view.

When the British Government heard the results of the Victoria Falls conference, it said that it could never accept such a federation as the one Huggins wanted. But there were many people in Britain who thought that the economic arguments in favour of federation were so strong that the idea ought to be looked at again. Perhaps Huggins's idea was unworkable in the form he proposed it, but it might work if it were modified so that the three provincial Governments had more power.

As we have seen, the Central African Council[1] which the Bledisloe commission recommended had been set up in 1944. In 1950, the Southern Rhodesian Government gave notice that it would leave the Council in a year's time, because the Council was only a discussion group and had no powers to do anything. This frightened many people in Britain into thinking that Southern Rhodesia was turning towards South Africa. *Apartheid* in South Africa was becoming harder and harder, and people in Britain thought it important that there should be one strong British state in central Africa to prevent *apartheid* and other South African ideas from coming further north.

But I thought you said that the whites in Southern Rhodesia were turning away from South Africa?

So they were. It is most unlikely that Huggins had any idea

[1] See page 117

of joining South Africa. Perhaps he made this move for the very purpose of frightening Britain into agreeing to the scheme of federation.

At any rate, Huggins's hopes of getting his federation were rising. The Secretary of State, James Griffiths, agreed that officials from the British and all three central African Governments should meet in London and discuss the idea of federation. No Government would be bound by anything that the officials recommended. But the officials were the people who would have to work any scheme of government; and if the officials agreed that a particular scheme would work, no politician would be able to stand up and say that it would not.

The officials' conference met in London in January 1951. Its report said that it was urgent that the three territories should be brought into some form of closer union, and that a federal system was the most workable method of doing so. This, the report said, was the only way of saving Southern Rhodesia from *apartheid* of the South African type. There were certainly differences between the Southern Rhodesian policy and the policy of the other two territories in the matters of land and labour; but the officials did not think the differences were big enough to make federation unworkable.

But did the officials who drew up this report think that the white settlers in Southern Rhodesia would give up their policy in matters of land and labour, and follow the policy of the other two countries?

It seems as if they must have thought so. Many people in Britain at that time thought that *apartheid* was invented by the Nationalist Party in South Africa. They did not realise that it was a policy which was likely to grow up among any Europeans, in any part of Africa, who did not like the idea of having Africans competing with them on equal terms. As we have seen, the whites in both the Rhodesias – the followers both of Huggins in the South and of Welensky in the North – wanted federation for the very opposite reason: not in order that the South might become liberal like the North, but in order that the North might get away from the control of the Colonial Office and be free to follow the land and labour policy of the South.

Anyhow, the officials worked out a detailed scheme for a federal constitution. Their idea was that all the services which specially affected the day-to-day life and work of the African peoples would be reserved to the three territorial Governments: examples of these were health, African primary and secondary education, labour, mines, and local government. The federal Government should control such matters as customs, immigration, postal services, railways, aviation, defence, external affairs, and higher education.

In all federations, it is an important question, who is to control the federal Government? The scheme which the officials worked out provided for a federal parliament of 35 members: 17 from the South, eleven from the North, and seven from Nyasaland. There were to be four elected Africans – Sir Godfrey Huggins had at first refused to have any African members, but he changed his mind and accepted this – five members nominated to represent African interests, and 26 elected members, who would presumably all be white, though the constitution said nothing about their race.

It was clear that the federal parliament would be controlled by Europeans; for not only were 31 of the 35 members to be European, but nearly all the voters too were European. This might not matter so very much provided that two conditions were satisfied: first, that the real power in matters that interested the African people was held by the territorial Governments, and second, that those territorial Governments were controlled by African voters and had enough African members in the territorial parliaments.

But these two conditions were not satisfied. In Southern Rhodesia, there were over 46,000 voters; only 380 were Africans. In Northern Rhodesia there were 30,000 voters, of whom eleven were Africans. In Nyasaland, all the members of the legislative council were nominated; there were no elected members, and so there were no voters, white or black. As for African members in the three legislative councils: in Southern Rhodesia there were none; in Northern Rhodesia two (increased to four in 1953); and in Nyasaland two. Thus the Africans had very little influence in the three territorial Governments. Nor did those Governments keep all the powers which the officials' scheme proposed to give them. In the course of discussions during the next two years, several matters which closely concerned Africans were taken away from the territorial Governments and handed over to the federal Government; they included marketing, health, income tax, and town planning.

Africans naturally opposed this scheme of federation. Huggins and Welensky, and most of the Europeans, welcomed it, though they thought the officials proposed to give too little power to the federal Government. Another conference was arranged at Victoria Falls for September 1951. It was to be attended by two British cabinet Ministers, James Griffiths and Gordon Walker; and this time Nyasaland and Northern Rhodesia were invited to send African representatives as well as European. Griffiths and Walker spent some time before the conference in going round the country to find what Africans and Europeans thought of federation. They found all the Africans opposed to it: not merely members of the three African congresses, but chiefs and elders and ordinary people everywhere. James Griffiths spoke of partnership between the two races, by which he meant that African and European interests should be treated alike, and that Europeans should help Africans forward until they were able to take a full share in the life of their country. But this was far from satisfying the Africans. When the conference met, the African members from Nyasaland said they would never agree to federation, and the African members from Northern Rhodesia said they would not consider federation until this 'partnership' had been more satisfactorily explained to them, and they had seen it actually working in their country. It had not begun to work yet; they felt that the progress which the Africans had made in Northern Rhodesia had been made with the help of the Government against the opposition of their 'partners', the Europeans.

The conference could not reach agreement. The Southern Rhodesian representatives wanted to change several points in the draft constitution drawn up by the officials. The Africans would not accept federation, and the two British Ministers said that they would never set up any federation while the Africans were opposed to it. The conference did however agree that if any form of federation were set up, Nyasaland and Northern Rhodesia should remain British protectorates; and that in those two countries, land and African political advance must be controlled by the protectorate Governments, not by the federal Government.

Britain decides to set up the Federation

Only a month after the conference, there was an election in Britain, and the Labour Government fell from power. The new Conservative Government said it believed that federation was necessary. It admitted that the Africans were opposed to the idea, but it hoped that if the two northern countries were kept as British protectorates, they would come to accept it.

In April 1952 another conference was held at Lancaster House in London. Two Africans came to it from Southern Rhodesia, two from Nyasaland, and three from Northern Rhodesia. But the Nyasaland and Northern Rhodesian Africans soon decided to take no part in the conference; their people had sent them to oppose federation, and they found that the British Government was determined to set up the federation, no matter what the Africans thought.

The conference produced another draft constitution; and nearly a year later, after the whole scheme of federation had been much discussed by the Press and the public both in Britain and in Africa, the final revision appeared.

THE FEDERAL CONSTITUTION

The constitution of the Federation of Rhodesia and Nyasaland, as published in 1953, was based on the first draft made by the conference of officials in January 1951. But the 1951 draft had been a good deal modified; and it is important to notice what the modifications were.

First of all, a preamble (or introduction) was added. Such preambles are sometimes unimportant, but this one was very important. It said that Northern Rhodesia and Nyasaland were to remain protectorates as long as their peoples wished; those two territorial Governments would remain responsible for land and the political advance of the Africans; and the Federation would become a fully self-governing member of

the Commonwealth only 'when the inhabitants of the territories so desire.'

**But what did the preamble mean by 'the inhabitants'? Did it
mean only the voters, that is to say the Europeans and only a
handful of Africans?**

No, it meant more than that. This is an important point;
and James Griffiths asked the Government in parliament
what it meant. He said that it ought to mean 'inhabitants,
without any qualification of colour, race, or creed.' He received
a satisfactory answer from the Government spokesman, Oliver
Lyttelton: 'By "the majority of the people", I agree with the
Right Honourable Gentleman that we mean the inhabitants
which he said are the inhabitants.' And Mr Lyttelton went on
to promise that the Government would not give up the Protectorates, or allow the Federation to become independent,
'without the agreement of the majority of the inhabitants.'
In other words, when the preamble spoke of 'the inhabitants',
it meant to include all the Africans, whether they had votes
or not.

The powers were divided between the federal and the
territorial Governments in the way we have described on pages
135 and 136. The chief powers which the territorial Governments
kept were African primary and secondary education, local
government, labour, mines, African land, and African coope-
rative societies.

The federal parliament had 35 members. Each territory sent
two elected African members and one European who was
nominated to represent African interests. The other 26 members were all elected (and all European): fourteen from Southern
Rhodesia, eight from Northern Rhodesia, and four from
Nyasaland.

There was one very important question which the conference
of officials had discussed. How was a federal parliament with
so few African members to be prevented from passing laws
against African interests? The officials had proposed that
for this purpose there should be a special Minister for African
Interests, appointed by the Governor. His duty would be to
watch everything the Government did. If he thought it was
being unfair to the Africans, he was to send word to the Govern-

ment in Britain, who would have power to stop the Federal Government's action. The Minister was to be helped by an African Affairs Board, which would have similar powers to warn the British Government if a Bill was introduced into the federal parliament which the Board thought unfair to Africans. The Board was to be appointed by the Governor; it was to have nine members, European and African, not more than three of whom were to be members of parliament.

This was the machinery which the officials had proposed in 1951 for protecting African interests. It was much disliked by the Europeans in the Rhodesias, and between 1951 and 1953 they succeeded in greatly weakening it, though not in abolishing it altogether. In the final constitution, there was no Minister for African Interests. But there was still an African Affairs Board. It was to have six members, not nine; all the six were to be members of parliament. Each territory would send its one European nominated member, and one of its two African members. The Governor was to appoint one of the six as chairman.

This gave the Africans much less protection than the machinery which the conference of officials had proposed.

Yes, especially as far as the Government's executive actions were concerned. There was no Minister with power to see what the Government proposed to do, and to warn London before the Government did it. But as far as proposed new laws were concerned, Africans still had some protection. Three of the six members of the Board were Africans, and the other three were supposed to be people in close touch with African views. The Board still had the power to warn the British Government about proposed laws; and as we shall see, it used its power.

So far, the constitution did not seem too bad. The territorial Governments had some important powers, and it was for them, and not for the Federal Government, to settle the way in which their African people should advance politically. But when Africans had been given the vote for territorial Government elections, they would naturally hope to be given the vote for federal elections also. And here the constitution gave them no help. It said that it would be for the federal parliament itself to decide who was to be given the vote for the federal elections. And not content with giving the federal parliament this power, it said that the constitution could be amended only by a two-thirds majority of the federal parliament. Thus, whatever advances Africans might make in the territorial Governments, they could not hope to advance towards power in the federal Government.

Many of the Europeans in Rhodesia disliked this constitution. They wanted to abolish the African Affairs Board altogether, to keep the Africans out of the federal parliament, and to bring land and labour policy in Nyasaland and Northern Rhodesia under federal control. All the voters in Southern Rhodesia were asked whether they approved of the constitution; 25,000 voted yes, but 16,000 voted no.

All the Africans disliked it. Mr Harry Nkumbula burned the printed constitution paper in Lusaka in front of a great crowd. Nyasaland sent three chiefs to London to ask the Queen not to force this constitution on their country. But the Queen has to be guided by the advice of her Ministers; and she was advised not to receive the chiefs. The legislative council in Northern Rhodesia approved of the constitution by 17 votes to four; the four who opposed it were the two Africans and the two Europeans representing African interests. In the Nyasaland legislative council, the one Asian member and the one European nominated member voted against the constitution, and the two African members walked out of the debate to show how strongly they opposed it. We do not know what the official members of these two legislative councils thought about the scheme; they were ordered to vote in favour of it, and they had to obey.

There was much opposition to the Federation in Britain. The Government did take one important step to meet the criticism of the opposition both in Britain and in Africa. It promised that there would be another conference of all the five Governments concerned (the British, the Federal, and the three territorial Governments), not sooner than 1960 but not later than 1963, to look at the constitution again and make whatever improvements seemed necessary. But this was not enough to satisfy those who disliked the constitution. The Labour and Liberal parties in parliament opposed it. Many Church leaders and people who knew something of Africa joined in saying to the Government, 'No doubt you honestly believe that this constitution will do the Africans, as well as the Europeans, a great deal of good; and that in seven years time the Africans will see this for themselves. But however good your scheme may be, it is wrong to force it on the Africans against their wishes; and if you do this, you will have trouble.'

But the Government had made up its mind. In March 1953 it carried its scheme through parliament by a majority of 44, and the Federation was formally set up on 1st August 1953.

10

CENTRAL AFRICA IN THE FEDERATION

The Federation was now in existence, but much work still had to be done to fill in the details. The first thing was to elect the federal parliament. Only British subjects were allowed to vote in the elections. But Nyasaland and Northern Rhodesia were British protectorates, and so their peoples were not British subjects, but 'British protected persons'. Consequently, they had no vote. In the Federation as a whole there were 66,000 voters; 444 were African, 1,100 Coloured and Asian, the rest European.

Parties and Elections

Three political parties developed among the European electors. The first was the Federal Party, which was led by Sir Godfrey Huggins and supported the constitution and the idea of partnership. No one could tell yet how it would carry out a policy of partnership; but at any rate, partnership was part of its programme.

For this reason, the Federal Party was opposed by a party which called itself the Confederate Party. This was the party which disliked the constitution because it gave too much power to the Africans. The party did not believe in partnership; it believed in keeping all power in European hands.

Against both these parties there was a small Progressive Party. This was a party which believed that much more should be done to provide education for Africans and to bring Africans forward as quickly as possible into a position of full equality with the Europeans. There should be no colour-bar of any kind, and the best man should be chosen, no matter what his race or creed.

When the elections were held, the Federal Party received 36,000 votes, the Confederate Party 15,000, other parties

2,000; three were 13,000 who did not trouble to vote. The Federal Party won 24 out of the 26 elected seats, and Huggins became Federal prime minister. His party in Southern Rhodesia called itself the United Party, and it was led by Mr Garfield Todd, who had been a missionary before entering politics. Garfield Todd himself was a liberal; he believed in helping forward the Africans and ending the colour-bar. He was too liberal for most of his colleagues; and as we shall see, before long they turned on him and threw him out of power. But for the moment it was a great support to the Federal Government that Garfield Todd and his United Party were in power in Southern Rhodesia; it made it seem possible that the Federal Government's talk of partnership really meant something.

The first test of what partnership really meant would be what the Government proposed to do about increasing the number of African voters. The Federal Government seemed in no hurry to do anything about this, and made no change in the arrangements for federal elections until 1957.

Changes however were made in Northern Rhodesia and Nyasaland. In Northern Rhodesia, the number of elected Europeans on the legislative council was raised from ten to twelve, and there were to be four nominated Africans instead of two. In Nyasaland, the legislative council in 1953 had ten official and ten unofficial members, three of whom were Africans and one an Asian. All the members were nominated. In 1955 the system was changed. There were now to be five African members instead of three, but they were still to be nominated by the African Protectorate Council and appointed by the Governor. At the same time, the Asian and European members, instead of being nominated, were now to be elected on a common roll. This change had the effect of causing the one Asian member to lose his seat, so that the council now had six elected European and five nominated African unofficial members. This change in the government of Nyasaland cannot be said to advance the position of the Africans very much. In fact, European elected members were likely to have more power than European nominated members.

These changes did not touch the important point, which was the question of voting. Africans in the Federation knew what was happening in other parts of Africa; they knew, for

example, that from 1954 onwards Ghana was governed
by a parliament of 104 members, all Africans and all directly
elected by the people. How could they be content to be power-
less in their own country?

It is true that in those early years of Federation, some
improvements were made in other matters. The colour-bar
was eased in shops and post offices. An African lawyer was
allowed to open an office in a part of Salisbury which had
been completely reserved for whites. And more important
than these, the British Government intended to provide money
under the Colonial Development and Welfare Act for a
university to be open to students of all races. The Federal
Government provided a site for the university at Salisbury;
but this meant that the university hostels as well as the lecture
rooms must be in an area reserved for whites, and this would not
be possible without an amendment to the Land Apportionment Act. Many Europeans opposed these changes; but the
Government carried them through.

In African eyes, these changes, though good in themselves,
were less important than changes in the voting system. In
1957 the Federal Government brought forward its proposals
for altering the law in this matter.

Sir Godfrey Huggins was now Lord Malvern. He knew that
he must be able to show the British Government some evidence
that his policy of partnership was really meant to help the
Africans forward; otherwise, the British Government was
likely to be very critical when the federal constitution was
revised in 1960 or later. On the other hand, he knew that the
majority of his Federal Party would never accept too big an
increase in the number of African voters; if he went too far, he
would lose the support of his party and would get nothing done.
On one thing, Huggins was determined: politics in the Federation must not be allowed to become racial, with Africans and
Europeans voting against each other. Both African and European voters must be placed on a common roll, so that Africans
and Europeans voted for the same candidate, and when the
candidate was elected, he would have to consider the interests
of the electors of both races.

Lord Malvern (Huggins) was thus in a difficulty. His way
of meeting it was to propose a common roll of voters, divided

into two parts, an upper and a lower. The upper part of the roll would include all citizens who satisfied certain requirements as to education or wealth. The lower part would include citizens who satisfied lower requirements in education or wealth; the voters in the lower part of the roll would have ess power than voters in the upper part. Both Africans and Europeans would be enrolled in both parts of the roll, but since most Europeans were better educated and richer than most Africans, most of the names on the upper roll would be European, and most of those on the lower roll would be African.

Having put out this suggestions, Lord Malvern resigned as prime minister, and was succeeded by his colleague Roy Welensky, now Sir Roy. This change did not mean any change of policy.

Lord Malvern's scheme was of course much discussed. The Africans, who were encouraged by what was happening in other parts of Africa to aim at 'One man, one vote', criticised it because it seemed to them a trick to keep the number of African voters down. Many Europeans on the other hand criticised it because they disliked the idea of fixing the qualifications for a vote. Once the qualifications were fixed, it seemed to them only a matter of time before with more education and more prosperity, African voters would outnumber European. To them this was a horrible thought, for they were so used to the idea that political power must be kept in European hands.

The Tredgold Commission

Lord Malvern had not worked out the details of his scheme, and the Southern Rhodesian Government appointed a commission under Sir Robert Tredgold to work out a detailed scheme for Southern Rhodesia, which should ensure that the Government should remain in the hands of 'civilized and responsible people'. In March 1957 the Tredgold commission published its report, and soon afterwards the Federal Government introduced an electoral law which was clearly based on the general principles of the Tredgold Report.

The Tredgold report recommended that the country should be divided into constituencies, each to be represented in

parliament by one member. There should be, as Lord Malvern
had proposed, one common roll of voters. Everybody should
have a vote who satisfied certain requirements both in education
and in wealth; a rich man would have a vote even if not very
well educated, and a poor man would have a vote if he had
more education. This was a long way from being 'One man,
one vote'. There is nothing specially sacred about the principle
of 'One man, one vote'; Britain itself came to this rule in slow
stages, and only achieved it in 1948; and politics and government in Britain have not been noticeably better since 1948
than before it. It would not be right to criticise the Tredgold
recommendations merely because they fell short of the principle
of 'One man, one vote.'

But they can be criticised on other grounds. For one thing,
the Commission took the phrase 'civilized and responsible
people' to include every European, but only those Africans
who had received a school education and were earning money
in European employment; thus it assumed that Africans in
the villages, however old and wise, were not fit to have a vote.
Next, it is all very well to say that to obtain a vote you must
earn so much money or pass such an examination. But if
there is no school to help you to pass the examination, and if
wages are so low that you have very little chance of earning
the money, the Commission is not giving you much hope of
ever obtaining the vote.

In fact, the Commission explained clearly that it intended
to give the vote only to a small proportion of the African
population: to those who

> have acquired a certain standing, such as that of
> an agricultural supervisor, building overseer, clerk,
> interpreter, minister of religion, chief, editor or
> journalist, medical orderly, building contractor,
> artisan or farmer (but only the most advanced
> representatives of these two occupations.)

These were the people the Commission considered sufficiently
'civilized and responsible' to be given a vote. No doubt as
time went on there would be more of such men; but the numbers would increase slowly unless much more money were
spent on African education. In 1950 there were fewer than
300 Africans in the whole of the Federation who were atten-

ding secondary school. The Africans felt that it would be easy for the Government to keep Africans from political power by limiting their education so that they could never qualify for a vote.

These were the details of the qualifications which the Tredgold commission recommended. There were to be three grades of qualifications for the upper roll[1]:

(a) Property of £1,500 or an income of £720 a year, with literacy in English;

(b) Property of £1,000 or an income of £480 a year, with a Standard VI education (that is, a full primary education);

(c) Property of £500 or an income of £300 a year, with two years of secondary education.

Anyone with one of these qualifications was entitled to a vote on the upper roll. The qualification for a vote on the lower roll was an income of £180 a year, with literacy in English. There was a limit placed on the lower-roll votes; they were not to count for more than one-third of the votes cast in any constituency.

These were the recommendations of the Tredgold commission. The Southern Rhodesian Government, which had appointed the commission, adopted most of its recommendations in its Electoral Amendment Act of 1957. It gave the vote on the lower roll to anyone who earned £120 a year and had completed the primary school course; but it limited the value of the lower-roll votes more than the Tredgold report had proposed. Instead of counting for not more than one-third of the total votes cast in any constituency, they were not to count for more than one-sixth of the total in the whole country. Thus, no matter how many Africans qualified for a vote on the lower roll, the lower-roll vote was limited to a fixed proportion of the total. The immediate effect of the Act was far from reaching this limit; it increased the number of African voters from 441 to 1,696.

[1] This idea of dividing the common roll into an upper and a lower roll lasted until Malawi and Zambia became independent, and is still (1967) in force in Rhodesia. The Tredgold report did not speak of upper and lower; it spoke of "ordinary" and "special". More recently in Rhodesia people speak of the A-roll and the B-roll. We shall use the terms upper and lower roll throughout.

The Federal Electoral Act, 1958

In that same year, 1957, the Federal Government passed a
Constitution Amendment Act which increased the size of the
Federal parliament from 35 members to 59. Next year it
passed a Federal Electoral Act which was based on the general principles of the Tredgold report. But this Federal Act set
up still stricter limitations on the value of the lower-roll
votes. Of the 59 members of parliament, 57 were to be elected,
and one each from Nyasaland and Northern Rhodesia nominated to represent African interests. Four of the 57 elected
members must be Africans, elected by the African voters in
Nyasaland and Northern Rhodesia. Forty-four members
were to be elected by upper-roll voters only; lower-roll votes
would not be counted in these constituencies. Five members
from Southern Rhodesia and two each from Northern Rhodesia and Nyasaland were to be elected by upper-roll and
lower-roll voters together; of these nine members, eight must
be Africans.

This is very complicated. What was the effect of it all?

About 6,500 African voters were placed on the Federal
roll of electors: 1,700 on the upper roll and 4,800 on the
lower. The lower-roll voters could use their votes only in 13
out of the 57 constituencies, and twelve of these thirteen
members must be Africans. Thus, of all the elected European
members, only one would depend at all on the lower-roll
votes. On the other hand, eight out of the twelve African
members would depend very largely on upper-roll votes,
nine-tenths of which were European. The general result of
the Act was to make a modest increase in the number of
African voters, but to set very narrow limits to the value of
their votes.

The African Affairs Board protests

These two Acts, the Constitution Act and the Federal Electoral
Act, were not passed without difficulty. The Africans of
course protested, but the Federal Government did not mind
their protests. What was more important to the Government
was that the African Affairs Board too protested. It said that
the new parliament did not represent African interests as well

as the old. In the old parliament, 29 members depended on European votes and four on African; in the new parliament, there would be 49 members depending on European votes, but still only four depending on African votes.

Here, then, is the African Affairs Board, though weaker than the Board which had originally been proposed, doing its duty in defending African interests. What would happen in London when the Board's protest was received?

Sir Roy Welensky had already seen to this. Before publishing his Constitution Amendment Bill, he had visited London. There he explained that his position as federal prime minister was not as strong as it looked. The opposition party[1], which wanted to keep all political power for ever in white hands, was growing. More and more people were looking on him with suspicion, fearing that he was going to let in large numbers of African voters and let power pass into African hands. If he was to hold his place, he must have 'something to take home' with him to show these critics that he did not intend to hand over power to the Africans. If the British Government were to block his two Bills, he would be greatly weakened. He might even fall from power altogether, and be replaced by someone who was far less friendly to the Africans than he was.

The British Government saw the difficult position he was in. To help him, the Government promised:

(a) that it would not oppose his two Bills;

(b) that it would hold the promised conference on the federal constitution at the earliest possible date, that is in 1960;

(c) that Britain would make laws for the Federation (which the constitution allowed her to do) only if the Federal Government asked her to do so;

(e) that all the civil service in the Federation would in the end be staffed by people who had their homes there; the Colonial Office would cease to send officials from Britain.

In return for all this, the British Government asked that 'a reasonable number' of British protected persons in the two

[1] Formerly called the Confederate Party, now called the Dominion Party.

protectorates should be allowed to vote in the federal elections; and this Welensky promised.

Sir Roy Welensky seems to have gained a great deal and to have given very little in return. It does not seem as if the Government ought to have trusted him as much as it did.

Yes, the British Government had given Welensky a good deal. In particular, by promising never to use its power of making laws for the Federation unless the Federal Government asked it to do so, the British Government had given up much of its power over the Federation. It trusted Welensky to do his best to make the idea of partnership a reality. It made up its mind that it must trust Welensky, for if he were to go, someone much worse might come into power instead of him.

Sir Roy Welensky seemed to the British Government the most liberal statesman in Federal politics. (Garfield Todd was more liberal, but he was not in Federal politics; he was in the territorial politics of Southern Rhodesia.) Welensky spoke as if he really meant to make partnership work; but there was not much that as Federal prime minister he could do about it, for African affairs were mainly in the hands of the territorial Governments. What Welensky could do, he did. His Federal Government service opened all senior posts to Africans on the same salary scale as Europeans; and it trained African nurses, who would earn European salaries when they were qualified. Welensky abolished the system which made Africans and Europeans use different doors in post offices and travel separately on the railway, and he abolished other small but irritating pieces of colour-bar rules. Africans of course thought he should have done more, and many Europeans thought he was doing too much. At any rate, he did enough in this way to make it sound reasonable when he said to the British Government, 'I know you want this partnership to work. So do I. You see what I am doing. I would do more if I could. But many members of my party think I am doing too much, and I have to go carefully. If you make things too difficult for me by interfering, I shall fall; and whoever takes my place will be harder on the Africans than I am.'

The result of Welensky's talks in London was that when

the African Affairs Board in Salisbury protested against the Constitution Amendment Act and the Federal Electoral Act, the Government in London overruled the African Affairs Board and approved the two Acts. The Opposition, the Labour and Liberal parties, protested; but of course they were in a minority.

When this news reached Africa, the African leaders felt that they had no hope as long as the Federation lasted. The African Affairs Board had done its duty, but the British and the Federal Governments had agreed to ignore it. Their only hope was to break up the Federation altogether: to show the 1960 conference that it was finished and dead. The African Congresses grew stronger, and their leaders attacked the Federation more bitterly. In Nyasaland, Mr Chipembere told the two Nyasaland African members of the Federal parliament that they ought to resign. He invited Dr Hastings Banda to come back home and take his place as leader of the Congress. Dr Banda had been away from Nyasaland for thirty years, but he had always kept in touch with his native country; he helped to set up the Nyasaland African National Congress, and was its leader from the beginning. The Africans in Nyasaland had been disappointed by the new constitution they had been given in 1955. They had hoped that the new legislative council in Nyasaland would have contained as many African members as there were unofficial European members. So they were already feeling bitter before the Federal Electoral Act.

Electoral changes in Northern Rhodesia

In Northern Rhodesia too, there was a constitutional change in 1958. The African members of the legislative council hoped that there would be a new council with as many African members as there were unofficial European members. The African Congress hoped for still more; it hoped for as many African members as all the European members, officials and unofficials together. But they were not given anything like this.

The Government followed the provisions of the Federal law in having upper and lower-roll voters. It went still further, and divided the country into ordinary and special constituen-

12. Dr Hastings Banda

cies. The twelve ordinary constituencies covered the main European areas. In these, lower-roll votes were not to count for more than a quarter of the total number of votes cast. The rest of the country was divided into six special constituencies; we might have expected that in these special constituencies, upper-roll votes would not count for more than a quarter of the total, but it was not so: upper and lower-roll votes were to count equally. Besides this, there were two extra seats in the European areas reserved for African members, and two seats in the African areas reserved for European members. (This shows that in Northern Rhodesia, the Government had given up any pretence that Africans came to the towns only as 'visitors'.) The new legislative council contained 14 elected European members and eight elected Africans, with two nominated members, one European and one African, and with six officials. The totals were 15 European members and nine Africans, plus the officials. Thus, the African members and the official members together equalled the elected and nominated European unofficial members; which was far from what the Africans had been hoping for. It was better than before; there were now nine Africans out of 30 instead of four out of 26. But it was not enough. In Northern Rhodesia there were now 7,600 African voters, of whom 800 were on the upper roll.

The African National Congress in Northern Rhodesia at once protested, and Mr Nkumbula burned the printed copy of the constitution, as he had previously burned the copy of the federal constitution. But some of his members, led by Mr Kaunda and Mr Kapwepwe, thought he should do more. They were in a minority, and the rest of the Congress was faithful to Mr Nkumbula and expelled them. They set up a new body, the Zambia African National Congress. The African Representative Council in Northern Rhodesia had already said that the country ought to leave the Federation, and the Zambia Congress agreed. It would take no part in working the new constitution, but would put all its energy into taking its country out of the Federation.[1]

In July 1958, Dr Banda came back from abroad to be leader of the Nyasaland African Congress. He began by asking for 'One man, one vote', so that Africans would have a majority in all the legislative councils and the federal parliament. In December he went further, and joined Mr Kaunda in saying that the Federation must be broken up.

---

[1] The name Zambia was formed from the name Zambesi. The congress at first thought of calling itself the Zambesia Congress. It was Mr Kapwepwe who said that the word Zambesia was too long, and ought to be shortened to Zambia.

Southern Rhodesia and the Land Husbandry Act

In Southern Rhodesia too, the Africans were asking for an end to the Federation. The Southern Rhodesian African National Congress was formed in 1957, with Mr Joshua Nkomo as president.

The Africans in the South were thinking about other grievances as well as about votes and representation in parliament. Two years before federation, in 1951, their Government had passed a Native Land Husbandry Act, and the bitter feeling this Act caused was still growing.

There was much to be said in favour of the Act. The Government saw that the African population was growing fast, and knew that the time would come when there would not be enough land to provide each African family with a plot of its own. The old African subsistence agriculture would have to be changed; it just could not go on for ever. Subsistence agriculture used to be practised all over Europe, including Britain; but it had to be given up long ago, because there is no longer enough land for it. The Southern Rhodesian Government wanted to train farmers in scientific agriculture, and give them farms of their own which they would work on modern scientific methods, so that they could grow food not only for their own families, but for sale.

The Government had already tried to encourage scientific agriculture in the African areas, and by 1950 there were already about 3,000 African farmers who were practising these modern ways. But this was not enough, and most African farmers were unwilling to change their old ways. The Native Land Husbandry Act set out to force them to do so. It proposed that gradually – the process would take several years – all the African reserves would be divided into individual farms, of different sizes up to twenty acres. Dams would be made to provide water, and tanks for dipping the cattle. The Government would do this work, and when the farms were ready, it would hand them over to farmers who would promise to farm them properly.

Many Europeans disliked the Act. They said that the new African farms were too small; and they looked ahead, and saw that if the Act were successful, there would be many African farmers who would be fit to take one of the new farms but would not be able to find one. And what would they do then? Why, they would ask to have a farm cut out for them from the European area; and that would end the whole of the Land Apportionment Act.

But the Africans disliked the Act much more. Agriculture to them was not merely a way of earning a living; it was their whole way of life. The life of the tribe depended on its links with the land; take away the land from the tribe's control, and the tribe would be weakened, if not quite destroyed. Africans who lived and worked in the towns still thought of themselves as members of their tribe, and liked to think that one day they could go back to the reserves and live on the family land. Again, when the land was cut up into individual farms, it would grow much more food, but it would not hold so many families. Many families would lose their land and would have to go to the towns to work. All these changes had taken place in Britain long ago, but they had caused trouble there. And in Rhodesia, there were large areas of land reserved for European farmers, and not all of this land was being used. It is not surprising that the Africans said, 'There is no need for this Act. There is plenty of land still freee; why do you not let us go and farm it?'

This land trouble in Southern Rhodesia was for the moment taking even more of the attention of the African National Congress than the question of votes. Even before the Native Land Husbandry Act was passed, the people there had been afraid of losing their land: not only because of the Land Apportionment Act but also of the Maize Control Act. Then again, the Government was making regulations to limit the number of cattle that were grazed in the reserves. The regulations were necessary, for the cattle were increasing, and the land was being spoilt by over-grazing. But it is not surprising again that the African farmers opposed the regulations, and said simply, 'There is plenty of empty land; why do you not let us take our cattle there?'

The Native Land Husbandry Act was passed by Mr Garfield Todd's Government. Many of Mr Todd's Ministers disliked his policy because they thought him too liberal towards Africans. He raised African minimum wages, he wanted to allow Africans to become members of trade unions, he wanted to spend much more money on improving African education. But the Africans disliked his electoral law, and they disliked his Native Land Husbandry Act. As he was losing his African support, his Ministers saw their chance of getting rid of him. In February 1958, 13 out of the 24 members of parliament who supported Mr Todd said that they would support him no more. They took the greater part of his party over to combine with Welensky's Federal Party, under the title of the United Federal Party. Mr Todd formed a new party of his own. There was a general election in Southern Rhodesia. Mr Todd's new party did not win a single seat; the United Federal Party won 17 and the Dominion Party (which stood for the policy of keeping all power in white hands) won 13. Sir Edgar Whitehead became prime minister.

This election was held in 1958; and in the same year, the Southern Rhodesian Government lost a chance of doing something to improve the life of Africans living in the towns. Garfield Todd's Government had set up the Plewman Commission to report on African housing in the towns, and its report came before the Whitehead Government. Much African housing was very bad; no one needed a commission to tell him that. But the Plewman report did make some wise recommendations. It said that African housing would never be improved until it was admitted that Africans were living permanently in the towns, and needed the same security as European town dwellers. Like European, they should buy or rent their own homes, instead of living in quarters provided by their employer; and their rates of pay should be increased to enable them to do this. The towns must not be considered separately from the country districts. More must be done to improve life in the African reserves so that they could produce more and support more people. In fact, Africans should be treated as human beings, and not as pieces of machinery. But the Government took very little notice of these recommendations.

The African Congress in Southern Rhodesia thus had other grievances in 1958 besides the electoral system.

In November 1958 fresh elections were held for the federal parliament. Nine-tenths of the electors were still European; so the election was fought over the one question which most interested the Europeans: which party would have the best chance of securing independence for the Federation when the 1960 review of the constitution was held? The Nyasaland Congress under Dr Banda and the Zambia Congress under Mr Kaunda boycotted the election altogether. In the election campaign, Sir Roy Welensky had a great advantage over his rival Mr Winston Field, the leader of the Dominion Party; Welensky was well-known and trusted, Field was a new man. Welensky's party, the United Federal Party, won 46 seats, the Dominion Party won eight, a new party called the Central Africa Party won three. This new party was led by Garfield Todd and Sir John Moffat of Northern Rhodesia. It was a liberal party, and hoped to win African votes and the votes of those Europeans who believed in a society in which race should not count. The three seats which it won were all in Northern Rhodesia.

Twelve African members were elected, but eight of them depended very much on European votes. One of the eight accepted Winston Field's leadership, the other seven followed Welensky.

THE 1959 EMERGENCY

The African Congress parties felt that time was short. The federal election was held in November 1958, and the future of the Federation was to be considered at a conference during 1960. The Congress parties wanted to show the British Government that the Federation had failed; they now had not much longer than one year to do this.

It was mainly because of this, not because of anything special which the three Governments had done at that moment, that there were disturbances in all three territories at the beginning of 1959.

In December 1958, a pan-African congress had been held at Accra in Ghana. Banda, Kaunda and Nkumbula had all attended it; and there all three of them agreed that they must work to get the Federation broken up. In January, a meeting of the Nyasaland African Congress talked of using violence, and in February the violence began. Large crowds gathered; at Karonga they opened the prison and let out the prisoners;

they attacked and wounded some Europeans (though they killed none); they threw stones at cars and at Government buildings – and so on. For a time, the whole of the northern part of Nyasaland was out of the Government's control. On 20 February, the Governor of Nyasaland, Sir Robert Armitage, asked for Federal troops to support his police, and the troops were flown in from Southern Rhodesia. At the beginning of March, the Governor declared a state of emergency; Dr Banda's Congress was declared illegal, and Dr Banda himself, with about six hundred other Africans, was arrested. This led to more trouble, especially at Nkata Bay. By the time the country was quiet again, 51 Africans had been killed.

Sir Edgar Whitehead in Southern Rhodesia declared a state of emergency earlier, on 26 February; and his Government arrested about five hundred people, including one European. The Congress was declared illegal, and in the next few months, several strong laws were passed, such as the Preventive Detention Act and the Unlawful Organizations Act. These Acts gave the Government power to arrest people and keep them in prison without trial, and made it an offence to belong to any organization which the Government declared illegal. A person could be regarded as belonging to an organization if he had attended one of its meetings, or had in his possession any of its papers or badges. No meeting of more than twelve Africans was to be held without Government permission, and it was to be an offence to say or do anything against the Government.

All Governments may sometimes have to take such sweeping powers; the Governments of Ghana and of other independent African countries have taken them and have used them against their own African people. The questions to be asked in each case are these: How serious is the emergency? Does the Government really need all these powers? When will the Government give them up and allow the ordinary law of the land to come inti force again? The Whitehead Government said that the danger was great; the leaders of the African Congress did not really represent the people, and the Congress was compelling people to join it, and meant to overthrow the Government by force. No lesser powers, it thought, would be enough to keep the peace. It had every hope that some at least of these laws

13. President Kaunda of Zambia

could be dropped after five years, and perhaps even sooner. But many people protested: the Churches and the lawyers in Southern Rhodesia, and many others both in Africa and in Britain. Some people in Britain said that the Whitehead Government was wrong in thinking that the Congress did not really represent the African people. Far from this: all Africans who were interested in politics supported the Congress: so said the Government's critics in Britain.

In Northern Rhodesia, things passed off more quietly. There was no declaration of emergency. Mr Kaunda and the Zambia Congress boycotted the territorial elections of April 1959, though Mr Nkumbula took part in them, and won one seat. Before the elections, the Zambia Congress was declared illegal, and Mr Kaunda was sent to be detained in a distant part of the country.

So during 1959, all the Congress leaders except Mr Nkumbula were detained, and their parties had to manage without them. It seemed as if there was nothing to be gained by setting up road-blocks, rioting, beating, and burning; the Governments were too strong. And moreover, violence of this kind was not likely to please the British Government. When it came to discuss the Federation in 1960, the Government might think that leaders who advised their people to behave like this were not suitable to become leaders of independent countries. So the Congress parties changed their ways. They had been declared illegal, so they could no longer operate openly. New parties were set up to replace them: the National Democratic Party in the South, the United National Independence Party in the North, the Malawi Congress in Nyasaland. They had the same members and the same leaders as the old parties; only the names were new. They were more careful. Some people were still beaten, some houses were still burnt, in order to make people join the Congress; but no one would give evidence, so the Governments could do little to stop this. If the new parties were to say that they spoke for the whole African population they must see to it that everyone belonged to them and bought a membership card. The Governments in Zomba, Lusaka and Salisbury would certainly tell the British Government that the African Congress parties spoke only for a few people, and that most Africans were quite content with their Governments. It was important for the Congress leaders that no Africans should speak up to say that the Governments were right in this.

THE DEVLIN COMMISSION

The troubles in Nyasaland had been so serious that the British Government sent out a commission to inquire into them. This commission, headed by a British judge (now Lord Devlin), reported in August 1959. Like all good commissions, it was not content to inquire into the immediate facts of the situation, but inquired also into the deeper causes of the trouble. On the immediate facts, it reported that the violence and disorder had been so bad that the Government was right in using troops to restore order; it had to 'act or abdicate' – that is, if it had not done what it did, it would have failed in its duty and given all power over to Dr Banda. It was not the fault of the Government, thought the Commission, that fifty people lost their lives.

But when the Devlin commission came to inquire into the deeper causes of the troubles, it blamed the Nyasaland Government very strongly: so strongly that the Governor protested. The Governor said that Dr Banda and the Congress had a plan to kill all the Europeans in Nyasaland. The Devlin commission did not believe a word of this. It said that the real trouble was that the Government and the Africans did not understand each other, and the Government took no pains to try and understand the African point of view. The Government meant to be kind and just; but it did not believe that Africans understood affairs of government. Therefore, it thought, the African people ought to be content to leave it alone to do what it thought best for them; and it was hurt and angry when leaders like Dr Banda were not content with this. The Commission was quite clear in its opinion that, whether they understood affairs of government or not, nearly all the Africans – educated and uneducated, chiefs and villagers – supported Dr Banda and the Congress and opposed the Federation. If so, said the Commission, the Government will sooner or later have to come to terms with the people; it cannot go on for ever imprisoning people because they have a Congress membership card. And the Commission used a phrase which made many Europeans angry; it said that Nyasaland at the moment was a police state.[1] It was an unhappy phrase, for it reminded people in Britain of Hitler's Germany, with its secret State police who were responsible to no law. People said, truly, that there were no such secret police in Nyasaland: only the ordinary police, who were responsible to the ordinary law of the land. What the Devlin commission

[1] "Nyasaland is – no doubt only temporarily – a police State, where it is not safe for anyone to express approval of the Congress party, to which before 3 March 1953 the vast majority of politically-minded Africans belonged, and where it is unwise to express any but the most restrained criticisms of Government policy."

meant was that during the state of emergency the police behaved in such a way that everyone was frightened of them; their powers under the emergency regulations were so great that, if they were cruel or unjust – and the Commission said that they sometimes had been – the ordinary citizen had little chance of getting justice against them.

The Devlin report was widely read in Britain, and it had a great effect on public opinion there. When the Government set up the Federation in 1953, it argued (a) that nine Africans out of ten knew nothing at all about federation, and had no opinion of their own either for it or against it; and (b) that the one African in ten who did oppose the idea would change his mind when he had had a few years experience of the Federation at work. Now the Devlin commission reported that after six years of the Federation, all the Nyasaland Africans were opposed to it. People in Britain knew that Nyasaland was the poorest of the three territories, and so should be receiving the greatest economic benefits from the Federation. They began to ask themselves, 'If, in spite of this, the people are so opposed to the Federation, have we the right to continue forcing it on them?'

In Africa, too, the troubles of 1959 and the Devlin report had an effect. The United Federal Party saw that it had no hope of being given independence unless it could do something to remove the bad impression which had been made in Britain. In Southern Rhodesia, the Whitehead Government passed an Education Act which planned to provide primary education for all African children by 1964, and a Trade Disputes Act which at last allowed trade unions to have African as well as European members. It began a programme of improving African housing in the towns, at last doing something about the Plewman report. It even set up a committee to inquire into the land situation, though Whitehead explained that he did not intend to do away with the Land Apportionment Act. There was similar activity in the other territories: the colour-bar was ended in shops and hotels in Northern Rhodesia, and two more African members were added to the legislative council in Nyasaland. If the Governments hoped that these steps would make the Africans change their minds and support the Federation, they were disappointed.

14. A Saw-mill in Zambia

THE MONCKTON COMMISSION

In February 1960, the British Government carried out its promise to look into the Federal constitution. It sent out a Royal Commission of 25 members (20 European and five African), headed by Lord Monckton. The Commission's task was to advise the British, the Federal, and the three territorial Governments what sort of constitution would best help to bring about the objects contained in the Constitution of the Federation of Rhodesia and Nyasaland of 1953, including the preamble.'

Before the Commission was set up, Welensky asked the British Government to make it clear that the Commission would have no power to say that the Federation had failed and must be broken up: its only power would be to recommend improvements in the constitution. In January, the British

prime minister, Harold Macmillan, passed through Salisbury on
his way to Cape Town. The two prime ministers talked together,
and Welensky said that during their talk, Macmillan had made
him the promise he wanted, namely that the Commission
would not have power to recommend that the Federation
should be broken up. The African leaders believed that the
Monckton commission would have power only to make
small changes. They were not interested in small changes;
nothing but the ending of the Federation interested them. So
they decided to boycott the Commission. But in spite of the
boycott, many Africans did give evidence before the Commission. It would have been a pity if the Commission had been
unable to learn what Africans were thinking.

It is important that the Commission was specially told to
remember the preamble to the constitution. The preamble, as we
have seen on pages 137 and 138, makes two things clear. The first
is that land and political advance in the two protectorates are
to be the responsibility of the protectorate Governments and
of the British Government – not of the Federal Government –
for as long as the African peoples of the protectorates wish.
The second is that the Federation will not be given independence until the majority of its people – African and European,
voters and non-voters – have asked for it. Thus, the Monckton
commission had to ask three questions: (1) Do the majority
of the people want independence now? (2) If they do not, are
they likely to want it after there have been changes in the
constitution, and a few more years trial of the federal system?
(3) If they are not likely to want independence after this, is
there anything else that will make them want it?

The Monckton commission reported in October 1960. It
said that for economic reasons, it would be a good thing if
the Federation could continue; but it could not continue if
the African people remained strongly opposed to it. The only
way of gaining African support was to make, not small changes,
but 'drastic and fundamental changes': not only in the federal
constitution, but in the policy of the Southern Rhodesian
Government.

The Commission recommended big changes in the Federal
constitution. First: there must be many more African members
in the Federal parliament; the Commission suggested a parlia-

ment of 30 African and 30 European members. Second: many more Africans must be given the vote, so that the African members of parliament should not depend mainly on European votes. Third: the common roll of voters should be kept, and a special committee should be set up to find ways of adding large numbers of African voters quickly. (The Commission did not want a communal roll, with Africans voting always for African candidates and Europeans voting always for Europeans.) Fourth: various powers which were in the hands of the Federal Government should be handed over to the territorial Governments; the Federal Government should be left responsible only for external affairs, defence, and certain economic matters. Fifth: all laws which were 'unfairly discriminatory' should be abolished all through the Federation; the Land Apportionment Act and the pass laws in Southern Rhodesia were specially mentioned as laws which ought to go. Sixth: in order that no such unfair laws could be made in the future, all three territories should set up Councils of State to watch for the danger. The constitutions must make it impossible for these Councils of State to be abolished or weakened, and for their opinion to be ignored.[1]

Sir Roy Welensky would not like these recommendations.

No, they were bad enough from his point of view, though perhaps no worse than he had expected. But then the Commission made another recommendation which he thought much worse. The Commission said that one reason why the Africans so hated the Federation was that it had been forced on them and they could not break it. Perhaps, the Commission thought, if they knew that they were free to leave it, they would not really wish to. So it advised the British Government to say that any one of the three member-states would be free to leave the Federation if it wished: either after a fixed number of years, or after it had reached a certain stage in its own constitution. This made Sir Roy very angry. He said that before the Commission was appointed, the British Government had promised him that it would not be free to suggest breaking

---

[1] See page 139, in which we see how the African Affairs Board had been weakened between 1951 and 1953.

up the Federation; but now it had done so. The British Government replied that it had made no such promise; and anyway, the Commission was not suggesting that the Federation should be broken up. On the contrary: it wished the Federation to continue, but thought it had more chance of continuing if the member-states knew they were free to leave it. Sir Roy was not content with this reply; he said that if the territories were free to leave the Federation, of course they would want to leave it, though afterwards they might be sorry they had done so. By making this recommendation, he said, the Commission was killing the Federation.

The Commission's report was not unanimous. Eight European members signed the whole report; twelve Europeans and three Africans signed the report but said that it contained some opinions which they did not accept. The two remaining members, Mr Chirwa from Nyasaland and Mr Habanyama from Northern Rhodesia, refused to sign the report at all. They said they would sign no report unless it proposed to break up the Federation at once, and to introduce big constitutional changes in the territories.

The African leaders had boycotted the Monckton Commission, and said they were not interested in its report; nothing would satisfy them but breaking up the Federation. It was something, of course, that a territory should be free to leave the Federation (to 'secede') if it wished; but Dr Banda said, 'Federation or no Federation, we want to get out of the Federation; we want to secede now, not in five years.' In the federal parliament, both the party leaders, Welensky and Winston Field, rejected the idea that a territory might be free to secede. In Southern Rhodesia, the Dominion Party decided to press for independence. Its leader, Mr Harper, said that he would not agree to having as many Africans as Europeans in the federal parliament. He wanted to bring in large numbers of white men from Britain to increase the white population of Southern Rhodesia and prevent the Africans from ever taking control there.

The British Government had to weigh all these opinions against each other. It still thought that there were strong economic reasons for continuing the Federation. Nyasaland was receiving much financial help. The river Zambesi was

15. The Kariba Dam

being dammed at the Kariba gorge, and the power station
there would send electricity both to the Northern Rhodesian
copper mines and to the industries of Southern Rhodesia.
The University College of Rhodesia and Nyasaland was
opened in March 1957, and the British Government gave
£1,400,000 to build and equip it. But the African leaders
were saying that political freedom was more important than
these economic benefits; it was better to be free and poor,
said Dr Banda, than rich but in slavery. Northern Rhodesian
leaders did not want the Zambesi dam to be built at Kariba;
they wanted a dam in their own country on the Kafue river,
and they thought that Southern Rhodesia would get more
than its fair share of the benefit from the Kariba dam. As for

the university college, the Africans pointed out that the Europeans in Salisbury had made great difficulty over allowing African students to live in hostels on the university site, because it was built on European land. The Africans did not think that Southern Rhodesia wanted the university to be truly multi-racial. So the economic benefits of Federation, which were very real, did not bring the Africans to support it.

So as 1959, 1966 and 1961 passed by, the British Government slowly made up its mind that there was no hope of keeping the Federation alive. It must give Nyasaland and Northern Rhodesia majority government, even though it knew that the first use the new Governments made of their powers would be to take their countries out of the Federation.

11

THE END OF
THE FEDERATION

The British Government now set itself to bring Nyasaland and
Northern Rhodesia forward towards self-government. Mr
Kaunda was released from detention in January 1960 and
Dr Banda in April; and both of them told the Government
that they must be given power to take their countries out of
the Federation.

Nyasaland

In August 1960 a conference was held in London to consider
a new constitution for Nyasaland. The Governor and eighteen
members came from Nyasaland, including Dr Banda, Mr
Chirwa, Mr Chinyama and other African leaders. It did not
take the conference long to reach agreement on a new constitution. Nyasaland was to have much more internal self-
government, but some power was still kept in the Governor's
hands. The Governor's executive council was to consist of
five officials and five unofficial members; the unofficial
members were to be chosen from the party in power in the
legislative council.

The legislative council was to consist of three officials who
sat *ex-officio* (that is to say, the holders of three particular
official posts) and two nominated officials; but it was to have
28 elected members. The vote was given to thousands of
people. In addition to the upper roll of voters, the vote on the
lower roll was given to anyone who (a) was literate in English
and earned £120 a year or had property of £250; or (b) had
been paying taxes regularly for ten years and was literate in
any language of Nyasaland; or (c) held certain positions, such
as a village headman or councillor; or (d) was a master farmer;
or (e) was a pensioner; or (f) was an ex-service man. All votes,
upper and lower, counted equally; Nyasaland broke away

from the system of allowing lower-roll votes to count only to a limited extent.

How is this constitution short of full internal self-government?

For one thing, the executive council was still responsible to the Governor, not to the legislative council. For another, it contained five official members, who were not party men and could not be dismissed by the prime minister. For a third, there were five officials still sitting in the legislative council. There were other less important ways in which the constitution fell short of self-government. However, for the time being, Dr Banda was content; like Dr Nkrumah in Ghana a few years earlier, he thought he could work this constitution and would soon be given full self-government.

Mr Chipembere however was not content, and blamed Dr Banda for being too easily satisfied. He wanted the Malawi Congress to fight harder to break up the Federation. In the autumn of 1960 he and his followers caused disturbances in Nyasaland, and he said that if the Congress remained quiet and orderly, he and Mr Chiume would resign from it. But the Government prosecuted Mr Chipembere for proposing violence, and he was imprisoned; and when Dr Banda came back from the London conference, he stopped the trouble.

The elections were held in August 1961. The Malawi Congress Party under Dr Banda won 94% of the votes, and 22 seats in the council out of 28. The United Federal Party won five upper-roll seats, and one seat was won by an independent candidate. Dr Banda said that this election result meant that the people of Malawi wanted the Government to secede from the Federation as soon as possible.

Northern Rhodesia

With the Nyasaland constitution, the British Government had had an easy task in August 1960. But in December, when it came to consider a new constitution for Northern Rhodesia, it found this a very different matter. In Northern Rhodesia there were two African parties instead of one, and there was also a very strong European population, with Sir Roy Welensky as its spokesman. The conference sat in London for two months, and could not come to an agreement. But the British

Government could not allow the matter to rest there. Welensky and the Europeans held the power in Northern Rhodesia, but the Government had made up its mind that much more power must be given to the Africans. So the Secretary of State, Mr Ian Macleod, decided that if the people of Northern Rhodesia could not agree on a constitution for themselves, the British Government must work out a constitution for them, and make them accept it.

The Government's scheme would add about 2,000 Africans to the upper roll of voters and about 70,000 to the lower roll. The legislative council should be divided into three equal parts: one part to be elected by the upper-roll voters only, one by the lower-roll voters only, and one by upper and lower-roll voters, voting together. This scheme produced an uproar in Northern Rhodesia. Welensky and the Europeans said it would give far too much power to the Africans; Nkumbula said it would leave far too much power to the Europeans; Kaunda and his United National Independence Party said nothing but went on making disorder in the country so as to take it out of the Federation.

The British Government thought that, since each party attacked its scheme because it gave the other party too much, the scheme was probably about right. Mr Macleod discussed the scheme with Mr Kaunda to see if he could be brought to agree. To meet Mr Kaunda's views, Mr Macleod made some modifications in the scheme. The seats in the council for which both upper and lower-roll electors would vote were called 'national' seats. The problem with these was how to keep them from becoming in effect European seats – in other words, to give enough weight to the lower-roll votes. The decision in the end was to require that each candidate for a national seat must obtain at least ten per cent of the votes on each roll; and to make the two rolls count equally, the candidate's vote would be calculated as the average of the figures he obtained on the two. For example, if a candidate obtained 68 per cent of the upper-roll votes and 24 per cent of the lower-roll, his total vote would be calculated as the average of these two figures, 46 per cent.

Mr Kaunda said he did not think that this complicated scheme would work. Nevertheless, he said he would try it, on four conditions. They were: (a) if no candidate succeeded in winning a national seat, the seat must not be left empty, but the Governor must nominate a candidate to fill it; (b) there must be an independent commission to mark out the limits of the constituencies; (c) all political parties and political leaders who had been forbidden to take part in politics must be allowed to resume; (d) the review of the federal constitution must not be held until Northern Rhodesia had obtained a representative majority in its legislative council. Mr Macleod accepted all these conditions, and Mr Kaunda then said that he and his U.N.I.P. would take part in the elections. Very fortunately, Mr Macleod and Mr Kaunda got on well together; the friendship between them was as important for Northern Rhodesia as the friendship Dr Nkrumah and his Governor, Sir Charles Arden-Clarke, was for the Gold Coast.

Why did Mr Kaunda want the limits of the constituencies to be marked out by an independent commission?

Because he did not trust the Government to mark them. A party which is in power can sometimes make its position even stronger by the way in which it marks out the limits of the constituencies. For example, there may be three neighbouring constituencies, two of which are safe to return a member of party X, and the third safe to return a member of party Y. Now if party X is in power, it may decide to do away with the third constituency altogether and divide it between the other two; in this case, the whole area will no longer be represented by two X members and one Y member, but by two members only, both of them X. Mr Kaunda was afraid that if the Government (which was mainly controlled by European votes) marked out the constituencies, it would mark them out so as to ensure that as many as possible returned European members.

The new constitution came into force in September 1962. The elections were held with 37,000 voters on the upper roll and 92,000 on the lower. The United Federal Party won nearly all the upper-roll seats, the U.N.I.P. and the A.N.C. shared all the lower-roll seats; the national seats were divided fairly evenly. The U.F.P. was thus the strongest single party, but if the U.N.I.P. and the A.N.C. were to join together, they would be stronger than the U.F.P. Clearly the right thing for these two parties to do was to join; so Mr Kaunda invited Mr Nkumbula to agree that they should do so. Mr Nkumbula agreed, on condition that the united party should drop all violence and disorder and have nothing to do with communism. He had always been against violence, whereas Mr Kaunda had made up his mind that without violence the Africans would get nowhere. Now the Africans were within sight of gaining power, so there was no more need of violence, and Mr Kaunda was glad to accept Mr Nkumbula's conditions.

Southern Rhodesia

All this time the Federation was still in existence; but the Europeans in Southern Rhodesia saw that it would not last much longer, and that the British Government was determined to give the Africans more power. They now had to ask themselves what they should do to move with the times. The Whitehead Government decided that when Nyasaland and Northern Rhodesia were receiving new constitutions which added many thousands of Africans to the roll of voters and gave their legislative councils an African majority, it would be unwise for Southern Rhodesia to continue with a council in which there was not a single African member.

The Government made other changes to ease the position of the Africans. In November 1960, a new Act allowed African villages to be built on Crown land in the European area, and allowed Africans to buy houses and land in these villages. The Act also allowed Africans to occupy Crown land in the European area if they were college students or hospital patients. In 1961 another change was made, which allowed Africans to buy land in industrial areas and to take part in multiracial clubs. Moreover, two million acres of farm land were transferred from the European to the African area, and another five million set aside as 'unreserved land', which might be used for farms held either by Europeans or by Africans. Besides this softening of the Land Apportionment Act, the Government softened the pass laws. Instead of a pass to be in a town, a pass to look for work, a pass to visit the European area, and a pass to be out late at night, an African would need only one paper, a certificate to show who he was.

But these changes still left the Africans worse off than the Europeans; the Government might have done much more.

True, the two million acres of land transferred from the European to the African area amounted to only about four per cent of the whole. Still, there had been very little change in Southern Rhodesia before this, and even a small change for the better was welcome. As we shall see, even this was enough to make the Government lose much support among the voters.

In that same year, 1961, the British Government consulted the Government of Southern Rhodesia and obtained its agreement to a new constitution. There was to be a parliament of 65 members. Fifty were to be elected by constituencies, in which votes on the lower roll counted for only a quarter of the votes on the upper roll. The other fifteen were elected by 'electoral districts', in which upper roll votes counted for only a quarter of lower roll. Since most African voters were on the lower roll, this meant that the fifteen members from the electoral districts were likely to be Africans. There had so far been no African members at all in the Southern Rhodesian parliament; so this was an improvement. All chiefs and head-men were given votes on the upper roll, and the lower roll was greatly enlarged: all heads of kraals containing over twenty families were put on the lower roll, all ministers of religion, and all men over thirty who were earning £180 a year, even if they had had no schooling at all.

But how many such people were there?

We do not know, for the African leaders, Mr Nkomo and the Rev. Ndabaningi Sithole, told their followers not to register themselves on the roll of electors; in the elections which were held in Uganda in that same year the Government of Buganda told its people the same. When the constitution was in force, the lower roll contained about 10,000 names, including some hundreds of Europeans; but there must have been thousands of Africans who might have registered but did not. Mr Nkomo and Mr Sithole, the leaders of the National Democratic Party, would take no part in discussing the constitution. They gave their reasons. They said that the constitution proposed to give the vote to Africans who possessed a certain amount of property. But what was the use of that? they asked. In the reserves, land and houses belonged to the tribe or the family, so no one could count them as his own property. As for the towns, Africans were not allowed to buy houses or land in towns[1]; so all this talk of giving the vote to Africans with property meant nothing. As for education, they said that there were at that time only 677 Africans in the whole country who had gone beyond the primary school.

Besides this, Nkomo and Sithole gave other reasons for walking out of the discussions. They wanted to hold meetings in the rural areas to explain the proposed constitution; but the Government would not let them. They wanted to discuss the whole of the land question with the chiefs; but the Government would not let them. They wanted the new constitution to reopen the whole land question, both of African and of European land; but the Government would not hear of it.

The new constitution did not propose the sort of big changes in the land system that the African leaders wanted, but it did propose some change. It proposed that all the African reserves and the Special Native Area should be put together and called Tribal Trust Land, with a board of trustees to look after it for the benefit of the African people. This was the sort of system which had been set up in Nyasaland in 1936. But the African National Democratic Party said that this change was of no importance: the African people did not want new machinery for looking after African land, they wanted more land and better land.

The constitution included a Bill of Rights, promising every Rhodesian life, liberty, law and so forth; family and private life was to be respected, and Rhodesians were free to think as they liked, to say what they thought, to join together in groups and to hold meetings. A Constitutional Council of twelve members (including two Africans and one Asian) was to be set up to see that the Government respected these human rights. The Governor's executive council was changed: the Governor was no longer free to ignore its advice, so that it became more like a cabinet.

This was the constitution which the British Government

---

[1] The Whitehead Government was just changing this law, but the change had not yet come into effect.

offered Rhodesia; would Rhodesia accept it? Sir Edgar Whitehead was in favour of accepting. In October, he visited New York and addressed the Trusteeship Council of the United Nations. He told the Council that his Government would remove all discrimination against Africans. Within twelve months, he said, Africans would be free to live anywhere they chose, for his Government would repeal the Land Apportionment Act. And, he added, 'I have no doubt that Africans will have a majority within fifteen years.' To the newspaper men he added something which he did not say in his public speech: all this was part of a careful plan to make Rhodesia a multi-racial state.

Having said all this in New York, Whitehead came home to Salisbury and held a meeting of his party to consider the new constitution. The majority of the party agreed to accept the constitution and repeal the Land Apportionment Act. But a section of the party, led by Mr Ian Smith, refused to agree and voted against him.

The constitution was put into force on 1st November 1961. The National Democratic Party would have nothing to do with it, and its leaders told all Africans not to register as voters. They held a referendum of their own, and told the Government that only 584 Africans had voted in favour of the constitution, but 467,189 had voted against it. There were riots in Salisbury and Bulawayo, and Sir Edgar Whitehead banned the National Democratic Party. His Government did not regard the African referendum as worth anything; for even if the votes were accurately counted, many people (it said) voted against the constitution because they were afraid of being beaten or of having their houses burned if they voted for it. Mr Nkomo denied this; and as the N.D.P. was now illegal he formed a new party, the Zimbabwe African People's Union. After more rioting in 1962, the Z.A.P.U. too was banned, and Mr Nkomo was restricted for a time; Mr Sithole took over the leadership of the party while Nkomo was unable to act. In July 1963, after Mr Nkomo had been set free, a meeting of the Z.A.P.U. council was held in Dar-es-Salaam. At this meeting there was a split; the majority supported Mr Sithole and a minority remained faithful to Mr Nkomo. As Z.A.P.U. was banned, Sithole set up a new party, the Zimbabwe African National

Union; Nkomo called his group the People's Caretaker Council.

In March 1962, Mr Ian Smith and his followers left the United Federal Party and joined with the Dominion Party and other opposition groups to form a new party which they called the Rhodesian Front. The leader of the Front was Mr Winston Field, leader of the old Dominion Party. The Rhodesian Front had a simple policy: it was to oppose all these liberal ideas which Whitehead had adopted, and keep all power in European hands. Africans were being allowed to build houses in European areas, to come and live in towns, and even to sit in parliament; really, this was too much!

When the first elections were held, the Rhodesian Front won 73,000 votes and had 35 seats; the U.F.P. won 60,000 with 29 seats; the one remaining seat was won by an independent candidate. Whitehead of course resigned, and Winston Field formed a Government, in which Ian Smith became Minister of Finance. Fifteen of the 29 United Federal Party seats were won by Africans; these were the first Africans ever to sit in the territorial parliament of Rhodesia, though there had been Africans sitting in the Federal parliament at Salisbury from the beginning of the Federation.

So Sir Edgar Whitehead was no longer in power. But why did he think that under the 1961 constitution there would soon be an African majority in parliament?

A great deal depends on the way in which a constitution is worked. If Africans were to be in a majority in parliament, there must be a great increase in the number of African voters. There are three ways in which such an increase might be brought about. One way would be for the Government to extend African education, so that more Africans would obtain the educational qualifications for a vote, and Africans could take better jobs and earn better pay. In this way, they would qualify for a vote under the existing regulations. Another way would be for the Government to ease the regulations, so that Africans could obtain the vote with less money or less education. And we must not forget the third way. It would be no use for the Government to do these things if Africans still refused to register as voters. Mr Nkomo and Mr Sithole would have to help by allowing their people to register.

Now if Sir Edgar Whitehead had remained in power, and really meant to bring about an African majority within fifteen years, there were various ways in which he could have done so. He could encourage Africans to buy property in towns, he could push ahead with African education, and he could also make it possible for Africans to take jobs which had hitherto always been held by Europeans. In other words, he would have been accepting, like Dr Banda and Mr Kaunda, a constitution which did not give him all be wanted, with the idea that in a few years time he would be able to improve it. The 1961 constitution made it possible for the Rhodesian Government, if it wished, to help the Africans forward to majority rule and political power. It is because the constitution made this possible that Mr Ian Smith and the Rhodesian Front disliked it; and they threw Whitehead from power because they feared that he might bring about African majority rule. The Rhodesian Front could not stop the constitution from coming into force; but they thought they could so work it that there need be no African majority rule in fifteen years – nor yet in fifty or a hundred.

Then why did the British Government give Rhodesia a constitution which provided for only fifteen African members in a parliament of 65? Would it not have been better to provide for thirty or forty African members from the beginning?

In politics. it is often wise to go one step at a time. Whitehead and most of his followers were ready to accept fifteen African members in 1961. and Whitehead and a minority were willing to increase the number gradually to (let us say) 35 African members by about 1975. But if the British Government had asked them to accept 35 African members all at once in 1961, they would probably have refused. We must remember that if 35 African followers of Mr Nkomo had taken their seats in parliament, Mr Nkomo would have become prime minister. It is not likely that Whitehead would have agreed to that in 1961; and the great majority of the voters would have voted against the constitution. No constitution will work well if the majority of the voters dislike it and do not want it to work.

But you have told us that in that very same year, the African and European members of the constitutional conference for Northern Rhodesia could not agree. The British Government then drew up its own constitution and made Northern Rhodesia accept it. When Mr Kaunda disliked certain points in the British Government's draft, Mr Macleod discussed them with him and made some modifications, so that Mr Kaunda accepted the constitution. That was good and wise. But if Britain could do that for the North, why could she not do it for the South also?

For one thing, the political situation in the two countries was different. In the North, there seemed no hope at all of any agreement: Welensky and Kaunda and their friends had been discussing for two months, and were no nearer agreement at the end than they had been at the beginning. In the South, Whitehead was the prime minister at the head of a strong Government; he was ready to accept fifteen members at once from the African parties, and was hoping for an African majority in fifteen years time. As we have seen, he was mistaken; but the British Government could not know this in 1961. As far as Britain could see, the door to an African majority was open; there was no need to kick at it.

But the main reason was that Northern Rhodesia was a British protectorate, and Britain was responsible for helping the Africans to advance towards political power. Southern Rhodesia was very largely self-governing, and had been so since 1923. Having given Southern Rhodesia so much power, Britain no longer had the power to enforce constitutional changes there, as she had in Northern Rhodesia and Nyasaland. Once you give away power, you cannot take it back again. In 1923, Britain had given Southern Rhodesia responsible government. It was for the Southern Rhodesian Government henceforth, not for Britain, to say who should have the vote in Southern Rhodesia, and how members should be elected to parliament. When Whitehead said that there would be an African majority within fifteen years, he did not mean that he would ask Britain to bring it about: he meant that his Government would bring it about by passing the necessary Acts of the Rhodesian parliament.

But Southern Rhodesia was still a colony; and in 1923 Britain had kept the right of disallowing any law which did not treat Africans the same as Europeans.

True: but in the Commonwealth, a 'colony' may be in any stage of government, ranging from a territory where the Governor rules with an almost absolute power, to a territory like Ghana in 1954 or Southern Rhodesia in 1962, where Britain has no power at all in internal affairs. All British colonies have advanced on the road which leads from complete British control towards full independence. Merely to say that a country is a 'colony' means very little; it means only that the country is not yet fully independent. But it may be very near independence; and Rhodesia was very near it.

As for the right of disallowing laws of Southern Rhodesia, Britain had never once exercised her right after 1923. Not even in the case of the Land Apportionment Act. Perhaps if the Africans had protested against that Act at the time, Britain might have exercised her right of disallowing the Act; but they did not protest, either in 1930 or in 1939 when the Bledisloe Commission visited the country.

So the situation in Southern Rhodesia was quite different from that in Northern. Britain had powers in the North which she no longer had in the South. And in 1961, with the Whitehead Government still in power, Britain had every reason for hoping that Africans in the South were at last about to begin their political advance. That hope was disappointed; but Britain could not use powers which she had long ago given up.

MALAWI AND ZAMBIA INDEPENDENT

Both Dr Banda and Mr Kaunda were working under constitutions which did not fully satisfy them, and both of them were quietly carrying their countries forward to independence. Malawi first. In November 1962 another constitutional conference for Malawi was held in London, and a new constitution was drawn up; part of it was put into force in February 1963 and the rest of it in May 1963. The legislative assembly was to have a Speaker and the financial secretary, and the same number of elected members as before. Dr Banda was prime minister again, and he formed a cabinet of eight African

and two European members, responsible to the legislative
assembly.

The Federation was dissolved on 31 December 1963, and
Nyasaland (now to be called Malawi) became an independent
member of the Commonwealth on 6 July 1964.

Dr Banda's Government faced great difficulties. Malawi is
a poor country. It has hardly any minerals, and only one-third
of it is suitable for agriculture. When Malawi left the Federation, it lost the help it had been receiving from the Federal
Government. So Malawi, like many other African countries,
had the great problem of poverty. One of the consequences
of poverty is that there is not enough education. Malawi in
1963 was very short of qualified men, and it still had to use
British and other officials from overseas.

In September 1964, this led to trouble. Some of Dr Banda's
old companions, Mr Chipembere, Mr Chiume, Mr Chirwa
and others, complained that Africans were not being appointed
quickly enough to posts held by Europeans; and they were
dissatisfied with Dr Banda's leadership in some other ways as
well. Dr Banda dismissed these three ministers and some
others, and appointed new men to fill their places. Some of
the dismissed ministers crossed the border into Zambia and
Tanzania, and from there they made disorder in Malawi
against Dr Banda's Government.

Zambia

In January 1964 Zambia was given a new constitution to
prepare the way for independence. The legislative assembly
was to contain 65 members elected on one roll, with ten more
members elected by special European constituencies. There
was to be a prime minister and a cabinet of 13 ministers,
responsible to the assembly. The constitution included a Bill
of Rights, and there was to be a constitutional council to
prevent any law or Government action which was contrary to
the Bill of Rights.

By this time, Mr Kaunda and his United National Independence Party had the support not only of most of the Africans
but also of many Europeans. Still, as ten seats were reserved
in the assembly for European members, a new European
party came into existence to fight for them. The party called
itself the National Progress Party, but though purely European,

its leaders said that it would support the policy of the U.N.I.P. The other African party, the African National Congress, was weaker; its leader Mr Nkumbula had been ill, and many of its members had left it and gone over to Mr Kaunda.

The elections were held in January. The U.N.I.P. won 55 seats and the A.N.C. ten; all the reserved European seats were won by the N.P.P., though one U.N.I.P. candidate, Sir John Moffat, was only narrowly beaten at Ndola. In one constituency there was a straight fight between an African candidate of the A.N.C. and a European of the U.N.I.P., and the European won. The Congress was strong in the southern part of the country, and Mr Nkumbula himself was elected with a very large majority. Mr Kaunda had won the elections, and of course formed a cabinet from his own party. He said that he meant to build 'one roll, one people, in one country'; he did not think that questions of race should be allowed to come into politics. As we have seen, his party included European as well as African candidates for election.

In May 1964 there was yet another conference in London, and Mr Kaunda got the constitution that he wanted. Zambia was to be an independent republic. The president's cabinet would consist of the vice-president and 14 ministers, chosen from the members of the assembly. The president would go out of office whenever the assembly was dissolved, and a new president would be elected with the new assembly. There were to be no special European seats in the assembly; there were to be 75 elected members, and five more nominated by the President.

Another matter settled at the London conference was the position of Barotseland in an independent Zambia. Ever since the early days, Barotseland had held a special position because of its agreements with Britain. The present paramount chief, Sir Mwanawina Lewanika III, agreed at the conference that when Zambia became independent, all his special agreements with Britain should come to an end. Barotseland would be part of Zambia, and would be treated like any other part of the country in financial and economic matters. But the Zambia Government would recognize the Litunga (paramount chief) and his council as the principal local government authority in Barotseland, and would allow him to keep his customary powers of holding courts of justice and of making laws for his people on certain subjects.

Under this new constitution, Zambia became an independent republic on 24 October 1964. Mr Kaunda was elected president ·and his cabinet of 14 U.N.I.P. members included one European as Minister of Justice.

When Northern Rhodesia became independent under the name Zambia, Southern Rhodesia became known simply as Rhodesia.

RHODESIA ASKS FOR INDEPENDENCE

When the Winston Field Government took office in December 1962, it saw plainly that the British Government meant to dissolve the Federation and give independence to Zambia and Malawi. It was natural that the Rhodesian Government should ask that Rhodesia too should be given independence. Winston Field had several talks in London and elsewhere to find out if this were possible. He found his position difficult. Britain had granted Rhodesia the 1961 constitution when Whitehead was in power and there was hope that he would use the constitution to help the Africans forward. The Africans had always opposed the 1961 constitution; and now Whitehead had been replaced in power by a party which disliked the constitution and believed that all political power should be kept in European hands. The British Government did not think it would be right to grant independence to Rhodesia while so few Africans had the vote, there were only fifteen African members of parliament out of 65, and a party was in power which had no intention of improving this position. The British Government had already given independence to some of its African colonies, and independence for the others was very near. In every case but one, the British Government had made sure before granting independence that every man had the vote. The one exception was South Africa; and the British Government did not think it should make another exception for Southern Rhodesia. Both parties in the British parliament agreed that it would be wrong to give Rhodesia independence under the 1961 constitution; some other constitution must first be adopted, under which the Africans would have more **power.**

In 1964 there was a general election in Britain, and the Conservative Government was replaced by a Labour Government under Mr Harold Wilson. The new Government was likely to be less favourable to the white settlers in Rhodesia than the old one had been.

The Rhodesian Front Government in Salisbury was angry that Britain did not think Rhodesia was yet ready for independence. One of its Ministers, Mr Clifford Dupont, said, 'Independence is our legal, logical and moral right after forty years of existence during which no one has been able to point a finger at us in criticism of our treatment of any Black Rhodesian. He went on to say that Britain had no right to lay down conditions as to what Rhodesia should or should not do in exchange for its independence. The prime minister, Winston Field, himself went so far as to say, 'We don't want to be members of the Commonwealth if this delays our independence.'

In February 1964, the Constitutional Council reported to the Government that the Land Apportionment Act was unfair to the Africans. As the Act was more than thirty years old, the Government was entitled under the constitution to ignore this report, and of course it did ignore it. In the election campaign, the Opposition had promised that if returned to power, it would repeal the Act. Sir Edgar Whitehead had lost the election; but he now introduced a motion in parliament calling for the repeal of the Act. He was defeated by 31 votes to 27.

Next month, March, the Rhodesian Government carried a motion in parliament, asking the Queen to agree that she would not use her powers of altering the Rhodesian constitution by an Order in Council unless two-thirds of the Rhodesian parliament asked her to do so. If the Queen (as advised by the British Government in London) had agreed to this, it would have meant that the Rhodesian parliament, by a two-thirds majority, could have declared the country independent, and the Queen would have promised not to interfere. By giving Southern Rhodesia internal self-government in 1923, the British Government had promised that it would not interfere in the country's constitutional development. But only the British Government could grant full independence; and it was most unlikely to advise the Queen to make the promise which the Rhodesian Government required. So the Rhodesian Government seemed to be faced with a choice: if it wished to become independent, it must either accept the conditions which Britain laid down, or it must break away from the authority of Britain and the Queen. This was a difficult decision.

Ian Smith becomes prime minister

In April, after what he called 'serious disagreements between my party and myself', Mr Winston Field resigned, and Mr Ian Smith became prime minister. No statement was made on the reasons for the disagreement; but it was supposed that Ian Smith and the majority of the cabinet wanted to press the British Government harder than Winston Field was prepared to do, and wanted to tell Britain that if Rhodesia was not given independence by a certain date, she would declare herself independent.

In July, a meeting of Commonwealth prime ministers was held in London. Mr Ian Smith thought that he should be invited; but the British Government told him that he could not be invited because Rhodesia was not a fully independent country. It was known moreover that if he had been invited, some Commonwealth countries (Ghana and India among them) would have been angry.

After this, Ian Smith began to talk openly of declaring independence without the British Government's permission. There were many more discussions between the Governments in London and in Salisbury. The Rhodesian Government said that most of the Africans would be content to see Rhodesia independent under the 1961 constitution. The British Government did not believe this. So now there were two questions to be answered: (1) How was Ian Smith to prove that most Africans were content with the 1961 constitution? (2) If he could not prove this, on what conditions would the British Government be ready to give Rhodesia its independence?

In October 1964, the Government held an *indaba* or meeting of chiefs. It was attended by 196 chiefs and 426 headmen, and they agreed that they would be content with independence under the 1961 constitution. But Sir Edgar Whitehead said that such a small meeting proved nothing; the Government ought to have consulted all the 38,000 heads of kraals. Another Rhodesian Statesman, Lord Malvern, called the *indaba* 'a swindle'. The British Government said that the vote at the *indaba* did not satisfy it as a test of African opinion. Next, the Government held a referendum of all registered voters, in which 58,000 voted in its favour and 6,000 against it. But this was a small poll, only 61 per cent of the voters; and the British Government knew that only about 13,000 Africans had registered. So again the British Government said it was not satisfied. A British cabinet Minister visited Salisbury, and had a meeting with 600 chiefs, who told him that they disagreed with Nkomo and Sithole. The ballot box, they said, was a foreign thing, contrary to African custom; and the Africans who voted for Nkomo and Sithole did so out of fear. But in spite of that, the British Government thought that Mr Nkomo and Mr Sithole represented African feelings better than the chiefs did.

During the discussion which were held in 1965, the British Government laid down five conditions which must be fulfilled before it could give Rhodesia independence. In these conditions, the Government was speaking with the full support of parliament; the Conservative Opposition agreed with them. The conditions were:

1. The Rhodesian Government must guarantee that Africans should progress towards majority rule, and that it would do nothing to hinder them.
2. It must guarantee that after it became independent, it would not amend its constitution so as to diminish African rights.
3. The Rhodesian Government must do something at once to improve the political position of the Africans.
4. It must do away with the racial discrimination which still existed.
5. Any constitution for an independent Rhodesia must be acceptable to the people of Rhodesia as a whole.

But what would these conditions really mean in practice?

That was what the two Governments now had to discuss. We can take the five conditions one by one.

1. The British Government no doubt remembered that

Whitehead had promised an African majority within fifteen years. It would have liked Ian Smith to promise an African majority within a fixed time – say fifteen years, or twenty, or twenty-five – and it would have been ready to give Rhodesia help with African education so as to make this possible. Ian Smith would make no such promise. He promised that after Rhodesia had been given independence – not before – he would increase the number of lower-roll seats in parliament, and would increase the number of lower-roll voters, by giving the vote to all taxpayers. (This would add about a million African votes to the lower roll.) But he would not lay down any time limit for majority rule; the Rhodesian Government must be left quite free to give the Africans more power gradually as it thought fit. He did not believe in 'educating people merely to qualify them for the vote.'

2. Ian Smith agreed to this. But he pointed out that the 1961 constitution could be amended by a two-thirds majority in parliament, and he would not agree that amending the constitution should be made more difficult than this. (We may remember that a two-thirds majority of the Rhodesian parliament needed 44 seats; Ian Smith's party held fifty[1].)

3. The British Government would have liked the fifteen lower-roll seats increased at once to 22. Ian Smith said that he would give no more seats to Africans while so many Africans who were qualified for the vote refused to register as voters. He offered to set up a Senate composed of twelve African chiefs, who would vote on all Bills which affected African rights. Since there was then no Senate in Rhodesia, he thought that the British Government should be satisfied to see a million voters added to the lower roll, and a new Senate without a single white member. But the British Government did not think this a sufficient improvement in the political position of the Africans.

4. Ian Smith agreed that one day all racial discrimination must be abolished. But his Government refused to be hurried over the Land Apportionment Act. It would repeal that Act when it thought the time had come; not before.

5. Ian Smith agreed that the independence constitution must

[1] See below, page 188

be acceptable to the Rhodesian people as a whole. But if the British Government was not satisfied with his referendum and his *indaba* of chiefs, he could not see what would satisfy it. In October 1965 Harold Wilson (the British prime minister) visited Salisbury and discussed this point with Ian Smith. Wilson suggested a new and larger referendum, to cover all the people, not merely the registered voters; and he suggested also that a Royal Commission should draw up an independence constitution. Ian Smith would not agree to these suggestions. He suggested that a commission of three men (one British and one Rhodesian member, with the Chief Justice of Rhodesia as chairman) should go round the country and report whether in its opinion the Rhodesian people as a whole were content with the 1961 constitution. Wilson would not accept this.

The meeting broke up without an agreement. The real point on which the two prime ministers disagreed was the same as the one on which the Devlin commission had disagreed with the Nyasaland Government.[1] Mr Ian Smith, like the Government of Nyasaland in 1959, thought that most Africans in Rhodesia understood nothing about politics and had no real opinions of their own; they followed Mr Nkomo and Mr Sithole blindly, and many of them followed only because they were afraid of being ill-treated if they refused. Mr Wilson took quite the opposite view. Like the Devlin commission, he thought that the Africans in Rhodesia, even if uneducated, understood enough about politics to have strong opinions; and that most of them were strongly opposed to the Smith Government and the 1961 constitution. No agreement was possible between statesmen who held such different views about the African people.

RHODESIA DECLARES ITSELF INDEPENDENT

In May 1965 there were fresh elections for the Rhodesian parliament. Whitehead and some other leaders retired from politics and did not stand for election. The Rhodesian Front won all the fifty upper-roll seats. It did not put up candidates for the fifteen lower-roll seats; ten of these were won by the

[1] See page 161

Opposition and five by independents. An African, Mr Josiah Gondo, was elected leader of the Opposition.

Mr Ian Smith had already said that he would not wait very long for independence; and he thought that this victory in the elections meant that the Rhodesian people supported him in this. After his talks with Mr Wilson in October, it was plain that the two Governments were far from any agreement, and that it would be a long time before Britain agreed to give Rhodesia independence. He decided to wait no longer. On 5 November 1965, the Rhodesian Government declared itself independent of Britain, though it said that it remained loyal to the Queen.

I have heard this called 'U.D.I.' What does U.D.I. mean?

The letters stand for the words 'unilateral declaration of independence'. 'Unilateral' means simply one-sided: that is, instead of independence being declared by agreement between both sides (Britain and Rhodesia), it was declared by one side only, without the agreement of the other.

The British Government at once declared that this was an act of rebellion, and that Mr Ian Smith and his Ministers were no longer the lawful Government of Rhodesia. The Governor, Sir Humphrey Gibbs, was the Queen's representative in Rhodesia. He dismissed Ian Smith and his Government from office. But they refused to accept his dismissal, and they drew up a new constitution, under which they continue to govern the country.

The British Government said that the Smith Government in Rhodesia must somehow be pulled down. It asked all other countries to refuse to recognize Rhodesia as an independent country and the Smith Government as its lawful Government. The United Nations, which had already been discussing the Rhodesia question, asked all its member states to do the same. The British Government said that it would not use armed force against Rhodesia; but it thought that economic sanctions would soon pull the Smith Government down.

What did it mean by economic sanctions?

A sanction is simply a punishment. What the Government did was to forbid anyone to buy Rhodesian goods or to sell to Rhodesia, to forbid anyone to lend money to Rhodesia or to use Rhodesian banking services, and to stop all payments to Rhodesia. The British Government of course had no power over people in foreign countries; but many foreign Governments agreed to support these economic sanctions. Britain thought that these steps would soon stop all business in Rhodesia, and bring about so much distress that the Smith Government would have to resign. Britain knew that there was an Opposition in Rhodesia, and the Government hoped that the Opposition would grow stronger and defeat the Government. Mr Wilson thought that all this might happen quite quickly, but it took much longer than he had expected. The Rhodesian Government was in a strong position. The laws which the Whitehead Government had passed enabled it to detain all the African leaders, and even such men as Mr Garfield Todd, a former prime minister. The Opposition was kept under such tight control that there was very little it could do.

But why would Britain not use armed force? She used armed force against Egypt in 1956.

Yes, Britain did use armed force against Egypt. But as far as we can see, it did no good; in fact, the British position after 1956 was worse than it would have been if force had not been used. The experience of 1956 did not encourage Britain to try using force again. There were two main reasons why Britain did not use armed force against Rhodesia. One was that it would have been a civil war. Thousands of people in Britain had sons or brothers living in Rhodesia, and no British Government could have persuaded the British people as a whole to agree to such a war.

There is another reason. Even if Britain had been willing to use force, it would have been extremely difficult. In the case of Egypt, there was the British island of Cyprus close by, in which an army could be gathered over a period of months. There was nothing of the kind in the case of Rhodesia. There were no British troops in Africa. A British army would have to be taken all the way from Britain to Zambia by air, and it would be several weeks before it was ready to attack Rhodesia.

But why Zambia? Why not direct to Rhodesia?

Because the Rhodesian army could gather much more quickly than the British army. If a few hundred British troops had been landed to capture the airfields near Salisbury, they would have been attacked by ten or twenty times their own numbers, and would have been destroyed long before fresh troops could come from Britain to support them. They would have had to land in the friendly country of Zambia and wait there until they were strong enough. But we may be sure that the Rhodesian army and air force would not wait patiently until the attack came. As soon as they saw a British army beginning to gather, they would move into Zambia to capture the airfields. No doubt other African countries would wish to help; but they could not help unless some country like Russia or the United States would provide aircraft to carry their troops. The danger in using armed force was that there might soon be a large-scale war, and most of the fighting would take place in Zambia, not in Rhodesia. No doubt Rhodesia would be crushed in the end, but both Rhodesia and Zambia would be ruined, and there would be terrible suffering among the people. The risk was too great.

So there was no fighting; but the economic sanctions went on. Even these were not easy to work, for Portugal and South Africa were on the side of the Rhodesian Government, so that Rhodesia was surrounded on three sides by friendly country. The British navy stopped some ships from delivering oil at Beira for pumping through the pipe line to Rhodesia. But Rhodesia got some oil by road from South Africa, and it seemed that some foreign business men bought part at least of the Rhodesian tobacco crop. It soon became plain that the sanctions would take longer to weaken the Rhodesian Government than Mr Wilson had believed. Some of the African countries, especially Zambia, became impatient. Zambia especially was suffering, because she needed the Kariba electricity to provide power for the copper mines, and needed the Rhodesian railway to take away her copper and bring in coal and oil. For a time, Britain supplied Zambia with oil by air, but could not send her enough. It is natural that Zambia should be anxious to get the affair over quickly.

In the end, the Wilson Government promised the African countries of the Commonwealth that if Rhodesia was still

16. Electric Transformers at Kariba

holding out at the end of 1966, Britain would go to the United
Nations and ask all member states of the United Nations to
order their people to support the economic sanctions against
Rhodesia. Since most states sympathised with the Africans
and disliked the policy of the Rhodesian Government, many
of them had already done this. But now, Britain proposed to
ask the United Nations to make a rule on the matter, so that
even states that did not wish to support the sanctions should
be compelled to do so.

But in making this promise, the Wilson Government lost
the support of the Conservative opposition in Britain. The
Conservatives (some of them unwillingly) had supported the
Government in its sanctions against Rhodesia; but they

were quite opposed to the idea of seeking help from the United Nations. Rhodesia, they held, was a British affair, or at most a Commonwealth affair; and Britain or the Commonwealth ought to settle it. Moreover, they quoted the charter of the United Nations to support their argument. They pointed out that the charter allowed the United Nations to declare economic sanctions against an independent country which was a danger to peace. But Rhodesia, they said, was not an independent country, and it was not proposing to attack any other country; so if the United Nations made the rule to compel its members to support economic sanctions, it would be going against its own charter.

In the last few weeks of 1966, Mr Wilson and Mr Ian Smith met on board a British warship in another attempt to reach agreement. But these talks also failed, and so Wilson had to fulfil his promise, and take the matter to the United Nations. He did this, and in December the United Nations agreed to the British request, and ordered all its member states to impose economic sanctions against Rhodesia.

EDUCATION SINCE 1939

The 1939 war and the 1945 Colonial Development and Welfare Act gave new hope for African education. During the war, secondary schools were opened at Zomba and Blantyre in Nysaland and at Lusaka in Northern Rhodesia; the Northern Rhodesian Government named its new school Munali, which was the name that Africans had given to David Livingstone. In 1946, the Methodists added a secondary class to their girls' primary school at Chipembe in Northern Rhodesia, and in the same year, Southern Rhodesia opened its Government secondary school at Goromonzi, to which both girls and boys were admitted. In 1947 education was made compulsory on the copper-belt for all children between the ages of 12 and 16; but this had to be dropped four years later, because the population of the copper-belt was increasing so fast that the Government could not provide schools and teachers fast enough to keep pace with it.

Africans were now demanding more and more education. In 1943, the Government in Southern Rhodesia reported

that a few years earlier, it had been difficult to find children
to fill the empty seats in school; now the difficulty was to
provide seats for all the children who wanted to come. In
1947, Northern Rhodesia complained that 'the education of
girls and women still advances at the pace of the ox'; but four
years later the pace was quickening: there were 5,000 more
girls in school in 1951 than there had been at the end of the
war in 1945. Not only was there now more African demand
for education, there was also more money to supply it. Some
of this extra money came from Britain under the Colonial
Development and Welfare Acts; but much of it came because
the produce of Central Africa was selling for much higher
prices than before the war. Government expenditure on African
education in Northern Rhodesia rose from £29,000 in 1937
to £190,000 in 1946 and nearly half a million in 1951. Even
Nyasaland, which spent only £11,000 in 1936, was able to
increase this tiny sum to £166,000 in 1951. This was before
Federation; under the Federation, Nyasaland's expenditure
rose to nearly £900,000. In the Federation's last year, the
copper mining companies in Northern Rhodesia gave
£1,300,000 to help the Government to provide education
for the children on the copper-belt; and in that same year,
Southern Rhodesia spent £3,250,000 on African education.

Even large sums of money like these will not satisfy the
educational authorities, for there is always room for improvement: for more trained teachers and for more thorough training, for smaller classes, for more varied secondary education,
for technical and adult and university education, for more
apparatus and equipment of all kinds. Very much still remained
to be done when the Federation ended. The university college
had been opened in 1957, but secondary education was still
lagging behind; and because of this, there were not many
African students ready to enter the university classes. Southern
Rhodesia had nearly 4,000 African children in secondary
school, but the other two countries had fewer still. There
were 5,200 teachers in training college: half of them in Rhodesia,
the other half divided between Malawi and Zambia. Many of
the training colleges were too small to be really effective:
those in Rhodesia averaged 55 students each, those in the
other two countries about twice as many.

In all three countries the problems still to be solved are much the same, and we may take Rhodesia as an example of how education departments are trying to solve them. In 1959, Rhodesia had for some years been trying to provide at least five years of schooling for all who wanted it. In that year, the department of education reckoned that 85 per cent of African children were getting some amount of schooling. But by then, more and more children were finishing the five years course, and a new problem was arising: there were not enough places in the sixth year, fewer than one-half of the number of children who were finishing their fifth year. So the Government started a new programme of building senior primary schools, so that all children who wanted to so so could stay at school for eight years instead of only five. The Government foresaw that this would raise a demand for junior secondary schools, and by 1966 it had already done so. In that year the Government began a programme of building more secondary schools, and it hoped that by the year 1974, one African child out of every five who finished the eight years primary course would be able to go on to secondary education.

This of course would not be the end. New problems would arise at once: what can be done for the other four children out of five? and how can more higher education be provided in universities and technical colleges for those who complete the secondary school course? But Governments have to take one step at a time; in education, as in other sides of human life, the journey we have made is only a small part of the journey that lies before us.

THINGS TO DO, TO DISCUSS, OR TO FIND OUT

1. Find out all you can about the Bushmen today. What help do you think an African Government could give them?
2. Draw a map of Central Africa; mark on it the journeys taken by the Bantu peoples mentioned in this book, and any other peoples whose history you know.
3. Find out all you can about the stone buildings (Zimbabwe and others) of Rhodesia and the objects that have been found in them.
4. Make a list of the crops and foodstuffs which are now grown in Central Africa. Find out how many of them were introduced into Africa by the Arabs and the Portuguese.
5. Read Thomas Mofolo's book *Chaka* and anything else you can find about king Chaka. Why did Dingiswayo and Chaka turn their peoples into constant warfare, and thus change their whole way of life?
6. Mark Livingstone's travels on a map. Read about Livingstone and find out what made Sebetwane and Sekeletu and other Africans admire him so much.
7. This book says that Livingstone could never have imagined large-scale industry in Africa like the copper-belt. What benefits and what evils has large-scale industry brought to Africa? Can African Governments hope in future to keep the benefits and get rid of the evils? If so, how?
8. Mark the principal missionary stations on a map of Central Africa. What benefits did the missionaries bring to Africa in the early days? Does Africa still need missionaries today?
9. Write and act a scene in which a great chief like Msilikazi is discussing with his elders what they are to say to a missionary who wants to come and live and preach in his capital town.
10. Suppose Cecil Rhodes met Gladstone in London and talked about his plans. Would Gladstone approve? Write an account of their conversation.
11. Try and put yourself in the place of (1) Rhodes, (2) Kruger, (3) Lobengula, (4) the British High Commissioner in

South Africa. Write a speech for each man, explaining and defending himself.

12. Write the history of Central Africa as it would have been if Rhodes had never lived to become rich and .powerful.

13. Did the British Government make a mistake in leaving so much responsibility to the British South Africa Company?

14. Write and act a scene in a village near lake Nyasa: the actors are the chief and his elders, Sir Harry Johnston, and a white man who says that the chief has sold him some land.

15. Do you think that John Chilembwe might have had more success if he had been less impatient?

16. How far is it true that the troubles of Rhodesia in the 1960s really had their beginnings in 1923?

17. We are told that African leaders did not protest against the Land Apportionment Act when it was first passed, or for some years later. If so, do you think that the Government in London should have used its power of disallowing the Act?

18. Indirect rule did not work as well as Lugard hoped. Many Africans in Nigeria think that indirect rule kept their country back. Do you think it kept Central Africa back?

19. Britain always allowed colonial Governments a good deal of freedom. The Government in London (as in the Passfield Memorandum) laid down the general lines of policy, but left the colonial Governments to carry it out, and did not attempt to control the details. Do you think it would have been better if closer control had been exercised from London? Can you suggest any disadvantages of closer control?

20. What economic advantage did Nyasaland gain from Federation?

21. 'A good idea, but carried out in the wrong way.' Would you agree with this description of the Federation? Do you think it likely that when all three countries are independent, they may decide to form a new Federation?

22. By demanding 'One man, one vote', Africans in multi-racial countries have got power into their hands. In Britain, the system of 'One man, one vote' was reached

only in 1948. Can you suggest any disadvantages in the system?

23. The population of Central Africa is increasing fast. What will happen when there is no longer enough land for each family to have its own farm?

24. Consider the way in which Nyasaland became separated from Northern Rhodesia in 1890. The line then drawn is still the boundary between Zambia and Malawi. Do you think it right to keep these two countries separate?

25. It has been said that British colonial Governments in Africa usually tried to govern justly and to help the Africans as much as they could; the trouble was that they were not strong enough to stand up to the commercial men and the settlers. Would you agree with this?

26. So far, only one African country south of the Sahara – South Africa – has succeeded in becoming a major manufacturing country. What problems face a Government in Africa which tries to develop manufacturing industry?

27. What place have the chiefs and the tribal system in modern Africa?

28. Agriculture in Central Africa depends largely on rainfall. If you have 15 inches of rain a year, you will have grass for cattle; if you have 30 inches a year, you can grow food crops. Draw a map of Central Africa, marking the areas with 30 inches or more and with 15 inches or more. What does your map suggest to you should be the agricultural policy of the Governments in Zambia, Malawi and Rhodesia?

29. Africans dislike the South African system of *apartheid*. But some independent African countries have recently begun to enter into close trading relations with South Africa. Do you approve of this?

30. Make a list of the exports of the three countries, and of their value. Find out what proportion these exports make of the total world supply of these products.

BOOK ONE
INDEX

i

Index

BOOK TWO
INDEX

v

BOOK THREE
INDEX

xi